Fodor's

SCOTLAND

23rd Edition

Where to Stay and Eat
for All Budgets

Must-See Sights
and Local Secrets

Ratings You Can Trust

Fodor's Travel Publications   New York, Toronto, London, Sydney, Auckland
www.fodors.com

FODOR'S SCOTLAND

Writers: Nick Bruno, Mike Gonzalez, Shona Main, Elizabeth Reeder

Editor: Linda Cabasin (lead project editor), Mark Sullivan

Production Editor: Jennifer DePrima

Maps & Illustrations: David Lindroth and Mark Stroud, *cartographers;* Bob Blake, Rebecca Baer, *map editors;* William Wu, *information graphics*

Design: Fabrizio La Rocca, *creative director;* Tina Malaney, Chie Ushio, Jessica Walsh, *designers;* Melanie Marin, *associate director of photography;* Jennifer Romains, *photo research*

Cover Photo: (Highland dancing competition, Highland Games, Portree, Isle of Skye): David Hughes/Robert Harding World Imagery

Production Manager: Angela L. McLean

COPYRIGHT

23rd Edition

ISBN 978-0-307-92841-2

ISSN 0743–0973

SPECIAL SALES

This book is available at special discounts for bulk purchases for sales promotions or premiums. Special editions, including personalized covers, excerpts of existing books, and corporate imprints, can be created in large quantities for special needs. For more information, write to Special Markets/Premium Sales, 1745 Broadway, MD 3-1, New York, NY 10019, or e-mail specialmarkets@randomhouse.com.

AN IMPORTANT TIP & AN INVITATION

Although all prices, opening times, and other details in this book are based on information supplied to us at press time, changes occur all the time in the travel world, and Fodor's cannot accept responsibility for facts that become outdated or for inadvertent errors or omissions. So **always confirm information when it matters**, especially if you're making a detour to visit a specific place. Your experiences—positive and negative—matter to us. If we have missed or misstated something, **please write to us.** Share your opinion instantly through our online feedback center at fodors.com/contact-us.

CONTENTS

1 EXPERIENCE SCOTLAND........7
   What's Where................. 8
   Welcome to Scotland.......... 12
   Scotland Top Attractions 14
   Quintessential Scotland........ 16
   If You Like................... 18
   Flavors of Scotland........... 22
   Great Itineraries............. 24

2 EDINBURGH AND THE
   LOTHIANS 27
   Orientation and Planning....... 29
   Exploring Edinburgh........... 35
   Where to Eat 56
   Best Bets for
   Edinburgh Dining 59
   Where to Stay................ 67
   Best Bets for
   Edinburgh Lodging............ 69
   Nightlife and the Arts.......... 74
   Sports and the Outdoors....... 81
   Shopping.................... 83
   Side Trips from Edinburgh 86

3 GLASGOW.................. 99
   Orientation and Planning...... 101
   Exploring Glasgow........... 107
   Where to Eat 121
   Best Bets for
   Glasgow Dining 123
   Where to Stay............... 134
   Best Bets for
   Glasgow Lodging 135
   Nightlife and the Arts......... 139
   Sports and the Outdoors...... 145
   Shopping................... 146
   Side Trips: Ayrshire, Clyde Coast,
   and Robert Burns Country..... 150
   Side Trips: The Clyde Valley.... 158

4 THE BORDERS AND
   THE SOUTHWEST 163
   Orientation and Planning...... 165
   The Borders 169
   Dumfries and Galloway 186

5 FIFE AND ANGUS 201
   Orientation and Planning...... 203
   St. Andrews and Fife's East
   Neuk Villages 206
   Dundee and Angus.......... 218

6 THE CENTRAL HIGHLANDS... 233
   Orientation and Planning...... 235
   Stirling.................... 239
   The Trossachs and
   Loch Lomond 246
   Perthshire.................. 257

7 ABERDEEN AND THE
   NORTHEAST................ 269
   Orientation and Planning...... 271
   Aberdeen 275
   Royal Deeside and
   Castle Country 286
   The Northeast and the
   Malt Whisky Trail 299

8 ARGYLL AND THE ISLES...... 313
   Orientation and Planning...... 315
   Around Argyll 320
   Arran...................... 329
   Islay and Jura............... 334
   Isle of Mull and Iona 340
   The Smaller Islands 344

9 AROUND THE GREAT GLEN... 347
   Orientation and Planning...... 349
   Inverness and Environs 353
   Speyside and the Cairngorms .. 362
   Loch Ness and Toward
   the Small Isles 369

10 THE NORTHERN HIGHLANDS
AND THE WESTERN ISLES ... 379
  Orientation and Planning...... 381
  The Northern Landscapes 385
  Torridon.................... 397
  Isle of Skye................. 400
  The Outer Hebrides 409

11 ORKNEY AND SHETLAND
ISLANDS.................... 417
  Orientation and Planning...... 418
  Around Orkney.............. 423
  Around Shetland............ 432

12 A GOLFER'S COUNTRY....... 443

UNDERSTANDING
SCOTLAND................. 457
  Scotland at a Glance 458
  Books and Movies 460
  Chronology................. 464

TRAVEL SMART SCOTLAND... 471
  Getting Here and Around...... 472
  Essentials 482

INDEX...................... 499

ABOUT OUR WRITERS 512

MAPS

Edinburgh 38–39
Where to Eat and Stay
in Edinburgh.............. 62–63
West Lothian and the
Forth Valley.................. 88
Midlothian and East Lothian 95
Glasgow 108–109
Where to Eat and Stay
in Glasgow 124–125
Ayrshire and the Clyde Coast .. 152
Clyde Valley 159

The Borders and the
Southwest.................. 167
The Borders 172
Dumfries and Galloway 189
Fife and Angus 205
St. Andrews................. 209
Fife 214
Dundee..................... 220
Angus Area................. 225
The Central Highlands 237
Stirling.................... 240
The Trossachs and
Loch Lomond 247
Perthshire.................. 258
Aberdeen and the Northeast... 273
Aberdeen 277
Royal Deeside............... 288
The Northeast............... 301
Argyll and the Isles 317
Argyll and Arran............. 322
Islay and Jura............... 336
Iona, Mull, and the
Smaller Islands.............. 341
Around the Great Glen........ 351
Inverness and Environs 354
Speyside and the Cairngorms .. 363
Loch Ness and Toward
the Small Isles 371
The Northern Highlands
and the Western Isles 383
The Northern Highlands....... 386
Isle of Skye................. 400
The Outer Hebrides 410
The Orkney Islands........... 424
The Shetland Islands 433
Great Golf Courses....... 448–449

ABOUT THIS BOOK

Our Ratings

As travelers we've all discovered a place so wonderful that its worthiness is obvious. And sometimes that place is so unique that superlatives don't do it justice: you just have to be there to know. These sights, properties, and experiences get our highest rating, **Fodor's Choice,** indicated by orange stars throughout this book. Black stars highlight sights and properties we deem **Highly Recommended.** By default, there's another category: any place we include in this book is by definition worth your time, unless we say otherwise. And we will. Disagree with any of our choices? Care to nominate a place or suggest that we rate one more highly? Visit our feedback center at www.fodors.com/feedback.

For expanded hotel reviews, visit **Fodors.com**

Hotels

Hotels have private bath, phone, TV, and air-conditioning, and do not include meals in the rate unless specified. We always list facilities but not whether you'll be charged an extra fee to use them.

Restaurants

Unless we state otherwise, restaurants are open for lunch and dinner daily. We mention dress only when there's a specific requirement and reservations only when they're essential or not accepted—it's always best to book ahead.

Credit Cards

We assume that restaurants and hotels accept credit cards. If not, we'll note it in the review.

Budget Well

Hotel and restaurant price categories from ¢ to $$$$ are defined in the opening pages of the respective chapters. For attractions, we always give standard adult admission fees; reductions are usually available for children, students, and senior citizens.

Listings		Hotels & Restaurants	Outdoors
★ Fodor's Choice	✍ E-mail	🏨 Hotel	⛳ Golf
★ Highly recommended	🎟 Admission fee	🛏 Number of rooms	⛺ Camping
✉ Physical address	⊙ Open/closed times	🛁 Facilities	**Other**
✣ Directions or Map coordinates	Ⓜ Metro stations	⏸ Meal plans	♥ Family-friendly
🏤 Mailing address	▭ No credit cards	✕ Restaurant	⇨ See also
☎ Telephone		✎ Reservations	✉ Branch address
🖷 Fax		🏛 Dress code	☞ Take note
⊕ On the Web		↘ Smoking	

Experience Scotland

WORD OF MOUTH

"I think that objectively Scotland offers . . . a variety of scenery and spectacular nature. Add to that two great cities and you have a brilliant destination. Skye was magical and we will return for a much longer stay there. . . . Midges didn't affect us too often. The single-track roads were huge fun and for the most part empty of traffic. B&Bs were much better than we thought they were going to be."

—tjhome1

WHAT'S WHERE

Numbers refer to chapters.

2 Edinburgh and the Lothians. Scotland's captivating capital is the country's most popular city, famous for its high-perched castle, Old Town and 18th-century New Town, ultramodern Parliament building, and Georgian and Victorian architecture. Among the city's highlights are superb museums, including the newly refurbished National Museum of Scotland, and the most celebrated arts festival in the world, the International Festival. If Edinburgh's crowds are too much, escape to the Lothians and visit coastal towns, beaches, ancient chapels, and castles.

3 Glasgow. The country's largest city has evolved from prosperous Victorian hub to depressed urban center to thriving modern city with a strong artistic, architectural, and culinary reputation. Museums and galleries such as the Kelvingrove and Burrell are here, along with the Arts and Crafts architecture of Charles Rennie Mackintosh and iconic institutions such as Glasgow University. Glasgow is also the place to shop in Scotland.

4 The Borders and the Southwest. Scotland's southern gateway from England, the Borders, with its moors and gentle hills and river valleys, is rustic but historically rich. It's known for being the home of Sir Walter Scott, and has impressive stately homes such as Floors Castle and ruined abbeys including Melrose. The Southwest, or Dumfries and Galloway region, is perfect for scenic drives, castles, and hiking.

5 Fife and Angus. The "kingdom" of Fife is considered the sunniest and driest part of Scotland, with sandy beaches, fishing villages, and stone cottages. St. Andrews has its world-famous golf courses, but this university town is worth a stop even for nongolfers. To the north in Angus is Glamis Castle, the legendary setting of Shakespeare's *Macbeth*, as well as the reviving city of Dundee.

6 The Central Highlands. Convenient to both Edinburgh and Glasgow, this area encompasses some of Scotland's most beautiful terrain, with rugged, dark landscapes broken up by lochs and fields. Not to be missed is Loch Lomond and the Trossachs, Scotland's first national park. Perth and Stirling are the main metropolitan hubs and worth a stop; Stirling Castle has epic views that stretch from coast to coast.

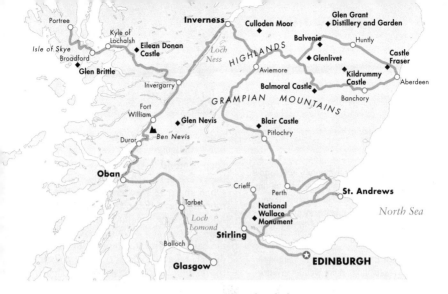

number of restaurants and entertainment venues.

Alternatives: Prefer whisky to castles? Explore distilleries both on and off the Malt Whisky Trail in Speyside, near Inverness. Balvenie, Glenlivet, and Glen Grant are good choices; check hours and tour times, and note that some distilleries require prebooking. Another option for the day is to visit Loch Ness, though it's not one of Scotland's prettiest lakes; still, perhaps you'll spot Nessie. It's a 20-minute drive from Inverness.

Logistics: A car is best for this part of your journey. Rent one in Inverness or sign up for an organized tour; public transportation is not a viable option. Castles are open seasonally, so many close in winter; check in advance. It's about two hours from Inverness to Kildrummy. Some sample distances are 30 mi (one hour) from Balmoral Castle to Kildrummy Castle; 20 mi (30 minutes) from Kildrummy Castle to Castle Fraser; and Castle Fraser to Balmoral, 40 mi (90 minutes). The distilleries are about 90 minutes from Inverness. Some distances between distilleries are 18 mi (50 minutes) from Balvenie to Glenlivet; 17 mi (30 minutes) from Glenlivet to Glen Grant; and 13 mi (30 minutes) from Glen Grant to Glenfiddich.

The Isle of Skye

Day 6. Leave Inverness early and head south to Skye. The drive to the island is peaceful, full of raw landscapes and big, open horizons. Stop at Eilean Donan Castle on the way; go in, walk around, and take a few photos. This castle set on an island among three lochs is the stuff postcards are made of. Explore Skye; Glen Brittle is the perfect place to enjoy mountain scenery, and Armadale is a good place to go crafts shopping. End up in Portree for dinner and the night.

Logistics: It's 80 mi (a two-hour drive) from Inverness to Skye. Public transportation is possible but connections can take time, so it's best to have the freedom of a car.

Oban via Ben Nevis

Day 7. Leave Skye no later than 9 am and head for Fort William. The town isn't worth stopping for, but the view of Britain's highest mountain, the 4,406-foot Ben Nevis, is. If time permits, take a hike in Glen Nevis. Continue on to Oban, a traditional Scottish resort town on the water. Outside Oban, stop by the Scottish Sealife Sanctuary. At night, feast on fish-and-chips in a local pub.

Logistics: It's nearly 100 mi from Skye to Oban; the drive is 3½ hours without stop-

TIPS

■ You can begin this itinerary in Glasgow and finish in Edinburgh, or adjust the timing to your interests. For example, if you enjoy castles, you might stay in Inverness longer; if you like golf, St. Andrews may deserve more time.

■ August is festival season in Edinburgh; make reservations there well in advance during that month.

■ Remember to drive on the left side of the road and keep alert, especially on small, narrow country roads. Travel will take longer on smaller roads.

■ Weather is unpredictable; always dress in layers. Hikers should carry a cell phone and tell someone where they're going. Golfers and everyone else should carry rain gear.

■ Pack bug repellent for the midges (small, biting insects that travel in swarms). These insects breed in stagnant water, but they are *everywhere* from May through September.

■ Check distillery tour times and book arrangements in advance. When visiting distilleries, choose a designated driver or take a bus tour. Drunken drivers aren't tolerated.

ping. Public transportation is an option but a challenging one.

Loch Lomond to Glasgow

Days 8 and 9. Enjoy a leisurely morning in Oban and take a waterfront stroll. Mid-morning, set off for Glasgow via Loch Lomond. Stop in Balloch on the loch for fresh oysters and a walk along the bonnie banks. Arrive in Glasgow in time for dinner; take in a play or concert. Spend the next day and night visiting the sights: Kelvingrove Art Gallery and Museum, Charles Rennie Mackintosh's Glasgow School of Art, and the new Riverside Museum are a few highlights.

Logistics: It's 127 mi (a three-hour drive) from Oban to Glasgow via Balloch. Traveling by train is a possibility, but you won't be able to go via Balloch. Return your rental car in Glasgow; it's easy to travel around the city by foot, subway, or train.

Glasgow and Home

Day 10. On your final day, leave your suitcases at your hotel and hit Buchanan and Sauchiehall Streets for some of Britain's best shopping. Clothes, whisky, and tartan items are good things to look for.

Logistics: It's less than 10 mi (15 minutes) by taxi to Glasgow's international airport in Paisley but more than 30 mi (40 minutes) to the international airport in Prestwick. Be sure you have the correct airport information.

PARLIAMENT AND POWER

Three centuries after the Union of Parliaments with England in 1707, Edinburgh is once again the seat of a Scottish parliament. A new parliament building, designed by the late Spanish architect Enric Miralles, stands adjacent to the Palace of Holyroodhouse, at the foot of the Royal Mile.

The first-time visitor to Scotland may be surprised that the country still has a capital city at all, perhaps believing the seat of government was drained of its resources and power after the union with England—but far from it. The Union of Parliaments brought with it a set of political partnerships—such as separate legal, ecclesiastical, and educational systems—that Edinburgh assimilated and integrated with its own surviving institutions.

Scotland now has significantly more control over its own affairs than at any time since 1707, and the 129 Members of the Scottish Parliament (MSPs), of whom 40% are women, have extensive powers in Scotland over education, health, housing, transportation, training, economic development, the environment, and agriculture. Foreign policy, defense, and economic policy, remain under the jurisdiction of the U.K. government in London. First Minister Alex Salmond, however, hopes to have a referendum in 2014 on independence.

to move your car by 8 the following morning, when the rush hour gets under way. Parking lots are clearly signposted; overnight parking is expensive and not always permitted.

TAXI TRAVEL
Taxi stands can be found throughout the downtown area. The following are the most convenient: the west end of Princes Street; South St. David Street and North St. Andrew Street (both just off St. Andrew Square); Princes Mall; Waterloo Place; and Lauriston Place. Alternatively, hail any taxi displaying an illuminated "for hire" sign.

TRAIN TRAVEL
Edinburgh's main train hub, Waverley Station, is downtown, below Waverley Bridge and around the corner from the unmistakable spire of the Scott Monument. Travel time from Edinburgh to London by train is as little as 4½ hours for the fastest service.

Edinburgh's other main station is Haymarket, about four minutes (by rail) west of Waverley. Most Glasgow and other western and northern services stop here. Haymarket can be more convenient if you're staying in hotels beyond the west end of Princes Street.

Train Contacts National Rail Enquiries ☏ *08457/484950* ⊕ *www.nationalrail. co.uk.* **ScotRail** ☏ *0845/601–5929* ⊕ *www.scotrail.co.uk.*

TRAM TRAVEL
Gone since 1956, trams are set to return to the streets of Edinburgh. They were slated to debut in 2012, but huge delays and cost overruns have slowed things down. At the time of this writing, the forecast for completion was 2014.

Supporters hope that the network, which will be integrated with buses, will finally provide the city with a world-class public transport system.

Tram Contact Edinburgh Trams ☎ *0800/328–3934* ⊕ *www.edinburghtrams. co.uk.*

TOURS

ORIENTATION TOURS

The best way to get oriented in Edinburgh is to take a bus tour, most of which are operated by Lothian Buses. Its "City Sightseeing" open-top bus tours (£9) include multilingual commentary; its "MacTours" (£12) are conducted in vintage open-top vehicles. All tours take you to the main attractions, including Edinburgh Castle, the Royal Mile, Palace of Holyroodhouse, and museums and galleries. Buses depart from Waverley Bridge, and are hop-on/hop-off services, with tickets lasting 24 hours. Lothian Buses' 60-minute Majestic Tour (£12) operates with a professional guide and takes you from Waverly Bridge to the New Town, past Charlotte Square, the Royal Botanic Garden, and Newhaven Heritage Museum until it reaches the royal yacht *Britannia* moored at Leith. Tickets for all tours are available from ticket sellers on Waverley Bridge or on the buses themselves.

If you want to get to know the area around Edinburgh, Rabbie's Trail Burners leads small groups on several different excursions, including a one-day trip to Rosslyn Chapel.

Orientation Tours Contacts Lothian Buses ☎ *0131/220–0770* ⊕ *www. edinburghtour.com.* **Rabbie's Trail Burners** ✉ *207 High St.* ☎ *0131/226–3133* ⊕ *www.rabbies.com.*

PERSONAL GUIDES

Scottish Tourist Guides can supply guides (in 19 languages) who are fully qualified and will meet clients at any point of entry into the United Kingdom or Scotland. They can also tailor tours to your interests.

Personal Guide Contacts Scottish Tourist Guides ✉ *18b Broad St., Stirling* ☎ *01786/451953* ⊕ *www.stga.co.uk.*

WALKING TOURS

Cadies and Witchery Tours, a member of the Scottish Tourist Guides Association, has built a reputation for combining entertainment and historical accuracy in its lively and enthusiastic Ghosts & Gore Tour and Murder & Mystery Tour (£7.50 each), which take you through the narrow Old Town alleyways and closes. Costumed guides and other theatrical characters show up en route. The Scottish Literary Tour Company takes you around Edinburgh's Old Town or New Town (£10 each), with guides invoking Scottish literary characters.

Walking Tour Contacts Cadies and Witchery Tours ✉ *84 West Bow* ☎ *0131/225–6745* ⊕ *www.witcherytours.com.* **Scottish Literary Tour Trust** ✉ *5 Wellington Pl.* ☎ *0131/226–6665* ⊕ *www.edinburghliterarypubtour.co.uk.*

VISITOR INFORMATION

The Edinburgh and Scotland Information Centre, next to Waverley Station (follow the "tic" signs in the station and throughout the city), offers an accommodations-booking service in addition to the more typical services. Complete information is also available at the information desk at the Edinburgh Airport. Information centers also sell the Edinburgh Pass, www.edinburgh.com, which offers sightseeing and other discounts.

Visitor Info Edinburgh and Scotland Information Centre ✉ *3 Princes St., East End* ☎ *08452/255121* ⊕ *www.edinburgh.org.*

2

EXPLORING EDINBURGH

Edinburgh's Old Town, which bears a great measure of symbolic weight as the "heart of Scotland's capital," is a boon for lovers of atmosphere and history. In contrast, if you appreciate the unique architectural heritage of the city's Enlightenment, then the New Town's for you. If you belong to both categories, don't worry—the Old and New towns are only yards apart. Princes Street runs east–west along the north edge of the Princes Street Gardens. Explore the main thoroughfares but don't forget to get lost among the tiny *wynds* and *closes*: old medieval alleys that connect the winding streets.

Like most cities, Edinburgh incorporates small communities within its boundaries, and many of these are as rewarding to explore as Old Town and New Town. Dean Village, for instance, even though it's close to the New Town, has a character all of its own. Duddingston, just southeast of Arthur's Seat, has all the feel of a country village. Then there's Corstorphine, to the west of the city center, famous for being the site of Murrayfield, Scotland's international rugby stadium. Edinburgh's port, Leith, sits on the shore of the Firth of Forth, and throbs with smart bars and restaurants.

OLD TOWN

East of Edinburgh Castle, the historic castle esplanade becomes the street known as the Royal Mile, leading from the castle down through Old Town to the Palace of Holyroodhouse. The Mile, as it's called, is actually made up of one thoroughfare that bears, in consecutive sequence, different names—Castlehill, Lawnmarket, Parliament Square, High Street, and Canongate. The streets and passages winding into their tenements, or "lands," and crammed onto the ridge in back of the Mile really *were* Edinburgh until the 18th century saw expansions to the south and north. Everybody lived here, the richer folk on the lower floors of houses, with less well-to-do families on the middle floors—the higher up, the poorer.

Time and progress (of a sort) have swept away some of the narrow closes and tall tenements of the Old Town, but enough survive for you to be able to imagine the original profile of Scotland's capital. There are many guided tours of the area, or you can walk around on your own. The latter is often a better choice in summer when tourists pack the area and large guided groups have trouble making their way through the crowds.

TIMING An exploration of the Old Town could be accomplished in a day, but to give the major sights—Edinburgh Castle, the Palace of Holyroodhouse, and the National Museum of Scotland—their due, you should allow more time. ■TIP➔ **Don't forget that some attractions have special hours during the Edinburgh International Festival. If you want to see something special, check the hours ahead of time.**

TOP ATTRACTIONS

☚ **Edinburgh Castle.** The crowning glory of the Scottish capital, Edinburgh Castle is popular not only because it's the symbolic heart of Scotland but also because of the views from its battlements: on a clear day the vistas—stretching to the "kingdom" of Fife—are breathtaking. ■TIP➔ **There's so much to see that you need at least three hours to do the site justice, especially if you're interested in military sites.**

Fodor's Choice ★

You enter across the **Esplanade,** the huge forecourt built in the 18th century as a parade ground. The area comes alive with color and music each August when it's used for the Military Tattoo, a festival of magnificently outfitted marching bands and regiments. Heading over the drawbridge and through the gatehouse, past the guards, you can find the rough stone walls of the **Half-Moon Battery,** where the 1 o'clock gun is fired every day in an impressively anachronistic ceremony; these curving ramparts give Edinburgh Castle its distinctive appearance from miles away. Climb up through a second gateway and you come to the oldest surviving building in the complex, the tiny 11th-century **St. Margaret's Chapel,** named in honor of Saxon queen Margaret (1046–93), who had persuaded her husband, King Malcolm III (circa 1031–93), to move his court from Dunfermline to Edinburgh. Edinburgh's environs—the Lothians—were occupied by Anglian settlers with whom the queen felt more at home, or so the story goes (Dunfermline was surrounded by Celts). The **Crown Room,** a must-see, contains the "Honours of Scotland"—the crown, scepter, and sword that once graced the Scottish monarch. Upon the **Stone of Scone,** also in the Crown Room, Scottish monarchs once sat to be crowned. In the section now called **Queen Mary's Apartments,** Mary, Queen of Scots, gave birth to James VI of Scotland. The **Great Hall** displays arms and armor under an impressive vaulted, beamed ceiling. Scottish parliament meetings were conducted here until 1840.

Military features of interest include the **Scottish National War Memorial,** the **Scottish United Services Museum,** and the famous 15th-century Belgian-made cannon *Mons Meg.* This enormous piece of artillery has been silent since 1682, when it exploded while firing a salute for the duke of York; it now stands in an ancient hall behind the Half-Moon Battery. Contrary to what you may hear from locals, it's not *Mons Meg*

Edinburgh's Castle Fit for a King

Archaeological investigations have established that the rock on which Edinburgh Castle stands was inhabited as far back as 1000 BC, in the latter part of the Bronze Age. There have been fortifications here since the mysterious people called the Picts first used it as a stronghold in the 3rd and 4th centuries AD. Anglian invaders from northern England dislodged the Picts in AD 452, and for the next 1,300 years the site saw countless battles and skirmishes.

In the castle you'll hear the story of how Randolph, Earl of Moray and nephew of freedom fighter Robert the Bruce, scaled the heights one dark night in 1313, surprised the English guard, and recaptured the castle for the Scots. During this battle he destroyed every one of the castle's buildings except for St. Margaret's Chapel, dating from around 1076, so that successive Stewart kings had to rebuild the castle bit by bit.

The castle has been held over time by Scots and Englishmen, Catholics and Protestants, soldiers and royalty. In the 16th century Mary, Queen of Scots, gave birth here to the future James VI of Scotland (1566–1625), who was also to rule England as James I. In 1573 it was the last fortress to support Mary's claim as the rightful Catholic queen of Britain, causing the castle to be virtually destroyed by English artillery fire.

but the battery's gun that goes off with a bang every weekday at 1 pm, frightening visitors and reminding Edinburghers to check their watches. ✉ *Castle Esplanade and Castlehill, Old Town* ☎ *0131/225–9846 Edinburgh Castle, 0131/226–7393 War Memorial* ⊕ *www.edinburghcastle. gov.uk* ✆ *£14* ⊙ *Apr.–Sept., daily 9:30–6; Oct.–Mar., daily 9:30–5; last entry 45 mins before closing.*

NEED A BREAK?

Red Coat Café. You can have lunch or afternoon tea with panoramic views of the city at the Red Coat Café. Cakes, sandwiches, soups, and drinks are all available at reasonable prices. ✉ *Edinburgh Castle, Castlehill, Old Town* ☎ *0131/225–9746.*

High Kirk of St. Giles. Sometimes called St. Giles's Cathedral, this is one of the city's principal churches. However, anyone expecting a rival to Paris's Notre Dame or London's Westminster Abbey will be disappointed: St. Giles is more like a large parish church than a great European cathedral. There has been a church here since AD 854, although most of the present structure dates from either 1120 or 1829, when the church was restored. The tower, with its stone crown towering 161 feet above the ground, was completed between 1495 and 1500. The most elaborate feature is the **Chapel of the Order of the Thistle,** built onto the southeast corner of the church in 1911 for the exclusive use of Scotland's only chivalric order, the Most Ancient and Noble Order of the Thistle. It bears the belligerent national motto "nemo me impune lacessit" ("No one provokes me with impunity"). Inside the church stands a life-size statue of the Scot whose spirit still dominates the

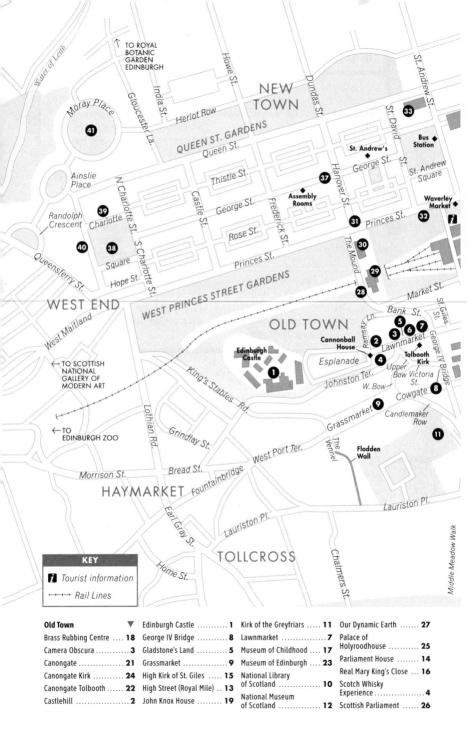

TO ROYAL
BOTANIC
GARDEN
EDINBURGH

Water of Leith

Moray Place

41

Gloucester La.

India St.

Howe St.

Heriot Row

Dundas St.

St. Andrew St.

**NEW
TOWN**

QUEEN ST. GARDENS

Queen St.

33

Bus
Station ◆

Ainslie
Place

N. Charlotte St.

Thistle St.

George St.

St. Andrew's

St. David St.

St. Andrew
Square

Randolph
Crescent

39

Charlotte

Castle St.

George St.

Frederick St.

Assembly
Rooms

Hanover St.

37

Princes St.

Waverley
Market

32

ℹ

40

38

Square

S. Charlotte St.

Rose St.

31

Queensferry St.

Hope St.

Princes St.

30

The Mound

29

WEST END

WEST PRINCES STREET GARDENS

28

Market St.

West Maitland

Bank St.

OLD TOWN

Ramsay Ln.

5

St. Giles St.

2

Cannonball
House

3 **6** **7**

Lawnmarket

George IV Bridge

TO SCOTTISH
NATIONAL
GALLERY OF
MODERN ART

Edinburgh
Castle

1

Esplanade

Johnston Ter.

4

Tolbooth
Kirk

Upper
Bow Victoria
St.

King's Stables Rd.

W. Bow

8

TO
EDINBURGH ZOO

Lothian Rd.

Grindlay St.

Cowgate

9

Grassmarket

Candlemaker
Row

11

Bread St.

West Port Ter.

The Vennel

Flodden
Wall

Morrison St.

Fountainbridge

HAYMARKET

Lauriston Pl.

Earl Gray St.

Lauriston Pl.

Middle Meadow Walk

TOLLCROSS

Home St.

Chalmers St.

KEY

ℹ *Tourist information*

┝━━━┿ *Rail Lines*

Old Town   ▼

Brass Rubbing Centre **18**

Camera Obscura **3**

Canongate **21**

Canongate Kirk **24**

Canongate Tolbooth **22**

Castlehill **2**

Edinburgh Castle **1**

George IV Bridge **8**

Gladstone's Land **5**

Grassmarket **9**

High Kirk of St. Giles ... **15**

High Street (Royal Mile) .. **13**

John Knox House **19**

Kirk of the Greyfriars **11**

Lawnmarket **7**

Museum of Childhood **17**

Museum of Edinburgh ... **23**

National Library
of Scotland **10**

National Museum
of Scotland **12**

Our Dynamic Earth **27**

Palace of
Holyroodhouse **25**

Parliament House **14**

Real Mary King's Close .. **16**

Scotch Whisky
Experience **4**

Scottish Parliament **26**

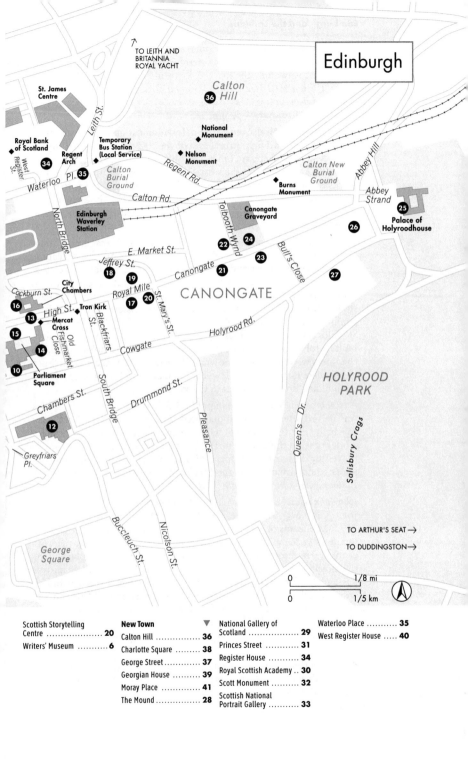

Edinburgh

TO LEITH AND
BRITANNIA
ROYAL YACHT

St. James Centre

Royal Bank of Scotland

Calton Hill **36**

National Monument

Regent Arch

Temporary Bus Station (Local Service)

Nelson Monument

West Register St.

34

Regent Rd.

Calton Burial Ground

Calton New Burial Ground

Abbey Hill

Waterloo Pl. **35**

Calton Rd.

Burns Monument

Abbey Strand

Palace of Holyroodhouse **25**

North Bridge

Edinburgh Waverley Station

Tolbooth Wynd

Canongate Graveyard

26

E. Market St.

22 **24**

Jeffrey St.

Canongate **21** **23**

Bull's Close

27

18 **19**

City Chambers

Cockburn St.

Royal Mile

CANONGATE

16

High St.

Tron Kirk

17 **20**

St. Mary's St.

13

Mercat Cross

Blackfriars St.

Holyrood Rd.

15

Old Fishmarket Close

14

Cowgate

10

Parliament Square

Chambers St.

South Bridge

Drummond St.

Pleasance

HOLYROOD PARK

12

Queen's Dr.

Salisbury Crags

Greyfriars Pl.

George Square

Buccleuch St.

Nicolson St.

TO ARTHUR'S SEAT →

TO DUDDINGSTON →

0   1/8 mi
0   1/5 km

Scottish Storytelling Centre **20**

Writers' Museum **6**

New Town

Calton Hill **36**

Charlotte Square **38**

George Street **37**

Georgian House **39**

Moray Place **41**

The Mound **28**

National Gallery of Scotland **29**

Princes Street **31**

Register House **34**

Royal Scottish Academy .. **30**

Scott Monument **32**

Scottish National Portrait Gallery **33**

Waterloo Place **35**

West Register House **40**

place—the great religious reformer and preacher John Knox, before whose zeal all of Scotland once trembled. The church lies about one-third of the way along the Royal Mile from Edinburgh Castle. ✉ *High St., Old Town* ☎ *0131/225–9442* ⊕ *www.stgilescathedral.org.uk* 🎟 *£3 suggested donation* ⊙ *May–Sept., weekdays 9–7, Sat. 9–5, Sun. 1–5; Oct.–Apr., Mon.–Sat. 9–5, Sun. 1–5.*

High Street (Royal Mile). Some of Old Town's most impressive buildings and sights are on High Street, one of the five streets making up the Royal Mile. Also here are other, less obvious historic relics. Near Parliament Square, look on the west side for a **heart** set in cobbles. This marks the site of the vanished Tolbooth, the center of city life from the 15th century until the building's demolition in 1817. The ancient civic edifice housed the Scottish parliament and was used as a prison—it also inspired Sir Walter Scott's novel *The Heart of Midlothian.*

Just outside Parliament House is the **Mercat Cross** (*mercat* means "market"), a great landmark of Old Town life. It was an old mercantile center, where in the early days executions were held, and where royal proclamations were—and are still—read. Most of the present cross is comparatively modern, dating from the time of William Ewart Gladstone (1809–98), the great Victorian prime minister and rival of Benjamin Disraeli (1804–81). Across High Street from the High Kirk of St. Giles stands the **City Chambers,** now the seat of local government. Built by John Fergus, who adapted a design of John Adam's in 1753, the chambers were originally known as the Royal Exchange and intended to be where merchants and lawyers could conduct business. Note how the building drops 11 stories to Cockburn Street on its north side.

A *tron* is a weigh beam used in public weigh houses, and the **Tron Kirk** was named after a salt tron that used to stand nearby. The kirk itself was built after 1633, when St. Giles's became an Episcopal cathedral for a brief time. In this church in 1693, a minister offered an often-quoted prayer for the local government: "Lord, hae mercy on a' [all] fools and idiots, and particularly on the Magistrates of Edinburgh." ✉ *Between Lawnmarket and Canongate, Old Town.*

John Knox House. It's not certain that Scotland's severe religious reformer John Knox ever lived here, but there's evidence that he died here in 1572. Mementos of his life are on view inside, and the distinctive dwelling gives you a glimpse of what Old Town life was like in the 16th century. The projecting upper stories were once commonplace along the Royal Mile, darkening and further closing in the already narrow passage. Look for the initials of former owner James Mossman and his wife, carved into the stonework on the marriage lintel. Mossman was goldsmith to Mary, Queen of Scots, and was hanged in 1573 for his allegiance to her. ✉ *45 High St., Old Town* ☎ *0131/556–9579* ⊕ *www. scottishstorytellingcentre.co.uk* 🎟 *£4.25* ⊙ *Mon.–Sat. 10–6; last admission ½ hr before closing.*

Kirk of the Greyfriars. Greyfriars Church, built circa 1620 on the site of a medieval monastery, was where the National Covenant, declaring that the Presbyterian Church in Scotland was independent of the monarch and not Episcopalian in government, was signed in 1638. The

THE BUILDING OF EDINBURGH

Towering over the city, Edinburgh Castle was actually built over the plug of an ancient volcano. Many thousands of years ago, an eastward-grinding glacier encountered the tough basalt core of the volcano and swept around it, scouring steep cliffs and leaving a trail of matter. This material formed a ramp gently leading down from the rocky summit. On this *crag* and *tail* would grow the city of Edinburgh and its castle.

CASTLE, WALLED TOWN, AND HOLYROODHOUSE

By the 12th century Edinburgh had become a walled town, still perched on the hill. Its shape was becoming clearer: like a fish with its head at the castle, its backbone running down the ridge, and its ribs leading briefly off on either side. The backbone gradually became the continuous thoroughfare now known as the Royal Mile, and the ribs became the closes (alleyways), some still surviving, that were the scene of many historic incidents.

By the early 15th century Edinburgh had become the undisputed capital of Scotland. The bitter defeat of Scotland at Flodden in 1513, when Scotland aligned itself with France against England, caused a new defensive city wall to be built. Though the castle escaped destruction, the city was burned by the English earl of Hertford under orders from King Henry VIII (1491–1547) of England. This was during a time known as the "Rough Wooing," when Henry was trying to coerce the Scots into allowing the young Mary, Queen of Scots (1542–87) to marry his son Edward. The plan failed and

Mary married Francis, the Dauphin of France.

By 1561, when Mary returned from France already widowed, the guesthouse of the Abbey of Holyrood had grown to become the Palace of Holyroodhouse, replacing Edinburgh Castle as the main royal residence. Mary's legacy to the city included the destruction of most of the earliest buildings of Edinburgh Castle; she was eventually executed by Elizabeth I.

ENLIGHTENMENT AND THE CITY

In the trying decades after the union with England in 1707, many influential Scots, both in Edinburgh and elsewhere, went through an identity crisis. Out of the 18th-century difficulties, however, grew the Scottish Enlightenment, during which educated Scots made great strides in medicine, economics, and science.

Changes came to the cityscape, too. By the mid-18th century it had become the custom for wealthy Scottish landowners to spend the winter in the Old Town of Edinburgh, in town houses huddled between the high Castle Rock and the Royal Palace below. Cross-fertilized in coffeehouses and taverns, intellectual notions flourished among a people determined to remain Scottish despite their parliament's having voted to dissolve itself. One result was a campaign to expand and beautify the city, to give it a look worthy of its future nickname, the Athens of the North. Thus was the New Town of Edinburgh built, with broad streets and gracious buildings creating a harmony that even today's throbbing traffic cannot obscure.

2

covenant plunged Scotland into decades of civil war. Informative panels tell the story, and there's a visitor center on-site. Be sure to search out the graveyard—one of the most evocative in Europe. Its old, tottering, elaborate tombstones mark the graves of some of Scotland's most respected heroes and despised villains. Nearby, at the corner of George IV Bridge and Candlemaker Row, stands one of the most photographed sites in Scotland, the Greyfriars Bobby statue. ⌧ *Greyfriars Pl., Old Town* ☎ *0131/225–1900* ⊕ *www.greyfriarskirk.com* ⌧ *Free* ⊗ *Easter–Oct., weekdays 10:30–4:30, Sat. 11–2; Nov.–Easter, Thurs. 1:30–3:30.*

ⓒ **National Museum of Scotland.** This museum traces the country's fascinating story from the oldest fossils to the most recent popular culture, making it a must-see for first-time visitors to Scotland or anyone interested in history. One of the most famous treasures is the Lewis Chessmen, 11 intricately carved ivory chess pieces found in the 19th century on one of Scotland's Western Isles: other pieces are in London's British Museum. An extensive renovation in 2011 freed up space in the basement, creating a dramatic, cryptlike entrance. Visitors now rise to the light-filled, birdcage wonders of the Victorian grand hall and the upper galleries in glass elevators. Highlights include the hanging hippo and sea creatures of the Wildlife Panorama, a life-size skeleton cast of a Tyrannosaurus rex, Viking brooches, Pictish stones, Jacobite relics, the Stevenson family's inventions, including lighthouse optics, and Queen Mary's *clarsach* (harp). All this is free, but donations are welcomed to help renovate 11 other galleries. ⌧ *Chambers St., Old Town* ☎ *0131/225–7534* ⊕ *www.nms.ac.uk* ⌧ *Free* ⊗ *Daily 10–5.*

Fodor's Choice

★

ⓒ **Our Dynamic Earth.** Using state-of-the-art technology, the 11 theme galleries at this interactive science gallery educate and entertain as they explore the wonders of the planet, from polar regions to tropical rain forests. Geological history, from the big bang to the unknown future, is also examined. ⌧ *Holyrood Rd., Old Town* ☎ *0131/550–7800* ⊕ *www.dynamicearth.co.uk* ⌧ *£10.80* ⊗ *Apr.–June, Sept., and Oct., daily 10–5:30; July and Aug., daily 10–6; Nov.–Mar., Wed.–Sun. 10–5:30; last admission 90 mins before closing.*

★ **Palace of Holyroodhouse.** Once the haunt of Mary, Queen of Scots, and the setting for high drama—including at least one notorious murder, several major fires, and centuries of the colorful lifestyles of larger-than-life, power-hungry personalities—this is now Queen Elizabeth's official residence in Scotland. A doughty and impressive palace standing at the foot of the Royal Mile in a hilly public park, it's built around a graceful, lawned central court at the end of Canongate. When the queen or royal family is not in residence you can tour it. The free audio guide is excellent.

Many monarchs, including Charles II, Queen Victoria, and George V, have left their mark on its rooms, but it's Mary, Queen of Scots, whose spirit looms largest. For some visitors, the most memorable room here is the little chamber in which David Rizzio (1533–66), secretary to Mary, Queen of Scots, met an unhappy end in 1566. In part because Rizzio was hated at court for his social-climbing ways, Mary's second husband, Lord Darnley (Henry Stewart, 1545–65), burst into the queen's rooms with his henchmen, dragged Rizzio into an antechamber, and stabbed him more than 50 times; a bronze plaque marks the spot. Darnley himself was murdered the next year, which made way for the queen's marriage to her lover, the Earl of Bothwell.

■ TIP→ **There's plenty to see here, so make sure you have at least two hours to tour the palace, gardens (in summer), and the ruins of the 12th-century abbey.** The **King James Tower** is the oldest surviving section, containing the rooms of Mary, Queen of Scots, on the second floor, and Lord Darnley's rooms below. Though much has been altered, there are fine fireplaces, paneling, plasterwork, tapestries, and 18th- and 19th-century furnishings throughout. At the south end of the palace front you can find the **Royal Dining Room,** and along the south side are the **Throne Room** and other drawing rooms now used for social and ceremonial occasions.

At the back of the palace is the **King's Bedchamber.** The 150-foot-long **Great Picture Gallery,** on the north side, displays the portraits of 110 Scottish monarchs. These were commissioned by Charles II, who was eager to demonstrate his Scottish ancestry—some of the royal figures here are fictional and the likenesses of others imaginary. All the portraits were painted by a Dutch artist, Jacob de Witt, who signed a contract in 1684 with the queen's cash keeper, Hugh Wallace. The contract bound him to deliver 110 pictures within two years, for which he received an annual stipend of £120.

The Queen's Gallery, in a former church and school at the entrance to the palace, holds rotating exhibits from the Royal Collection. There is a separate admission charge.

Holyroodhouse has its origins in an Augustinian monastery founded by David I (1084–1153) in 1128. In the 15th and 16th centuries, Scottish royalty, preferring the comforts of the abbey to the drafty rooms of Edinburgh Castle, settled into Holyroodhouse, expanding and altering the buildings until the palace eventually eclipsed the monastery. You can still walk around some ruins though.

After the Union of the Crowns in 1603, when the Scottish royal court packed its bags and decamped for England, the building fell into decline. It was Charles II (1630–85) who rebuilt Holyrood in the architectural style of Louis XIV (1638–1715), and this is the style you see today.

In 1688 an anti-Catholic faction ran riot within the palace, and in 1745, during the last Jacobite campaign, Charles Edward Stuart occupied the palace, followed a short while later by the duke of Cumberland, who defeated Charles at Culloden. After the 1822 visit of King George IV (1762–1830), at a more peaceable time, the palace sank into decline once again. But Queen Victoria (1819–1901) and her grandson King George V (1865–1936) renewed interest in the palace: the buildings were once more refurbished and made suitable for royal residence. Behind the palace lie the open grounds and looming crags of Holyrood Park, the hunting ground of early Scottish kings. From the top of Edinburgh's mini mountain, **Arthur's Seat** (822 feet), views are breathtaking. ✉ *Abbey Strand, Old Town* ☎ *0131/556–5100* ⊕ *www.royalcollection. org.uk* 🖾 *£10.75, £6 Queen's Gallery, £15.10 joint ticket* ☉ *Apr.–Oct.,* *daily 9:30–6; Nov.–Mar., daily 9:30–4:30; last admission 1 hr before closing. Closed during royal visits.*

⟳ **Real Mary King's Close.** Hidden beneath the City Chambers, this nar-
★ row, cobbled *close*, or lane, named after a former landowner, is said
to be one of Edinburgh's most haunted sites. The close was sealed off
in 1645 to quarantine residents who became sick when the bubonic
plague swept through the city, and many victims were herded there
to die. After the plague passed, the bodies were removed and buried,
and the street was reopened. A few people returned, but they soon
reported ghostly goings-on and departed, leaving the close empty for
decades. In 1753 city authorities built the Royal Exchange (later the
City Chambers) directly over the close, sealing it off and, unwittingly,
ensuring it remained intact, except for the buildings' upper stories,
which were destroyed. Today you can walk among the remains of the
shops and houses. People still report ghostly visions and eerie sounds,
such as the crying of a young girl. Over the years visitors have left small
offerings for her, such as dolls, pieces of ribbon, or candy. ■ **TIP➜ Although kids like the spookiness of this attraction, it's not for the youngest
ones. In fact, children under age five are not admitted.** ✉ *Writers' Court,
Old Town* ☎ *0845/070–6244* ⊕ *www.realmarykingsclose.com* 💷 *£12*
⊙ *Apr.–Oct., daily 10–9; Aug., daily 9–9; Nov.–Mar., weekdays 10–5,
weekends 10–9.*

**NEED A
BREAK?**

Always Sunday. In a white-walled, light-filled space near the cathedral
and opposite the City Chambers, Always Sunday offers fresh, flavorful fare,
including great breakfasts (salmon and eggs), lunches (hearty soups, meat
pies, salads), and cakes and coffee or tea. It's open daily until 6. ✉ *170 High
St., Old Town* ☎ *0131/622–0667.*

★ **Scottish Parliament.** Scotland's somewhat controversial Parliament building is dramatically modern, with irregular curves and angles that mirror the twisting shapes of the surrounding landscape. The structure's
artistry is most apparent when you step inside, where the gentle slopes,
forest's worth of oak, polished concrete and granite, walls of glass,
water features, and subtle imagery create an understated magnificence.
It's worth taking a free tour to see the main hall and debating chamber,
a committee room, and other areas. Call ahead for the tour schedule,
as it changes frequently. Another option is to call well in advance to
get a free ticket to view Parliament in action. Originally conceived by
the late Catalan architect Enric Miralles, who often said the building was "growing out of the ground," the design was completed by
his widow, Benedetta Tagliabue, in August 2004. ✉ *Horse Wynd, Old
Town* ☎ *0131/348–5200* ⊕ *www.scottish.parliament.uk* 💷 *Free* ⊙ *Public areas Mon.–Sat. 10–5:30.*

WORTH NOTING

⟳ **Brass Rubbing Centre.** No experience is necessary for you to make your
own souvenirs of Scotland at this center. You can explore the past by
creating do-it-yourself replicas (£2 to £6) from original Pictish stones
and markers, rare Scottish brasses, and medieval church brasses, or you
can buy them in the shop for anywhere between £2 and £20. All the

A GOOD WALK IN THE OLD TOWN

A perfect place to start your stroll through the Old Town is Edinburgh Castle. After exploring its extensive complex of buildings and admiring the view from the battlements, set off down the first part of the Royal Mile. The Camera Obscura's Outlook Tower affords more splendid views of the city. The six-story tenement known as Gladstone's Land, a survivor of 16th-century domestic life, is on the left as you head east. Near Gladstone's Land, down another close, stands the Writers' Museum, in a fine example of 17th-century urban architecture called Lady Stair's House. Farther down on the right are the Tolbooth Kirk (a *tolbooth* was a town hall or prison, and *kirk* means "church") and Upper Bow.

Turn right down George IV Bridge to reach the historic Grassmarket, where parts of the old city walls still stand. Turn left up Candlemaker Row and you can see the Kirk of the Greyfriars, and the little statue of faithful Greyfriars Bobby. On Chambers Street, at the foot of George IV Bridge, are the impressive galleries of the National Museum of Scotland.

Returning to the junction of George IV Bridge with the Royal Mile, turn right (east) down High Street to visit the old Parliament House; the High Kirk of St. Giles; the Mercat Cross; and the elegant City Chambers, bringing a flavor of the New Town's neoclassicism to the Old Town's severity. Beneath the chambers is the eerie Real Mary King's Close, a lane that was closed off in the 17th century when the bubonic plague struck the city.

A short distance down Canongate on the left is Canongate Tolbooth. The Museum of Edinburgh stands opposite, and the Canongate Kirk and Acheson House are nearby. This walk draws to a close, as it started, on a high note, at the Palace of Holyroodhouse, full of historic and architectural interest and some fine paintings, tapestries, and furnishings to admire, in Holyrood Park.

TIMING

This walk can expand greatly in length depending on how often you stop to explore different sights, so plan accordingly. You can walk the Royal Mile in an hour, take a day to stop and visit points of interest, or even spend a couple of days exploring the area.

materials are here, and children find the pastime quite absorbing. The center occupies the surviving piece of a Gothic church down a close opposite the Museum of Childhood. ⊠ *Trinity Apse, Chalmers Close, Old Town* ☎ *0131/556–4364* ⊕ *www.cac.org.uk* ⊠ *Free* ☉ *Apr.–Sept., Mon.–Sat. 10–5.*

↻ **Camera Obscura and World of Illusions.** Want to view Edinburgh as Victorian travelers once did? Then head for the 17th-century Outlook Tower's camera obscura, where an optical instrument—a sort of projecting periscope—affords bird's-eye views of the whole city (on a clear day, that is) illuminated onto a concave table. The tower was significantly altered in the 1840s and 1850s with the installation of the telescopic "magic lantern." Other attractions include a Magic Gallery with optical illusions, holograms, pin-hole photography, and rooftop views.

⊠ *Castlehill, Old Town* ☎ *0131/226–3709* ⊕ *www.camera-obscura. co.uk* ◎ *£9.95* ☉ *Apr.–June, Sept., and Oct., daily 9:30–6; July–Aug., daily 9:30–7:30; Nov.–Mar., daily 10–5.*

Canongate. This section of the Royal Mile takes its name from the canons who once ran the abbey at Holyrood. Canongate—in Scots, *gate* means "street"—was originally an independent town, or *burgh*, another Scottish term used to refer to a community with trading rights granted by the monarch. Here you'll find **Canongate Kirk** and its graveyard, **Canongate Tolbooth,** and the **Museum of Edinburgh.** ⊠ *Royal Mile, between High St. and Abbey Strand, Old Town.*

Canongate Kirk. This unadorned building, built in 1688, is run by the Church of Scotland and has an interesting graveyard. Although you can find information about the graveyard in the church, local authorities actually oversee it. This is the final resting place of some notable Scots, including economist Adam Smith (1723–90), author of *The Wealth of Nations* (1776), who once lived in the nearby 17th-century Panmure House. Also buried here are Dugald Stewart (1753–1828), the leading European philosopher of his time, and the undervalued Scots poet Robert Fergusson (1750–74). That Fergusson's grave is even marked is the result of efforts by the much more famous Robert Burns (1759–96), who commissioned an architect—by the name of Robert Burn—to design one. Burn also designed the Nelson Monument, the tall column on Calton Hill to the north, which you can see from the graveyard.

Against the eastern wall of the graveyard is a bronze sculpture of the head of Mrs. Agnes McLehose, the "Clarinda" of the copious correspondence in which Robert Burns engaged while confined to his lodgings with an injured leg in 1788. Burns and McLehose—a highborn, talented woman who had been abandoned by her husband—exchanged passionate letters for some six weeks that year. The missives were dispatched across town by a postal service that delivered them within the hour for one penny. The curiously literary affair ended when Burns left Edinburgh in 1788 to take up a farm tenancy and to marry Jean Armour. ⊠ *Canongate, Old Town* ☎ *0131/556–3515* ⊕ *www. canongatekirk.com* ◎ *Free* ☉ *Daily.*

Canongate Tolbooth. Nearly every city and town in Scotland once had a tolbooth. Originally a customhouse where tolls were gathered, a tolbooth came to mean town hall and later prison because detention cells were in the basement. The building where Canongate's town council once met now has a museum, the **People's Story,** which focuses on the lives of "ordinary" people from the 18th century to today. Exhibits describe how Canongate once bustled with the activities of the tradespeople needed to supply life's essentials in the days before superstores. Special displays include a reconstruction of a cooper's workshop and a 1940s kitchen. ⊠ *163 Canongate, Old Town* ☎ *0131/529–4057* ⊕ *www.cac.org.uk* ◎ *Free* ☉ *Mon.–Sat. 10–5.*

NEED A BREAK?

Clarinda's. You can get a good cup of tea and a scone, a quintessentially Scottish indulgence, at Clarinda's homey tearoom. ⊠ *69 Canongate, Old Town* ☎ *0131/557–1888.*

The Hub. For soups, sandwiches, and vegetarian options head to The Hub, housed in the grand Tolbooth Kirk. Its comfy seats, stained-glass windows, and inviting terrace create a relaxing atmosphere to refuel and hear the latest cultural chatter. ⊠ *Castlehill, Old Town* ☎ *0131/473–2067.*

Castlehill. In the late 16th century, alleged witches were brought to what is now a street in the Royal Mile to be burned at the stake, as a bronze plaque here recalls. The cannonball embedded in the west gable of Castlehill's **Cannonball House** was, according to legend, fired from the castle during the Jacobite Rebellion of 1745, led by Charles Edward Stuart (also known as Bonnie Prince Charlie, 1720–88), the most romantic of the Stuart pretenders to the British throne. Most authorities agree on a more prosaic explanation, however; they say it was a height marker for Edinburgh's first piped water-supply system, installed in 1681. Atop the Gothic **Tolbooth Kirk,** built in 1842–44 for the General Assembly of the Church of Scotland, stands the tallest spire in the city, at 240 feet. The church now houses the cheery Edinburgh Festival offices and a café known as **The Hub.**

The **Upper Bow,** running from Lawnmarket to Victoria Street, was once the main route westward from the town and castle. Before Victoria Street was built in the late 19th century, the Upper Bow led down into a narrow dark thoroughfare coursing between a canyon of tenements. All traffic struggled up and down this steep slope from the Grassmarket, which joins the now-truncated West Bow at its lower end. ⊠ *East of Esplanade and west of Lawnmarket, Old Town.*

OFF THE BEATEN PATH

Duddingston. Tucked behind Arthur's Seat, and about an hour's walk from Princes Street via Holyrood Park, this little community, formerly of brewers and weavers, still seems like a country village. The Duddingston Kirk has a Norman doorway and a watchtower that was built to keep body snatchers out of the graveyard. The church overlooks Duddingston Loch, popular with bird-watchers, and moments away is an old-style pub called the Sheep's Heid Inn, which serves a wide selection of beers and hearty food. For £12.50 you can have a go on the oldest skittle (bowling) alley in Scotland. To get here, take Lothian Bus #42.

George IV Bridge. It's not immediately obvious that this is in fact a bridge, as buildings are closely packed most of the way along both sides. At the corner of the bridge stands one of the most photographed sculptures in Scotland, *Greyfriars Bobby.* This statue pays tribute to the legendary Skye terrier who kept vigil beside his master John Gray's grave in the Greyfriar's churchyard for 14 years after Gray died in 1858. The 1961 Walt Disney film *Greyfriars Bobby* tells a version of the heartrending tale that some claim to be a shaggy-dog story. ⊠ *Bank St. and Lawnmarket, Old Town.*

Gladstone's Land. This narrow, six-story tenement, next to the Assembly Hall, is a survivor from the 17th century. Typical Scottish architectural features are evident on two floors, including an arcaded ground floor (even in the city center, livestock sometimes inhabited the ground floor). The house has magnificent painted ceilings and is furnished in the style of a 17th-century merchant's home. ⊠ *477B Lawnmarket, Old Town*

☎ *0131/226–5856*   ⊕ *www.nts. org.uk/visits* 🎫 *£6* ⊙ *Apr.–Oct., daily 10–5; July and Aug., daily 10–6:30; last admission 30 mins before closing.*

Grassmarket. For centuries an agricultural marketplace, Grassmarket now is the site of numerous shops, bars, and restaurants, making it a hive of activity at night. Sections of the Old Town wall can be traced on the north side by a series of steps that ascend from Grassmarket to Johnston Terrace. The best-preserved section of the wall can be found by crossing to the south side and climbing the steps of the lane called the Vennel. Here the 16th-century **Flodden Wall** comes in from the east and turns south at Telfer's Wall, a 17th-century extension.

GRASSMARKET GALLOWS

Grassmarket's history is long and gory. The **cobbled cross** at the east end marks the site of the town gallows. Among those hanged here were many 17th-century Covenanters, members of the Church of Scotland who rose up against Charles I's efforts to enforce Anglican or "English" ideologies on the Scottish people. Judges were known to issue the death sentence for these religious reformers with the words, "Let them glorify God in the Grassmarket."

From the northeast corner of the Grassmarket, **Victoria Street,** a 19th-century addition to the Old Town, leads to the George IV Bridge. Shops here sell antiques and designer clothing.

Lawnmarket. A corruption of "land market," Lawnmarket is the second of the streets that make up the Royal Mile. It was formerly the site of the produce market for the city, with a once-a-week special sale of wool and linen. Now it's home to **Gladstone's Land** and the **Writers' Museum.** At different times the Lawnmarket Courts housed James Boswell, David Hume, and Robert Burns. In nearby Brodie's Close in the 1770s lived the infamous Deacon Brodie, pillar of society by day and a murdering gang leader by night. Robert Louis Stevenson (1850–94) may well have used Brodie as the inspiration for his *Strange Case of Dr. Jekyll and Mr. Hyde.* ⊠ *Between Castlehill and High St., Old Town.*

NEED A BREAK?

Jolly Judge. Several atmospheric pubs and restaurants bustle on this section of the Royal Mile. Try the friendly Jolly Judge, where firelight brightens the dark-wood beams and a mixed crowd of university professors and students sip ale and eat light lunches of soup, pasta, or baked potatoes. ⊠ *7 James Ct., Old Town* ☎ *0131/225–2669.*

🔄 **Museum of Childhood.** Even adults tend to enjoy this cheerfully noisy museum—a cacophony of childhood memorabilia, vintage toys, and dolls, as well as a reconstructed schoolroom, street scene, fancy-dress party, and nursery. The museum claims to have been the first in the world devoted solely to the history of childhood. It's two blocks past the North Bridge–South Bridge junction on High Street. ⊠ *42 High St., Old Town* ☎ *0131/529–4142* ⊕ *www.cac.org.uk* 🎫 *Free* ⊙ *Mon.–Sat. 9–5, Sun. noon–5.*

Museum of Edinburgh. A must-see if you're interested in the details of Old Town life, this former home, dating from 1570, is a fascinating museum of local history, displaying Scottish pottery and Edinburgh silver and glassware. One of the museum's most impressive documents is the National Covenant, signed by Scotland's Presbyterian leadership in 1639. This "profession of faith" begins with not one, but three verses from the Bible. ⊠ *142 Canongate, Old Town* ☎ *0131/529–4143* ⊕ *www.cac.org.uk* ⊠ *Free* ☉ *Mon.–Sat. 10–5.*

National Library of Scotland. Founded in 1689, the library has a superb collection of books and manuscripts on the history and culture of Scotland, and also mounts regular exhibitions. Genealogists investigating family trees come here, and amateur family sleuths will find the staff helpful in their research. ⊠ *George IV Bridge, Old Town* ☎ *0131/623–3700* ⊕ *www.nls.uk* ⊠ *Free* ☉ *Library Mon., Tues., Thurs., and Fri. 9:30–8:30, Wed. 10–8:30, Sat. 9:30–1. Exhibitions weekdays 10–8, Sat. 10–5, Sun. 2–5.*

Parliament House. This was the seat of Scottish government until 1707, when the governments of Scotland and England were united, 104 years after the union of the two crowns. Partially hidden by the bulk of the High Kirk of St. Giles, it now houses the Supreme Law Courts of Scotland. Interesting exhibits are displayed under the hammer-beam roof of cavernous Parliament Hall. ⊠ *11 Parliament Sq., Old Town* ☎ *0131/225–2595* ⊕ *www.scotcourts.gov.uk* ⊠ *Free* ☉ *Weekdays 9–4:30.*

Scotch Whisky Experience. The mysterious process that turns malted barley and springwater into one of Scotland's most important exports is revealed in this museum. Although whisky making is not in itself packed with drama, the center manages an imaginative presentation using models and tableaux viewed while you ride in low-speed barrel cars. Explore Scotland's diverse whisky regions and the flavors they impart. Sniff the various aromas and decide whether you like fruity, sweet, or smoky, and afterward experts will help you select your perfect dram. Your guide will then allow you access to a vault containing the Diageo Claive Vidiz Scotch Whisky Collection, the world's largest collection of Scotch whiskies. ⊠ *354 Castlehill, Old Town* ☎ *0131/220–0441* ⊕ *www.whisky-heritage.co.uk* ⊠ *£12* ☉ *Tours Sept.–May, daily 10–6, last tour 5; June–Aug. daily 10–7, last tour 5:45.*

Scottish Storytelling Centre. This arts center is housed in a modern building that manages to blend seamlessly with the historic structures on either side. It hosts a year-round program of storytelling, theater, and literary events. A café serves lunch and tea. ⊠ *43 High St., Old Town* ☎ *0131/556–9579* ⊕ *www.scottishstorytellingcentre.co.uk* ⊠ *Free* ☉ *Sept.–June, Mon.–Sat. 10–6; July and Aug., Mon.–Sat. 10–6, Sun. noon–6.*

Writers' Museum. Down a close off Lawnmarket is Lady Stair's House, built in 1622 and a fine example of 17th-century urban architecture. Inside, the Writer's Museum evokes Scotland's literary past with such exhibits as the letters, possessions, and original manuscripts of Sir Walter Scott, Robert Louis Stevenson, and Robert Burns. The Stevenson collection is particularly compelling. ⊠ *Lady Stair's Close, Old Town* ☎ *0131/529–4901* ⊕ *www.cac.org.uk* ⊠ *Free* ☉ *Mon.–Sat. 10–5, last admission 4:45.*

NEW TOWN

It was not until the Scottish Enlightenment, a civilizing time of expansion in the 1700s, that the city fathers decided to break away from the Royal Mile's rocky slope and create a new Edinburgh below the castle. This was to become the New Town, with elegant squares, classical facades, wide streets, and harmonious proportions. Clearly, change had to come. At the dawn of the 18th century, Edinburgh's unsanitary conditions—primarily a result of overcrowded living quarters—were becoming notorious. The well-known Scots fiddle tune "The Flooers (flowers) of Edinburgh" was only one of many ironic references to the capital's unpleasant environment, which greatly embarrassed the Scot James Boswell (1740–95), biographer and companion of the English lexicographer Dr. Samuel Johnson (1709–84). In his *Journal of a Tour of the Hebrides,* Boswell recalled that on retrieving Johnson from his grubby inn in the Canongate, "I could not prevent his being assailed by the evening effluvia of Edinburgh. . . . Walking the streets at night was pretty perilous and a good deal odoriferous."

To help remedy this sorry state of affairs, in 1767 James Drummond, the city's lord provost (the Scots term for mayor), urged the town council to hold a competition to design a new district for Edinburgh. The winner was an unknown young architect named James Craig (1744–95). His plan called for a grid of three main east–west streets, balanced at either end by two grand squares. These streets survive today, though some of the buildings that line them have been altered by later development. Princes Street is the southernmost, with Queen Street to the north and George Street as the axis, punctuated by St. Andrew and Charlotte squares. A look at the map will reveal a geometric symmetry unusual in Britain. Even the Princes Street Gardens are balanced by the Queen Street Gardens, to the north. Princes Street was conceived as an exclusive residential address, with an open vista facing the castle. It has since been altered by the demands of business and shopping, but the vista remains.

The New Town was expanded several times after Craig's death and now covers an area about three times larger than Craig envisioned. Indeed, some of the most elegant facades came later and can be found by strolling north of the Queen Street Gardens.

TIMING   If you want to get the most out of the museums of the New Town, take a whole day and allow at least an hour for each one.

TOP ATTRACTIONS

OFF THE
BEATEN
PATH

Britannia. Moored on the waterfront at Leith, Edinburgh's port north of the city center, is the former Royal Yacht *Britannia*, launched in Scotland in 1953 and now retired to her home country. The Royal Apartments and the more functional engine room, bridge, galleys, and captain's cabin are all open to view. The land-based visitor center within

A GOOD WALK IN THE NEW TOWN

Start your walk on the Mound, the sloping street that joins the Old and New towns. Two museums immediately east of this great linking ramp, the National Gallery of Scotland and the Royal Scottish Academy, are the work of William Playfair (1789–1857), an architect whose neoclassical buildings contributed greatly to Edinburgh's title: the Athens of the North.

At the foot of the Mound is the city's most famous thoroughfare, Princes Street, the humming center of modern-day Edinburgh. Residents lament the disappearance of the dignified old shops that once lined this street; now a long sequence of chain stores has replaced them, although there is still a grand vista of the castle to the south. A block north is George Street, another row of shops, then one block farther lies Queen Street and the grand National Portrait Gallery.

The essence of the New Town spirit survives in Charlotte Square, at the west end of George Street, and especially in the beautiful Georgian House and West Register House. To explore further, choose your own route northward, down to the wide and elegant streets centering on Moray Place, a fine example of an 1820s development.

the huge Ocean Terminal shopping mall has exhibits and photographs about the yacht's history. ⊠ *Ocean Terminal, Leith* ☎ *0131/555–5566* ⊕ *www.royalyachtbritannia.co.uk* 🎟 *£11* ⊙ *Mar.–Oct., daily 10–4; Nov.–Feb., daily 10–3:30.*

★ **Georgian House.** The National Trust for Scotland has furnished this house in period style to show the elegant domestic arrangements of an affluent family of the late 18th century. The hallway was designed to accommodate sedan chairs, in which 18th-century grandees were carried through the streets. ⊠ *7 Charlotte Sq., New Town* ☎ *0844/493–2117* ⊕ *www.nts.org.uk/visits* 🎟 *£6* ⊙ *Mar., daily 11–4; Apr.–June, Sept., and Oct., daily 10–5; July and Aug., daily 10–6; Nov., daily 11–3; last admission ½ hr before closing.*

Fodor's Choice **National Gallery of Scotland.** Opened to the public in 1859, the National ★ Gallery presents a wide selection of paintings from the Renaissance to the postimpressionist period within a grand neoclassical building designed by William Playfair. Most famous are the old-master paintings bequeathed by the Duke of Sutherland, including Titian's *Three Ages of Man*. Many masters are here; works by Velázquez, El Greco, Rembrandt, Goya, Poussin, Turner, Degas, Monet, and Van Gogh, among others, complement a fine collection of Scottish art, including Sir Henry Raeburn's *Reverend Robert Walker Skating on Duddingston Loch* and other works by Ramsay, Raeburn, and Wilkie. The Weston Link connects the National Gallery of Scotland to the Royal Scottish Academy and provides expanded gallery space as well as a restaurant, bar, café, shop, and information center. ⊠ *The Mound, New Town* ☎ *0131/624–6336* ⊕ *www.nationalgalleries.org* 🎟 *Free* ⊙ *Fri.–Wed. 10–5, Thurs. 10–7.*

Royal Botanic Garden Edinburgh. Britain's largest rhododendron and azalea gardens are part of the varied and comprehensive collection of plant and flower species in this 70-acre garden, just north of the city center. An impressive Chinese garden has the largest collection of wild-origin Chinese plants outside China. There's a cafeteria, a visitor center with exhibits exploring biodiversity, and a fabulous gift shop selling plants, books, and gifts. Handsome 18th-century Inverleith House hosts art exhibitions. ■ **TIP→ Don't miss the soaring palms in the glass-domed Temperate House and the steamy Tropical Palm House.** The hilly rock garden and stream are magical on a sunny day. Guided tours are available. Take a taxi to the garden, or ride Bus 27 from Princes Street or Bus 23 from Hanover Street. To make the 20-minute walk from the New Town, take Dundas Street (the continuation of Hanover Street) and turn left at the clock tower onto Inverleith Row. ⊠ *23 Inverleith Row, Inverleith* ☎ *0131/552–7171* ⊕ *www.rbge.org.uk* ✉ *Free; greenhouses £4* ☉ *Nov.–Jan., daily 10–4; Feb.–Oct., daily 10–6.*

Scott Monument. What appears to be a Gothic cathedral spire chopped off and planted in the east end of the Princes Street Gardens is the nation's tribute to Sir Walter—a 200-foot-high monument looming over Princes Street. Built in 1844 in honor of Scotland's most famous author, Sir Walter Scott, the author of *Ivanhoe, Waverley,* and many other novels and poems, it's centered on a marble statue of Scott and his favorite dog, Maida. It's worth taking the time to explore the immediate area, including Princes Street Gardens, one of the prettiest city parks in Britain. In the open-air theater, amid the park's trim flower beds, stately trees, and carefully tended lawns, brass bands occasionally play. Here, too, is the famous **monument to David Livingstone,** whose African meeting with H. M. Stanley is part of Scots-American history. ⊠ *Princes St., New Town* ☎ *0131/529–4068* ⊕ *www.cac.org.uk* ✉ *£3* ☉ *Apr.–Sept., Mon.–Sat. 10–7, Sun. 10–6; Oct.–Mar., Mon.–Sat. 9–4, Sun. 10–6.*

Scottish National Gallery of Modern Art. This handsome former school building, close to the New Town, displays paintings and sculptures by Pablo Picasso, Georges Braque, Henri Matisse, and André Derain, among others. The gallery houses an excellent restaurant in the basement. Across the street in a former orphanage is the **Gallery of Modern Art Two** (formerly the Dean Gallery), which has Scots-Italian Sir Eduardo Paolozzi's re-created studio. ⊠ *Belford Rd., Dean Village* ☎ *0131/624–6200* ⊕ *www.nationalgalleries.org* ✉ *Free* ☉ *Daily 10–5.*

Scottish National Portrait Gallery. A magnificent red-sandstone Gothic building dating from 1889 houses this must-see institution. Conceived as a gift to the people of Scotland, the recently revamped gallery is organized under five broad themes: Reformation, Enlightenment, Empire, Modernity, and Contemporary. The refurbished complex features a photography gallery, a gallery for contemporary art, and a fancy glass elevator. New spaces hold exhibits on various aspects of Scots history and life, including "The Visual Culture of the Jacobite Cause" and "Playing for Scotland: The Making of Modern Sport." ⊠ *1 Queen St., New Town* ☎ *0131/624–6200* ⊕ *www.nationalgalleries.org* ✉ *Free* ☉ *Fri.–Wed. 10–5, Thurs. 10–7.*

CLOSE UP

Leith, Edinburgh's Seaport

Edinburgh's port has a rich history all its own. While not as rambunctious as it used to be, Leith is still a good bet for an authentically Scottish night out. Ample restaurants and bars make this a good alternative to staying in the center of town.

Just north of the city, Leith sits on the south shore of the Firth of Forth and was a separate town until it merged with the city in 1920. After World War II and up until the 1980s, the declining seaport had a reputation for poverty and crime. In recent years, however, it has been revitalized with the restoration of commercial buildings as well as the construction of new luxury housing, bringing a buzz of trendiness. All of the docks have been redeveloped; the Old East and West docks are now the administrative headquarters of the Scottish Executive. Plans are afoot to make the docks a hub of renewable energy industries.

In earlier times, Leith was the stage for many historic happenings. In 1560 Mary of Guise, the mother of Mary, Queen of Scots, ruled Scotland from Leith; her daughter landed in Leith the following year to embark on her infamous reign. A century later, Cromwell led his troops to Leith to root out Scots royalists. An arch of the Leith Citadel reminds all of the Scots' victory. Leith also prides itself on being a "home of golf" because official rules to the game were devised in 1744, in what is today Links Park. The rolling green mounds here hide the former field and cannon sites of past battles.

It's worth exploring the lowest reaches of the Water of Leith (the river that flows through the town), an area where restaurants, shops, and pubs proliferate. The major attraction for visitors here is the former royal yacht *Britannia,* moored outside the huge Ocean Terminal shopping mall. Reach Leith by walking down Leith Street and Leith Walk, from the east end of Princes Street (20 to 30 minutes), or take Lothian Bus 22 (Britannia Ocean Drive, Leith).

WORTH NOTING

Calton Hill. Robert Louis Stevenson's favorite view of his beloved city was from the top of this hill. The architectural styles represented by the extraordinary collection of monuments here include mock Gothic—the Old Observatory, for example—and neoclassical. Under the latter category falls the monument by William Playfair (1789–1857) designed to honor his talented uncle, the geologist and mathematician John Playfair (1748–1819), as well as his cruciform **New Observatory.** The piece that commands the most attention, however, is the so-called **National Monument,** often referred to as "Scotland's Disgrace." Intended to mimic Athens's Parthenon, this monument to the dead of the Napoleonic Wars was started in 1822 to the specifications of a design by Playfair. But in 1830, only 12 columns later, money ran out, and the facade became a monument to high aspirations and poor fund-raising. The tallest monument on Calton Hill is the 100-foot-high **Nelson Monument,** completed in 1815 in honor of Britain's naval hero Horatio Nelson (1758–1805); you can climb its 143 steps for sweeping city views. The **Burns Monument** is the circular Corinthian temple below

Regent Road. Devotees of Robert Burns may want to visit one other grave—that of Mrs. Agnes McLehose, or "Clarinda," in the Canongate Graveyard. ⊠ *Bounded by Leith St. to the west and Regent Rd. to the south, New Town* ☎ *0131/556–2716* ⊕ *www.cac.org.uk* ✍ *Nelson Monument £3* ⊙ *Nelson Monument Oct.–Mar., Mon.–Sat. 10–3; Apr.–Sept., daily 10–6.*

Charlotte Square. At the west end of George Street is the New Town's centerpiece—an 18th-century square with one of the proudest achievements of Robert Adam, Scotland's noted neoclassical architect. On the north side, Adam designed a palatial facade to unite three separate town houses of such sublime simplicity and perfect proportions that architects come from all over the world to study it. Happily, the Age of Enlightenment grace notes continue within, as the center town house is now occupied by the **Georgian House** museum, and to the west stands **West Register House.** ⊠ *West end of George St., New Town.*

OFF THE
BEATEN
PATH

☾ **Edinburgh Zoo.** Children love to visit the some 1,000 animals that live in Edinburgh Zoo. You can even handle some of the animals from April to September. In late 2011, two giant pandas—Tian Tian and Yang Gaung—became the talk of the town when they were flown in from China. Free 20-minute viewing sessions must be booked in advance. The ever-popular Penguin Parade begins at 2:15 (but since penguin participation is totally voluntary, the event is unpredictable). The zoo spreads over an 80-acre site on the slopes of Corstorphine Hill. Take buses 12, 26, or 31. ⊠ *Corstorphine Rd., next to Holiday Inn Edinburgh, Corstorphine ✛ 3 mi west of city center* ☎ *0131/334–9171* ⊕ *www. edinburghzoo.org.uk* ✍ *£15.50* ⊙ *Apr.–Sept., daily 9–6; Oct. and Mar., daily 9–5; Nov.–Feb., daily 9–4:30.*

George Street. With its upscale shops and handsome Georgian frontages, this is a more pleasant, less crowded street for wandering than Princes Street. The **statue of King George IV,** at the intersection of George and Hanover streets, recalls the visit of George IV to Scotland in 1822. He was the first British monarch to do so since King Charles II, in the 17th century. By the 19th century, enough time had passed since the Jacobite Uprising of 1745 for Scotland to be perceived at Westminster as being safe enough for a monarch to visit.

The ubiquitous Sir Walter Scott turns up farther down the street. It was at a grand dinner in the **Assembly Rooms,** between Hanover and Frederick streets, that Scott acknowledged having written the Waverley novels (the name of the author had hitherto been a secret, albeit a badly kept one). You can meet Scott once again, in the form of a plaque just downhill, at 39 Castle Street, his Edinburgh address before he moved to Abbotsford, in the Borders region, where he died in 1832. ⊠ *Between Charlotte and St. Andrew Squares, New Town.*

Moray Place. Moray Place—with its "pendants" of Ainslie Place and Randolph Crescent—was laid out in 1822 by the earl of Moray. From the start the homes were planned to be of particularly high quality, with lovely curving facades, imposing porticos, and a central secluded garden reserved for residents. ⊠ *Between Charlotte Sq. and Water of Leith, New Town.*

2

The Mound. This rising street originated from the need for a dry-shod crossing of the muddy quagmire left behind when Nor' Loch, the body of water below the castle, was drained (the railway now cuts through this area). The work is said to have been started by a local tailor, George Boyd, who tired of struggling through the mud en route from his New Town house to his Old Town shop. The building of a ramp was under way by 1781, and by the time of its completion, in 1830, "Geordie Boyd's mud brig [bridge]," as the street was first known, had been built up with an estimated 2 million cartloads of earth dug from the foundations of the New Town. ⊠ *From Princes St. to George IV Bridge, New Town.*

Princes Street. The south side of this well-planned street is occupied by the well-kept Princes Street Gardens, which act as a wide green moat to the castle on its rock. The north side is now one long sequence of chain stores with unappealing modern fronts apart from the handsome Victorian facade that holds Jenners department store. ⊠ *Waterloo Pl. to Lothian Rd., New Town.*

Register House. Scotland's first custom-built archives depository, Register House, designed by the great Robert Adam, was partly funded by the sale of estates forfeited by Jacobite landowners after their last rebellion in Britain (1745–46). Work on the Regency-style building, which marks the end of Princes Street, started in 1774. The statue in front is of the first duke of Wellington (1769–1852). The recently installed **ScotlandsPeople Centre** lets you conduct genealogical research. Free weekday research sessions, from 10 to 2 and 2 and 4, meet growing interest in Scots family history. Access to public records and the library is £15 per day. ⊠ *2 Princes St., New Town* ☎ *0131/314–4300* ⊕ *www. scotlandspeoplehub.gov.uk* ⊠ *Free* ⊗ *Weekdays 9–4:30.*

NEED A BREAK?

Café Royal. Immediately west of Register House, Café Royal serves good Scottish lagers and ales, and simple lunch items and, of course, oysters. The 18th-century building has bags of character, with ornate tiles, stained-glass windows and—allegedly—its own ghost. ⊠ *19 W. Register St., New Town* ☎ *0131/556–1884* ⊕ *www.caferoyal.org.uk.*

Royal Scottish Academy. The William Playfair–designed Academy hosts temporary art exhibitions (Monet paintings, for example), but is also worth visiting for a look at the imposing, neoclassic architecture. The underground Weston Link connects the museum to the National Gallery of Scotland. ⊠ *The Mound, New Town* ☎ *0131/225–6671* ⊕ *www. royalscottishacademy.org* ⊠ *Free* ⊗ *Mon.–Sat. 10–5, Sun. noon–5.*

Waterloo Place. The fine neoclassical architecture on this street was designed as a piece by Archibald Elliot (d. 1823) in 1815. Waterloo Place extends over Regent Bridge, bounded by the 1815 **Regent Arch,** a simple, triumphal Corinthian-column war memorial at the center of Ionic screens bordering the bridge. ⊠ *Eastern extension of Princes St., New Town.*

West Register House. The former St. George's Church, in the middle of the west side of Charlotte Square, today fulfills a different role, as an extension of the original Register House on Princes Street. Much of

Ancestor Hunting

Are you a Cameron or a Campbell, Mackenzie or Macdonald? If so, you may be one of the more than 25 million people of Scottish descent around the world. It was the Highland clearances of the 18th and 19th century, in which tenant farmers were driven from their homes and replaced with sheep, that started the mass emigration to North America and Australia. Before or during a trip, you can do a little genealogical research or pursue your family tree more seriously.

VisitScotland (⊕ www. ancestralscotland.com) has information about clans and surnames, books, and family-history societies. At the Register House, the new ScotlandsPeople Centre (⊕ www. scotlandspeople.gov.uk) is the place to dip into the past or conduct in-depth genealogical research.

Willing to pay for help? Companies such as Scottish Ancestral Trail (⊕ www.scottish-ancestral-trail. co.uk) do the research and plan a trip around your family history. Throughout Scotland, you can check bookstores for information and visit clan museums and societies.

the material is historical, with documents including clan maps and trial records. ⊠ *17 Charlotte Sq., New Town* ☎ *0131/535–1400* ⊕ *www.nas. gov.uk* ⊠ *Free* ⊙ *Weekdays 9–4:45.*

WHERE TO EAT

Edinburgh's eclectic restaurant scene has attracted a brigade of well-known chefs, including the award-winning trio of Martin Wishart, Tom Kitchin, and Paul Kitching. They and dozens of others have abandoned the tried-and-true recipes for more adventurous cuisine. Of course, you can always find traditional fare, which usually mean the Scottish-French style that harks back to the historical "Auld Alliance" of the 13th century. The Scots element is the preference for fresh and local foodstuffs; the French supply the sauces. In Edinburgh you can sample anything from Malaysian *rendang* (a thick, coconut-milk stew) to Kurdish kebabs, while the long-established French, Italian, Chinese, Pakistani, and Indian communities ensure that the majority of the globe's most treasured cuisines are well represented.

PRICES AND HOURS

It's possible to eat well in Edinburgh without spending a fortune. Multicourse prix-fixe options are common, and almost always less expensive than ordering à la carte. Even at restaurants in the highest price category, you can easily spend less than £30 per person. People tend to eat later in Scotland than in England—around 8 pm on average—or rather they finish eating and then drink on in leisurely Scottish fashion.

WHAT IT COSTS IN POUNDS					
	¢	$	$$	$$$	$$$$
AT DINNER	under £10	£10–£14	£15–£19	£20–£25	over £25

Prices are per person for a main course at dinner.

OLD TOWN

Use the coordinate (✛ B2) at the end of each listing to locate a site on the corresponding map.

The most historic part of the city houses the grander restaurants that many people associate with this city. It is also home to some of Edinburgh's oldest pubs, which serve informal meals.

$$
MODERN BRITISH
✕ **Angels with Bagpipes.** The name may amuse or bemuse you, but there's no doubt this relaxed spot with windows overlooking the Royal Mile provides good-value, refined dining. Within the 16th-century building, the understated decor includes a sculptural centerpiece of an angel with bagpipes copied from a carving in St. Giles Cathedral, opposite. Menus are straightforward and not overlong, the service is slick, and the atmosphere is warm. Seafood and game dominate, with dishes such as hake with chorizo and venison with red cabbage. For the best value, opt for the table d'hôte menu, available between noon and 6, with two courses for £11.95 and three for £15.95. ⊠ *343 High St., Old Town* 🕾 *0131/220–1111* ⊕ *www.angelswithbagpipes.co.uk* ✛ *G4.*

$
VEGETARIAN
✕ **David Bann.** In the heart of the Old Town, this ultrahip eatery serving vegetarian and vegan favorites attracts young locals with its light, airy, modern dining room. Drinking water comes with mint and strawberries; the sizable and creative dishes include mushroom risotto and Jerusalem artichoke in puff pastry. The food is so flavorful that carnivores may forget they're eating vegetarian. Try the spinach-and-smoked-cheese strudel and the malt-whisky panna cotta. The plentiful weekend brunch, served until 5 pm, is a great value. ⊠ *56–58 St. Mary's St., Old Town* 🕾 *0131/556–5888* ⊕ *www.davidbann.com* ✛ *H4.*

$
BRITISH
✕ **Doric Tavern.** Edinburgh's original gastropub offers a languid bistro environment and serves reliable Scots favorites. The menu has such daily-changing items as honey-baked salmon with oatcakes, and specialties include haggis, neeps and tatties, and chicken curry. Try the creamy Cullen skink soup for a filling, good-value lunchtime choice. The stripped-wood interiors upstairs have been spruced up. The Doric is handy, as it's near Waverley Station. ⊠ *15/16 Market St., Old Town* 🕾 *0131/225–1084* ⊕ *www.the-doric.com* ⚑ *Reservations essential* ✛ *G3.*

$
MIDDLE EASTERN
✕ **Hanam's.** A stone's throw from the castle, this enticing place transports you to the Middle East. Kurdish cuisine may not be as exalted as others in that region, but the *bayengaan surocrau* (marinated eggplant) and the lamb *tashreeb* (a kind of casserole) will convince you that it's among the best. There's also a great range of kebabs and more familiar Lebanese options. The deep-red interiors have a relaxed Middle Eastern vibe. It's possible to smoke a hookah pipe on the heated terrace,

and you can bring your own alcohol. ⊠ *3 Johnston Terr., Old Town* ☎ *0131/225–1329* ⊕ *www.hanams.com* ✣ *F4.*

$$ ✕ **Howie's.** This chain of stylish neighborhood bistros serves comtempo-
BRITISH rary Scottish fare—think lots of fresh local produce, fish, and game. The
steaks are tender Aberdeen beef, and the Loch Fyne herring is sweet-
cured to Howie's own recipe. The decor includes modern wood furnish-
ings and warm colors—it's smart and understated. Try the fixed-price
two-course lunch, a bargain at £8.95. ⊠ *10–14 Victoria St., Old Town*
☎ *0131/225–1721* ✣ *B3* ⊠ *29 Waterloo Pl., East End* ☎ *0131/556–
5766* ✣ *F4* ⊠ *208 Bruntsfield Pl., South Side* ☎ *0131/221–1777*
✣ *G2* ⊠ *10-14 Victoria Street, West End* ☎ *0131/225 1721* ⊕ *www.
howies.uk.com* ✣ *H6.*

$$ ✕ **La Garrigue.** Edinburgh is blessed with several affordable French bis-
FRENCH tros, and this is one of the best. Although the modern decor evokes
Paris, the food has the rustic flavor of the Languedoc region. Regional
favorites include a starter of croquette of slow-cooked pig's head and
such main dishes as braised lamb shank and a casserole of shin of beef
in a red wine sauce. Desserts such as a lavender crème brûlée offer a
light finale to a heady dining experience. Check out the fixed-price two-
course meal that's £12.95 for lunch and £25 for dinner. ⊠ *31 Jeffrey
St., Old Town* ☎ *0131/557–3032* ⊕ *www.lagarrigue.co.uk* ⊘ *Closed
Sun.* ✣ *G3.*

¢ ✕ **Mother India Cafe.** Despite its popularity, good Indian food is hard to
INDIAN find in Scotland. Not so at this humble eatery, where the emphasis is
on home-style cooking. Meals are served tapas-style, with lots of small,
reasonably priced dishes, making it possible to sample a little of everything. The lamb *karahi* (a Pakistani curry made in a woklike pot) is
particularly recommended, as are any of the fish dishes. The split-level
dining area is smart and contemporary. ⊠ *3–5 Infirmary St., Old Town*
☎ *0131/524–9801* ⊕ *www.motherindiaglasgow.co.uk* ✣ *H4.*

$$ ✕ **Petit Paris.** Even in typical Scottish weather it's possible to get a taste
FRENCH of warmer climes at this little bistro on the cobbled Grassmarket, cheer-
fully decorated with checked tablecloths, copper pots, and bunches
of garlic. The staff is predominantly French, and the emphasis is on
casual dining, local produce, and home cooking. Try the traditional
French blood sausage and slow-baked rabbit with Dijon-mustard sauce.
The £11.90 two-course lunch is a bargain. ⊠ *38/40 Grassmarket, Old
Town* ☎ *0131/226–2442* ⊕ *www.petitparis-restaurant.co.uk* ⊘ *Closed
Mon.* ✣ *E5.*

$ ✕ **Thai Orchid.** A golden Buddha, beautiful flowers, a traditionally
THAI dressed staff, and spicy cuisine transport you to Thailand, if only for a
few hours. To start, try the *todd mun kao pode* (deep-fried corn cakes
with a sweet-and-sour peanut-and-coriander dip). Good main courses
include *pla priew wan* (monkfish poached with coconut milk) or *pedt
Orchid,* duck stir-fried with mango, chili, garlic, and red peppers. The
sticky rice with coconut milk and mango is a dessert not to be missed.
The decor is contemporary, with banquette seating and lots of natu-
ral wood. ⊠ *5A Johnston Terr., Old Town* ☎ *0131/225–6633* ⊕ *www.
thaiorchid.uk.com* ✣ *F4.*

BEST BETS FOR EDINBURGH DINING

Where can you find the best food Edinburgh has to offer? Fodor's writers and editors have selected their favorite restaurants by price, cuisine, and experience in the lists below. In the first column, the Fodor's Choice properties represent the "best of the best" across price categories. You can also search by neighborhood for excellent eating experiences—just peruse our complete reviews on the following pages.

2

MOST ROMANTIC

Le Café St. Honore, $$$, p. 61

The Witchery, $$$$, p. 60

BEST PRETHEATER EATS

La Garrigue, $$, p. 58

Fodor's Choice ★

Kalpna, ¢, p. 66
The Kitchin, $$$$, p. 67
Martin Wishart, $$$$, p. 67
Number One, $$$$, p. 61
Wedgwood, $$, p. 60

By Price

¢

Kalpna, p. 66
Mother India Cafe, p. 58

$

Al Dente, p. 66
David Bann, p. 57

$$

Santini, p. 65
Wedgwood, p. 60

$$$

Forth Floor, p. 60

$$$$

The Kitchin, p. 67
Martin Wishart, p. 67
Number One, p. 61
The Witchery, p. 60

By Cuisine

MODERN BRITISH

Howie's, $$, p. 58
21212, $$$$, p. 64
Wedgwood, $$, p. 60

CHINESE

Chop Chop, $, p. 65
Jasmine, $, p. 65

FRENCH

La Garrigue, $$, p. 58
L'escargot Bleu, $$, p. 61
Martin Wishart, $$$$, p. 67

INDIAN

Kalpna, ¢, p. 66

Mother India Cafe, ¢, p. 58

SPANISH

Rafael's, $$, p. 61

SEAFOOD

Fishers Bistro, $$, p. 66

VEGETARIAN

David Bann, $, p. 57
Henderson's, ¢, p. 60

By Experience

MOST KID-FRIENDLY

Al Dente, $, p. 66
Howie's, $$, p. 58

BEST VIEW

Forth Floor, $$$, p 60
Oloroso, $$$, p. 61

HOT SPOTS

Forth Floor, $$$, p. 60
L'escargot Bleu, $$, p. 61

$$ ✕**Wedgwood.** Rejecting the idea that fine dining should be a stuffy
BRITISH   affair, owners Paul Wedgwood and Lisa Channon opened this Royal
Fodor's Choice   Mile gem. The dining space is smart but informal, and the professional
★   staff has mastered the tricky task of giving guests space to relax while
remaining attentive. But Wedgwood's food is the standout. The best
local produce is taken in some surprising directions with Asian, French,
and traditional Scottish influences apparent in dishes such as monkfish
tail with shellfish paella and ham, or panfried pigeon with haggis, neeps
(turnips), and tatties (potatoes). Save space for seasonal sweets like
rhubarb-and-vanilla trifle infused with gin and pink pepper. ⊠ *267 Can-
ongate, Old Town* ☎ *0131/558–8737* ⊕ *www.wedgwoodtherestaurant.
co.uk* ⌕ *Reservations essential* ✛ *H3.*

$$$$ ✕**The Witchery.** The hundreds of "witches" who were executed on Cas-
MODERN BRITISH   tlehill, just yards from where you'll be seated, are the inspiration for
this outstanding and atmospheric restaurant. The cavernous interior,
complete with flickering candlelight, is festooned with cabalistic insignia
and tarot-card characters. Gilded and painted ceilings reflect the close
links between France and Scotland, as does the menu, which includes
steak tartare, roasted quail with braised endive, shellfish bisque, and
herb-baked scallops. Two-course pre- and posttheater (5:30–6:30 and
10:30–11:30) specials are an inexpensive way to sample the exceptional
cuisine. ⊠ *Castlehill, Old Town* ☎ *0131/225–5613* ⊕ *www.thewitchery.
com* ✛ *F4.*

NEW TOWN

*Use the coordinate (✛ B2) at the end of each listing to locate a site on
the corresponding map.*

The New Town, with its striking street plan, ambitious architecture,
and professional crowd, has restaurants where you can get everything
from a quick snack to a more formal dinner.

$$$ ✕**Forth Floor.** Harvey Nichols has become synonymous with chic shop-
MODERN BRITISH   ping, so it stands to reason that the department store's restaurant is no
slouch when it comes to style. The decor pulls off the trick of being
minimalist without being too severe. Factor in a glorious view over
Princes Street Gardens and the Edinburgh Castle and it's a winner from
the moment you walk in the door. The imaginative menu devised by chef
Stuart Muir lives up to the lofty location. Scallops served with spring
cabbage and pea mousse, and clam-and-cider chowder make for healthy
starters, while the braised shin of beef with globe artichoke, shallots,
and lobster is memorable. Ask for a window or terrace table—weather
permitting, of course. ⊠ *Harvey Nichols, 30–34 St. Andrew Sq., New
Town* ☎ *0131/524–8350* ⊕ *www.harveynichols.com* ⌕ *Reservations
essential* ✛ *F2.*

¢ ✕**Henderson's.** This vegetarian restaurant opened in 1962, long before it
VEGETARIAN   was fashionable to serve healthful, meatless creations. The salad bar has
more than a dozen different offerings each day; a massive plateful costs
£7. Tasty hot options include Moroccan stew with couscous and mous-
saka. Live mellow music plays six nights a week, and there's an art gallery as well. Around the corner on Thistle Street is the Bistro, from the

2

same proprietors; it serves snacks, meals, and decadent desserts such as chocolate fondue. Drop by the fabulous deli for picnic supplies, including wonderful bread. ⊠ *94 Hanover St., New Town* ☎ *0131/225–2605* ⊕ *www.hendersonsofedinburgh.co.uk* ⦾ *Closed Sun* ✛ *E2.*

$$$
FRENCH

✕ **Le Café St Honoré.** Quintessentially Parisian in style, this restaurant reflects all that is charming about French café dining. From the moment you enter the beautifully lighted room you're transported into the decadently stylish belle epoque. A concise menu leaves more time for chatting. You might start off with a warm salad of scallops, monkfish, chorizo, and pine nuts, followed by lamb confit or panfried turbot cooked with cider, green peppercorns, and prawns. ⊠ *34 N.W. Thistle Street La., New Town* ☎ *0131/226–2211* ⊕ *www.cafesthonore.com* ✛ *D2.*

$$
FRENCH

✕ **L'escargot Bleu.** Anyone still laboring under the misconception that French cuisine is pretentious should pay a visit to this gem. In one of the city's trendiest quarters, this venture from the former co-owner of Petit Paris would make anyone from France feel at home. The welcome is warm, the stripped wooden floors and period French posters add to a convivial atmosphere that is loud and proud, and the food is as authentic as a gendarme whistling "La Marseillaise." Dishes like snails in parsley butter and beef bourguignon fly the flag proudly. Follow your nose to the French deli in the basement. ⊠ *56A Broughton St., New Town* ☎ *0131/557–1600* ⊕ *www.lescargotbleu.co.uk* ⚇ *Reservations essential* ✛ *G1.*

$$$$
BRITISH
Fodor's Choice
★

✕ **Number One.** Clublike but unstuffy, this basement restaurant with a thoughtful layout perfect for intimate dining serves the best of Scottish seafood and meat within the Edwardian splendor of the Balmoral Hotel. The regular three-course prix-fixe is £64; for special occasions, choose the chef's six-course tasting menu (£70) with amuse-bouche delights, gourmet breads, and exquisite creations highlighting west-coast scallops, halibut, monkfish, beef, and lamb. Desserts include a rich, bitter chocolate and orange soufflé, and the lighter, candy-store-inspired hibiscus panna cotta. Service is impeccable and friendly. ⊠ *Balmoral Hotel, Princes St., New Town* ☎ *0131/557–6727* ⊕ *www.restaurantnumberone.com* ⚇ *Reservations essential* ✛ *G2.*

$$$
MODERN BRITISH

✕ **Oloroso.** In the heart of the New Town and close to the main shopping streets, this is the perfect spot for a revitalizing lunch or dinner after exploring the city. The contemporary international cooking reflects influences from Europe and Asia, the service is efficient and friendly, and the bar serves some of the best cocktails in Britain. Try the roasted duck breast with braised red cabbage and apples, or the aubergine galette (eggplant tart) with a tomato-and-cinnamon sauce. The wine list has about 230 selections, including champagne. The dining room and roof terrace have stunning views across the Firth of Forth to the hills of Fife on one side, and the castle and city rooftops on the other. Check out the lunch deals: two courses for £19.50 or three courses for £24.50. ⊠ *33 Castle St., New Town* ☎ *0131/226–7614* ⊕ *www.oloroso.co.uk* ✛ *D3.*

$$
SPANISH

✕ **Rafael's.** All great restaurants should be as laid back as Rafael's. Situated in a quaint pink-hued basement room replete with eccentric trinkets, the restaurant is clearly not in thrall to prevailing trends and is

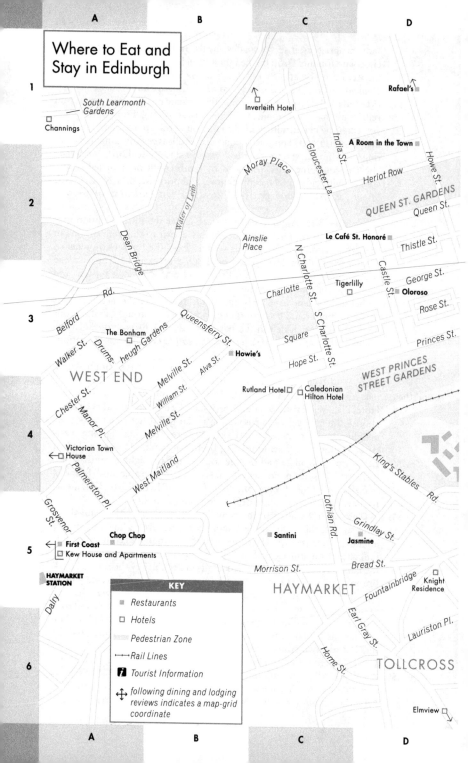

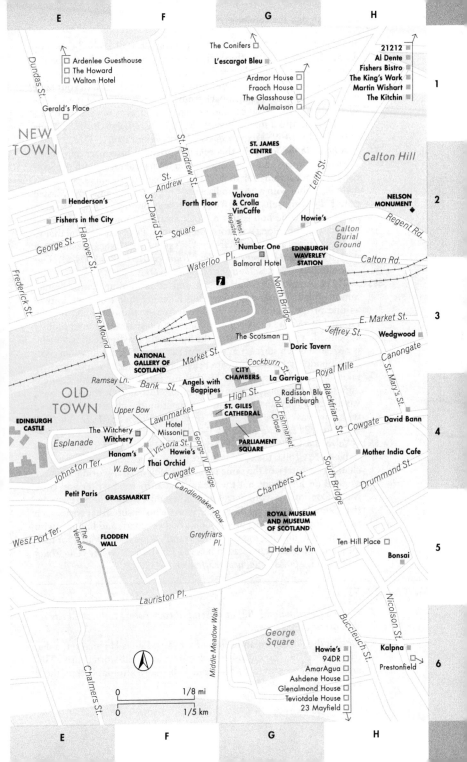

E   **F**   **G**   **H**

The Conifers □

L'escargot Bleu ■

21212 ■
Al Dente ■
Fishers Bistro ■
The King's Wark ■
Martin Wishart ■
The Kitchin ■

Ardenlee Guesthouse □
The Howard □
Walton Hotel □

Gerald's Place □

Ardmor House □
Fraoch House □
The Glasshouse □
Malmaison □

1

NEW TOWN

St. Andrew St.

ST. JAMES CENTRE

Leith St.

Calton Hill

Henderson's ■

St. Andrew

Valvona & Crolla VinCaffe

West Register St.

NELSON MONUMENT ◆

Fishers in the City ■

Forth Floor

Howie's ■

Regent Rd.

2

George St.

Hanover St.

St. David St.

Square

Number One

Calton Burial Ground

Frederick St.

Waterloo Pl.

Balmoral Hotel

EDINBURGH WAVERLEY STATION

Calton Rd.

🛈

North Bridge

E. Market St.

3

The Mound

The Scotsman □

Jeffrey St.

Wedgwood ■

Doric Tavern ■

Canongate

NATIONAL GALLERY OF SCOTLAND

Market St.

Cockburn St.

Royal Mile

St. Mary's St.

OLD TOWN

Ramsay Ln.

Bank St.

Angels with Bagpipes

CITY CHAMBERS

La Garrigue ■

High St.

Old Fishmarket Close

Blackfriars St.

EDINBURGH CASTLE

Upper Bow

Lawnmarket

Hotel Missoni □

Radisson Blu Edinburgh

Cowgate

David Bann ■

4

Esplanade

The Witchery ■
Witchery

ST. GILES CATHEDRAL

Victoria St.

George IV Bridge

Johnston Ter.

Hanam's ■

Howie's ■

PARLIAMENT SQUARE

South Bridge

Mother India Cafe ■

W. Bow

Thai Orchid ■

Cowgate

Candlemaker Row

Chambers St.

Drummond St.

Petit Paris ■

GRASSMARKET

West Port Ter.

The Vennel

FLODDEN WALL

Greyfriars Pl.

ROYAL MUSEUM AND MUSEUM OF SCOTLAND

Ten Hill Place □

Bonsai ■

5

Hotel du Vin □

Lauriston Pl.

Chalmers' St.

Middle Meadow Walk

George Square

Nicolson St.

Buccleuch St.

0   1/8 mi
0   1/5 km

Howie's ■
94DR □
AmarAgua □
Ashdene House □
Glenalmond House □
Teviotdale House □
23 Mayfield □

Kalpna ■

Prestonfield □

6

E   **F**   **G**   **H**

all the better for it. Not only does chef/proprietor/all-around-good guy Rafael Torrubia create affordably priced masterpieces with an Iberian twist, he's also likely to deliver dishes such as a sea bass and salmon duo with pesto or a wonderfully authentic tortilla with chorizo to your table himself. Despite his Spanish background, Torrubia's use of ingredients such as curry in his sauces shows that as well as being a man of the people, he is also a man of the world. ⊠ *2 Deanhaugh St., New Town* ☎ *0131/332–1469* ⊕ *www.rafaels-bistro.wikidot.com* ✣ *D1.*

$$
BRITISH ✕ **A Room in the Town.** At this relaxed, friendly bistro serving Scots-French fare, there's a strong emphasis on fresh local meat, with the Scottish touch accounting for slightly sweeter-than-usual sauces. Standouts include halibut with a horseradish-and-chervil cream, and slow-roasted pork belly with fruity relish. You may bring your own bottle of wine—an excellent wineshop is just a block away—although the restaurant serves wine, too, along with top-notch brandy. Plain but cheerful thanks to bright colors and wooden fixtures, it's perfect for a sociable night out with friends. ⊠ *18 Howe St., New Town* ☎ *0131/225–8204* ⊕ *www. aroomin.co.uk* ⟍ *Reservations essential* ✣ *D1.*

$$$$
MODERN BRITISH ✕ **21212.** Abandoning the Michelin-starred restaurant that made him famous might sound risky, but Paul Kitching didn't become known as one of the region's most innovative chefs without being daring. Housed in a grand old Georgian house, this restaurant is sumptuously appointed, with prices to match; the five-course fixed-price dinner menu is £67, and lunch starts at £26 for three courses.The dining room combines boudoir-style comfort with belle-epoque grandeur. Expect creative takes on old classics, such as his deconstructed fish-and-chips. Kitching's fearlessness is apparent in dishes like turbot with chorizo, dates, vanilla, and rutabaga puree—not to mention the cheesecake flavored with caraway seeds. ⊠ *3 Royal Terr., New Town* ☎ *0131/523–1030* ⊕ *www.21212restaurant.co.uk* ✣ *H1.*

$$
ITALIAN ✕ **Valvona & Crolla VinCaffe.** Every Scot with a passion for food knows Valvona & Crolla, the country's first Italian delicatessen and wine merchant. This eatery of the same name may lack the old-world feel of the original on Elm Row, but the menu created by food writer and cook Mary Contini is as wonderful as you would expect. The fare is relatively simple, but the quality of the ingredients ensures that treats such as the white pizza with cured bacon, fried calamari, and linguine with crab meat do nothing to tarnish the brand's reputation. Watch for tastings and cultural events staged here. ⊠ *11 Multrees Walk, New Town* ☎ *0131/557–0088* ⊕ *www.vincaffe.com* ✣ *G2.*

HAYMARKET

Use the coordinate (✣ B2) at the end of each listing to locate a site on the corresponding map.

West of the Old Town and south of the West End is Haymarket, a district with its own down-to-earth character and well-worn charm. This area has many restaurants that tend to be more affordable than those in the center of town.

$ ✕**Chop Chop.** Authentic Chinese cuisine created by skilled chefs and
CHINESE served in a friendly dining room make this place especially popular.
Since arriving in Edinburgh from northern China, Jian Wang has won
many awards and has opened two restaurants. Expect flavorful, robust
creations like the trademark dumplings with spiced minced meat or vegetables, spicy squid with garlic, and lamb with cumin. The large eatery
has splashes of Chinese red and is suitably relaxed. ✉ *248 Morrison St.,
Haymarket* ☎ *0131/221–1155* ⊕ *www.chop-chop.co.uk* ✛ *A5.*

$ ✕**First Coast.** This laid-back bistro, just a few minutes from Haymar-
BRITISH ket Station, is a favorite with locals. Hardwood floors, stone walls,
soft blue hues, and seaside paintings add to the coastal theme. Savory
temptations include roasted butternut squash with chestnut-and-apple
salad; panfried sea bass with fennel, mustard, and ginger; and Aberdeen
Angus sirloin with tomato-and-red-onion salad. The international wine
list is as varied as the daily specials. ✉ *99–101 Dalry Rd., Haymarket*
☎ *0131/313–4404* ⊕ *www.first-coast.co.uk* ✛ *A5.*

WEST END AND POINTS WEST

*Use the coordinate (✛ B2) at the end of each listing to locate a site on
the corresponding map.*

Even after business hours, the city's commercial center is the place to
find a variety of international restaurants.

$ ✕**Jasmine.** Seafood is the specialty of this small, friendly Cantonese
CHINESE restaurant. Delicious dishes include mixed seafood on a bed of let-
tuce, and the chicken served inside the two halves of a mango. The
staff doesn't break a sweat as it serves a constant stream of customers.
Flickering candles add a relaxing feel to the interior, although tables
are quite closely spaced. Prix-fixe lunches, starting at £8.95 for three
courses, are a good value. A take-out menu is available. ✉ *32 Grindlay
St., West End* ☎ *0131/229–5757* ⊕ *www.jasminechinese.co.uk* ✛ *D5.*

$$ ✕**Santini.** Fine food and cheery surroundings gives Santini an edge over
ITALIAN other Italian eateries on Lothian Road. The decor is crisp and vibrant,
with lots of stone, wood, and contemporary furnishings. Classic dishes
include osso buco (Piemontese-style braised veal shank) and steamed
wild sea bass with mixed herbs and balsamic vinegar. The simple pizza
margherita will keep kids happy, while the pizza *fiorentina* with moz-
zarella, tomatoes, spinach, and egg is *deliziosa.* The fixed two-course
lunch (antipasto and primo) is a good value at £10. ✉ *8 Conference
Sq., West End* ☎ *0131/221–7788* ⊕ *www.santiniedinburgh.co.uk* ✛ *C5.*

SOUTH SIDE

*Use the coordinate (✛ B2) at the end of each listing to locate a site on
the corresponding map.*

The presence of university professors and students means eateries that
are both affordable and interesting.

$ ✕**Bonsai.** The owners of Bonsai regularly visit Tokyo to research the
JAPANESE casual dining scene, and their expertise is setting a high standard for Jap-
anese cuisine in Edinburgh. The succulent *gyoza* (steamed dumplings)

are pliant and tasty, while the wide variety of noodle and teriyaki dishes and the classy sushi balance sweet and sour deliciously. Try the raw prawns and scallops served with radish noodles and wasabi for refreshing, briny mouthfuls with a kick. The dining area has a bright informality, but the tiny tables may be a tad cramped for some. ⊠ *46 West Richmond St., South Side* ☎ *0131/668–3847* ⊕ *www.bonsaibarbistro. co.uk* ✛ *H5.*

¢   INDIAN   Fodor's Choice   ★

✗ **Kalpna.** Amid an ordinary row of shops, the facade of this vegetarian Indian restaurant may be unremarkable, but the food is exceptional and a superb value. Try the *dam aloo kashmiri*, a medium-spicy potato dish with a sauce made from honey, pistachios, and almonds. *Bangan mirch masala* is spicier, with eggplant and red chili peppers. Thaali, a variety of dishes served in bowls on a tray, is particularly appetizing, and a bargain at £13.50. The interior is enlivened by exotic Indian mosaics. Check out the lunchtime buffet for under £10. With lots of meatless options on the menu, veggies and vegans flock here. ⊠ *2–3 St. Patrick Sq., South Side* ☎ *0131/667–9890* ⊕ *www.kalpnarestaurant. com* ⊗ *Closed Sun. Jan.–Mar.* ✛ *H6.*

LEITH

Use the coordinate (✛ B2) at the end of each listing to locate a site on the corresponding map.

Seafood lovers are drawn to the old port of Leith to sample the freshest seafood and to admire the authentic seafaring feel of the docklands.

$ ITALIAN

✗ **Al Dente.** This tiny neighborhood favorite serves authentic Italian cuisine in friendly surroundings. Chef Graziano Spano, from Puglia, is attuned to the freshness and flavors that typify food from the Bel Paese. Fresh pasta and local produce feature prominently. Try the Puglian favorite, pasta orecchiette (little-eared pasta), served with lamb ragu, or sample classic dishes from the regions of Sardinia, Liguria, Lazio, Emilia-Romagna, and Tuscany. Leave room for dessert by ordering a half portion of pasta for £5.40. ⊠ *139 Easter Rd., Leith* ☎ *0131/652– 1932* ⊕ *www.al-dente-restaurant.co.uk* ⌕ *Reservations essential* ✛ *H1.*

$$ SEAFOOD

✗ **Fishers Bistro.** Locals and visitors flock to this laid-back pub-cum-bistro down on the waterfront, and to its sister restaurant, **Fishers in the City,** in the New Town. The menu is the same, but Fishers Leith has the better reputation and vibe. Bar meals are served, although for more comfort and elegance, sit in the cozy blue-walled dining room. Seafood is the specialty—the Loch Fyne oysters and queenie scallops from Tarbert are wonderful. Watch for the daily specials: perhaps a seafood or vegetarian soup followed by huge North African prawns. It's wise to reserve ahead for the bistro. ⊠ *1 The Shore, Leith* ☎ *0131/554– 5666* ⊕ *www.fishersbistros.co.uk* ✛ *H1* ⊠ *58 Thistle St., New Town* ☎ *0131/225–5109* ✛ *E2.*

$ BRITISH

✗ **The King's Wark.** Along the shoreline at Leith is a gastropub with a pleasant atmosphere and quality food that continues to win plaudits. At lunchtime, the dark-wood bar does a roaring trade in simple fare such as gourmet burgers and fish cakes, but in the evening the kitchen ups the ante with such dishes as sea trout stuffed with smoked mackerel risotto. Old stone walls attest to the building's 15th-century origins. Book early to sample the legendary breakfast. ⊠ *36 The Shore, Leith* ☎ *0131/554–9260* ✛ *H1*.

$$$$ ✕ **The Kitchin.** One of the Edinburgh's most popular eateries, Tom
FRENCH Kitchin's award-winning venture has packed in the crowds since open-
Fodor's Choice ing in 2006. It's not difficult to see why. Kitchin, who trained in France,
★ runs a tight ship, and his passion for using seasonal and locally sourced produce to his own creative ends shows no sign of waning. Unfashionable ingredients such as ox tongue, tripe, and pig's head emerge heroic after Kitchin's alchemy, and he works his magic equally dexterously on more familiar elements such as seafood and venison. To sample this verified culinary world affordably, try the three-course lunch for £26.50. ⊠ *78 Commercial Quay, Leith* ☎ *0131/555–1755* ⊕ *www.thekitchin. com* ◿ *Reservations essential* ✆ *Closed Sun. and Mon.* ✛ *H1*.

$$$$ ✕ **Martin Wishart.** Slightly out of town but worth every penny of the taxi
FRENCH fare and the cost (three courses for £65), this rising culinary star woos
Fodor's Choice diners with an impeccable and varied menu of beautifully presented,
★ French-influenced dishes. Terrine of foie gras, compote of Agen prunes, and sole Murat (a glazed fillet with baby onions, artichoke, parsley, and lemon) with *pommes en cocotte* (potatoes cooked in a casserole) typify the cuisine. Reservations are essential on Friday and Saturday night. ⊠ *54 The Shore, Leith* ☎ *0131/553–3557* ⊕ *www.martin-wishart.co.uk* ✆ *Closed Sun. and Mon. No lunch Sat.* ✛ *H1*.

WHERE TO STAY

For expanded hotel reviews, visit Fodors.com.

From stylish boutique hotels to homey B&Bs, Edinburgh has a world-class array of accommodations to suit every taste. Its status as one of Britain's most attractive and fascinating cities ensures a steady influx of visitors, but the wealth of overnight options means there's no need to compromise on where you stay. Grand old hotels are rightly renowned for their regal bearing and old-world charm. If your tastes are a little more contemporary, the city's burgeoning contingent of chic design hotels offers an equally alluring alternative. For those on a tighter budget, the town's B&Bs are the most likely choice. If you feel B&Bs can be restrictive, keep in mind that Scots are trusting people—many proprietors provide front-door keys and few impose curfews.

Rooms are harder to find in August and September, when the Edinburgh International Festival and the Fringe Festival take place, so reserve at least three months in advance. Bed-and-breakfast accommodations may be harder to find in December, January, and February, when some proprietors close for a few weeks.

PRICES

Weekend rates in the larger hotels are always much cheaper than midweek rates, so if you want to stay in a plush hotel, come on the weekend. To save money and see how local residents live, stay in a B&B in one of the areas away from the city center, such as Pilrig to the north, Murrayfield to the west, or Sciennes to the south. Public buses can whisk you to the city center in 10 to 15 minutes.

WHAT IT COSTS IN POUNDS				
¢	$	$$	$$$	$$$$
FOR TWO PEOPLE	under £70	£70–£120	£121–£180	£181–£250	over £250

Prices are for two people in a standard double room in high season, usually including 20% V.A.T.

OLD TOWN

Use the coordinate (✛ B2) at the end of each listing to locate a site on the corresponding map.

The narrow *pends* (alleys), cobbled streets, and steep hills of the Old Town remind you that this is a city with many layers of history. Medieval to modern, these hotels all are within a stone's throw of the action.

$$ **Hotel Du Vin.** This is one of the U.K.'s most forward-thinking hotel chains, so it's no surprise that they haven't missed a trick here. **Pros:** trendy design; youthful feel. **Cons:** some rooms are better than others; in a noisy neighborhood. ⊠ *11 Bristo Pl., Old Town* ☎ *0131/247–4900* ⊕ *www.hotelduvin.com* ↪ *37 rooms, 10 suites* ⚘ *In-room: no a/c, Wi-Fi. In-hotel: restaurant, parking* ⦿ *Breakfast* ✛ *G5.*

$$$
Fodor's Choice
★
Hotel Missoni. Glasgow is regarded as Scotland's most stylish city, but the capital has beaten its rival by becoming the site of Italian fashion house Missoni's first boutique hotel. **Pros:** perfect location; in the thick of the action; as far from staid as you can get. **Cons:** it's a little Austin Powers in places; some find it hard to relax in such chichi surrounds. ⊠ *1 George IV Bridge, Old Town* ☎ *0131/220–6666* ⊕ *www. hotelmissoni.com* ↪ *129 rooms, 7 suites* ⚘ *In-room: no a/c, safe, Wi-Fi. In-hotel: restaurant, bar, gym, parking* ⦿ *Breakfast* ✛ *F4.*

$$
☾
Knight Residence. Ten minutes from the Grassmarket, the Knight is made up of 19 different apartments that offer good value and convenient locations. **Pros:** comfortable apartments; secure location; good for families needing space and privacy. **Cons:** lack of staff won't suit everyone; better for stays of two or more nights. ⊠ *12 Lauriston St., Old Town* ☎ *0131/622–8120* ⊕ *www.theknightresidence.co.uk* ↪ *19 apartments* ⚘ *In-room: no a/c, kitchen, Wi-Fi. In-hotel: parking* ⦿ *Breakfast* ✛ *D5.*

$$$
Radisson Blu Hotel, Edinburgh. Built in the late 1980s, this city-center hotel was designed to blend in among the 16th-, 17th-, and 18th-century buildings on the Royal Mile; rooms are spacious and contemporary, with muted colors—practical rather than luxurious. **Pros:** central location; can-do staff. **Cons:** expensive breakfast; difficult to reach by car. ⊠ *80 High St., Royal Mile, Old Town* ☎ *0131/557–9797* ⊕ *www. radissonblu.co.uk/hotel-edinburgh* ↪ *238 rooms, 10 suites* ⚘ *In-room: Internet, Wi-Fi. In-hotel: restaurant, bar, pool, gym, parking* ⦿ *Breakfast* ✛ *G4.*

BEST BETS FOR EDINBURGH LODGING

Fodor's Choice★

Balmoral Hotel, $$$$,
p. 70
Hotel Missoni, $$$, p. 68
The Howard, $$$, p. 70
Rutland Hotel, $$, p. 72
The Scotsman, $$$$,
p. 69

By Price

$

Elmview, p. 73
Gerald's Place, p. 70

$$

The Bonham, p. 71
Hotel Du Vin, p. 68
Rutland Hotel, p. 72

$$$

Channings, p. 72
Hotel Missoni, p. 68
Kew House and Apartments, p. 71
The Howard, p. 70

$$$$

Balmoral Hotel, p. 70
The Glasshouse, p. 70
Prestonfield, p. 73
The Scotsman, p. 69

By Experience

BEST SPAS

Balmoral Hotel, $$$$,
p. 70

The Scotsman, $$$$,
p. 69

BEST HISTORIC HOTELS

Balmoral Hotel, $$$$,
p. 70
Elmview, $, p. 73

BEST CONCIERGE

The Howard, $$$, p. 70
Malmaison, $$, p. 74

MOST ROMANTIC

Prestonfield, $$$$, p. 73
The Witchery, $$$$, p. 69

MOST KID-FRIENDLY

Caledonian Hilton Hotel,
$$$, p. 70
Knight Residence, $$,
p. 68

$$$$ ▦ **The Scotsman.** A magnificent turn-of-the-20th-century building, with

Fodor's Choice a marble staircase and a fascinating history—it was once the headquar-

★ ters of the *Scotsman* newspaper—now houses this modern, luxurious hotel. **Pros:** gorgeous surroundings; personalized service. **Cons:** no air-conditioning; spa can be noisy. ⊠ *20 N. Bridge, Old Town* ☎ *0131/ 556–5565* ⊕ *www.thescotsmanhotel.co.uk* ⤶ *56 rooms, 13 suites* ♿ *In-room: no a/c, Internet, Wi-Fi. In-hotel: restaurant, bar, pool, gym, spa* ▯⊙▮ *Breakfast* ✛ *G3.*

$$ ▦ **Ten Hill Place.** This stylish hotel just around the corner from the Fes-tival Theatre has impeccable service. **Pros:** well kept; close to every-thing but not in the midst of the brouhaha. **Cons:** rooms can be too dark; peekaboo glass doors on the bathrooms. ⊠ *10 Hill Pl., Old Town* ☎ *0131/662–2080* ⊕ *www.tenhillplace.com* ⤶ *78 rooms* ♿ *In-room: Internet. In-hotel: bar, parking* ▯⊙▮ *Breakfast* ✛ *H5.*

$$$$ ▦ **The Witchery.** This lavishly theatrical lodging promises a night to remember. **Pros:** the Gothic drama and intriguing antiques; sumptuous dining. **Cons:** can be noisy at night; rooms may feel too cluttered for some. ⊠ *Castlehill, Royal Mile, Old Town* ☎ *0131/225–5613* ⊕ *www. thewitchery.com* ⤶ *8 suites* ♿ *In-room: no a/c. In-hotel: restaurant* ▯⊙▮ *Breakfast* ✛ *F4.*

NEW TOWN

Use the coordinate (⊕ B2) at the end of each listing to locate a site on the corresponding map.

$ **Ardenlee Guest House.** An exquisite Victorian-tile floor is one of many original features at this gem of a guesthouse tucked away from the hustle and bustle of the city center. **Pros:** family-run establishment; good value, especially for long-term stays. **Cons:** few amenities; uphill walk to the city center. ⊠ *9 Eyre Pl., New Town* ☎ *0131/556–2838* ⊕ *www.ardenlee.co.uk* ⟿ *9 rooms, 7 with bath* ⚫ *In-room: no a/c, Wi-Fi* ⟨◎⟩ *Breakfast* ⊕ *E1.*

$$$$ **Balmoral Hotel.** The attention to detail in the elegant rooms—colors
Fodor's Choice   were picked to echo the country's heathers and moors—and the sheer
★   élan that has re-created the Edwardian splendor of this grand, former railroad hotel make staying at the Balmoral a special introduction to Edinburgh. **Pros:** big and beautiful building; top-hatted doorman; quality bathroom goodies. **Cons:** small pool; spa books up fast; restaurants can be very busy. ⊠ *1 Princes St., New Town* ☎ *0131/556–2414* ⊕ *www.thebalmoralhotel.com* ⟿ *168 rooms, 20 suites* ⚫ *In-room: Internet. In-hotel: restaurant, bar, pool, gym, spa, business center, parking* ⟨◎⟩ *Breakfast* ⊕ *G2.*

$$$ **Caledonian Hilton Hotel.** "The Caley," a conspicuous block of red sand-
☾   stone beyond the west end of West Princes Street Gardens, has imposing Victorian decor that has been faithfully preserved. **Pros:** service with a smile; lots of choices at breakfast. **Cons:** Internet access is extra; decor looks a bit tired in places. ⊠ *Princes St., New Town* ☎ *0131/222–8888* ⊕ *www.hilton.co.uk/caledonian* ⟿ *254 rooms, 20 suites* ⚫ *In-room: Internet, Wi-Fi. In-hotel: restaurant, bar, pool, parking* ⟨◎⟩ *Breakfast* ⊕ *C4.*

$ **Gerald's Place.** Although he is not a native of the city, Gerald Della-Porta is one of those B&B owners to whom Edinburgh owes so much: forget the clichés—you really are welcomed into his home and treated like a most honored guest. **Pros:** the advice and thoughtfulness of the owner; spacious rooms. **Cons:** stairs are difficult to manage; an uphill walk to the city center; cash only. ⊠ *21B Abercromby Pl.* ☎ *0131/558–7017* ⊕ *www.geraldsplace.com* ⟿ *2 rooms* ⚫ *In-room: no a/c* ▤ *No credit cards* ⟨◎⟩ *Breakfast* ⊕ *E1.*

$$$$ **The Glasshouse.** Glass walls extend from the 19th-century facade of a former church, foreshadowing the daring interior of one of the city's chicest boutique hotels. **Pros:** near all the attractions; very modern and stylish. **Cons:** perhaps a little sterile for some; nightclub downstairs is noisy. ⊠ *2 Greenside Pl., New Town* ☎ *0131/525–8200* ⊕ *www.theetoncollection.com* ⟿ *65 rooms, 18 suites* ⚫ *In-room: safe, Internet, Wi-Fi. In-hotel: bar* ⟨◎⟩ *Breakfast* ⊕ *G1.*

$$$ **The Howard.** This hotel is in a classic New Town building, elegantly
Fodor's Choice   proportioned and superbly outfitted; antique furniture and original art
★   throughout make the Howard like a swank private club. **Pros:** small but grand building; staff has a great attitude; special afternoon tea. **Cons:** not for younger travelers; noisy neighborhood. ⊠ *34 Great King St., New Town* ☎ *0131/557–3500* ⊕ *www.thehoward.com* ⟿ *18*

2

rooms, 5 suites ⚼ *In-room: no a/c, Wi-Fi. In-hotel: restaurant, parking* ⫿◉⫿ *Breakfast* ✢ *E1.*

$ 🏨 **Inverleith Hotel.** Across from the Royal Botanical Gardens, this renovated Victorian town house has cozy, well-lighted rooms with velour bedspreads, dark wooden furniture, and pale-gold curtains. **Pros:** quiet surroundings; knowledgeable staff. **Cons:** some rooms are small; narrow passageways; uphill walk to the city center. ⊠ *5 Inverleith Terr., New Town* ☎ *0131/556–2745* ⊕ *www.inverleithhotel.co.uk* ⟿ *12 rooms, 2 apartments* ⚼ *In-room: no a/c, Wi-Fi. In-hotel: bar, parking* ⫿◉⫿ *Breakfast* ✢ *C1.*

$$$ 🏨 **Tigerlilly.** On hip George Street, this boutique hotel has everything a girl could imagine—bowls of fresh fruit, designer candles, hair straighteners—for a night away from home: but there's plenty for the guys, too. **Pros:** chic yet not intimidating; laid-back but efficient staff. **Cons:** no views; can be noisy. ⊠ *125 George St., New Town* ☎ *0131/225–5005* ⊕ *www.tigerlilyedinburgh.co.uk* ⟿ *33 rooms* ⚼ *In-room: Wi-Fi. In-hotel: restaurant, bar, laundry facilities* ⫿◉⫿ *Breakfast* ✢ *C3.*

$ 🏨 **Walton Hotel.** This B&B in a Georgian town house is a 10-minute walk from the city center. **Pros:** top-class staff; bountiful breakfasts. **Cons:** limited parking; some rooms are below street level. ⊠ *79 Dundas St., New Town* ☎ *0131/556–1137* ⊕ *www.waltonhotel.com* ⟿ *10 rooms* ⚼ *In-room: no a/c, Internet, Wi-Fi. In-hotel: parking* ⫿◉⫿ *Breakfast* ✢ *E1.*

HAYMARKET

Use the coordinate (✢ B2) at the end of each listing to locate a site on the corresponding map.

$$$ 🏨 **Kew House and Apartments.** With such sumptuous rooms, you might think that Kew House was a full-service hotel. **Pros:** as clean as a whistle; thoughtful touches throughout; close to Water of Leith walk. **Cons:** longish walk to the city center; traffic noise on street side. ⊠ *1 Kew Terr., Haymarket* ☎ *0131/313–0700* ⊕ *www.kewhouse.com* ⟿ *6 rooms, 2 apartments* ⚼ *In-room: no a/c, Wi-Fi. In-hotel: parking* ⫿◉⫿ *Breakfast* ✢ *A5.*

$ 🏨 **Victorian Town House.** In a leafy crescent, this house once belonged to David Alan Stevenson, cousin of Robert Louis Stevenson. **Pros:** serene surroundings; gracious staff. **Cons:** no parking nearby ⊠ *14 Eglinton Terr., Haymarket* ☎ *0131/337–7088* ⊕ *www.thevictoriantownhouse. co.uk* ⟿ *3 rooms* ⚼ *In-room: no a/c, Wi-Fi* ⫿◉⫿ *Breakfast* ✢ *A4.*

WEST END

Use the coordinate (✢ B2) at the end of each listing to locate a site on the corresponding map.

$$ 🏨 **The Bonham.** This hotel in the elegant West End carries out a successful, sophisticated flirtation with modernity that makes it stand out from its neighbors. **Pros:** thorough yet unobtrusive service; excellent restaurant. **Cons:** not many common areas; can have a business-hotel feel. ⊠ *35 Drumsheugh Gardens, West End* ☎ *0131/226–6050* ⊕ *www.*

thebonham.com ⟳ *42 rooms, 6 suites* ⚯ *In-room: no a/c, Wi-Fi. In-hotel: restaurant, parking* |⦿| *Breakfast* ✛ *A3.*

$$$ ⊞ **Channings.** Five Edwardian terraced town houses make up this intimate, elegant hotel in an upscale West End neighborhood just minutes from Princes Street. **Pros:** near Stockbridge shops and eateries; inventive color schemes. **Cons:** not all rooms are equal; breakfasts are a bit meager and cost £5 extra. ⊠ *12–16 S. Learmonth Gardens, West End* ☎ *0131/315–2226* ⊕ *www.channings.co.uk* ⟳ *36 rooms, 5 suites* ⚯ *In-room: no a/c, Wi-Fi. In-hotel: restaurant, bar* |⦿| *Breakfast* ✛ *A1.*

$$ ⊞ **Rutland Hotel.** The building may have once been the residence of Sir
Fodor's Choice   Joseph Lister—known as the "father of antiseptic surgery"—but there's
★   nothing clinical about this acclaimed boutique hotel at the west end of Princes Street. **Pros:** friendly staff; not pretentious; great bar and restaurant. **Cons:** the nearby taxi rank can harbor some unsavory characters on weekend evenings. ⊠ *1–3 Rutland St., West End* ☎ *0131/229–3402* ⊕ *www.therutlandhotel.com* ⟳ *12 rooms* ⚯ *In-room: no a/c, Wi-Fi. In-hotel: restaurant, bar, parking* |⦿| *Breakfast* ✛ *C4.*

SOUTH SIDE

Use the coordinate (✛ B2) at the end of each listing to locate a site on the corresponding map.

$ ⊞ **94DR.** This is hardly your average guesthouse; like owners Paul Lightfoot and John MacEwan—a self-described "high-octane" couple—94DR reaches for the stars with its stylish decor and contemporary trappings. **Pros:** warm welcome; gay-friendly vibe; smashing breakfast. **Cons:** monochromatic color schemes; a long walk to the city center. ⊠ *94 Dalkeith Rd., South Side* ☎ *0131/662–9265* ⊕ *www.94dr. com* ⟳ *7 rooms* ⚯ *In-room: Wi-Fi. In-hotel: business center, parking* |⦿| *Breakfast* ✛ *H6.*

$$ ⊞ **23 Mayfield.** A self-styled "boutique guest house," 23 Mayfield is a cut above your average B&B; the Victorian villa features lots of original elements expertly complemented by dark wood furniture, lovely artwork, and antiquarian books to create a sumptuous atmosphere. **Pros:** relaxing atmosphere; helpful yet unobtrusive service; gourmet breakfast featuring famed porridge. **Cons:** need to book well in advance. ⊠ *23 Mayfield Gardens, South Side* ☎ *0131/667–5806* ⟳ *9 rooms* ⚯ *In-hotel: parking* |⦿| *Breakfast* ✛ *H6.*

$ ⊞ **AmarAgua.** Deep-pile carpets, floral drapes with plenty of swags, and well-designed furniture create restrained opulence in this Victorian town house 10 minutes by bus from the city center. **Pros:** quiet setting; snug rooms. **Cons:** far from the city center; minimum stay. ⊠ *10 Kilmaurs Terr., Newington* ☎ *0131/667–6775* ⊕ *www.amaragua. co.uk* ⟳ *5 rooms, 4 with bath* ⚯ *In-room: no a/c, Wi-Fi* ☾ *Closed Jan.* |⦿| *Breakfast* ✛ *H6.*

$ ⊞ **Ashdene House.** On a quiet residential street sits this Edwardian house, one of the city's first-class B&Bs, and still a worthy choice. **Pros:** homemade breads at breakfast; spacious rooms. **Cons:** not within walking distance of the center. ⊠ *23 Fountainhall Rd., The Grange* ☎ *0131/667–*

6026 ⊕ *www.ashdenehouse.com* ➲ *5 rooms* ♿ *In-room: no a/c, Wi-Fi. In-hotel: parking* ⟨○⟨ *Breakfast* ✛ *H6.*

$ ⬚ **Elmview.** Near Bruntsfield Links, the Elmview has a verdant location that completely justifies the name. **Pros:** next to the historic golf course; superb breakfasts; helpful owners. **Cons:** books up in advance; doesn't cater to families with young children; closed in winter months. ✉ *15 Glengyle Terr., Bruntsfield* ☎ *0131/228–1973* ⊕ *www.elmview.co.uk* ➲ *5 rooms* ♿ *In-room: no a/c, Wi-Fi. In-hotel: some age restrictions* ☾ *Closed Nov.–Apr.* ⟨○⟨ *Breakfast* ✛ *D6.*

$ ⬚ **Glenalmond House.** Longtime hoteliers Jimmy and Fiona Mackie are well schooled in making guests happy. **Pros:** knowledgeable owners; breakfast fit for champions. **Cons:** smallish bathrooms; in a sleepy residential area that's a little bit of a walk to the New Town. ✉ *25 Mayfield Gardens, South Side* ☎ *0131/668–2392* ⊕ *www.glenalmondhouse.com* ➲ *10 rooms* ♿ *In-room: no a/c, Wi-Fi. In-hotel: parking* ⟨○⟨ *Breakfast* ✛ *H6.*

$$$$ ⬚ **Prestonfield.** The cattle grazing on the hotel's 20-acre grounds let you know that you've entered a different world, even though you're five minutes by car from the Royal Mile. **Pros:** eccentric grandeur; comfortable beds. **Cons:** slightly haphazard service; brooding decor can look gloomy. ✉ *Priestfield Rd., Prestonfield* ☎ *0131/225–7800* ⊕ *www. prestonfield.com* ➲ *18 rooms, 5 suites* ♿ *In-room: Wi-Fi. In-hotel: restaurant, bar, parking* ⟨○⟨ *Breakfast* ✛ *H6.*

$ ⬚ **Teviotdale House.** The lavish interior of this 1848 town house includes canopy beds and miles of festive fabrics. **Pros:** the kind of porridge that builds a nation; owners take pride in their hospitality. **Cons:** a long walk from the city center; not all bathrooms have tubs. ✉ *53 Grange Loan, The Grange* ☎ *0131/667–4376* ⊕ *www.teviotdalehouse.com* ➲ *7 rooms* ♿ *In-room: no a/c, Wi-Fi* ⟨○⟨ *Breakfast* ✛ *H6.*

LEITH

Use the coordinate (✛ B2) at the end of each listing to locate a site on the corresponding map.

$$ ⬚ **Ardmor House.** This low-key guesthouse combines the original features of a Victorian home with stylish contemporary furnishings. **Pros:** warm and friendly owner; decorated with great style; gay-friendly environment. **Cons:** a bit out of the way; double room on the ground floor is tiny. ✉ *74 Pilrig St., Leith* ☎☎ *0131/554–4944* ⊕ *www.ardmorhouse. com* ➲ *5 rooms* ♿ *In-room: no a/c, Wi-Fi* ⟨○⟨ *Breakfast* ✛ *G1.*

$ ⬚ **The Conifers.** This trim B&B in a red-sandstone town house north of the New Town offers simple, traditionally decorated rooms. **Pros:** nice mix of old and new; many original fittings; hearty breakfasts. **Cons:** a long walk to the city center; not all rooms have en-suite bathrooms. ✉ *56 Pilrig St., Leith* ☎ *0131/554–5162* ⊕ *www.conifersguesthouse. com* ➲ *4 rooms, 3 with bath* ♿ *In-room: no a/c* ▭ *No credit cards* ⟨○⟨ *Breakfast* ✛ *G1.*

$ ⬚ **Fraoch House.** A popular option, this B&B manages to combine a homey feel and stylish decor without leaning too far in either direction. **Pros:** a warm welcome; great DVD library. **Cons:** uphill walk to the city center. ⊠ *66 Pilrig St., Leith* ☎ *0131/554–1353* ⊕ *www. fraochhouse.com* ⇩ *9 rooms* ⚬ *In-room: no a/c, Wi-Fi. In-hotel: parking* |⊙| *Breakfast* ✛ *G1.*

$$ 🎏 **Malmaison.** Once a seamen's hostel, the Malmaison now draws a more refined clientele to this chic conversion. **Pros:** impressive building; great location. **Cons:** not as immaculate as it was; bar can be rowdy at night; long way from the center of town. ⊠ *1 Tower Pl., Leith* ☎ *0131/468–5000* ⊕ *www.malmaison-edinburgh.com* ⇩ *100 rooms, 9 suites* ⚬ *In-room: no a/c, Internet. In-hotel: restaurant, bar, gym, parking* |⊙| *Breakfast* ✛ *G1.*

NIGHTLIFE AND THE ARTS

THE ARTS

Those who think Edinburgh's arts scene consists of just the elegiac wail of a bagpipe and the twang of a fiddle or two will be proved wrong by the hundreds of performing-arts options. The jewel in the crown, of course, is the famed Edinburgh International Festival, which now attracts the best in music, dance, theater, painting, and sculpture from all over the globe during three weeks from mid-August to early September. The *Scotsman* and *Herald,* Scotland's leading daily newspapers, carry listings and reviews in their arts pages every day, with special editions during the festival. Tickets are generally available from box offices in advance; in some cases they're also available from certain designated travel agents or at the door, although concerts by national orchestras often sell out long before the day of the performance.

DANCE

Festival Theatre. Scottish Ballet productions and other dance acts appear at the Festival Theatre. ⊠ *13–29 Nicolson St., Old Town* ☎ *0131/529–6000* ⊕ *www.eft.co.uk.*

Royal Lyceum. Visiting contemporary dance companies perform in the Royal Lyceum. ⊠ *Grindlay St., West End* ☎ *0131/248–4848* ⊕ *www. lyceum.org.uk.*

FESTIVALS

Edinburgh Festival Fringe. The Edinburgh Festival Fringe presents many theatrical and musical events, some by amateur groups (you have been warned), and is more of a grab bag than the official festival. Many events are free but some do require tickets; prices start at £2 and go up to £15. During festival time—roughly the same as the International Festival—it's possible to arrange your own entertainment program from morning to midnight and beyond, if you don't feel overwhelmed by the variety available. ⊠ *Edinburgh Festival Fringe Office, 180 High St., Old Town* ☎ *0131/226–0026* ⊕ *www.edfringe.com.*

☾ **Edinburgh International Book Festival.** The Edinburgh International Book Festival, a two-week-long event in August, pulls together a heady mix of the biggest-selling and the most challenging authors from around the world and gets them talking about their work in a magnificent tent

CLOSE UP

Festivals in Edinburgh

Walking around Edinburgh in late July, you'll likely feel the first vibrations of the earthquake that is festival time, which shakes the city throughout August and into September. You may hear reference to an "Edinburgh Festival," but this is really an umbrella term for five separate festivals all taking place around the same time. For an overview, check out ⊕ www. edinburghfestivals.co.uk.

Edinburgh International Festival. The best-known and oldest of the city's festivals is the Edinburgh International Festival, founded in 1947 when Europe was recovering from World War II. In recent years the festival has drawn as many as 400,000 people to Edinburgh, with more than 100 acts by world-renowned music, opera, theater, and dance performers, filling all the major venues in the city. Tickets for the festival go on sale in April, and many sell out within the month. However, you may still be able to purchase tickets, which range from £6 to £60, during the festival.

Edinburgh Festival Fringe. If the Edinburgh International Festival is the parent of British festivals, then the Edinburgh Festival Fringe is its unruly child. The Festival Fringe started in 1947 at the same time as the International Festival, when eight companies that were not invited to perform in the latter decided to attend anyway. Knowing there would be an audience,

these companies found small, local theaters to host them. By 2005 there were 1,800 shows and 27,000 performances of those shows at the Fringe, making it the largest festival of its kind in the world. Its events range from the brilliant to the impossibly mundane, badly performed, and downright tacky.

While the Fringe is going on, most of the city center becomes one huge performance area, with fire-eaters, sword swallowers, unicyclists, jugglers, string quartets, jazz groups, stand-up comics, and magicians all thronging into High Street and Princes Street. Every available theater and pseudo performance space is utilized—church halls, community centers, parks, sports fields, putting greens, and nightclubs. In 1954 the Edinburgh Festival Fringe Society was formed, and it oversees everything from ticket sales to publicity.

Festivals for all interests. Edinburgh festival time can fill almost any artistic need. Besides the International Festival and Festival Fringe, look for the Edinburgh Jazz and Blues Festival, the International Book Festival, and the Military Tattoo, which includes reenactments of historic events, military marching bands, Highland dancing, and more. The Edinburgh International Film Festival used to take place in August, but it moved to June when the calendar is less congested.

2

village. Workshops for would-be writers and children are hugely popular. ⊠ *Charlotte Sq. Gardens, New Town* ☎ *0131/718–5666* ⊕ *www. edbookfest.co.uk.*

Fodor'sChoice ★ **Edinburgh International Festival.** The Edinburgh International Festival, the flagship arts event of the year, attracts performing artists of international caliber to a celebration of music, dance, drama, and artwork. Advance information, programs, tickets, and reservations are available from the impressive Victorian-Gothic Tolbooth Kirk. Tickets range from £7 to £60, depending on the event, and some can sell out quickly in late March when they are first available. The festival runs from mid-August through early September. ⊠ *Edinburgh Festival Centre, Castlehill, Old Town* ☎ *0131/473–2009 information, 0131/473–2000 tickets* ⊕ *www.eif.co.uk.*

Edinburgh International Film Festival. The Edinburgh International Film Festival has grown into one of Europe's foremost film festivals. It is held in late June. ⊠ *Edinburgh Film Festival Office, 88 Lothian Rd., West End* ☎ *0131/228–2688* ⊕ *www.edfilmfest.org.uk.*

☼ **Edinburgh International Science Festival.** The Edinburgh International Science Festival, held around Easter each year, aims to make science accessible, interesting, but above all fun. Children's events turn science into entertainment and are especially popular. ⊠ *The Hub, Castlehill* ☎ *0131/553–0320* ⊕ *www.sciencefestival.co.uk.*

★ **Edinburgh Military Tattoo.** The Edinburgh Military Tattoo may not be art, but it is certainly Scottish culture. It's sometimes confused with the Edinburgh International Festival, partly because both events take place in August (though the Tattoo starts and finishes a week earlier). This celebration of martial music and skills with bands, gymnastics, and stunt motorcycle teams is on the castle esplanade, and the dramatic backdrop augments the spectacle. Dress warmly for late-evening performances. Even if it rains, the show most definitely goes on. ⊠ *Edinburgh Military Tattoo Office, 32 Market St., Old Town* ☎ *0131/225–1188* ⊕ *www.edintattoo.co.uk.*

Edinburgh Jazz and Blues Festival. Edinburgh Jazz and Blues Festival, held in late July, attracts international top performers and brings local enthusiasts out of their living rooms and into the pubs and clubs to listen and play. ⊠ *89 Giles St., Leith* ☎ *0131/467–5200* ⊕ *www.edinburghjazzfestival.co.uk.*

FILM

Cameo. The Cameo has one large and two small auditoriums, both of which are extremely comfortable, plus a bar with late-night specials. ⊠ *38 Home St., Tollcross* ☎ *0871/902–5723* ⊕ *www.picturehouses.co.uk.*

Filmhouse. Apart from cinema chains, Edinburgh has the excellent three-screen Filmhouse, the best venue for modern, foreign-language, offbeat, or simply less commercial films. ⊠ *88 Lothian Rd., West End* ☎ *0131/228–2688 box office* ⊕ *www.filmhousecinema.com.*

MUSIC

Festival Theatre. The Festival Theatre hosts performances by the Scottish Ballet and the Scottish Opera. ⊠ *13–29 Nicolson St., Old Town* ☎ *0131/529–6000* ⊕ *www.fctt.org.uk.*

Playhouse. The Playhouse leans toward popular artists, comedy acts, and musicals. ⊠ *Greenside Pl., East End* ☎ *0131/524–3333.*

Queen's Hall. The intimate Queen's Hall hosts small recitals. ⊠ *Clerk St., Old Town* ☎ *0131/668–2019.*

Usher Hall. Edinburgh's grandest venue, Usher Hall hosts national and international performers and groups, including the Royal Scottish National Orchestra. ⊠ *Lothian Rd., West End* ☎ *0131/228–1155.*

THEATER

MODERN **Traverse Theatre.** With its specially designed space, the Traverse Theatre has developed a solid reputation for new, stimulating Scottish plays and dance productions. ⊠ *10 Cambridge St., West End* ☎ *0131/228–1404.*

TRADITIONAL Edinburgh has three main theaters—the Festival Theatre, King's, and the Royal Lyceum—as well as others.

Brunton Theatre. On the eastern outskirts of Edinburgh, the Brunton Theatre presents a regular program of repertory, touring, and amateur performances. ⊠ *Ladywell Way, Musselburgh* ☎ *0131/665–2240.*

Church Hill Theatre. The Church Hill Theatre hosts high-quality productions by local dramatic societies. ⊠ *Morningside Rd., Morningside* ☎ *0131/447–7597.*

Festival Theatre. This popular venue presents opera and ballet, as well as the occasional excellent touring play. ⊠ *13–29 Nicolson St., Old Town* ☎ *0131/529–6000.*

King's. The King's has a program of contemporary and traditional dramatic works. ⊠ *2 Leven St., Tollcross* ☎ *0131/529–6000.*

Playhouse. Popular concerts and musicals, along with the occassional ballet and opera production, are staged at the Playhouse. ⊠ *Greenside Pl., East End* ☎ *0844/871–3014.*

Royal Lyceum. The Royal Lyceum presents traditional plays and contemporary works, often transferred from or prior to their London West End showings. ⊠ *Grindlay St., West End* ☎ *0131/248–4848* ⊕ *www. lyceum.org.uk.*

NIGHTLIFE

The nightlife scene in Edinburgh is vibrant—whatever you're looking for, you'll most certainly find it here, and you won't have to go far. Expect old-style pubs as well as cutting-edge bars and clubs. Live music pours out of many watering holes on weekends, particularly folk, blues, and jazz. Well-known artists perform at some of the larger venues.

Edinburgh's 400-odd pubs are a study in themselves. In the eastern and northern districts of the city you can find some grim, inhospitable-looking places that proclaim that drinking is no laughing matter. But throughout Edinburgh many pubs have deliberately traded in their old spit-and-sawdust images for atmospheric revivals of the warm, oak-paneled, leather-chaired howffs of a more leisurely age. Most pubs and bars are open weekdays and Saturday from 11 am to midnight, and from 12:30 to midnight on Sunday.

The List and *The Skinny* carry the most up-to-date details about cultural events. *The List* is available at newsstands throughout the city, while *The Skinny* is free and can be picked up at a number of pubs, clubs, and shops around town. The *Herald* and *Scotsman* newspa-

Hogmanay: Hello, New Year

In Scotland, New Year's Eve is called Hogmanay. Other places in Scotland have public celebrations, but Edinburgh's multiday event at sites in the heart of town is famous throughout Europe and beyond, with something for everyone. Yes, it's still winter and cold, but joining the festivities with up to 80,000 other people can be memorable.

Around Scotland, celebrations continue the next day with customs such as "first-footing"—visiting your neighbors with gifts that include whisky, all with the purpose of bringing good fortune. It's so important that January 2 as well as January 1 is a holiday in Scotland; the rest of the United Kingdom settles for recuperating on January 1.

WHAT TO EXPECT

Edinburgh's Hogmanay extends over several days with spectacles and performances (music, dance, and more); the yearly-changing lineup includes many free events. Festivities featuring fire add a dramatic motif; buildings may open for rare night tours; a *ceilidh* offers dancing outdoors to

traditional music; and family concerts and serious discussions during the day round out the agenda. At the heart of Hogmanay, though, is the evening street party on New Year's Eve, with different music stages, food and drink (and people do drink), and the heart-lifting—despite the cold— sight of glowing fireworks over Edinburgh Castle and the singing of "Auld Lang Syne," written by Scotland's own Robert Burns.

PLANNING BASICS

Costs vary: entering the New Year's Eve street party costs around £10, and certain entertainments that night will cost more: a concert may be £30 or so, including the street party fee. Other events are included in the basic entrance cost, or may even be free if they are not part of the street party. Book rooms ahead. Prices may go up, but look for multiday packages; it's also easy to take buses outside the center. Obvious but essential is warmth: crazy hats and the bundled-up look are de rigueur. Check out ⊕ *www.edinburghshogmanay. com* for full details, and have a happy Hogmanay!

---

pers are good for reviews and notices of upcoming events throughout Scotland.

OLD TOWN

BARS AND PUBS **Black Bo's.** One of the coziest places in town, Black Bo's has a decent selection of beers from around the world, vegetarian food, and an eclectic soundtrack. ⊠ *57–61 Blackfriars St., Old Town* ☎ *0131/557–6136.*

Canons' Gait. Canons' Gait has a fine selection of local real ales and malts. It stages live jazz and blues, as well as fringe comedy in the cellar bar. ⊠ *232 Canongate, Old Town* ☎ *0131/556–4481.*

The Last Drop. There's plenty of atmosphere amid the nooks and crannies at The Last Drop, which takes its name from a nearby site of public hangings. ⊠ *74-78 Grassmarket, Old Town* ☎ *0131/225–4851.*

FOLK CLUBS You can usually find folk musicians performing in pubs throughout Edinburgh, although there's been a decline in the live-music scene because of dwindling profits and the predominance of popular theme bars.

Royal Oak. The friendly "folk at the Oak" are what make the Royal Oak so special. This cozy bar presents live blues and folk most nights. ⊠ *1 Infirmary St., Old Town* ☎ *0131/557–2976.*

Whistle Binkies Pub. Whistle Binkies Pub is a friendly basement bar with great rock and folk music every night of the week. ⊠ *4–6 South Bridge, Old Town* ☎ *0131/557–5114.*

NIGHTCLUBS **Bongo Club.** The bohemian Bongo Club stages indie, rockabilly, and techno gigs, as well as various club and comedy nights. ⊠ *37 Holyrood Rd., Old Town* ☎ *0131/558–7604* ⊕ *www.thebongoclub.co.uk.*

Cabaret Voltaire. This subterranean club hosts everything from cheesy raves to cutting-edge bands and DJs. ⊠ *36–38 Blair St., Old Town* ☎ *0131/220–6176* ⊕ *www.thecabaretvoltaire.com.*

NEW TOWN

BARS AND PUBS **Abbotsford.** A handsome Victorian-era island bar serves an ever-changing selection of five real ales at the Abbotsford. ⊠ *3 Rose St., New Town* ☎ *0131/225–5276.*

The Basement. The Basement is a longtime pre-club favorite with the younger crowd. The Hawaiian-shirted bar staff adds to the general amiability. ⊠ *10A–12A Broughton St., New Town* ☎ *0131/557–0097.*

Blue Blazer. This cozy, dark-wood bar has a top-notch selection of real ale, 50 malt whiskies, and 75 rums, all of which are enjoyed by a friendly, diverse crowd. ⊠ *2 Spittal St., West End* ☎ *0131/229–5030.*

★ **Café Royal Circle Bar.** Famed for its atmospheric Victorian interiors—think ornate stucco, etched mirrors, tiled murals, stained glass, and leather booths—the Café Royal Circle Bar draws a cast of Edinburgh characters for its drinks and its seafood platters. ⊠ *19 W. Regent St., New Town* ☎ *0131/556–1884.*

Cask and Barrel. A spacious, busy pub, Cask and Barrel lets you sample hand-pulled ales at the horseshoe-shaped bar, reflected in a collection of brewery mirrors. ⊠ *115 Broughton St., New Town* ☎ *0131/556–3132.*

Cumberland Bar. Fine ales on tap, wood trim, typical pub mirrors, and a beer garden are the draws at the Cumberland Bar. ⊠ *1–3 Cumberland St., New Town* ☎ *0131/558–3134.*

Guildford Arms. This place is worth a visit just for its interior. Ornate plasterwork, cornices, friezes, and wood paneling form the backdrop for some excellent draft ales, including Orkney Dark Island. ⊠ *1 W. Register St., east end of Princes St., New Town* ☎ *0131/556–4312.*

Joseph Pearce's. One of four Swedish-owned pubs in Edinburgh, Joseph Pearce's has a continental feel, thanks to the cosmopolitan staff and Scandinavian-themed cocktails. ⊠ *23 Elm Row, New Town* ☎ *0131/556–4140.*

Kay's Bar. Housed in a former Georgian coach house is this friendly spot serving 50 single-malt whiskies, seven guest ales, and decent bottled beers. ⊠ *39 Jamaica St., New Town* ☎ *0131/225–1858.*

Milne's Bar. This spot is known as the poets' pub because of its popularity with Edinburgh's literati. Pies and baked potatoes go well with seven real ales and various guest beers (meaning anything besides the house brew). Victorian advertisements and photos of old Edinburgh give the place an old-time feel. ⊠ *35 Hanover St., New Town* ☎ *0131/225–6738.*

Star Bar. Tucked away but well worth seeking out, Star Bar has a beer garden, table soccer, and—a rarity—a good jukebox. ⊠ *1 Northumberland Pl., New Town* ☎ *0131/539–8070.*

Teuchters. With more than 80 whiskies for sale and comfy sofas, Teuchters is a fine place to relax with a dram. ⊠ *26 William St., West End* ☎ *0131/226–1036.*

Tonic. A stylish basement bar with bouncy stools and comfy sofas, Tonic advertises more than 200 cocktails from which to choose. ⊠ *34A Castle St., New Town* ☎ *0131/225–6431.*

CEILIDHS AND SCOTTISH EVENINGS
Thistle King James Hotel. For those who feel a trip to Scotland is not complete without hearing the "Braes of Yarrow" or "Auld Robin Gray," several hotels present traditional Scottish-music evenings in the summer season. Head for the Thistle King James Hotel to see *Jamie's Scottish Evening,* an extravaganza of Scottish song, tartan, plaid, and bagpipes that takes place nightly from April to October. The cost is £55, including a four-course dinner. ⊠ *Thistle King James Hotel, 107 Leith St., New Town* ☎ *0131/556–0111.*

COMEDY CLUBS
Stand. The Edinburgh Festival Fringe has become one of the world's most famous events for comedy. But throughout the year you can laugh until your sides split at the Stand, which hosts both famous names and up-and-coming acts. ⊠ *5 York Pl., East End* ☎ *0131/558–7272.*

GAY AND LESBIAN
There's a burgeoning gay and lesbian scene in Edinburgh, and the city has many predominantly gay clubs, bars, and cafés. However, don't expect the scene to be as open as in London, New York, or even Glasgow. *The List* and *The Skinny* have sections that focus on gay and lesbian venues.

Blue Moon Café. Edinburgh's longest-running gay café, the Blue Moon Café has a cozy basement bar and a friendly diner. ⊠ *36 Broughton St., New Town* ☎ *0131/556–2788.*

CC Blooms. Modern, colorful, and open nightly, CC Blooms plays a mix of musical styles. Once a month there's an icebreaker evening for those new to the gay scene. ⊠ *23–24 Greenside Pl., New Town* ☎ *0131/556–9331.*

GHQ. More refined than the other gay spots, GHQ hosts a number of the city's best DJs. ⊠ *4 Picardy Pl., New Town* ☎ *0845/166–6024.*

Regent. The Regent has a very homey vibe—dogs are welcome—and is renowned for its real ales. ⊠ *2 Montrose Terr., Abbeyhill* ☎ *0131/661–8198.*

NIGHTCLUBS
Liquid Room. Top indie bands and an eclectic mix of club nights (techno, hip-hop, and alternative, to name a few) make the Liquid Room a superb venue. ⊠ *9C Victoria St., New Town* ☎ *0131/225–2564* ⊕ *www.liquidroom.com.*

Opal Lounge. The Opal Lounge is a casual but stylish nightspot with a glam VIP lounge that was favored by Prince William while he attended university. ⊠ *51A George St., New Town* ☎ *0131/226–2275* ⊕ *www. opallounge.co.uk.*

SOUTH SIDE

BARS AND
PUBS

Cloisters. The Cloisters prides itself on the absence of music, gaming machines, and all other modern pub gimmicks. Instead, it specializes in real ales, malt whiskies, and good food, all at reasonable prices. ⊠ *26 Brougham St., Tollcross* ☎ *0131/221–9997.*

Leslie's Bar. An unspoiled Victorian establishment near the hotels and guesthouses of Newington, Leslie's Bar has a good range of traditional Scottish ales and whiskies. ⊠ *45 Ratcliffe Terr., South Side* ☎ *0131/667–7205.*

Under the Stairs. As you might guess from the name, Under the Stairs is situated below street level. This cozy, low-ceilinged place with quirky furniture specializes in cocktails and excellent bar food. ⊠ *3A Merchant St., Old Town* ☎ *0131/466–8550.*

LEITH

BARS AND
PUBS

★

The King's Wark. A 15th-century building houses The King's Wark, a popular pub with decent ales that is renowned for its food. Breakfasts are legendary, and are worth booking in advance. ⊠ *36 The Shore, Leith* ☎ *0131/554–9260.*

Malt and Hops. More than 260 years old, Malt and Hops overlooks the waterfront and has its own cask ales and is haunted by its own ghost. ⊠ *45 The Shore, Leith* ☎ *0131/555–0083.*

Robbie's. This classic pub with friendly regulars is a great place for catching big sporting events. ⊠ *367 Leith Walk, Leith* ☎ *0131/554–6850.*

SPORTS AND THE OUTDOORS

BICYCLING

Edinburgh is not the friendliest city for bikes; there's a lot of traffic, even on weekends. The tourist information center can point you toward some quieter routes just beyond the city center. Rentals cost £75 per week for a 21-speed or mountain bike. Daily rates (24 hours) are about £16, with half days costing £12.

Bike Trax. A variety of rental bikes is available at Bike Trax. ⊠ *11–13 Lochrin Pl., Tollcross* ☎ *0131/228–6633* ⊕ *www.biketrax.co.uk.*

Edinburgh Cycle Tours. Edinburgh Cycle Tours leads guided bicycle tours of the city from April to October. A three-hour tour runs twice a day and costs £20, which includes bike rental, a helmet, and waterproof gear. ☎ *0796/644–7206.*

CRICKET

Surprising even to many Scots, the game of bat and ball has a long history and healthy club scene in Scotland.

Grange Cricket Club. Between April and September, the beautiful old Grange Cricket Club ground, established in 1832, stages county cricket games and hosts various Scots league matches. Local club games are free to watch and make for a civilized introduction to the game. ⊠ *Port-gower Pl., Stockbridge* ☎ *0131/332–2148* ⊕ *www.grangecricket.org.*

GOLF

In Scotland, SSS indicates the "standard scratch score," the score a scratch golfer could achieve in ideal conditions.

Edinburgh and Scotland Information Centre. VisitScotland provides a free leaflet on golf in Scotland, available from the Edinburgh and Scotland Information Centre. ⊠ *3 Princes St., East End* ☎ *0131/625–8625* ⊕ *www.edinburgh.org.*

Braid Hills. Known to locals as Braids, this 18-hole course first opened in 1897 and extends over several small hills 3 mi south of Edinburgh. Expect wonderful views on a clear day of Arthur's Seat, Edinburgh Castle, North Berwick Law, and the Forth to Fife. The nearby 9-hole Princes course, which opened in 2003, is fun for beginners and families. ⊠ *Braids Hill Rd., Braidburn* ☎ *0131/447–6666* ⊕ *www.edinburghleisuregolf.co.uk/courses/braid-hills* 🖃 *£20–£24* ⁑ *Braids: 18 holes, 5,865 yds, par 70; Princes: 9 holes, 2,006 yds, par 31.*

Bruntsfield Links. Several tournaments are held each year at this championship course, opened in 1898 a couple of miles northwest of the city. ⊠ *32 Barnton Ave., Davidson's Mains* ☎ *0131/336–2006* ⊕ *www.bruntsfieldlinks.co.uk* 🖃 *Weekdays £65, weekends £70* ⁑ *18 holes, 6,446 yds, par 71.*

Duddingston. You can find this public parkland course, founded in 1895, 2 mi east of the city. A key feature and a perilous golfing hazard amid its undulating terrain is the Braid Burn. ⊠ *Duddingston Rd. W, Duddingston* ☎ *0131/661–7688* ⊕ *www.duddingstongolfclub.co.uk* 🖃 *£38* ⁑ *18 holes, 6,525 yds, Par 72.*

Liberton. This rolling public parkland course built in 1920 has tight fairways and smallish greens. ⊠ *Kingston Grange, 297 Gilmerton Rd., Liberton* ☎ *0131/664–3009* ⊕ *www.libertongc.co.uk* 🖃 *Weekdays £31, weekends £36* ⁑ *18 holes, 5,344 yds, Par 67.*

Lothianburn. You can see fine views of the Midlothian countryside from this hillside course, founded in 1893. It's located 6 mi south of the city. ⊠ *Biggar Rd., Fairmilehead* ☎ *0131/445–2288* ⊕ *www.lothianburngc.co.uk* 🖃 *Weekdays £15, weekends £20* ⁑ *18 holes, 5,692 yds, Par 71.*

Murrayfield. Only five minutes from the city center, this heathland-style course is kept in fine condition and commands outstanding views over Edinburgh. ⊠ *43 Murrayfield Rd., Murrayfield* ☎ *0131/337–3478* ⊕ *www.murrayfieldgolfclub.co.uk* 🖃 *£40* ⁑ *18 holes, 5,781 yds, Par 70.*

RUGBY

Murrayfield Stadium. At Murrayfield Stadium, home of the Scottish Rugby Union, Scotland's international rugby matches are played in early spring and fall. During that time of year, crowds of good-humored rugby fans from all over the world add greatly to the sense of excitement in the streets of Edinburgh. ⊠ *Roseburn Terr., Murrayfield* ☎ *0131/346–5000.*

RUNNING

Holyrood Park. In Holyrood Park, stick to jogging on the road around the volcanic mountain for a 2¼-mi trip. For a real challenge, charge up to the summit of Arthur's Seat, or to the halfway point, the Cat's Nick.

West Princes Street Gardens. The most convenient spot downtown for joggers is West Princes Street Gardens, which is separated from traffic by a 30-foot embankment. It has a half-mile loop on asphalt paths.

SOCCER

Like Glasgow, Edinburgh is soccer-mad, and there's an intense rivalry between the city's two professional teams. Remember, the game is called football in Britain.

Heart of Midlothian ("Hearts") Football Club. The Heart of Midlothian ("Hearts") Football Club plays in maroon and white and is based at Tynecastle. ☎ *0871/663–1874.*

Hibernian ("Hibs") Club. The green-bedecked Hibernian ("Hibs") Club plays its home matches at Easter Road. ☎ *0131/661–2159.*

SHOPPING

Despite its renown as a shopping street, **Princes Street** in the New Town may disappoint some visitors with its dull modern architecture, average chain stores, and fast-food outlets. One block north of Princes Street, **Rose Street** has many smaller specialty shops; part of the street is a pedestrian zone, so it's a pleasant place to browse. The shops on **George Street** in New Town tend to be fairly upscale. London names, such as Laura Ashley and Penhaligons, are prominent, though some of the older independent stores continue to do good business.

The streets crossing George Street—Hanover, Frederick, and Castle—are also worth exploring. **Dundas Street,** the northern extension of Hanover Street, beyond Queen Street Gardens, has several antiques shops. **Thistle Street,** originally George Street's "back lane," or service area, has several boutiques and more antiques shops.

As may be expected, many shops along the **Royal Mile** in Old Town sell what may be politely or euphemistically described as tourist-ware—whiskies, tartans, and tweeds. Careful exploration, however, will reveal some worthwhile establishments. Shops here also cater to highly specialized interests and hobbies. Close to the castle end of the Royal Mile, just off George IV Bridge, is **Victoria Street,** with specialty shops grouped in a small area. Follow the tiny West Bow to **Grassmarket** for more specialty stores.

Stafford and William streets form a small, upscale shopping area in a Georgian setting. Walk to the west end of Princes Street and then along its continuation, Shandwick Place, then turn right onto Stafford Street. William Street crosses Stafford halfway down.

North of Princes Street, on the way to the Royal Botanic Garden Edinburgh, is **Stockbridge,** an oddball shopping area of some charm, particularly on St. Stephen Street. To get here, walk north down Frederick

Street and Howe Street, away from Princes Street, then turn left onto North West Circus Place.

OLD TOWN

SPECIALTY SHOPS

BOOKS, PAPER, MAPS, AND GAMES

Armchair Books. Near the Grassmarket, Armchair Books is a chaotic secondhand bookshop heaving with tomes from your youth. ⊠ 72–74 W. Port, Old Town ☎ 0131/229–5927.

Carson Clark Gallery. Carson Clark Gallery specializes in antique maps, sea charts, and prints. ⊠ 181–183 Canongate, Old Town ☎ 0131/556–4710.

Main Point Books. This bibliophile's haven is stacked high with obscure first editions and bargain tomes. ⊠ 8 Lauriston St., Old Town ☎ 0131/228–4837.

CLOTHING BOUTIQUES

Bill Baber. One of the most imaginative of the many Scottish knitwear designers, Bill Baber is a long way from the conservative pastel woolies sold at some of the large mill shops. ⊠ 66 Grassmarket, Old Town ☎ 0131/225–3249.

Ragamuffin. If you don't make it up to the main shop on the Isle of Skye, the local outpost of Ragamuffin sells the funkiest and brightest knits produced in Scotland. ⊠ 278 Canongate, Old Town ☎ 0131/557–6007.

JEWELRY

Clarksons. A family firm, Clarksons handcrafts a unique collection of jewelry, including Celtic styles. The pieces here are made with silver, gold, platinum, and precious gems, with a particular emphasis on diamonds. ⊠ 87 W. Bow, Old Town ☎ 0131/225–8141.

SCOTTISH SPECIALTIES

Edinburgh Old Town Weaving Company. At the Edinburgh Old Town Weaving Company, you can watch and even talk to the cloth and tapestry weavers as they work, then buy the products. The company can also provide information on clan histories and which tartan to wear. ⊠ 555 Castlehill, Old Town ☎ 0131/226–1555.

Geoffrey (Tailor) Highland Crafts. This shop can clothe you in full Highland dress, with kilts made in its own workshops. ⊠ 57–59 High St., Old Town ☎ 0131/557–0256.

NEW TOWN

DEPARTMENT STORES

Harvey Nichols. Affectionately known as Harvey Nicks, this high-style British chain has opened a Scots outpost. ⊠ 30–34 St. Andrew Sq., New Town ☎ 0131/524–8388.

Jenners. Traditional china and glassware are a specialty here, as is Scottish clothing (upscale tweeds and tartans). Its famous food hall, run by Valvona & Crolla, stocks Scots staples like shortbread, Dundee cakes, honey, and marmalade, alongside quality Continental groceries. ⊠ 48 Princes St., New Town ☎ 0844/800–3725.

Marks & Spencer. Well-priced, stylish clothes and accessories are on offer at Marks & Spencer. You can also buy quality food and household goods. ✉ *54 Princes St., New Town* ☎ *0131/225–2301.*

SPECIALTY SHOPS

ANTIQUES **Unicorn Antiques.** This basement is crammed with fascinating antiques, including artworks, ornaments, pots, and drawerfuls of aged cutlery. ✉ *65 Dundas St., New Town* ☎ *0131/556–7176.*

JEWELRY **Hamilton and Inches.** Established in 1866, Hamilton and Inches is a silver- and goldsmith worth visiting not only for its modern and antique gift possibilities, but also for its late-Georgian interior. Designed by David Bryce in 1834, it's all columns and elaborate plasterwork. ✉ *87 George St., New Town* ☎ *0131/225–4898.*

Joseph Bonnar. Tucked behind George Street, Joseph Bonnar stocks Scotland's largest collection of antique jewelry, including 19th-century agate jewels. ✉ *72 Thistle St., New Town* ☎ *0131/226–2811.*

LINENS, **And So To Bed.** This shop has a wonderful selection of embroidered and TEXTILES, embellished bed linens, cushion covers, and the like. ✉ *30 Dundas St.,* AND HOME *New Town* ☎ *0131/652–3700.* FURNISHINGS

Hannah Zakari. Quirky handmade pieces, including embroidered cushions, are a specialty at Hannah Zakari. Also look for unusual jewelry, artworks, and accessories that make wonderful gifts. ✉ *43 Candlemaker Row, New Town* ☎ *0131/516–3264.*

In House. This shop sells designer furnishings and collectibles at the forefront of modern design. ✉ *28 Howe St., New Town* ☎ *0131/225–2888.*

Studio One. Studio One has a well-established and comprehensive inventory of gifts. ✉ *10–16 Stafford St., New Town* ☎ *0131/226–5812.*

OUTDOOR **Tiso.** This shop stocks outdoor clothing, boots, and jackets ideal for SPORTS GEAR hiking or camping in the Highlands. ✉ *123–125 Rose St., New Town* ☎ *0131/225–9486* ✉ *41 Commercial St., Leith* ☎ *0131/554–0804.*

WEST END

SPECIALTY SHOPS

CLOTHING **Concrete Wardrobe.** For an eclectic mix of quirky knitwear and accesBOUTIQUES sories, dive into Concrete Wardrobe. You can also find vintage furnishings. ✉ *50a Broughton St., West End* ☎ *0131/558–7130.*

Extra Inch. The Extra Inch stocks a full selection of clothes in European sizes 16 (U.S. size 14) and up. ✉ *12 William St., West End* ☎ *0131/226–3303.*

Herman Brown's. This secondhand clothing store is where cashmere twinsets and classic luxe labels are sought and found. ✉ *151 W. Port, West End* ☎ *0131/228–2589.*

EAST END

ARCADES AND SHOPPING CENTERS

St. James Centre. The St. James Centre has Dorothy Perkins, Past Times, Thorntons, HMV, and other chain stores. ✉ *Princes St., East End.*

DEPARTMENT STORES

John Lewis. Part of a U.K.–wide chain, John Lewis specializes in furniture and household goods, but also stocks designer clothes. ⊠ *69 St. James Centre, East End* ☎ *0131/556–9121.*

SOUTH SIDE

ARCADES AND SHOPPING CENTERS

Cameron Toll. On the city's South Side, Cameron Toll caters to local residents with food stores and High Street brand names. ⊠ *Bottom of Dalkeith Rd., Mayfield.*

DEPARTMENT STORES

★ **Aitken and Niven.** An Edinburgh institution, Aitken and Niven is where the well-heeled come to buy upscale clothing, shoes, and accessories. ⊠ *6 Falcon Rd. W, Morningside* ☎ *0131/477–3922.*

SPECIALTY SHOPS

ANTIQUES **Courtyard Antiques.** Courtyard Antiques stocks a mixture of high-quality antiques, toys, and militaria. ⊠ *108A Causewayside, Sciennes* ☎ *0131/662–9008.*

LEITH

ARCADES AND SHOPPING CENTERS

Ocean Terminal. The Ocean Terminal houses a large collection of shops, as well as bars and eateries. Here you can also visit the former royal yacht *Britannia.* ⊠ *Ocean Dr., Leith.*

SPECIALTY SHOPS

SCOTTISH **Clan Tartan Centre.** Here you'll find a database containing details of all
SPECIALTIES known tartans, plus information on clan histories. ⊠ *70–74 Bangor Rd., Leith* ☎ *0131/553–5161.*

SIDE TRIPS FROM EDINBURGH

If you stand on an Edinburgh eminence—the castle ramparts, Arthur's Seat, Corstorphine Hill—you can plan a few Lothian excursions without even the aid of a map. The Lothians is the collective name given to the swath of countryside south of the Firth of Forth and surrounding Edinburgh. Many courtly and aristocratic families lived here, and the region still has the castles and mansions to prove it. The rich arrived and with them came deer parks, gardens in the French style, and Lothian's fame as a seed plot for Lowland gentility.

Although the region has always provided rich pickings for historians, it also used to offer even richer pickings for coal miners—for a century after the start of the industrial revolution, gentle streams steamed and stank with pollution. Although some black spots still remain, most of the rural countryside is once again a lovely setting for excursions.

You can explore a number of historic houses and castles of West Lothian and the Forth Valley, and territory north of the River Forth, in a day or two, or you can just pick one excursion. Stretching east to the sea and south to the Lowlands from Edinburgh, Midlothian and East Lothian are no more than one hour from Edinburgh. The inland river valleys, hills, and castles of Midlothian and East Lothian's delightful waterfronts, dunes, and golf links offer a taste of Scotland close to the capital.

WEST LOTHIAN AND THE FORTH VALLEY

West Lothian comprises a good bit of Scotland's central belt. The River Forth snakes across a widening floodplain on its descent from the Highlands, and by the time it reaches the western extremities of Edinburgh, it has already passed below the mighty Forth bridges and become a broad estuary. Castles and stately homes sprout thickly on both sides of the Forth.

GETTING HERE AND AROUND

BUS TRAVEL First Bus services link most of this area, but working out a detailed itinerary by bus isn't always easy.

CAR TRAVEL If you're headed from Edinburgh to Linlithgow Palace, take the M9 westward. The Queensferry Road, also known as the A90, is the main artery north towards the Forth Bridge heading to Hopetoun House, the House of the Binns, and Blackness Castle. North of the Forth Bridge, the A985 goes to Culross, the M9 and A823 head to Dunfermiline, and the A91 passes Ochil Hills and Castle Campbell.

TRAIN TRAVEL Dalmeny, Linlithgow, and Dunfermline all have rail stations and can be reached from Edinburgh stations.

VISITOR INFORMATION

VisitScotland has an information center about West Lothian in the town of Bo'ness, close to Blackness Castle and the House of Binns. It's open April to October. Visit West Lothian runs an information center at Burgh Halls in Linlithgow.

ESSENTIALS

Bus Contacts First ☎ *0870/872–7271* ⊕ *www.firstgroup.com.*

Train Contacts National Rail Enquiries ☎ *08457/484950* ⊕ *www.nationalrail. co.uk.*

Visitor Info Visit West Lothian ✉ *Burgh Halls, The Cross, Linlithgow* ☎ *01506/282720.* **VisitScotland** ✉ *Bo'ness Station, Union St., Bo'ness* ☎ *0845/225–5121.*

DALMENY HOUSE
6 mi west of Edinburgh.

EXPLORING

Dalmeny House. The first of the stately houses clustered on the western edge of Edinburgh, Dalmeny House is the home of the earl and countess of Rosebery. This 1815 Tudor Gothic mansion displays among its sumptuous contents the best of the family's famous collection of 18th-century French furniture. Highlights include the library, the Napoléon Room, the Vincennes and Sevres porcelain collections, and the drawing room, with its tapestries and intricately wrought French furniture. Admission is only by guided tour. ✉ *B924, South Queensferry* ☎ *0131/331–1888* ⊕ *www. dalmeny.co.uk* 💷 *£6* ☉ *Tours June–July, Sun.–Tues. 2:15 and 3:30.*

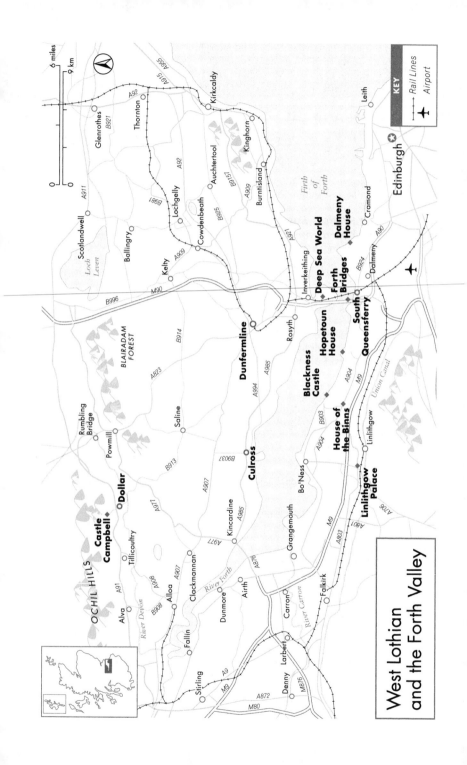

West Lothian and the Forth Valley

SOUTH QUEENSFERRY

7 mi west of Edinburgh.

This pleasant little waterside community, a former ferry port, is completely dominated by the Forth Bridges, dramatic structures of contrasting architecture that span the Firth of Forth at this historic crossing point.

EXPLORING

★ **Forth Rail Bridge.** The Forth Rail Bridge was opened in 1890 and at the time hailed as the eighth wonder of the world, at 2,765 yards long; on a hot summer's day it expands by about another yard. Its neighbor is the 1,993-yard-long **Forth Road Bridge,** in operation since 1964.

WHERE TO EAT

$$ ✕ **The Boat House.** Scotland's natural larder is on display at this romantic
SEAFOOD restaurant on the banks of the Forth. Seafood is the star of the show, and chef Paul Steward is the man behind the imaginative yet unfussy recipes. Standouts include halibut with an orange, ginger, and peppercorn reduction, panfried Oban scallops, and choice cuts of steak. If you want a less formal affair, the bistro and bar next door has a friendly buzz. ✉ *22 High St.* ☎ *0131/331–5429* ⊕ *www.theboathouse-sq.co.uk.*

HOPETOUN HOUSE

10 mi west of Edinburgh.

EXPLORING

★ **Hopetoun House.** The palatial premises of Hopetoun House, probably Scotland's grandest courtly seat and home of the Marquesses of Linlithgow, are considered to be among the Adam family's finest designs. The enormous house was started in 1699 to the original plans of Sir William Bruce (1630–1710), then enlarged between 1721 and 1754 by William Adam (1689–1748) and his sons Robert and John. There's a notable painting collection, and the house has decorative work of the highest order, plus all the trappings to keep you entertained: a nature trail, a restaurant in the former stables, farm shop, and a museum. Much of the wealth that created this sumptuous building came from the family's mining interests in the surrounding regions. The house is 6 mi west of South Queensferry. ✉ *Off A904, South Queensferry* ☎ *0131/331–2451* ⊕ *www.hopetounhouse.com* ✉ *£9.20* ☉ *Apr.–Sept., daily 10:30–5, last admission at 4.*

HOUSE OF THE BINNS

12 mi west of Edinburgh.

EXPLORING

House of the Binns. The 17th-century general "Bloody Tam" Dalyell (circa 1599–1685) transformed a fortified stronghold into a gracious mansion, the House of the Binns (the name derives from *bynn,* the old Scottish word for hill). The present exterior dates from around 1810 and shows a remodeling into a kind of mock fort with crenellated battlements and turrets. Inside, magnificent plaster ceilings are done in the Elizabethan style. Cared for by the National Trust for Scotland, the house is 4 mi east of Linlithgow. ✉ *Off A904, Linlithgow* ☎ *0844/493–2127* ⊕ *www. nts.org.uk/visits* ✉ *£9* ☉ *June–Sept., Sat.–Wed. 2–5.*

BLACKNESS CASTLE
12 mi west of Edinburgh.

EXPLORING

Blackness Castle. Standing like a grounded ship on the very edge of the Forth, this curious 15th-century structure has had a varied career as a strategic fortress, state prison, powder magazine, and youth hostel. The countryside is gently green and cultivated, and open views extend across the blue Forth to the distant ramparts of the Ochil Hills. The castle is 4 mi northeast of Linlithgow. ✉ *B903, Linlithgow* ☎ *01506/834807* ⊕ *www.historic-scotland.gov.uk/places* 💷 *£5* 🕑 *Apr.–Sept., daily 9:30–5:30; Oct., daily 9:30–4:30; Nov.–Mar., Sat.–Wed. 9:30–4:30.*

LINLITHGOW PALACE
12 mi west of Edinburgh.

EXPLORING

Linlithgow Palace. On the edge of Linlithgow Loch stands the splendid ruin of Linlithgow Palace, the birthplace of Mary, Queen of Scots, in 1542. Burned, perhaps accidentally, by Hanoverian troops during the last Jacobite rebellion in 1746, this impressive shell stands on a site of great antiquity, though it's not certain anything survived an earlier fire in 1424. The palace gatehouse was built in the early 16th century, and the central courtyard's elaborate fountain dates from around 1535. The halls and great rooms are cold, echoing stone husks now in Historic Scotland's care. ✉ *A706, south shore of Linlithgow Loch* ☎ *01506/842896* ⊕ *www.historic-scotland.gov.uk/places* 💷 *£5.50* 🕑 *Apr.–Sept., daily 9:30–5:30; Oct.–Mar., daily 9:30–4:30.*

OCHIL HILLS
24 mi northwest of Edinburgh.

The scarp face of the Ochil Hills looms unmistakably. It's an old fault line that yields up hard volcanic rocks and contrasts with the quantities of softer coal immediately around the River Forth. The steep Ochils provided grazing land and water power for Scotland's second-largest textile area.

EXPLORING

Alva Glen. There's a breathtaking gorge at Alva Glen, and walking paths (some are steep, so be prepared) which follow the gushing Alva Burn and pass many abandoned woolen mills. ✉ *A91, Alva* ⊕ *www.alvaglen. org.uk.*

Mill Glen. Behind Tillicoultry (pronounced tilly-*coot*-ree), Mill Glen has a giant quarry, fine waterfalls, and interesting plants, making it a good hiking option for energetic explorers. ✉ *A91, Tillicoultry.*

Mill Trail Visitor Centre. Some mills still survive in the so-called Hillfoots towns, on the scarp edge east of Stirling. The Mill Trail Visitor Centre, has information about the area's mill shops. ✉ W. Stirling St., Alva ☎ 01259/769696.

Ochil Hills Woodland Park. East of Alva is the Ochil Hills Woodland Park, which provides access to lovely Silver Glen, so-called because the precious metal was mined here in the 18th century. ✉ *A91, Alva* ☎ *01259/450000* ⊕ *www.clacksweb.org.uk/visiting/ochilhillswoodlandpark.*

DOLLAR

30 mi northwest of Edinburgh.

This *douce* (Scots for well-mannered or gentle) and tidy town below the Ochil Hills lies at the mouth of Dollar Glen.

EXPLORING

Castle Campbell. With green woods below, bracken hills above, and a view that on a clear day stretches right across the Forth Valley to the tip of Tinto Hill near Lanark, Castle Campbell is certainly the most atmospheric fortress within easy reach of Edinburgh. Formerly known as Castle Gloom, Castle Campbell stands out among Scottish castles for the sheer drama of its setting. The sturdy square of the tower house survives from the 15th century, when the site was fortified by the first Earl of Argyll (died 1493). Other buildings and enclosures were subsequently added, but the sheer lack of space on this rocky eminence ensured that there would never be any drastic changes. John Knox, the fiery religious reformer, once preached here. In 1654 the castle was captured by Oliver Cromwell and garrisoned with English troops. It's now cared for by Historic Scotland. To get here, follow a road off the A91 that angles sharply up the east side of the wooded defile. ⊠ *Off A91, Dollar Glen* ☎ *01259/742408* ⊕ *www.historic-scotland.gov.uk/places* 🖾 *£5* ⊙ *Apr.–Sept., daily 9:30–5:30; Oct., daily 9:30–4:30, Nov.–Mar., Mon.–Wed. and weekends 9:30–4:30.*

CULROSS

17 mi northwest of Edinburgh.

EXPLORING

★ **Culross.** With its Mercat Cross, cobbled streets, tolbooth, and narrow wynds (alleys), Culross, on the muddy shores of the Forth, is now a living museum of a 17th-century town and one of the most remarkable little towns in Scotland. It once had a thriving industry and export trade in coal and salt (the coal was used in the salt-panning process). It also had, curiously, a trade monopoly in the manufacture of baking *girdles* (griddles). As local coal became exhausted, the impetus of the industrial revolution passed Culross by, and other parts of the Forth Valley prospered. Culross became a backwater town, and the merchants' houses of the 17th and 18th centuries were never replaced by Victorian developments or modern architecture. In the 1930s the National Trust for Scotland started to buy up the decaying properties. With the help of other agencies, these buildings were brought to life. Today ordinary citizens live in many of the National Trust properties. A few—the Palace, Study, and Town House—are open to the public. ⊠ *Off A985, 8 mi south of Dollar* ☎ *0844/493–2189* ⊕ *www.nts.org.uk/visits* 🖾 *£9* ⊙ *June–Aug., daily noon–5; Apr., May, and Sept., Thurs.–Mon. noon–5; Oct., Fri.–Mon. noon–4; last admission 1 hr before closing.*

DUNFERMLINE

16 mi northwest of Edinburgh.

Dunfermline was once the world center for the production of damask linen, but the town is better known today as the birthplace of millionaire industrialist and philanthropist Andrew Carnegie (1835–1919). Undoubtedly Dunfermline's most famous son, Carnegie endowed the town with a park, library, health and fitness center, and, naturally, a Carnegie Hall, still the focus of culture and entertainment.

EXPLORING

Andrew Carnegie Birthplace Museum. The 18th-century weaver's cottage where Carnegie was born in 1835 is now the Andrew Carnegie Birthplace Museum. Don't be misled by the cottage's simple exterior. Inside it opens into a larger hall, where documents, photographs, and artifacts relate Carnegie's fascinating life story. You can learn such obscure details as the claim that Carnegie was one of only three men in the United States then able to translate Morse code by ear as it came down the wire. ⊠ *Moodie St.* ☎ *01383/724302* ⊕ *www.carnegiebirthplace. com* 🖃 *Free* ☉ *Mar.–Nov., Mon.–Sat. 10–5, Sun. 2–5.*

Dunfermline Abbey and Palace. The Dunfermline Abbey and Palace complex was founded in the 11th century by Queen Margaret, the English wife of the Scots king Malcolm III. Some Norman work can be seen in the present church, where Robert the Bruce (1274–1329) lies buried. The palace grew from the abbey guesthouse and was the birthplace of Charles I (1600–49). Dunfermline was the seat of the royal court of Scotland until the end of the 11th century, and its central role in Scottish affairs is explored by means of display panels dotted around the drafty but hallowed buildings. ⊠ *Monastery St.* ☎ *01383/739026* ⊕ *www. historic-scotland.gov.uk/places* 🖃 *£4* ☉ *Apr.–Sept., daily 9:30–5:30; Oct.–Mar., daily 9:30–4:30; Nov.–Mar., Mon.–Wed. and weekends 9:30–4:30; last admission ½ hr before closing.*

Pittencrieff House Museum. Housed in a 17th-century laird's mansion surrounded by beautiful parkland dotted with picnic areas and resident peacocks, the Pittencrieff House Museum explores the town's history. The recently installed Magic of the Glen section features a family-friendly natural-history exhibit that includes dinosaurs, fossils, and the like. ⊠ *Pittencrieff Park* ☎ *01383/722935* ⊕ *www.scottishmuseums. org.uk* 🖃 *Free* ☉ *Apr.–Sept., daily 11–5; Oct.–Mar., daily 11–4.*

DEEP SEA WORLD
9 mi northwest of Edinburgh.

EXPLORING

🌣 **Deep Sea World.** The former ferry port in North Queensferry dropped almost into oblivion after the Forth Road Bridge opened, but was dragged abruptly back into the limelight by the hugely popular Deep Sea World. This sophisticated aquarium on the Firth of Forth offers a fascinating view of underwater life. Go down a clear acrylic tunnel for a diver's-eye look at more than 5,000 fish, including 250 sharks (some more than 9 feet long); and visit the exhibition hall, which has an Amazon-jungle display and an audiovisual presentation on local marine life. Ichthyophobes will feel more at ease in the adjacent café and gift shop. ⊠ *Forthside Terr.* ☎ *01383/411880* ⊕ *www.deepseaworld. com* 🖃 *£12.50* ☉ *Weekdays 10–5, weekends 10–6; last admission 1 hr before closing.*

MIDLOTHIAN AND EAST LOTHIAN

In spite of the finest stone carving in Scotland at Rosslyn Chapel, associations with Sir Walter Scott, outstanding castles, and miles of rolling countryside, Midlothian, the area immediately south of Edinburgh, for years remained off the beaten path. Perhaps a little in awe of sophisticated Edinburgh to the north and the well-manicured charm of the stockbroker belt of nearby upmarket East Lothian, Midlothian was quietly preoccupied with its own workaday little towns and dormitory suburbs.

As for East Lothian, it started with the advantage of golf courses of world rank, most notably Muirfield, plus a scattering of stately homes and interesting hotels. It's an area of glowing grain fields in summer and quite a few discreetly polite "strictly private" signs at the end of driveways. Still, it has plenty of interest, including photogenic villages, active fishing harbors, and vistas of pastoral Lowland Scotland, seemingly a world away (but much less than an hour by car) from bustling Edinburgh.

GETTING HERE AND AROUND

BUS TRAVEL City buses travel as far as Swanston and the Pentland Hills. First buses serve towns and villages throughout Midlothian and East Lothian. For details of all services, inquire at the St. Andrew Square bus station in Edinburgh.

CAR TRAVEL A quick route to Rosslyn Chapel follows the A701, while the A7 heads towards Gorebridge and the Scottish Mining Museum. The A1 passes Newhailes, Haddington, and Dunbar. Take the A198 to North Berwick, Dirleton Castle, and Tantallon Castle.

TRAIN TRAVEL There is no train service in Midlothian. In East Lothian, the towns of North Berwick, Drem, and Dunbar have train stations with regular service from Edinburgh.

ESSENTIALS

Bus Contacts First ☎ *0871/200–2233* ⊕ *www.firstgroup.com.*

NEWHAILES

5 mi east of Edinburgh.

EXPLORING

Newhailes. This fine late-17th-century house (with 18th-century additions), owned and run by the National Trust for Scotland, was designed by Scottish architect James Smith (circa 1645–1731) in 1686 as his own home. He later sold it to Lord Bellendon, and in 1707 it was bought by Sir David Dalrymple (c. 1665–1721), first baronet of Hailes, who improved and extended the house, adding one of the finest rococo interiors in Scotland. The library played host to many famous figures from the Scottish Enlightenment, including inveterate Scot-basher Dr. Samuel Johnson, who dubbed the library "the most learned room in Europe." Most of the original interiors and furnishings remain intact, creating great authenticity. ⊠ *Newhailes Rd.* ☎ *0844/493–2125* ⊕ *www.nts.org. uk/visits* 🎟 *£11* ⊙ *House Apr.–Sept., Thurs.–Mon. noon–5; grounds daily year-round.*

ROSLIN
7 mi south of Edinburgh.

Although the town is overshadowed by its chapel, Roslin is a pleasant place to while away some time. There are some nice walks by the North River Esk.

EXPLORING

Fodor'sChoice
★

Rosslyn Chapel. Rosslyn Chapel has always beckoned curious visitors intrigued by the various legends surrounding its magnificent carvings, but today it pulses with tourists as never before. Dan Brown's bestselling novel *The Da Vinci Code* has made visiting this Episcopal chapel (services continue to be held here) an imperative stop for many of its enthusiasts. Whether you're a fan of the book or not—and of the book's theory that the chapel has a secret sign that can lead you to the Holy Grail—this is a site of immense interest. Originally conceived by Sir William Sinclair (circa 1404–80) and dedicated to St. Matthew in 1446, the chapel is outstanding for the quality and variety of the carving inside. Covering almost every square inch of stonework are human figures, animals, and plants. The meaning of these remains subject to many theories; some depict symbols from the medieval order of the Knights Templar and from Freemasonry. The chapel's design called for a cruciform structure, but only the choir and parts of the east transept walls were completed. ⊠ *Chapel Loan* ☎ *0131/440-2159* ⊕ *www. rosslynchapel.com* 🖼 *£8.75* ⊗ *Apr.–Sept., Mon.–Sat. 9:30–5:30, Sun. noon–4:15; Oct.–Mar., Mon.–Sat. 9:30–4:30, Sun. noon–4:15.*

SCOTTISH MINING MUSEUM
9 mi southeast of Edinburgh.

EXPLORING

The Scottish Mining Museum. In the former mining community of Newtongrange, the Scottish Mining Museum provides a good introduction to the history of Scotland's mining industry. With the help of videos you can experience life deep below the ground. There are also interactive displays and "magic helmets" that bring the tour to life and relate the power that the mining company had over the lives of the individual workers here, in Scotland's largest planned-mining village. This frighteningly autocratic system survived well into the 1930s—the company owned the houses, shops, and even the pub. The scenery is no more attractive than you would expect, though the green Pentland Hills hover in the distance. ⊠ *A7* ☎ *0131/663-7519* ⊕ *www. scottishminingmuseum.com* 🖼 *£7.50* ⊗ *Apr.–Sept., daily 10–5; Oct.– Mar., daily 10–4; last admission 1½ hrs before closing.*

BORTHWICK CASTLE
12 mi southeast of Edinburgh.

EXPLORING

Borthwick Castle. Set in green countryside with scattered woods and lush hedgerows, the village of Borthwick is dominated by Borthwick Castle, which dates from the 15th century and is still occupied. Mary, Queen of Scots, came to this stark, tall, twin-towered fortress on a kind of honeymoon with her ill-starred third husband, the Earl of Bothwell. Their already-dubious bliss was interrupted by Mary's political opponents,

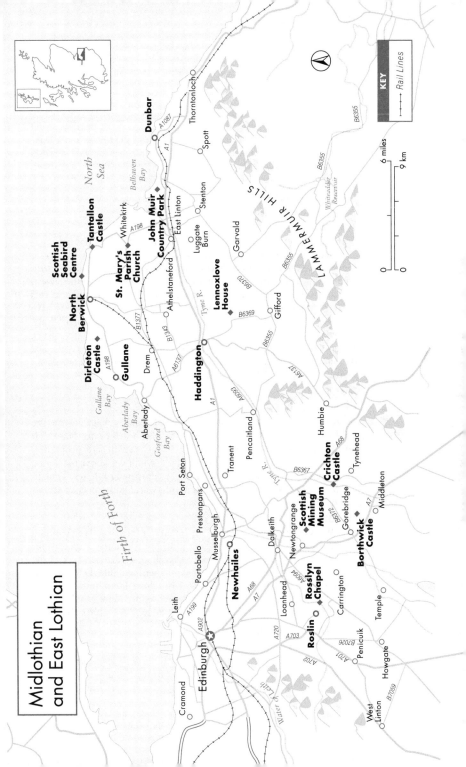

Midlothian and East Lothian

KEY
↦ Rail Lines

North Sea

Firth of Forth

Water of Leith

Edinburgh

Cramond
Leith
Portobello
Musselburgh
Prestonpans
Port Seton
Aberlady
Gullane
Dirleton Castle
North Berwick
Scottish Seabird Centre
Tantallon Castle
St. Mary's Parish Church
John Muir Country Park
Dunbar
Thorntonloch
Spott
Belhaven Bay
Whitekirk
East Linton
Stenton
Luggate Burn
Garvald
Athelstaneford
Lennoxlove House
Gifford
Haddington
Drem
Tranent
Pencaitland
Humbie
Tynehead
Middleton
Crichton Castle
Gorebridge
Borthwick Castle
Scottish Mining Museum
Newtongrange
Dalkeith
Newhailes
Loanhead
Roslin
Rosslyn Chapel
Carrington
Temple
Penicuik
Howgate
West Linton

LAMMERMUIR HILLS

Whiteadder Reservoir

Gullane Bay
Aberlady Bay
Gosford Bay

Tyne R.

Tyne R.

A1087
A1
A198
B1377
B1343
A6137
B1343
Tyne R.
B6370
B6369
B6355
B6355
B6355
B6355
A6093
A6137
B6367
A68
A7
B6372
A6094
A68
A7
A720
A703
A702
A701
A7026
B7059
A199
A902
A1

6 miles
9 km

often referred to as the Lords of the Congregation, a confederacy of powerful nobles who favored the crowning of her young son, James. Rather insensitively, they laid siege to the castle while the newlyweds were there. Mary subsequently escaped disguised as a man. She was not free for long, however. It was only a short time before she was defeated in battle and imprisoned. She languished in prison for 21 years before Queen Elizabeth I of England (1558–1603) signed her death warrant in 1587. Bothwell's fate was equally gloomy: he died insane in a Danish prison. The castle now functions as a hotel, but it's well worth a look around. ✦ *1 mi south of Gorebridge* ☎ *01875/820514* ⊕ *www. borthwickcastlehotel.com* 🔄 *Free* ☉ *Tour hrs vary.*

CRICHTON CASTLE
11 mi southeast of Edinburgh.

EXPLORING
Crichton Castle. Crichton Castle stands amid rolling hills that are interrupted here and there by patches of woodland. Crichton was a Bothwell family castle; Mary, Queen of Scots, attended the wedding here of Bothwell's sister, Lady Janet Hepburn, to Mary's brother, Lord John Stewart. The curious arcaded range reveals diamond-faceted stonework; this particular geometric pattern is unique in Scotland and is thought to have been inspired by Renaissance styles on the Continent, particularly Italy. The oldest part of the work is the 14th-century keep (square tower). Do note that there are no toilets at the castle. ✉ *B6367, 7 mi southeast of Dalkeith, Pathhead* ☎ *01875/320017* ⊕ *www.historic-scotland.gov. uk/places* 🔄 *£4* ☉ *Apr.–Sept., daily 9:30–5:30.*

DUNBAR
25 mi east of Edinburgh.

In the days before tour companies started offering package deals to the Mediterranean, Dunbar was a popular holiday beach resort. Now a bit faded, the town is still lovely for its spacious Georgian-style properties, characterized by the astragals, or fan-shape windows, above the doors; the symmetry of the house fronts; and the parapeted rooflines. Though not the popular seaside playground it once was, Dunbar has an attractive beach and a picturesque harbor.

EXPLORING
John Muir Country Park. Taking in the estuary of the River Tyne winding down from the Moorfoot Hills, the John Muir Country Park encompasses varied coastal scenery: rocky shoreline, golden sands, and the mixed woodlands of Tyninghame, teeming with wildlife. Dunbar-born conservationist John Muir (1838–1914), whose family moved to the United States when he was a child, helped found Yosemite and Sequoia national parks in California. The park is 2 mi west of Dunbar. ✉ *A1087.*

NORTH BERWICK
20 mi northeast of Edinburgh.

The pleasant little seaside resort of North Berwick manages to retain a small-town personality even when it's thronged with city visitors on warm summer Sunday afternoons. Eating ice cream, the city folk stroll on the beach and in the narrow streets or gaze at the sailing craft in the small harbor. The town is near a number of castles and other sights.

EXPLORING

Dirleton Castle. In the center of tiny Dirleton sits the 12th-century Dirleton Castle, surrounded by a high outer wall. Within the wall you can find a 17th-century bowling green, set in the shade of yew trees and surrounded by a herbaceous flower border that blazes with color in high summer. The castle, now in Historic Scotland's care, was occupied in 1298 by King Edward I of England as part of his campaign for the continued subjugation of the unruly Scots. It's 2 mi west of North Berwick. ⊠ *A198* ☎ *01620/850330* ⊕ *www.historic-scotland.gov.uk/places* ⌨ *£5* ☉ *Apr.–Sept., daily 9:30–5:30; Oct.–Mar., daily 9:30–4:30; last admission ½ hr before closing.*

☪ **Scottish Seabird Centre.** An observation deck, exhibits, and films at the Scottish Seabird Centre provide a captivating introduction to the world of the gannets and puffins that nest on nearby Bass Rock. Live interactive cameras let you take an even closer look at the bird colonies and marine mammals at Craigleith and the Isle of May. There are plenty of family-friendly activities, nature walks, and photography shows. ⊠ *The Harbour* ☎ *01620/890202* ⊕ *www.seabird.org* ⌨ *£7.95* ☉ *Apr.–Sept., daily 10–6; Feb., Mar., and Oct., weekdays 10–5, weekends 10–5:30; Nov.–Jan., weekdays 10–4, weekends 10–5; last admission 45 mins before closing.*

St. Mary's Parish Church. The unmistakable red-sandstone St. Mary's Parish Church, with its Norman tower, stands in the village of Whitekirk, 6 mi south of North Berwick, on a site occupied since the 6th century. It was a place of pilgrimage in medieval times because of its healing well. Behind the kirk, in a field, stands a tithe barn. Tithe barns originated with the practice of giving to the church a portion of local produce, which then required storage space. In the 15th century, the church was visited by a young Italian nobleman, Aeneas Sylvius Piccolomini, after he was shipwrecked off the East Lothian coast. Two decades later, Piccolomini became Pope Pius II. At one end of the barn stands a 16th-century tower house, which at one point in its history accommodated visiting pilgrims. The large three-story barn was added to the tower house in the 17th century. ⊠ *A198, Whitekirk* ⌨ *Free* ☉ *Daily 9am–sunset.*

Tantallon Castle. Rising on a cliff beyond the flat fields east of North Berwick, Tantallon Castle is a substantial ruin defending a headland with the sea on three sides. The red sandstone is pitted and eaten by time and sea spray, with the earliest surviving stonework dating from the late 14th century. The fortress was besieged in 1529 by the cannons of King James V (1512–42). Rather inconveniently, the besieging forces ran out of gunpowder. Cannons were used again, to deadlier effect, in a later siege during the Civil War in 1651. Twelve days of battering with the heavy guns of Cromwell's General Monk greatly damaged the flanking towers. Fortunately much of the curtain wall of this former Douglas stronghold, now cared for by Historic Scotland, survives. ⊠ *A198* ☎ *01620/892727* ⊕ *www.historic-scotland.gov.uk/places* ⌨ *£5*

Apr.–Sept., daily 9:30–5:30; Oct., daily 9:30–4:30; Nov.–Mar., Sat.–Wed. 9:30–4:30; last admission ½ hr before closing.

WHERE TO STAY

$$ 🏨 **Glebe House.** This dignified 18th-century manse sits amid its own secluded grounds, yet it's in the heart of town, a 10-minute walk east of the station. **Pros:** peaceful atmosphere; interesting antiques; sociable breakfast around a mahogany table. **Cons:** books up well in advance; too twee for some. ✉ *Law Rd.* ☎ *01620/892608* ⊕ *www.glebehouse-nb.co.uk* 🛏 *4 rooms* ⚬ *In-room: no a/c, no TV* ⊟ *No credit cards* 🍽 *Breakfast.*

GULLANE

15 mi northeast of Edinburgh.

Noticeable along this coastline are the golf courses of East Lothian, laid out wherever there is available links space. Gullane is surrounded by them, and its inhabitants are typically clad in expensive golfing sweaters. Apart from golf, you can enjoy restful summer evening strolls at Gullane's beach, well within driving distance of the village.

HADDINGTON

15 mi east of Edinburgh.

One of the best-preserved medieval street plans in the country can be explored in Haddington. Among the many buildings of architectural or historical interest is the Town House, designed by William Adam in 1748 and enlarged in 1830. A wall plaque at the Sidegate recalls the great heights of floods from the River Tyne. Beyond is the medieval Nungate footbridge, with the Church of St. Mary a little way upstream.

EXPLORING

Lennoxlove House. Just to the south of Haddington stands Lennoxlove House, the grand ancestral home of the very grand dukes of Hamilton since 1947 and the Baird family before them. A turreted country house, part of it dating from the 15th century, Lennoxlove is a cheerful mix of family life and Scottish history. The beautifully decorated rooms house portraits, furniture, porcelain, and items associated with Mary, Queen of Scots, including her supposed death mask. Sporting activities from falconry to fishing take place on the stunning grounds. ✉ *B6369* ☎ *01620/823720* ⊕ *www.lennoxlove.com* 💷 *£5* ⊙ *Tours Apr.–Sept., Wed., Thurs, and Sun. 1:30–3:30.*

Glasgow

WORD OF MOUTH

"Glasgow often gets short shrift, but it really is a great place to spend some time. The Burrell Collection is an eclectic treasure house and one of Great Britain's best museums. Also worth a visit are Glasgow Cathedral, the Hunterian Art Gallery, St. Mungo's Museum of Religious Life and Art, and the Tall Ship; the Glasgow Science Centre is fun, especially for kids."

—historytraveler

"Glasgow has some wonderful areas, and I love shopping on Buchanan Street. The Kelvingrove is a great museum."

—palmettoprincess

Updated
by Mike
Gonzalez

Trendy stores, a booming cultural life, and stylish restaurants reinforce Glasgow's claim to be Scotland's most exciting city. After decades of decline, it has experienced an urban renaissance uniquely its own. The city's grand architecture reflects a prosperous past built on trade and shipbuilding. Today buildings by Charles Rennie Mackintosh hold pride of place along with the Zaha Hadid–designed Riverside Museum. In recent years, visitors have rediscovered Glasgow, and the announcement that the Commonwealth Games will be held here in 2014 has given the city a new luster.

Glasgow (the "dear green place," as it was known) was founded some 1,500 years ago. Legend has it that the king of Strathclyde, irate about his wife's infidelity, had a ring he had given her thrown into the river Clyde. (Apparently she had passed it on to an admirer.) When the king demanded to know where the ring had gone, the distraught queen asked the advice of her confessor, St. Mungo. He suggested fishing for it—and the first salmon to emerge had the ring in its mouth. The moment is commemorated on the city's coat of arms.

The medieval city expanded when it was given a royal license to trade; the current High Street was the main thoroughfare at the time. The vast profits from American cotton and tobacco built the grand mansions of the Merchant City. In the 19th century the river Clyde became the center of a vibrant shipbuilding industry, fed by the city's iron and steel works. The city grew again, but its internal divisions grew at the same time. The West End harbored the elegant homes of the newly rich shipyard owners. Down by the river, areas like the infamous Gorbals, with its crowded slums, sheltered the laborers who built the ships. They came from the Highlands, expelled to make way for sheep, or from Ireland, where the potato famines drove thousands from their homes.

During the 19th century, the population grew from 80,000 to more than a million. And the new prosperity gave Glasgow its grand neoclassical buildings, such as those built by Alexander 'Greek' Thomson, as well as the adventurous visionary buildings designed by Charles Rennie Mackintosh and others who produced Glasgow's Arts and Crafts movement. The City Chambers, built in 1888, are a proud statement in marble and gold sandstone, a clear symbol of the wealthy and powerful Victorian industrialists' hopes for the future.

The decline of shipbuilding and the closure of the factories led to much speculation as to what direction the city would take now. The curious thing is that, at least in part, the past gave the city a new lease of life. It was as if people looked at their city and saw Glasgow's beauty for the

TOP REASONS TO GO

Design and architecture: The ambitious Victorians left a legacy of striking architecture, and Glasgow's buildings manifest the city's enduring love of grand artistic statements—just remember to look up. The Arts and Crafts buildings and interiors by Charles Rennie Mackintosh are reason alone to visit the city.

Artistic treasures: Some of Britain's best museums and art galleries are in Glasgow. The Burrell Collection and the eclectic Kelvingrove Art Gallery and Museum are definitely worth a visit, even on a sunny day.

Gorgeous parks and gardens: From Kelvingrove Park to the Botanic Gardens, Glasgow has more parks per square mile than any other city in Europe. Stop by the Botanic Gardens for outdoor theatrical productions in summer, or Bellahouston Park for the annual piping festival.

Pints and great grub: Whether you fancy a Guinness in a traditional old-man's pub like the Scotia or one of the churches-turned-pubs like Òran Mór, there's a pub to fit all thirsts. Locals love their cafés and tearooms; stop by the Willow Tearoom or Where the Monkey Sleeps for cake and a rest from sightseeing.

Retail therapy: The city has become known for cutting-edge design. Look for everything from Scottish specialties to stylish fashions on the city center's hottest shopping streets, Ingram or Buchanan, or at the elegant Princes Square.

Burns country: Scotland's national poet lived, wrote, and drank in Ayrshire. The new Robert Burns Birthplace Museum in Alloway is fitting tribute to his life and work.

first time: its extraordinarily rich architectural heritage, its leafy parks, its artistic heritage, and its complex social history. Today, Glasgow is a cultural center and a commercial hub, as well as a launching pad from which to explore the rest of Scotland, which, as it turns out, is not so far away. In fact, it takes only 40 minutes to reach Loch Lomond, where the other Scotland begins.

ORIENTATION AND PLANNING

GETTING ORIENTED

Glasgow's layout is hard to read in a single glance. The city center is roughly defined by the M8 motorway to the north and west, the River Clyde to the south, and High Street to the east. Glaswegians tend to walk a good deal, and the relatively flat and compact city center, most of which follows a grid pattern, is perfect for pedestrians. The West End has Glasgow University and lovely Kelvingrove Park. The River Clyde, around which Glasgow grew up as a trading city, runs through the center of the city—literally cutting it in two.

City Center and the Merchant City. The central area includes some of city's most treasured and historic sights: Glasgow Cathedral, the Necropolis, City Chambers, and the Gallery of Modern Art, as well as top-notch eateries. Most of the city's theaters are here, along with many of the best shops.

The West End. In this quieter, slightly hillier western part of the city is Glasgow University and the more bohemian side of Glasgow. The West End's treasures include the Botanic Gardens, Kelvingrove Park, and the Kelvingrove Art Gallery and Museum. There are also plenty of well-priced restaurants and lively bars.

The South Side. Often overlooked, this less visited side of the city is home to the spectacular Burrell Collection set in Pollok Park.

PLANNING

WHEN TO GO

The best times to visit Glasgow are spring and summer. Although you may encounter crowds, the weather is more likely to be warm and dry. In summer the days are long and pleasant—that is, if the rain holds off—and festivals and outdoor events are abundant. Fall can be nice, although cold weather begins to set in after mid-September and the days grow shorter. From November to February it is cold, wet, and dark. Although thousands of people flock to Glasgow for New Year's celebrations, the winter months are relatively quiet in terms of crowds.

PLANNING YOUR TIME

You could quite easily spend five comfortable days here, although in a pinch, two would do and three would be pleasant. The best strategy for seeing the city is to start in the center and work your way out. On the first day explore the city center, taking in Glasgow Cathedral, the Museum of Religious Life, and Provand's Lordship, as well as the Necropolis with its fascinating crumbling monuments. It is a gentle walk from here to the Merchant City and George Square, around which spread the active and crowded shopping areas. The Mackintosh Trail will take you to the many buildings designed by this outstanding Glasgow designer and architect. Another day could be well spent between the Kelvingrove Art Gallery (you can lunch here and listen to the daily concert on its magnificent organ) and the nearby Hunterian Museum and Gallery. From here it's only minutes to lively Byres Road and its shops, pubs, and cafés. Another option is to make a beeline to the Burrell Collection and the House for an Art Lover, on the south side of the city.

If you have a few extra days, head out to Burns country in Ayrshire. It's a scenic 45-minute drive from Glasgow, and you can use the city as a base. Most destinations on the Clyde Coast are easily accessible from Glasgow. Direct trains from Central Station take you to Paisley, Irvine, Largs, Troon, Kilmarnock, and Lanark in less than an hour. These small towns need no more than a day to explore. To get a flavor of island life, take the hour-long train ride to Wemyss Bay and then the ferry to the Isle of Bute.

GETTING HERE AND AROUND

AIR TRAVEL

Airlines flying from Glasgow Airport to the rest of the United Kingdom and to Europe include Aer Lingus, Air Malta, bmi, British Airways, easyJet, Icelandair, and KLM. Several carriers fly from North America, including Air Canada, American Airlines, United, and Icelandair (service via Reykjavík).

Ryanair offers rock-bottom airfares between Prestwick and London's Stansted Airport. Budget-minded easyJet has similar services from Glasgow to London's Stansted and Luton airports. Loganair flies to the islands.

Air Contacts Aer Lingus 📞 0871/718–2020 ⊕ www.aerlingus.com. **Air Canada** 📞 0871/220-1111 ⊕ www.aircanada.com. **Air Malta** 📞 0845/607–3710 ⊕ www.airmalta.com. **American Airlines** 📞 0844/499–7300 ⊕ www.aa.com. **bmi/ British Midland** 📞 0844/848–4888 ⊕ www.flybmi.com. **British Airways** 📞 0844/493–0787 ⊕ www.britishairways.com. **United** 📞 0845/844–4777 ⊕ www.united.com. **easyJet** 📞 0871/244–2366 ⊕ www.easyjet.com. **Icelandair** 📞 0844/811–1190 ⊕ www.icelandair.com. **KLM** 📞 0871/231–0000 ⊕ www.klm. com. **Loganair** 📞 0141/848–7594 ⊕ www.loganair.co.uk. **Ryanair** 📞 0871/246– 0000 ⊕ www.ryanair.com.

AIRPORTS Glasgow Airport is about 7 mi west of the city center on the M8 to Greenock. The airport serves international and domestic flights, and most major European carriers have frequent and convenient connections (some via airports in England) to many cities on the Continent. There's a frequent shuttle service from London, as well as regular flights from Birmingham, Bristol, East Midlands, Leeds/Bradford, Manchester, Southampton, Isle of Man, and Jersey. There are also flights from Wales (Cardiff) and Ireland (Belfast, Dublin, and Londonderry). Local Scottish connections can be made to Aberdeen, Barra, Benbecula, Campbeltown, Inverness, Islay, Kirkwall, Shetland (Sumburgh), Stornoway, and Tiree.

Prestwick Airport sits on the Ayrshire coast about 30 mi southwest of Glasgow. Eclipsed for some years by Glasgow Airport, Prestwick has grown in importance, not least because of lower airfares from Ryanair.

Airport Contacts Glasgow Airport 📞 0844/481–5555 ⊕ www.glasgowairport. com. **Prestwick Airport** 📞 0871/223–0700 ⊕ www.gpia.co.uk.

TRANSFERS **From Glasgow Airport:**

Although there's a railway station about 2 mi from Glasgow Airport (Paisley Gilmour Street), most people travel to the city center by bus or taxi. It takes about 20 minutes, slightly longer at rush hour. Metered taxis are available outside domestic arrivals, and cost around £22.

Express buses run from Glasgow Airport (outside departures lobby) to Central and Queen Street stations and to the Buchanan Street bus station. They depart every 15 minutes throughout the day. The fare is £4.50.

The drive from Glasgow Airport into the city center is normally quite easy, even if you're used to driving on the right. The M8 motorway runs beside the airport (Junction 29) and takes you straight into the Glasgow city center. Thereafter Glasgow's streets follow a grid pattern, at least in the city center. A map is useful—get one from the car-rental company.

Most companies that provide chauffeur-driven cars and tours will also do limousine airport transfers. Companies that are currently members of the Greater Glasgow and Clyde Valley Tourist Board include Charlton and Little's.

From Prestwick Airport:

An hourly coach service makes trips to Glasgow, but takes much longer than the train. There's a rapid half-hourly train service (hourly on Sunday) direct from the terminal to Glasgow Central. Strathclyde Passenger Transport and ScotRail offer a discount ticket that allows you to travel for half the standard fare; just show a valid airline ticket for a flight to or from Prestwick Airport.

By car, the city center is reached via the fast M77 in about 40 minutes (longer in rush hour). Metered taxis are available at the airport. The fare to Glasgow is about £40.

Airport Transfer Contacts **Charlton** ☎ 0870/058–9500 ⊕ www.charltonlimo. com. **Little's** ☎ 0141/883–2111 ⊕ www.littles.co.uk.

BUS TRAVEL

The main intercity operators are National Express and Scottish Citylink, which serve numerous towns and cities in Scotland, Wales, and England, including London and Edinburgh. Glasgow's bus station is on Buchanan Street, not far from Queen Street Station.

When traveling from the city center to either the West End or the South Side, it's easy to use the city's integrated network of buses, subways, and trains. Service is reliable and connections are convenient from buses to trains and the subway. Many buses require exact fare, which is usually around £1.50.

Traveline Scotland provides information on schedules and fares, as does the Strathclyde Passenger Transport Travel Centre, which has an information center.

Bus Contacts **Buchanan Street bus station** ⊠ Killermont St., City Center ☎ 0141/333-3708 ⊕ www.spt.co.uk. **National Express** ☎ 0871/781–8181 ⊕ www.nationalexpress.co.uk. **Scottish Citylink** ☎ 0871/266–3333 ⊕ www. citylink.co.uk. **Strathclyde Passenger Transport Travel Centre** ⊠ 12 W. George St., City Center ☎ 0141/332-6811 ⊕ www.spt.co.uk ⊙ Mon.–Thurs. 8:30–4:45, Fri. 8:30–4. **Traveline Scotland** ☎ 0871/200-2233 ⊕ www. travelinescotland.com.

CAR TRAVEL

If you're driving to Glasgow from England and the south of Scotland, you'll probably approach the city via the M6, M74, and A74. The city center is clearly marked from these roads. From Edinburgh, the M8 leads to the city center. From the north, the A82 from Fort William and the A82/M80 from Stirling join the M8 in the city center.

You don't need a car in Glasgow, and you're probably better off without one. Although most modern hotels have their own lots, parking can be trying. In the city center, meters are expensive, running about £2.40 per hour during the day. In the West End they cost 40 pence per hour, but you often have to feed the meter until 10 pm. Don't even consider parking illegally, as fines are upward of £30. Multistory garages are open 24 hours a day at the following locations: Anderston Centre, George Street, Waterloo Place, Mitchell Street, Cambridge Street, and Concert Square. Rates run between £1 and £2 per hour. More convenient are the park-and-ride operations at some subway stations (Kelvinbridge, Bridge Street, and Shields Road). You'll be downtown in no time.

SUBWAY TRAVEL

Glasgow's small subway system—it has just 15 stations—is useful for reaching all the city center and West End attractions. Starting in 2012, stations are slated to be marked by a prominent letter "S." You can choose between flat fares (£1.20), a one-day pass (£3.50), or a 12-journey ticket (£11.50). Trains run regularly from Monday through Saturday with more limited Sunday service. The distance between many central stops is no more than a 5- to 10-minute walk. More information is available from Strathclyde Passenger Transport Travel Centre.

Subway Contacts National Rail ☎ 08457/484950 ⊕ www.nationalrail.co.uk. **Strathclyde Passenger Transport Travel Centre** ✉ 12 W. George St., City Center ☎ 0141/332–6811 ⊕ www.spt.co.uk ☾ Mon.–Thurs. 8:30–4:45, Fri. 8:30–4.

TAXI TRAVEL

Taxis are a fast and cost-effective way to get around. You'll find metered taxis (usually black and of the London sedan type) at stands all over the city center. Most have radio dispatch. Some have also been adapted to take wheelchairs. You can hail a cab on the street if its "for hire" sign is illuminated. A typical ride from the city center to the West End or the South Side costs around £6.

Taxi Contact Glasgow Taxis ☎ 0141/429–7070 ⊕ www.glasgowtaxisltd.co.uk.

TRAIN TRAVEL

Glasgow has two main rail stations: Central and Queen Street. Central serves trains from London's Euston station (five hours), which come via Crewe and Carlisle in England. Some trains arrive via Edinburgh from London's King's Cross station. Central also serves other cities in the northwest of England and towns in the southwest of Scotland: Kilmarnock, Dumfries, Ardrossan (for the island of Arran), Gourock (for Dunoon), Wemyss Bay (for the Isle of Bute), and Stranraer (for Ireland). Trains also run from here to Prestwick Airport.

Queen Street station has frequent connections to Edinburgh (50 minutes), where you can head north to Aberdeen or south to Newcastle, York, and King's Cross. Other trains from Queen Street head to Stirling, Perth, and Dundee; northward to Inverness, Kyle of Lochalsh, Wick, and Thurso; and on the scenic West Highland line to Oban, Fort William, and Mallaig. For details contact National Rail.

A regular bus service links the Queen Street and Central stations. Queen Street is near the Buchanan Street subway station, and Central is close to St. Enoch. Taxis are available at both stations.

The Glasgow area has an extensive network of suburban railway services. Locals still call them the Blue Trains, even though most are now painted maroon and cream. For more information and a free map, contact the Strathclyde Passenger Transport Travel Centre or National.

Train Contacts National Rail ☎ *08457/484950* ⊕ *www.nationalrail.co.uk.* **Strathclyde Passenger Transport Travel Centre** ⊠ *12 W. George St., City Center* ☎ *0141/332–6811* ⊕ *www.spt.co.uk* ⊙ *Mon.–Thurs. 8:30–4:45, Fri. 8:30–4.*

TOURS

You can sign on for a sightseeing tour to get a different perspective on the city and the surrounding area.

BOAT TOURS

Cruises are available on Loch Lomond and to the islands in the Firth of Clyde; contact the Greater Glasgow and Clyde Valley Tourist Board for details. Contact the *Waverley* paddle steamer from June through August.

Contacts Greater Glasgow and Clyde Valley Tourist Board ⊠ *11 George Sq., near Queen Street station, City Center* ☎ *0141/204–4400* ⊕ *www.visitscotland. com/glasgow.* **Waverley** ☎ *0141/221–8152* ⊕ *www.waverleyexcursions.co.uk.*

BUS TOURS

The popular City Sightseeing bus tours leave daily from the west side of George Square. The Greater Glasgow and Clyde Valley Tourist Board can give information about city tours and about longer tours northward to the Highlands and Islands.

Day trips in minivans (16 people maximum) to the surrounding areas, including Loch Lomond and Oban, are available from Rabbie's Trail Burners.

Contacts City Sightseeing ☎ *0141/204–0444* ⊕ *www.citysightseeingglasgow. co.uk.* **Greater Glasgow and Clyde Valley Tourist Board** ⊠ *11 George Sq., near Queen Street station, City Center* ☎ *0141/204–4400* ⊕ *www.visitscotland. com/glasgow.* **Rabbie's Trail Burners** ☎ *0845/643–2248* ⊕ *www.rabbies.com.*

PRIVATE GUIDES

Little's Chauffeur Drive arranges personally tailored car-and-driver tours, both locally and throughout Scotland. The Scottish Tourist Guides Association also provides a private-guide service.

Glasgow Taxis offers city tours. If you allow the driver to follow a set route, the cost is £38 for up to five people and lasts around an hour. A two-hour tour costs £59. You can book tours in advance and be picked up and dropped off wherever you like.

Contacts Glasgow Taxis ☎ *0141/429–7070* ⊕ *www.glasgowtaxisltd.co.uk.* **Little's Chauffeur Drive** ☎ *0141/883–2111* ⊕ *www.littles.co.uk.* **Scottish Tourist Guides Association** ☎ *01786/447784* ⊕ *www.stga.co.uk.*

WALKING TOURS

The Greater Glasgow and Clyde Valley Tourist Board can provide information on special walks on a given day. Glasgow Walking Tours organizes specialized tours of the city's architectural treasures.

Contacts Glasgow Walking Tours ☎ *07751/978935* ⊕ *www.greetingglasgow. com.* **Greater Glasgow and Clyde Valley Tourist Board** ⊠ *11 George Sq., near*

Queen Street station, City Center ☎ *0141/204–4400* ⊕ *www.visitscotland.com/ glasgow.*

VISITOR INFORMATION

The Greater Glasgow and Clyde Valley Tourist Board provides information about different types of tours and has an accommodations-booking service, a currency-exchange office, and a money-transfer service. Books, maps, and souvenirs are also available. The tourist board has a branch at Glasgow Airport, too.

Contacts Greater Glasgow and Clyde Valley Tourist Board ✉ *11 George Sq., near Queen Sreet Station, City Center* ☎ *0141/204–4400* ⊕ *www.visitscotland. com/glasgow.*

EXPLORING GLASGOW

As cities go, Glasgow is contained and compact. It's set up on a grid system, so it's easy to navigate and explore, and the best way to tackle it is on foot. In the eastern part of the city, start by exploring Glasgow Cathedral and other highlights of the oldest section of the city. Next you can either walk (it takes a good 45 minutes) or take the subway to the West End. If you walk, head up Sauchiehall Street and visit Mackintosh's Glasgow School of Art (buy a £16 one-day Mackintosh Trail Ticket if you're exploring multiple sites). Once in the West End, visit the Botanic Gardens, Glasgow University, and the Kelvingrove Art Gallery and Museum. Then take a taxi to the South Side to experience the Burrell Collection.

If you break your sightseeing up into neighborhoods, it's completely manageable to explore all three neighborhoods in three days. Glasgow's pubs and clubs serve up entertainment until late in the evening; there's something for everyone.

CITY CENTER AND THE MERCHANT CITY

Although relatively few medieval buildings survive, many of the city's most important historical buildings are found here. Along the streets of the city center are some of the best examples of the architectural confidence and exuberance that so characterized the burgeoning Glasgow of the turn of the 20th century. There are also plenty of shops, trendy eateries, and pubs.

GETTING HERE Every form of public transportation can bring you here, from bus to train to subway. Head to George Square and walk from there.

TOP ATTRACTIONS

Barras. Scotland's largest indoor market—named for the barrows, or pushcarts, formerly used by the stall holders—is a must-see for anyone addicted to searching through piles of junk for bargains. The century-old institution, open weekends, consists of nine markets. The atmosphere is always good-humored, and you can find just about anything here, in any condition, from dusty model railroads to antique jewelry. Haggling is compulsory. You can reach the Barras by walking from the

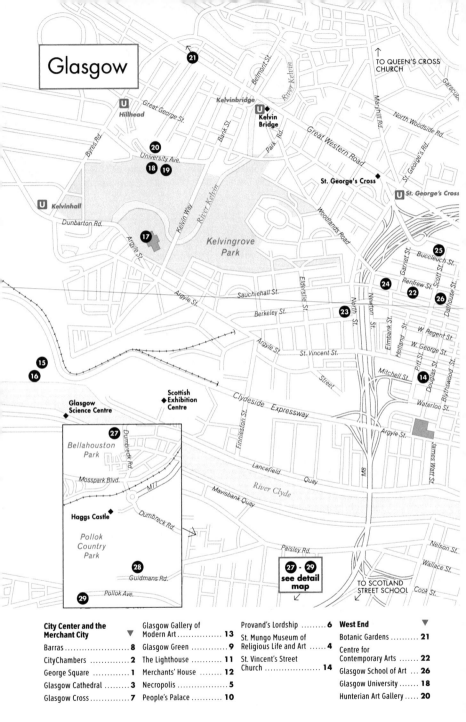

Glasgow

TO QUEEN'S CROSS CHURCH

Kelvinbridge

Hillhead

Great George St.

Kelvin Bridge

Belmont St.

Great Western Road

River Kelvin

Maryhill Rd.

North Woodside Rd.

St. George's Rd.

Garscu...

Byres Rd.

University Ave.

Bank St.

Park Rd.

St. George's Cross

St. George's Cross

Kelvinhall

Dunbarton Rd.

Kelvin Way

River Kelvin

Woodlands Road

Kelvingrove Park

Elderslie St.

Garnet St.

Buccleuch St.

Scott St.

Stanhope Dr.

Argyle St.

Sauchiehall St.

Newton

Renfrew St.

Argyle St.

Berkeley St.

North St.

Elmbank St.

Holland

W. Regent St.

W. George St.

Argyle St.

St. Vincent St.

Street

Pitt St.

Douglas St.

Blythswood...

Mitchell St.

Waterloo St.

Clydeside Expressway

Finnieston St.

Argyle St.

James Watt St.

Glasgow Science Centre

Scottish Exhibition Centre

Bellahouston Park

Dumbreck Rd.

Lancefield

Quay

M8

Mosspark Blvd.

M77

River Clyde

Haggs Castle

Dumbreck Rd.

Mavisbank Quay

Paisley Rd.

Nelson St.

Wallace St.

Pollok Country Park

27 - 29 see detail map

TO SCOTLAND STREET SCHOOL

Cook St.

Guidmans Rd.

Pollok Ave.

City Center and the Merchant City ▼

Barras **8**
CityChambers **2**
George Square **1**
Glasgow Cathedral **3**
Glasgow Cross **7**

Glasgow Gallery of Modern Art **13**
Glasgow Green **9**
The Lighthouse **11**
Merchants' House **12**
Necropolis **5**
People's Palace **10**

Provand's Lordship **6**
St. Mungo Museum of Religious Life and Art **4**
St. Vincent's Street Church **14**

West End ▼

Botanic Gardens **21**
Centre for Contemporary Arts **22**
Glasgow School of Art ... **26**
Glasgow University **18**
Hunterian Art Gallery **20**

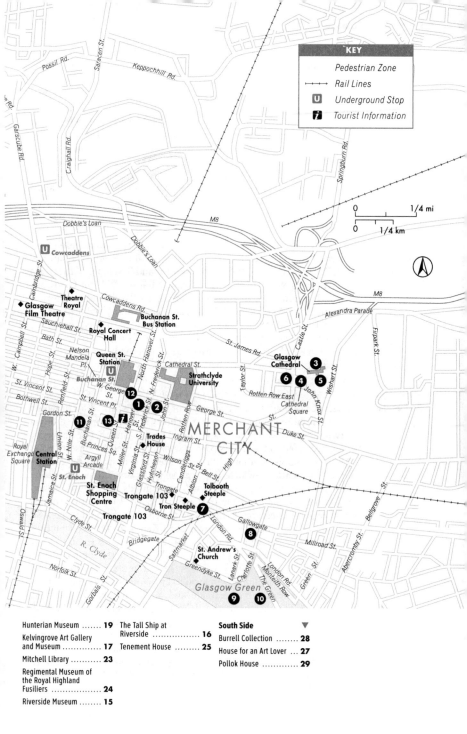

KEY

Pedestrian Zone
Rail Lines
U Underground Stop
i Tourist Information

0   1/4 mi
0   1/4 km

Possil Rd.
Saracen St.
Keppochhill Rd.
Garscube Rd.
Craighall Rd.
Springburn Rd.
Dobbie's Loan
M8
Dobbie's Loan
U Cowcaddens
Cambridge St.
Theatre Royal
Glasgow Film Theatre
Cowcaddens Rd.
Buchanan St. Bus Station
Alexandra Parade
M8
Sauchiehall St.
Bath St.
Royal Concert Hall
Nelson Mandela Pl.
Queen St. Station
St. James Rd.
Glasgow Cathedral
Castle St.
3
U Buchanan St.
W. Campbell St.
Hope St.
Renfield St.
St. Vincent St.
W. George St.
Cathedral St.
Strathclyde University
Taylor St.
6 4 5
Wishart St.
Flipark St.
Bothwell St.
St. Vincent Pl.
12
1
North Hanover St.
N. Frederick St.
John St.
George St.
Rotten Row
Rotten Row East
Cathedral Square
John Knox St.
Gordon St.
11
Buchanan St.
13
i
Queen St.
MERCHANT CITY
Duke St.
Royal Exchange Square
Central Station
U
W. Nile St.
Princes Sq.
Miller St.
Virginia St.
Glassford St.
Hutcheson St.
Trades House
Ingram St.
Wilson St.
Candleriggs
Albion St.
Bell St.
St. Enoch
Argyll Arcade
St. Enoch Shopping Centre
Trongate 103
Trongate
Tron Steeple
7
Tolbooth Steeple
Jamaica St.
Oswald St.
Clyde St.
Trongate 103
Osborne St.
Bridgegate
Saltmarket
London Rd.
Gallowgate
8
Millroad St.
Bellgrove St.
Abercromby St.
R. Clyde
Norfolk St.
Gorbals
St. Andrew's Church
Greendyke St.
Lanark St.
Charlotte St.
Monteith Row
The Green
Green St.
Glasgow Green
9   10

Hunterian Museum **19**
Kelvingrove Art Gallery and Museum **17**
Mitchell Library **23**
Regimental Museum of the Royal Highland Fusiliers **24**
Riverside Museum **15**

The Tall Ship at Riverside **16**
Tenement House **25**

South Side ▼
Burrell Collection **28**
House for an Art Lover ... **27**
Pollok House **29**

Argyle Street train station or the St. Enoch subway station. ⊠ *Gallow-gate, ¼ mi east of Glasgow Cross, Glasgow Cross* ☎ *0141/552–4601* ⊕ *www.glasgow-barras.com* ✉ *Free* ☺ *Weekends 10–5* Ⓜ *St. Enoch.*

★ **City Chambers.** Dominating the east side of George Square, this exuberant expression of Victorian confidence, built by William Young in Italian Renaissance style, was opened by Queen Victoria in 1888. Among the interior's outstanding features are the entrance hall's vaulted ceiling, sustained by granite columns topped with marble, the marble-and-alabaster staircases, and Venetian mosaics. The enormous banqueting hall has murals illustrating Glasgow's history. Free guided tours lasting about an hour depart weekdays at 10:30 and 2:30. ■TIP➔ **Note that the building is closed to visitors during civic functions.** ⊠ *80 George Sq., City Center* ☎ *0141/287–4020* ⊕ *www.glasgow.gov.uk* ✉ *Free* ☺ *Weekdays 9–5* Ⓜ *Buchanan St.*

George Square. The focal point of Glasgow is lined with an impressive collection of statues of worthies: Queen Victoria; Scotland's national poet, Robert Burns (1759–96); the inventor and developer of the steam engine, James Watt (1736–1819); Prime Minister William Gladstone (1809–98); and towering above them all, Scotland's great historical novelist, Sir Walter Scott (1771–1832). The column was intended for George III (1738–1820), after whom the square is named, but when he was found to be insane toward the end of his reign, his statue was never erected. On the square's east side stands the magnificent Italian Renaissance–style **City Chambers**; the handsome **Merchants' House** fills the corner of West George Street, crowned by a globe and a sailing ship. ⊠ *Between St. Vincent and Argyle Sts., City Center* Ⓜ *Buchanan St.*

Fodor's Choice **Glasgow Cathedral.** The most complete of Scotland's cathedrals (it would
★ have been more complete had 19th-century vandals not pulled down its two rugged towers), this is an unusual double church, one above the other, dedicated to Glasgow's patron saint, St. Mungo. Consecrated in 1136 and completed about 300 years later, it was spared the ravages of the Reformation—which destroyed so many of Scotland's medieval churches—mainly because Glasgow's trade guilds defended it. A late-medieval open-timber roof in the nave and lovely 20th-century stained glass are notable features. In the lower church is the splendid crypt of St. Mungo, who was originally known as St. Kentigern (*kentigern* means "chief word"), but who was nicknamed St. Mungo (meaning "dear one") by his early followers in Glasgow. The site of the tomb has been revered since the 6th century, when St. Mungo founded a church here. Mungo features prominently in local legends; one such legend is about a pet bird that he nursed back to life, and another tells of a bush or tree, the branches of which he used to miraculously relight a fire. The bird, the tree, and the salmon with a ring in its mouth (from another story about him) are all to be found on the city of Glasgow's coat of arms, together with a bell that Mungo brought from Rome. ⊠ *Cathedral St., City Center* ☎ *0141/552–8198* ⊕ *www.glasgow-cathedral.com* ✉ *Free* ☺ *Apr.–Sept., Mon.–Sat. 9:30–5:30, Sun. 1–5; Oct.–Mar., Mon.–Sat. 9:30–4:30, Sun. 1–4:30* Ⓜ *Buchanan St.*

3

Peckham's. Perfect for lunch, afternoon coffee, or a light evening meal, the street-level Peckham's serves a range of soups, sandwiches, and quiches. The prices are very reasonable, too. In the basement is a deli and wineshop. ⊠ *61–65 Glassford St., City Center* ☎ *0141/553–0666* ⊕ *www.peckhams. co.uk.*

★ **Glasgow School of Art.** The exterior and interior, structure, furnishings, and decoration of this art-nouveau building, built between 1897 and 1909, form a unified whole, reflecting the inventive genius of Charles Rennie Mackintosh, who was only 28 years old when he won the competition for its design. Architects and designers from all over the world come to admire it. Book ahead for daily guided tours, which cost £8.75 and begin at 11 and 3 (sometimes more frequently in the summer). Otherwise, you can visit four galleries that host frequently changing exhibitions. A visitor center has a small Mackintosh exhibition and sells a good selection of prints, postcards, and books. ⊠ *11 Dalhousie St., City Center* ☎ *0141/353–4526* ⊕ *www.gsa.ac.uk/tours* ☜ *£8.75* ☉ *Building daily 10:30–5. Exhibitions Mon.–Sat. 10:30–4:30, Sat. 10–2.* Ⓜ *Cowcaddens.*

★ **Glasgow Gallery of Modern Art.** One of Glasgow's boldest, most innovative galleries occupies the neoclassical former Royal Exchange building. The modern art, craft, and design collections include works by Scottish conceptual artists such as David Mach, and also paintings and sculptures from around the world, including Papua New Guinea, Ethiopia, and Mexico. Each floor of the gallery reflects the elements—air, fire, earth, and water—which creates some unexpected juxtapositions and also allows for various interactive exhibits. In the basement is a café and an extensive library. The exchange building, designed by David Hamilton (1768–1843) and finished in 1829, was a meeting place for merchants and traders; later it became Stirling's Library. It incorporates the mansion built in 1780 by William Cunninghame, one of the wealthiest tobacco lords. ⊠ *Queen St., City Center* ☎ *0141/229–1996* ⊕ *www.glasgowmuseums.com* ☜ *Free* ☉ *Mon.–Wed. and Sat. 10–5, Thurs. 10–8, Fri. and Sun. 11–5* Ⓜ *Buchanan St.*

Ⓒ **Glasgow Green.** Glasgow's oldest park, on the north side of the River Clyde, has a long history as a favorite spot for public recreation and political demonstrations. Note the Nelson Column, erected long before London's; the McLennan Arch, originally part of the facade of the old Assembly Halls in Ingram Street; and the Templeton Business Centre, a former carpet factory built in the late 19th century in the style of the Doge's Palace in Venice. The most significant building in the park is the **People's Palace.** ⊠ *North side of River Clyde between Green St. and Saltmarket St., Trongate and East End* Ⓜ *St. Enoch.*

The Lighthouse. Charles Rennie Mackintosh designed these former offices of the *Glasgow Herald* newspaper in 1893, with its emblematic Mackintosh Tower. Today it serves as Scotland's **Centre for Architecture, Design and the City,** which celebrates all facets of the architectural field. Regular and changing exhibitions on its second floor address issues of urban design and sustainability. On the third floor, the **Mackintosh**

Interpretation Centre is a great starting point for discovering more about this groundbreaking architect's work, illustrated in a glass wall with alcoves containing models of his buildings. From here you can climb the more than 130 steps up the tower and, once you have caught your breath, look out over Glasgow. The fifth-floor Doocot Café is a great place to take a break from sightseeing. ✉ *11 Mitchell La., City Center* ☎ *0141/271–5365* ⊕ *www.thelighthouse.co.uk* ✉ *Free* ⊗ *Mon–Sat. 10:30–5* Ⓜ *St. Enoch.*

> ### MACKINTOSH TRAIL
>
> **Mackintosh Trail Ticket.** If you're interested in the work of architect Charles Rennie Macintosh, buy a £16 one-day Mackintosh Trail Ticket at major sites, visitor centers, or online from the Mackintosh Society. It includes bus and subway transportation and one-day admission to many sites. ⊕ *www.glasgowmackintosh.com.*

Merchant City. Many of the city's most important Georgian and Victorian buildings, many built by the tobacco merchants, are found here, as well as elegant designer boutiques and trendy eateries and pubs. The city and county buildings on Ingram Street were built in 1842 to house civil servants; note the impressive arrangement of bays and Corinthian columns. To see more interesting architecture, explore the roads off Ingram Street—including Candleriggs, Wilson, and Glassford. It tends to be a little more rundown and remote toward the southeast. Stick to well-lit, well-traveled areas after sunset. ✉ *Between George, Argyle, Buchanan, and High sts., Merchant City* Ⓜ *St. Enoch.*

★ **Necropolis.** A burial ground since the beginning of recorded history, the large Necropolis, modeled on the famous Père-Lachaise Cemetery in Paris, contains some extraordinarily elaborate Victorian tombs. A statue of John Knox (circa 1514–72), leader of the Scottish Reformation, watches over the cemetery, which includes the tomb of 19th-century Glasgow merchant William Miller (1810–72), author of the "Wee Willie Winkie" nursery rhyme. The main gates are behind the St. Mungo Museum of Religious Art and Life. Call ahead for free guided tours. ✉ *Behind Glasgow Cathedral, City Center* ☎ *0141/287–5064* ⊕ *www.glasgownecropolis.org* ✉ *Free* ⊗ *Daily 7–dusk* Ⓜ *Buchanan St.*

☺ **People's Palace.** An impressive Victorian red-sandstone building dating from 1894 houses an intriguing museum dedicated to the city's social history. Included among the exhibits is one devoted to the ordinary folk of Glasgow, called the *People's Story.* Also on display are the writing desk of John McLean (1879–1923), the "Red Clydeside" political activist who came to Lenin's notice, and the famous banana boots worn on stage by Glasgow-born comedian Billy Connolly. On the top floor a sequence of fine murals by Glasgow artist Ken Currie tells the story of Glasgow's working-class citizens. Behind the museum are the restored Winter Gardens and a popular café. To get here from the St. Enoch subway station, walk along Argyle Street past Glasgow Cross. ✉ *Glasgow Green, Trongate and East End* ☎ *0141/276–0788* ⊕ *www.glasgowmuseums.com* ✉ *Free* ⊗ *Tue.–Thurs. and Sat. 10–5, Fri. and Sun. 11–5* Ⓜ *St. Enoch.*

UNION AND GROWTH

Glasgow flourished quietly during the Middle Ages. Its cathedral was the center of religious life, its university a center of serious academia. Although the city was made a burgh (meaning that it was granted trading rights) in 1175 by King William the Lion, its population never numbered more than a few thousand people.

What changed Glasgow irrevocably was the 1707 Treaty of Union between Scotland and England, which allowed Scotland to trade with the essentially English colonies in America. Glasgow, with its advantageous position on Scotland's west coast, prospered. In came cotton, tobacco, and rum; out went various Scottish manufactured goods and clothing. The key to it all was tobacco. The prosperous merchants known as tobacco lords ran the city, and their wealth laid the foundation for the manufacturing industries of the 19th century. You can still see some of the buildings they created in the renovated neighborhood called the Merchant City.

Provand's Lordship. Glasgow's oldest house was built in 1471 by Bishop Andrew Muirhead as a residence for churchmen. Mary, Queen of Scots (1542–87), is said to have stayed here. After her day, however, the house fell into decline and was used as a sweetshop, a soft-drink factory, the home of the city hangman, and a junk shop. The city finally rescued it and turned it into a museum. Exhibits show the house as it might have looked in its heyday, with period rooms and a spooky re-creation of the old hangman's room. The St. Nicholas Garden behind the house is a medicinal herb garden, with the famous Tontine carved stone faces. ⊠ *3 Castle St., City Center* ☎ *0141/552–8819* ⊕ *www.glasgowmuseums. com* ⊡ *Free* ⊗ *Mon.–Thurs. and Sat. 10–5, Fri. and Sun. 11–5* Ⓜ *Buchanan St.*

St. Mungo Museum of Religious Life and Art. An outstanding collection of artifacts, including Celtic crosses and statuettes of Hindu gods, reflects the many religious groups that have settled throughout the centuries in Glasgow and the west of Scotland. This rich history is depicted in the stunning Sharing of Faiths Banner, which celebrates the city's many different faiths. A Zen Garden creates a peaceful setting for rest and contemplation, and elsewhere stained-glass windows include a depiction of St. Mungo himself. ⊠ *2 Castle St., City Center* ☎ *0141/276–1625* ⊕ *www.glasgowmuseums.com* ⊡ *Free* ⊗ *Tues.–Thurs. and Sat. 10–5, Fri. and Sun. 11–5* Ⓜ *Buchanan St.*

WORTH NOTING

Centre for Contemporary Arts. This arts, film, and performance venue is housed in a modern building constructed around the facade of the older center. The Café Saramago sits between old and new, under a glass roof that feels a little like an open courtyard. It has a very good lunch and pretheater two-course menu. The center hosts a range of activities, including cutting-edge art exhibitions, film screenings, and educational activities for community groups. There's a small theater on the first floor and a small bookshop specializing in art books. ⊠ *350 Sauchiehall St., City Center* ☎ *0141/352–4900* ⊕ *www.cca-glasgow.*

com Free ☉ *Tues.–Fri. 11–6, Sat. 10–6* Ⓜ *Cowcaddens.*

Glasgow Cross. This crossroads was the center of the medieval city. The Mercat Cross (*mercat* means "market"), topped by a unicorn, marks the spot where merchants met, where the market was held, and where criminals were executed. Here, too, was the *tron,* or weigh beam, installed in 1491 and used by merchants to check weights. The Tolbooth Steeple dates from 1626 and served as the civic center and the place where travelers paid tolls. ⊠ *Intersection of Saltmarket, Trongate, Gallowgate, and London Rds., Glasgow Cross* Ⓜ *St. Enoch.*

GETTING AROUND

Family Day Tripper Ticket. For £10.20 for one adult and up to two children, or £18.20 for two adults and up to four children, the Family Day Tripper Ticket gets you around the whole area, from Loch Lomond to Ayrshire. The tickets are a good value and are available from rail, bus, and subway stations and from the Strathclyde Passenger Transport Travel Centre. ⊠ *12 W. George St., City Center* ☎ *0141/332–6811* ⊕ *www.spt. co.uk.*

Merchants' House. A golden sailing ship, a reminder of the importance of sea trade to Glasgow's prosperity, tops this handsome 1874 Victorian building, home to Glasgow's chamber of commerce. The interior isn't open to the public, but the exterior is impressive. ⊠ *West side of George Sq., Merchant City* Ⓜ *Buchanan St.*

Regimental Museum of the Royal Highland Fusiliers. Exhibits of medals, badges, and uniforms relate the history of a famous, much-honored regiment and the men who served in it. ⊠ *518 Sauchiehall St., City Center* ☎ *0141/332–0961* ⊕ *www.rhf.org.uk* Free ☉ *Mon.–Thurs. 9–4, Fri. 9–3* Ⓜ *Cowcaddens.*

St. Vincent's Street Church. Dating from 1859, this church, the work of Alexander Thomson, exemplifies his Greek Revival style, replete with Ionic temple, sphinx-esque heads, Greek ornamentation, and rich interior color. There are no tours; you can see the interior only by attending a service Sunday at 11 am or 6:30 pm. ⊠ *Pitt and St. Vincent Sts., City Center* ⊕ *www.greekthomsonchurch* Ⓜ *Buchanan St.*

Tenement House. This ordinary first-floor apartment is anything but ordinary inside: it was occupied from 1937 to 1982 by Agnes Toward (and before that by her mother), who seems never to have thrown anything away. Her legacy is this fascinating time capsule, painstakingly preserved with her everyday furniture and belongings. The red-sandstone building dates from 1892 and can be found in the Garnethill area north of Charing Cross station. A small museum explores the life and times of its careful occupant. ⊠ *145 Buccleuch St., City Center* ☎ *0844/493–2197* ⊕ *www.nts.org.uk* £6 ☉ *Mar.–Oct., daily 1–5; last admission at 4:30* Ⓜ *Cowcaddens.*

A GOOD WALK IN THE WEST END

This tranquil stroll, taking about an hour if you don't poke into the museums, showcases all of the beauty of the West End. Start in Kelvingrove Park, at the junction of Sauchiehall (pronounced socky-hall) and Argyle streets, where you'll find the city's main art museum, the Kelvingrove Art Gallery and Museum. The impressive red-sandstone building and its leafy surroundings are well worth a visit. From here stroll up tree-lined Kelvin Way; the skyline to your left is dominated dramatically by Glasgow University. Turn left onto University Avenue and walk past the Memorial Gates. On the south side of University Avenue is the Hunterian Museum, and across the street is the even more interesting Hunterian Art Gallery. From here make your way to the Botanic Gardens, where 12 Victorian conservatories and their fragrant collections await. To get there, continue west along University Avenue, turn right at Byres Road, and walk as far as Great Western Road. The 40 acres of gardens are across the busy intersection. Its peaceful garden makes you feel a million miles away from the city center.

THE WEST END

Founded in 1451, Glasgow University is the third oldest in Scotland, after St. Andrews and Aberdeen. (It's at least 130 years ahead of the University of Edinburgh.) Needless to say, its presence dominates the West End. The industrialists and merchants who built their grand homes on Great Western Road and the adjacent streets endowed museums and art galleries and commissioned artists to decorate and design their homes, as a stroll around the area will quickly reveal. In the summer, the beautiful Botanical Gardens, with the iconic glasshouse that is the Kibble Palace, become a stage for new and unusual versions of Shakespeare's plays. A good way to save money is to picnic in the park (weather permitting, of course). You can buy sandwiches, salads, and other portable items at shops on Byres Road.

GETTING HERE The best way to get to the West End from the city center is by subway; get off at the Hillhead station. A taxi is another option.

TOP ATTRACTIONS

Botanic Gardens. The Royal Botanical Institute of Glasgow began to display plants here in 1842. At the heart of the gardens is the spectacular circular glasshouse, the **Kibble Palace,** a favorite haunt of Glaswegian families. Originally built in 1873, it was the conservatory of a Victorian eccentric named John Kibble. Its domed, interlinked greenhouses contain tree ferns, palm trees, temperate plants, and the Tropicarium, where you can experience the lushness of a rain forest and briefly forget the weather outside. Two other greenhouses have comprehensive displays of cacti, tropical plants, and a world-famous collection of orchids. When the sun shines, the gardens quickly fill up with people enjoying the extensive lawns, the beautiful flower displays, and the herb garden. In July the park becomes a stage for presentations of Shakespeare's plays. ⊠ *730 Great Western Rd., West End* ☎ *0141/276–1614* ⊕ *www.*

glasgow.gov.uk ☒ *Free* ☉ *Gardens daily 7–dusk; Kibble Palace Mar.–mid-Oct., daily 10–6; mid-Oct.–Feb., daily 10–4:15* Ⓜ *Hillhead.*

OFF THE
BEATEN
PATH

☾**Glasgow Science Centre.** Families with children love this museum, which has a fun-packed Science Mall, an IMAX theater, and the futuristic Glasgow Tower. The 417-foot spire—with an aerodynamic profile that twists 360 degrees—is a marvel. In the three-level Science Mall, state-of-the-art displays educate kids and adults about exploration, discovery, and the environment. The ScottishPower Planetarium has a fantastic Zeiss Starmaster projector, which allows visitors to gaze at the glittering stars. Set aside half a day to see everything. IMAX screenings and planetarium visits are extra. ☒ *50 Pacific Quay, South Side* ☎ *0141/420–5000* ⊕ *www.glasgowsciencecentre.org.uk* ☒ *£9.95* ☉ *Oct.–Mar., Wed.–Fri. 10–3, weekends 10–5; Apr.–Sept, daily 10–5* Ⓜ *Cessnock.*

Glasgow University. The architecture, grounds, and great views of Glasgow all warrant a visit to the university. The Gilbert Scott Building, the university's main edifice, was built more than a century ago and is a good example of the Gothic Revival style. **Glasgow University Visitor Centre,** near the main gate on University Avenue, has exhibits on the university, a small coffee bar, and a gift shop; it's the starting point for one-hour guided walking tours of the campus. A self-guided tour starts at the visitor center and takes in the east and west quadrangles, the cloisters, Professor's Square, Pearce Lodge, and the not-to-be-missed University Chapel. ☒ *University Ave., West End* ☎ *0141/330–5511* ⊕ *www.glasgow.ac.uk* ☒ *Tour £10* ☉ *May–Sept., Mon.–Sat. 9:30–5* Ⓜ *Hillhead.*

★ **Hunterian Art Gallery.** Opposite Glasgow University's main gate, this gallery houses William Hunter's (1718–83) collection of paintings (his antiquarian collection is housed in the nearby Hunterian Museum). You'll also find prints, drawings, and sculptures by Tintoretto, Rembrandt, and Auguste Rodin, as well as a major collection of paintings by James McNeill Whistler, who had a great affection for the city that bought one of his earliest paintings. Also in the gallery is a replica of **Charles Rennie Mackintosh's town house,** which once stood nearby. The rooms contain Mackintosh's distinctive art-nouveau chairs, tables, beds, and cupboards, and the walls are decorated in the equally distinctive style devised by him and his artist wife, Margaret. The gallery is free, but the Mackintosh House and occasional special exhibitions are £5. ☒ *Hillhead St., West End* ☎ *0141/330–5431* ⊕ *www.hunterian.gla.ac.uk* ☒ *Free, Mackintosh house £5* ☉ *Tues.–Sat. 10–5, Sun. 11–4* Ⓜ *Hillhead.*

Hunterian Museum. Set within Glasgow University, the city's oldest museum (opened in 1807) showcases part of the collections of William Hunter, an 18th-century Glasgow doctor who assembled a staggering quantity of valuable material. (The doctor's art treasures are housed in the nearby Hunterian Art Gallery.) The museum displays Hunter's hoards of coins, manuscripts, scientific instruments, and archaeological artifacts in a striking Gothic building. A new permanent exhibit chronicles the building of the Antonine Wall, the Roman's northern-

Charles Rennie Mackintosh

Not so long ago, the furniture of innovative Glasgow-born architect Charles Rennie Mackintosh (1868–1928) was broken up for firewood. Today art books are devoted to his distinctive, astonishingly elegant Arts and Crafts– and art nouveau–influenced interiors, and artisans around the world look to his theory that "decoration should not be constructed, rather construction should be decorated" as holy law. Mackintosh's stripped-down designs ushered in the modern age with their deceptively stark style.

AN ARCHITECT'S CAREER

Mackintosh trained in architecture at the Glasgow School of Art and was apprenticed to the Glasgow firm of John Hutchison at the age of 16. Early influences on his work included the Pre-Raphaelites, James McNeill Whistler (1834–1903), Aubrey Beardsley (1872–98), and Japanese art. But by the 1890s a distinct Glasgow style developed.

The building for the *Glasgow Herald* newspaper, which he designed in 1893 and which is now the Lighthouse Centre for Architecture, Design and the City, was soon followed by other major Glasgow buildings: Queen Margaret's Medical College; the Martyrs Public School; tearooms including the Willow Tearoom; the Hill House, in Helensburgh, now owned by the National Trust for Scotland; and Queen's Cross Church, completed in 1899 and now the headquarters of the Charles Rennie Mackintosh Society. In 1897 Mackintosh began work on a new home for the Glasgow School of Art, recognized as one of his major achievements.

Mackintosh married Margaret Macdonald in 1900, and in later years her decorative work enhanced the interiors of his buildings. In 1904 he became a partner in Honeyman and Keppie and designed Scotland Street School, now the Scotland Street School Museum, in the same year. Until 1913, when he left Honeyman and Keppie and moved to England, Mackintosh's projects included buildings over much of Scotland. He preferred wherever possible to include interiors as part of his overall design.

Commissions in England after 1913 included design challenges not confined to buildings, such as fabrics, furniture, and even bookbindings. Mackintosh died in London in 1928.

After 1904 architectural taste had turned against Mackintosh's style; his work was seen as strange. Mackintosh could not conform to the times; he lost commissions, drank heavily, and ended up poor and sick. His reputation revived only in the 1950s with the publication of his monographs.

HOW TO SEE HIS WORK

Glasgow is the best place in the world to admire Mackintosh's work: in addition to the buildings mentioned above, most of which can be visited, the Hunterian Art Gallery contains magnificent reconstructions of the principal rooms at 78 Southpark Avenue, Mackintosh's Glasgow home, and original drawings, documents, and records, plus the re-creation of a room at 78 Derngate, Northampton.

Mackintosh Trail Ticket. Purchase a Mackintosh Trail Ticket for £16, available at visitor centers, the Strathclyde Passenger Transport Centre, or online at the Mackintosh Society. ⊕ *www. glasgowmackintosh.com.*

most defense. ⊠ *University Ave., West End* ☎ *0141/330–4221* ⊕ *www. hunterian.gla.ac.uk* ☑ *Free* ⊙ *Mon.–Sat. 9:30–5* Ⓜ *Hillhead.*

↻ **Kelvingrove Art Gallery and Museum.** Worthy of its world-class reputation, **Fodor's Choice** the Kelvingrive Art Gallery and Museum attracts local families as well ★ as international visitors. This combination of cathedral and castle was designed in the Renaissance style and built between 1891 and 1901. The stunning red-sandstone edifice is an appropriate home for works by Botticelli, Rembrandt, Monet, and others; the museum has been hailed as "one of the greatest civic collections in Europe." The Glasgow Room houses extraordinary works by local artists. There's a Mackintosh and the Glasgow Style room, a picture promenade, and a natural-history exhibit on creatures of the past. Whether the subject is Scottish culture, design, or storytelling, every wall and room begs you to look deeper; labels are thought provoking and sometimes witty. You could spend a weekend here, but in a pinch three hours would do one level justice—there are three. Leave time to visit the gift shop and the attractive base-ment restaurant. ⊠ *Argyle St., West End* ☎ *0141/276–9599* ⊕ *www. glasgowmuseums.com* ☑ *Free* ⊙ *Mon.–Thurs. and Sat. 10–5, Fri. and Sun. 11–5* Ⓜ *Kelvinhall.*

↻ **Kelvingrove Park.** A peaceful retreat, the park was purchased by the city in 1852 and takes its name from the River Kelvin, which flows through it. Among the numerous statues of prominent Glaswegians is one of Lord Kelvin (1824–1907), the Scottish mathematician and physicist who pioneered a great deal of work in electricity. The park also has a massive fountain commemorating a lord provost of Glasgow from the 1850s, a duck pond, play areas, a skate park, and lots of exotic trees. ⊠ *Bounded by Sauchiehall St., Woodlands Rd., and Kelvin Way, West End* Ⓜ *Kelvinhall.*

Mitchell Library. The largest public reference library in Europe houses more than a million volumes, including what's claimed to be the world's largest collection about Robert Burns. A bust in the entrance hall com-memorates the library's founder, Stephen Mitchell, who died in 1874. Minerva, goddess of wisdom, looks down from the library's dome, encouraging the library's users and frowning at the drivers thundering along the motorway just in front of her. The western facade (at the back), with its sculpted figures of Mozart, Beethoven, Michelangelo, and other artistic figures, is particularly beautiful. The Aye Write Litera-ture Festival takes place here every March, as do many other events cel-ebrating Glasgow's history. ⊠ *North St., West End* ☎ *0141/287–2999* ⊕ *www.mitchelllibrary.org* ☑ *Free* ⊙ *Mon.–Thurs. 9–8, Fri. and Sat. 9–5* Ⓜ *St. George's Cross.*

↻ **Riverside Museum: Scotland's Museum of Transport and Travel.** An extraor-**Fodor's Choice** dinary new riverside museum designed by Zaha Hadid celebrates the ★ area's industrial heritage with flair. Its huge metal structure with curving walls echoes the covered yards where ships were built on the Clyde. Glasgow's history of shipbuilding is celebrated in the world-famous collection of Clyde-built ship models. Some of the locomotives built at the nearby St. Rollox yards are also on display. There are cars from every age and many countries suspended on a kind of flying roadway above the main museum. You can wander down Main Street, circa 1930, without leaving the building: the pawnbroker and the Italian café, the subway train and the funeral parlor are frozen in time. Relax with a coffee in the café, wander out onto the expansive riverside walk, or board the tall ship that is moored permanently behind the museum. Bus 100 from George Square brings you here, or you can walk from the Partick subway station in 10 minutes. ⊠ *100 Poundhouse Pl., West End* ☎ *0141/ 287–2720* ⊕ *www.glasgowlife. org.uk/museums* 💷 *Free* ⊗ *Mon.– Thurs. and Sat. 10–5, Fri. and Sun. 11–5* Ⓜ *Partick.*

WORTH NOTING

OFF THE BEATEN PATH
Queen's Cross Church. Head for the Charles Rennie Mackintosh Society Headquarters, housed in the only church Mackintosh designed, to learn more about the famous Glasgow-born architect and designer. Although one of the leading lights in the art-nouveau movement, Mackintosh died in relative obscurity in 1928. Today he's widely accepted as a brilliant innovator. The church has beautiful stained-glass windows and a light-enhancing, carved-wood interior. The center's library and shop provide further insight into Glasgow's other Mackintosh-designed buildings, which include Scotland Street School, the Martyrs Public School, and the Glasgow School of Art. The church sits on the corner of Springbank Street at the junction of Garscube Road with Maryhill Road; a cab ride can get you here, or you can take a bus toward Queen's Cross from stops along Hope Street. ⊠ *870 Garscube Rd., West End* ☎ *0141/946–6600* ⊕ *www.crmsociety.com* 💷 *£4* ⊗ *Apr.–Oct., Mon., Wed., and Fri. 10–5; Nov.–Mar., Mon., Wed., and Fri. 10–4.*

OFF THE BEATEN PATH
The Tall Ship. Built in 1896, this fine tall sailing ship now sits on the river Clyde immediately behind the Riverside Museum. The *Glenlee* once belonged to the Spanish Navy (under a different name), but carried cargo all over the world in her day. She returned to Glasgow and the river Clyde in 1993, and now forms part of the museum. You can wander throughout this surprisingly large cargo ship with or without a £2 audio guide, peer into cabins and holds, and stand on the forecastle as you gaze down the river. Bus 100 from George Square brings you here, or you can walk from the Partick subway station in 10 minutes. ⊠ *150 Pointhouse Pl., West End* ☎ *0141/357–3699* ⊕ *www.thetallship. com* 💷 *£5* ⊗ *Mar.–Oct., daily 10–5, last admission 4:15; Nov.–Feb., daily 10–4, last admission 3:15* Ⓜ *Partick.*

GLASGOW'S UNDERGROUND

Glasgow is the only city in Scotland with a subway—or underground, as it's called here. The system was built at the end of the 19th century and takes the simple form of two circular routes, one going clockwise and the other counterclockwise. All trains eventually bring you back to where you started, and the complete circle takes 24 minutes. The tunnels are small, and so are the trains. This, together with the affection in which the system is held and the bright-orange paint of the trains, gave the system its nickname, the "Clockwork Orange."

3

THE SOUTH SIDE

Just southwest of the city center in the South Side are two of Glasgow's dear green spaces—Bellahouston Park and Pollok Country Park—which have important art collections: Charles Rennie Mackintosh's House for an Art Lover in Bellahouston and the Burrell Collection, and Pollok House. A respite from the buzz of the city can also be found in the parks, where you can have a picnic or ramble through greenery and gardens.

GETTING HERE   Both parks are off Paisley Road, about 3 mi southwest of the city center. You can take a taxi or car, city bus, or a train from Glasgow Central Station to Pollokshaws West Station or Dumbreck.

TOP ATTRACTIONS

Fodor's Choice   **Burrell Collection.** An elegant, ultramodern building of pink sandstone
★   and stainless steel houses thousands of items of all descriptions, from ancient Egyptian, Greek, and Roman artifacts to Chinese ceramics, bronzes, and jade. You can also find medieval tapestries, stained-glass windows, Rodin sculptures, and exquisite French-impressionist paintings—Degas's *The Rehearsal* and Sir Henry Raeburn's *Miss Macartney*, to name two. Eccentric millionaire Sir William Burrell (1861–1958) donated this collection of some 8,000 pieces to the city in 1944. The 1983 building was designed with large glass walls so that the items on display could relate to their surroundings in Pollok Country Park: art and nature, supposedly in perfect harmony. You can get here via Buses 45, 48, and 57 from Union Street, or it's a leisurely 15-minute walk from the Pollokshaws West rail station. ⊠ *2060 Pollokshaws Rd., South Side* ☎ *0141/287-2550* ⊕ *www.glasgowmuseums.com* ☒ *Free* ⊙ *Mon.–Thurs. and Sat. 10–5, Fri. and Sun. 11–5.*

House for an Art Lover. Within Bellahouston Park is a "new" Mackintosh house, based on a competition entry Charles Rennie Mackintosh submitted to a German magazine in 1901. The house was never built in his lifetime, but took shape between 1989 and 1996. The building houses the Glasgow School of Art's postgraduate study center, and exhibits designs for the various rooms and decorative pieces by Mackintosh and his wife, Margaret. The main lounge is spectacular. There's also a café and shop filled with art. Buses 9, 53, and 54 from Union Street will get you here. Call ahead, as opening times can vary. ⊠ *Bellahouston Park, 10 Dumbreck Rd., South Side* ☎ *0141/353–4770* ⊕ *www. houseforanartlover.co.uk* ☒ *£4.50* ⊙ *Apr.–Sept., Mon.–Wed. 10–4, Thurs.–Sun. 10–1; Oct.–Mar., weekends 10–1* Ⓜ *Ibrox.*

WORTH NOTING

OFF THE
BEATEN
PATH

Holmwood House. The National Trust for Scotland has undertaken the restoration of this large mansion house, designed by Alexander "Greek" Thomson for the wealthy owner of a paper mill. Its classical Greek architecture and stunningly ornamented wood and marble features are among his finest. You can witness the ongoing restoration process one or two days a week; call to check for times. ⊠ *61–63 Netherlee Rd., South Side* ☎ *0141/637–2129* ⊕ *www.nts.org.uk* ☒ *£6* ⊙ *Apr.–Oct., Thurs.–Mon. noon–5:30; last admission at 5.*

Pollok House. This classic Georgian house, dating from the mid-1700s, sits amid landscaped gardens and avenues of trees that are now part of Pollok Country Park. It still has the tranquil air of an expensive but unpretentious country house. The Stirling Maxwell Collection includes paintings by Blake and a strong grouping of Spanish works by El Greco, Murillo, and Goya. Lovely examples of 18th- and early-19th-century furniture, silver, glass, and porcelain are also on display. The house has lovely gardens that overlook the White Cart River. The downstairs servants' quarters now house the restaurant's kitchen, still hung with the cooking implements of its times. Eat in the small, pleasant garden if the weather allows. You can take Buses 45, 47, or 57 to the gate of Pollok County Park. ⊠ *Pollok County Park, 2060 Pollokshaws Rd., South Side* ☎ *0141/616–6410* ⊕ *www.nts.org.uk* 🖭 *£6, free Nov.–Mar.* ☉ *Daily 10–5.*

OFF THE BEATEN PATH

Scotland Street School Museum. A former school designed by Charles Rennie Mackintosh, this building houses a fascinating museum of education. Classrooms re-create school life in Scotland during Victorian times and World War II, and a cookery room recounts a time when education for Scottish girls consisted of little more than learning how to become a housewife. An exhibition space and café are also here. The building sits opposite Shields Road underground station. ⊠ *225 Scotland St., South Side* ☎ *0141/287–0500* ⊕ *www.glasgowmuseums.com* 🖭 *Free* ☉ *Tues.–Thurs. and Sat. 10–5, Fri. and Sun. 11–5* Ⓜ *Shields Rd.*

WHERE TO EAT

In the past few years, restaurants have been popping up all around Glasgow that emphasize the best that Scotland has to offer: grass-fed beef, free-range chicken, wild seafood, venison, duck, and goose—not to mention superb fruits and vegetables. The growing emphasis on organic food is reflected on menus that increasingly provide detailed information about the source of their ingredients. No wonder Glasgow is garnering a reputation among food lovers.

You can eat your way around the world in Glasgow. Chinese and Indian foods are longtime favorites, and Thai and Japanese restaurants have become very popular. Spanish-style tapas are now quite common. Glasgow has a large Italian community, and its traditional cafés have been joined by a new generation of eateries serving updated versions of the classics. And seafood restaurants have moved well beyond the fish-and-chips wrapped in newspaper that were always a Glasgow staple.

Smoking isn't allowed in any enclosed space in Scotland, so many restaurants have placed tables outside under awnings during the warmer summer months. With this type of outdoor dining comes more Mediterranean-style meals.

PRICES

Eating in Glasgow can be casual or lavish. For inexpensive dining, consider the benefit of lunch or pretheater set menus. Beer and spirits cost much the same as they would in a bar, but wine is relatively expensive in restaurants. ■TIP→ Some restaurants allow you to bring your own bottle of wine, charging just a small corkage fee. It's worth the effort.

WHAT IT COSTS IN POUNDS					
	¢	$	$$	$$$	$$$$
AT DINNER	under £10	£10–£14	£15–£19	£20–£25	over £25

Prices are per person for a main course at dinner.

CITY CENTER AND MERCHANT CITY

Use the coordinate (✢ B2) at the end of each listing to locate a site on the corresponding map.

The city center has restaurants catering to the 9-to-5 crowd, meaning there are a lot of fine-dining establishments catching people as they leave work. You can, however, always find a fish-and-chips shop on any busy street corner.

$$
CHINESE ✕ **Amber Regent.** This may not be the cheapest Chinese restaurant in town, but it's certainly one of the finest and most formal. For a start, the meticulously sculpted vegetables that accompany the hors d'oeuvres seem almost too artful to eat. Succulent king prawns or duck with mashed prawns in an oyster sauce readily attest to the kitchen's skill in preparing excellent Cantonese and Szechuan cuisine. Its reputation means that the restaurant can get very busy, so do make reservations, especially on weekends. For the best value, try the £9.50 two-course menus served between noon and 2:15. ⊠ *50 W. Regent St., City Center* ☎ *0141/331–1655* ⊕ *www.amberregent.com* ⊗ *No lunch Sun.* ✢ *F3.*

$$
SPANISH ✕ **Arta.** The narrow entrance doesn't prepare you for this huge, spacious venue—restaurant, bar, dance club—nor for its extravagant decor. The interior is like an enormous hacienda somewhere in southern Spain, and the menu is made to match. There's an elaborate tapas menu, accentuated by resident musicians and salsa dancing. Paellas (with the usual meat and fish, and there's even a vegetarian version) are substantial and delicious. ⊠ *13–19 Wallis St., City Center* ☎ *0845/166–6018* ⊗ *No lunch. Closed Sun.–Wed.* ✢ *H5.*

$$
FRENCH ✕ **Brasserie.** This basement restaurant was once the crypt of a church, and its vaulted wood ceiling and dark accents create an intimate, relaxed vibe. Kick back and enjoy locally sourced steaks or something from the game menu: perhaps partridge, venison, or game pie with roasted root vegetables. The desserts are tempting—who could resist chocolate-and-chestnut cake with milk-and-honey sorbet? There are some tantalizing cocktails and a long wine list. ⊠ *Malmaison Hotel, 278 W. George St., City Center* ☎ *0141/572–1001* ⊕ *www.malmaison-glasgow.com* ⬧ *Reservations essential* ✢ *E3.*

¢
BRITISH ✕ **The Butterfly and the Pig.** Down an innocuous-looking flight of stairs, this intimate restaurant is the type of place the locals love: flickering candles, mix-and-match crockery, and food that is inventive, inexpensive, and original. The menu reads like a comedic narrative, with descriptions like "traditional fish and chips, battered to death" served

BEST BETS FOR GLASGOW DINING

Where can I find the best food Glasgow has to offer? Fodor's writers and editors have selected their favorite restaurants by price, cuisine, and experience in the lists below. In the first column, the Fodor's Choice properties represent the "best of the best" across price categories. You can also search by neighborhood for excellent eating experiences—just peruse our complete reviews on the following pages.

Fodor's Choice ★

Balbir's, $, p. 130
The Corinthian Club, $$, p. 126
Hotel du Vin Bistro, $$$, p. 131
Mussel Inn, $$, p. 127
Number Sixteen, $$, p. 132
Rogano, $$$, p. 128
Ubiquitous Chip, $$$$, p. 133

By Price

¢

Willow Tearoom, p. 129

$

Balbir's, p. 130
Café-Gallery Cossachok, p. 126
Café Gandolfi, p. 126
Crabshakk, p. 130
Kool Ba, p. 127
Mother India Cafe, p. 132

$$

The Brasserie at Òran Mór, p. 130
Cafezique, p. 130
The Corinthian Club, p. 126
Number Sixteen, p. 132
The Sisters, p. 132
Two Fat Ladies, p. 129

$$$

Hotel du Vin Bistro, p. 131
Rogano, p. 128

$$$$

Ubiquitous Chip, p. 133

By Cuisine

MODERN BRITISH

Café Gandolfi, $, p. 126
City Merchant, $$, p. 126
Number Sixteen, $$, p. 132

Pelican Café Bistro, $$, p. 132
Stravaigin, $$, p. 133

ASIAN

Amber Regent, $$, p. 122
Opium, $$, p. 128
Wudon, ¢, p. 133

FRENCH

Brasserie, $$, p. 122
Hotel du Vin Bistro, $$$, p. 131
La Vallée Blanche, $$, p. 131

INDIAN

Balbir's, $, p. 130
Kool Ba, $, p. 127
Mother India Cafe, $, p. 132

ITALIAN

Battlefield Rest, $ p. 133
Fratelli Sarti, $, p. 127
La Parmigiana, $$, p. 131

Little Italy, ¢, p. 131
Spuntini, $, p. 132

SEAFOOD

Crabshakk, $, p. 130
Mussel Inn, $$, p. 127
Rogano, $$$, p. 128
Two Fat Ladies, $$, p. 129

SPANISH

Arta, $$, p. 122
Café Andaluz, $, p. 130

VEGETARIAN

Stereo, ¢, p. 128

By Experience

MOST KID-FRIENDLY

Fratelli Sarti, $, p. 127
Fressh, ¢, p. 127
Little Italy, ¢, p. 131
Pancho Villa's, $, p. 128
Spuntini, $, p. 132

HOTSPOTS

Café-Gallery Cossachok, $, p. 126
Cafezique, $$, p. 130
The Left Bank, $, p. 131
Stereo, ¢, p. 128

MOST ROMANTIC

Hotel du Vin Bistro, $$$, p. 131
Kool Ba, $, p. 127
La Vallée Blanche, $$, p. 131
Rogano, $$$, p. 128

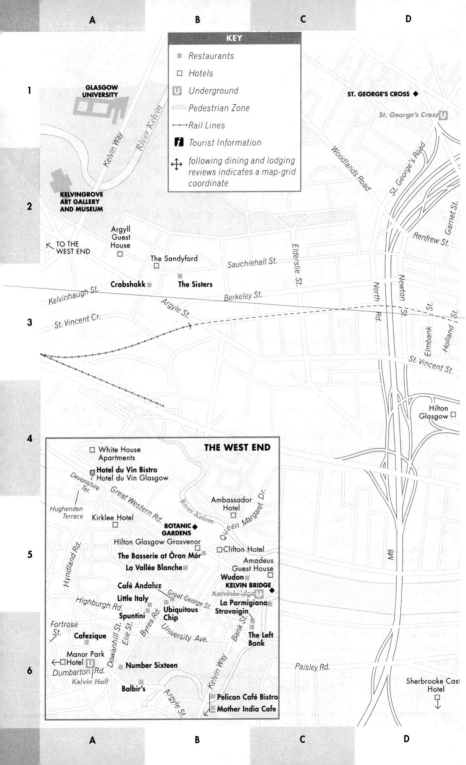

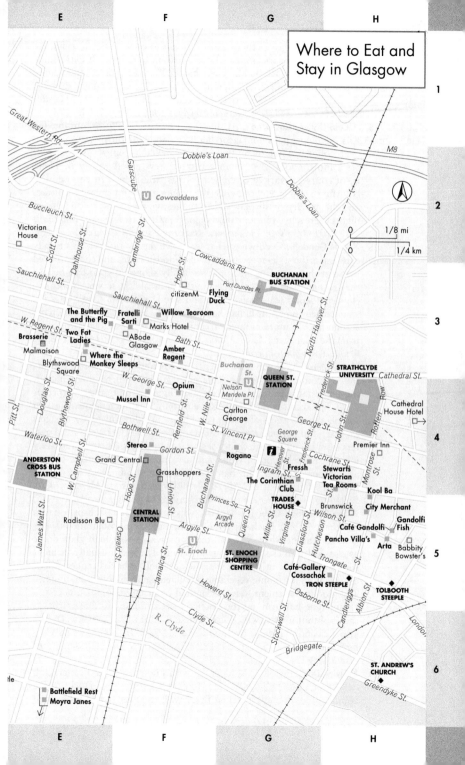

Where to Eat and Stay in Glasgow

with "beans today, as the peas don't want to cook." Worth trying are dishes such as hearty portobello-mushroom burgers with extra-thick potato chips or black pudding with bacon, Parmesan cheese, and apples. The chef uses only local ingredients, so the menu changes daily. A tea shop upstairs serves wonderful cakes. ⊠ *153 Bath St., City Center* ☎ *0141/221–7711* ⊕ *www.thebutterflyandthepig.com* ✢ *E3*.

$

EASTERN EUROPEAN

✕ **Café-Gallery Cossachok.** At this spacious and quirky restaurant, the Russian owner pays homage to her homeland (and other Eastern European countries) in a menu that includes delicious blintzes, savory beef Stroganoff, and a Moldavian vegetable stew called *gouvetch*. There is, of course, a variety of chilled vodkas from which to choose. The colorful shawls stretched across the ceiling, the hand-carved furniture, and the jewelry on display add to the festive atmosphere. On Sunday nights there's live music, from tango to jazz. ⊠ *10 King St., Merchant City* ☎ *0141/553–0733* ⊕ *www.cossachok.com* ⊗ *Closed Mon.* ✢ *H5*.

$

BRITISH

✕ **Café Gandolfi.** Occupying what was once the tea market, this trendy café draws the style-conscious crowd. Wooden tables and chairs crafted by Scottish artist Tim Stead are so fluidly shaped it's hard to believe they're inanimate. The café opens early for breakfast, serving croissants, eggs *en cocotte* (casserole-style), and strong espresso. Don't miss the smoked venison or the finnan haddie (smoked haddock). The bar on the second floor is more intimate and much less busy—and lets you order from the same menu. ⊠ *64 Albion St., Merchant City* ☎ *0141/552–6813* ⊕ *www.cafegandolfi.com* ✢ *H5*.

$$

MODERN BRITISH

✕ **City Merchant.** If you have a penchant for fresh and flavorful cuisine, this welcoming spot with simple but traditional furnishings, including white tablecloths, dark wood, soft lighting, and tartan carpets is a joy. The secret is the kitchen's use of only local ingredients. You can sample the tasty cuts of venison and beef (including fillet with a haggis mousse), but seafood remains the star attraction. The mussels and oysters from Loch Etive are wondrous, as is the sea bass. There's a relatively inexpensive selection of wines and a wonderful cheese board served, as the locals like it, with oatcakes, celery, and quince. A fixed-price lunch is a bargain at £12.50. ⊠ *97–99 Candleriggs St., Merchant City* ☎ *0141/553–1577* ⊕ *www.citymerchant.co.uk* ⊗ *No lunch Sun.* ✢ *H5*.

$$

BRITISH

Fodor's Choice

★

✕ **The Corinthian Club.** Inside what was once the mansion of tobacco merchant George Buchanan, the Corinthian has an ostentatiously elegant restaurant where you can dine under a 26-foot-high glass dome as classical statues stare in your direction. The menu usually includes such staples of Scottish cuisine as rack of lamb or baked salmon fillets, as well as an intriguing vegetable bouillabaisse with potato dumplings. The gloomy basement, once a criminal court, now houses a beer and champagne bar. Among the other on-site drinking establishments is the Prohibition Bar, which uses teacups rather than glasses. There's also a casino that stays open until 6 am. ⊠ *191 Ingram St., City Center* ☎ *0141/552–1101* ⊕ *www.thecorinthianclub.co.uk* ⌫ *Reservations essential* ✢ *G4*.

¢

VEGETARIAN

✕ **Flying Duck.** Imagine a student flat with a doorway into the nightclub next door, and you'll know what to expect at the Flying Duck. At the comfortable, homey "Kitchen Bar," with its mismatched tables and chairs and shelves stacked with books, you can get nachos, stuffed baked potatoes, and various other vegetarian dishes to sustain you through an extended game of Scrabble, or a long night in the club next door. ✉ *142 Renfield St., Merchant City* ☎ *0141/564–1450* ⊕ *www. flyingduckclub.com* ✛ *F3.*

$ ✗ **Fratelli Sarti.** Glasgow's large Italian population is never more visible—
ITALIAN   or audible—than here. The cavernous surroundings are cluttered and
☾   the tables are pressed close together, so this is not really the place for an intimate dinner, but the food is authentic, with Tuscan and Ligurian specialties as well as other classic dishes on an extensive menu. If you like seafood, try the wonderfully fresh and piquant pasta *vongole* (with small clams). Finish off with the light, creamy tiramisu. Note that the service can be a bit leisurely. ✉ *121 Bath St., City Center* ☎ *0141/204–0440* ⊕ *www.sarti.co.uk* ✛ *F3.*

¢   ✗ **Fressh.** Settle in at one of the tables at this airy café for a quick,
CAFÉ   healthy, and well-priced breakfast or lunch. The food is simple, but
☾   hearty and fresh. Warm baguettes come filled with Brie, grapes, and cranberries, and the seeded rolls stuffed with pastrami, cream cheese, and dill pickles hit the spot. Several homemade soups and salads are offered daily, as well as straight-from-the-blender low-fat smoothies. There are also several varieties of coffee. ✉ *51 Cochrane St., City Center* ☎ *0141/552–5711* ⊕ *www.fresshglasgow.com* ⤳ *Reservations not accepted* ☾ *No dinner* ✛ *G4.*

$$ ✗ **Gandolfi Fish.** With the same owner as its well-established neighbor,
SEAFOOD   Café Gandolfi, this local favorite offers a range of fish and shellfish dishes that varies according to the season. Each comes with your choice of sauces, such as garlic butter or tequila, lime, and coriander. For sheer luxury try the steak accompanied by langoustines and scallops. The bright, minimalist environment provides a good backdrop for the food. Reservations are advisable, especially on the weekends. ✉ *84–86 Albion St., City Center* ☎ *0141/552–9475* ⊕ *www.cafegandolfi.com/ gandolfi-fish* ✛ *H5.*

$ ✗ **Kool Ba.** Thick wooden tables, Persian tapestries, and soft candlelight
ECLECTIC   make you feel at home in this small yet atmospheric haven that serves an intriguing mix of Indian and Persian fare. It's all about healthy, flavorful cooking: chicken tikka masala in a yogurt sauce or lamb korma with coconut cream and fruit are good picks. Accompany your meal with bowls of basmati saffron rice and fluffy naan bread. This popular place continues to win award after award; reserve ahead on Friday and Saturday. ✉ *109–113 Candleriggs, Merchant City* ☎ *0141/552–2777* ⊕ *www.koolba.com* ✛ *H5.*

$$ ✗ **Mussel Inn.** West coast shellfish farmers own this restaurant and feed
SEAFOOD   their customers incredibly succulent oysters, scallops, and mussels. The
Fodor's Choice   kilo pots of mussels, beautifully steamed to order and served with any
★   of a number of sauces, are revelatory. The surroundings are simple but stylish, with cool ceramic tiles, wood floors, and plenty of sleek wooden furniture. Another plus is the staff, which is helpful yet unpretentious. This is the type of place locals take their favorite out-of-towners. ✉ *157 Hope St., City Center* ☎ *0141/572–1405* ⊕ *www.mussel-inn.com* ☾ *No lunch Sun.* ✛ *F4.*

$$ ✕ **Opium.** This eatery has completely rethought Asian cuisine, taking
ASIAN Chinese, Malaysian, and Thai cooking in new directions. Sauces are
fragrant and spicy, but never overpowering. The speciality of the house
is dim sum, prepared by a chef who knows his dumplings. The wontons
are fresh and crisp, with delicious combinations of crab, shrimp, and
chicken peeking through the almost transparent pastry. But leave room
for the main dishes, especially the tiger prawns and scallops in a sauce
made from dried shrimp and fish. Familiar dishes like beef in black bean
sauce are astonishingly delicate and aromatic. The vegetarian menu is
adventurous, too. There are also capitivating cocktails. ✉ *191 Hope
St., City Center* ☎ *0141/332–6668* ✛ *F4.*

$ ✕ **Pancho Villa's.** If you have a craving for a margarita, look no further.
MEXICAN Images of Pancho Villa and Emiliano Zapata are everywhere in this fes-
☺ tive Mexican eatery, whose pink, yellow, and blue walls are decorated with
authentic papier-mâché masks. Locals can't get enough of the cocktails or
the food, which includes all the old favorites—enchiladas, burritos, tacos,
and fajitas—as well as some new dishes. Try the flour tortillas filled with
marinated lamb, or the chipotle chicken in a dark, spicy sauce. ✉ *26 Bell
St., Merchant City* ☎ *0141/552–7737* ⊕ *www.panchovillas.co.uk* ✛ *H5.*

$$$ ✕ **Rogano.** Modeled after the *Queen Mary,* this restaurant's spacious
SEAFOOD art-deco interior—maple paneling, chrome trim, and dramatic ocean
Fodor's Choice murals—is enough to recommend it. Portions are generous in the main
★ dining area, where you'll find impeccably prepared seafood dishes like
pan-seared scallops, as well as classics like roast rack of lamb. You can
eat very well in the less expensive ($) Café Rogano, where the brasserie-
style food is more modern and imaginative. The gorgeous bar serves
wonderful cocktails along with elegant sandwiches and a lovely fish
soup. You can even sit on the terrace, obligingly warmed by open-air
heaters throughout the winter. Few people know that between 3 and
6 you get a free starter or dessert with a main dish. ✉ *11 Exchange
Pl., City Center* ☎ *0141/248–4055* ⊕ *www.roganoglasgow.com* ✛ *G4.*

¢ ✕ **Stereo.** Down a quiet lane near Central Station, this ultracool eatery
VEGETARIAN dishes up a fantastic range of vegan food from paella to gnocchi to a
colorful platter with hummus, red-pepper pâté, and home-baked flat-
bread. Roasted sweet-potato chips are the perfect side dish. The decor
is homey and relaxed, and there always seems to be someone nearby
reading or writing. The walls are lined with paintings, posters, and
announcements of upcoming concerts in the space downstairs. The
music in the restaurant is excellent, but never so loud as to disturb the
serious business of eating. Service is laid-back but very friendly. ✉ *20–
28 Renfield La., City Center* ☎ *0141/222–2254* ⊕ *www.stereocafebar.
com* ⊜ *Reservations not accepted* ✛ *F4.*

$ ✕ **Stewarts Victorian Tea Rooms.** Afternoon tea, complete with cakes and
BRITISH tiny sandwiches served on a three-tier stand, has become very popular
in Glasgow. In this city-center tearoom, decorated with the obliga-
tory large potted plants and floral teapots, you can enjoy afternoon
tea (dainty sandwiches and cakes) or high tea, an old-time ritual that
includes a meal (fish cakes, for example) along with scones, cakes,
and tea. ✉ *89 Glassford St., City Center* ☎ *0141/552–0646* ⊕ *www.
stewartsvictoriantearooms.com* ✛ *H4.*

$$ ✕ **Two Fat Ladies.** It might have the
BRITISH same name as the owner's other
restaurants at 88 Dumbarton Road
and 652 Argyle Street, but this
branch of Two Fat Ladies deserves
a visit because it has more space,
more light, and a better location.
The menu is predominantly fish,
from the delicate smoked salmon,
crab, and asparagus salad to the
fresh whole sea bream stuffed with
red pepper, oregano, and garlic
salsa. But if fish doesn't rock your
boat, then a choice such as fillet of
Angus beef with wild mushrooms
and spinach jus is also delicious.
The trio of berry crème brûlées is
the perfect dessert. The set menu
for lunch is £16 for two courses.
✉ *118A Blythswood St., City Center* ☎ *0141/847–0088* ⊕ *www.
twofatladiesrestaurant.com* ✛ *E3.*

TAKE TIME FOR TEA
In the Victorian tradition, while men went to pubs, Glasgow women's social interaction would take place in the city's many tea-rooms and cafés. Today *everyone* goes to the café. Glaswegians have succumbed to the worldwide love for Italian-style, espresso-based coffees, but they'll never give up the comfort of a nice cup of tea, so you'll find both at most tearooms, along with scones, Scot-tish pancakes, other pastries, and light lunch fare like sandwiches and soup.

¢ ✕ **Where the Monkey Sleeps.** This quirky basement café serves huge
BRITISH sandwiches with amusing names—the "Wytchfinder" has chorizo sau-
sage and cheese, while the "Serious Operation" contains practically
everything on the menu. Enjoy your choice with one of the wonderful
smoothies. The café consists of a series of small rooms with brightly
colored sofas that encourage intimate conversation or just a long read.
It's just around the corner from Blythswood Square. ✉ *182 West Regent
St., City Center* ☎ *0141/226–3406* ✛ *E3.*

¢ ✕ **Willow Tearoom.** This Sauchiehall Street eatery takes up part of a
BRITISH department store originally designed by Charles Rennie Mackintosh.
The original tearoom is now reduced to a gallery at the back of the Mack-
intosh-themed jewelry and gift shop, but it retains his trademark fur-
nishings, including high-back chairs with elegant lines and subtle curves.
The St. Andrew's Platter is an exquisite selection of trout, salmon, and
prawns. Scottish and Continental breakfasts are available throughout
the day, and the scrambled eggs with salmon is traditional Scots food
at its finest. The in-house baker guarantees fresh scones, cakes, and
pastries. ✉ *217 Sauchiehall St., City Center* ☎ *0141/332–0521* ⊕ *www.
willowtearooms.co.uk* ☻ *No dinner* ✛ *F3.*

WEST END AND ENVIRONS

*Use the coordinate (✛ B2) at the end of each listing to locate a site on
the corresponding map.*

Because of Glasgow University, the food in this area was once just for
students. That has changed in recent years. You can still find fast food
at any hour of the day, but you'll discover some of the best food from
around the world served at some of the city's most respected restaurants
in the West End.

$ — INDIAN — Fodor'sChoice ★

✕ **Balbir's.** Don't let the tinted windows discourage you: this place is a temple for pure, healthy Indian food that's impressive in taste and presentation. Twinkling chandeliers, immaculate white tablecloths, and perfectly polished silverware set the stage, and the waitstaff tends to your every need. All food is prepared with cholesterol-free canola oil; no artificial colors or additives are used. Try the chicken *tikka chasni* (with mango chutney, lemon juice, and mint) or lamb *korma* (with coconut, cream, and mild spices). The tandoori salmon is also a good bet. ⊠ *7 Church St., West End* ☎ *0141/339–7711* ⊕ *www.balbirsrestaurants. co.uk* ⊗ *No lunch* ✛ *A6.*

$$ — BRITISH

✕ **Brasserie at Òran Mór.** This is the more formal eatery (the other being the bistro-style Conservatory) within this handsome church turned cultural center. There's lots of elegantly curved dark wood and high-backed bench seating, as well as some Alasdair Gray murals to savor. The food is equally well crafted. Expect contemporary treats using Angus beef, Gressingham duck, and sea bass. The restaurant has also introduced small plates for sharing. There's a very busy bar just beyond the door. ⊠ *731–735 Great Western Rd., West End* ☎ *0141/357–6226* ⊕ *www. oran-mor.co.uk* ⚑ *Reservations essential* ✛ *B5.*

$ — SPANISH

✕ **Cafe Andaluz.** With its Spanish flair, this beautifully designed basement eatery is always busy and lively. The first tapas place to make an impact in Glasgow, it has been followed by others (and has opened a second branch of its own in the city center) but remains the most successful. This is an ideal way to dine with friends: sharing the dishes as they arrive and as you down some good Spanish wine. (Rioja is always a reliable choice.) Booking ahead is strongly advised. ⊠ *2 Cresswell Ln., West End* ☎ *0141/339–1111* ✛ *B5.*

$$ — BRITISH

✕ **Cafezique.** Small but inviting, this West End magnet has a vibrant, changing breakfast, lunch, and dinner menu that is always fresh and exciting. The food is divided on the dinner menu into "wee things," "big things," and "sweet things." Try the roasted globe artichoke as your wee thing (if it's in season), the roast lamb with Mediterranean vegetables as your big thing, and fruit crumble with custard as your sweet thing. The curved wooden bar that snakes around the belly of the restaurant allows you to watch your food being prepared. Soft music, twinkling lights, and sepia photographs of seaside scenes help create a cozy but lively scene. ⊠ *66 Highland St., West End* ☎ *0141/339–7180* ✛ *A6.*

$ — SEAFOOD

✕ **Crabshakk.** This place is anything but a shack. The intimate dining room has heavy wooden tables and chairs and a bar so shiny and inviting that it seems to almost insist you have a drink. The lamps are like half-moons, and the ceiling is elegantly ornate. Mirrors make the place feel bigger, though it's fine the way it is. The food comes from the sea—oysters, lobster, and squid—and you can have your choice served iced, grilled, roasted, or battered. The fish sandwich and crab cakes (no fillers, just crab) are favorites on the lunch menu. In the evening, the mussels and scallops draw the eye. Only local and sustainably sourced Scottish seafood is featured. ⊠ *1114 Argyle St., West End* ☎ *0141/334–6127* ⊕ *www.crabshakk.com* ⚑ *Reservations essential* ⊗ *Closed Mon.* ✛ *B3.*

$$$ ✕ **Hotel du Vin Bistro.** A kilted doorman, crystal chandeliers, and stylish
FRENCH blue-and-green tartan carpets beckon you into the city's most elegant
Fodor'sChoice eatery. The service is impeccable from beginning to end, and all the food
★ is locally sourced from a 35-mi radius. It's the perfect place for cold,
wet days, as romantic fires flicker in the background and stained-glass
murals twist the natural light into colorful new shades. From the menu
of French and Scottish fare, try the lamb with bean-and-pea puree or the
halibut with asparagus and herb gnocchi. The starters are seductive, and
the coffee-and-chocolate soufflé with caramel ice cream is a truly indul-
gent dessert. Ask for a tour of the superb wine cellar. ⊠ *1 Devonshire
Gardens, West End* ☎ *0141/339–2001* ⊕ *www.hotelduvin.com* ✛ *A4.*

$$ ✕ **La Parmigiana.** The refreshing elegance of the surroundings is mir-
ITALIAN rored by the consistently exquisite fare at this longtime favorite. The
Giovanazzis pride themselves on using the freshest ingredients—this
means you may be able to enjoy simply prepared sea bass or veal one
day, guinea fowl or scallops the next. Expertise in the kitchen is reflected
in the well-balanced wine list and the impeccable attentiveness of the
black-jacketed waiters in this small restaurant. The pretheater menu
is £16.10 for two courses and £18.25 for three. ⊠ *447 Great Western
Rd., West End* ☎ *0141/334–0686* ⊕ *www.laparmigiana.co.uk* ☾ *Closed
Sun.* ✛ *C5.*

$$ ✕ **La Vallée Blanche.** Above a record store, this fine-dining restaurant
FRENCH has an alpine atmosphere, with dark wood eaves that you might find
in a chalet. The theme is rustic, and the food is hearty and adventur-
ous. The partridge comes with celery-root puree, chestnut mash, and
savoy cabbage, for example, while the pigs' cheeks are accompanied
by saffron potatoes. Good lunch and pretheater menus are £14.95 for
two courses. ⊠ *360 Byres Rd., West End* ☎ *0141/334–3333* ⊕ *www.
lavalleeblanche.com* ✛ *B5.*

¢ ✕ **Little Italy.** This busy, noisy, and extremely friendly Italian café sits in
MODERN ITALIAN the heart of the West End. You can perch on a stool by the window with
a cappuccino while watching the world go by, or grab a seat at one of
the crowded tables and enjoy one of the fine pizzas, probably the best
around. Create your own combination from the many topping options
and wait while it's made; or skip the pizza and the pasta and move
straight to the tiramisu. ⊠ *205 Byres Rd., West End* ☎ *01451/339–6287*
⊕ *www.littleitalyglasgow.com* ✛ *B5.*

$ ✕ **The Left Bank.** Close to Glasgow University and Kelvingrove Park, this
ECLECTIC popular hangout attracts a more mature student crowd. It's an airy spot
with high ceilings, leather sofas, and wood floors, and the specialty is
good, eclectic food at reasonable prices. Breakfast is your best bet, with
thick-sliced French toast, or eggs served on an English muffin with spin-
ach and smoked salmon. Tapas-style plates are an option: try roasted
eggplant and wild-garlic hummus with wholegrain flatbread, or sticky
pork ribs cooked in maple syrup and sesame. Moroccan spiced free-
range chicken with walnut-and-beet quinoa salad carries you across the
sea to Africa. This is also a nice place for a beer after walking around
Kelvingrove Park. ⊠ *33–35 Gibson St., West End* ☎ *0141/339–5969*
⊕ *www.theleftbank.co.uk* ✛ *C6.*

$ ✕**Mother India Cafe.** Overlooking the Kelvingrove Art Gallery and

INDIAN   Museum, this quaint, casual eatery has a spectacular view as well as an impressive menu. It's quite crowded, so don't expect much intimacy. The food is served tapas-style in small dishes—the idea is that you get to try lots of different flavors. Chili king prawns, chicken *achari* (cooked with lime and chili pickle) and *aloo saag dosa* (potato and spinach stuffed in a rice-and-lentil pancake) are all rich in flavor and presentation. The popular café doesn't accept reservations, so be prepared for a (fast-moving) line. It's worth it to bring your own wine, as there's just a small corkage charge. ✉ *1355 Argyle St., West End* ☎ *0141/339–9145* ⊕ *www.motherindiaglasgow.co.uk* ⊹ *B6.*

$$ ✕**Number Sixteen.** This tiny, intimate restaurant serves only the freshest

BRITISH   ingredients, superbly prepared. There's room for only 40 diners, and the

Fodor's Choice   result is cozy but never cramped. Seared mullet is served with risotto,

★   chorizo, broad beans, and artichokes—a typically unpredictable meeting of flavors. The venison with braised red cabbage is tantalizing, and desserts like treacle tarts with poached kumquats are equally seductive. A good deal is the pretheater menu, which includes two courses for £12.95 or three courses for £15.95. Book ahead, particularly on weekends. ✉ *16 Byres Rd., West End* ☎ *0141/339–2544* ⊕ *www.number16. co.uk* ⊹ *A6.*

$$ ✕**Pelican Café Bistro.** The hum of conversation and a glimpse of the busy

ECLECTIC   kitchen through the open hatch give this restaurant a relaxed vibe. A horseshoe bar in dark wood contrasts with the cream-colored walls displaying local art. The food is adventurous and resolutely fresh, with the source of the ingredients carefully listed on the menu. The dishes vary with the seasons and the conditions on the high seas, but you might find delicious sea bream with saffron-herb mash, or monkfish tails with a delicate pea risotto. There are always unusual and exciting options for vegetarians and vegans. The owner has a passion for wine, which shows in the huge wine list. ✉ *1377 Argyle St., West End* ☎ *0844/573–0670* ⊕ *www.thepelicancafe.co.uk* ⚄ *Reservations essential* ⊹ *B6.*

$ ✕**Spuntini.** A relative newcomer to the Byres Road scene, Spuntini has tapped successfully into the small-plates market with its Italian tapas (£4.95 each). It's furnished in dark wood, and large booths at the back of the restaurant are sought after. The restaurant is particularly popular with families since it offers a good kids' menu as well as a value menu (£6.99 for three tapas) from noon–6. ✉ *199–201 Byres Rd., West End* ☎ *0141/339–4222* ⊹ *B6.*

$$ ✕**The Sisters.** Walk up the smooth sandstone steps to this restaurant

BRITISH   that inspires both your palate and heart. Douglas Gray tartan pads the pristine room, and polished floorboards reflect the natural light shining in from the long windows around the unusual oval-shaped room. Wild seascape paintings are a nice touch in a space that feels both wide open and contained. The food is locally sourced and ever changing: all meat comes from Smitten Farm (in Galloway) and is prepared using seasonal vegetables. A typical dish is chicken with haggis in a whisky-mustard cream. The homegrown Arran gooseberry fool is the ultimate Scottish pudding. ✉ *36 Kelvingrove St., West End* ☎ *0141/564–1157* ⊕ *www. thesisters.co.uk* ⊹ *B3.*

$$
ECLECTIC

✕ **Stravaigin.** The busy bar and eatery on street level draws crowds with its buzz of conversation and its warm, inviting interior. Wooden tables, booths, and assorted chairs create a lively and informal atmosphere. Stravaigin takes pride in its wide-ranging cuisine, with regular nights featuring less familiar cuisines. Look for fine fish dishes like hake and mussels in a lemongrass broth. There's always a curry plate on the menu, as well as reliable Scottish favorites like haggis and neeps. For dessert, the kitchen makes its own ice cream. Good lunch and pretheater specials are a bargain. ✉ *28 Gibson St., West End* ☎ *0141/334–2665* ⊕ *www.stravaigin.com* ✛ *C6.*

$$$$
BRITISH
Fodor's Choice
★

✕ **Ubiquitous Chip.** Occupying a converted stable behind the Hillhead underground station, this restaurant is an institution among members of Glasgow's media and theater communities, who most days can be found in the busy bar. The more informal upstairs brasserie serves imaginative starters and luxurious ciabatta "pieces" (the local term for sandwiches). The ground-floor restaurant has a large cobbled yard with a glass roof, much greenery, and a fish pond. The menu offers fish and game dishes that vary from week to week. Try the poached halibut with watercress and spinach pistou, or the roast wood pigeon with cauliflower puree. There's an excellent lunch and pretheater set menu for £19.95. The fixed-price dinner menu is £34.95 for two courses and £39.95 for three. Booking ahead is well advised. ✉ *12 Ashton La., West End* ☎ *0141/334–5007* ⊕ *www.ubiquitouschip.co.uk* ✛ *B5.*

¢
ASIAN FUSION

✕ **Wudon.** A welcome addition to Glasgow's restaurant scene, this pleasant and relaxed Japanese restaurant offers beautifully prepared food presented with great charm by the staff. Whether your taste is for hearty broths or for savory rice and noodle dishes, the chef will combine the elements to your taste. Vegetarians are well served here. The lunchtime bento boxes (£6.50) are a particularly good value, with miso soup, rice or noodles, meat or fish, and a piece of fresh fruit. Asian beers and a range of drinks are available, too. ✉ *535 Great Western Rd., West End* ☎ *0141/357–3039* ⊕ *www.wudon-noodle.co.uk* ✛ *B5.*

SOUTH SIDE

Use the coordinate (✛ B2) at the end of each listing to locate a site on the corresponding map.

$
ITALIAN

✕ **Battlefield Rest.** Built in 1915, this former tram station has been lovingly transformed into a very popular Italian restaurant where the walls of windows are framed by heavy cream drapes. The food is authentic, well seasoned, and full of flavor; try the chicken stuffed with goat cheese and wrapped in Parma ham, or the panfried duck with figs. There are plenty of pastas and pizzas from which to choose. To get to this restaurant near Queen's Park, take Bus 66 from the St. Enoch underground station. ✉ *55 Battlefield Rest, South Side* ☎ *0141/636–6955* ⊕ *www.battlefieldrest.co.uk* ⊘ *Closed Sun.* ✛ *E6.*

$
BRITISH

✕ **Moyra Janes.** Pull up a chair to one of the marble-topped tables in this former bank building and soak up the genteel Scots charm. This South Side favorite serves a splendid tea with mouthwatering cakes. There's a healthy dash of cosmopolitan flair to boot: alongside the all-day breakfast menu are lamb tagine and chicken dopiazza. The £11.95 two-course dinner is a real bargain. ⊠ *20 Kildrostan St., Pollokshields* ☎ *0141/423–5628* ✢ *E6.*

WHERE TO STAY

For expanded hotel reviews, visit Fodors.com.

Glasgow's city center never sleeps, so downtown hotels will be noisier than those in the leafy and genteel West End. Downtown hotels are within walking distance of all the main sights, while West End lodgings are more convenient for museums and art galleries. Over the past few years the hotel scene has become noticeably more stylish, with new hotels opening, including Blythswood Square, citizenM, and Grand Central.

Although big hotels are spread out all around the city, B&Bs are definitely a more popular, personal, and cheaper option. For country-house luxury you should look beyond the city—try Mar Hall, near Paisley. Regardless of the neighborhood, hotels are about the same in price. Some B&Bs as well as the smaller properties may also offer discounts for longer stays.

Make your reservations in advance, especially when there's a big concert, sporting event, or holiday (New Year's Eve is very popular). Glasgow is busiest during summer, but it can fill up when something special is going on. If you arrive in town without a place to stay, contact the Glasgow Tourist Board.

PRICES AND MONEY-SAVING OPTIONS

It is always worthwhile to inquire about special deals or rate, especially if you book online and in advance. Another money-saving option is to rent an apartment. B&Bs are the best-priced short-term-lodging option, and you're sure to get breakfast.

Most smaller hotels and all guesthouses include breakfast in the room rate. Larger hotels usually charge extra for breakfast. Also note that the most expensive hotels often exclude V.A.T. (Value Added Tax, the sales tax) in the initial price quote but budget places include it.

WHAT IT COSTS IN POUNDS				
	¢	$	$$	$$$	$$$$
FOR TWO PEOPLE	under £70	£70–£120	£121–£180	£181–£250	over £250

Hotel prices are for two people in a standard double room in high season, generally including the 20% V.A.T.

CITY CENTER AND THE MERCHANT CITY

Use the coordinate (✢ B2) at the end of each listing to locate a site on the corresponding map.

Here you'll be close to everything—the main sights, shops, theaters, restaurants, and bars—the pulse of the city. You don't have to worry

BEST BETS FOR GLASGOW LODGING

Fodor's Choice ★	$	By Experience
Blythswood Square, $$$$, p. 135	**Cathedral House Hotel,** p. 136	BEST HISTORIC HOTELS
CitizenM, ¢, p. 136	**Kirklee Hotel,** p. 138	**ABode Glasgow,** $$, p. 135
Hotel du Vin Glasgow, $$$, p. 138	**$$**	**Blythswood Square,** $$$$, p. 135
Malmaison, $$, p. 137	**ABode Glasgow,** p. 135	**Hotel du Vin Glasgow,** $$, p. 138
By Price	**Carlton George,** p. 136	
	Grand Central Hotel, $$, p. 136	BEST CONCIERGE
¢	**Malmaison,** p. 137	**Hilton Glasgow,** $, p. 137
Amadeus Guest House, p. 137	**Sherbrooke Castle Hotel,** p. 139	**Hotel du Vin Glasgow,** $$$, p. 138
Babbity Bowster's, p. 135	**$$$**	**Radisson Blu,** $$$, p. 137
Brunswick, p. 136	**Hotel du Vin Glasgow,** p. 138	MOST ROMANTIC
CitizenM, ¢, p. 136	**Radisson Blu,** p. 137	**CitizenM,** ¢, p. 136
Victorian House, p. 137	**$$$$**	**Grand Central Hotel,** $$, p. 136
The White House Apartments, p. 139	**Blythswood Square,** p. 135	**Hotel du Vin Glasgow,** $$$, p. 138
		Malmaison, $$, p. 137

about transportation in the center of town, but it can get noisy on weekend nights.

$$ 🏨 **ABode Glasgow.** This stylish hotel was once the home of a prime minister, and it has retained architectural features like the wrought-iron elevator and walls lined with gold-leaf lions (2,000 of them). **Pros:** stylish rooms; great location; nice mix of old and new in public areas. **Cons:** some front rooms can be noisy; parking is a pricey £12 a day. ✉ *129 Bath St., City Center* ☎ *0141/221–6789* ⊕ *www.abodehotels. co.uk* ↘ *59 rooms, 1 suite* ⚅ *In-room: a/c, Internet, Wi-Fi. In-hotel: restaurant, bar, parking* |◯| *No meals* ✛ *F3.*

¢ 🏨 **Babbity Bowster's.** It takes its name from a Scottish dance, but the sound you mainly hear at this comfortable and friendly establishment is the buzz of conversation and, on Saturday afternoon, the melodies of Scotland played by the musicians who drop by and jam together. **Pros:** centrally located; quiet street; fine selection of real ales. **Cons:** gets noisy on the weekends; no elevator. ✉ *16–18 Blackfriars St., Merchant City* ☎ *0141/552–5055* ⊕ *www.babbitybowster.com* ↘ *6 rooms* ⚅ *In-room: no a/c. In-hotel: restaurant, bar* |◯| *Breakfast* ✛ *H5.*

$$$$ 🏨 **Blythswood Square.** History and luxury come together at this smart Fodor's Choice conversion of the former headquarters of the Royal Automobile Club ★ of Scotland, which occupies a classical building on peaceful Blythswood

Square. **Pros:** airy and luxurious; glorious bathrooms; lovely common areas that retain the original gold-topped columns. **Cons:** room lighting may be too dim for some; some street noise. ⊠ *11 Blythswood Sq., City Center* ☎ *0141/248–8888* ⊕ *www.blythswoodsquare.com* ⟿ *100 rooms, 6 suites* ⚴ *In-room: a/c, safe, Wi-Fi. In-hotel: restaurant, bar, gym, spa, parking* ⦅◎⦆ *Breakfast* ✛ *E3.*

¢ ⛆ **Brunswick.** In a contemporary town house, this six-story hotel is modest but comfortable. **Pros:** excellent value; hip downstairs café; free Wi-Fi. **Cons:** the area can be noisy, especially on weekends; some rooms are very small; rooms at the back have an unappealing view over neighboring roofs. ⊠ *106–108 Brunswick St., Merchant City* ☎ *0141/552–0001* ⊕ *www.brunswickhotel.co.uk* ⟿ *18 rooms, 1 suite* ⚴ *In-room: no a/c. In-hotel: restaurant, bar* ⦅◎⦆ *Breakfast* ✛ *H5.*

$$ ⛆ **Carlton George.** The narrow revolving doorway, a step back from busy West George Street, creates the illusion of a secret passageway into this lavish boutique hotel. **Pros:** near city-center attractions; discounted parking nearby. **Cons:** breakfast is extra during the week; only top-level rooms can access the residents' lounge. ⊠ *44 W. George St., City Center* ☎ *0141/353–6373* ⊕ *www.carltonhotels.co.uk/george* ⟿ *64 rooms* ⚴ *In-room: a/c, safe, Wi-Fi. In-hotel: restaurant* ✛ *G4.*

$ ⛆ **Cathedral House Hotel.** Adjacent to Glasgow Cathedral, this Scottish Baronial–style building dating to 1867 once served as the church's ecclesiastical headquarters—hence the name of this small hotel. **Pros:** historic atmosphere; quiet location; good views. **Cons:** no elevator; a long 10-minute walk to the center of town. ⊠ *28–32 Cathedral Sq., Merchant City* ☎ *0141/552–3519* ⊕ *www.cathedralhouse.org* ⟿ *7 rooms* ⚴ *In-hotel: bar, parking* ⦅◎⦆ *Breakfast* ✛ *H4.*

¢ ⛆ **CitizenM.** There's no lobby at the futuristic CitizenM; instead you'll
Fodor'sChoice find elegant and comfortable "living rooms" with bookshelves and
★ sofas. **Pros:** wonderful design and ultramodern comfort. **Cons:** not for the claustrophobic. ⊠ *60 Renfrew St., corner of Hope St., City Center* ☎ *01782/488–3490* ⊕ *www.citizenm.com* ⟿ *198 rooms* ⚴ *In-room: a/c, Wi-Fi. In-hotel: restaurant, bar, business center* ⦅◎⦆ *Some meals* ✛ *F3.*

$$ ⛆ **Grand Central Hotel.** This recently refurbished hotel certainly deserves
Fodor'sChoice its name, as everything about it, from the magnificent marble-floor
★ champagne bar to the ballroom fully restored to its original glory, is grand. **Pros:** a real air of luxury; spacious, comfortable rooms; champagne bar is a wonderful place to linger. **Cons:** some noise from street; parking is a couple of blocks away. ⊠ *99 Gordon St., City Center* ☎ *0141/240–3700* ⊕ *www.principal-hayley.com/grandcentralhotel* ⟿ *186 rooms, 3 suites* ⚴ *In-room: no a/c, Wi-Fi. In-hotel: restaurant, bar* ⦅◎⦆ *No meals* ✛ *F4.*

$ ⛆ **Grasshoppers.** Not visible from the street, this hotel occupies the sixth floor above Central Station (look for the door marked "Caledonian Chambers" and take the elevator). **Pros:** bright and clean; quiet despite its location. **Cons:** no lobby; rooms are quite small. ⊠ *87 Union St., City Center* ☎ *0141/222–2666* ⊕ *www.grasshoppersglasgow.com* ⟿ *30 rooms* ⚴ *In-room: Wi-Fi* ⦅◎⦆ *Breakfast* ✛ *F4.*

$ **Hilton Glasgow.** On first impression this is a typical international hotel, but Glasgow friendliness permeates its professional facade. **Pros:** fabulous service; great pool; interesting bar. **Cons:** uninspiring room decor; mediocre location beside motorway and more than a mile from Merchant City shops. ⊠ *1 William St., City Center* ☎ *0141/204–5555* ⊕ *www.hilton.com* ↝ *319 rooms* ⬧ *In-room: safe, Internet. In-hotel: restaurant, bar, pool, gym, parking* ❣*Breakfast* ✛ *D4.*

$$ **Malmaison.** Housed in a converted church, this modern boutique

Fodor's Choice hotel prides itself on personal service and outstanding amenities: each

★ room has nice touches like plasma televisions and music systems. **Pros:** stunning lobby; attention to detail; five-minute walk to Sauchiehall Street. **Cons:** bland views; dark hallways; no on-site parking. ⊠ *278 W. George St., City Center* ☎ *0141/572–1000* ⊕ *www.malmaison.com* ↝ *64 rooms, 8 suites* ⬧ *In-room: Wi-Fi. In-hotel: restaurant, bar, gym, spa, some pets allowed* ❣*Breakfast* ✛ *E3.*

$$ **Marks Hotel.** This hotel's small reception area doesn't prepare you for its sheer size; the 108 rooms and suites are plain and fairly compact. **Pros:** good location; free Wi-Fi; great views from front rooms. **Cons:** very busy wallpaper; parking garage is a brisk five-minute walk away; restaurant is windowless and slightly enclosed. ⊠ *110 Bath St., City Center* ☎ *0141/353–0800* ⊕ *www.markshotels.com* ↝ *103 rooms, 5 suites* ⬧ *In-room: no a/c, Wi-Fi. In-hotel: restaurant, bar* ✛ *F3.*

¢   **Premier Inn.** It may be part of a chain, but this hotel's bright rooms and low prices appeal to savvy travelers. **Pros:** great location; bargain rates; modern rooms. **Cons:** some front rooms are noisy; extra charges for parking and Wi-Fi. ⊠ *187 George St., Merchant City* ☎ *0870/238–3320* ⊕ *www.premierinn.com* ↝ *239 rooms* ⬧ *In-room: no a/c. In-hotel: restaurant, bar* ✛ *H4.*

$$$ **Radisson Blu.** You can't miss this eye-catching edifice behind Central Station in the city's up-and-coming financial quarter. **Pros:** kilted doorman; great gym; free Wi-Fi; impeccable service. **Cons:** neighborhood can get noisy; most rooms have poor views; constant traffic on the doorstep; no on-site parking. ⊠ *301 Argyle St., City Center* ☎ *0141/204–3333* ⊕ *www.radissonblu.com* ↝ *247 rooms, 3 suites* ⬧ *In-room: safe, Wi-Fi. In-hotel: restaurant, bar, pool, gym, parking* ❣*Breakfast* ✛ *E5.*

¢   **Victorian House.** Compared with the bright-yellow entrance hall, the rooms in this hotel are rather plain. **Pros:** next to the Glasgow School of Art; great front patio; basement rooms very spacious. **Cons:** some rooms need to be freshened up; no elevator; on-street parking can be difficult to find. ⊠ *212 Renfrew St., City Center* ☎ *0141/332–0129* ⊕ *www. thevictorian.co.uk* ↝ *58 rooms* ⬧ *In-room: no a/c* ❣*Breakfast* ✛ *E2.*

WEST END AND ENVIRONS

Use the coordinate (✛ *B2) at the end of each listing to locate a site on the corresponding map.*

¢   **Amadeus Guest House.** This adorable, newly remodeled Victorian town house is on a leafy residential street overlooking the river Kelvin. **Pros:** near West End attractions; two-minute walk from subway; kids under six stay free. **Cons:** some rooms are small; finding parking can be difficult. ✉ *411 N. Woodside Rd., West End* ☎ *0141/339–8257* ⊕ *www. amadeusguesthouse.co.uk* 🛏 *9 rooms* & *In-room: no a/c* ⦿ *Breakfast* ✛ *C5.*

$ 🏨 **Ambassador Hotel.** Opposite the West End's peaceful Botanic Gardens, the Ambassador is part of a string of elegant town houses on the banks of the river Kelvin. **Pros:** views of Botanic Gardens; great for kids; five-minute walk to public transportation and West End amenities. **Cons:** no elevator; on-street parking can be difficult after 6 pm; staff a little frosty. ✉ *7 Kelvin Dr., West End* ☎ *0141/946–1018* ⊕ *www. glasgowhotelsandapartments.co.uk* 🛏 *16 rooms* & *In-room: no a/c, safe, Wi-Fi. In-hotel: bar, laundry facilities, parking* ⦿ *Breakfast* ✛ *B5.*

¢   🏨 **Argyll Guest House.** At this small hotel, the rooms are plainly furnished and fairly basic but scrupulously clean. **Pros:** close to Kelvingrove Park; near public transportation; bargain prices. **Cons:** front rooms noisy on weekends; decor is bland and uninspiring; no elevator. ✉ *966–970 Sauchiehall St., West End* ☎ *0141/357–5155* ⊕ *www. argyllguesthouseglasgow.co.uk* 🛏 *20 rooms* & *In-room: no a/c, Wi-Fi. In-hotel: bar, parking* ⦿ *Breakfast* ✛ *A2.*

¢   🏨 **Clifton Hotel.** Occupying two of the grand houses along a terrace above Great Western Road, this is a popular hotel. **Pros:** conveniently located; attentive staff. **Cons:** some rooms are small and look out on to the parking lot; no elevator. ✉ *26–27 Buckingham Terr., West End* ☎ *0141/334–8080* 🛏 *25 rooms* & *In-room: Wi-Fi* ⦿ *Breakfast* ✛ *B5.*

$ 🏨 **Hilton Glasgow Grosvenor.** Behind a row of grand terrace houses, this modern hotel overlooks the Botanical Gardens. **Pros:** close to Byres Road; some rooms have good views over the Botanic Gardens. **Cons:** rooms at the back overlook a parking lot; a rather institutional feel. ✉ *1–9 Grosvenor Terr., West End* ☎ *0141/339–8811* ⊕ *www.hilton. com/glasgowgrosvenor* 🛏 *96* & *In-room: Wi-Fi. In-hotel: restaurant, bar, business center* ⦿ *Breakfast* ✛ *B5.*

$$$ 🏨 **Hotel du Vin Glasgow.** Once the legendary One Devonshire Gardens, **Fodor's Choice**   frequented by such celebrities as Luciano Pavarotti and Elizabeth Taylor, ★   the Hotel Du Vin Glasgow is still a destination for those in search of luxury. **Pros:** stunning Scottish rooms; doting service; complimentary whisky upon arrival. **Cons:** no elevator; on-street parking can be difficult after 6 pm. ✉ *1 Devonshire Gardens, West End* ☎ *0141/339–2001* ⊕ *www. hotelduvin.com/glasgow* 🛏 *41 rooms, 8 suites* & *In-room: no a/c, Wi-Fi. In-hotel: restaurant, bar, gym, spa, parking* ⦿ *Breakfast* ✛ *A4.*

$ 🏨 **Kirklee Hotel.** This West End B&B occupies a cozy Edwardian town house with dark paneling and tartan carpets in the public areas. **Pros:** friendly service; quiet street; close to West End attractions. **Cons:** on-street parking is challenging; city center is 2 mi away. ✉ *11 Kensington Gate, West End* ☎ *0141/334–5555* ⊕ *www.kirkleehotel.co.uk* 🛏 *9 rooms* & *In-room: no a/c, Wi-Fi* ⦿ *Breakfast* ✛ *A5.*

¢   🏨 **Manor Park Hotel.** On a quiet street close to Victoria Park, one of Glasgow's most idyllic public spaces, this stately terraced town house is spacious and has charm to spare. **Pros:** quiet residential area; helpful staff; delicious breakfast. **Cons:** an hour walk to the city center and at least a 20-minute walk from the nearest subway station; close to motorway. ✉ *28 Balshagray Dr., West End* ☎ *0141/339–2143* ⊕ *www.*

manorparkhotel.com ➷ *10 rooms* ⚴ *In-room: no a/c, Wi-Fi. In-hotel: parking* ⦾ *Breakfast* ✛ *A6.*

¢ ⊡ **The Sandyford.** The Victorian exterior of this hotel anticipates the colorful interior. **Pros:** on the doorstep of Kelvingrove Park; minutes from several good eateries; newly refurbished rooms. **Cons:** front rooms can get late-night noise; no elevator. ✉ *904 Sauchiehall St., West End* ☎ *0141/334–0000* ⊕ *www.sandyfordhotelglasgow.com* ➷ *55 rooms* ⚴ *In-room: no a/c, Wi-Fi. In-hotel: business center, some pets allowed* ⦾ *Breakfast* ✛ *B3.*

¢ ⊡ **The White House Apartments.** On a tranquil crescent just west of the
⟳ Botanic Gardens, this well-managed group of Victorian town houses has more than 30 apartments—studios to two bedrooms—that can be rented from a night to as long as a year, with considerable reductions along the way. **Pros:** large rooms; fully equipped kitchens; courtyard gardens; good for families. **Cons:** an old-fashioned feel in places; bathrooms are fairly basic. ✉ *11–13 Cleveden Crescent, West End* ☎ *0141/339–9375* ⊕ *www.whitehouse-apartments.com* ➷ *33 apartments, 2 suites* ⚴ *In-room: no a/c, kitchen, Wi-Fi. In-hotel: laundry facilities, business center, parking* ✛ *A4.*

SOUTH SIDE

Use the coordinate (✛ B2) at the end of each listing to locate a site on the corresponding map.

$$ ⊡ **Sherbrooke Castle Hotel.** Set high above the road, the Sherbrooke is one the grand homes built by the newly prosperous industrialists of the 19th century. **Pros:** relaxed atmosphere; top-notch service; large bathrooms. **Cons:** some rooms are small; weekend functions can get very loud; no elevator. ✉ *11 Sherbrooke Ave., South Side* ☎ *0141/427–4227* ⊕ *www. sherbrooke.co.uk* ➷ *14 rooms* ⚴ *In-room: no a/c, Wi-Fi. In-hotel: restaurant, bar* ⦾ *Breakfast* ✛ *D6.*

NIGHTLIFE AND THE ARTS

Glasgow's music scene is vibrant and creative, and many successful pop artists began their careers in its pubs and clubs. Celtic Connections is probably one of the world's most important festivals of its kind, and the city's summer Jazz Festival has attracted some of the world's finest players.

When it comes to nightlife, the city center and the West End are alive with pubs and clubs offering an eclectic mix of everything from bagpipes to salsa to punk. The biweekly magazine *The List,* available at newsstands and many cafés and arts centers, is an indispensable guide to Glasgow's bars and clubs.

THE ARTS

Because the Royal Scottish Conservatoire is in Glasgow, there is always a pool of impressive young talent that's pressing the city's artistic boundaries in theater, music, and film. The city has a well-deserved reputation for its theater, with everything from cutting-edge plays to over-the-top pantomimes. The Citizens Theatre is one of Europe's leading companies, and the Kings and the Theatre Royal play host to touring productions.

Scottish Music Centre. As well as a library, the Scottish Music Centre is the main ticket office for all music events at venues like the Royal Concert Hall and for annual events like the Glasgow Jazz Festival. ⊠ *Candleriggs, City Center* ☎ *0141/353–8000* ⊕ *www.glasgowconcerthalls. com.*

ARTS CENTER

Glasgow Print Studio. Essentially an artists' cooperative, the Glasgow Print Studio's facilities have launched a generation of outstanding painters, printers, and designers. The work of members past and present can be seen (and bought) at the Print Studio Gallery on King Street. ⊠ *103 Trongate* ☎ *0141/552–0704* ⊕ *www.gpsart.co.uk.*

↻ **Tramway.** South of the city center, this innovative arts center is well worth seeking out. It hosts regular exhibitions in its two galleries, and plays—often of a very experimental nature—in its flexible theater space. It has a café and a more formal restaurant on the first floor. Don't miss the Hidden Garden, which has transformed a lot behind the building into a sculpture park. This is a great place to go with kids. ⊠ *25 Albert Dr., Pollokshields* ☎ *0141/276–0950.*

Trongate 103. This vibrant contemporary arts center, housed in a converted Edwardian warehouse, is home base for diverse groups producing film, photography, paintings, and prints. It contains the Russian Cultural Centre and the Sharmanka Kinetic Theatre, as well as the Glasgow Print Studio and the Transmission Gallery. It also offers a range of workshops. ⊠ *103 Trongate, Merchant City* ☎ *0141/276–8380* ⊕ *www.trongate103.com.*

CONCERTS

City Halls. One of the top music venues in the city center, the stone-fronted City Halls hosts orchestral concerts, jazz, and folk. ⊠ *Candleriggs, City Center* ☎ *0141/353–8000* ⊕ *www.glasgowconcerthalls. com.*

Glasgow Royal Concert Hall. The 2,500-seat Glasgow Royal Concert Hall is the venue for a wide range of concerts, from classical to pop. It also hosts the very popular late-night club. ⊠ *2 Sauchiehall St., City Center* ☎ *0141/353–8000.*

The Old Fruitmarket. A wonderful venue for almost every type of music, this was once the city's fruit and vegetable market. The first-floor balcony, with its intricate iron railings, still carries some of the original merchants' names. It's adjacent to City Halls. ⊠ *Candleriggs, City Center* ☎ *0141/353–8000* ⊕ *www.glasgowconcerthalls.com.*

O2 ABC. One of the city's major music venues, O2 ABC houses inside what was once a cinema. It's the city's main showcase for popular pop and rock bands. ⊠ *300 Sauchiehall St., City Center* ☎ *0141/332–2232.*

Royal Scottish Conservatoire. This is an important venue for music and drama. It has regular concerts by well-known performers, as well as by its own students. It hosts a popular lunchtime concert series. ⊠ *100 Renfrew St., City Center* ☎ *0141/332–4101* ⊕ *www.rcs.ac.uk.*

Scottish Exhibition and Conference Centre. Beside the river Clyde, the Scottish Exhibition and Conference Centre hosts major exhibitions and large-scale pop concerts in its iconic building. ⊠ *Exhibition Way, West End* ☎ *0141/248–3000.*

St. Andrew's in the Square. A beautifully restored 18th-century church close to Glasgow Cross, the glorious St. Andrew's in the Square is a popular arts venue. Drop by to see fiddle players on Monday evening or take traditional Scottish dance classes on Wednesday night. Chamber concerts are held here from time to time. The downstairs café serves a good range of Scottish food for lunch or dinner. ⊠ *1 St. Andrew's in the Square, Trongate and East End* ☎ *0141/559–5902* ⊕ *www.standrewsinthesquare.com.*

DANCE AND OPERA

★ **Theatre Royal.** Glasgow is home to the Scottish Opera and Scottish Ballet, both of which perform at the Theatre Royal. Visiting dance and theater companies from many countries appear here as well. ⊠ *282 Hope St., City Center* ☎ *0141/332–9000.*

FESTIVALS

Celtic Connections. This ever-expanding music festival is held in the second half of January in a number of venues across the city. Musicians from Scotland, Ireland, and other countries celebrate Celtic music, both traditional and contemporary. There are a series of hands-on workshops and a popular late-night club at the Royal Concert Hall. ☎ *0141/353–8000* ⊕ *www.celticconnections.com.*

Glasgay. Held between November and December, Glasgay is the United Kingdom's largest arts festival focusing on gay and lesbian issues. The international lineup is always impressive and draws a huge audience. ☎ *0141/552–7575* ⊕ *www.glasgay.co.uk.*

Glasgow Jazz Festival. In late June and early July, Glasgow hosts jazz musicians from around the world in venues throughout the city, though mainly in the city center. ⊠ *81 High St., City Center* ☎ *0141/552–3552* ⊕ *www.jazzfest.co.uk.*

FILM

Center for Contemporary Arts. The Center for Contemporary Arts screens classic, independent, and children's films. ⊠ *350 Sauchiehall St., City Center* ☎ *0141/352–4900.*

Cineworld Glasgow. An 18-screen facility, this is Glasgow's busiest movie complex. At 170 feet tall, it's also the world's tallest cinema building. If you're going to the upper floors, take the glass-walled elevator. ⊠ *7 Renfrew St., City Center* ☎ *0871/200–2000.*

Glasgow Film Theatre. An independent operation, the Glasgow Film Theatre has two cinemas that screen the best new releases, documentaries, and classic films. It has several programs for young people and hosts the annual Glasgow Film Festival. ⊠ *12 Rose St., City Center* ☎ *0141/332–6535* ⊕ *www.glasgowfilm.org.*

★ **Grosvenor.** This popular, compact cinema has two screens and extremely comfortable leather seats (some of them double sofas). It's part of a small complex that includes two street-level bars and a spacious upstairs café and bar. ⊠ *Ashton La., West End* ☎ *0141/339–8444* ⊕ *www. grosvenorcafe.co.uk.*

THEATER

Ticketmaster. Tickets for theatrical performances can be purchased at theater box offices or online through Ticketmaster (⊕ *www.ticketmaster. co.uk*).

★ **Arches.** The labyrinth of passageways under Central Station has become the Arches, a flexible space for theater, music, and regular club nights. It hosts various festivals through the year, including October's Glasgay celebration of gay arts. There's also a basement café-bar that's open throughout the day and into the evening. ⊠ *253 Argyle St., City Center* ☎ *0141/565–1000* ⊕ *www.thearches.co.uk.*

★ **Citizens' Theatre.** Some of the most exciting theatrical performances take place at the internationally renowned Citizens' Theatre, where productions, and their sets, are often of hair-raising originality. Behind the theater's striking contemporary glass facade is a glorious Victorian red-and-gilded auditorium. ⊠ *119 Gorbals St., South Side* ☎ *0141/429– 0022* ⊕ *www.citz.co.uk.*

Cottier's Arts Theatre. Contemporary works are staged at Cottier's Arts Theatre, which is housed in a converted church. ⊠ *93 Hyndland St., West End* ☎ *0141/357–5825.*

King's Theatre. Dramas, variety shows, and musicals are staged at the King's Theatre. ⊠ *297 Bath St., City Center* ☎ *0141/240–1111.*

★ **Òran Mór.** Head to Òran Mór at lunchtime for the hugely successful series called "A Play, Pie and Pint" (and you do get all three). The series, which showcases new writing from Scotland and elsewhere, has included more than 250 plays. It sells out quickly, particularly late in the week, so book well in advance. ⊠ *731 Great Western Rd., West End* ☎ *0141/357–6200* ⊕ *www.playpiepint.com.*

Pavilion. The Pavilion hosts family variety entertainment along with rock and pop concerts. ⊠ *121 Renfield St., City Center* ☎ *0141/332–1846.*

Sharmanka Kinetic Theatre. A unique spectacle, Sharmanka Kinetic Theatre is the brainchild of Eduard Bersudsky, who came to Glasgow from Russia in 1989 to continue making the mechanical sculptures that are his stock in trade. They are witty and sometimes disturbing, and move in a kind of ballet to specially composed music punctuated by a light show. ⊠ *103 Trongate, Merchant City* ☎ *0141/552–7080* ⊕ *www. sharmanka.com* ⊠ *£5–£8* ⊘ *Wed. at 3, Thurs. and Fri. at 3 and 7, Sat. at 1 and 3, Sun. at 1, 3, and 7.*

Theatre Royal. The Theatre Royal hosts performances of major dramas by visiting theatre companies. ⊠ *282 Hope St., City Center* ☎ *0141/ 332–9000.*

Tron Theatre. Come here for contemporary theater from Scotland and around the world. ⊠ *63 Trongate, Merchant City* ☎ *0141/552–4267.*

NIGHTLIFE

Glasgow's busy nightlife scene is impressive and varied. Bars and pubs often close at midnight on the weekends, but nightclubs often stay open until 3 or 4 am. Traditional *ceilidh* (a mix of country dancing, music, and song; pronounced *kay-lee*) is not as popular as it used to be (unless you're at a wedding), but you can still find it at many establishments.

Glasgow's pubs were once hangouts for serious drinkers who demanded few comforts. Times have changed, and many of these gritty establishments have been transformed into trendy cocktail bars or cavernous spaces with multiple video monitors, though a few traditional bars do survive. Bars and pubs vary according to location; many of those in the city center cater to business types, although some still draw a more traditional clientele.

As elsewhere in Britain, electronic music—from house to techno to drum and bass—is par for the course in Glasgow's dance clubs. Much of the scene revolves around the city center, as a late-night walk down Sauchiehall Street on Friday or Saturday will reveal.

CITY CENTER AND THE MERCHANT CITY
BARS AND PUBS

Babbity Bowster's. A busy, friendly spot, Babbity Bowster's serves real ales and excellent, mainly Scottish food, prepared for more than a decade now by a French chef, who adds his own very special touch. The atmosphere is lively and very friendly; there is an outside terrace in summer and a fireplace in winter. If you like Scottish traditional music, make a point of coming on Saturday afternoon. ⊠ *16–18 Blackfriars St., Merchant City* ☎ *0141/552–5055.*

Baby Grand. One of Glasgow's best-kept secrets, this intimate piano bar is hidden behind the Theatre Royal. It serves good food all day, and it somehow manages to be crowded but never overcrowded, even at the busiest times. The pretheater menu is a good value, especially when accompanied by a discounted bottle of wine. ⊠ *3 Elmbank Gardens, City Center* ☎ *0141/248–4942* ⊕ *www.babygrandglasgow.com.*

Black Sparrow. A cool Charles Bukowski theme bar named after the American writer's publishing company, the Black Sparrow has plenty of tall plants and cocktails as well as sophisticated bar food. There's also a great outdoor beer garden. ⊠ *241 North St., City Center* ☎ *0141/221–5530.*

Bloc. At Bloc, you can step behind a curious version of the Iron Curtain where Tex-Mex diner food mixes with an eclectic musical mash of DJs and live rock and folk bands. ⊠ *117 Bath St., City Center* ☎ *0141/574–6066.*

King Tut's Wah Wah Hut. Hosting live music most nights, King Tut's Wah Wah Hut claims to have been the venue that discovered the U.K. pop band Oasis. It's a favorite with students, but the cozy and traditional pub setting draws people of all ages. ✉ *227a St. Vincent St., City Center* ☎ *0141/221–5279.*

Moskito. For a splash of Mediterranean style, head to Moskito. Amid the cool, aquatic hues you can see people dancing to laid-back tunes Thursday to Sunday nights. ✉ *200 Bath St., City Center* ☎ *0141/331–1777.*

Rogano. Famous for its champagne cocktails, Rogano has a general air of 1920s decadence. ✉ *11 Exchange Pl., City Center* ☎ *0141/248–4055.*

Fodor's Choice ★ **Scotia Bar.** The Scotia Bar serves up a taste of an authentic Glasgow pub, with some traditional folk music occasionally thrown in. ✉ *112 Stockwell St., Merchant City* ☎ *0141/552–8681.*

★ **Sloans.** One of Glasgow's oldest and most beautiful pubs, the wood-paneled Sloans is always lively and welcoming and serves traditional pub food like fish-and-chips throughout the day. The upstairs ballroom is a magnificent mirrored affair, and on the floor above that is a basic dance floor. There's a good selection of beers and spirits, and the outdoor area is always lively on a dry night. ✉ *108 Argyle St., City Center* ☎ *0141/221–8886* ⊕ *www.sloansglasgow.com.*

NIGHTCLUBS

★ **Arches.** One of the city's largest arts venues, the Arches thumps with house and techno on Friday and Saturday nights. The club welcomes big music names like Colours and Inside Out at legendary parties. A few times a month it holds dressed-up gay nights. ✉ *253 Argyle St., City Center* ☎ *0141/565–1000* ⊕ *www.thearches.co.uk.*

Polo Lounge. Oozing with Edwardian style, the Polo Lounge is Glasgow's largest gay club. Upstairs is a bar that resembles an old-fashioned gentlemen's club; downstairs two dance floors play something for everyone. The festivities run until 3 am. ✉ *84 Wilson St., Merchant City* ☎ *0141/553–1221.*

Stereo. You'll find a wide range of live music Sunday through Thursday nights (9 to 11:30) and DJ club nights on Friday and Saturday (11 pm to 3 am). The small downstairs music venue gets crowded quickly, but that only adds to the electric atmosphere. Upstairs, a café-bar serves tasty vegan food and organic drinks as well as fabulous tapas. ✉ *20–28 Renfield La., City Center* ☎ *0141/222–2254* ⊕ *www.stereocafebar.com.*

Sub Club. This atmospheric underground venue has staged cutting-edge music events since its jazz club days in the '50s. Legendary favorites like Saturday's SubCulture (House) and Sunday's Optimo (a truly eclectic mix for musical hedonists) pack in friendly and sweaty crowds. ✉ *22 Jamaica St., City Center* ☎ *0141/248–4600.*

WEST END
BARS AND PUBS

78. The 78 has cozy sofas, vegan food, and a real coal fire. There's live music every night, with jazz on Sunday. ✉ *10–14 Kelvinhaugh St., West End* ☎ *0141/576–5018.*

Ben Nevis. This eccentric pub is full of Highland artifacts. There are more than 180 whiskies from which to choose and traditional live music just about every night. ✉ *1147 Argyle St., West End* ☎ *0141/576–5204.*

Cottiers. Despite its former austere existence as a church, the always-busy Cottiers is a famous haunt of the young, particularly in the summer months. The best seats are outside in the popular beer garden. ✉ *93 Hyndland St., West End* ☎ *0141/357–5825.*

Dram. This cozy spot has a strong connection to Gaelic culture, and not only because of its vast selection of whiskies and the knowledgeable staff to go with it. Decorated in a witty style that can only be described as "ultra eclectic," the four large rooms have everything from recycled furnishings to the odd stag's head on the wall. There's a wide range of beers and good, cheap food until 8 pm. On Thursday and Sunday, musicians gather in an informal jam session. ✉ *232–246 Woodlands Rd., West End* ☎ *0141/332–1622* ⊕ *www.dramglasgow.co.uk.*

Halt. There's often a good lineup of established and up-and-coming rock groups at the Halt, which attracts an older clientele as well as younger rock fans. ✉ *160 Woodlands Rd., West End* ☎ *0141/564–1527.*

Òran Mór. At the top of Byres Road, Òran Mór is popular with all ages. Situated in a massive church, the bar has beautiful stained-glass windows. The beer garden fills up quickly in good weather. It caters to different crowds at different times, and is open until 3 am. ✉ *731 Great Western Rd., West End* ☎ *0141/357–6200.*

Rio Cafe. With the feel of a 1950s diner, the Rio Cafe is all things to all people. You can eat economical breakfasts or lunches here, or drop by in the evening to listen to musicians, DJs, and poets (or even play poker on some nights). The standards are high despite the laid-back atmosphere. ✉ *27 Hyndland St., West End* ☎ *0141/334–9909.*

★ **Tennents.** A spacious street-corner bar, Tennents prides itself on its comprehensive selection of beers, lively conversation, and a refreshing lack of loud music. ✉ *191 Byres Rd., West End* ☎ *0141/341–1021.*

COMEDY CLUBS

Stand Comedy Club. With live shows every night of the week, the Stand Comedy Club is most popular on Thursday and Friday. Prices vary according to who is appearing, and the doors open at 7:30. ✉ *333 Woodlands Rd., West End* ☎ *0844/335–8879* ⊕ *www.thestand.co.uk.*

SPORTS AND THE OUTDOORS

You can't go far these days without seeing a runner or cyclist; because of the city's numerous parks, there is plenty of space. Rarely is the weather conducive to outdoor exercise; it rains a lot in Glasgow, but don't let that deter you. It doesn't deter the locals who play soccer, tennis, hike, bike, run, swim, and walk in the rain.

GOLF

Several municipal courses are operated within Glasgow proper by the local authorities. Bookings are relatively inexpensive and should be made directly to the course 24 hours in advance to ensure prime tee times (courses open at 7 am). A comprehensive list of contacts, facilities, and greens fees of the 30 or so other courses near the city is available from the tourist board. The abbreviation SSS means standard scratch score, which is often used here instead of par.

Douglas Park. North of the city near Milngavie, Douglas Park is a long, attractive course set among birch and pine trees with masses of rhododendrons blooming in early summer. ⊠ *Hillfoot, Bearsden* ☎ *0141/942– 0985* ⊕ *www.douglasparkgolfclub.co.uk* ⌕ *18 holes, 5,962 yds, par 69.*

Lethamhill. The fairways of this city-owned parkland course overlook Hogganfield Loch. To get here, take the M8 north to Junction 12, and drive up the A80 about a quarter mile. ⊠ *1240 Cumbernauld Rd., North City* ☎ *0141/276–0810* ⌕ *18 holes, 5,836 yds, SSS 68.*

Littlehill. Level fairways and greens make this municipal course not too difficult to play. It's about 4 mi north of the city center. ⊠ *Auchinairn Rd., North City* ☎ *0141/276–0704* ⌕ *18 holes, 6,240 yds, SSS 70.*

FOOTBALL

The city has been sports mad, especially for football (soccer), for more than 100 years. The rivalry between its two main football clubs, the Rangers and the Celtic, is legendary. Matches are held usually on Saturday in winter. Admission prices start at about £20. Don't go looking for a family-day-out atmosphere; football remains a fiercely contested game attended mainly by males, though the stadiums at Ibrox and Celtic Park are fast becoming family-friendly.

Ibrox. The Rangers wear blue and play at Ibrox, pronounced *eye*-brox, on the south side of the Clyde. Stadium tours on Friday and Sunday cost £8. Booking is essential. ⊠ *150 Edmiston Dr., South Side* ☎ *0871/702–1972.*

Celtic Park. Celtic wear white and green stripes and play in the east at Celtic Park. There are regular stadium tours, which must be booked ahead. ⊠ *18 Kerrydale St., East End* ☎ *0141/551–4308.*

Firhill Park. The game in Glasgow isn't just blue or green, nor is it dominated by international players and big money. Partick Thistle (the Jags) wear red and yellow and their ground is Firhill Park. ⊠ *80 Firhill Rd., West End* ☎ *0141/579–1971.*

SHOPPING

You'll find the mark of the fashion industry on the city center's hottest shopping streets. In the Merchant City, Ingram Street is lined on either side by high-fashion and designer outlets like Cruise. Buchanan Street, in the city center, is home to many chains geared toward younger people, including Diesel, Monsoon, and USC, and the adjacent Argyle Street Arcade is filled with jewelry stores. Antiques tend be found on and around West Regent Street in the city center.

The West End has a number of small shops selling crafts, vintage clothing, and trendier fashions—punctuated by innumerable cafés and restaurants. The university dominates the area around West End, and many shops cater to students. The easiest way to get here is by taking the subway to Hillhead.

CITY CENTER AND THE MERCHANT CITY

ARCADES AND SHOPPING CENTERS

Buchanan Galleries. The Buchanan Galleries, at the top end of Buchanan Street next to the Glasgow Royal Concert Hall, is packed with high-quality shops; its magnet attraction is the John Lewis department store. ⊠ *220 Buchanan St., City Center* ☎ *0141/333–9898.*

Fodor'sChoice
★ **Princes Square.** By far the best shopping center is the art-nouveau Princes Square, with high-quality shops alongside pleasant cafés and restaurants. Look for the Scottish Craft Centre, which carries an outstanding collection of work created by some of the nation's best craftspeople. ⊠ *48 Buchanan St., City Center* ☎ *0141/221–0324.*

St. Enoch's Shopping Centre. St. Enoch's Shopping Centre is eye-catching if not especially pleasing—it's a modern glass building that resembles an overgrown greenhouse. It houses various stores, but most are also found elsewhere. ⊠ *55 St. Enoch Sq., City Center* ☎ *0141/204–3900.*

SHOPPING DISTRICTS

Argyle Street. On the main, often-crowded pedestrian area of Argyle Street, you'll find chain stores such as Debenham's.

Argyll Arcade. An interesting diversion off Argyle Street is the covered Argyll Arcade, which has the largest collection of jewelers under one roof in Scotland. The L-shape edifice, built in 1904, houses several locally based jewelers and a few shops specializing in antique jewelry.

Barras. This indoor market, on London Road in the Glasgow Cross neighborhood east of the city center, prides itself on selling everything "from a needle to an anchor." Stalls hawk antique (and not-so-antique) furniture, bric-a-brac, good and not-so-good jewelry, and textiles—you name it, it's here.

Buchanan Street. Buchanan Street is Glasgow's premier shopping street and almost totally a pedestrian area. The usual suspects are here: Monsoon, Topshop, Burberry, Jaeger, and other household names, some with premises in Buchanan Galleries, at the top end of the street. There are usually plenty of street entertainers to accompany you from shop to shop.

Merchant City. Many of Glasgow's young and upwardly mobile make their home in Merchant City, on the edge of the city center. Shopping here is expensive, but the area is worth visiting if you're seeking the youthful Glasgow style. There are plenty of stylish restaurants and cafés here as well.

West Regent Street. If you're an antiques connoisseur and art lover, a walk along West Regent Street, particularly its **Victorian Village,** is highly recommended, as there are various galleries and shops, some specializing in Scottish antiques and paintings.

DEPARTMENT STORES

Debenham's. One of Glasgow's principal department stores, Debenham's has fine china and crystal as well as women's and men's clothing. ⊠ *97 Argyle St., City Center* ☎ *0844/561–6161.*

House of Fraser. A Glasgow institution, the House of Fraser stocks wares that reflect the city's material aspirations—leading European designer clothes and fabrics combined with home-produced articles, such as tweeds, tartans, glass, and ceramics. The magnificent interior, set off by the grand staircase rising to various floors and balconies, is itself worth a visit. ⊠ *21–45 Buchanan St., City Center* 🕾 *0141/221–3880.*

★ **John Lewis.** This shop is a favorite for its stylish mix of clothing, household items, electronics, and practically everything else. John Lewis claims to have "never been knowingly undersold" and prides itself on its customer service. It has a very elegant second-floor balcony café. ⊠ *Buchanan Galleries, 220 Buchanan St., City Center* 🕾 *0141/353–6677.*

Marks & Spencer. With sturdy, practical clothes and accessories at moderate prices, Marks & Spencer also offers foods and household goods. There's a second location at 172 Sauchiehall Street. ⊠ *2–12 Argyle St., City Center* 🕾 *0141/552–4546* ⊠ *172 Sauchiehall St., City Center* 🕾 *0141/332–6097.*

SPECIALTY SHOPS
ANTIQUES AND FINE ART

★ **Compass Gallery.** The gallery is something of an institution, having opened in 1969 to provide space for young and unknown artists. It now shares space with Cyril Gerber Fine Arts. ⊠ *178 W. Regent St., City Center* 🕾 *0141/221–3095* ⊕ *www.compassgallery.co.uk.*

Cyril Gerber Fine Art. This gallery specializes in British paintings from 1880 to the present; it will ship your purchase for you, as will most galleries. ⊠ *178 W. Regent St., City Center* 🕾 *0141/221–3095* ⊕ *www.gerberfineart.co.uk.*

BOOKS, PAPER, AND MUSIC

Art Store. Selling cards, books, and games, the Art Store has a wonderful array of all things connected with art—paper, paints, pens—as well as craft items like beads for stringing. ⊠ *94 Queen St., City Center* 🕾 *0141/221–1101* ⊕ *www.artstore.co.uk.*

Glasgow School of Art. The Glasgow School of Art sells books, cards, jewelry, and ceramics. Students often display their work during the degree shows in June. ⊠ *167 Renfrew St., City Center* 🕾 *0141/353–4526.*

Monorail Music. For the latest on the city's ever-thriving music scene try Monorail Music, inside a café-bar called Mono. The shop specializes in indie music and has a large collection of vinyl with everything from rock to jazz. ⊠ *12 Kings Ct., City Center* 🕾 *0141/552–9458* ⊕ *www.monorailmusic.com.*

Waterstone's. In an age of online sales, bookstores seem to be becoming scarcer. Waterstone's remains, and it has an excellent selection on its four floors. There's also a good basement café. ⊠ *153-57 Sauchiehall St., City Center* 🕾 *0141/248–4814* ⊕ *www.waterstones.com.*

CLOTHING BOUTIQUES

Cruise. Male and female fashionistas shouldn't miss Cruise, which caters to those at the high end of fashion. ⊠ *180 Ingram St., City Center* 🕾 *0141/572–3200* ⊕ *www.cruisefashion.co.uk.*

Mr. Ben. A funky selection of vintage clothing is what you'll find at Mr. Ben. ⊠ *6 King's Ct., City Center* ☎ *0141/553–1936.*

HOME FURNISHINGS AND TEXTILES

Linens Fine. This shop carries wonderful embroidered and embellished bed linens and other textiles. ⊠ *The Courtyard, Princes Sq., City Center* ☎ *0141/248–7082.*

SCOTTISH SPECIALTIES

Catherine Shaw. For high-quality gifts in Charles Rennie Mackintosh style, head to Catherine Shaw. ⊠ *32 Argyll Arcade, City Center* ☎ *0141/ 221–9038* ⊠ *32 Argyll Arcade, City Center* ☎ *0141/221–9038.*

Hector Russell Kiltmakers. Hector Russell Kiltmakers specializes in Highland outfits, wool and cashmere clothing, and women's fashions. ⊠ *110 Buchanan St., City Center* ☎ *0141/221–0217.*

MacDonald MacKay Ltd. MacDonald MacKay Ltd. makes, sells, and exports Highland dress and accessories. ⊠ *161 Hope St., City Center* ☎ *0141/204–3930.*

SPORTS GEAR

Tiso Glasgow Outdoor Experience. You'll find good-quality outerwear at Tiso Glasgow Outdoor Experience, handy if you're planning some Highland walks. There's a second location on Couper Street in the West End. ⊠ *129 Buchanan St., City Center* ☎ *0141/248–4877* ⊕ *www.tiso. com* ⊠ *50 Couper St., West End* ☎ *0141/559–5450.*

WEST END

SPECIALTY SHOPS

BOOKS, PAPER, AND MUSIC

Caledonia Books. This well-organized and well-stocked secondhand bookstore fills the gap left by the departure of other bookstores. The owners are knowledgeable and willing to search for even the most obscure volumes. ⊠ *483 Great Western Rd., West End* ☎ *0141/334–9663.*

Papyrus. Here you'll find designer cards as well as a selection of books. There's a second location in the city center on Sauchiehall Street. ⊠ *374 Byres Rd., West End* ☎ *0141/334–6514* ⊕ *www.papyrusgifts.co.uk* ⊠ *10 Sauchiehall St., City Center* ☎ *0141/332–6788.*

CLOTHING BOUTIQUES

Pink Poodle. This stylish fashion boutique is mainly for younger dressers, and sells some lovely and often quirky accessories. ⊠ *181–183 Byres Rd., West End* ☎ *0141/357–3344* ⊕ *www.lovelaboutique.com.*

Strawberry Fields. The high-end Strawberry Fields sells colorful children's wear. ⊠ *517 Great Western Rd., West End* ☎ *0141/339–1121.*

FOOD

Demijohn. Specializing in infused wines, spirits, oils, and vinegars, Demijohn calls itself a "liquid deli." ⊠ *382 Byres Rd., West End* ☎ *0141/337–3600.*

★ **Iain Mellis Cheesemonger.** This shop has a superb, seemingly endless selection of fine Scottish cheeses, as well as others from England and across Europe. ⊠ *492 Great Western Rd., West End* ☎ *0141/339–8998.*

Peckham's Delicatessen. This deli is *the* place for Continental sausages, cheeses, and anything else you'd need for a delicious picnic. ✉ *61–65 Glassford St., Merchant City* ☎ *0141/553–0666* ✉ *43 Clarence Dr., West End* ☎ *0141/357–2909* ✉ *61–65 Glassford St., Merchant City* ☎ *0141/553–0666.*

HOME FURNISHINGS AND TEXTILES
Nancy Smillie. Local to the floorboards, Nancy Smillie is a one-of-a-kind boutique that sells unique glassware, jewelry, and furnishings. ✉ *53 Cresswell St., West End* ☎ *0141/334–0055.*

JEWELRY
Orro. The beautiful and contemporary jewelry here uses modern designs and new materials in unexpected ways. The shop has a gallery feel, and you can browse uninterrupted. ✉ *12 Wilton St., West End* ☎ *0141/552–7888* ⊕ *www.orro.co.uk.*

SOUTH SIDE

ARCADES AND SHOPPING CENTERS
Silverburn. One of Europe's largest shopping malls, Silverburn is a good option on a rainy day. The interior feels like a village with streams, waterfalls, and restaurants galore, plus everything from small boutiques to retail giants like Marks & Spencer. Direct buses from Buchanan Street Station leave every 20 minutes. ✉ *Barrhead Rd., Pollock* ☎ *0141/880–3200.*

SIDE TRIPS: AYRSHIRE, CLYDE COAST, AND ROBERT BURNS COUNTRY

The jigsaw puzzle of firths and straits and interlocking islands that you see as you fly into Glasgow Airport harbors numerous tempting one-day excursion destinations. You can travel south to visit the fertile farmlands of Ayrshire—Robert Burns country—or west to the Firth of Clyde, or southeast to the Clyde Valley, all by car or by public transportation. Besides the Burns sites, key treasures in this area include the Marquess of Bute's Mount Stuart House on the Isle of Bute, and Culzean Castle, as famous for its Robert Adam (1728–92) design as it is for its spectacular seaside setting and grounds.

For many people, a highlight of this region is Robert Burns country, a 40-minute drive from Glasgow. The poet was born in Alloway, beside Ayr, and the towns and villages where he lived and loved make for an interesting day out. English children learn that Burns (1759–96) is a good minor poet. But Scottish children know that he's Shakespeare, Dante, Rabelais, Mozart, and Karl Marx rolled into one. As time goes by, it seems that the Scots have it more nearly right. As poet and humanist, Burns increases in stature. When you plunge into Burns country, don't forget that he's held in extreme reverence by Scots of all backgrounds. They may argue about Sir Walter Scott and Bonnie Prince Charlie, but there's no disputing the merits of the author of "Bonnie Doon."

On your way here you travel beside the estuary and firth of the great River Clyde and will be able to look across to Dumbarton and its Rock, a nostalgic farewell point for emigrants leaving Glasgow. The river is surprisingly narrow here, considering that the *Queen Elizabeth II* and the other great ocean liners sailed these waters from the place of their birth.

GETTING HERE AND AROUND

From Glasgow, you can take the bus to Ayr for the Burns Heritage Trail; and Troon, Prestwick, and Ayr to play golf. Bus companies also operate one-day guided excursions; for details, contact the tourist information center in Glasgow or the Strathclyde Passenger Transport Travel Centre. Traveline Scotland has a helpful website.

If you're driving from Glasgow, there are two main routes to Ayr. The quickest is to take the M77 to the A77, which takes you all the way to Ayr. Alloway is well signposted when you get to Ayr. The alternative and much slower route is the coast road; take the M8 to Greenock and continue down the coast on the A78 until you meet the A77 and continue on into Burns Country.

You can travel by train to Ayr for the Burns Heritage Trail; and Troon, Prestwick, and Ayr to play golf.

PAISLEY

7 mi south of Glasgow.

The industrial prosperity of Paisley came from textiles and, in particular, from the woolen paisley shawl. The internationally recognized paisley pattern is based on the shape of a palm shoot, an ancient Babylonian fertility symbol brought from Kashmir. Today you can explore this history at several attractions.

GETTING HERE AND AROUND

Paisley-bound buses depart from the Buchanan Street bus station in Glasgow. Traveline Scotland provides information on schedules and fares. Trains to Paisley depart daily every 5 to 10 minutes from Glasgow Central Station. If you're driving, take the M8 westbound and turn off at Junction 27, which is clearly signposted to Paisley.

ESSENTIALS

Visitor Information Paisley Visitor Information Centre ✉ *9A Gilmour St.* ☎ *0141/889–0711* ⊕ *www.visitscotland.com/paisley.*

EXPLORING

Abbey. Paisley's 12th-century Cluniac Abbey dominates the town center. Almost completely destroyed by the English in 1307, the abbey was not totally restored until the early 20th century. It's associated with Walter Fitzallan, the high steward of Scotland, who gave his name to the Stewart monarchs of Scotland (Stewart is a corruption of "steward"). Outstanding features include the vaulted stone roof and stained glass of the choir. Paisley Abbey is today a busy parish church; if you're visiting with a large group you should call ahead. ✉ *13 High St.* ☎ *0141/889–7654* ⊕ *www.paisleyabbey.org.uk* ✉ *Free* ☉ *Mon.–Sat. 10–3:30, Sun. services at 11, 12:15, and 6:30.*

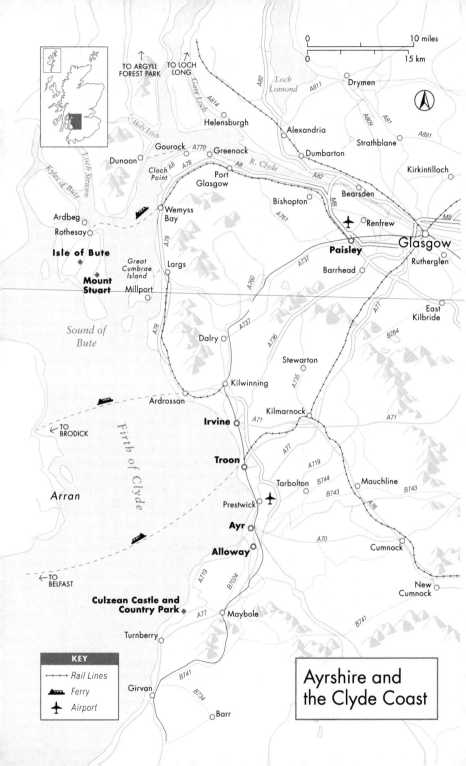

★ **Paisley Museum & Art Gallery.** The full story of the pattern and of the innovative weaving techniques introduced in Paisley is told in the Paisley Museum & Art Gallery, which has a world-famous shawl collection. ⊠ *High St.* ☎ *0141/887–1010* 🖼 *Free* ⏰ *Tues.–Sat. 10–5, Sun. 2–5.*

Sma' Shot Cottages. To get an idea of the life led by textile-industry workers, visit the Sma' Shot Cottages. These re-creations of mill workers' houses contain displays of linen, lace, and paisley shawls. An 18th-century weaver's cottage is also open to visitors. ⊠ *11–17 George Pl.* ☎ *0141/889–1708* 🖼 *Free* ⏰ *Apr.–Sept., Wed. and Sat. noon–4; Oct.–Mar. by appointment.*

WHERE TO STAY
For expanded hotel reviews, visit Fodors.com.

$$$$ ★ 🏨 **Mar Hall.** This imposing baronial house sits amid formal gardens and overlooks the river Clyde and verdant woodlands. **Pros:** spacious rooms; fantastic pool; wonderful setting. **Cons:** quite remote; an expensive treat. ⊠ *Earl of Mar Estate, Mar Hall Dr., Bishopton* ☎ *0141/812–9999* ⊕ *www.marhall.com* 🛏 *53 rooms* 🔌 *In-room: Internet. In-hotel: restaurant, bar, golf course, pool, gym, spa* 🍽 *Breakfast.*

ISLE OF BUTE

75 mi west of Glasgow.

The Isle of Bute affords a host of relaxing walks and scenic vistas. Mount Stuart, a stately home, is a popular attraction. Like the nearby Isle of Arran *(see Chapter 8)*, the Isle of Bute was a Victorian holiday favorite convenient for Glaswegians.

Rothesay, a faded but appealing resort, is the main town. Some of the ornate Victorian architecture is striking. In the old Victorian village of Wemyss Bay there's ferry service to the island. The many handsome buildings, especially the station, are a reminder of the grandeur and style of a century ago.

ESSENTIALS
Visitor Information Isle of Bute Discovery Centre ⊠ *The Winter Garden, Victoria St., Rothesay* ☎ *08452/255121* ⊕ *www.isle-of-bute.com.*

EXPLORING
Mount Stuart. Bute's biggest draw is spectacular Mount Stuart, ancestral home of the marquesses of Bute. The massive Victorian Gothic palace, built in red sandstone, has ornate interiors, including the Marble Hall, with a star-studded vault, stained glass, arcaded galleries, and magnificent tapestries woven in Edinburgh in the early 20th century. The paintings and furniture throughout the house are equally outstanding. Even if you don't like Victorian style, you may appreciate the lovely gardens and grounds here. ⊠ *Off A844, Rothesay* ☎ *01700/503877* ⊕ *www. mountstuart.com* 🖼 *Gardens £5; house and gardens £10* ⏰ *Gardens May–Sept., daily 10–6; house May–Sept., Sun.–Fri. 11–5, Sat. 10–2:30.*

Rothesay. Rothesay, a faded but appealing resort, is the main town. Some of the ornate Victorian architecture is striking.

WHERE TO STAY

For expanded hotel reviews, visit Fodors.com.

$ ⊞ **Munro's Bed and Breakfast.** Surrounded by colorful gardens, this small B&B in a peaceful residential area has a home-away-from-home feel. **Pros:** beautiful location; nicely remodeled; environmentally aware. **Cons:** hilltop location a problem for those with trouble walking; no restaurant; sea-view rooms cost extra. ⊠ *Ardmory Rd., Ardbeg* ☎ *01700/ 502346* ⊕ *www.visitmunros.co.uk* ⟿ *6 rooms* ⌂ *In-room: no a/c, Wi-Fi* ¶⊙ *Breakfast.*

IRVINE

24 mi south of Glasgow.

Beyond Irvine's cobbled streets and grand Victorian buildings, look for a peaceful crescent-shape harbor and fishermen's cottages huddled in solidarity against the Atlantic winds. The Scottish Maritime Museum pays homage to the town's seafaring past. Scotland's national poet, Robert Burns, lived here in 1781.

ESSENTIALS

Visitor Information Irvine Tourist Information Centre ⊠ *New St.* ☎ *01294/313886.*

EXPLORING

Irvine Burns Club. Founded in 1826, the Irvine Burns Club is one of the oldest Burns clubs in the world. Today its gallery displays a collection of original manuscripts, plus murals and stained-glass windows that narrate Burns's life and work. The author lived in Irvine when he was 22. ⊠ *28 Eglinton St.* ☎ *01294/274511* ⊕ *www.irvineburnsclub.org* ⊠ *Free* ⊙ *Apr.–Sept., Mon., Wed., Fri., and Sat. 2:30–4:30; Oct.–Mar., Sat. 2:30–4:30.*

Scottish Maritime Museum. On the waterfront in the coastal town of Irvine, this museum brings together ships and boats—both models and the real thing—to tell the tale of Scotland's maritime history, as well as chronicle the lives of its boatbuilders, its fishermen, its sailors. The atmospheric Linthouse Engine Building, part of a former shipyard, hosts most of the displays. The museum also includes a shipyard worker's tenement home that you can explore. ⊠ *6 Gottries Rd.* ☎ *01294/278283* ⊕ *www. scottishmaritimemuseum.org* ⊠ *£4* ⊙ *Apr.–Sept., daily 10–5.*

Vennel Art Gallery. The Vennel Art Gallery occupies the 18th-century cottage where poet Robert Burns lived and the shed where he learned to heckle—or dress—flax (the raw material for linen). Both buildings have on display paintings, photographs, and sculpture by mainly Scottish artists. ⊠ *10 Glasgow Vennel* ☎ *01294/275059* ⊠ *Free* ⊙ *Thurs.– Sat. 10–1 and 2–5.*

TROON

4 mi south of Irvine, 30 mi south of Glasgow, 6 mi north of Ayr.

The small coastal town of Troon is famous for its outstanding golf course, Royal Troon. You can easily see that golf is very popular here and in this area: at times, the whole 60-mi-long Ayrshire coast seems one endless course. *(For more about the best courses in this area, see Chapter 12.)* The town's several miles of sandy beaches provide other diversions. It's easy to get to Troon by train or bus from both Glasgow and Ayr.

WHERE TO EAT AND STAY
For expanded hotel reviews, visit Fodors.com.

$$ ✕ **MacCallums Oyster Bar.** Finding McCallums is a bit of an adventure,
SEAFOOD but it's well worth it. The menu varies according to the day's catch, but
★ you can usually count on lobster in garlic butter, seared scallops, or grilled langoustines, which taste of the sea. The fish pie is justly famous, and excellent light white wines match the freshness of the food. Solid wooden tables and other simple furnishings add a rustic touch to the dining room. For a more modest price, or if you prefer to take out and watch the fishing boats bob in the harbor, try the adjacent Wee Hurrie, very possibly one of the best fish-and-chips shops in Scotland, serving monkfish and oysters with chips as well as the usual fare. It's the same food served in the restaurant, without the wine list. ✉ *Harbour Rd.* ☎ *01292/319339* ☉ *Closed Mon. No dinner Sun.*

¢ ⌂ **Piersland House Hotel.** A late-Victorian mansion on the southern edge of town, formerly the home of a whisky magnate, is now a country-house hotel. **Pros:** gorgeous gardens and grounds; close to golf courses; near Prestwick Airport. **Cons:** helps to have a car to get around; can get crowded with private functions. ✉ *15 Craigend Rd.* ☎ *01292/314747* ⊕ *www.piersland.co.uk* ⌫ *37 rooms* ♿ *In-room: no a/c, Wi-Fi. In-hotel: restaurant, bar* |○| *Breakfast.*

GOLF
Royal Troon. Founded in 1878, Royal Troon has two 18-hole courses: the Old, or Championship, Course and the Portland Course. The views are magnificent, but the courses can get windy. Access for nonmembers is limited between May and mid-October to Monday, Tuesday, and Thursday only; day tickets cost £220 and include two rounds, morning coffee, and a buffet lunch, but there are cheaper options. ✉ *Craigend Rd.* ☎ *01292/311555* ⊕ *www.royaltroon.co.uk* ⚐ *Old Course: 18 holes, 7,150 yds, SSS 74. Portland Course: 18 holes, 6,289 yds, SSS 70.*

SHOPPING
Regalia Fashion Salon. Many Glaswegians frequent Regalia Fashion Salon for its unusual collection of designer clothing for women. ✉ *46–48 Church St.* ☎ *01292/312162.*

Tantalus Antiques. For a fascinating look at local antiquities, visit Tantalus Antiques. ✉ *79 Temple Hill* ☎ *01292/315999.*

AYR AND ALLOWAY

6 mi south of Troon, 34 mi south of Glasgow.

The commercial port of Ayr is Ayrshire's chief town, a peaceful and elegant place with an air of prosperity. Poet Robert Burns was baptized in the Auld Kirk (Old Church) here and wrote a humorous poem about the Twa Brigs (Two Bridges) that cross the river nearby. Burns described

Ayr as a town unsurpassed "for honest men and bonny lasses." If he were to visit today, he might also mention the good shopping.

If you're on the Robert Burns trail, head for Alloway, on B7024 in Ayr's southern suburbs. A number of sights here are part of the **Burns National Heritage Park**, including the magnificent new Robert Burns Birthplace Museum.

GETTING HERE AND AROUND

From Glasgow you can take the bus or train to Ayr; travel time is about an hour (a bit less by train). Drivers can use the A78 and A77 near the coast; a car would provide more flexibility to see the Burns sites around Alloway.

ESSENTIALS

Visitor Information Ayr ⊠ *22 Sandgate* ☎ *01292/288688* ⊕ *www. ayrshire-arran.com.*

EXPLORING

Auld Kirk Alloway. Auld Kirk Alloway is where Tam o' Shanter, in Robert Burns's eponymous poem, unluckily passed a witches' revel—with Old Nick himself playing the bagpipes—on his way home from a night of drinking. Tam, in flight from the witches, managed to cross the medieval **Brig o' Doon** (*brig* is Scots for *bridge*; you can still see the bridge) just in time. His gray mare, Meg, lost her tail to the closest witch. (Any resident of Ayr will tell you that witches cannot cross running water.) The church is in ruins, but the graveyard includes the tomb of Burns's father, William. ⊠ *Murdoch's La., Alloway* ⊕ *www.burnsheritagepark.com.*

Bachelors' Club. About 8 mi northeast of Ayr is the Bachelors' Club, the 17th-century house where Robert Burns learned to dance, founded a debating and literary society, and became a Freemason. ⊠ *Sandgate St., Tarbolton* ☎ *01292/541940* ⊕ *www.nts.org.uk* ⊠ *£5* ⊗ *Apr.–late Sept., Fri.–Tues. 1–5.*

★ **Burns Cottage.** In the delightful Burns Heritage Park, this thatched cottage is where Scotland's national poet lived for his first seven years. It has a living room, a kitchen, and a stable, one behind the other. The life and times of Burns, born in 1759, are beautifully and creatively illustrated, particularly in the videos of daily life in the 18th century. The garden is lush with the types of vegetables the poet's father might have grown. Take the Poet's Path through the village to the Robert Burns Birthplace Museum, the spooky churchyard where Tam o' Shanter faced fearsome ghosts, and the Brig o' Doon. ⊠ *Greenfield Ave., Alloway* ☎ *01292/441215* ⊕ *www.burnsmuseum.org.uk* ⊠ *£8, includes Burns Monument and Robert Burns Birthplace Museum* ⊗ *Apr.–Sept., daily 10–5:30; Oct.–Mar., daily 10–5.*

Burns Monument. A tall neoclassical structure built in 1823, the Burns Monument overlooks the Brig o' Doon. Entry is included with a Robert Burns Birthplace Museum ticket. ⊠ *Murdoch's Lone, Alloway* ☎ *No phone* ⊕ *www.burnsmuseum.org.uk* ⊠ *£8, includes Burns Cottage and Robert Burns Birthplace Museum* ⊗ *Apr.–Sept., daily 9:30–5; Oct.– Mar., daily 10–4.*

Fodor's Choice

★ **Robert Burns Birthplace Museum.** Besides being a poet of delicacy and depth, Robert Burns was also a rebel, a thinker, a lover, a good companion, and a man of the countryside. This wonderful new museum, opened in 2011, explains why the Scots so admire this complex "man o' pairts." The imaginative museum presents each of his poems in context, with commentaries sensitively written in a modern version of the Scots language in which he spoke and wrote. Headsets let you hear the poems sung or spoken. The exhibit is vibrant and interactive, with touch screens that allow you to debate his views on politics, love, taxation, revolution, and Scottishness. An elegant café offers a place to pause, while the kids can play in the adjoining garden. ⊠ *Murdoch's Lone, Alloway* ☎ *0844/493–2601* ⊕ *www.burnsmuseum.org.uk* ⊠ *£8, includes Burns Cottage and Burns Monument* ☉ *Apr.–Sept. daily 10–5:30; Oct.–Mar. daily 10–5.*

> **REMEMBERING MR. BURNS**
>
> Born in Ayrshire, Robert Burns (1759–96) is one of Scotland's treasures. The poet and balladeer had a style that was his and his alone. His most famous song, "Auld Lang Syne," is heard everywhere on New Year's Day. Burns's talent, charisma, and good looks made him an icon to both the upper and lower classes (and made him quite popular with the ladies). Today his birthday (January 25) is considered a national holiday; on "Burns Night" young and old alike get together for Burns Suppers and recite his work over neeps, tatties, and drams of the country's finest whisky.

WHERE TO EAT

$$
BRITISH
★
✕**Brig o' Doon House.** Originally built in 1827, this attractive restaurant often has a piper by the door to greet hungry travelers. The setting is very Scottish, with tartan carpets, dark wood paneling, and buck heads mounted on the walls. The bar is a shrine to Robert Burns, and the surrounding gardens overlook the Brig o' Doon as well as a small, rushing river. The food keeps to the Scottish theme: try panfried scallops with citrus butter to start, and venison casserole with juniper berries and creamed potatoes, or haggis with neeps and tatties (served with a dram) as a main course. There are several rooms for rent upstairs. ⊠ *High Maybole Rd., Alloway* ☎ *01292/442466.*

$$
BRITISH
★
✕**Fouter's Bistro.** In the center of Ayr, Fouter's is in a long and narrow cellar that was an 18th-century bank vault, yet its white walls and decorative stenciling create a sense of airiness. The cuisine is light and skillful—no heavy sauces here. Try the roast Ayrshire lamb with pan juices, red wine, and mint, or sample the Taste of Scotland appetizer—smoked salmon, trout, and other goodies. This is modern Scottish and French cooking at its best. ⊠ *2A Academy St.* ☎ *01292/261391* ☉ *Closed Sun. and Mon.*

SHOPPING

Ayr has a good range of shops.

Begg & Co. Upscale Begg & Co. sells a good selection of scarves, stoles, plaids, and travel rugs handmade on the premises. ⊠ *Viewfield Rd.* ☎ *01292/267615* ⊕ *www.beggscotland.com.*

Diamond Factory. You can watch craftspeople at work at the jewelry workshop Diamond Factory. Particularly coveted are the handmade Celtic wedding bands. The store will happily ship your purchases. ✉ *26 Queen's Ct.* ☎ *01292/280476.*

CULZEAN CASTLE AND COUNTRY PARK

12 mi south of Ayr, 50 mi south of Glasgow.

GETTING HERE AND AROUND

Stagecoach buses run from Ayr to the park entrance; the nearest train station from Glasgow is at Maybole, 4 mi to the east, but there is Stagecoach bus service to the park entrance. Note that the park entrance is a mile walk from the castle visitor center.

EXPLORING

Ⓒ **Culzean Castle and Country Park.** The dramatic cliff-top castle of Culzean
★ (pronounced ku-*lain*) is the National Trust for Scotland's most popular property, yet it remains unspoiled. Robert Adam designed the neoclassical mansion, complete with a walled garden, in 1777. Guided tours are available at 11 and at 3, without extra charge; the tour includes an armory display, the library, dining room, several drawing rooms, and the kitchen. In addition to its marvelous interiors, the house contains the National Guest Flat, donated by the people of Scotland in appreciation of General Dwight D. Eisenhower's (1890–1969) services during World War II; as president he stayed here once or twice. On the estate grounds (which are as memorable as the house), shrubberies reflect the essential mildness of this coast, though some visitors, meeting the full force of a westerly gale, might think otherwise. Culzean's perpendicular sea cliff affords views across the Firth of Clyde to Arran and the Irish coast. Not a stone's throw away, it seems, the pinnacle of Ailsa Craig, a rock, rears from midchannel. It's easy to spend a day here. ✉ *A719, Maybole* ☎ *0844/493–2149* ⊕ *www.culzeanexperience.org* 🎫 *Park £9, park and castle £14* ⊙ *Park daily 9:30–sunset; castle, Apr.–Oct., daily 10:30–5; last admission at 4.*

SIDE TRIPS: THE CLYDE VALLEY

The River Clyde is (or certainly was) famous for its shipbuilding, yet its upper reaches flow through some of Scotland's most fertile farmlands, rich with tomato crops. It's an interesting area with some museums, most notably at New Lanark, that tell the story of manufacturing and mining prosperity.

GETTING HERE AND AROUND

If you're driving from Glasgow, head south on the M74 and turn on to the A72. This is the main road through the Clyde Valley, ending at Lanark. The A702 is the turnoff to Biggar. Train service runs from Glasgow Central Station to Hamilton (near Blantyre) and Lanark; for details check National Rail. There are no trains to Biggar, but there's a connecting bus from Hamilton to Biggar.

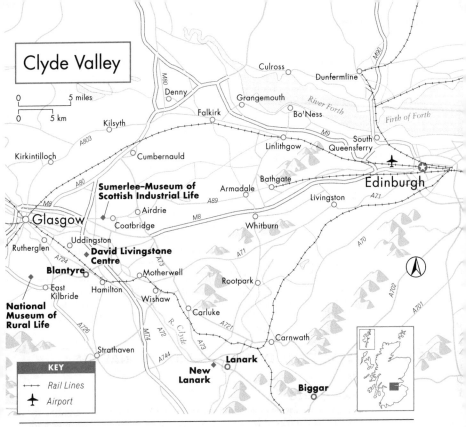

BLANTYRE

8 mi southeast of Glasgow.

Blantyre, a suburb of Hamilton, is not a pretty town. The explorer David Livingstone was born here.

EXPLORING

David Livingstone Centre. Set among gardens above the river bank, the David Livingstone Centre is based partly in the tiny one-room tenement apartment where the explorer-missionary (1813–73) spent his first 23 years. The rest of the museum is devoted to his travels across Africa, depicted in small, framed tableaux that light up as you walk past them. His meeting with Henry Stanley, sent by *The New York Times* to find him and bring him back, is commemorated. On meeting him, Stanley famously said, "Dr Livingstone, I presume." Livingstone refused the invitation and died in Africa. Copies of Livingstone's letters are displayed, and there is plenty of opportunity for youngsters to interact with the exhibits. ⊠ *165 Station Rd.* ☎ *0844/493–2207* ⊕ *www.nts.org.uk* ⊠ *£6* ⊙ *Mon.–Sat. 10–5:30, Sun. 12:30–5:30.*

Chatelherault Country Park. The grand building at the heart of this 500-acre estate served only as hunting lodge and dog kennel for the immensely wealthy dukes of Hamilton, who lived in a palace that disappeared into the mine beneath (the source of the family's wealth). The park contains the ruins of Cadzow Castle and some beautiful walks, as well as a wonderfully designed children's park. There are guided tours around the lodge and the surrounding gardens, but it's just as satisfying to take in the fabulous view of Glasgow from the front of the house and then wander around independently. ⊠ *Carlisle Rd., Ferniegar* ☎ *01698/426213* 🖃 *Free* 🕙 *Mon.–Sat. 10–5, Sun. noon–5.*

NATIONAL MUSEUM OF RURAL LIFE

9 mi south of Glasgow.

EXPLORING

National Museum of Rural Life. This lovely museum, a 20-minute drive from Glasgow, is slightly off the beaten track but well worth the trip. Set in a rural area, it explores every aspect of the country's agricultural heritage. In a modern building resembling a huge barn you learn about how farming transformed the land, experience the life and hardships of those who worked it, and see displays of tools and machines from across the ages. Take a tractor ride to a fully functioning 1950s farmhouse. There are also some great exhibits geared toward children. ⊠ *Philipshill Rd., East Kilbride* ☎ *0300/123–6789* ⊕ *www.nms.ac.uk/rural* 🖃 *£6.50* 🕙 *Daily 10–5.*

SUMMERLEE–MUSEUM OF SCOTTISH INDUSTRIAL LIFE

10 mi east of Glasgow.

EXPLORING

Summerlee–Museum of Scottish Industrial Life. On the site of the old Summerlee Ironworks, this vast and exciting museum re-creates a mine and the miners' rows (the cottages where miners and their families lived). An electric tram transports you to the huge hall where industrial machines vie with exhibits about ordinary life. Later you can stroll along the canal and take the kids to a fine playground. The drive from Glasgow takes less than 15 minutes. ⊠ *Heritage Way, Coatbridge* ☎ *01236/638460* ⊕ *www.visitlanarkshire.com* 🖃 *Free.*

LANARK

19 mi east of Glasgow.

Set in pleasing, rolling countryside, Lanark is a typical old Scottish town. It's now most often associated with its unique neighbor New Lanark, a model workers' community about a mile to the south.

ESSENTIALS

Visitor Information Lanark Visitor Information Centre ⊠ *Horsemarket, Ladyacre Rd.* ☎ *01555/661661.*

EXPLORING

🔿 **New Lanark.** Now a World Heritage Site, New Lanark was home to a social experiment at the beginning of the Industrial Revolution. Robert Owen (1771–1858), together with his father-in-law David Dale

Fodor's Choice
★

(1739–1806), set out to create a model industrial community with well-designed workers' homes, a school, and public buildings. Owen went on to establish other communities on similar principles, both in Britain and in the United States. Robert Owen's son, Robert Dale Owen (1801–77), helped found the Smithsonian Institution.

After many changes of fortune, the mills eventually closed. One of the buildings has been converted into a visitor center that tells the story of this brave social experiment. You can also explore Robert Owen's house, the school, and a mill worker's house, and enjoy the Annie McLeod Experience, a fairground ride that takes you through the story of one mill worker's life. Other restored structures hold various shops and eateries; one has a rooftop garden with impressive views of the entire site.

The river Clyde powers its way through a beautiful wooded gorge here, and its waters were once harnessed to drive textile-mill machinery. Upstream it flows through some of the finest river scenery anywhere in Lowland Scotland, with woods and spectacular waterfalls. ⊠ *New Lanark Rd., New Lanark* ☎ *01555/661345* ⊕ *www.newlanark.org* ☞ *£8.50* ☉ *Oct.–Mar., daily 11–5; Apr.–Sept., daily 10–5.*

WHERE TO STAY
For expanded hotel reviews, visit Fodors.com.

$ 🏨 **New Lanark Mill Hotel.** Housed in a converted cotton mill in the 18th-century village of New Lanark, this hotel is decorated in a spare, understated style that allows the impressive architecture of barrel-vaulted ceilings and elegant Georgian windows to speak for itself. **Pros:** beautiful views of the river; large rooms; impressive spa. **Cons:** bland bar; some rooms can get cold. ⊠ *New Lanark Rd., New Lanark* ☎ *01555/667200* ⊕ *www.newlanarkmillhotel.co.uk* ☞ *38 rooms, 8 cottages* ☖ *In-room: no a/c. In-hotel: restaurant, pool, gym* ⦿ *Breakfast.*

SHOPPING
Lanark has an interesting selection of shops within walking distance of each other; there are also some shops such as the Edinburgh Woollen Mill at New Lanark.

McKellar's. McKellar's sells Charles Rennie Mackintosh–inspired designs in gold and silver. ⊠ *41 High St.* ☎ *01555/661312.*

Strands. Strands carries yarns and knitwear, including Arran designs and one-of-a-kind creations by Scottish designers. ⊠ *8 Bloomgate* ☎ *01555/665757.*

BIGGAR

34 mi southeast of Glasgow.

A pleasant town built of stone, Biggar is a rewarding place to spend an hour or two, out of all proportion to its size, thanks to an excellent collection of small, specialized museums. At Biggar you are near the headwaters of the Clyde, on the moors in the center of southern Scotland. The Clyde flows west toward Glasgow and the Atlantic Ocean, and the Tweed, only a few miles away, flows east toward the North

Sea. There are fine views around Biggar to Culter Fell and to the Border Hills in the south.

ESSENTIALS

Visitor Information Biggar ⊠ *155 High St.* ☎ *01899/221066.*

EXPLORING

Biggar Gasworks. The Biggar Gasworks, built in 1839, is a fascinating reminder of the efforts once needed to produce gas for light and heat. ⊠ *Gasworks Rd.* ☎ *01899/221050* ⊕ *www.biggarmuseumtrust.co.uk* ⊠ *£2* ⊙ *June–Sept., daily 2–5.*

☾ **Biggar Puppet Theatre.** Purves Puppets, famous for its "black box" puppetry, regularly performs at the Biggar Puppet Theatre. Before and after performances, puppeteers lead two half-hour hands-on tours (£3). One tour ducks backstage, while the other explores the puppet museum. These tours should be booked well in advance, as should tickets for very popular performances. ⊠ *Broughton Rd.* ☎ *01899/220631* ⊕ *www. purvespuppets.com* ⊠ *Tours £3; performances £8* ⊙ *Call ahead for tours.*

Gladstone Court Museum. Gladstone Court Museum paints a fascinating picture of life in the town in years past, with reconstructed Victorian-era shops, a bank, a phone exchange, and a school. ⊠ *Northback Rd.* ☎ *01899/221050* ⊕ *www.biggarmuseumtrust.co.uk* ⊠ *£2.50* ⊙ *Easter weekend and Apr.–Oct., Mon.–Sat. 11–4:30, Sun. 2–4:30.*

Greenhill Covenanters' House. This farmhouse is filled with 17th-century furnishings, costume dolls, and rare farm breeds. The Covenanters were breakaway supporters of Presbyterianism in the 17th century. ⊠ *Burn Braes* ☎ *01899/221050* ⊕ *www.biggarmuseumtrust.co.uk* ⊠ *£1.50* ⊙ *May–Sept., first Sat. of each month by appointment 2–4:30.*

Moat Park Heritage Centre. For a look at Biggar's geology and prehistory, plus an interesting embroidery collection (including samplers and fine patchwork coverlets), visit the Moat Park Heritage Centre, housed in a former church. ⊠ *Kirkstyle* ☎ *01899/221050* ⊕ *www. biggarmuseumtrust.co.uk* ⊠ *£2.50* ⊙ *May–Sept., Mon.–Sat. 11–4:30, Sun. 2–5.*

The Borders and the Southwest

WORD OF MOUTH

"There are some wonderful old houses in the Borders. Mellerstain and Floors Castle come to mind. Both are near Kelso and, to my mind, are much better to visit than yet another ruined abbey. Manderston house is another great place. It is near Duns and has a silver-plated staircase."

—almcd

"The Borders abbeys like Melrose will fulfill your dreams. Melrose Abbey was not my favorite because it is surrounded by a town, but Dryburgh Abbey was in the country on the River Tweed. Jedburgh Abbey, like Melrose, is in a town; these three abbeys in a small area are great."

—PalenQ

www.fodors.com/community

Updated
by Mike
Gonzalez

The Borders region embraces the whole 90-mi course of one of Scotland's greatest rivers, the Tweed. Passing woodlands luxuriant with game birds, the river flows in rushing torrents through this fertile land. In this area south of Edinburgh you'll find more stately homes, fortified castles, and medieval abbeys than in any other part of Scotland. This is also Sir Walter Scott territory, including his pseudo-baronial home at Abbotsford. To the west of the Borders is Dumfries and Galloway, a low-key area with gentle coastal and upland areas.

For centuries, the Borders was a battlefield where English and Scottish troops remained locked in a struggle for its possession. At different times, parts of the region have been in English hands, just as slices of northern England (Berwick-upon-Tweed, for example) have been in Scottish hands. The castles and fortified houses across the Borders are the surviving witnesses to those times. After the Union of 1707, fortified houses gradually gave way to the luxurious country mansions that pepper the area. And by the 19th century they had become grand country houses built by fashionable architects.

All the main routes between London and Edinburgh traverse the Borders, whose hinterland of undulating pastures, woods, and valleys is enclosed within three lonely groups of hills: the Cheviots, the Moorfoots, and the Lammermuirs. Hamlets and prosperous country towns dot the land, giving valley slopes a lived-in look, yet the total population is still sparse. The sheep that are the basis of the region's prosperous textile industry outnumber human beings by 14 to 1.

To the west is the region of Dumfries and Galloway, on the shores of the Solway Firth. It might appear to be an extension of the Borders, but the southwest has a history all its own. From these ports ships sailed to the Americas, carrying country dwellers driven from their land to make room for the sheep that still roam the hills across southern Scotland. Inland, the earth rises toward high hills, forest, and bleak but captivating moorland, whereas nearer the coast you can find pretty farmlands, small villages, and unassuming towns. The shoreline is washed by the North Atlantic Drift (Scotland's answer to the Gulf Stream), and first-time visitors are always surprised to see palm trees and exotic plants thriving in gardens and parks along the coast.

At the heart of the region is Dumfries, the "Queen o' the South." Once a major port and commercial center, its glamour is now slightly faded. But the memory of poet Robert Burns, who spent many years living and working here and who is buried in the town, burns as bright as ever.

TOP REASONS TO GO

Ancient abbeys: The great abbeys of the Border regions, and the Whithorn Priory and the wonderful Sweetheart Abbey in the Southwest, are in ruins, but they retain hints of their former grandeur.

Walking and cycling: You can walk or bicycle your way across Galloway or through the Borders. Abandoned railway tracks make good paths, and there are forests and moorlands if you prefer wilder country. Most towns have bike-rental shops.

Stately homes and castles: The landed aristocracy still lives in these grand mansions, and most of the homes are open to visitors. Try Floors Castle or the wonderful

Traquair House in the east. Threave, Drumnlarig, and the magical Caerlaverock Castle near Dumfries evoke grander times.

Literary Scotland: The Borders region has enough monuments dedicated to Sir Walter Scott that you could make him a theme of your visit. Abbotsford House, which he built for himself, is unmissable. The poet Robert Burns spent much of his working life in Dumfries.

Things to wear: The sheep you see everywhere explain why so many locals became involved in textile production. Mill shops are abundant, and are well worth a visit for their wonderful woolens.

ORIENTATION AND PLANNING

GETTING ORIENTED

Once a battleground region separating Scotland and England, today the Borders area is a gateway between the two countries. This is a place of upland moors and hills, fertile farmland, and forested river valleys. Yet it also embraces the rugged coastline between Edinburgh and Berwick. It's rustic and peaceful, with century-old textile mills, abbeys, castles, and gardens. The area is a big draw for hikers and walking enthusiasts, too. The Borders region is also steeped in history, with Mary, Queen of Scots, a powerful presence despite the relatively short time she spent here.

The Borders. Borders towns cluster around and between two rivers—the Tweed and its tributary, the Teviot. These are mostly textile towns with plenty of personality, where residents take fierce pride in their local municipalities. The area's top attractions include Jedburgh Abbey, Floors Castle in Kelso, and Abbotsford House just outside Melrose.

Dumfries and Galloway. Easygoing and peaceful, towns in this southwestern region are usually very attractive, with wide streets and colorful buildings. The Solway Firth is a vast nature preserve, and the climate of the west sustains the surprising tropical plants at the Logan Botanic Gardens and the gardens at Threave Castle.

PLANNING

WHEN TO GO

Because many lodgings and some sights are privately owned and shut down from early autumn until early April, the area is less suited to off-season touring than some other parts of Scotland. The best time to visit is between Easter and late September. The region does look magnificent in autumn, especially along the wooded river valleys of the Borders. Late spring is the time to see the rhododendrons in the gardens of Dumfries and Galloway.

PLANNING YOUR TIME

If you are driving north along the A1 toward Edinburgh, take a tour around the prosperous Borders towns. Turn onto the A698 at Berwick-upon-Tweed, which will take you along the Scottish–English border toward Coldstream, and from there to Kelso, Jedburgh, Dryburgh, and Melrose. It's 36 mi from Jedburgh to Peebles, a good place to stay overnight. Another day might begin with a visit to Walter Scott's lovely Abbotsford House, and then some shopping in any of these prosperous towns.

From here, Dumfries and Galloway beckon. Travel east on the A708 to Moffat and across the A74 toward Dumfries. Two days would give you time to explore Burns sites and more in Dumfries. From Dumfries you can visit Sweetheart Abbey (8 mi away), Caerlaverock Castle (9 mi away), and Threave Gardens (20 mi away). Castle Douglas is a good place to stop for lunch. The A710 and A711 take you along the dramatic coastline of the Solway Firth. Farther west along the A75 are the towns of Newton Stewart, Portpatrick, and Glen Trool.

GETTING HERE AND AROUND

AIR TRAVEL

The nearest Scottish airports are at Edinburgh, Glasgow, and Prestwick (outside of Glasgow).

BOAT AND FERRY TRAVEL

P&O European Ferries and Stena Line operate from Larne, in Northern Ireland, to Cairnryan, near Stranraer, several times daily. The crossing takes one hour on the Superstar Express, two hours on other ferries.

Boat and Ferry Contacts P&O European Ferries ☎ 08716/642020 ⊕ *www. poferries.com.* **Stena Line** ☎ 08447/707070 ⊕ *www.stenaline.co.uk.*

BUS TRAVEL

If you're approaching from the south, check with Scottish Citylink, National Express, or First about buses from Edinburgh and Glasgow. In the Borders, Munro's of Jedburgh offers services within the region; Perryman's also has some services in the area. Stagecoach Western is the main bus company serving Dumfries and Galloway.

Bus Contacts First ☎ 08708/727271 ⊕ *www.firstgroup.com.* **Munro's of Jedburgh** ☎ 01835/862253 ⊕ *www.munrosofjedburgh.co.uk.* **National Express** ☎ 08717/818178 ⊕ *www.nationalexpress.com.* **Perryman's Buses** ☎ 01289/308719 ⊕ *www.perrymansbuses.co.uk.* **Scottish City-link** ☎ 0871/266–3333 ⊕ *www.citylink.co.uk.* **Stagecoach Western**

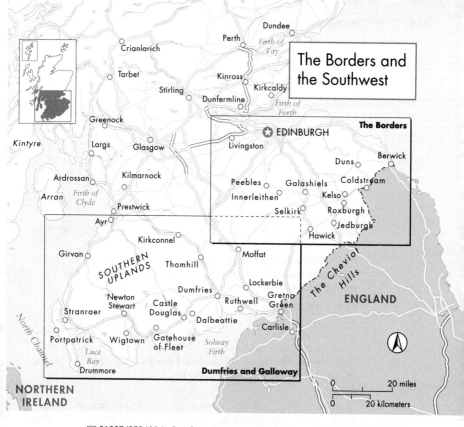

The Borders and the Southwest

☎ 01387/253496 in Dumfries, 01563/525192 in Kilmarnock, 01776/704484 in Stranraer ⊕ www.stagecoachbus.com.

CAR TRAVEL

Traveling by car is the best way to explore the area. The main route into both the Borders and Galloway from the south is the M6, which becomes the M74 at the border. Or take the scenic and leisurely A7 northwestward through Hawick toward Edinburgh, or the A75 and other parallel routes westward into Dumfries, Galloway, and the ferry ports of Stranraer and Cairnryan.

There are, in addition, several other routes: starting from the east, the A1 brings you from the English city of Newcastle to the border in about an hour. The A1 has the added attraction of Berwick-Upon-Tweed, on the English side of the border, but traffic on the route is heavy. Moving west, the A697, which leaves the A1 north of Morpeth (in England) and crosses the border at Coldstream, is a leisurely back-road option. The A68 is probably the most scenic route to Scotland: after climbing to Carter Bar, it reveals a view of the Borders hills and windy skies before dropping into the ancient town of Jedburgh.

The best way to explore the region is to get off the main, and often crowded, arterial roads and onto the little back roads. You may occasionally be delayed by a herd of cows on their way to the milking parlor, or a pheasant fluttering across the road, but this is often far more pleasant than, for example, tussling on the A75 with heavy-goods vehicles rushing to make the Irish ferries.

TRAIN TRAVEL
There is no train service in the Borders, apart from the main east coast London King's Cross–Edinburgh line (although there is a plan to restore the rail network within the next few years). Trains stop at Berwick-Upon-Tweed, just south of the border.

In the southwest, trains headed from London's Euston to Glasgow stop at Carlisle, just south of the border, and some also stop at Lockerbie. Trains between Glasgow and Carlisle stop at Gretna Green, Annan, and Dumfries. From Glasgow, there is service on the coastal route to Stranraer.

First Edinburgh has buses linking Hawick, Selkirk, and Galashiels with train service at Carlisle, Edinburgh, and Berwick.

Train Contacts First Edinburgh ☎ *0131/663–9233, 0871/200–2233* ⊕ *www. firstgroup.com.* **National Rail** ☎ *08457/484950* ⊕ *www.nationalrail.co.uk.* **ScotRail** ☎ *08457/550033* ⊕ *www.scotrail.co.uk.*

RESTAURANTS
In the past, most good restaurants in the region were located in hotels, but today things are changing. Good independent eateries are popping up in small (and sometime unlikely) towns and villages, and many of these new establishments specialize in fresh local ingredients. Seasonal menus are now very popular in the area.

HOTELS
From top-quality, full-service hotels to quaint 18th-century drovers' inns to cozy bed-and-breakfasts, the Borders has all manner of lodging options. Choices in Dumfries and Galloway may be a little less expensive than in the Borders (with the same full range of services). These days many establishments have a shifting scale and are willing to lower their rates depending on availability.

WHAT IT COSTS IN POUNDS				
¢	$	$$	$$$	$$$$
RESTAURANTS under £10	£10–£14	£15–£19	£20–£25	over £25
HOTELS under £70	£70–£120	£121–£160	£161–£220	over £220

Restaurant prices are for a main course at dinner. Hotel prices are for two people in a standard double room in high season, generally including the 20% V.A.T.

VISITOR INFORMATION
The Scottish Borders Tourist Board has offices in Jedburgh, Hawick, and Peebles. The Dumfries & Galloway Tourist Board can be found in Dumfries and Stranraer. Seasonal information centers are at Castle Douglas, Coldstream, Eyemouth, Galashiels, Gretna Green, Kelso, Kirkcudbright, Langholm, Melrose, Moffat, Newton Stewart, Sanquhar, and Selkirk.

Contacts Scottish Borders Tourist Board ✉ *Murray's Green, Jedburgh* ☎ *01835/863170* ⊕ *www.scot-borders.co.uk.* **Dumfries & Galloway Tourist Board** ✉ *64 Whitesands, Dumfries* ☎ *01387/245550* ⊕ *www.visitscotland.com/ dumfries.*

THE BORDERS

Although the Borders has many attractions, it's most famous for being the home base for Sir Walter Scott (1771–1832), the early-19th-century poet, novelist, and creator of *Ivanhoe,* who single-handedly transformed Scotland's image from that of a land of brutal savages to one of romantic and stirring deeds and magnificent landscapes. The novels of Scott are not read much nowadays—frankly, some of them are difficult to wade through—but the mystique that he created, the aura of historical romance, has outlasted his books and is much in evidence in the ruined abbeys, historical houses, and grand vistas of the Borders.

A visit to at least one of the region's four great ruined abbeys makes the quintessential Borders experience. The monks in these powerful, long-abandoned religious orders were the first to work the fleeces of their sheep flocks, thus laying the groundwork for what is still the area's main manufacturing industry.

Borders folk take great pride in the region's fame as Scotland's main woolen-goods manufacturing area. Its main towns—Jedburgh, Hawick, Selkirk, Peebles, Kelso, and Melrose—retain an air of prosperity and confidence with their solid stone houses and elegant town squares. And the pride in local identity is expressed in the fiercely contested Melrose Sevens rugby competition in April and the annual Common Ridings— local events commemorating the time when towns needed to patrol their borders—throughout June and July.

JEDBURGH

50 mi south of Edinburgh, 95 mi southeast of Glasgow, 14 mi northeast of Hawick.

The town of Jedburgh (*-burgh* is always pronounced *burra* in Scots) was for centuries the first major Scottish target of invading English armies. In more peaceful times it developed textile mills, most of which have since languished. The large landscaped area around the town's tourist information center was once a mill but now provides an encampment for the armies of modern tourists. The past still clings to this little town, however. The ruined abbey dominates the skyline, a reminder of the formerly strong governing role of the Borders abbeys.

GETTING HERE AND AROUND

The best and easiest way to travel in this region is by car. From Edinburgh you can take the A68 (about 45 minutes) or the A7 (about an hour). From Glasgow take the M8, then the A68 direct to Jedburgh (about two hours).

There are fairly good bus connections from all major Scottish cities to Jedburgh. From Edinburgh, direct routes to Melrose take about two hours. From Glasgow it takes 3½ hours to reach Melrose. From Melrose it's just 20 minutes to Jedburgh. There is no direct train service. The closest station is in Dumfries.

ESSENTIALS

Visitor Information Jedburgh Visitor Centre ⊠ *Murray's Green* ☎ *01835/863170* ⊕ *www.visitscotland.com/jedburgh.*

EXPLORING

TOP ATTRACTIONS

⟳ **Harestanes Countryside Visitor Centre.** Housed in a former farmhouse 3 mi north of Jedburgh, this visitor center portrays life in the Scottish Borders through changing art exhibitions and interpretive displays on the natural history of the region. Crafts such as woodworking and tilemaking are taught at the center, and finished projects are often on display. There's a gift shop and tearoom, and outside are paths for countryside walks, plus the biggest children's play area in the Borders. The quiet roads are suitable for bicycle excursions. ⊠ *Junction of A68 and B6400, 4 mi north of Jedburgh, Ancrum* ☎ *01835/830306* ▭ *Free* ⊙ *Apr.–Oct., daily 10–5.*

★ **Jedburgh Abbey.** The most impressive of the Borders abbeys towers above Jedburgh. The abbey was nearly destroyed by the English earl of Hertford's forces in 1544–45, during the destructive time known as the Rough Wooing. This was English king Henry VIII's (1491–1547) armed attempt to persuade the Scots that it was a good idea to unite the kingdoms by the marriage of his young son to the infant Mary, Queen of Scots (1542–87); the Scots disagreed and sent Mary to France instead. The full story is explained in vivid detail at the visitor center, which also provides information on interpreting the ruins. Ground patterns and foundations are all that remain of the once-powerful religious complex. ⊠ *High St.* ☎ *01835/863925* ⊕ *www.historic-scotland.gov.uk/ places* ▭ *£5.50* ⊙ *Apr.–Sept., daily 9:30–5; Oct.–Mar., daily 9:30–4:30.*

Mary, Queen of Scots House. This *bastel* (from the French *bastille*) was the fortified town house in which, as the story goes, Mary stayed before embarking on her famous 20-mi ride to Hermitage Castle to visit her wounded lover, the earl of Bothwell (circa 1535–78). Interpretative displays relate the tale and illustrate other episodes in her life. Some of her possessions are also on display, as are tapestries and furniture of the period. The ornamental garden surrounding the house has ranks of pear trees leading down to the river. ⊠ *Queen St.* ☎ *01835/863331* ▭ *Free* ⊙ *Mar.–Nov., Mon.–Sat. 10–4:30, Sun. 11–4.*

WORTH NOTING

OFF THE BEATEN PATH

Hermitage Castle. To appreciate the famous 20-mi ride of Mary, Queen of Scots, to visit her wounded lover, the earl of Bothwell, travel southwest from Jedburgh to this, the most complete remaining example of the bare and grim medieval border castles. Restored in the early 19th century, it was built in the 14th century to guard what was at the time one of the important routes from England into Scotland. The original owner, Lord Soulis, notorious for diabolical excess, was captured by the local populace, who wrapped him in lead and boiled him in a cauldron—or so the tale goes. ⊠ *2 mi west of B6399, about 15 mi south of Hawick, Liddesdale* ☎ *01387/376222* ⊕ *www.historic-scotland.gov.uk/places* ⊠ *£4* ⊙ *Apr.–Sept., daily 9:30–5:30; last admission ½ hr before closing.*

Jedburgh Castle Jail. This was the site of the Howard Reform Prison established in 1820; it sits behind the front of the castle that previously stood in the same spot. Today you can inspect prison cells, rooms arranged with period furnishings, and costumed figures. Audiovisual displays recount the history of the Royal Burgh of Jedburgh. ⊠ *Castlegate* ☎ *01835/864750* ⊠ *Free* ⊙ *Mar.–Oct., Mon.–Sat. 10–4:30, Sun. 1–4; last admission ½ hr before closing.*

Waterloo Monument. From Harestanes Countryside Visitor Centre you can see the Waterloo Monument on the horizon about 3 mi to the northeast. The imposing tower is an enduring reminder of the power of the landowning gentry: a marquis of Lothian built the monument in 1815, with the help of his tenants, in celebration of the victory of Wellington at Waterloo. If you have time, you can walk to the tower from the visitor center in about an hour. ⊠ *Off B6400, 5 mi north of Jedburgh.*

THE COMMON RIDINGS

Borders communities have reestablished their identities through the gatherings known as the Common Ridings. Long ago it was essential that each town be able to defend its area, and this need became formalized in mounted gatherings to "ride the marches," or patrol the boundaries. The Common Ridings, which celebrate this history, possess much more authenticity than the concocted Highland Games, so often taken to be the essence of Scotland. You can watch the excitement of clattering hooves and banners proudly displayed, but this is essentially a time for native Borderers.

WHERE TO EAT

$ × **Cross Keys.** This cozy, traditional pub is a national treasure and is BRITISH full of history (the aerial railway lines that once carried beer from cellar to bar still remain). The kitchen utilizes fresh, local ingredients; ★ salmon, sausages, and lamb are perfectly cooked and come accompanied with a colorful array of seasonal vegetables. Local Broughton Brewery supplies Cross Keys with the finest microbrews this side of the border. This is the quintessential village inn, right down to the green outside the front door. ⊠ *The Green, Ancrum* ☎ *01835/830340* ⊕ *www.ancrumcrosskeys.co.uk.*

$$ × **Vino y Tapas.** Mediterranean colors warm the interior of this Spanish-SPANISH style eatery. The modern tapas menu was inspired by the years that the Scottish owners spent in Spain. The simple and authentic dishes have an occasional dramatic touch, like the "carne de chocolate" (literally, chocolate meat), a beef stew with a touch of chocolate. The tapas are generous, and cost between £5 and £6. There's a good, if modest, wine list. ⊠ *23 Castlegate* ☎ *01835/862380* ⊕ *www.theforrestersrestaurantsb.com* ⊙ *No lunch.*

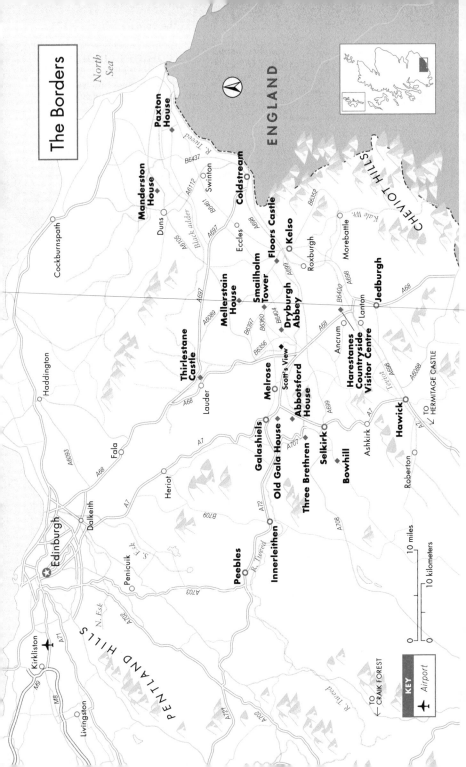

WHERE TO STAY

For expanded hotel reviews, visit Fodors.com.

¢ ⚇ **Hundalee House.** This B&B in an 18th-century manor has richly decorated Victorian-style rooms with nice touches like four-poster beds and
cozy fireplaces. **Pros:** fantastic views of apple orchards; hearty breakfasts with homemade jams and honey; good children's facilities. **Cons:**
farm aromas; far from shops and restaurants. ⊠ *Off A68, 1 mi south of
Jedburgh* ☎ *01835/863011* ⊕ *www.accommodation-scotland.org* ⤶ *5
rooms* ⏧ *In-room: no a/c, Wi-Fi* ⊟ *No credit cards* ⊘ *Closed Christmas,
Jan.–Mar.* ⍩ *Breakfast.*

¢ ⚇ **Meadhon House.** On the medieval row that is Castlegate, Meadhon
House is a charming 17th-century house with a history to match. **Pros:**
central; pleasant rooms; welcoming atmosphere. **Cons:** rooms on the
small side. ⊠ *48 Castlegate* ☎ *01835/862504* ⊕ *www.meadhon.co.uk*
⤶ *5 rooms* ⏧ *In-room: Wi-Fi* ⍩ *Breakfast.*

¢ ⚇ **Spinney Guest House.** A converted farm cottage, this B&B offers simple
but carefully decorated rooms; there are also two one-bedroom wood
cabins that are perfect for couples who like privacy, and a two-bedroom
cabin where three people can sleep comfortably. **Pros:** close to Jedburgh;
plenty of peace and quiet; pristine cabins. **Cons:** nearest restaurant is
2 mi away; dated decor; no Wi-Fi. ⊠ *The Spinney* ☎ *01835/863525*
⊕ *www.thespinney-jedburgh.co.uk* ⤶ *3 rooms, 3 cabins* ⏧ *In-room:
no a/c, kitchen* ⍩ *Breakfast.*

BICYCLING

Christopher Rainbow Tandem & Bike Hire. This company rents tandem
bikes, mountain bikes, and touring bikes. It's on the A698 between
Jedburgh and Ancrum, making it ideal for exploring the four abbeys
as well as the Tweed Cycleway and Borderloop Cycleway. The company provides tour itineraries, as well as extra services such as luggage forwarding. ■TIP➜ **Remember that cars drive on the left side of
the road; this rule applies to cyclists as well.** ⊠ *8 Timpendean Cottages*
☎ *01835/830326.*

SHOPPING

Jedburgh Woollen Mill. This shop has shelves bursting with sweaters,
kilts, tartan knitwear, and scarves. It's a good place to stock up on gifts.
⊠ *Bankend North, Edinburgh Rd.* ☎ *01835/863585.*

Scottish Tradition. The knitwear and hats here are of the finest quality.
Scottish Tradition also sells beautiful cashmere items, as well as Scottish
tartan goods. ⊠ *New Bongate Mill* ☎ *01835/863306* ⊕ *www.cashmere-
in-scotland.com.*

KELSO

12 mi northeast of Jedburgh.

One of the most charming Borders burghs, Kelso is often described
as having a Continental flavor—some people think its broad, paved
square makes it resemble a Belgian market town. The community has
some fine examples of Georgian and Victorian Scots town architecture.

GETTING HERE AND AROUND

There are direct bus routes from Jedburgh to Kelso. Edinburgh has direct buses to Jedburgh; buses from Glasgow aren't direct. Your best option is to travel by car. From Jedburgh to Kelso take the A698, which is 12 mi, or about 20 minutes. Alternatively, the A699 is a scenic half-hour drive.

ESSENTIALS

Visitor Information Kelso ⊠ *The Square* ☎ *01835/863170* ⊕ *www.visitscotland.com.*

EXPLORING

Fodor'sChoice
★
Floors Castle. On the outskirts of Kelso stands the palatial Floors Castle, the largest inhabited castle in Scotland. The ancestral home of the dukes of Roxburghe, Floors is an architectural extravagance bristling with pepper-mill turrets and towers. It stands on the "floors," or flat terrain, on the banks of the River Tweed opposite the barely visible ruins of Roxburghe Castle. The enormous home was built in 1721 by William Adam (1689–1748) and modified by William Playfair (1789–1857), who added the turrets and towers in the 1840s. A holly tree in the deer park marks the place where King James II of Scotland (1430–60) was killed by a cannon that "brak in the shooting." ⊠ *A6089* ☎ *01573/223333* ⊕ *www.floorscastle.com* ⊠ *Grounds £4, castle and grounds £8* ☉ *Mid-Apr.–Oct., daily 11–5; last admission ½ hr before closing.*

Kelso Abbey. The least intact ruin of the four great abbeys, Kelso Abbey is just a bleak fragment of what was once the largest of the group. It was here in 1460 that the nine-year-old James III was crowned king of Scotland. On a main invasion route, the abbey was burned three times in the 1540s alone, on the last occasion by the English earl of Hertford's forces in 1545, when the 100 men and 12 monks of the garrison were butchered and the structure all but destroyed. ⊠ *Bridge St.* ☎ *0131/668–8800* ⊕ *www.kelso.bordernet.co.uk* ⊠ *Free* ☉ *Apr.–Dec., daily 24 hrs.*

Mellerstain House. One fine example of the Borders area's ornate country homes is Mellerstain House. Begun in the 1720s, it was finished in the 1770s by Robert Adam (1728–92) and is considered one of his finest creations. Sumptuous plasterwork covers almost all interior surfaces, and there are outstanding examples of 18th-century furnishings. The beautiful terraced gardens (open an hour before the house itself) are as renowned as the house. ⊠ *Off A6089, 7 mi northwest of Kelso, Gordon,* ☎ *01573/410225* ⊕ *www.mellerstain.com* ⊠ *Gardens £5, house and gardens £8* ☉ *Apr.–Oct., Sun., Mon., and Wed. 12:30–5; last admission ½ hr before closing.*

Smailholm Tower. The characteristic Borders structure Smailholm Tower stands uncompromisingly on top of a barren, rocky ridge in the hills south of Mellerstain. The 16th-century peel was built solely for defense, and its unadorned stones contrast with the luxury of Mellerstain House. If you let your imagination wander in this windy spot, you can almost see the flapping pennants and rising dust of an advancing raiding party and hear the anxious securing of doors and bolts. Sir Walter Scott found this spot inspiring. His grandfather lived nearby, and the young Scott visited the tower often during his childhood. A museum here displays costumed figures and tapestries relating to Scott's Borders folk ballads. A free audio tour is available. ⊠ *Off B6404, 4½ mi south of Mellerstain House* ☎ *01573/460365* ⊕ *www.historic-scotland.gov.uk* 🎫 *£4.50* ⊘ *Apr.–Sept., daily 9:30–5:30; Oct.–Mar., weekends 9:30–4:30; last admission ½ hr before closing.*

WHERE TO EAT AND STAY

For expanded hotel reviews, visit Fodors.com.

¢ ✕ **Cobbles Inn.** A lively bar and restaurant off the town square, Cobbles
BRITISH is much favored by locals. The bar menu is an excellent value, and includes such dishes as breaded pork fillets with perfectly prepared root vegetables in a red wine sauce. The dinner menu features a savory cheesecake starter made with chestnuts and balsamic vinegar, and lamb cutlets with parsnips and artichokes. Desserts are well made and come in generous portions. ⊠ *7 Bowmont St.* ☎ *01573/223548* ⊕ *www. thecobblesinn.co.uk.*

$ ✕ **Oscar's Wine Bar and Restaurant.** Winner of numerous culinary and
MEDITERRANEAN entrepreneurial awards, this establishment is a local favorite. The space is well lit, with bright yellow walls, contemporary furniture, and the work of local artists lining the walls. In season, try the medallions of venison with black pudding or char-grilled monkfish and salmon kebabs. The homemade banoffee pie (with banana, toffee, and cream) is to die for. The staff is attentive and well-informed. ⊠ *35–37 Horsemarket* ☎ *01573/224008* ⊕ *www.oscars-kelso.com.*

$ 🏨 **Edenwater House.** This handsome stone house overlooks Edenwater,
★ a trout stream that runs into the River Tweed. **Pros:** excellent food; romantic atmosphere; peaceful surroundings. **Cons:** not good for families with small children; far from urban amenities. ⊠ *Off B6461, Ednam* ☎ *01573/224070* ⊕ *www.edenwaterhouse.co.uk* 🛏 *4 rooms* ⚘ *In-room: no a/c, Internet. In-hotel: restaurant, bar* ⊘ *Restaurant closed Sun.–Tues.* ⫶⊘⫶ *Breakfast.*

$$ 🏨 **Ednam House Hotel.** People return again and again to this large, stately
★ hotel on the banks of the River Tweed, close to Kelso's grand abbey and sprawling Market Square. **Pros:** great outdoor activities; atmospheric lobby; impressive restaurant. **Cons:** some rooms need a makeover. ⊠ *Bridge St.* ☎ *01573/224168* ⊕ *www.ednamhouse.com* 🛏 *32 rooms* ⚘ *In-room: no a/c. In-hotel: restaurant, bar* ⊘ *Closed late Dec. to early Jan.* ⫶⊘⫶ *Breakfast.*

SHOPPING

John Moody. This shop sells soft cashmere and lambs wool sweaters, along with purses, scarves, and gloves. It's a real treat for knitwear fanatics, or those simply looking for something Scottish to keep them warm. ⊠ *38 The Square* ☎ *01573/224400.*

COLDSTREAM

9 mi east of Kelso.

Three miles west of Coldstream, the England–Scotland border comes down from the hills and runs beside the Tweed for the rest of its journey to the sea. Coldstream itself is still a small town, with a mix of attractive 18th- and 19th-century buildings. Like Gretna Green, this was once a place where runaway couples from the south could come to get married in a time when the marriage laws of Scotland were more lenient than those of England. A plaque on the former bridge tollhouse recalls this fact.

The town is also celebrated in military history: in 1659 General Monck raised a regiment of foot guards here on behalf of his exiled monarch, Charles II of England (1630–85). Known as the Coldstream Guards, the successors to this regiment have become an elite corps in the British army.

GETTING HERE AND AROUND

There is no direct bus service from Jedburgh or Kelso to Coldstream. Your best bet is to drive. From Jedburgh, take the A68/A698/A697 (30 minutes). From Kelso, take the A698 (15 minutes).

ESSENTIALS

Visitor Information Coldstream ⊠ *76 High St.* ☎ *08706/080404* ⊕ *www. visitscottishborders.com.*

EXPLORING

Coldstream Museum. In the Coldstream Guards' former headquarters, the Coldstream Museum examines the history of the regiment and the community. You can see 18th-century marriage contracts, pieces of masonry from the village's lost medieval convent, weapons, uniforms, and photographs. A children's play area has toys and costumes, including a child-size Coldstream Guard uniform and bearskin hat made by the regimental tailor. ⊠ *12 Market Sq.* ☎ *01890/882630* ⊕ *www. scotborders.gov.uk* 🖃 *Free* ☉ *Mar.–Sept., Mon.–Sat. 10–4, Sun. 2–4; Oct., Mon.–Sat. 1–4.*

Hirsel. Dignified houses and gardens line the stretch of the Tweed near Coldstream. The best-known house is the Hirsel, where a complex of farmyard buildings now serves as a crafts center and museum, with interesting walks on the extensive grounds. It's a favorite spot for bird-watchers, and superb rhododendrons bloom here in late spring. The house itself is not open to the public. ⊠ *A697* ☎ *01890/882834* ⊕ *www.hirselcountrypark.co.uk* 🖃 *Free* ☉ *Grounds daily sunrise–sunset; museum and crafts center weekdays 10–5, weekends noon–5.*

OFF THE BEATEN PATH

Manderston House. Built by a family that made its fortune selling herring to Russia, Manderston is a good example of the grand, no-expense-spared Edwardian country house. A Georgian house from the 1790s was completely rebuilt from 1903 to 1905 to the specifications of John Kinross. The silver-plated staircase was modeled after the one in the Petit Trianon, at Versailles. Look for the collection of late-19th- and early-20th-century cookie tins. There's much to see downstairs in the kitchens, and outside, among a cluster of other buildings, is the octagonal, one-of-a-kind marble dairy where lunch, dinner, or afternoon tea can be arranged for groups. You can reach the house by traveling northeast from Coldstream along the A6112 to Duns, then taking the A6105 east. ⊠ *Off A6105, Duns* ☎ *01361/882636* ⊕ *www.manderston.co.uk*

Grounds £5, house and grounds £9 ⊙ Mid-May–Sept., Thurs. and Sun. 1:30–5; last entry 4:15.

OFF THE
BEATEN
PATH

Paxton House. Stately Paxton House is a comely Palladian mansion designed in 1758 by James and John Adam, with interiors designed by their brother Robert. There's Chippendale and Trotter furniture, and the splendid Regency picture gallery, an outstation of the National Galleries of Scotland, has a magnificent collection of paintings. The garden is delightful, with a squirrel hide and a restored boathouse containing a museum of salmon fishing. The adjacent crafts shop and tearoom are open April to October, daily 9 to 5. ⊠ B6461, 15 mi northeast of Coldstream, Paxton ☎ 01289/386291 ⊕ www.paxtonhouse.co.uk ☜ Grounds £4, house and grounds £7.50 ⊙ Apr.–Oct., daily 11–5; last tour at 4.

WHERE TO EAT

$$
BRITISH
★

✕ **Wheatsheaf Hotel and Restaurant.** The Wheatsheaf is a dining establishment that also provides accommodations—an important distinction, according to the owner. You can have an outstanding casual meal in the black-beamed bar, but the real treat is the formal restaurant. Here, the sheer excellence of the Scottish cuisine, whether you order beef, salmon, or venison, has won widespread praise yet neither the food nor the small but carefully chosen wine list is overpriced. Extend your stay in one of the 10 country-style bedrooms; room prices include breakfast and/or dinner. The inn is in Swinton, 6 mi north of Coldstream. ⊠ Main St., Swinton ☎ 01890/860257 ⊕ www.wheatsheaf-swinton.co.uk ⊙ Closed first 2 wks of Jan.

MELROSE

24 mi west of Coldstream, 4 mi southeast of Galashiels.

Though it's small, there is nevertheless a bustle about Melrose, the perfect example of a prosperous Scottish market town and one of the loveliest in the Borders. It's set round a square lined with 18th- and 19th-century buildings housing myriad small shops and cafés. Despite its proximity to the much larger Galashiels, Melrose has rejected industrialization. You'll likely hear local residents greet each other by first name in the square.

GETTING HERE AND AROUND

Buses do go to Melrose. However, driving is the easiest, fastest, and most efficient way to travel here. From Coldstream, take the A699 (40 minutes). From Galashiels, take the A6091 (10 minutes).

ESSENTIALS

Visitor Information Melrose ⊠ Abbey St. ☎ 01896/822283 ⊕ www.visitscottishborders.com.

EXPLORING
TOP ATTRACTIONS

Fodor's Choice
★

Abbotsford House. In 1811 Sir Walter Scott, already an established writer, bought a farm on this site named Cartleyhole, which was a euphemism for the real name, Clartyhole (clarty is Scots for "muddy" or "dirty"). The name was surely not romantic enough for Scott, who renamed the property after a ford in the nearby Tweed used by the abbot of Melrose. Scott eventually had the house entirely rebuilt in the Scots baronial style. The result was called "the most incongruous pile that gentlemanly modernism ever devised" by art critic John Ruskin. That was Mr. Ruskin's idiosyncratic take; most people have found this to be one of the most fetching of all Scottish abodes. It's worth visiting just to feel the atmosphere that the most successful writer of his day created and to see the condition in which he wrote, driving himself to pay off his endless debts. To Abbotsford came most of the famous poets and thinkers of Scott's day, including Wordsworth and Washington Irving. With some 9,000 volumes in the library, Abbotsford is the repository for the writer's collection of Scottish memorabilia and historic artifacts. The house is undergoing a major renovation, slated to be completed by 2013. The lovely gardens will remain open, as will a new visitor center. To get here, take the A6091 from Melrose. ⊠ *B6360, Galashiels* ☎ *01896/752043* ⊕ *www.scottsabbotsford.co.uk* ☙ *£3* ⊗ *Mid-Mar.–Oct., Mon.–Sat. 9:30–5, Sun. 2–5; Nov.–mid-Mar., weekdays by appointment only.*

★ **Melrose Abbey.** Just off the square sit the ruins of Melrose Abbey, one of the four Borders abbeys. "If thou would'st view fair Melrose aright, go visit it in the pale moonlight," wrote Scott in *The Lay of the Last Minstrel*, and so many of his fans took the advice literally that a sleepless custodian begged him to rewrite the lines. Today the abbey is still impressive: a red-sandstone shell with slender windows, delicate tracery, and carved capitals, all carefully maintained. Among the carvings high on the roof is one of a bagpipe-playing pig. An audio tour is included in the admission price. ⊠ *Abbey St.* ☎ *01896/822562* ⊕ *www.historic-scotland.gov.uk* ☙ *£5.50* ⊗ *Apr.–Sept., daily 9:30–5:30; Oct.–Mar., daily 9:30–4:30; last entry ½ hr before closing.*

☺ **Thirlestane Castle.** This large, turreted, and castellated house, part of which was built in the 13th century and part in the 16th century, looks for all the world like a French château, and it brims with history. The former home of the Duke of Lauderdale (1616–82), one of Charles II's advisors, Thirlestane is said to be haunted by the duke's ghost. Exquisite 17th-century plaster ceilings and rich collections of paintings, porcelain, and furniture fill the rooms. In the nursery, children are invited to play with Victorian-style toys and to dress up in masks and costumes. Guided tours are available 11 to 2. ⊠ *Off A68, 9 mi north of Melrose, Lauder* ☎ *01578/722430* ⊕ *www.thirlestanecastle.co.uk* ☙ *£10* ⊗ *Apr.–June and Sept., Wed., Thurs., and Sun. 10–5; July and Aug., Sun.–Thurs. 10–5.*

WORTH NOTING

Dryburgh Abbey. The final resting place of Sir Walter Scott and his wife, and the most peaceful and secluded of the Borders abbeys, the "gentle ruins" of Dryburgh Abbey sit on parkland in a loop of the Tweed. The abbey suffered from English raids until, like Melrose, it was abandoned in 1544. The style is transitional, a mingling of rounded Romanesque and pointed early English. The north transept, where the Haig and Scott families lie buried, is lofty and pillared, and once formed part of the abbey church. ⊠ *B6404* ☎ *01835/822381* ⊕ *www.historic-scotland.*

The World of Sir Walter Scott

Sir Walter Scott (1771–1832) was probably Scottish tourism's best propagandist. Thanks to his fervid "Romantik" imagination, his long narrative poems—such as "The Lady of the Lake"—and a long string of historical novels, including *Ivanhoe, Waverley, Rob Roy, Redgauntlet,* and *The Heart of Midlothian,* the world fell in love with the image of heroic Scotland. Scott wrote of Scotland as a place of Highland wilderness and clan romance, shaping outsiders' perceptions of Scotland in a way that to an extent survives even today.

Scott was born in College Wynd, Edinburgh. A lawyer by training, he was an assiduous collector of old ballads and tales. "The Lay of the Last Minstrel," a romantic poem published in 1805, brought him fame. In 1811 Scott bought the house that was to become Abbotsford, his Borders mansion near Melrose.

Scott started on his series of Waverley novels in 1814, at first anonymously, and by 1820 had produced *Waverley, Guy Mannering, The Antiquary, Tales of My Landlord* (three series), and *Rob Roy.* Between 1820 and 1825

there followed an additional 11 titles, including *Ivanhoe* and *The Pirate.* Many of his verse narratives and novels focused on real-life settings, in particular the Trossachs, northwest of Stirling, an area that rapidly became, and still remains, popular with visitors.

Apart from his writing, Scott is also remembered for rediscovering the Honours of Scotland—the crown, scepter, and sword of state of the Scottish monarchs—in 1819. These symbols had languished at the bottom of a chest in Edinburgh Castle since 1707, when Scotland lost its independence. Today they're on display in the castle.

Abbotsford is under renovation until 2013, but several other houses associated with Scott can be seen in Edinburgh: 25 George Square, which was his father's house, and 39 Castle Street, where he lived from 1801 to 1826. The site of his birthplace, in College Wynd, is marked with a plaque. The most obvious structure associated with Scott in Edinburgh is the Scott Monument on Princes Street, which looks like a Gothic rocket ship with a statue of Scott and his pet dog as passengers.

4

---

gov.uk/places 🔲 *£5* ⊙ *Apr.–Sept., daily 9:30–5:30; Oct.–Mar., daily 9:30–4:30; last entry ½ hr before closing.*

Priorwood Gardens. The National Trust for Scotland's Priorwood Gardens, next to Melrose Abbey, specializes in flowers for drying. Dried flowers are on sale in the shop. Next to the gardens is an orchard with some old apple varieties. The nearby walled Harmony Garden is also included in the entry price. ✉ *Abbey St.* ☎ *0844/493–2257* ⊕ *www.nts. org.uk* 🔲 *£6* ⊙ *Apr.–Oct., Mon.–Sat. 10–5, Sun. 1–5; Nov. and Dec., Mon.–Sat. 10–4.*

Scott's View. This is possibly the most photographed rural view in the south of Scotland. (It's almost as iconic as Eilean Donan Castle, far to the north). The sinuous curve of the River Tweed and the gentle landscape unfolding to the triple peaks of the Eildons are certainly worth seeing. ✉ *B6356, Dryburgh.*

Three Hills Roman Heritage Centre. On exhibit here are such artifacts as tools, weapons, and armor retrieved from the largest Roman settlement in Scotland, which was at nearby Newstead. A blacksmith's shop, several examples of pottery, and scale models of the fort are also on display. A guided four-hour walk along the 5-mi trail to the site departs at 1:30 on Thursday (also on Tuesday in July and August). The cost is £3. ⊠ *The Ormiston, Market Sq.* ☎ *01896/822651* ⊕ *www.trimontium. org.uk/wb* 🖃 *£2* ☉ *Apr.–Oct., daily 10:30–4:30.*

WHERE TO EAT AND STAY
For expanded hotel reviews, visit Fodors.com.

$$ ✕ **Hoebridge Inn.** Whitewashed walls, oak-beamed ceilings, and an open
BRITISH   fire welcome you into this converted 19th-century bobbin mill. The cui-
Fodor'sChoice sine is a blend of British and Mediterranean styles with occasional Asian
★   influences. You might have lamb served with rosemary mashed pota-
toes and red-currant sauce or panfried tiger prawns with chili and lime syrup, accompanied by a salad of bean sprouts and *mangetout* (peas in their edible pods). The inn lies in Gattonside, Melrose's across-the-river neighbor, but a 2-mi drive is required to cross to the other side; you can reach the inn more easily via a footbridge. ⊠ *B6360, Gattonside* ☎ *01896/823082* ☉ *Closed Mon. No dinner Sun.*

$$ 🛏 **Burts Hotel.** This charming whitewashed building dating from the 18th century sits in the center of Melrose. **Pros:** walking distance to restaurants and pubs; good menu in restaurant. **Cons:** some rooms are tiny; bland room decor. ⊠ *Market Sq.* ☎ *01896/822285* ⊕ *www.burtshotel. co.uk* 🛏 *20 rooms* ☖ *In-room: no a/c, Wi-Fi. In-hotel: restaurant, bar* ⦿| *Breakfast.*

$$ 🛏 **Dryburgh Abbey Hotel.** Mature woodlands and verdant lawns surround this imposing, 19th-century mansion, which is adjacent to the abbey ruins on a sweeping bend of the River Tweed. **Pros:** beautiful grounds; romantic setting. **Cons:** some rooms need to be freshened up; service can be on the slow side; not much nightlife. ⊠ *Off B6404, St. Boswells* ☎ *01835/822261* ⊕ *www.dryburgh.co.uk* 🛏 *36 rooms, 2 suites* ☖ *In-room: no a/c, Wi-Fi. In-hotel: restaurant, pool* ⦿| *Breakfast.*

THE ARTS
Wynd Theatre. The Wynd Theatre has a monthly program of four nights of drama from national touring companies, two concerts of folk, blues, jazz, or classical from touring national and international companies, plus screenings of classic films on two Fridays. There's an art gallery highlighting top contemporary Scottish artists. Tickets cost £10 to £12 for performances or £5 to £7 for films. ⊠ *3 Buccleuch St.* ☎ *01896/823854.*

SHOPPING
Abbey Mill. Take a break from sightseeing at Abbey Mill, where you'll find hand-woven knitwear as well as homemade jams and fudge. There's also a wee tearoom. ⊠ *Annay Rd.* ☎ *01896/822138.*

GALASHIELS

5 mi northwest of Melrose.

A busy gray-stone Borders town, Galashiels is still active with textile mills and knitwear factories (be aware that these mills and factories do not offer tours or have visitor centers or shops).

GETTING HERE AND AROUND

There is regular bus service from Melrose to Galashiels (20 minutes). You can also drive; from Melrose, take the B6374 or the A6091 (both 10 minutes).

EXPLORING

Old Gala House. Dating from 1583, Old Gala House is the former home of the lairds (landed proprietors) of Galashiels. It now serves as a museum with displays on the building's history and the town of Galashiels, as well as a contemporary art gallery. You can trace your family history at a comprehensive genealogy facility. The house is a short walk from the town center. ⊠ *Scott Crescent* ☎ *01896/75611* ⊕ *www.galashiels.bordernet.co.uk/oldgalahouse* ◩ *Free* ⊙ *Apr.–Sept., Tues.–Sat. 10–4; July–Aug., Mon.–Sat. 10–4, Sun. 2–4; Oct., Tues.–Sat. 1–4.*

SHOPPING

Books Plus. A fun place to get lost is Books Plus, which carries all forms of literature (from rare books to current best-sellers), as well as toys and art supplies. ⊠ *2 Channel St.* ☎ *01896/752843.*

SELKIRK

6 mi southwest of Galashiels, 11 mi north of Hawick.

Selkirk is a hilly outpost with a smattering of antiques shops and an assortment of bakers selling Selkirk bannock (fruited sweet bread) and other cakes. It is the site of one of Scotland's iconic battles, Flodden Field, commemorated here with a statue in the town. Sir Walter Scott was sheriff (judge) of Selkirkshire from 1800 until his death in 1832, and his statue stands in Market Place. The town is also near Bowhill, a stately home.

GETTING HERE AND AROUND

If you're driving, take the A7 south to Galashiels. The scenic journey is less than 7 mi and takes around 10 minutes. First Edinburgh Bus offers a regular service between Galashiels and Selkirk.

ESSENTIALS

Visitor Information Selkirk ⊠ *Halliwell's House, Market Pl.* ☎ *08706/080404* ⊕ *www.visitscotland.com.*

EXPLORING

Bowhill. One of the stately homes in the Borders, and home of the Duke of Buccleuch, Bowhill dates from the 19th century and houses an outstanding collection of works by Gainsborough, Van Dyck, Canaletto, Reynolds, and Raeburn, as well as porcelain and period furniture. The house itself is open only in July and August; the grounds have slightly more friendly hours. A combined pass for Bowhill and Abbotsford is available for £12. ⊠ *Off A708, 3 mi west of Selkirk* ☎ *01750/22204* ⊕ *www.bowhill.org* 🖾 *Grounds £3.50, house and grounds £8* ⊘ *House: July, daily 11–5; Aug., daily 2–3:30. Grounds: May and June, weekends 11–4; July and Aug., daily 10–5.*

Halliwell's House Museum. Tucked off the main square, Halliwell's House Museum was once an ironmonger's shop, which is now re-created downstairs. Upstairs, an exhibit tells the town's tale, with useful background information on the Common Ridings. ⊠ *Market Pl.* ☎ *01750/720096* ⊕ *www.scotborders.gov.uk* 🖾 *Free* ⊘ *Apr.–June and Sept., Mon.–Sat. 10–5, Sun. 10–noon; July and Aug., Mon.–Sat. 10–5:30, Sun. 10–noon; Oct., Mon.–Sat. 10–4.*

Lochcarron of Scotland Cashmere and Wool Centre. Love tartans and tweeds? The Lochcarron of Scotland Cashmere and Wool Centre houses a museum where you can tour a mill and learn about the manufacturing process. ⊠ *Waverley Mill, Dinsdale Rd.* ☎ *01750/726000* ⊕ *www.lochcarron.com* 🖾 *Museum free, tour £2.50* ⊘ *Mon.–Sat. 9–5. Guided tours Mon.–Thurs. at 10:30, 11:30, 1:30, and 2:30.*

Philiphaugh Salmon Centre. The site of a famous battle in 1645 in which the Scottish Covenanters drove off the pro-English armies under the Earl of Montrose, the Philiphaugh Salmon Centre is now devoted to more peaceful pursuits. Its salmon-viewing platforms allow you to follow the life cycle of the salmon. There are also country walks and cycling routes to follow on the estate, and the Waterwheel Tea Room is open all year. ⊠ *A708* ☎ *01750/21766* ⊕ *www.salmonviewingcentre.com* 🖾 *Free* ⊘ *Daily 10–4.*

Sir Walter Scott's Courtroom. The historic courtroom, where Sir Walter Scott presided as sheriff from 1804–32, contains a display examining his life, writings, and time on the bench. It includes an audiovisual presentation. ⊠ *Market Sq.* ☎ *01750/720096* ⊕ *www.scotborders.gov.uk* 🖾 *Free* ⊘ *Mar. and Apr., weekdays 10–4, Sat. 11–3; May–Sept., Mon.–Sat. 11–3; Oct., Mon.–Sat. noon–3.*

WHERE TO EAT AND STAY

For expanded hotel reviews, visit Fodors.com.

¢   ✕ **Court Coffee Shop.** This modest, old-fashioned café serves house-made
CAFÉ   soup, tasty scones, and locally made cakes on floral crockery. It sits beside Selkirk's Old Court House. ⊠ *28 Market St.* ☎ *01750/21766.*

$$ 🏨 **Best Western Philipburn House Hotel.** West of Selkirk, this alpine-style hotel enjoys a lovely setting among the woods and hills. **Pros:** pleasant rural setting; bright rooms; on-site parking. **Cons:** no elevator; restaurant closes rather early. ⊠ *Off A708* ☎ *01750/20747* ⊕ *www.philipburnhousehotel.co.uk* 🛏 *12 rooms, 4 lodges* ⚒ *In-room: Wi-Fi. In-hotel: restaurant, bar* ⦿ *Breakfast.*

SHOPPING

Waverly Mill. You can take an informative tour of this world-renowned mill and also purchase some of the best woolen goods on offer, from knitwear to tartans and tweeds. The shop also sells Scottish jewelry. ⊠ *Dinsdale Rd.* ☎ *01750/726100.*

HAWICK

10 mi south of Selkirk, 14 mi southwest of Jedburgh.

Hawick (pronounced *hoyk*) is a busy town at the center of the region's textile industry, commemorated in the interesting Borders Textile Towerhouse. The Victorian buildings along its High Street recall the town's heyday. The largest community in the Borders, it's a good place to buy the delicate cashmere and wool goods that made the region famous. Hawick's Common Riding festival, held each June, draws onlookers from all over Scotland.

GETTING HERE AND AROUND

Driving here from Selkirk or Jedburgh is no trouble—it's a straight shot on major roads. There is also bus service from many of the other Borders towns.

ESSENTIALS

Visitor Information Hawick Visitor Centre ⊠ *Kirkstyle* ☎ *01450/373993* ⊕ *www.visitscotland.com.*

EXPLORING

Borders Textile Towerhouse. This museum in the former Drumlanrig Tower at the southern end of High Street in Hawick includes a good exhibition about the textile industry, once the lifeblood of the Borders, but brings it up to the present. Plenty of interactive elements make it interesting for children as well. One room commemorates the demonstrations by textile workers who were demanding the right to vote in the 1880s. On the upper floor are up-to-the-minute fabrics that define the 21st century. Check out the shop, too. ⊠ *1 Tower Knowe* ☎ *01450/377615* ⊕ *www.heartofhawick.co.uk* ✉ *Free* ⊙ *Apr.–Oct., Mon.–Sat. 10–4:30, Sun. noon–3; Nov.–Mar., Mon. and Wed.–Sat. 10–4.*

WHERE TO EAT

CAFÉ **✕ Damascus Drum.** This lovely café and bookshop was established as a place to talk, tell stories, and buy beautiful Oriental rugs. The café's name comes from a traditional folktale, and the menu includes some Middle Eastern dishes like baba ghanoush. ⊠ *2 Silver St.* ☎ *07707/856123* ⊕ *www.damascusdrum.co.uk.*

SHOPPING

Hawick Factory Visitor Centre. This is a good place to see knitwear in the making—literally. In the shop you can buy Hawick knitwear and cashmere goods for discounted prices. ⊠ *Arthur St.* ☎ *01450/371221* ⊕ *www.hawickcashmere.com.*

White of Hawick. There's a room here exclusively dedicated to cashmere, and it's a good place to stock up on warm outerwear. White of Hawick also sells an extensive range of lambswool and knitted garments. ⊠ *Victoria Rd.* ☎ *01450/373206* ⊕ *www.whiteofhawick.co.uk.*

INNERLEITHEN

17 mi northwest of Hawick.

Innerleithen is one of the larger Borders towns; you'll feel like you've entered a hub of activity when you arrive. It's also dramatically beautiful. Surrounded by hills and glens, the town is where the Tweed and Leithen rivers join then separate. Historically, Innerleithen dates back to pre-Roman times, and there are artifacts all around for you to see. Once a booming industrialized town of wool mills, today it's a great destination for outdoor activities including hiking, biking, and fly-fishing.

GETTING HERE AND AROUND
To drive to Innerleithen, take the A7 north from Hawick and then the A707 northwest from Selkirk. There are no trains between the two towns.

EXPLORING
⟳ **Robert Smail's Printing Works.** A popular reason to come to Innerleithen is to see this printing works. The fully operational, restored print shop with a reconstructed waterwheel fascinates adults and older children, who can try their hand at old-fashioned typesetting. ⊠ *7–9 High St.* ☎ *01896/830206* ⊕ *www.nts.org.uk/Visits* ⊡ *£6* ⊙ *Apr.–Oct., Thurs.–Mon. noon–5, Sun. 1–5; last admission at 4:15.*

Fodor's Choice **Traquair House.** Near the town of Innerleithen stands Traquair House,
★ said to be the oldest continually occupied home in Scotland. Inside you're free to discover secret stairways, more than 3,000 books, secret passageways, and a bed used by Mary, Queen of Scots, in 1566. Outside there is a maze and extensive grounds and gardens.The 18th-century brew house still makes highly recommended ale. You may even spend the night, if you wish. Traquair Fair in August is a major event in the regional calendar. ⊠ *B709* ☎ *01896/830323* ⊕ *www.traquair.co.uk* ⊡ *Grounds £4, house and grounds £7.60* ⊙ *Apr., May, and Sept. daily noon–5; June–Aug., daily 10:30–5; Oct., daily 11–4; Nov., weekends 11–3; last admission ½ hr before closing.*

WHERE TO STAY
For expanded hotel reviews, visit Fodors.com.

$$$ ⊞ **Traquair House.** To stay in one of the guest rooms in the 12th-century part of Traquair House is to experience a slice of Scottish history. **Pros:** stunning grounds; spacious rooms; great breakfast. **Cons:** nearly 2 mi to restaurants and shops; rooms fill up quickly in summer. ⊠ *B709* ☎ *01896/830323* ⊕ *www.traquair.co.uk* ⇔ *3 rooms* ⌂ *In-room: no a/c* ⦿| *Breakfast.*

PEEBLES

6 mi west of Innerleithen.

Thanks to its excellent though pricey shopping, Peebles gives the impression of catering primarily to leisured country gentlefolk. Architecturally, the town is nothing out of the ordinary, just a very pleasant burgh. Don't miss the splendid dolphins ornamenting the bridge crossing the River Tweed.

GETTING HERE AND AROUND

Because of its size and location, direct buses run from both Edinburgh and Glasgow to Peebles. There are also buses here from Innerleithen, though driving from here is more direct. (Take the A72; it's about a 10-minute drive.)

ESSENTIALS

Visitor Information Peebles Visitor Information Centre ⊠ *23 High St.* ☎ *01721/723159* ⊕ *www.scot-borders.co.uk.*

EXPLORING

Neidpath Castle. A 15-minute walk upstream along the banks of the Tweed, Neidpath Castle perches artistically above a bend in the river. It comes into view as you approach through the tall trees. The castle is a medieval structure remodeled in the 17th century, with dungeons hewn from solid rock. You can return on the opposite riverbank after crossing an old, finely skewed railroad viaduct. ⊠ *Off A72* ☎ *01875/870201* ⊕ *www.discovertheborders.co.uk* 🎟 *£3* ⊙ *May–Sept., Mon.–Sat. 10:30–5, Sun. 12:30–5; last admission ½ hr before closing.*

Peebles War Memorial. The exotic, almost Moorish mosaics of the Peebles War Memorial are unique in Scotland, although most towns have a memorial to honor those killed in service. It's a remarkable tribute to the 225 Peebleans killed in World War II. ⊠ *Chambers Quadrangle, High St.*

WHERE TO EAT

$$$
FRENCH
✕ **Bardoulet's Restaurant.** The color theme here is gold, and the inviting dining room has large gold-framed mirrors and heavy hanging drapes. A lot of care is put into the classic French food, which consists of local ingredients with rich sauces, perfectly presented. Scottish lobster and Jersey potato salad and Gressingham duck breast with eggplant and foie gras are good choices, and crispy haggis with caramelized apple puree, sweet-potato gratin, and whisky sauce is a real treat. The set menu is £40 for four courses. The bar-bistro also has top-notch food, and the prices are a little easier to swallow (about £10 cheaper per entrée). ⊠ *The Horseshoe Inn, A703, Eddleston* ☎ *01721/730225* ⊕ *www.horseshoeinn.co.uk.*

$
ECLECTIC
✕ **The Sunflower Restaurant.** Quaint and bright, this unique little café has something for everyone. It serves fresh in-house baked breads, and uses only local meats, vegetables, and dairy products. The owner puts a lot of love into her cooking, whether it's breakfast, lunch, or dinner. The Thai fish cakes with coriander salad and lemon sauce are full of flavor, as is the Moroccan lamb with couscous. Oatcakes and homemade

chutney are a light and unusual way to end your meal. ⊠ *4 Bridgegate* ☎ *01721/722420* ☾ *Closed Sun. No dinner Mon.–Wed.*

WHERE TO STAY
For expanded hotel reviews, visit Fodors.com.

$$ 🛏 **Cringletie House.** With medieval-style turrets and crow-step gables, this
★   small-scale, peaceful retreat manages to be fancy *and* homey, Victorian (it was built in the 1860s) and modern (flat-screen TVs). **Pros:** elegant bedrooms; cozy fireplaces; decadent dining. **Cons:** some bedrooms have low ceilings; atmosphere can be almost too quiet. ⊠ *Edinburgh Rd., off A703* ☎ *01721/725750* ⊕ *www.cringletie.com* ⇝ *13 rooms* ☖ *In-room: no a/c, Wi-Fi. In-hotel: restaurant, bar, some pets allowed* ⦿ *Breakfast.*

$$ 🛏 **Park Hotel.** An intimate retreat on the banks of the River Tweed at the northern tip of the Ettrick Forest, the Park Hotel offers tranquil surroundings and airy, modern rooms. **Pros:** homey feel; great views of golf course; complimentary sherry upon arrival. **Cons:** needs to be redecorated; some rooms have a slight doggy smell. ⊠ *Innerleithen Rd.* ☎ *01721/720451* ⊕ *www.parkpeebles.co.uk* ⇝ *24 rooms* ☖ *In-room: no a/c, Wi-Fi. In-hotel: restaurant, bar, some pets allowed* ⦿ *Breakfast.*

$$$$ 🛏 **Peebles Hydro.** One of the great "hydro hotels" built in the 19th century for those anxious to "take the waters," Peebles Hydro has something for everyone, and in abundance: pony rides, a putting green, and a giant chess game are just a few of the diversions. **Pros:** plenty of activities; good children's programs; delicious breakfast. **Cons:** can feel impersonal; some rooms have bland decor; reception area in need of a makeover. ⊠ *Innerleithen Rd.* ☎ *01721/720602* ⊕ *www. peebleshotelhydro.com* ⇝ *132 rooms* ☖ *In-room: no a/c, Wi-Fi. In-hotel: restaurant, bar, pool, tennis court, gym, children's programs* ⦿ *All-inclusive.*

SHOPPING
Be prepared for temptations at every turn as you browse the shops on High Street and in the courts and side streets leading off it.

Caledonia. For all things Scottish, look no further than Caledonia, where you'll find everything from kilts to throws, and jams to tablecloths. ⊠ *61 High St.* ☎ *01721/722343.*

Head to Toe. This shop stocks natural beauty products, handmade pine furniture, and handsome linens—from patchwork quilts to silk flowers. ⊠ *43 High St.* ☎ *01721/722752.*

Keith Walter. Among the many jewelers on High Street is Keith Walter, a gold- and silversmith who makes items on the premises. He also stocks jewelry made by other local designers. ⊠ *28 High St.* ☎ *01721/720650.*

DUMFRIES AND GALLOWAY

Galloway covers the southwestern portion of Scotland, west of the main town of Dumfries. Here a gentle coastline gives way to farmland and then breezy uplands that gradually merge with coniferous forests. Use caution when negotiating the A75—you're liable to find aggressive trucks bearing down on you as these commercial vehicles race for the ferries at Stranraer and Cairnryan. Things are far more relaxed once you leave the main highway; take the coastal A710/A711 instead. Dumfries and Galloway offer some of the most pleasant drives in Scotland—though the occasional herd of cows on the way to be milked is a potential hazard.

GRETNA GREEN

10 mi north of Carlisle, 87 mi south of Glasgow, 92 mi southwest of Edinburgh.

GETTING HERE AND AROUND
From Glasgow you can reach Gretna Green via the M74 and A74; it's an hour-and-a-half drive. From Edinburgh, take the A74 (about two hours). Buses and trains travel to Gretna Green from Glasgow and Edinburgh daily.

ESSENTIALS
Visitor Information Gretna Green/Ruthwell ⊠ *Gretna Gateway Outlet Village, Glasgow Rd.* ☎ *01461/337834* ⊕ *www.visitdumfriesandgalloway.co.uk.*

EXPLORING
Gretna Green. Gretna Green is tied to the reputation this community developed as a refuge for runaway couples from England, who once came north to take advantage of Scotland's more lenient marriage laws. This was the first place they reached on crossing the border. At one time anyone could perform a legal marriage in Scotland, and the village blacksmith (known as the "anvil priest") did the honors in Gretna Green. The blacksmith's shop is still standing, and today it contains a collection of blacksmithing tools, including the anvil over which many weddings were conducted. The town is highly commercialized rather than atmospheric, though, with plenty of shops.

RUTHWELL

21 mi west of Gretna Green, 83 mi south of Glasgow, 88 mi southwest of Edinburgh.

North of the upper Solway Firth the countryside is flat, fertile farmland. Progressing west, however, a pleasant landscape of low, round hills begins to take over. But there are historical features among the flatlands that should not be ignored.

GETTING HERE AND AROUND
There is no train station in Ruthwell; however, buses—both local and national—do frequent the town. But the best way to get here is via car. From Glasgow, take the M74 then A74; the trip is just under two hours. From Edinburgh take the A74; your journey will take just over two hours. Gretna Green is just under a half hour away via the A75.

EXPLORING
Fodor's Choice ★ **Caerlaverock Castle.** The stunningly beautiful moated Caerlaverock Castle stands in splendid isolation amid the surrounding wetlands that form the Caerlaverock Nature Reserve. It's a pretty 7-mi drive from Ruthwell. Built in a unique triangular design, this 13th-century fortress

4

has solid-sandstone masonry and an imposing double-tower gatehouse. King Edward I of England (1239–1307) besieged the castle in 1300, when his forces occupied much of Scotland at the start of the Wars of Independence. A spendid residence was built inside in the 1600s. ⊠ *Off B725, 8 mi southeast of Dumfries* ☎ *01387/770244* ⊕ *www. historic-scotland.gov.uk/places* ▤ *£5.50* ⊗ *Apr.–Sept., daily 9:30–5:30; Oct.–Mar., daily 9:30–4:30.*

Caerlaverock Wildfowl and Wetlands Centre. You can observe wintering wildfowl, including various species of geese, ducks, swans, and raptors. Free guided walks are available in the afternoons throughout the year. ⊠ *Eastpark Farm, off B725, Dumfries* ☎ *01387/770200* ▤ *Free* ⊗ *Daily 24 hrs.*

Ruthwell Parish Church. Inside Ruthwell Parish Church is the 8th-century Ruthwell Runic Cross, a Christian sculpture admired for the detailed biblical scenes carved onto its north and south faces. The east and west faces have carvings of vines, birds, and animals, plus verses from an Anglo-Saxon poem called "The Dream of the Rood." Considered an idolatrous monument, it was removed and demolished by Church of Scotland zealots in 1642 but was later reassembled. The church is at the end Kirklands Loaning, in Ruthwell village. ⊠ *Northern end of Kirklands Loaning* ☎ *No phone.*

DUMFRIES

15 mi northwest of Ruthwell, 76 mi south of Glasgow, 81 mi southwest of Edinburgh.

The River Nith meanders through Dumfries, and the pedestrian-only town center makes wandering and shopping a pleasure. Author J. M. Barrie (1860–1937) spent his childhood in Dumfries, and the garden of Moat Brae House is said to have inspired his boyish dreams in *Peter Pan*. But the town also has a justified claim to Robert Burns, who lived and worked here for several years. His house and his favorite *howff* (pub), The Globe Inn, are here too, as is his final resting place in St Michael's Churchyard.

The Dumfries & Galloway Tourist Board has a lodging service, and also sells golf passes for the region at £120 for six rounds.

GETTING HERE AND AROUND

Public transportation is a good option for reaching Dumfries—there's a good train station here, and most major Scottish cities have regular daily bus routes to the town. If you're driving from Ruthwell, take the B724 (15 mi). From Glasgow, take the M74 then A701 (76 mi). From Edinburgh, take the A701 (81 mi).

ESSENTIALS

Visitor Information Dumfries & Galloway Tourist Board ⊠ *64 Whitesands* ☎ *01387/245550* ⊕ *www.visitdumfriesandgalloway.co.uk.*

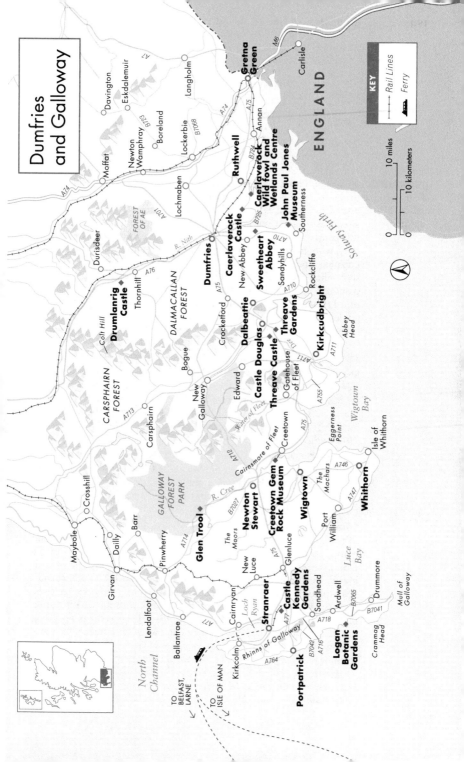

Dumfries and Galloway

KEY
━━ *Rail Lines*
⛴ *Ferry*

10 miles
10 kilometers

ENGLAND

Carlisle

Gretna Green

M6

A74

A7

Eskdalemuir

Davington

Langholm

Boreland

B723

Newton Wamphray

Moffat

Lockerbie

B7068

Lochmaben

Durisdeer

FOREST OF AE

A701

R. Nith

A74

A75

B722

Annan

Ruthwell

Caerlaverock Wild fowl and Wetlands Centre

John Paul Jones Museum

Southerness

Sandyhills

Solway Firth

Coh Hill

Thornhill

A76

Drumlanrig Castle

DALMACALLAN FOREST

Bogue

New Galloway

Crocketford

Dumfries

New Abbey Road

B725

Caerlaverock Castle

Sweetheart Abbey

A710

Rockcliffe

Abbey Head

Dalbeattie

Castle Douglas

Threave Castle

Threave Gardens

Gatehouse of Fleet

Kirkcudbright

A711

A755

CARSPHAIRN FOREST

A713

Carsphairn

Crosshill

Barr

Edward

Water of Fleet

Cairnsmore of Fleet

A712

Creetown

A75

Eggerness Point

Wigtown Bay

Isle of Whithorn

GALLOWAY FOREST PARK

A714

Glen Trool

R. Cree

B7027

The Moors

Newton Stewart

Creetown Gem Rock Museum

Wigtown

The Machars

A746

A747

Whithorn

Port William

Maybole

Dailly

Pinwherry

Girvan

Lendalfoot

Ballantrae

North Channel

A77

New Luce

Glenluce

A75

Stranraer

Cairnryan

Loch Ryan

Kirkcolm

Castle Kennedy Gardens

Sandhead

A718

Ardwell

B7065

Luce Bay

Drummore

Mull of Galloway

Cranmag Head

Rhinns of Galloway

Portpatrick

A764

B7042

A716

Logan Botanic Gardens

Crammag Head

TO BELFAST, LARNE

TO ISLE OF MAN

EXPLORING
TOP ATTRACTIONS

Burns House. Poet Robert Burns lived here, on what was then called Mill Street, for the last three years of his life, when his salary from the customs service allowed him to improve his living standards. Many distinguished writers of the day visited him here, including William Wordsworth. The house contains some of his writings and letters, some furniture, and some family memorabilia. ✉ *Burns St.* ☎ *01387/255297* ⊕ *www.dumgal.gov.uk/museums* ✉ *Free* ⊙ *Apr.–Sept., Mon.–Sat. 10–5, Sun. 2–5; Oct.–Mar., Tues.–Sat. 10–1 and 2–5.*

OFF THE BEATEN PATH

Drumlanrig Castle. This spectacular estate is as close as Scotland gets to the treasure houses of England—which is not surprising, since it's owned by the dukes of Buccleuch, one of the wealthiest British peerages. Resplendent with romantic turrets, this pink-sandstone palace was constructed between 1679 and 1691 by the first Duke of Queensbury, who, after nearly bankrupting himself building the place, stayed one night and never returned. The Buccleuchs inherited the palace and soon filled the richly decorated rooms with a valuable collection of paintings by Holbein, Rembrandt, and Murillo. Because of the theft of a Leonardo da Vinci painting in 2003, all visits are conducted by guided tour. There's also a playground, a gift shop, and a tearoom. The house is about 18 mi northwest of Dumfries. ✉ *Off A76, Thornhill* ☎ *01848/600283* ⊕ *www.drumlanrig.com* ✉ *Park £5, castle and park £9* ⊙ *Grounds Apr.–Sept., daily 10–5. Castle Apr.–Aug., daily 11–4.*

Robert Burns Centre. Not surprisingly, Dumfries has its own Robert Burns Centre, housed in a sturdy former mill overlooking the river. The center has an audiovisual program and an extensive exhibit on the life of the poet. There's a restaurant upstairs. ✉ *Mill Rd.* ☎ *01387/264808* ✉ *Free* ⊙ *Apr.–Sept., Mon.–Sat. 10–5, Sun. 2–5; Oct.–Mar., Tues.–Sat. 10–1 and 2–5.*

St. Michael's Churchyard. When he died in 1796, poet Robert Burns was buried in a modest grave in St. Michael's Churchyard. English poet William Wordsworth, visiting a few years later, was horrified by the small gravestone and raised money to build the present, much grander, monument. ✉ *39 Cardiness St.* ☎ *01387/253849.*

Sweetheart Abbey. At the center of the village of New Abbey, 7 mi south of Dumfries, is the red-tinted and roofless Sweetheart Abbey. The odd name is a translation of the abbey's previous name, St. Mary of the Dolce Coeur. The abbey was founded in 1273 by the Lady of Galloway, Devorgilla (1210–90), who, it is said, had her late husband's heart placed in a tiny casket that she carried everywhere. After she died, she was laid to rest in Sweetheart Abbey with the casket resting on her breast. The couple's son John (1249–1315) was the puppet king installed in Scotland by Edward of England when the latter claimed sovereignty over Scotland. After John's appointment the Scots gave him a scathing nickname that would stay with him for the rest of his life: Toom Tabard (Empty Shirt). ✉ *A710, New Abbey* ☎ *01387/253849* ⊕ *www. historic-scotland.com* ✉ *£4* ⊙ *Apr.–Sept., daily 9:30–5:30; Oct., daily 9:30–4:30; Nov.–Mar., Mon.–Wed. and weekends 9:30–4:30.*

WORTH NOTING

Dumfries Museum and Camera Obscura. A camera obscura is essentially a huge reflecting mirror that projects an extraordinarily clear panoramic view of the surrounding countryside on an internal wall. The one at the Dumfries Museum is housed in the old Windmill Tower, built in 1836. The museum itself covers the culture and daily life of the people living in the Dumfries and Galloway region. ⊠ *Rotchell Rd.* ☎ *01387/253374* 🖃 *Museum Free; Camera Obscura £2.40* ⊘ *Apr.–Sept., Mon.–Sat. 10–5; Oct.–Mar., Tues.–Sat. 10–1 and 2–5.*

Globe Inn. Poet Robert Burns spent quite a lot of time at the Globe Inn, where he frequently fell asleep in the tack room beside the stables. He later graduated to the upstairs bedroom where he slept with his wife, Jean Armour, and scratched some lines of poetry on the window. The room is preserved (or at least partly re-created) and the staff will happily show you around if you ask. ⊠ *56 High St.* ☎ *01387/252335* ⊕ *www. globeinndumfries.co.uk.*

John Paul Jones Museum. The little community of Kirkbean (blink and you'll miss it), 12 mi south of Dumfries, is the backdrop for Arbigland Estate. It was in a cottage, now the John Paul Jones Museum, in this bright green landscape that John Paul (1747–92), the son of an estate gardener, was born. He eventually left Scotland, added "Jones" to his name, and became the founder of the U.S. Navy. The cottage where he was born is furnished as it would have been when he was a boy. Jones returned to raid the coastline of his native country in 1778, an exploit recounted in an adjoining visitor center. ⊠ *Off A710, Kirkbean* ☎ *01387/880613* 🖃 *£2.50* ⊘ *Apr.–June and Sept., Tues.–Sun. 10–5; July and Aug., daily 10–5.*

WHERE TO EAT AND STAY

For expanded hotel reviews, visit Fodors.com.

$ | ECLECTIC | ✕ **Cavens Arms.** This lively, welcoming, traditional pub has a separate bar and dining area, comfortable seating, and a large selection of beers. The restaurant seems to always be busy, a testimony to the quality of its food (as well as the large portions). As for favorite dishes, grilled pork loin with fruity red cabbage vies with panfried sea bass with couscous. The excellent desserts are made on the premises. ⊠ *20 Buccleuch St.* ☎ *01387/252896* 🖃 *Reservations not accepted.*

$ | BRITISH | ✕ **Hullabaloo.** Occupying the top floor of the Robert Burns Centre, this restaurant serves a substantial and varied dinner menu, including wild game like venison and pheasant. Homey dishes include fish pie and pigs' cheeks braised in cider. There are some very interesting vegetarian options. Try to get a window table overlooking the River Nith. ⊠ *Robert Burns Centre, Mill Rd.* ☎ *01387/259679* ⊕ *www.hullaboorestaurant. co.uk* ⊘ *No lunch Nov.–Mar.*

$ | ▦ **Aston Hotel.** With the secluded feel of a grand country hotel, the Aston Hotel is less than 2 mi from the center of Dumfries. **Pros:** beautiful setting; easy access to Dumfries; rooms for people with disabilities. **Cons:** slightly institutional feel. ⊠ *Bankend Rd., Crichton* ☎ *01387/272410* ⊕ *www.astonhotels.co.uk/dumfries* 🛏 *71 rooms* 🛎 *In-room: a/c, Wi-Fi. In-hotel: restaurant, bar, parking* ❘⊙❘ *Breakfast.*

¢ ⊡ **Ferintosh Guest House.** Directly across from the train station, this handsome sandstone guesthouse sits on a leafy street in a quiet part of town. **Pros:** dog friendly; great robes; helpful owners. **Cons:** no children under 10; some rooms share bathrooms. ⊠ *30 Lovers Walk* ☎ *01387/252262* ⊕ *www.ferintosh.net* ☞ *6 rooms* ♿ *In-room: no a/c, safe, Wi-Fi. In-hotel: some pets allowed, some age restrictions* ⊠ *Breakfast.*

THE ARTS

Dumfries & Galloway Arts Festival. This festival, celebrated every year since 1979, is usually held at the end of May at several venues throughout the region. ☎ *01387/260447* ⊕ *www.dgartsfestival.org.uk.*

Gracefield Arts Centre. With galleries hosting constantly changing exhibits, Gracefield Arts Centre also has a well-stocked crafts shop. ⊠ *28 Edinburgh Rd.* ☎ *01387/262084.*

BICYCLING

G&G Cycle Centre. Bicycles can be rented from G&G Cycle Centre. The staff gives good advice on where to ride. ⊠ *10–12 Academy St.* ☎ *01387/259483* ⊕ *www.cycle-centre.com.*

7stanes Mountain Biking. This company manages seven different mountain-biking routes around the area that were built by cyclists themselves. There are a number of bike-rental shops nearby. ⊠ *Campbell House, Bankhead Rd* ☎ *01387/702228* ⊕ *www.7stanesmountainbiking.com.*

SHOPPING

Dumfries is the main shopping center for the region, with all the big-name chain stores as well as specialty shops.

Greyfriars Crafts. This shop sells mainly Scottish goods, including glass, ceramics, and jewelry. ⊠ *56 Buccleuch St.* ☎ *01387/264050.*

Loch Arthur Creamery and Farm Shop. This lively and active farm in the charmingly named village of Beeswing has organic foods of the highest quality, particularly its butter and cheese, which are sold in the farm shop. ⊠ *A711, 6 mi from Dumfries, Beeswing* ☎ *01387/760296* ⊕ *www.locharthur.org.uk.*

DALBEATTIE

14 mi southwest of Dumfries, 89 mi south of Glasgow, 95 mi southwest of Edinburgh.

Like the much larger Aberdeen far to the northeast, Dalbeattie contains buildings constructed with local gray granite from the town's quarry. The well-scrubbed gray glitter makes Dalbeattie atypical of Galloway towns, where housefronts are usually painted in pastels.

GETTING HERE AND AROUND

There are no direct bus routes from Dumfries to Dalbeattie; your best mode of transport is car. From Dumfries, take the A711 (about 25 minutes). From Glasgow take the M74, A74, then A701 (about two hours). From Edinburgh, take the A701 and A702 (about 2¼ hours).

WHERE TO STAY

For expanded hotel reviews, visit Fodors.com.

¢ 🖼 **Kerr Cottage.** This 165-year-old house is holding up quite well, thank you very much; bedrooms are fresh, spacious, and newly renovated with contemporary wood furniture, comfy beds, and large, tiled bathrooms. **Pros:** close to biking and hiking trails; great storage space for outdoor gear; comfortable lounge. **Cons:** no pets allowed; no children under 12. ⊠ *Port Rd.* ☎ *01556/612245* ⊕ *www.kerrcottage.co.uk* 🖎 *3 rooms* 🖔 *In-room: no a/c, Wi-Fi. In-hotel: some age restrictions* 🍴 *Breakfast.*

SPORTS AND THE OUTDOORS
Barend Riding School and Trekking Centre. You'll be helped to a "horse-high" view of the beautiful coast and countryside. ⊠ *A710, 6 mi south-east of Dalbeattie, Sandyhills* ☎ *01387/780–6533.*

CASTLE DOUGLAS

6 mi west of Dalbeattie, 84 mi south of Glasgow, 90 mi southwest of Edinburgh.

A quaint town that sits beside Carlingwark Loch, Castle Dougles is a popular base for exploring the surrounding countryside. The loch sets off the city perfectly, reflecting its dramatic architecture of sharp spires and soft sandstone arches. Its main thoroughfare, King Street, has unique shops and eateries.

GETTING HERE AND AROUND
There's no train station in Castle Douglas, and buses from Dumfries make several stops along the way. The best way to get to Castle Douglas is by car. From Dalbeattie, take the A711/A745 (10 minutes). From Glasgow, take the A713 (just under two hours). From Edinburgh, take the A70 (2 hours).

ESSENTIALS
Visitor Information Castle Douglas ⊠ *Market Hill* ☎ *01556/502611* ⊕ *www. visitdumfriesandgalloway.co.uk.*

EXPLORING
Threave Castle. Not to be confused with the mansion in Threave Gardens, Threave Castle was an early home of the Black Douglases, who were the earls of Nithsdale and lords of Galloway. The castle was dismantled in the religious wars of the mid-17th century, though enough of it remains to have housed prisoners from the Napoleonic Wars of the 19th century. It's a few minutes from Castle Douglas by car and is signposted from the main road. To get here, leave your car in a farmyard and make your way down to the edge of the river. Ring a bell, and, rather romantically, a boatman will come to ferry you across to the great stone tower looming from a marshy island in the river. ⊠ *A75, 3 mi west of Castle Douglas* ☎ *07711/223101* ⊕ *www.historic-scotland.com* 🖃 *£4.20, includes ferry* ⊗ *Castle Apr.–Sept., daily 9:30–5:30.*

★ **Threave Gardens.** The National Trust for Scotland cares for the gently sloping parkland around the 1867 mansion built by William Gordon, a Liverpool businessman. The house, fully restored in the 1930s, gives a glimpse into the daily life of a prosperous family in the 19th century. The foliage demands the employment of many gardeners—and it's here that the gardeners train, thus ensuring there's always some fresh development or experimental planting. Entry to the house is by timed guided tour, and it's wise to book ahead. There's an on-site restaurant. ⊠ *South of A75, 1 mi west of Castle Douglas* ☎ *0844/493–2245* ⊕ *www.nts. org.uk* 🖾 *Gardens £6, house and gardens £11* ⏱ *House Apr.–Oct., Wed.–Fri. and Sun. 11–3:30. Visitor center Feb., Mar., Nov., and Dec., daily 10–4; Apr.–Oct., daily 10–5.*

WHERE TO EAT

¢ ✕ **The Café at Designs Gallery.** For a good balance of art and food, look
CAFÉ   no further. You'll find the freshest ingredients here, from soup to salads, sandwiches to quiches. Everything is made on-site, including the bread, and it's all organic. The soup of the day is always a good choice, as are the seasonal fruit pies. The café is downstairs, beneath the shop and gallery, and is full of light and wooden tables and chairs. You can also choose to sit in the well-kept garden or conservatory, when weather permits. ⊠ *179 King St.* ☎ *01556/504552* ⊕ *www.designsgallery.co.uk* ⏱ *No dinner. Closed Sun.*

SPORTS AND THE OUTDOORS

BICYCLING   **Castle Douglas Cycle Centre.** You can rent bicycles from Castle Douglas Cycle Centre. ⊠ *Church St.* ☎ *01556/504542* ⊕ *www.cdbikes.co.uk.*

BOATING   **Galloway Activity Centre.** With dinghies, kayaks, and canoes for rent, the center specializes in water sports. "Dry" sports include mountain biking, archery, and rock climbing. It's about 10 mi northwest of Castle Douglas. ⊠ *Off A713, Parton* ☎ *01644/420626* ⊕ *www.lochken.co.uk.*

SHOPPING

Galloway Gems. This glittery shop sells mineral specimens, polished stone slices, and a range of Celtic- and Nordic-inspired jewelry. ⊠ *130–132 King St.* ☎ *01556/503254.*

Posthorn. The Posthorn is renowned for its display of figurines by Border Fine Art as well as Scotland's biggest display of Moorcroft glazed and enamel pottery. ⊠ *5 St. Andrew St.* ☎ *01556/502531* ⊕ *www.posthorn. co.uk.*

KIRKCUDBRIGHT

9 mi southwest of Castle Douglas, 89 mi south of Glasgow, 99 mi southwest of Edinburgh.

Kirkcudbright (pronounced kirk-*coo*-bray) is an 18th-century town of Georgian and Victorian houses, some of them washed in pastel shades and roofed with the blue slate of the district. Since the early 20th century it has been known as a haven for artistic types, and its L-shape main street is full of crafts and antiques shops.

GETTING HERE AND AROUND

Driving is your best and only real option. From Castle Douglas take the A711 (15 minutes). From Glasgow, take the A713 (about two hours). From Edinburgh, take the A701 (about 2½ hours).

ESSENTIALS

Visitor Information Kirkcudbright ⊠ *Harbour Sq.* ☎ *01557/330494* ⊕ *www. visitdumfriesandgalloway.co.uk.*

EXPLORING

Broughton House. The 18th-century Broughton House was once the home of the artist E. A. Hornel, one of the "Glasgow Boys" of the late 19th century. Many of his paintings hang in the house, which is furnished in period style and contains an extensive library specializing in local history. There's also a Japanese garden. ⊠ *12 High St.* ☎ *0844/493–2246* ⊕ *www.nts.org.uk* ⊠ *£6* ⊙ *House: Apr.–Oct., daily noon–5; Garden: Feb. and Mar., weekdays 11–4; Apr.–Oct., daily noon–5.*

MacLellan's Castle. Conspicuous in the center of town are the stone walls of MacLellan's Castle, a once-elaborate castellated mansion dating from the 16th century. You can walk around the interior, although the rooms are bare. The "Lairds Lug," behind the fireplace, allowed the *laird* (lord) to listen in to what his guests were saying about him. There are lovely views over the town from the windows. ⊠ *Off High St.* ☎ *01557/331856* ⊕ *www.historic-scotland.gov.uk* ⊠ *£4* ⊙ *Apr.–Sept., daily 9:30–5:30.*

Stewartry Museum. Stuffed with all manner of local paraphernalia, the delightfully old-fashioned Stewartry Museum allows you to putter and absorb as much or as little as takes your interest in the display cases. Stewartry is the former name of Kirkcudbright. ⊠ *St Mary St.* ☎ *01557/331643* ⊠ *Free* ⊙ *May, June, and Sept., Mon.–Sat. 11–5, Sun. 2–5; July and Aug., Mon.–Sat. 10–5, Sun. 2–5; Oct., Mon.–Sat. 11–4, Sun. 2–5; Nov.–Apr., Mon.–Sat. 11–4.*

Tolbooth Arts Centre. In the 17th-century tollbooth (a combination town hall–courthouse–prison), the Tolbooth Arts Centre gives a history of the town's most famous artists, including E. A. Hornel, Jessie King, and Charles Oppenheimer. Some of their paintings are on display, as are works by modern artists and craftspeople. The facility is evidence that the town has always been as it still is, a magnet for artists. ⊠ *High St.* ☎ *01557/331556* ⊕ *www.kirkcudbright.co.uk* ⊠ *Free* ⊙ *Oct.–May, Mon.–Sat. 11–4; June–Sept., Mon.–Sat. 11–4, Sun. 2–5.*

WHERE TO EAT AND STAY

For expanded hotel reviews, visit Fodors.com.

$$ ✕**Artistas.** Paintings of Scotland, starched white tablecloths, and giant
BRITISH windows overlooking the well-kept garden beckon you into this highly praised eatery. Locals love that the food is locally sourced and full of imagination. You can choose from two courses for £24 or three courses for £29. In season, try the globe artichoke and asparagus salad, then the braised fillet of turbot over saffron-and-shrimp quinoa. The "posh" fish-and-chips is one of the best around. For a less expensive, more casual dining experience try the hotel's bistro, where the à la carte menu is just as imaginative and delicious. ⊠ *Best Western Selkirk Arms, High St.* ☎ *01557/330402* ⚑ *Reservations essential.*

$ 🛏 **Best Western Selkirk Arms.** Bursting with charm, this elegant 18th-century hotel has a lot going for it. **Pros:** attentive service; massive breakfast; lively traditional pub. **Cons:** rooms closest to restaurant get some noise; bar can get crowded during sporting events. ☒ *High St.* ☎ *01557/330402* ⊕ *www.selkirkarmshotel.co.uk* ⟵ *17 rooms* ⬧ *In-room: no a/c, Wi-Fi. In-hotel: restaurant, bar, some pets allowed* ⊙ *Breakfast.*

NEWTON STEWART

18 mi northwest of Kirkcudbright, 77 mi southwest of Glasgow, 105 mi southwest of Edinburgh.

The bustling town of Newton Stewart is a good place to stop when touring the western region of Galloway.

GETTING HERE AND AROUND
Newton Stewart does not have a train station, but the town is served by regular buses from Glasgow and Edinburgh as well as local buses from neighboring towns. From Glasgow, take the A77 (about two hours). From Edinburgh, take the A702 (about 2¾ hours).

ESSENTIALS
Visitor Information Newton Stewart ☒ *Dashwood Sq.* ☎ *01671/402431* ⊕ *www.newtonstewart.org.*

EXPLORING
Creetown Gem Rock Museum. In the nearby village of Creetown, the Creetown Gem Rock Museum has an eclectic mineral collection, a dinosaur egg, an erupting volcano, and a crystal cave. There's also an Internet café, a tearoom, and a shop selling stones and crystals—both loose and in settings. ☒ *Chain Rd., off A75, Creetown* ☎ *01671/820357* ⊕ *www. gemrock.net* ⬧ *£4* ☉ *Easter–Sept., daily 9:30–5:30; Sept.–Easter, daily 10–4; last admission ½ hr before closing.*

Galloway Forest Park. You can walk or bicycle along the paths at the Galloway Forest Park. At the Clatteringshaws Visitor Centre there are exhibits about the region's wildlife and a reconstruction of an Iron Age dwelling. The park is 7 mi northeast of Newton Stewart. ☒ *A712* ☎ *01644/420285* ⊕ *www.forestry.gov.uk/gallowayforestpark* ⬧ *Free* ☉ *May–Sept., daily 10:30–5:30; Oct.–Apr., daily 10:30–4:30.*

Machars. The Machars is the name given to the triangular promontory south of Newton Stewart. This is an area of pretty rolling farmlands, yellow-gorse hedgerows, rich grazing for dairy cattle, and stony prehistoric sites. Fields are bordered by dry *stane dykes* (walls) of sharp-edge stones, and small hills and hummocks give the area its characteristic frozen-wave look, a reminder of the glacial activity that shaped the landscape.

Wood of Cree Nature Reserve. Birders will love the Wood of Cree Nature Reserve, owned and managed by

GOLF GETAWAYS

There are more than 30 courses in Dumfries and Galloway and 21 in the Borders. The Freedom of the Fairways Pass (five-day pass, £120; three-day pass, £88) allows play on all 21 Borders courses and is available from the Scottish Borders Tourist Board. The Gateway to Golf Pass (six-round pass, £120; three-round pass, £80) is accepted by all clubs in Dumfries and Galloway.

the Royal Society for the Protection of Birds. In the reserve you can see such species as the redstart, pied flycatcher, and wood warbler. To get there, take the minor road that travels north from Newton Stewart alongside the River Cree east of the A714. The entrance is next to a small parking area at the side of the road. ✉ *Off A714, 4 mi north of Newton Stewart* ☎ *01556/670464* ⊕ *www.rspb.org.uk* ✉ *Donations accepted* ☉ *Daily 24 hrs.*

GLEN TROOL

9 mi north of Newton Stewart, 86 mi southwest of Glasgow, 113 mi southwest of Edinburgh.

GETTING HERE AND AROUND

Driving is really the only way to get to Glen Trool. From Newton Stewart, take the A714 (about 15 minutes). From Glasgow, take the A77 (about 2¼ hours). From Edinburgh, take the A702 (about three hours).

EXPLORING

★ **Glen Trool.** Part of Galloway's Forest Park, Glen Trool is one of Scotland's best-kept secrets. With high purple-and-green hilltops shorn rockbare by glaciers, and with a dark, winding loch and thickets of birch trees sounding with birdcalls, the setting almost looks more highland than the real Highlands. Note **Bruce's Stone,** just above the parking lot, marking the site where in 1307 Scotland's champion Robert the Bruce (King Robert I, 1274–1329) won his first victory in the Scottish Wars of Independence. To get here, follow the A714 north and turn right at the signpost for Glen Trool. A little road leads through increasingly wild woodland scenery to a parking lot. Only after you have climbed for a few minutes onto a heathery knoll does the full, rugged panorama become apparent. ✉ *Off A714, Bargrennan* ☎ *01671/840302* ⊕ *www.forestry.gov.uk* ✉ *Free* ☉ *Visitor center Mar.–June and Sept.–Nov., daily 10:30–4:30; July and Aug., daily 10:30–5:30.*

WIGTOWN

7 mi south of Newton Stewart, 84 mi southwest of Glasgow, 111 mi southwest of Edinburgh.

More than 20 bookshops, mostly antiquarian and secondhand stores, have sprung up on the brightly painted main street of Wigtown, voted Scotland's national book town. The 10-day Wigtown Book Festival is held in late September and early October.

GETTING HERE AND AROUND

There is no train station in Wigtown, and you must make several transfers when traveling by bus to and from Scotland's larger cities. Driving is your best option. Take the A714 from Newton Stewart (15 minutes). From Glasgow, take the A77 (about two hours). From Edinburgh, take the A702 (about three hours).

EXPLORING

Bladnoch Distillery. Wigtown's Bladnoch Distillery is Scotland's southernmost malt-whisky producer. It has a visitor center and a gift shop, and tours are available. Tours are given on the hour between 10 and 4. ☒ *A714* ☎ *01988/402605* ⊕ *www.bladnoch.co.uk* ✉ *Distillery free, tours £3* ☺ *Easter–June, Sept., and Oct., weekdays 9–5; July and Aug., weekdays 9–5, Sat. 11–5, Sun. noon–5.*

Wigtown Book Festival. The 10-day Wigtown Book Festival, held in late September and early October, has readings, performances, and other events around town. ☎ *01988/402036* ⊕ *www.wigtown-booktown. co.uk.*

SHOPPING

Bookshop. One of the country's largest secondhand bookstores, the Bookshop offers temptingly full shelves. The narrow entrance, flanked by two tottering towers of books, belies the huge stock within. ☒ *17 N. Main St.* ☎ *01988/402499.*

WHITHORN

11 mi south of Wigtown, 94 mi southwest of Glasgow, 121 mi southwest of Edinburgh.

Whithorn is a tremendously historic town, known for its early Christian settlement. The main street is notably wide, with cute pastel buildings nestled up against each other, their low doorways and small windows creating images of years long past. It's still mainly a farming community, but is fast becoming a popular tourist destination. Several scenes from the original *Wicker Man* were shot in and around the area. During the summer months, it's a popular place for festivals. The Isle of Whithorn, just beyond the town, is not an island at all but a fishing village of great charm.

GETTING HERE AND AROUND

There's no train station in Whithorn, and most of the buses are local (getting to main Scottish cities from Whithorn takes careful planning and several transfers). To drive from Wigtown, take the A746 (about 20 minutes). From Glasgow, take the A77 (about 2½ hours). From Edinburgh, take the A702 (about three hours).

EXPLORING

St. Ninian's Chapel. The Isle of Whithorn (a small port, not an island) holds the ruins of St. Ninian's Chapel, where pilgrims who came by sea prayed before traveling inland to Whithorn Priory. Some people claim that this, and not Whithorn Priory, is the site of the Candida Casa. This 14th-century structure seems to have been built on top of a much older chapel.

Whithorn Priory. The road that is now the A746 was a pilgrims' path that led to the royal burgh of Whithorn, where sat Whithorn Priory, one of Scotland's great medieval cathedrals, now an empty shell. It was built in the 12th century and is said to occupy the site of a former stone church, the Candida Casa, built by St. Ninian in the 4th century. As the story goes, the church housed a shrine to Ninian, the earliest of Scotland's saints, and kings and barons sought to visit the shrine at least once in their lives. As you approach the priory, observe the royal arms of pre-1707 Scotland—that is, Scotland before the Union with England—carved and painted above the *pend* (covered walkway).

Whithorn Story and Visitor Centre. The center explains the significance of what is claimed to be the site of the earliest Christian community in Scotland. A museum has a collection of early Christian crosses. ✉ *45–47 George St.* ☎ *01988/ 500508* ⊕ *www.whithorn.com* 🎫 *£4.50* ⊙ *Apr.–Oct., daily 10:30– 5; last tour at 4.*

> **HIKING THE SOLWAY FIRTH**
>
> Mostly undiscovered by travelers, the Solway Firth is a must for walkers, cyclists, bird-watchers, and stone-circle seekers. This lovely and protected inlet is a haven for a great variety of seabirds, which you can spot from the coastal paths that link Sandyhills, Rockcliffe, and Kippford. To get here, take the A710 from Dumfries, continuing on to the A711. Park where you choose and take the coastal path from any of the three villages.

WHERE TO EAT

$ ✕ **Steam Packet Inn.** This lovely, old-fashioned inn is always full, mainly
BRITISH because of its hearty, well-cooked food and good beer, but also because of its location on the harbor of this quaint fishing village. You can walk the headland behind the pub to the rocky shore of the Solway Firth. Fish-and-chips and lamb shanks can be followed by some excellent house-made desserts. When weather permits you can eat at tables in the garden. If you like it so much you want to stay, there are also a couple of rooms. ✉ *Harbour Row, Isle of Whithorn* ☎ *01988/500334* ⊕ *www.steampacketinn.co.uk.*

STRANRAER

31 mi northwest of Whithorn, 86 mi southwest of Glasgow via A77, 131 mi southwest of Edinburgh.

Stranraer has a lovely garden and is also the main ferry port to Northern Ireland—if you make a purchase in one of its shops, you may wind up with some euro coins from Ireland in your change.

GETTING HERE AND AROUND

Stranraer has a busy train station that serves all major lines, and the buses are good as well (with many connections to smaller towns). If you're driving, take the A747 from Whithorn (about 45 minutes). From Glasgow, take the M77/A77 (two hours), and from Edinburgh, take the A77 (three hours).

ESSENTIALS

Visitor Information Stranraer ✉ *28 Harbour St.* ☎ *01776/702595* ⊕ *www. dumfriesandgalloway.co.uk.*

EXPLORING

★ **Castle Kennedy Gardens.** The lovely Castle Kennedy Gardens surround the shell of the original Castle Kennedy, which was burned in 1716. Parks scattered around the property were built by the second Earl of

Stair in 1733. The earl was a field marshal and used his soldiers to help with the heavy work of constructing banks, ponds, and other major landscape features. When the rhododendrons are in bloom, the effect is kaleidoscopic. There's also a pleasant tearoom. ⊠ *North of A75, 3 mi east of Stranraer* ☎ *01776/702024* ⊕ *www.castlekennedygardens.co.uk* 🖃 *£4* ⊙ *Easter–Sept., daily 10–5.*

PORTPATRICK

8 mi southwest of Stranraer, 94 mi southwest of Glasgow, 139 mi southwest of Edinburgh.

The holiday town of Portpatrick lies across the Rhinns of Galloway from Stranraer. Once an Irish ferry port, Portpatrick's harbor eventually proved too small for larger vessels.

GETTING HERE AND AROUND
Direct buses travel between Portpatrick to Stranraer and some of the neighboring towns, but travel to and from the larger Scottish cities can prove more difficult. There is no train station in Portpatrick (though there is one in Stranraer). Driving is probably your best bet. From Stranraer, take the A77; it's about a 15-minute journey. Take the M77/A77 from Glasgow (just over two hours) and the M8/A77 from Edinburgh (about three hours).

EXPLORING
Dunskey Castle. Just south of Portpatrick are the lichen-yellow ruins of 16th-century Dunskey Castle, accessible from a cliff-top path off the B7042.

★   **Logan Botanic Gardens.** The spectacular Logan Botanic Gardens, one of the National Botanic Gardens of Scotland, are a must-see for garden lovers. Displayed here are plants that enjoy the prevailing mild climate, especially tree ferns, cabbage palms, and other Southern Hemisphere exotica. There are free guided walks every second Tuesday of the month at 10:30 am. ⊠ *Off B7065, Port Logan* ☎ *01776/860231* 🖃 *£4* ⊙ *Mar. and Oct., daily 10–5; Apr.–Sept., daily 10–6.*

Mull of Galloway. If you wish to visit the southern tip of the Rhinns of Galloway, called the Mull of Galloway, follow the B7065/B7041 until you run out of land. The cliffs and seascapes here are rugged, and there's a lighthouse and a bird reserve.

Southern Upland Way. The village of Portpatrick is the starting point for Scotland's longest official long-distance footpath, the Southern Upland Way (⊕ www.southernuplandway.gov.uk/cms), which runs a switchback course for 212 mi to Cockburnspath, on the east side of the Borders. The path begins on the cliffs just north of the town and follows the coastline for 1½ mi before turning inland.

Fife and Angus

Updated by
Shona Main

Breezy cliff-top walkways, fishing villages, and open beaches characterize Fife and Angus. They sandwich Scotland's fourth-largest—and often overlooked—city, Dundee. Scotland's east coast has only light rainfall throughout the year; northeastern Fife, in particular, may claim the record for the most sunshine and the least rainfall in Scotland, which all adds to the enjoyment when you're touring the coast or the famous golf center of St. Andrews.

Fife proudly styles itself as a "kingdom," and its long history—which really began when the Romans went home in the 4th century and the Picts moved in—lends some substance to the boast. From medieval times its earls were first among Scotland's nobility and crowned her kings. For many, however, the most historic event in the region was the birth of golf, in the 15th century, which, legend has it, occurred in St. Andrews, an ancient university town with stone houses and seaside ruins. The Royal & Ancient Golf Club, the ruling body of the game worldwide, still has its headquarters here.

Not surprisingly, fishing and seafaring have also played a role in the history of the East Neuk coastal region. From the 16th through the 19th centuries, a large population lived and worked in the small ports and harbors that form a continuous chain around Fife's coast, which James V once called "a beggar's mantle fringed with gold." When the sun shines, this golden fringe—particularly at Tentsmuir, St Andrews, and Elie—gleams like the beaches of Normandy. Indeed, the houses of the East Neuk villages have a similar character, with color-washed fronts, rusty charm, fishy weather vanes, outdoor stone stairways to upper floors, and crude carvings of anchors and lobsters on their lintels. All of the houses are crowded on steep *wynds* (narrow streets), hugging pint-size harbors that in the golden era supported village fleets of 100 ships apiece.

North, across the Firth of Tay, lies the region of Angus, whose charm is its variety: in addition to its seacoast and pleasant Lowland market centers, there's also a hinterland of lonely rounded hills with long glens running into the typical Grampian Highland scenery beyond. One of Angus's interesting features, which it shares with the eastern Lowland edge of Perthshire, is its fruit-growing industry, which includes raspberries. The chief fruit-growing area is Strathmore, the broad vale between the northwesterly Grampian Mountains and the small coastal hills of the Sidlaws behind Dundee. Striking out from this valley, you can make a number of day trips to uplands or seacoast.

TOP REASONS TO GO

Seeing St. Andrews: With its medieval streets, ruined cathedral and castle, and peculiarly posh atmosphere, St. Andrews is one of the most incongruous yet beguiling places in Scotland—even without its famous golf course.

Hitting the links: If you can't get on the Old Course in St. Andrews by ballot or by any other means, Fife and Angus have fabulous fairways aplenty, including the famous links course at Carnoustie *(see Chapter 12 for the best courses).*

Exploring East Neuk: As you take in crowstep-gabled fishermen's cottages, winding cobbled lanes, seaside harbor scenes, and lovely beaches, you can almost imagine

the harsh lives of the hardworking Fifers who lived in tiny hamlets such as Crail, Anstruther, Pittenweem, and Elie. Today artists and visitors make it all pleasantly picturesque.

Discovering Dundee: This formerly industrial city is becoming better known for its vibrant arts, music, theater, restaurant, and nightlife scenes. It's in a spectacular natural setting by Britain's most powerful river, the Tay.

Roaming the glens: The long Angus glens (such as Glen Clova) that run into the wild Grampian Mountains are magical places beloved by outdoors enthusiasts and those just wanting to rediscover nature.

5

ORIENTATION AND PLANNING

GETTING ORIENTED

Fife lies north of the Lothians, across the iconic bridges of the Firth of Forth. A headland, Fife's northeastern coast (or East Neuk) is fringed with golden sands, rocky shores, fishermen's cottages, and, of course, the splendor of St. Andrews, home of golf. Northwest of Fife and across the glorious Firth of Tay, the city of Dundee is undergoing a postindustrial reinvention. Its rural hinterland, Angus, hugs the city, which, stretching north toward the foothills of the Grampian Mountains, houses agricultural and fishing communities, and Glamis, one of Scotland's best-loved castles.

St. Andrews and Fife's East Neuk Villages. St. Andrews isn't just a playground for golfers. This religious and academic center is steeped in history and prestige, with grand buildings, a palpable air of prosperity, and the cachet of being the place where a riveting 21st-century royal romance began. Beyond St. Andrews, the colorful fishing villages of the East Neuk are a day-tripper's (and fish eater's) delight.

Dundee and Angus. Dundee has a knockout setting beside Britain's mightiest river, historical sights—including Captain Scott's ship, RRS *Discovery*—and a vibrant social life. The tree-lined country roads of the Angus heartlands roll through strawberry and raspberry fields, to busy market towns, wee villages, and Glamis Castle.

PLANNING

WHEN TO GO

Spring in the Angus glens can be quite captivating, with the hills along Angus's northernmost boundary still covered in snow. Similarly, the moorland colors of autumn are appealing. However, Fife and Angus are really summer destinations, when most of the sights are open to visitors. St. Andrews hosts a number of international golf tournaments that effectively take over the town. Nongolfers may become incredibly frustrated when searching for accommodations or places to eat during these times, so check ahead.

PLANNING YOUR TIME

St. Andrews, 52 mi from Edinburgh, is not to be missed, for its history and atmosphere as much as for the golf; allot an overnight stop and at least a whole day if you can. The nearby East Neuk of Fife has some of Scotland's finest coastline, now becoming gentrified by the Edinburgh second-home set but still evoking Fife's past. A day's drive along A917 (allow for exploring and stops for ice cream and fish) will take you through the fishing villages of Elie, Pittenweem, Anstruther, and Crail. Dundee, with a rich maritime history and a grand museum, is an ideal base for a drive round the Angus towns of Arbroath, Kirriemuir, and Alyth; if you make a three-hour stop at Glamis Castle, this trip will take about a day.

GETTING HERE AND AROUND

AIR TRAVEL

Dundee Airport is off A85, 2 mi west of the city center. Air France operates a popular direct flight from London City Airport. Flybe flies here from Birmingham and Belfast.

BUS TRAVEL

Buses connect Edinburgh's St. Andrew Square bus station and Glasgow's Buchanan Street bus station to Fife and Angus. Megabus operates hourly service to Dundee from both Glasgow and Edinburgh. Stagecoach Fife serves Fife and St. Andrews, and Travel Dundee provides bus service in and around Dundee.

Stagecoach connects St. Andrews and Dundee to many of the smaller towns throughout Fife and Angus. A Day Rover ticket (£7.20 for Fife only) is a good value. An even better value is the £12.50 Super Dayrider ticket, which covers Fife and Angus and will even take you as far as Edinburgh and Glasgow.

Traveline Scotland is a service that helps you plan all public-transport journeys.

Bus Contacts Megabus ☎ 0901/331–0031 ⊕ www.uk.megabus.com. **Stagecoach Fife** ☎ 0871/200–2233 ⊕ www.stagecoachbus.com. **National Express Dundee** ☎ 0871/200–2233 ⊕ www.nxbus.co.uk/dundee. **Traveline Scotland** ☎ 08706/082608 ⊕ www.travelinescotland.com.

CAR TRAVEL

The fastest route to Angus and northeast Fife is the M90 motorway from Edinburgh. Exit onto the A90 at Perth (45 minutes), and travel an additional 20 minutes to reach Dundee; 15 minutes later, you'll arrive in

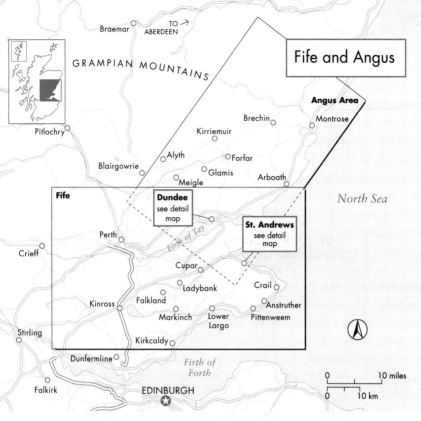

St. Andrews. If you're coming from Fife, you can also take the A91 and the A914, and cross the Tay Bridge to reach Dundee. This is a slower route, but does take you through the heartland of Fife.

Fife and Angus cover a compact area, so getting around is straightforward. You can visit everything via a series of excursions off the main north–south artery, the A90/M90, which leads from Edinburgh to Aberdeen. From here you can easily make day trips to Edinburgh, Glasgow, or Perthshire. Aberdeenshire and the Central Highlands are not too far away either.

Fife is easy to navigate—although it can be difficult to find a place to park in St. Andrews. The most interesting sights are in the east, which is served by a network of cross-country roads. Angus is also an easy region to explore. It's serviced by a fast main road (the A90), a gentler road (the A92), and several rural roads that run between the Grampians and the A90.

TRAIN TRAVEL
ScotRail stops at Kirkcaldy, Cupar, Leuchars (for St. Andrews), Dundee, Arbroath, and Montrose.

Train Contacts ScotRail ☎ *08457/484950* ⊕ *www.scotrail.co.uk*

RESTAURANTS

With an affluent population, St. Andrews supports several stylish hotel restaurants. Because it's a university town and popular tourist destination, there are also many good cafés and bistro-style restaurants. Bar lunches are the rule in large and small hotels throughout the region, and in seaside places the carry-*oot* (to-go) meal of fish-and-chips is an enduring tradition.

HOTELS

If you're staying in Fife, the obvious choice for a base is St. Andrews, with ample accommodations of all kinds. Another good option is the Howe of Fife, between Strathmiglo and Cupar, where there are some excellent country-house hotels, many with their own restaurants. Dundee and its hinterlands have a number of diverse accommodations, all of which offer good value.

WHAT IT COSTS IN POUNDS					
	¢	$	$$	$$$	$$$$
RESTAURANTS	under £10	£10–£14	£15–£19	£20–£25	over £25
HOTELS	under £70	£70–£120	£121–£160	£161–£220	over £220

Restaurant prices are for a main course at dinner. Hotel prices are for two people in a standard double room in high season, generally including the 20% V.A.T.

TOURS

From June to August, Scottish Express, run by Fishers Tours, operates bus tours both within and outside the region. Lochs and Glens operates bus tours of Scotland year-round. Heritage Golf Tours Scotland specializes in golf vacations that include hotel and car rental and course reservations. Links Golf St. Andrews tailors tours to individual requirements.

Bus Tours Fishers Tours ⊠ *16 W. Port, Dundee* ☎ *01382/227290* ⊕ *www. fisherstours.co.uk.* **Lochs and Glens** ⊠ *School Rd., Gartocharn* ☎ *01389/713713* ⊕ *www.lochsandglens.com.*

Golf Tours Heritage Golf Tours Scotland ⊠ *Swilken House, 21 Loch Dr., Helensburgh* ☎ *01436/674630* ⊕ *www.golftours-scotland.co.uk.* **Links Golf St. Andrews** ⊠ *7 Pilmour Links, St. Andrews* ☎ *01334/478639* ⊕ *www. linksgolfstandrews.com.*

VISITOR INFORMATION

The Arbroath, Dundee, and St. Andrews tourist offices are open year-round. Smaller tourist information centers operate seasonally in Anstruther, Brechin, Crail, Forfar, Kirriemuir, and Montrose.

ST. ANDREWS AND FIFE'S EAST NEUK VILLAGES

In its western parts Fife still bears the scars of heavy industry, especially coal mining, but these signs are less evident as you move east. Northeastern Fife, around the town of St. Andrews, seems to have played no part in the Industrial Revolution; instead, its residents earned a living from the grain fields or from the sea. Fishing has been a major industry, and in the past a string of Fife ports traded across the North Sea. Today the legacy of Dutch-influenced architecture, such as crowstep gables (the stepped effect on the ends of the roofs)—gives these East Neuk villages a distinctive character.

St. Andrews is unlike any other Scottish town. Once Scotland's most powerful ecclesiastical center as well as the seat of the country's oldest university and then, much later, the very symbol and spiritual home of golf, the town has a comfortable, well-groomed air, sitting almost smugly apart from the rest of Scotland. Its latest boast, being the town where Prince William first kissed Kate Middleton, has boosted university applications.

ST. ANDREWS

52 mi northeast of Edinburgh, 83 mi northeast of Glasgow.

It may have a ruined cathedral and a grand university—the oldest in Scotland—but the modern claim to fame for St. Andrews is mainly its status as the home of golf. Forget that Scottish kings were crowned here, or that John Knox preached here, or that Reformation reformers were burned at the stake here. Thousands flock to St. Andrews to play at the Old Course, home of the Royal & Ancient Club, and to follow in the footsteps of Hagen, Sarazen, Jones, and Hogan.

The layout is pure Middle Ages: its three main streets—North, Market, and South—converge on the city's earliest religious site, near the cathedral. Like most of the ancient monuments, the cathedral ruins are impressive in their desolation—but this town is no dusty museum. The streets are busy, the shops are stylish, the gray houses sparkle in the sun, and the scene is particularly brightened during the academic year by bicycling students in scarlet gowns.

GETTING HERE AND AROUND

If you arrive by car, be prepared for an endless drive round the town as you look for a parking space. The parking lots around Rose Park (behind the bus station and a short walk from the town center) are your best bet. If you arrive by local or national bus, the bus station is a five-minute walk from town. The nearest train station, Leuchars, is 10 minutes away by taxi (£13) or bus (£2), both of which can be found outside the station. St. Andrews can be fully enjoyed on foot without too much exertion.

ESSENTIALS

Visitor Information **St. Andrews** ⊠ *70 Market St.* ☎ *01334/472021* ⊕ *www. visitfife.com.*

EXPLORING

TOP ATTRACTIONS

British Golf Museum. This museum explores the centuries-old relationship between St. Andrews and golf and displays golf memorabilia from the 18th century to the 21st century. It's just opposite the Royal & Ancient Golf Club. ⊠ *Bruce Embankment* ☎ *01334/460046* ⊕ *www. britishgolfmuseum.co.uk* 🎫 *£6* 🕐 *Apr.–Oct., Mon.–Sat. 9:30–5, Sun. 10–5; Nov.–Mar., daily 10–4.*

St. Andrews Castle. On the shore north of the cathedral stands ruined St. Andrews Castle, begun at the end of the 13th century. The remains include a rare example of a cold and gruesome bottle-shape dungeon, in which many prisoners spent their last hours. Even more atmospheric is the castle's mine and countermine. The former was a tunnel dug by besieging forces in the 16th century; the latter, a tunnel dug by castle defenders in order to meet and wage battle below ground. You can stoop and crawl into this narrow passageway—an eerie experience, despite the addition of electric light. The visitor center has a good audiovisual presentation on the castle's history. The beach below is popular with sun bathers, weather permitting. ⊠ *N. Castle St.* 🕾 *01334/477196* ⊕ *www.historic-scotland.gov.uk* 🖾 *£5.50, £7.60 with St. Rule's Tower and St. Andrews Cathedral* ☉ *Apr.–Sept., daily 9:30–5:30; Oct.–Mar., daily 9:30–4.*

St. Andrews Cathedral. Near St. Rule's Tower, St. Andrews Cathedral is a ruined, poignant fragment of what was once the largest and most magnificent church in Scotland. Work on it began in 1160, and after several delays it was finally consecrated in 1318. The church was subsequently damaged by fire and repaired, but fell into decay during the Reformation. Only ruined gables, parts of the nave's south wall, and other fragments survive. The on-site museum helps you interpret the remains and gives a sense of what the cathedral must once have been like. ⊠ *Off Pends Rd.* 🕾 *01334/472563* ⊕ *www.historic-scotland.gov.uk* 🖾 *£4.50, £7.60 with St. Rule's Tower and St. Andrews Castle* ☉ *Apr.–Sept., daily 9:30–5:30; Oct.–Mar., daily 9:30–4:30.*

St. Rule's Tower. Local legend has it that St. Andrews was founded by St. Regulus, or Rule, who, acting under divine guidance, carried relics of St. Andrew by sea from Patras in Greece. He was shipwrecked on this Fife headland and founded a church. The holy man's name survives in the cylindrical tower, consecrated in 1126 and the oldest surviving building in St. Andrews. Enjoy dizzying views of town from the top of the tower, reached via steep stairs. ⊠ *Off Pends Rd.* 🕾 *01334/472563* ⊕ *www. historic-scotland.gov.uk* 🖾 *£4.20, £7.60 with St. Andrews Cathedral and St. Andrews Castle* ☉ *Apr.–Sept., daily 9:30–5:30; Oct.–Mar., daily 9:30–4:30.*

WORTH NOTING

OFF THE BEATEN PATH

Leuchars. This small town has a 12th-century church with some of the finest Norman architectural features to be seen anywhere in Scotland.

Leuchars Air Show. On the second Saturday of September 2012, the Royal Air Force will stage the last Leuchars Air Show. (Defense budget cuts mean the RAF is moving out.) The event promises to be a spectacular farewell, with dramatic flights by historic aircraft and their contemporary counterparts. ⊠ *A919, 5 mi northwest of St. Andrews* 🕾 *01334/839000* ⊕ *www.airshow.co.uk*

🌣 **Tentsmuir Forest.** Just 2 mi east of Leuchars, this pine forest fringes the long, sandy Kinshaldy Beach. Popular with families, kite flyers, beachcombers, and naturalists, it's 5 mi long and has enough space for everyone. ⊠ *B945, Leuchars* 🕾 ⊕ *www.forestry.gov.uk/tentsmuir* 🖾 *Parking £2* ☉ *9–sunset.*

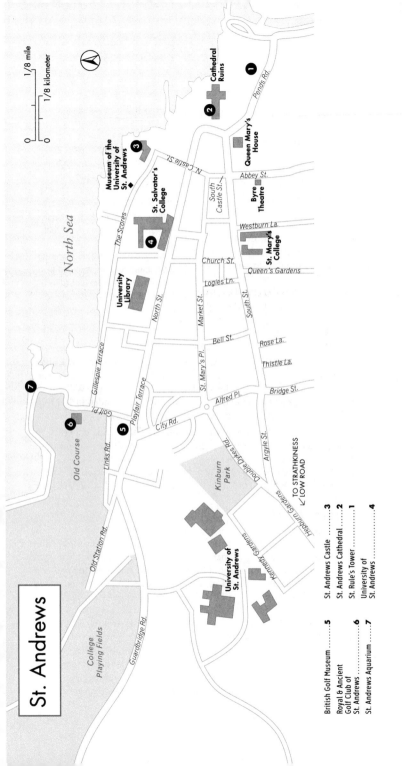

St. Andrews

North Sea

College Playing Fields

Old Course

University of St. Andrews

Kinburn Park

TO STRATHKINESS
LOW ROAD

British Golf Museum **5**

Royal & Ancient
Golf Club of
St. Andrews **6**

St. Andrews Aquarium **7**

St. Andrews Castle **3**

St. Andrews Cathedral **2**

St. Rule's Tower **1**

University of
St. Andrews **4**

Cathedral Ruins

Queen Mary's House

Museum of the University of St. Andrews

St. Salvator's College

University Library

Byre Theatre

St. Mary's College

1/8 mile
1/8 kilometer

Royal & Ancient Golf Club of St. Andrews. The ruling house of golf worldwide is the spiritual home of all who play or follow the game. Founded in 1754, its clubhouse on the dunes—open to members only, who must be male—is a mix of classical, Victorian, and neoclassical styles; it's adjacent to the famous Old Course. ⊠ *The Scores* ☏ *01334/ 460000* ⊕ *www.randa.org.*

☾ **St. Andrews Aquarium.** This modest aquarium is run by real enthusiasts whose passion for all things oceanic is infectious. Seals, fish, crustaceans, and many other forms of marine life inhabit aquariums and pool gardens designed to simulate their natural habitats. The seals are fed at midday and 3 pm. ⊠ *The Scores* ☏ *01334/474786* ⊕ *www. standrewsaquarium.co.uk* ⊠ *£7.10* ⊙ *Easter–Oct., daily 10–5:30; Nov.–Easter, hrs vary.*

University of St. Andrews. St. Andrews is the site of Scotland's oldest university, and *alma mater* of John Knox (Protestant reformer), King James II of Scotland, the Duke and Duchess of Cambridge (William and Kate), and Chris Hoy, Scotland's Olympic cyclist. Founded in 1411, the university's buildings and residences pepper the town.

Museum of the University of St. Andrews. With four galleries, the museum tells the history of this grand institution all the way up to the present day. It also has sweeping views over St. Andrews Bay. ⊠ *7A The Scores* ☏ *01334/461660* ⊕ *www.st-andrews.ac.uk/musa* ⊠ *Free* ⊙ *Apr.–Sept., Mon.–Sat. 10–5, Sun. noon–4; Oct.–Mar., Thurs.–Sun. noon–4.*

WHERE TO EAT

$$$$ ✕ **The Seafood Restaurant.** This glass-walled building is perched on the
SEAFOOD banks of the West Sands. Formerly the site of an open-air theater,
★ the kitchen, visible to all diners, creates a sense of drama all its own. The food is adventurous without being flashy: start with lemon and coriander Pittenweem crab, then move on to sea bass with celeriac puree. ⊠ *Bruce Embankment* ☏ *01334/479475* ⊕ *www.theseafoodrestaurant. com.*

¢ ✕ **West Port Bar & Kitchen.** It's easy to forget that St. Andrews is a univer-
ECLECTIC sity town when the students are on summer break, but this modern bar and eatery remains vibrant and youthful year-round. The reasonably priced menu offers nicely prepared pub grub—everything from gourmet burgers to smoked haddock fishcakes—making this a satisfying stop for lunch or dinner. Upstairs are four bright B&B rooms that go for £95. ⊠ *170 South St.* ☏ *01334/473186.*

WHERE TO STAY

For expanded hotel reviews, visit Fodors.com.

$ ▦ **Aslar Guest House.** This terraced town house dating from 1865 has large rooms with ornate cornicing and antique reproduction furniture. **Pros:** homey feel; exceptional breakfast. **Cons:** books up quickly. ⊠ *120 North St.* ☎ *01334/473460* ⊕ *www.aslar.com* ⇖ *6 rooms* ☌ *In-room: no a/c, Wi-Fi* ⦿*Breakfast.*

$$$$ ▦ **Fairmont St Andrews.** Just 2 mi from St. Andrews, this modern hotel has spectacular views of the bay and superb golf. **Pros:** spacious feel; excellent spa; golf at your doorstep. **Cons:** the huge atrium feels like a shopping center; paintings made to match the decor. ⊠ *A917, St. Andrews Bay* ☎ *01334/837000* ⊕ *www.fairmont.com/standrews* ⇖ *192 rooms, 17 suites* ☌ *In-room: safe, Wi-Fi. In-hotel: restaurant, bar, golf course, pool, gym, spa* ⦿*Breakfast.*

$$$$ ▦ **Old Course Hotel.** Regularly hosting international golf stars and jet-
Fodor's Choice setters, the Old Course Hotel is experiencing a renaissance. **Pros:** fabu-
★ lous location and lovely views; unpretentious service; golfer's heaven. **Cons:** breakfast is not as lavish as you'd expect; patchy air-conditioning. ⊠ *Old Station Rd.* ☎ *01334/474371* ⊕ *www.oldcoursehotel.co.uk* ⇖ *109 rooms, 35 suites* ☌ *In-room: no a/c. In-hotel: restaurant, bar, pool, gym, spa* ⦿*Breakfast.*

$$$$ ▦ **Rufflets Country House Hotel.** Ten acres of formal and informal gardens
★ surround this creeper-covered country house just outside St. Andrews. **Pros:** attractive gardens; cozy drawing room. **Cons:** too far to walk to St. Andrews; guest rooms too fussy for some tastes. ⊠ *Strathkinness Low Rd.* ☎ *01334/472594* ⊕ *www.rufflets.co.uk* ⇖ *24 rooms, 4 suites* ☌ *In-room: no a/c. In-hotel: restaurant, bar, business center* ⦿*Breakfast.*

NIGHTLIFE AND THE ARTS

PUBS **Central Bar.** Unlike a lot of local places, the Central Bar hasn't gone down the minimalist-decor-and-cocktails road. You'll find a good range of beers (bottled and on tap) and decent pub food. ⊠ *77 Market St.* ☎ *01334/478296.*

THEATER **Byre Theatre.** Experimental plays, small-scale operatic performances, contemporary dance, and Sunday-night jazz (in the foyer) are on the bill at the Byre. The Kingarroch, its handsome café-bar and bistro, serves excellent food. ⊠ *Abbey St.* ☎ *01334/475000* ⊕ *www.byretheatre.com.*

GOLF

What serious golfer doesn't dream of playing at world-famous St. Andrews? Seven St. Andrews courses, all part of the St. Andrews Trust, are open to visitors, and more than 40 other courses in the region offer golf by the round or by the day.

ST. ANDREWS LINKS TRUST COURSES

For information about availability—there's usually a waiting list, which varies according to the time of year—contact St. Andrews Links Trust. Greens fees range from £64 to £130 for a round on the Old Course and from £8 to £65 for a round on the five other courses. ⊠ *Pilmour House, St. Andrew* ☎ *01334/466666* ⊕ *www.standrews.org.uk.*

Balgove Course. At the beginner-friendly Balgove you can turn up and tee off without prior reservation. ✆ *£12 for two rounds* ⛳ *9 holes, 1,520 yds, par 30.*

Castle Course. Designed by David McLay Kidd in 2008, the Castle Course hugs the coast and has jaw-dropping views. It's 2 mi from the town center. ✆ *£120 per round.* ⛳ *18 holes, 6,759 yds, par 71.*

Eden Course. The inland and aptly named Eden, designed in 1914 by Harry S. Colt, has an easy charm compared with the other St. Andrews Links courses. ✆ *£40 per round.* ⛳ *18 holes, 6,250 yds, par 70.*

Jubilee Course. This windswept course, opened in 1897, offers quite a challenge even for experienced golfers. ✆ *£65 per round.* ⛳ *18 holes, 6,742 yds, par 72.*

★ **New Course.** Not exactly new—it opened in 1895—the New Course is rather overshadowed by the Old Course, but it has a firm following of golfers who appreciate the loop design. ✆ *£65 per round.* ⛳ *18 holes, 6,625 yds, par 71.*

Old Course. Believed to be the oldest golf course in the world, the Old Course was first played in the 15th century. Each year, more than 44,000 rounds are teed off, and no doubt most get stuck in one of its 112 bunkers. A handicap certificate is required. ✆ *£130 per round.* ⛳ *18 holes, 6,721 yds, par 72.*

Strathtyrum Course. Those with a high handicap will enjoy a toddle around this course, opened in 1993, without the worry or embarrassment of holding up more experienced golfers. ■ TIP➜ This course is for novices, rather than serious golfers. ✆ *£25 per round.* ⛳ *18 holes, 5,620 yds, par 69.*

SHOPPING

Artery. Artery sells work by local, Scottish, and British artists, including jewelry, ceramics, paintings, and intriguing handmade clocks. ⊠ *43 South St.* ☎ *01334/478221.*

Di Gilpin. A magnet for the knitters in the east coast of Scotland, where the finest wools are sold, Di Gilpin offers fantastic hand-knitted jumpers, cardigans, and accessories. ⊠ *Burghers Close, 141 South St.* ☎ *01334/476193.*

Mellis. Mellis is a cheese-lover's mecca. Look for a soft, crumbly local cheese called Anster. ⊠ *149 South St.* ☎ *01334/471410.*

CRAIL

Fodor'sChoice   *10 mi south of St. Andrews.*

★   The oldest and most aristocratic of East Neuk burghs, pretty Crail is where many fish merchants retired and built cottages. The town landmark is a picturesque Dutch-influenced town house, or *tolbooth,* which contains the oldest bell in Fife, cast in Holland in 1520. Crail is an artists' colony but remains a working harbor; take time to walk the streets and beaches and to sample fish by the harbor. ■ TIP➜ As you head into East Neuk from this tiny port, look about for market crosses, merchant houses, and little doocots (dovecotes, where pigeons were kept)—typical picturesque touches of this region.

GETTING HERE AND AROUND

Stagecoach bus number 63 operates between Crail and St. Andrews. However, the number 95 is more regular and also takes you to Anstruther, Pittenweem, and Lower Largo. Crail is about 15 minutes from St. Andrews by car via A917.

EXPLORING

Crail Museum & Heritage Centre. The story of this trading and fishing town can be found in the delightfully crammed Crail Museum & Heritage Centre, entirely run by local volunteers. There is a small tourist information desk within the center. ✉ *62–64 Marketgate* ☎ *01333/450869* ⊕ *www.crailmuseum.org.uk* ⌖ *Free* ⊘ *June–Sept., Mon.–Sat. 10–1 and 2–5, Sun. 2–5.*

WHERE TO STAY

For expanded hotel reviews, visit Fodors.com.

$ ▦ **Hazelton.** Beautifully polished wood, exquisitely restored period features, and gentle hues put the Hazelton head and shoulders above the typical seaside B&B. **Pros:** handsome building; excellent location; nothing is too much of a problem for the generous-spirited staff. **Cons:** you have to be a meat eater to make the most of the breakfast. ✉ *29 Marketgate N* ☎ *01333/450250* ⊕ *www.thehazelton.co.uk* ⌖ *5 rooms* ⌖ *In-room: Wi-Fi* ¶ *Breakfast.* ⊘ *Closed Jan.*

ANSTRUTHER

4 mi southwest of Crail.

Anstruther, locally called Ainster, has a lovely waterfront with a few shops brightly festooned with children's pails and shovels, a gesture to summer vacationers.

GETTING HERE AND AROUND

Strgecoach bus number 95 operates between St. Andrews, Crail, Anstruther, Pittenweem, and Lower Largo. Anstruther is 5 to 10 minutes from Crail by car via A917.

ESSENTIALS

Visitor Information Anstruther ✉ *Scottish Fisheries Museum, Harbour Head* ☎ *01333/311073* ⊕ *www.visitfife.com.*

EXPLORING

★ **Scottish Fisheries Museum.** Facing Anstruther Harbor is the Scottish Fisheries Museum, in a colorful cluster of buildings, the earliest of which dates from the 16th century. The museum illustrates the life of Scottish fisherfolk through documents, artifacts, model ships, paintings, and displays (complete with the reek of tarred rope and net). There are also floating exhibits at the quayside. Visit Fife has a small desk here with tourism information. ✉ *Harbourhead* ☎ *01333/310628* ⊕ *www. scotfishmuseum.org* ⌖ *£6* ⊘ *Apr.–Sept., Mon.–Sat. 10–5:30, Sun. 11–5; Oct.–Mar., Mon.–Sat. 10–4:30, Sun. noon–4:30; last admission 1 hr before closing.*

5

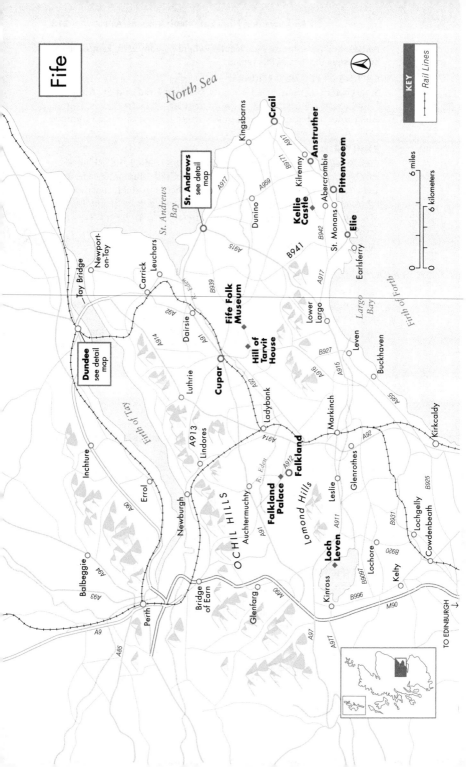

Anstruther Fish Bar and Restaurant. Next door to the Scottish Fisheries Museum, this popular fish-and-chip shop has space to eat, but most people order take-out. Try Pittenweem-landed prawns in batter or the catch of the day, which could be mackerel (line caught by the owners), skate wings, or lobster. ⊠ *42–44 Shore St.* ☎ *01333/310518* ⊕ *www.anstrutherfishbar. co.uk.*

WHERE TO EAT

$$$$
BRITISH

✕ **The Cellar.** Entered through a cobbled courtyard, this unpretentious, old-fashioned restaurant is hugely popular. The low ceiling and exposed beams create a cozy atmosphere. Specializing in seafood, as well as local beef and lamb, owner and chef Peter Jukes serves three-course meals cooked simply in modern Scottish style. The crayfish bisque served with Gruyère is known all over the region, as is the excellent wine list. ⊠ *24 E. Green* ☎ *01333/310378* ⊕ *www.cellaranstruther.co.uk* ⊙ *Closed Sun. and Mon. Nov.–Easter.*

NIGHTLIFE

Dreel Tavern. A 16th-century coaching inn, the Dreel Tavern is famous for its hand-drawn ales. ⊠ *16 High St.* W ☎ *01333/310727.*

BICYCLING

East Neuk Outdoors. The back roads of Fife make pleasant places for biking. You can rent bicycles from East Neuk Outdoors, which also has equipment for archery, climbing, and canoeing. ⊠ *Cellardyke Park* ☎ *01333/311929* ⊕ *www.eastneukoutdoors.co.uk.*

PITTENWEEM

1½ mi southwest of Anstruther.

Many examples of East Neuk architecture serve as the backdrop for the working harbor at Pittenweem. Look for the crowstep gables, white *harling* (the rough mortar finish on walls), and red pantiles (roof tiles with an S-shape profile). The *weem* part of the town's name comes from the Gaelic *uaime*, meaning cave.

GETTING HERE AND AROUND

Stagecoach bus number 95 operates hourly between St. Andrews, Crail, Anstruther, Pittenweem, and Lower Largo. Pittenweem is about five minutes from Anstruther by car via A917.

EXPLORING

The Cocoa Tree Shop & Café. Open daily, the Cocoa Tree Shop & Café is a former bakery that stocks the most imaginative and comprehensive range of fine chocolates you'll find in this part of the world. There is also a lovely café, with cakes and, of course, handmade chocolates from the Pittenweem Chocolate Company. ⊠ *9 High St.* ☎ *01333/311495* ⊕ *www.thecocoatreeshop.com* ⊙ *Daily 10–6.*

Kellie Castle and Garden. Dating from the 16th to 17th centuries and restored in Victorian times, Kellie Castle stands among the grain fields and woodlands of northeastern Fife. Four acres of pretty gardens surround the castle, which is in the care of the National Trust for Scotland.

In summer you can buy berries grown in the walled garden, and baked goods are sold in the tearoom. ⊠ *B9171, 3 mi northwest of Pittenweem* ☎ *0844/493–2184* ⊕ *www.nts.org.uk* ⊠ *£9* ⊙ *Castle Apr., May, Sept., and Oct., Thurs.–Mon. 12:30–5; June–Aug., daily 12:30–5; garden Apr.–Oct., daily 10–6, Nov.–Mar., daily 10–3:30.*

Pittenweem Arts Festival. There is nothing quite like the Pittenweem Arts Festival. Exhibitions, which involve hundreds of local and international artists, take place in the town's public buildings and in private homes and gardens. It's a week of events, workshops, and live music. ☎ *01333/313903* ⊕ *www.pittenweemartsfestival.co.uk.*

St. Fillan's Cave. This town's cavern is called St. Fillan's Cave, which contains the shrine of St. Fillan, a 6th-century hermit who lived here. It's up a *close* (alleyway) behind the waterfront. If the cave isn't open, ask at the Gingerbread Horse Café on High Street. ⊠ *Cove Wynd* ⊠ *£1* ⊙ *Mon.–Sat. 10–5.*

WHERE TO EAT

$$$$ ✕ **16 West End.** The big sister of the Seafood Restaurant in St. Andrews, this eatery put St. Monans on Scotland's culinary map. The menu has
SEAFOOD   vegetarian and meat options, but this is really a place for those who love the taste of the sea. The Thai mussel broth and seared scallops are fabulously fishy. ⊠ *16 West End, 2 mi west of Pittenweem, St. Monans* ☎ *01333/730327* ⚠ *Reservations essential* ⊙ *Closed Mon. and Tues.*

ELIE

5 mi south of Pittenweem.

To give it its full name, the Royal Burgh of Elie and Earlsferry is an old trading port with a handsome harbor that loops around one of the most glorious stretches of sand in the British Isles. Since Victorian times, when a railway (sadly defunct since the 1960s) linked it with the capital, Elie has been a weekend and summer retreat for the great and the good of Edinburgh. The beach to the south of the harbor is a mile long and has clean sands, clear waters, and just enough flotsam and jetsam to interest a beachcomber.

WHERE TO EAT

$ ✕ **Ship Inn.** Sports lovers visit Elie on Sunday to watch cricket matches
BRITISH   played on the beach outside the Ship Inn. The staff fires up a barbecue and cooks simple fare, including burgers and chicken. On the side are salads and lots of chips. The relaxed atmosphere and the beauty of this slow, cerebral game makes for an afternoon you'll never forget, especially if the sun shines. ⊠ *The Toft* ☎ *01333/330246* ⊕ *www.ship-elie.com.*

FALKLAND

Fodor'sChoice   *24 mi northwest of Pittenweem, 15 mi northwest of Elie.*

★   One of the loveliest communities in Scotland, Falkland is a royal burgh of twisting streets and crooked stone houses.

GETTING HERE AND AROUND

Stagecoach bus number 64A connects Falkland to St. Andrews as well as Cupar and Ladybank (both of which are train stations on the Edinburgh to Dundee line). Falkland is about 15 minutes from Cupar and a half hour from St. Andrews by car via A91 and A912, or A91 to A914 to A912.

EXPLORING

★ **Falkland Palace.** A former hunting lodge of the Stuart monarchs, Falkland Palace dominates the town. The castle is one of the earliest examples in Britain of the French Renaissance style. Overlooking the main street is the palace's most impressive feature, the walls and chambers on its south side, all rich with buttresses and stone medallions, built by French masons in the 1530s for King James V (1512–42). He died here, and the palace was a favorite resort of his daughter, Mary, Queen of Scots (1542–87). In the beautiful gardens, overlooked by the palace turret windows, you may easily imagine yourself back at the solemn hour when James on his deathbed pronounced the doom of the house of Stuart: "It cam' wi' a lass and it'll gang wi a lass." ⊠ *Main St.* ☎ *01337/857397, 0844/493–2186* ⊕ *www.nts.org.uk* ⌧ *£11* ⊘ *Mar.– Oct., Mon.–Sat. 10–5, Sun. 1–5.*

LOCH LEVEN

10 mi southwest of Falkland.

Scotland's largest Lowland loch, Loch Leven is famed for its fighting trout. The area is also noted for abundant birdlife, particularly its wintering wildfowl. Mary, Queen of Scots, was forced to sign the deed of abdication in her island prison in the loch.

GETTING HERE AND AROUND

If you're driving from St. Andrews or Cupar, take A91 to Kinross and follow the signs from there. From Falkland, take A911.

EXPLORING

Vane Farm Nature Reserve. On the southern shore overlooking the lock, Vane Farm Nature Reserve, a visitor center run by the Royal Society for the Protection of Birds, provides information about Loch Leven's ecology. It's the best place in Britain to see lapwings, pink-footed geese, tufted ducks, and shovelers. ⊠ *Rte. B9097, off M90 and B996* ☎ *01577/862355* ⊕ *www.rspb.org.uk* ⌧ *£3* ⊘ *Daily 10–5.*

CUPAR

21 mi northwest of Loch Leven, 10 mi west of St. Andrews.

Cupar is a busy market town with several interesting sites, including a museum about Fife.

GETTING HERE AND AROUND

Cupar has a train station on the Edinburgh–Aberdeen line (which passes through Dundee), and there are trains almost every hour. Stagecoach buses serve the town as well. By car, you can reach Cupar from Loch Leven via M90 and A91; take A91 if you're traveling from St. Andrews.

EXPLORING

Hill of Tarvit House. On rising ground near the town stands the National Trust for Scotland's Hill of Tarvit House. Originally a 17th-century mansion, the house was altered in the high-Edwardian style in the late 1890s and early 1900s by the Scottish architect Sir Robert Lorimer (1864–1929). The extensive wood and parklands offer an enjoyable place for a picnic or stroll, and the house itself is well worth a visit. Golfers will also want to play a round on the old Lorimer family course, the Hickory, which was brought back to life in 2008 after being ploughed up for agricultural use during World War II. ⊠ *Off A916, 2 mi south of Cupar* ☎ *0844/493–2185* ⊕ *www.nts.org.uk* ⌨ *£9* ⊙ *House Apr.–Oct., Thurs.–Mon. 1–5; gardens daily 9:30–sunset.*

Fife Folk Museum. To learn more about the history and culture of rural Fife, visit the Fife Folk Museum. The life of local rural communities is reflected in artifacts and documents housed in a former weigh house and adjoining weavers' cottages. The museum is 3 mi southeast of Cupar via A916 and B939. ⊠ *High St., Ceres* ☎ *01334/828180* ⊕ *www. fifefolkmuseum.org* ⌨ *£4* ⊙ *Apr.–Oct., daily 10:30–4:30.*

☺ **Scottish Deer Centre.** At the Scottish Deer Centre, many types of deer can be seen at close quarters or on ranger-guided tours. There are nature trails, falconry displays, an adventure playground (a wood-and-tire fortress suitable for older children), a handful of shops, and a café. The center, west of Cupar, is one of the few places you can spot red squirrels. ⊠ *A91* ☎ *01337/810391* ⊕ *www.tsdc.co.uk* ⌨ *£7.45* ⊙ *July and Aug., daily 10–5:30; Sept.–June, daily 10–4:30.*

WHERE TO EAT AND STAY

For expanded hotel reviews, visit Fodors.com.

$$$ ✕ **Ostlers Close Restaurant.** It's thoroughly unpretentious, but this cot-
BRITISH   tage-style restaurant with plain painted walls and stick-back chairs has earned a well-deserved reputation for top-quality cuisine that is imaginative without trying to be too trendy. The chef's light touch means the flavors are simple, with especially fresh shellfish and vegetables. This longtime favorite is tucked away in an alley off the main street. It's a good idea to reserve ahead, particularly for lunch. ⊠ *25 Bonnygate* ☎ *01334/655574* ⊙ *Closed Sun. and Mon. No lunch Tues.–Thurs.*

$$$ ⚏ **The Peat Inn.** With eight bright and contemporary two-room suites,
Fodor'sChoice   this popular "restaurant with rooms" is perhaps best known for its
★   outstanding, modern, Scottish-style restaurant ($$$). **Pros:** exceptional restaurant; super-efficient but easygoing staff. **Cons:** booking is essential; you need a car to get here. ⊠ *B941, at intersection of B940* ☎ *01334/840206* ⊕ *www.thepeatinn.co.uk* ⤳ *8 suites* ⚷ *In-room: no a/c. In-hotel: restaurant, parking* ⊙ *Closed Sun. and Mon.* ⏀ *Breakfast.*

DUNDEE AND ANGUS

The small city of Dundee sits near the mouth of the River Tay surrounded by the farms and glens of rural Angus and the coastal grassy banks and golf courses of northeastern Fife. A vibrant, industrious city that's off the main tourist track, Dundee plays a significant role in the biotech and computer-games industries. Dundee has a large student population; a lively arts and nightlife scene; and several historical and nautical sights. Its waterfront is slated to become home to the first outpost of London's Victoria and Albert Museum, a repository of decorative arts. This honor acknowledges Dundee's history in the textile trade.

Angus combines coastal agriculture on rich, red soils with dramatic inland glens that pierce their way into the foothills of the Grampian mountain ranges to the northwest. ■TIP➜ **The main road from Dundee to Aberdeen—the A90—requires drivers to take special care, with its mix of fast cars, trucks, and unexpectedly slow farm traffic.**

DUNDEE

14 mi northwest of St. Andrews, 58 mi north of Edinburgh, 79 mi northeast of Glasgow.

Dundee makes an excellent base for exploring Fife and Angus at any time of year. The West End—especially its main thoroughfare Perth Road—pulses with life, with intimate cafés and excellent bars. The Dundee Contemporary Arts center has gained the city some attention. As you walk the cobbled streets, you may glimpse the 1888 Tay Rail Bridge, and if you head southwest you can reach Magdalen Green, where landscape artist James McIntosh Patrick (1907–98) found inspiration from the views and ever-changing skyscapes. The popular comic strips *The Beano* and *The Dandy* were first published here in the 1930s, so statues depicting Desperate Dan, Dawg, and a catapult-wielding Minnie the Minx were erected in the City Square.

GETTING HERE AND AROUND
The East Coast train line runs through the city, linking it to Edinburgh (and beyond, to London), Glasgow (and the West Coast of England), and Aberdeen, with trains to all every hour or half-hourly at peak times. Cheaper bus service is available to all of these locations, as well as St. Andrews and several other towns in Fife and Angus.

If you're traveling by car, the A92 will take you from Fife, over the road bridge, and north to Abroath and the Angus coast towns. The A90, from Perth, heads north to Aberdeen.

Most of the sights in Dundee are clustered together, so you can easily walk around the city. If the weather is bad or your legs are heavy, hail one of the many cabs on the easy-to-find taxi ranks for little more than a few pounds.

ESSENTIALS
Visitor Information Dundee. ⊠ *Discovery Point, Riverside Dr.* ☎ *01382/527527* ⊕ *www.angusanddundee.co.uk.*

EXPLORING
TOP ATTRACTIONS
RRS *Discovery*. Dundee's urban-renewal program—the city is determined to celebrate its industrial past—was motivated in part by the arrival of the RRS (Royal Research Ship) *Discovery*, the vessel used by Captain Robert Scott (1868–1912) on his polar explorations. The steamer was originally built and launched in Dundee; now it's a permanent resident.

Broughty
Castle **10**

Dundee
Botanic Garden .. **8**

Dundee
Contemporary
Arts **4**

The Law **1**

McManus
Galleries **3**

Mills
Observatory **9**

North Carr
Lightship **7**

RRS
Discovery **5**

Unicorn **6**

Verdant
Works **2**

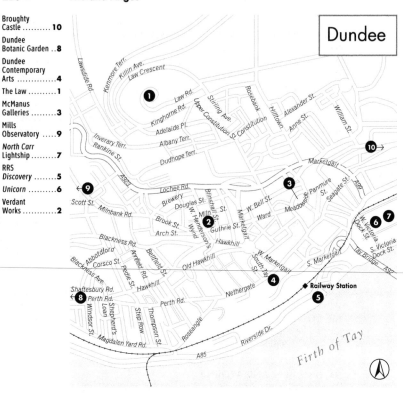

At Discovery Point, under the handsome cupola, the story of the ship
and its famous expedition unfold; you can even feel the Antarctic chill as
if you were there. The ship, berthed outside, is the star: wander the deck,
then explore the quarters to see the daily existence endured by the ship's
crew and captain. ⊠ *Discovery Quay, Riverside Dr.* ☎ *01382/309060*
⊕ *www.rrsdiscovery.com* ⊠ *£8, £12 with Verdant Works, £14.50 with
Glamis Castle* ⊗ *Apr.–Sept., Mon.–Sat. 10–6, Sun. 11–6; Oct.–Mar.,
Mon.–Sat. 10–5, Sun. 11–5; last admission 1 hr before closing.*

Dundee Botanic Garden. This renowned botanical garden contains an
extensive collection of native and exotic plants outdoors and in tropical
and temperate greenhouses. There are some beautiful areas for picnick-
ing, as well as a visitor center, an art gallery, and a coffee shop. ⊠ *Riverside Dr.* ☎ *01382/381190* ⊕ *www.dundeebotanicgarden.co.uk* ⊠ *£3.50*
⊗ *Mar.–Oct., daily 10–4:30; Nov.–Feb., daily 10–3:30.*

Dundee Contemporary Arts. Between a 17th-century mansion and a cathedral, this strikingly modern building houses one of Britain's most exciting artistic venues. The huge gallery houses up to six shows a year by
internationally acclaimed contemporary artists. There are children's
workshops and meet-the-artist events throughout the year. There are
also two movie theaters showing mainly independent, revival, and children's films, a craft shop, and a buzzing café-bar called Jute that's open

until midnight. ⊠ *152 Nethergate* ☎ *01382/909252* ⊕ *www.dca.org. uk* 🎫 *Free* ⊙ *Tues., Wed., Fri., and Sat. 10–6:30, Thurs. 11–8, Sun. noon–6.*

McManus Galleries. Dundee's principal museum and art gallery, housed in a striking Gothic Revival–style building, has an engaging collection of artifacts that document the city's history and the working, social, and cultural lives of Dundonians throughout the Victorian period and the 20th century. Its varied fine-art collection includes paintings by Rossetti, Raeburn, and Peploe as well as some thought-provoking yet accessible contemporary works. ⊠ *Albert Sq.* ☎ *01382/432350* ⊕ *www.mcmanus. co.uk* 🎫 *Free* ⊙ *Mon.–Sat. 10–5, Sun. 12:30–4:30.*

🕑 **Verdant Works.** In a former jute mill, Verdant Works houses a multi-faceted exhibit on the story of jute and the town's involvement in the jute trade. Restored machinery, audiovisual displays, and tableaux all illustrate the hard, noisy life of the jute worker. ⊠ *W. Hendersons Wynd* ☎ *01382/309060* ⊕ *www.verdantwork.co.uk* 🎫 *£7.25, £12 with RRS Discovery* ⊙ *Apr.–Oct., Mon.–Sat. 10–6, Sun. 11–6; Nov.–Mar., Wed.– Sat. 10:30–4:30, Sun. 11–4:30.*

WORTH NOTING

OFF THE
BEATEN
PATH

Broughty Castle. Originally built to guard the Tay Estuary, Broughty Castle is now a museum focusing on fishing, ferries, and the history of Broughty Ferry's whaling industry. The canons and ramparts make for fine photo opportunities, and inside (up a very narrow stairway) are four floors of displays, including the lovely art collection of the Victorian inventor and engineer Sir James Orchar. To the north of the castle lies beautiful Broughty Ferry Beach, which, even in mid-winter, is enjoyed by the locals; there is regular bus service here from Dundee's city center. ⊠ *King St., Broughty Ferry* ✛ *4 mi east of city center* ☎ *01382/436916* ⊕ *www.dundeecity.gov.uk/broughtycastle* 🎫 *Free* ⊙ *Apr.–Sept., Mon.– Sat. 10–4, Sun. 12:30–4; Oct.–Mar., Tues.–Sat. 10–4, Sun. 12:30–4.*

The Law. For sweeping views of the city, the Angus Glens to the north, and Fife's coastline to the south, head here. This hill (*law* means hill in Scottish) is actually an extinct volcano whose summit reaches 1,640 feet above sea level. A World War II memorial, parking lot, and seating area are at the top. ⊠ *Law Rd..*

Mills Observatory. At the top of a thickly forested hill, Mills Observatory is the only full-time public observatory in Britain. There are displays on astronomy, space exploration, scientific instruments, and a 12-inch refracting telescope for night viewing of the stars and planets. ⊠ *Balgay Hill, 2 mi west of city center* ☎ *01382/435967* 🎫 *Free* ⊙ *Oct.–Mar., weekdays 4–10 pm, weekends 12:30–4; Apr.–Sept., Tues.–Fri. 11–5, weekends 12:30–4.*

🕑 **North Carr Lightship.** After playing a significant role in World War II, Scot-land's only remaining lightship was wrecked on the Fife shore during a storm in 1959; seven crew members were lost. At this writing, the ship is closed for refurbishment. The charity Taymara, which looks after the *North Carr*, runs exhilarating trips on its other vessels, the *Badger* and the *Marigold*. Excursions include a half-day trip along the River Tay to Perth or an hour around the mouth of the delta, where dolphins jump

Fodor's Choice
★

and play. Prior booking is essential. ⊠ *Victoria Dock* ☎ *01382/562497* ⊕ *www.tayrivertrips.org* ✉ *One-hour trip £12.50, half-day trip £36.*

♻ **Unicorn.** It's easy to spot this 46-gun wood warship, as it's fronted by a figurehead of a white unicorn. This frigate has the distinction of being the oldest British-built warship afloat, having been launched in 1824 at Chatham, England. You can clamber right down into the hold, or see the models and displays about the Royal Navy's history. The ship's hours vary in winter, so call ahead. ⊠ *Victoria Dock, east of Tay Rd. bridge* ⊕ *www.frigateunicorn.org* ✉ *£5.25* ☉ *Apr.–Oct., daily 10–5; Nov.–Mar., Wed.–Fri. noon–4, weekends 10–4; last admission 20 mins before closing.*

WHERE TO EAT

$ ✕ **Jute.** Part of Dundee Contemporary Arts, this lively café-bar serves
BRITISH   gourmet burgers and tasty snacks by the bar (and on the terrace in
★   fine weather). The modish menu, including mains like teriyaki salmon with spring-onion noodles, is available in the dining area. The business lunch offers fabulous value: £15.50 for three courses. You can watch local artists at work while you eat, thanks to the huge windows that look onto the printmaking studio. ⊠ *152 Nethergate* ☎ *01382/909246.*

$ ✕ **Piccolo.** This small basement eatery, with sound wooden tables and
ITALIAN   chairs and a quirky staff, attracts a diverse clientele. It serves surprisingly good pizzas, crepes, and a fine plate of pappardelle with chicken in a light, lemony cream sauce. Reservations are recommended on weekends. ⊠ *21 Perth Rd.* ☎ *01382/201419* ⊕ *www.piccolodundee.co.uk* ⚑ *Reservations essential* ☉ *Closed Sun. and Mon.*

$$$ ✕ **Playwright.** This stylish restaurant is one of the city's more expensive,
BRITISH   but it's worth the price. A glass floor looks into the wine cellar, and the
★   staff is laid back but totally efficient. The menu is well put together, offering a range of flavors and textures and each dish, such as seared salmon with prawn risotto. Portions are a decent size, and everything is perfectly presented. There's a beautiful bar, too, for pre- or post-dinner tippling. ⊠ *11 Tay Sq.* ☎ *01382/223113* ⊕ *www.theplaywright.co.uk* ⚑ *Reservations essential* ☉ *Closed Sun.*

WHERE TO STAY

For expanded hotel reviews, visit Fodors.com.

$$ ⊡ **Apex City Quay.** Sleek, Scandinavian-style rooms with easy chairs, satiny pillows, and CD/DVD players help you unwind at this contemporary quayside hotel. **Pros:** stylish rooms; excellent brasserie. **Cons:** you have to cross a highway to get into town; often mobbed with conferences. ⊠ *1 W. Victoria Dock Rd.* ☎ *01382/202404* ⊕ *www.apexhotels. com* ➽ *145 rooms, 8 suites* ⚹ *In-room: no a/c, Wi-Fi. In-hotel: restaurant, bar, pool, gym, spa, parking* ❘◉❘ *Breakfast.*

$ ⊡ **Fisherman's Tavern Hotel.** One of Broughty Ferry's oldest pubs—it opened in 1827—still has its wooden, cabinlike bar, but it now stands in stark contrast to the comfortable minimalism of its bedrooms. **Pros:** quaint inn; short walk from the esplanade; a great breakfast served with a smile. **Cons:** you have to park on the street. ⊠ *10–16 Fort St., Broughty Ferry* ☎ *01382/775941* ➽ *7 rooms* ⚹ *In-room: no a/c, Wi-Fi. In-hotel: restaurant, bar* ❘◉❘ *Breakfast.*

$ ⛫ **Grampian Hotel.** This Georgian townhouse, right on the artery of the hip end of town, has undergone a few transformations over the years, but it has finally become the guesthouse it has always wanted to be. **Pros:** a few steps away from the lively West End; the loft room has wondrous views of the Tay. **Cons:** downstairs rooms feel rather tight. ✉ *295 Perth Rd.* ☎ *01382/667785* ⊕ *www.grampianhotel.com* ⮌ *10 rooms* ⚲ *In-room: no a/c, Wi-Fi* ⍾ *Breakfast.*

NIGHTLIFE AND THE ARTS

BARS AND PUBS Dundee's pub scene, centered in the West End–Perth Road area, is one of the liveliest in Scotland.

Fisherman's Tavern. If you find yourself in Broughty Ferry, you can't leave without a tipple here. ✉ *10–16 Fort St., Broughty Ferry* ☎ *01382/ 775941.*

Jute Café Bar. Better known as the bar at Dundee Contemporary Arts, this places attracts film fans (the art-house cinema's entrance is next door), students, and the well-heeled for European beers, wine, cocktails, or coffee. It serves tasty bar snacks every night until 9:30. ✉ *152 Nethergate* ☎ *01382/909246.*

Speedwell Bar. Called Mennie's by locals, the Speedwell Bar is in a mahogany-paneled building brimming with Dundonian characters. It's renowned for its superb cask beers and its whalebonelike Armitage Shanks urinals. ✉ *165–168 Perth Rd.* ☎ *01382/667783.*

DANCE CLUBS **Fat Sam's.** Fat Sam's attracts clubbers of all ages to its various club nights, which feature DJs spinning everything from indie to deep house. It has become the city's premier venue for live music, hosting up-and-coming bands as well as established acts who like to play more intimate gigs. ✉ *31 S. Ward Rd.* ☎ *01382/228181* ⊕ *www.fatsams.co.uk.*

MUSIC **Caird Hall.** Caird Hall is one of Scotland's finest concert halls, staging a wide range of music and events. ✉ *City Sq.* ☎ *01382/434451* ⊕ *www. cairdhall.co.uk.*

THEATER **Dundee Repertory Theatre.** The Dundee Repertory Theatre is home to the award-winning Dundee Rep Ensemble as well as Scotland's pre-eminent contemporary-dance group, Scottish Dance Theatre. Popular with locals, the restaurant and bar welcome late-night comedy shows and jazz bands. ✉ *Tay Sq.* ☎ *01382/223530* ⊕ *www.dundeerep.co.uk.*

Whitehall Theatre. The Whitehall Theatre has mostly comedy and musical theater productions, including light opera. ✉ *12 Bellfield St.* ☎ *01382/434940* ⊕ *www.whitehalldundee.co.uk.*

SHOPPING

BOOKS **Big Bairn Books.** There is no better place than Big Bairn Books to find old annuals of *The Beano, The Broons,* and *Oor Wullie,* all published by cult—and local—publisher D.C. Thomson. ✉ *17 Exchange St.* ☎ *01382/220225.*

COFFEE AND TEA **J. Allan Braithwaite.** This shop carries 13 types of freshly roasted coffees and more than 30 blended teas that you can pop into one of the quaint teapots you'll find here. ✉ *6 Castle St.* ☎ *01382/322693.*

5

Westport Gallery. The Westport Gallery stocks contemporary designer housewares, including ceramics and glass, plus highly stylized clothing and jewelry. ⊠ *44 West Port* ☎ *01382/221751.*

Queen's Gallery. The gallery has a compelling selection of jewelry, ceramics, and paintings by Scottish artists. ⊠ *160 Nethergate* ☎ *01382/ 220600.*

ARBROATH

15 mi north of Dundee.

You can find traditional boatbuilding in the fishing town of Arbroath. It also has several small curers and processors, and shops sell the town's most famous delicacy, Arbroath smokies—whole haddock gutted and lightly smoked. A few miles north along the coast is the old fishing village of Auchmithie, with a beautiful little beach that you can walk to via a short path. The jagged, reddish cliffs and caves are home to a flourishing seabird population.

GETTING HERE AND AROUND

The East Coast train line stops at Arbroath. The Abbey and Signal Tower are all within walking distance, but you'll need a car to get to Auchmithie. If you're driving from Dundee, take A92.

ESSENTIALS

Visitor Information Arbroath ⊠ *Fish Market Quay, A92* ☎ *01241/872609* ⊕ *www.angusanddundee.co.uk.*

EXPLORING

Arbroath Abbey. Founded in 1178, Arbroath Abbey is an unmistakable presence in the town center; it seems to straddle whole streets, as if the town were simply ignoring the red-stone ruin in its midst. Surviving today are remains of the church, as well as one of the most complete examples in existence of an abbot's residence. From here in 1320 a passionate plea was sent by King Robert the Bruce (1274–1329) and the Scottish Church to Pope John XXII (circa 1245–1334) in far-off Rome. The pope had until then sided with the English kings, who adamantly refused to acknowledge Scottish independence. The Declaration of Arbroath stated firmly, "It is in truth not for glory, nor riches, nor honours that we are fighting, but for freedom—for that alone, which no honest man gives up but with life itself." Some historians describe this plea, originally drafted in Latin, as the single most important document in Scottish history. The pope advised English king Edward II (1284–1327) to make peace, but warfare was to break out along the border from time to time for the next 200 years. The excellent visitor center recounts this history in well-planned displays. ⊠ *Abbey St.* ☎ *01241/878756* ⊕ *www.historic-scotland.gov.uk* ⌛ *£5.50* ☽ *Apr.–Sept., daily 9:30–5:30; Oct.–Mar., daily 9:30–4:30.*

Signal Tower Museum. In the early 19th century, Arbroath was the base for the construction of the Bell Rock lighthouse on a treacherous, barely exposed rock in the Forth of Tay. A signal tower was built to facilitate communication with the builders working far from shore. That structure now houses the Signal Tower Museum, which tells the story of

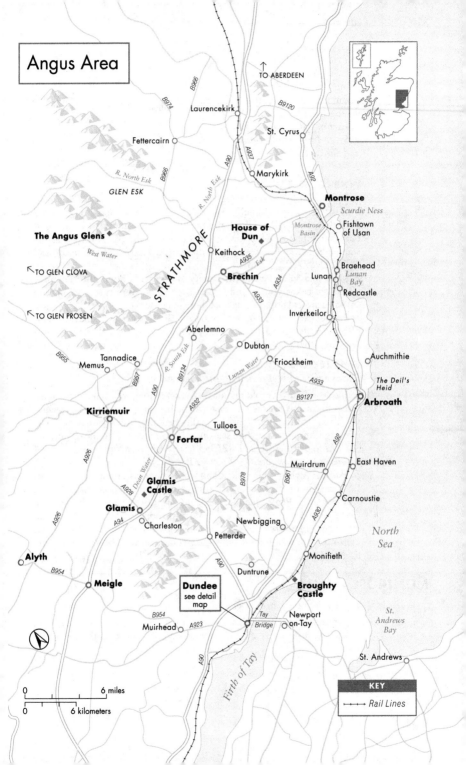

the lighthouse, built by Robert Stevenson (1772–1850) in 1811. The museum also houses a collection of items related to the history of the town, its customs, and the local fishing industry. ✉ *Ladyloan, west of harbor* ☎ *01241/435329* 🖥 *Free* ☉ *Sept.–June, Mon.–Sat. 10–5; July and Aug., Mon.–Sat. 10–5 and Sun. 2–5.*

WHERE TO EAT

¢ ✕ **But 'n' Ben.** This homey restaurant offers a taste of quality Scottish home cooking, including smokie
BRITISH pancakes, crab salad, mince and tatties, and lemon drizzle cake, all at reasonable prices. After lunch, stroll down to the Auchmithie's lovely shingle beach. ✉ *Ethie St., Auchmithie* ✛ *Near Arbroath, 3 mi off A92* ☎ *01241/877223* ☉ *Closed Tues.*

¢ ✕ **Sugar and Spice.** Peruse the sweets of your childhood and reminisce
BRITISH about the cakes your grandmother used to make in this combination café and sweet shop. Locals flock here to enjoy the meringues, sponges, and other desserts. There are soups and sandwiches for lunch and simple dishes like roast beef and Yorkshire pudding for dinner. ✉ *9–13 High St.* ☎ *01241/437500.*

WHERE TO STAY

For expanded hotel reviews, visit Fodors.com.

$ 🏨 **The Brucefield.** This old manor house, set among well-tended grounds, offers luxurious rooms for very reasonable rates. **Pros:** all the touches you'd expect in a five-star hotel; quality bedding; friendly owners. **Cons:** two-night minimum in high season; a 20-minute walk to the city center. ✉ *Cliffburn Rd.* ☎ *01241/875393* ⊕ *www.brucefieldbandb.com* ⇆ *4 rooms* ⚐ *In-room: no a/c, Wi-Fi* ❤️ *Breakfast.*

$ 🏨 **Harbour Nights.** An excellent and somewhat plush budget option, this B&B is right on the harbor, affording you the most authentic Arbroath stay possible. **Pros:** splendid seafront location; delicious breakfasts. **Cons:** only one room with a private bathroom; you must book far in advance. ✉ *4 Shore* ☎ *01421/434343* ⊕ *www.harbournights-scotland. com* ⇆ *5 rooms, 1 with bath* ⚐ *In-room: no a/c. In-hotel: parking* ❤️ *Breakfast.*

MONTROSE

14 mi north of Arbroath via A92.

An unpretentious and attractive town with a museum and a selection of shops, Montrose sits beside a wide estuary known as the Montrose Basin.

GETTING HERE AND AROUND

On the main East Coast train line and local bus route (the Stagecoach Strathtay 39 and 73 from Dundee and Arbroath), the town is easily accessed by public transportation. However, you'll need a car to get to attractions outside town.

ESSENTIALS

Visitor Info **Montrose Museum and Tourist Information Centre.** ⊠ *Panmure Pl.* ☎ *01674/673232* ⊕ *www.angusanddundee.co.uk* ⊠ *Free* ⊙ *Mon.–Sat. 10–5.*

EXPLORING

★ **House of Dun.** The National Trust for Scotland's leading attraction in this area is the House of Dun, which overlooks the Montrose Basin. The mansion was built in the 1730s for lawyer David Erskine, otherwise known as Lord Dun (1670–1755). Designed by architect William Adam (1689–1748), the house is particularly noted for its ornate plasterwork and curious Masonic masonry. Some of Lord Dun's heirlooms, including samples from the family's collection of embroidery, tell the story of the Seat of Dun and the eminent family's history. The sprawling grounds have restored workshops, plus an enchanting walled Victorian garden. ⊠ *A935, 4 mi west of Montrose* ☎ *0844/493–2144* ⊕ *www.nts.org.uk/ Visits* ⊠ *£9* ⊙ *House July and Aug., daily 11–5; Sept. and Oct., Wed.– Sun. noon–5. Garden year-round, daily 9–sunset.*

Montrose Basin Wildlife Centre. Run by the Scottish Wildlife Trust, this nature reserve has geese, ducks, and swans. Several nature trails can take you up close to the reserve's residents if you're quiet. ⊠ *Rossie Braes* ☎ *01674/676336* ⊕ *www.montrosebasin.org.uk* ⊠ *£4* ⊙ *Visitor center Mar.–Oct., daily 10:30–5; Nov.–Feb., Fri.–Sun. 10:30–4.*

Montrose Museum. The town's museum—housed in a neoclassical building that also contains the tourist information center—exhibits some fascinating bequests by the local gentry, including an early-19th-century ship carved from bone by French prisoners in the Napoleonic war. ⊠ *Panmure Pl.* ☎ *01674/673232* ⊕ *www.angus.gov.uk/history/ museums/montrose* ⊠ *Free* ⊙ *Mon.–Sat. 10–5.*

BRECHIN

10 mi southwest of Montrose.

The small market town of Brechin has a cathedral that was founded around 1200 and contains an interesting selection of antiquities, including the Mary Stone, a Pictish relic.

GETTING HERE AND AROUND

Brechin is not on the East Coast train line but can be reached by bus from Montrose or Arbroath (the Stagecoach Strathtay number 30). It's on the A935, just off the main A90 road between Dundee and Aberdeen.

EXPLORING

Brechin Town House Museum. Located in the old courtroom which had cells in its cellars, the Brechin Town House Museum houses a small but interesting collection of objects from as far back as the Bronze Age. There is a small tourist information desk within the museum.

BEAUTIFUL BEACHES

Scotland's east coast enjoys many hours of sunshine, compared with its west coast, and is blessed with lots of sandy beaches under the ever-changing backdrop of the sky. Take time to explore the beaches and walk along the coast for a change of pace whatever the time of year.

In Fife, Tentsmuir's Beach near St. Andrews is popular with kite fly-ers and horseback riders, and the famous and lovely West Sands in St. Andrews is where the running sequences in the movie *Chariots of Fire* were filmed. The small cove beach at Elie, south of Crail, hosts cricket matches in summer.

In Angus, the beach at Broughty Ferry, near the city of Dundee, fills with families and children on week-ends and during school holidays—even on the most blustery of days.

North of Arbroath lies Auchmithie Beach, more shingly (pebbly) than the others and offering a bracing breath of North Sea air. And finally, near the Montrose Basin, you can discover the enchanting crescent of Lunan Bay, home to many species of seabirds.

✉ *28 High St.* ☎ *01356/625536* ⊕ *www.angus.gov.uk/history/museums/ brechin* 🎟 *Free* ☉ *Mon.–Sat. 9–5.*

Pictavia. The first arrivals in this part of Scotland were the Picts, who came sometime in the first millennium. Pictavia explores what is known about this race of Celts using actual artifacts, replicas, and interactive exhibits. ✉ *Brechin Castle Centre, Off A90* ☎ *01307/626241* ⊕ *www. pictavia.org.uk* 🎟 *£3.25* ☉ *Mon.–Sat. 9–5, Sun. 10–5.*

Round Tower. The town's 10th-century Brechin Cathedral and Round Tower is on the site of a former Celtic monastery (prior of the Culdee monks) and has some unusual examples of Medieval sculpture. The tower is one of only two on mainland Scotland. This type of structure is more frequently found in Ireland. ✉ *6 Church St.* ☎ *01356/629360* ⊕ *www.brechincathedral.org* 🎟 *Free* ☉ *Daily 9–5.*

WHERE TO EAT

¢   ✕ **Rosie's Bakehouse.** It's exciting to discover such a great bakery in a
CAFÉ small Scottish town. You'll find all the classics, from traditional Vic-toria sponge cake to much-loved scones. If you're in the mood for something more substantial, try the soups, panini, and sandwiches, all served by the cheerful staff. ✉ *26 High St.* ☎ *01356/625254* ☉ *Closed Sun. No lunch.*

THE ANGUS GLENS

25 mi southwest of Brechin.

You can rejoin the hurly-burly of the A90 for the return journey south from Montrose or Brechin; the more pleasant route, however, leads southwesterly on minor roads (there are several options) that travel along the face of the Grampians, following the fault line that separates Highland and Lowland. The **Angus Glens** extend north from points on A90. Known individually as the glens of Isla, Prosen, Clova, and

Esk, these long valleys run into the high hills of the Grampians and some clearly marked walking routes. Those in Glen Clova are especially appealing.

Be aware that Thursday is a half day in Angus; many shops and attractions close at lunch.

GETTING HERE AND AROUND

You really need a car to reach the Angus Glens and enjoy the gentle (and not so gentle) inclines here. Glamis and Kirriemuir are both on the A928 (just off the A90), and the B955—which loops round at Glen Clova—is one of the loveliest Scottish roads to drive along, especially when the heather is blooming in late summer.

WHERE TO STAY

For expanded hotel reviews, visit Fodors.com.

$ 🔲 **Glen Clova Hotel.** Since the 1850s, the hospitality of this hotel has lifted the spirits of many a bone-tired hill walker. **Pros:** stunning location; great base for outdoor pursuits; spacious accommodations. **Cons:** lack of decent public transportation; rooms are booked well in advance. ⊠ *B955, Glen Clova* ☎ *01575/550350* ⊕ *www.clova.com* ➷ *10 rooms* ⚐ *In-room: no a/c. In-hotel: restaurant, bar* ⦾ *Breakfast.*

KIRRIEMUIR

15 mi southeast of Brechin.

Kirriemuir stands at the heart of Angus's red-sandstone countryside and was the birthplace of the writer J.M. Barrie (1860–1937), best known abroad as the author of *Peter Pan* (a statue of whom you can see in the town's square).

GETTING HERE AND AROUND

A number of roads lead to Kirriemuir, but A928 (off A90), which also passes Glamis Castle, is one of the loveliest. Stagecoach Strathtay runs buses to this area; the 20 and 22 from Dundee are the most regular.

EXPLORING

Camera Obscura. J.M. Barrie donated the Camera Obscura to the town. The device—a dark room with a small hole in one wall that projects an image of the outside world onto the opposite wall—is one of only three in the country. It affords magnificent views of the surrounding area on a clear day. It sits in a cricket pavilion on Kirrie Hill, just northeast of Kirriemuir. ⊠ *Kirrie Hill* ☎ *0844/493-2143* 🖾 *£3, £6 with J.M. Barrie's Birthplace* ⊙ *Apr.–June, Sept., and Oct., Sat.–Wed. 10–5; July and Aug., daily 11–5:30.*

J.M. Barrie's Birthplace. At the J.M. Barrie's Birthplace, the National Trust pays tribute to the man who sought to preserve the magic of childhood more than any other writer of his age. The house's upper floors are furnished as they might have been in Barrie's time, complete with domestic necessities, while downstairs is his study, replete with manuscripts and personal mementos. The outside washhouse is said to have been Barrie's first theater. ⊠ *9 Brechin Rd.* ☎ *0844/493-2142* ⊕ *www.*

nts.org.uk/visits 🖼 *£6, includes Camera Obscura* ⊗ *Apr.–June, Sept., and Oct., Sat.–Wed. 10–5; July and Aug., daily 11–5:30.*

Kirriemuir Gateway to the Glens Museum. As is the style in Angus, the local museum doubles as the visitor center, meaning you can get all the information you need and admire a few stuffed birds and artifacts at the same time. Rock fans will appreciate the exhibit celebrating local lad made good (or rather bad), the late Bon Scott, lead singer of the rock band ACDC. ⊠ *32 High St.* ☎ *01575/575479* ⊕ *www.angus.gov. uk/history/museums/kirriemuir* 🖼 *Free* ⊗ *Apr.–Sept., Mon.–Sat. 10–5; Oct.–Mar., Mon.–Wed., Fri., and Sat. 10–5, Thurs. 1–5.*

NEED A BREAK?

88 Degrees. If you're not in a rush (the service can be slow), you'll enjoy the best coffee in town and temple-achingly sweet cakes and handmade chocolates at 88 Degrees. ⊠ *17 High St.* ☎ *01575/570888.*

FORFAR

7 mi east of Kirriemuir.

Forfar goes about its business of being the center of a farming hinterland without being preoccupied (or even that interested in) tourism.

GETTING HERE AND AROUND

Buses are slow here. The quickest route is by car: take the A90 north, then the A926 turnoff. Alternatively, the A932/A933 route from Arbroath takes you through farmland and Angus villages.

EXPLORING

OFF THE BEATEN PATH

Aberlemno. You can see excellent examples of Pictish stone carvings about 5 mi northeast of Forfar alongside the B9134. Carvings of crosses, angels, serpents, and other animals adorn the stones, which date from the 7th to the early 9th centuries. Note the stone in the nearby churchyard—one side is carved with a cross and the other side depicts the only known battle scene in Pictish art, complete with horsemen and foot soldiers.

Meffan Museum and Art Gallery. A high point of the town is the Meffan Museum and Art Gallery, which displays an interesting collection of Pictish carved stones. Two galleries host frequently changing exhibitions by local and Scottish artists. The museum also houses a tourist information desk. ⊠ *20 W. High St.* ☎ *01307/476482* ⊕ *www.angus. gov.uk/history/museums/meffa* 🖼 *Free* ⊗ *Mon.–Sat. 10–5.*

GLAMIS

5 mi southwest of Forfar, 6 mi south of Kirriemuir.

Set in rolling countryside is the little village of Glamis (pronounced *glahms*).

GETTING HERE AND AROUND

The drive to Glamis Castle, along beech- and-yew-lined roads, is as majestic as the castle itself. Take the A90 north from Dundee, then off onto the A928 (just of the A90). The village of Glamis can be reached by the Stagecoach Strathtay number 22, but service is rather infrequent.

EXPLORING

Angus Folk Museum. A row of 19th-century cottages with unusual stone-slab roofs makes up the Angus Folk Museum, whose exhibits focus on the tools of domestic and agricultural life in the region during the past 200 years. ⊠ *Off A94* ☎ *0844/493–2141* ⊕ *www.nts.org.uk/visits* 🎫 *£6* ⊘ *Apr.–June and Sept.–Oct., weekends noon–5; July and Aug., daily noon–5.*

Fodor's Choice

★

Glamis Castle. One of Scotland's best-known and most beautiful castles, Glamis Castle connects Britain's royalty through 10 centuries, from Macbeth (Thane of Glamis) to the late Queen Mother and her daughter, the late Princess Margaret, born here in 1930 (the first royal princess born in Scotland in 300 years). The property of the earls of Strathmore and Kinghorne since 1372, the castle was largely reconstructed in the late 17th century; the original keep, which is much older, is still intact. One of the most famous rooms in the castle is Duncan's Hall, the legendary setting for Shakespeare's *Macbeth*. Guided tours allow you to see fine china, tapestries, and furniture. Within the castle is the delightful Castle Kitchen restaurant; the grounds contain a huge gift shop, a food shop selling Glamis Castle produce, and a pleasant picnic area. ⊠ *A94, 1 mi north of Glamis* ☎ *01307/840393* ⊕ *www.glamis-castle. co.uk* 🎫 *£9.75* ⊘ *Mar.–Oct., daily 10–6; Nov. and Dec., daily 11–5.*

MEIGLE

7 mi southwest of Glamis, 11 mi northwest of Dundee.

The historic village of Meigle, nestled in the rich agricultural land of the Strathmore Valley, is well known to those with an interest in Pictish stones. Said to be built upon an 11th-century Pictish monastery, the village has a number of elaborate Victorian buildings.

GETTING HERE AND AROUND

Meigle is an easy and pleasant drive from Glamis on the A94 (or from Dundee on the B954). The hourly Stagecoach Strathtay from Dundee (number 57) stops here.

EXPLORING

Meigle Sculptured Stone Museum. The town of Meigle, in the wide swathe of Strathmore, has one of the most notable collections of sculpted stones in Western Europe housed at this museum. It consists of some 25 monuments from the Celtic Christian period (8th to 11th centuries), nearly all of which were found in or around the local churchyard. ⊠ *A94* ☎ *01828/640612* ⊕ *www.historic-scotland.gov.uk* 🎫 *£4* ⊘ *Apr.–Sept., daily 9:30–5:30.*

ALYTH

10 mi west of Glamis, 15 mi northwest of Dundee.

Dating back to the Dark Ages, this market town was completely transformed by the Industrial Revolution, which lined its streets with mills and factories. The 20th century saw the closing of most of these companies, but the town had never forgotten its agricultural heritage. To this day it holds on to its rural appeal.

GETTING HERE AND AROUND

Just 4 mi farther along the B954 from Meigle, Alyth is also served by Stagecoach Strathtay number 57.

EXPLORING

Alyth Museum. This small but intriguing museum about the region's history displays nearly every type of tool and implement put to use by the resourceful and hardy locals. ⊠ *Commercial St.* ☎ *01828/632488* ⊠ *Free* ☉ *May–Sept., Wed.–Sun. 1–5.*

WHERE TO STAY

For expanded hotel reviews, visit Fodors.com.

$ ⊡ **Tigh Na Leigh.** This grand house, now a B&B, was originally built by the Earl of Airlie for his doctor. **Pros:** lovingly restored building; luxurious rooms; exceptional food. **Cons:** only five rooms; books up quickly. ⊠ *22–24 Airlie St.* ☎ *01828/632372* ⊕ *www.tighnaleigh.com* ⇖ *5 rooms* ⚘ *In-room: no a/c. In-hotel: business center* ⎟◎⎟ *Breakfast.*

The Central Highlands

WORD OF MOUTH

"I would highly recommend a walk on the West Highland Way. My family did a portion of this long-distance walk in June, and it was one of the best days we had during our week in the Highlands."

—pavot

"The day was still comparatively young so we then went back the way we came at a much slower pace, using the back roads, and made our way to Loch Katrine. Although the boats had stopped working, the scenery en route was stunning. It was good to stretch our legs with a short walk along the loch—definitely a place to return to."

—tjhome1

Updated
by Mike
Gonzalez

Central Scotland is a bridge between Highland Scotland and the cities of Glasgow and Edinburgh. From Stirling Castle, on a good day, you can see from coast to coast, before you travel north to the glens and the rising hills of the Trossachs. From there you can choose to seek out the tranquil waters of Loch Lomond to the west or the open country and darker peaks of Rannoch Moor to the north.

Central Scotland sits between the Glasgow–Edinburgh axis, marked by the M8 motorway and the dramatic natural divide that is the gateway to the Highlands—the Highland Boundary. The Carse of Stirling, the wide plain guarded by Stirling Castle, was the scene of many of the important moments in Scotland's history—from the Roman invasion commemorated by the Antonine Wall, to the castles that mark the site of medieval kingdoms and the battles to preserve them. Look up at Stirling Castle from the valley and you can see why so many battles were fought over its possession.

North from Stirling, past Dunblane, are the highland hills and valleys of the Trossachs, whose high peaks attract walkers and a tougher breed of cyclist. From Callander, a neat tourist town, the hills stretch westward to the "bonnie bonnie banks" of Loch Lomond, a national park since 2001. From the peaks of the Trossachs, on a good day, you can see Edinburgh Castle to the east and the tower blocks of Glasgow's housing projects to the west.

Farther north is Perth, once Scotland's capital; its wealthy mansions reflect the prosperous agricultural land that surrounds the city, and it is still an important market town today. Overlooking the River Tay, the city can reasonably claim to be the gateway to the Highlands, sitting as it does on the Highland Fault that divides Lowlands from Highlands. From Perth the landscape begins to change on the road to Pitlochry and the unforgiving moors of Rannoch.

For many years Stirling was the starting point for visitors from Edinburgh and Glasgow who were setting out to explore the Trossachs, with their lochs and hills hung with shaggy birch, oak, and pinewoods. Perhaps they were drawn by the lyrical descriptions of the area by Romantic poets like Sir Walter Scott (1771–1832), who set his dramatic verse narrative of 1810, "The Lady of the Lake," in the landscape of the Trossachs. Scott's poem was an immediate and huge success, and the poem is still a comprehensive guide to the area, though some bridges and farms have disappeared.

For those in search of more dramatic landscapes, the Highland fault line runs northeast above Perth, and into the old county of Angus and the high, rough country of Rannoch Moor and the towering Ben Lawers, near Killin, the ninth-highest peak in Scotland.

TOP REASONS TO GO

Exploring Loch Lomond: You can see the sparkling waters of Scotland's largest loch by car, by boat, or on foot. A popular option is the network of bicycle tracks that creep around Loch Lomond and the Trossachs National Park, offering every conceivable terrain.

Take in a castle or two: Choosing between Scotland's most splendid fortresses and mansions is a challenge. Among the highlights are Stirling Castle, with its palace built by James V, and Scone Palace, near Perth, with its grand aristocratic acquisitions. By contrast, Doune Castle is an atmospheric reminder of life in a fortification.

Bag a Munro: The way to experience the Central Highlands is to head out on foot. The fit and well equipped can "bag a Munro" (hills over 3,000 feet, named after the mountaineer who listed them). The less demanding woodland paths and gentle rambles of the Trossachs will stir even the least adventurous rambler.

Sample whisky, the water of life: The Scots love their whisky, and what better way to participate in Scottish life and culture than to learn about the land's finest? There are some exceptional distilleries in this region, from the Edradour Distillery to Glenturret, home of the Famous Grouse.

Jump on a bike: This region claims excellent biking trails, ranging from a gentle pedal through Stirling to a wind-in-your-face journey on the Lowland/Highland Trail. Whatever your preference, biking is a beautiful way to tour the countryside.

Loch Lomond, Scotland's largest loch in terms of surface area, lies just half an hour north of Glasgow. Its waters reflect the crags and dark woods that surround it, and attract those in search of a more romantic and nostalgic Scotland enshrined in the verses of the famous song that bears its name.

The region is full of reminders of heroic struggles, particularly against the English, from the monument to William Wallace to the field at Bannockburn (near Stirling), where Robert the Bruce took on the invader. In nearby Callander, Rob Roy MacGregor, the Scottish Robin Hood, lived (and looted and terrorized) his way into the storybooks.

ORIENTATION AND PLANNING

GETTING ORIENTED

The twin reference points for your trip are Stirling, an ancient historic town from whose castle you can see central Scotland laid out before you, and Perth, 36 mi away, the gateway to the Highlands. North from Stirling, you cross the fertile open plain (the Carse of Stirling) dotted with historic cathedral towns like Dunblane and Doune. The Trossachs are the Scotland of the Romantic imagination, lochs and woodland glens, drovers' inns and grand country houses. The small towns of the region, like Callander, Aberfoyle, and Pitlochry, are bases from which to explore this changing countryside. To the west lies the beautiful and tranquil Loch Lomond, along whose banks the road leads from industrial Glasgow to the hills and glens of the Highlands.

Stirling. Stirling is a city vibrant with history. The old town is quite a small area on the hill, and is worth covering on foot. Look down from the Stirling Castle crag that dominates the plains below and you can see the stages of its growth descending from the hill. The town is a good center from which to explore the changing landscape of central Scotland.

The Trossachs and Loch Lomond. This area is small, but incredibly varied—from dramatic mountain peaks that attract walkers and climbers, to the gentler slopes and forests that stretch from Perth eastward to Aberfoyle and the shores of Loch Lomond. The glens and streams that pepper the region create a romantic landscape that is a perfect habitat for the figure of Rob Roy McGregor—Robin Hood or bandit according to taste, but undeniably Scottish. Loch Lomond's western side is more accessible, if busier, but the views across the loch are always beautiful.

Perthshire. The prosperous air of Perth, once the capital of Scotland, testifies to its importance as a port exporting wool, salmon, and whisky to the world. Scone Palace serves as a monument to that era. The route northward leads across the Highland Boundary and into the changing landscapes beyond Pitlochry to Rannoch Moor, where the wind sweeps across the hardy heather.

PLANNING

WHEN TO GO

The Trossachs and Loch Lomond are in some ways a miniature Scotland, from the tranquil east shore of Loch Lomond to the hills and glens of the Trossachs and the mountains of the Arrochar Alps to the west—and all within a few hours' drive. In the spring and summer, despite the erratic weather, the area is always crowded; this is a good time to go. However, the landscape is notably dramatic when the trees are turning red and brown in autumn, and evening skies are spectacular. Scotland in winter has a different kind of beauty, especially for skiers and climbers. ■ TIP➔ Whatever the season, always carry clothes for wet and dry weather; the weather can change quickly.

PLANNING YOUR TIME

Scotland's beautiful interior is excellent touring country, though the cities of Stirling and Perth are worth your time too; Stirling in particular is worth a day. Two (slightly rushed) days would be enough to explore the Trossachs loop, to gaze into the waters of Loch Venachar and Loch Achray. The glens, in some places, run parallel to the lochs, including those along Lochs Earn, Tay, and Rannoch, making for satisfying loops and round-trips. Loch Lomond is easily accessible from either Glasgow or Stirling, and is well worth exploring. Don't miss the opportunity to take a boat trip on a loch, especially on Loch Lomond or on Loch Katrine in the Trossachs.

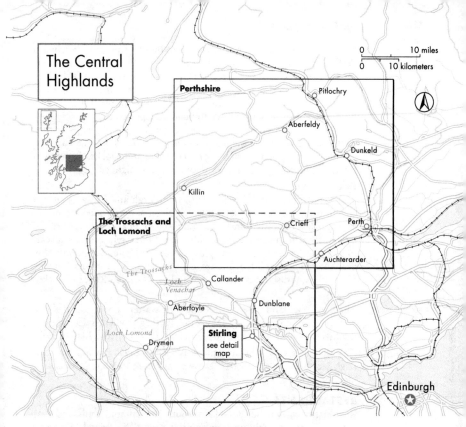

The Central Highlands

Perthshire
Pitlochry
Aberfeldy
Dunkeld
Killin
The Trossachs and Loch Lomond
Crieff
Perth
Auchterarder
The Trossachs
Loch Venachar
Callander
Aberfoyle
Dunblane
Loch Lomond
Drymen
Stirling
see detail map
Edinburgh

GETTING HERE AND AROUND

AIR TRAVEL

Perth and Stirling can be reached easily from the Edinburgh, Dundee, and Glasgow airports by train, car, or bus.

BUS TRAVEL

A good network of buses connects with the central belt via Edinburgh and Glasgow. For more information, contact Scottish Citylink or National Express. The Perth and Kinross Council supplies a map (available in tourist information centers) showing all public transport routes in Perthshire, marked with nearby attractions.

First, Scottish Citylink, and Stagecoach organize reliable service on routes throughout the Central Highlands.

Bus Contacts First ☎ 08708/727271 ⊕ www.firstgroup.com. **National Express** ☎ 08717/818181 ⊕ www.nationalexpress.com. **Scottish Citylink** ☎ 0871/266–3333 ⊕ www.citylink.co.uk. **Stagecoach** ☎ 01292/613502 ⊕ www.stagecoachbus.com.

CAR TRAVEL

You'll find easy access to the area from the central belt of Scotland via the motorway network. The M80 connects Glasgow to Stirling, and then briefly joins the M9 from Edinburgh, which runs within sight of the walls of Stirling Castle. From there, the A9 runs from Stirling to Perth, and onwards to Pitlochry; it is a good road but a little too fast for its own good (so take care). Perth can also be reached via the M90 over the Forth Bridge from Edinburgh. Three signed touring routes are useful: the Perthshire Tourist Route, the Deeside Tourist Route, and the Pitlochry Tourist Route, a beautiful and unexpected trip via Crieff and Loch Tay. Local tourist information centers can supply maps of these routes. Once you leave the major motorways, roads become narrower and slower, with many following the contours of the lochs. Be prepared for your journey to take longer than distances might suggest.

TRAIN TRAVEL

The Central Highlands are linked to Edinburgh and Glasgow by rail, with through routes to England (some direct-service routes from London take less than five hours). Several discount ticket options are available, although in some cases on the ScotRail system a discount card must be purchased before your arrival in the United Kingdom. Note that families with children and travelers under 26 or over 60 are eligible for significant discounts. Contact Trainline, National Rail, or ScotRail for details.

The West Highland Line runs through the western portion of the area. Services also run to Stirling, Dunblane, Perth, and Gleneagles; stops on the Inverness–Perth line include Dunkeld, Pitlochry, and Blair Atholl.

Train Contacts **National Rail Enquiries** ☎ *08457/484950* ⊕ *www.nationalrail. co.uk.* **ScotRail** ☎ *08457/550033* ⊕ *www.scotrail.co.uk.* **Trainline** ⊕ *www. thetrainline.com.*

RESTAURANTS

Regional country delicacies—loch trout, river salmon, lamb, and venison—appear regularly on even modest menus in Central Highlands restaurants. In all the towns and villages in the area you will find simple pubs, often crowded and noisy, many of them serving substantial food at lunchtime and in the evening until about 9 (eaten balanced on your knee, perhaps, or at a shared table).

HOTELS

There is a wide selection of accommodations available throughout the region, especially in Stirling and Callander. They range from bed-and-breakfasts to private houses with a small number of rooms to rural accommodation (often on farms). The grand houses of the past—family homes to the landed aristocracy—have for the most part become country-house hotels. Their settings, often on ample grounds, offer an experience of grand living—but there are also modern hotels in the area, for those who prefer 21st-century amenities.

WHAT IT COSTS IN POUNDS					
	¢	$	$$	$$$	$$$$
RESTAURANTS	under £10	£10–£14	£15–£19	£20–£25	over £25
HOTELS	under £70	£70–£120	£121–£160	£161–£220	over £220

Restaurant prices are for a main course at dinner. Hotel prices are for two people in a standard double room in high season and generally include the 20% V.A.T.

VISITOR INFORMATION
The tourist offices in Stirling and Perth are year-round, as are offices in larger towns; others are seasonal (generally from April to October).

STIRLING

26 mi northeast of Glasgow, 36 mi northwest of Edinburgh.

Stirling is one of Britain's great historic towns. An impressive proportion of the Old Town walls can be seen from Dumbarton Road, a cobbled street leading to Stirling Castle, built on a steep-sided plug of rock. From its esplanade there is a commanding view of the surrounding Carse of Stirling. The guns on the castle battlements are a reminder of the military advantage to be gained from its position.

GETTING HERE AND AROUND
Stirling's central position in the area makes it an ideal point for travel to and from Glasgow and Edinburgh (or north to Perth and the Highlands) by rail, train, or bus. The town itself is compact and easily walkable, though a shuttle bus travels to and from the town center up the steep road to Stirling Castle every 20 minutes. The Back Walk takes the visitor on a circuit around the base of the castle walls.

TIMING
The historic part of town is tightly nestled around the castle—everything is within easy walking distance. The Bannockburn Heritage Centre (3 mi away) and the National Wallace Monument (2 mi away) are on the outskirts of the town and can be reached by taxi or, for the more energetic, on foot. ■TIP➜ **The weather is always changing in this part of the country. Bring sunscreen, a hat, and a waterproof jacket with you wherever you go.**

ESSENTIALS
Visitor Information Stirling ⊠ *Old Town Jail, St. John St.* ☏ *01786/479901* ⊠ *Stirling Castle esplanade, Castlehill* ☏ *01786/472857.*

EXPLORING STIRLING

TOP ATTRACTIONS
★ **Bannockburn Heritage Centre.** In 1298, the year after William Wallace's victory, Robert the Bruce (1274–1329) emerged as the nation's champion, and the final bloody phase of the Wars of Independence began. Bruce's rise resulted from the uncertainties and timidity of the great lords of Scotland (ever unsure of which way to jump and whether or not to bow

6

Argyll's
Lodging 5

Church of the
Holy Rude 3

Mar's Wark 4

Old Town Jail 2

Smith Art Gallery
and Museum 1

Stirling
Castle 6

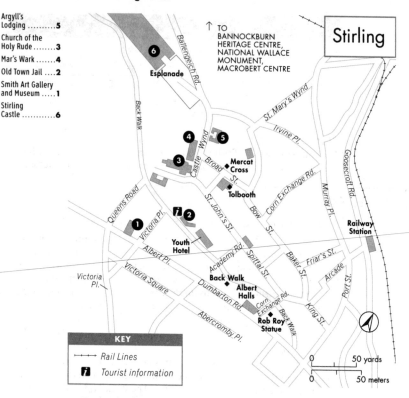

↑ TO
BANNOCKBURN
HERITAGE CENTRE,
NATIONAL WALLACE
MONUMENT,
MACROBERT CENTRE

Stirling

KEY

┝━━━┥ Rail Lines

🛈 Tourist information

0 ____ 50 yards

0 ____ 50 meters

to England's demands). The story is told at the Bannockburn Heritage Centre, hidden among the sprawl of housing and commercial development on the southern edge of Stirling. This was the site of the famed Battle of Bannockburn in 1314. In Bruce's day the Forth had a shelved and partly wooded floodplain, so he cunningly chose this site, where the heavy horses of the English would founder in the boggy ground. You can learn about events of this time with a 10-minute audiovisual presentation, hands-on exhibits, and costumed figures. At the time of this writing, the building was being modernized for the 700th anniversary of the battle. ✉ *Glasgow Rd., Bannockburn* ☎ *0844/493–2139* ⊕ *www.nts.org.uk/ Visits* 🖭 *£6* ☉ *Mar., daily 10:30–4; Apr.–Oct., daily 10–5:30.*

National Wallace Monument. It was near Old Stirling Bridge that the Scottish freedom fighter William Wallace (circa 1270–1305) and a ragged army of Scots won a major victory in 1297. The movie *Braveheart*, starring Mel Gibson, was based on Wallace's life. A more accurate version of events is told in an exhibition and audiovisual presentation at this pencil-thin museum on the Abbey Craig. Up close, this Victorian shrine to William Wallace, built between 1856 and 1869, becomes less slim and soaring, revealing itself to be a substantial square tower with a creepy spiral stairway. To reach the monument, follow the Bridge of Allan signs (A9) northward, crossing the River Forth by Robert

Stephenson's (1772–1850) New Bridge of 1832, next to the historic old one. The National Wallace Monument is signposted at the next traffic circle. ⊠ *Abbey Craig, Hillfoot Rd.* ☎ *01786/472140* ⊕ *www. nationalwallacemonument.com* ⊠ *£7.75* ☉ *Mar.–May and Oct., daily 10–5; June, daily 10–6; July and Aug., daily 9–6; Sept., daily 9:30–5:30; Nov.–Feb., daily 10:30–4.*

☺ **Old Town Jail.** The original town jail, now restored, has exhibitions about life in a 19th-century Scottish prison. Furnished cells, models, and staff—dressed as prisoners, wardens, and prison reformers—bring the gruesome prison to life. The irony is it that it was seen as an improvement on previous prisons. Guided tours are offered every half hour. ⊠ *St. John's St.* ☎ *01786/450050* ⊕ *www.oldtownjail.com* ⊠ *£6.65* ☉ *Apr.–Sept., daily 9–6; Oct.–Mar., weekends 9–4; last admission 1 hr before closing.*

Fodor's Choice **Stirling Castle.** Its magnificent strategic position on a steep-sided crag
★ made Stirling Castle the grandest prize in the Scots Wars of Independence in the late 13th and early 14th centuries. The Battle of Bannockburn in 1314 was fought within sight of its walls, and the victory by Robert the Bruce yielded both the castle and freedom from English subjugation for almost four centuries. Take time to visit the **Castle Exhibition** in the Queen Anne Garden beyond the lower gate to get an overview of its long history and evolution as a stronghold and palace.

The daughter of King Robert I (Robert the Bruce), Marjory, married Walter Fitzalan, the high steward of Scotland. Their descendants included the Stewart dynasty of Scottish monarchs (Mary, Queen of Scots, was a Stewart, though she preferred the French spelling, *Stuart*). The Stewarts were responsible for many of the works that survive within the castle walls today. They made Stirling Castle their court and power base, creating fine Renaissance-style buildings that were not completely obliterated, despite reconstruction for military purposes.

Enter the castle through its outer defenses, which consist of a great curtained wall and batteries from 1708, built to bulwark earlier defenses by the main gatehouse. From this lower square the most conspicuous feature is the **Palace,** built by King James V (1512–42) between 1538 and 1542. The decorative figures festooning the ornate outer walls show the influence of French masons. A new orientation center in the basement lets you try out the clothes and musical instruments of the time. Then you are led across a terace to the newly refurbished **Royal Apartments,** which re-create the furnishings and tapestries found here during the reign of James V and his French queen, Mary of Guise. The queen's bedchamber contains copies of the beautiful tapestries in which the hunt for the white unicorn is clearly an allegory for the persecution of Christ. Overlooking the upper courtyard is the **Great Hall,** built by King James IV (1473–1513) in 1503. Before the Union of Parliaments in 1707, when the Scottish aristocracy sold out to England, this building had been used as one of the seats of the Scottish Parliament. It has since been restored to its original splendor, with sparse but impressive furnishings. Here the king once ordered a full-size galleon to be placed in the hall during the fish course of a major banquet.

Among the later works built for regiments stationed here, the **Regimental Museum** stands out; it's a 19th-century baronial revival on the site of an earlier building. Nearby, the **Chapel Royal** is unfurnished but was the site of a visit by Charles I in 1633. The oldest building on the site is the **Mint,** or **Coonzie Hoose,** perhaps dating as far back as the 14th century. Below is an arched passageway leading to the westernmost section of the ramparts, the **Nether Bailey.** You'll have the distinct feeling of being in the bow of a warship sailing up the *carselands* (valley plain) of the Forth Valley.

To the castle's south lies the hump of the Touch and the Gargunnock Hills (part of the Campsie Fells), which diverted potential direct routes from Glasgow and the south. For centuries all roads into the Highlands across the narrow waist of Scotland led through Stirling. If you look carefully northward, you can still see the Old Stirling Bridge, once the lowest and most convenient place to cross the river. ⊠ *Castlehill* ☎ *01786/450000* ⊕ *www.historic-scotland.gov.uk/places* ⊠ *£13, includes admission to Argyll's Lodging* ⊙ *Apr.–Sept., daily 9:30–5:15; Oct.–Mar., daily 9:30–4:15.*

WORTH NOTING

Argyll's Lodging. A nobleman's town house built in three phases from the 16th century onward, this building is actually older than the name it bears—that of Archibald, the ninth earl of Argyll (1629–85), who bought it in 1666. It was for many years a military hospital, then a youth hostel. It has now been refurbished to show how the nobility lived in 17th-century Stirling. Specially commissioned reproduction furniture and fittings are based on the original inventory of the house's contents at that time. Entry is by guided tour only. ⊠ *Castle Wynd* ☎ *01786/431319* ⊕ *www.historic-scotland.gov.uk/places* ⊠ *£13, includes admission to Stirling Castle* ⊙ *Tours daily every ½ hr, 9:30–4.*

Church of the Holy Rude. The nave of this handsome church survives from the 15th century, and a portion of the original medieval timber roof can also be seen. This is the only Scottish church still in use to have witnessed the coronation of a Scottish monarch—James VI (1566–1625) in 1567. ⊠ *Top of St. John's St.* ⊙ *Apr.–Sept., daily 11–4.*

Mar's Wark. These distinctive windowless and roofless ruins are the stark remains of a Renaissance palace built in 1570 by Lord Erskine (died 1572), Earl of Mar and Stirling Castle governor. The name means "Mar's work," or building. Look for the armorial carved panels, the gargoyles, and the turrets flanking a railed-off *pend* (archway). During the 1745 Jacobite rebellion, Mar's Wark was besieged and severely damaged, but its admirably worn shell survives. The ruins are enclosed by a fence, so you can view them only from the outside. ⊠ *Castle Wynd* ☎ *01667/460232* ⊕ *www.historic-scotland.gov.uk/places.*

Smith Art Gallery and Museum. This Romanesque-style museum, founded in 1874, details the history of the town through artworks and objects, the oldest of which are 7,000-year-old whale bones. There are also temporary exhibits and a café. ⊠ *Dumbarton Rd.* ☎ *01786/471917* ⊕ *www.smithartgallery.demon.co.uk* ⊠ *Free* ⊙ *Tues.–Sat. 10:30–5, Sun. 2–5.*

WHERE TO EAT

$$ ✕**Hermann's Restaurant.** Run by Austrian Hermann Aschaber and his
ECLECTIC Glaswegian wife, the restaurant presents the cuisines of both countries.
The Black Watch–tartan carpet and alpine murals are as successfully
matched as the signature Scottish dishes like *cullen skink* (a fish and
potato soup) and chicken with Stornaway black pudding and Drambuie
cream, and Austrian staples like Wiener schnitzel and cheese spaetzle.
⊠ *58 Broad St.* ☎ *01786/450632.*

$$ ✕**River House.** Behind Stirling Castle, this restaurant sits by its own
ECLECTIC tranquil little loch and is built in the style of a Scottish *crannog* (ancient
loch dwelling). It's relaxed and friendly, with tables on a deck overlooking the water. Local produce dominates the menu, yet the food
reflects French and Mediterranean influences. Try the curried Scottish
lamb with lime yogurt. You can get here directly from the M9 motorway: follow the Stirling sign at Junction 10. From Aberfoyle it's on
A84, or follow B8051 around the Castle towards the Castle Business
Park. ⊠ *The Castle Business Park, B8051* ☎ *01786/465577* ⊕ *www.
riverhouse-restaurant.co.uk.*

WHERE TO STAY

For expanded hotel reviews, visit Fodors.com.

$$$ ▦ **Barceló Stirling Highland Hotel.** This hotel occupies what was once the
★ town's high school, and several of the rooms preserve that history (the
headmaster's study, for example). **Pros:** near train station; excellent res-
taurant. **Cons:** slightly institutional feel. ⊠ *Spittal St.* ☎ *01786/272727*
⊕ *www.barcelo-hotels.co.uk* ☞ *96 rooms* ☖ *In-room: Wi-Fi. In-hotel:
restaurant, bar, pool, gym, some pets allowed* �†☉† *Breakfast.*

¢ ▦ **Castlecroft.** Tucked beneath Stirling Castle, this comfortable modern
house welcomes you with freshly cut flowers everywhere and home-
made breakfasts. **Pros:** great location; lovely views; hearty breakfasts.
Cons: a little hard to find if you are not arriving directly from the
motorway. ⊠ *Ballengeich Rd.* ☎ *01786/474933* ⊕ *www.castlecroft-uk.
com* ☞ *5 rooms* ☖ *In-room: Wi-Fi* �†☉† *Breakfast.*

¢ ▦ **Kilronan House.** In Bridge of Allan, this granite-walled B&B has high
ceilings and other details that recall the house's genteel Victorian ori-
gins. **Pros:** lovely gardens; spacious rooms; close to bus stops. **Cons:**
not all rooms have bathrooms; steep driveway. ⊠ *15 Kenilworth Rd.,
Bridge of Allan* ☎ *01786/831054* ⊕ *www.kilronan.co.uk* ☞ *3 rooms*
☖ *In-room: no a/c, Wi-Fi* ▭ *No credit cards* �†☉† *Breakfast.*

$ ▦ **Park Lodge Hotel.** This elegant 18th-century country-house hotel
gives you a taste of French-inspired design and cuisine. **Pros:** great
views of park; homey feel; recently renovated. **Cons:** too many floral
prints. ⊠ *32 Park Terr.* ☎ *01786/474862* ⊕ *www.parklodge.net* ☞ *9
rooms* ☖ *In-room: no a/c. In-hotel: restaurant, bar, some pets allowed*
�†☉† *Breakfast.*

$ ▦ **West Plean.** More than 200 years old, this handsome, rambling B&B
★ is part of a working farm. **Pros:** beautiful gardens; plenty of peace
and quiet; huge and hearty breakfast. **Cons:** a little off the beaten

track; a long walk to Stirling. ⊠ *Denny Rd.* ☎ *01786/812208* ⊕ *www. westpleanhouse.com* ⇆ *4 rooms* ⚬ *In-room: no a/c. In-hotel: business center* ⊗ *Closed Dec.* |◎| *Breakfast.*

THE ARTS

Macrobert Arts Centre. The center has a theater, art gallery, and cinema with programs that range from films to pantomime. It's on the campus of the University of Stirling, off the A9 as you're heading toward Bridge of Allan. ⊠ *University of Stirling, W. Link Rd.* ☎ *01786/466666* ⊕ *www.macrobert.org.*

Tolbooth. Built in 1705, the Tolbooth has been many things: courthouse, jail, meeting place. At one time the city's money was kept here. It has retained its traditional Scottish steeple and gilded weathercock, and now has a newly built tower from which to survey the surrounding country. Today it serves as an art gallery and an arts venue with a 200-seat auditorium and a bar that is open for performances. ⊠ *Broad St.* ☎ *01786/274000* ⊕ *www.stirling.gov.uk/tolbooth.*

SHOPPING

Stirling Arcade. Built in the 19th century, Stirling Arcade has about 20 shops. You'll find everything from toys to fine clothing. ⊠ *King St.* ☎ *01786/474888.*

CERAMICS AND GLASSWARE

Barbara Davidson Pottery. South of Stirling, Barbara Davidson Pottery is run by one of the best-known potters in Scotland. Demonstrations can be arranged by appointment. Signs point the way from the A9. ⊠ *Muirhall Farm, Muirhall Rd., Larbert* ☎ *01324/554430* ⊕ *www. barbara-davidson.com.*

Heart of Glass. This shop sells original works made by local glassblowers. ⊠ *14 Henderson St., Bridge of Allan* ☎ *01786/832137* ⊕ *www. heartofglass.co.uk.*

CLOTHING

House of Henderson. A Highland outfitter, House of Henderson sells tartans, woolens, and accessories, and offers a made-to-measure kilt service. ⊠ *6–8 Friars St.* ☎ *01786/473681* ⊕ *www.houseofhenderson. co.uk.*

Mill Trail. East of Stirling is Mill Trail country, along the foot of the Ochil Hills. A leaflet from any local tourist information center will lead you to the delights of a real mill shop and low mill prices—even on cashmere—at Tillicoultry, Alva, and Alloa.

GIFTS

Fotheringham Gallery. The upscale Fotheringham Gallery stocks fine jewelry and paintings. ⊠ *78 Henderson St., Bridge of Allan* ☎ *01786/ 832861.*

Stirling Bagpipes. This small shop sells bagpipes of every type and at every price, including antiques by legendary craftspeople that are displayed in glass cases. In the room behind the shop, the owner lovingly turns the chanters and drones, but he will happily take time to talk you through the history of these instruments. ⊠ *8 Broad St.* ☎ *01786/448886.*

SIDE TRIP FROM STIRLING

FALKIRK

14 mi southeast of Stirling, along the M9 motorway.

Falkirk has a fascinating history. It was here, at the impressive Antonine Wall, that the Roman occupiers fought back the warlike Picts. You can visit parts of the wall and imagine the fierce battles over this strategic location.

In the late 18th century, Falkirk was an important industrial town because of its network of canals linking Glasgow and Edinburgh. But with the arrival of the railways, Falkirk's fortunes flagged. The canals have been brought back to life with the £78 million Millennium Link Project, which added a range of cycling and walking routes and the spectacular Falkirk Wheel, a boat lift.

GETTING HERE AND AROUND

The M9 from Stirling to Falkirk follows the widening estuary of the River Forth, the view dominated by the huge Grangemouth oil refinery in the distance.

EXPLORING

Antonine Wall. West of Falkirk, Bonnybridge is home to the most extensive remains of the Antonine Wall, a 37-mi Roman fortification built to defend against the warlike Picts to the north. A UNESCO World Heritage Site, the wall was also the site of a famous battle in 1298, when William Wallace was defeated by the English. To get here from Falkirk, take the A803 west. ⊠ *Off A803, 2 mi west of Falkirk, Bonnybridge* ☎ ⊕ *www.antoninewall.org* ☜ *Free* ☉ *Open 24 hrs.*

Callendar House. Near the town center, Callendar House is an attractive local-history museum where you get a glimpse of a family's daily life in the early 1800s. Entry is through the impressive wooden hallway, and the first-floor morning and drawing rooms are in the grandest of country-house traditions. The large kitchen will often have local interpreters to explain cooking in the early 19th century. There are also exhibits on the Romans and the Antonine Wall, as well as on the history of Falkirk. The second floor is a gallery space and houses the town's archives. The surrounding park has a boating lake and a Georgian herb garden. ⊠ *Callendar Park, off Callendar Rd.* ☎ *01324/503773* ⊕ *www.falkirk.gov.uk/cultural* ☜ *Free* ☉ *Mon.–Sat. 10–5, Sun. 2–5.*

Falkirk Wheel. In 2002, British Waterways opened the Falkirk Wheel, the only rotating boatlift in the world, linking two major waterways, the Forth and Clyde Canal and the Union Canal, between Edinburgh and Glasgow. This extraordinary engineering achievement lifts and lowers boats using four giant wheels shaped like Celtic axes. The wheel transports eight or more boats at a time from one canal to the other in about 45 minutes. Boats float into a cradlelike compartment full of water; as the wheel turns, they're transported up or down to the other canal. The Falkirk Wheel replaced 11 locks that were once the only way of moving between the two bodies of water. Several companies offer excursions on the waterways; call ahead. ⊠ *Lime Rd.* ☎ *01324/619888* ⊕ *www. thefalkirkwheel.co.uk* ⊒ *£7.95* ⊘ *Apr.–Oct., daily 10–5; Nov.–Mar., Wed.–Sun. 11–4.*

THE TROSSACHS AND LOCH LOMOND

Immortalized by Wordsworth and Sir Walter Scott, the Trossachs (the name means "bristly country") contains some of Scotland's loveliest forest, hills, and glens, well justifying the area's designation as a national park. The area has a special charm, combining the wildness of the Highlands with the prolific vegetation of an old Lowland forest. Its open ground is a dense mat of bracken and heather, and its woodland is of silver birch, dwarf oak, and hazel—trees that fasten their roots into the crevices of rocks and stop short on the very brink of lochs. There are also many small towns to visit along the way, some with their roots in a medieval world; others sprang up and expanded in the wake of the first tourists who came to Scotland in the late 19th century in search of wild country or healing waters. Dunblane has a magnificent cathedral; Doune's castle will make you stare in awe.

The most colorful season is fall, particularly October, a lovely time when most visitors have departed, and the hares, deer, and game birds have taken over. Even in rainy weather the Trossachs of "darksome glens and gleaming lochs" are memorable: the water filtering through the rocks by Loch Lomond comes out so pure and clear that the loch is like a sheet of glass.

The best way to explore this area is by car, by bike, or on foot; the latter two depend, of course, on the weather. Keep in mind that roads in this region of the country are narrow and winding, which can make for dangerous conditions in all types of weather.

DUNBLANE

7 mi north of Stirling.

The small, quiet town of Dunblane, just 4 mi from Stirling, has long been an important religious center; it is dominated by its cathedral, which dates mainly from the 13th century. The town also boasts one of Scotland's most impressive libraries, the Leighton Library.

GETTING HERE AND AROUND

Dunblane station is on the main line to Perth and Inverness, and regular bus service links the town to Stirling. For drivers it is easily reached along the main A9 artery.

ESSENTIALS

Visitor Information Dunblane ⊠ *Stirling Rd.* ☎ *01786/824428* ⊕ *www. perthshire-scotland.co.uk.*

EXPLORING

Cathedral. The oldest part of Dunblane—with its narrow winding streets—huddles around this church's square. The cathedral was built by Bishop Clement in the early 13th century on the site of St. Blane's

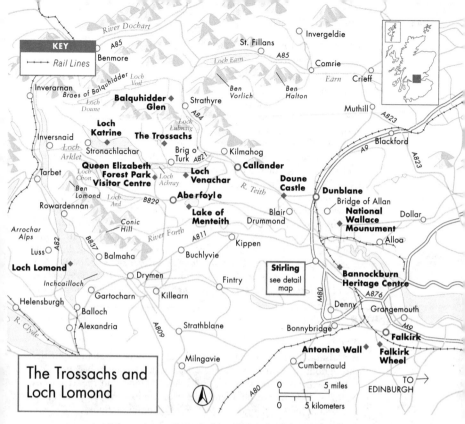

The Trossachs and Loch Lomond

tiny 8th-century cell; with the Reformation of the 16th century, it ceased to be a cathedral. In 1996 it was the scene of a moving memorial service for the 15 children killed in the local school by Thomas Hamilton. ✉ *The Cross* ☎ *01667/460232* ⊕ *www.historic-scotland.gov.uk/places* 🖼 *Free* ⊙ *Apr.–Sept., Mon.–Sat. 9:30–12:30 and 1:30–5, Sun. 2–5; Oct.–Mar., Mon.–Sat. 9:30–4, Sun. 2–4.*

★ **Doune Castle.** Once no self-respecting Highland chief's attire was complete without an ornate pair of pistols made in the community of Doune, 5 mi west of Dunblane. Today Doune is more widely known for having one of the best-preserved medieval castles in Scotland. It's also a place of pilgrimage for fans of *Monty Python and Holy Grail*, which was filmed here. Doune Castle is grim and high-walled, with a daunting central keep and echoing, drafty stairways up to the curtain-wall walk. The views make the climb well worthwhile. There is a good audio guide narrated by Monty Python's Terry Gilliam. The best place to photograph this squat, walled fort is from the bridge, a little way upstream. ✉ *Castle Rd., Doune* ☎ *01786/841742* ⊕ *www.historic-scotland.gov. uk* 🖼 *£5* ⊙ *Apr.–Sept., daily 9:30–5:30; Oct., daily 9:30–4; Nov.–Mar., Sat.–Wed. 9:30–4.*

WHERE TO EAT AND STAY
For expanded hotel reviews, visit Fodors.com.

$ ✕ **Sheriffmuir Inn.** The road to Sheriffmuir from Dunblane is too narrow
ECLECTIC to be numbered, and you may be concerned you have taken a wrong
turn until you reach this splendidly isolated, whitewashed inn. Inside
there is a warm fire at a friendly bar filled with wooden furniture. The
restaurant is unpretentious, with views onto the moor beyond. Owner
and chef Geoff Cook keeps to local produce wherever possible, but
with an international touch; try the monkfish with chili-crab crème
and basmati rice or the twice-cooked belly pork with black pudding.
⊠ *Off A9, Sheriffmuir* ☎ *01786/823285* ⊕ *www.sheriffmuirinn.co.uk*
☉ *Closed Tues.*

$$$ ⊞ **Cromlix House Hotel.** A long, narrow drive leads to this mansion on
a 2,000-acre estate just beyond the village of Kinbuck. **Pros:** beautiful
and extensive grounds; comfortable large rooms; attentive staff. **Cons:**
a little hard to find; not much for children; some old-fashioned plumb-
ing. ⊠ *B8033, 3 mi northeast of Dunblane, Kinbuck* ☎ *01786/822125*
⊕ *www.cromlixhouse.com* ⤳ *6 rooms, 8 suites* ⚹ *In-room: no a/c,
Wi-Fi. In-hotel: restaurant, tennis court, business center* ⦿ *Breakfast.*

CALLANDER

8 mi northwest of Doune.

A traditional Highland-edge resort, the little town of Callander bustles
throughout the year, even during off-peak times, simply because it's a
gateway to Highland scenery, and Loch Lomond and the Trossachs
National Park. As a result, there's plenty of window-shopping here, plus
nightlife in pubs and a good selection of accommodations.

GETTING HERE AND AROUND
The railway that brought visitors to Callander in the 19th century no
longer reaches the town. Today you can access Callander by bus from
Stirling, Glasgow, or Edinburgh. If you're traveling by car from Stirling,
take the M8 to Dunblane, then the A820 (which becomes the A84) to
Callander. If you are coming from Glasgow, take the A81 through Aber-
foyle to Callander; an alternative route (longer but more picturesque) is
to take the A821 around Loch Venachar, then the A84 east to Callander.

ESSENTIALS
Visitor Information Callander ⊠ *Ancaster Sq.* ☎ *01877/330342* ⊕ *www.
visitscotland.com.*

EXPLORING
☉ **Hamilton Toy Collection.** Here you'll find one of the most extensive toy col-
lections in Britain, with all conceivable types of toys grouped through-
out the house, ranging from teddy bears to porcelain dolls, toy soldiers
to Matchbox cars. There's a wonderful selection of model railways and
an Edwardian nursery complete with dollhouses. The shop is defiantly
divided into girls' and boys' sections. ⊠ *111 Main St.* ☎ *01877/330004*
⊡ *£2* ☉ *Apr.–Oct., Mon.–Sat. 10–4:30, Sun. noon–4:30.*

WHERE TO EAT AND STAY
For expanded hotel reviews, visit Fodors.com.

¢ ✕ **Lade Inn.** A traditional pub in Kilmahog, just a mile from Callander
BRITISH on the A85, the Lade Inn offers good, solid, pub fare in the bar. Steaks,
burgers, and chicken are locally sourced, and there are elements of
international cuisine, such as tagines. The establishment specializes in
ales, and there's quite a selection. Staff are friendly and attentive, and
traditional music (live or recorded) plays much of the time. ⊠ *Off A821,
Kilmahog* 🕾 *01877/330152* ⊕ *www.theladeinn.com.*

¢ ✕ **Pip's Coffee House.** Come to this cheerful little place just off the main
CAFÉ street for imaginative soups and salads, as well as exquisite Scottish
home baking, including fresh scones. And then, of course, there's great
coffee. ⊠ *21–23 Ancaster Sq.* 🕾 *01877/330470* ⊟ *No credit cards* ☉ *No
dinner.*

$$ 🏨 **Roman Camp.** Turn off the main street of Callander, and within a
hundred yards you will find this pink-washed 17th-century hunting
lodge surrounded by ornate gardens. **Pros:** beautiful grounds; luxuri-
ous rooms. **Cons:** restaurant is quite expensive; no Internet facilities
in rooms. ⊠ *Off Main St.* 🕾 *01877/330003* ⊕ *www.romancamphotel.
co.uk* ↩ *12 rooms, 3 suites* ⊘ *In-room: no a/c. In-hotel: restaurant, bar,
business center, some pets allowed* ⑩ *Breakfast.*

$ 🏨 **Westerton B and B.** A large Victorian stone-built house with a large gar-
den, the Westerton has gold, blue, and green rooms that are elegant and
bright. **Pros:** welcoming atmosphere; large comfortable rooms; in town
center. **Cons:** awkward entrance and exit into the drive; no phones in
room; price is a bit high for what you get. ⊠ *Leny Rd.* 🕾 *01877/330147*
⊕ *www.westerton.co.uk* ↩ *3 rooms* ⊘ *In-room: no a/c, Wi-Fi. In-hotel:
some age restrictions* ☉ *Closed Nov.–Feb.* ⑩ *Breakfast.*

SPORTS AND THE OUTDOORS

BICYCLING **Wheels/Trossachs Backpackers.** This is a friendly firm that rents bikes
of every sort by the hour, the half day, or the day. Most popular are
the mountain bikes (£18 per day). The staff will help you find the
best mountain-bike routes around the Trossachs. ⊠ *Invertrossachs Rd.*
🕾 *01877/331100* ⊕ *www.scottish-cycling.com.*

GOLF **Callander Golf Club.** The course at the Callander Golf Club, designed by
Tom Morris in 1890, has fine views and a tricky moorland layout. Keep
between the trees on the 15th hole and you may end up with a hole in
one. ⊠ *Aveland Rd.* 🕾 *01877/330090* ⊕ *www.callandergolfclub.co.uk*
🎫 *£35 per round.* ⚑ *18 holes, 5,151 yds, par 66.*

HIKING **Bracklinn Falls.** A walk is signposted from the east end of Callander's
main street to the Bracklinn Falls, over whose lip Sir Walter Scott once
rode a pony to win a bet.

Callander Crags. It's a 1½-mi walk through the woods up to the Cal-
lander Crags, with views of the Lowlands as far as the Pentland Hills
behind Edinburgh. The walk begins at the west end of Callander's main
street.

Pass of Leny. Just north of Callander, the mountains squeeze both the
road and rocky river into the narrow Pass of Leny. An abandoned rail-
way—now a pleasant walking or biking path—also goes through the
pass, past Ben Ledi and Loch Lubnaig.

6

TEEING OFF IN THE TROSSACHS

There are many beautiful golf courses within the Loch Lomond area and the Trossachs National Park. The National Park Golf Pass (£50 for three rounds, £80 for five) allows play at Callander, St. Fillans, Aberfoyle, Killin, and Buchanan Castle (£10 supplement). The Loch Lomond Pass (£90 for three rounds) covers the Cardos, Helensburgh, and Buchanan Castle courses.

Aberfoyle Golf Club ⊠ Braeval, Aberfoyle ☎ 01877/382493 ⊕ www. aberfoylegolf.com.

Buchanan Castle Golf Club ⊠ A809, Drymen ☎ 01360/660330 ⊕ www.buchanancastlegolfclub. co.uk.

Callander Golf Club ⊠ Aveland Rd. ☎ 01877/330090 ⊕ www. callandergolfclub.co.uk.

Killin Golf Club ⊠ Off A827, Killin ☎ 01567/820312 ⊕ www. killingolfclub.co.uk.

St. Fillans Golf Club ⊠ S. Loch Earn Rd., St. Fillans ☎ 01764/685312 ⊕ www.st-fillans-golf.com.

SHOPPING

Trossachs Woollen Mill. The Edinburgh Woollen Mill Group owns this mill shop in Kilmahog. It has a vast selection of woolens on display, including luxurious cashmere and striking tartan throws, and will provide overseas mailing and tax-free shopping. ⊠ Trossachs Woollen Mill, Main St., Kilmahog ☎ 01877/330268 ⊕ www.ewm.co.uk ⊘ Mar.–Oct. daily 9–5; Nov. daily 9–4:30; Dec.–Feb. daily 9–4.

BALQUHIDDER GLEN

12 mi north of Callander.

A 20-minute drive from Callander, through the Pass of Leny and beyond Strathyre, is Balquhidder Glen (pronounced *bal*-whidd-er), a typical Highland glen that runs westward. The glen has characteristics seen throughout the north: a flat-bottom U-shape profile, formed by prehistoric glaciers; extensive Forestry Commission plantings replacing much of the natural woodlands above; a sprinkling of farms; and, farther up the glen, hill roads bulldozed into the slopes to provide access for foresters. You may notice the boarded-up look of some of the area's houses, many of which are second homes for affluent residents of the south. The glen is also where Loch Voil and Loch Doune spread out, adding to the stunning vistas.

GETTING HERE AND AROUND

To reach Balquhidder Glen by car, take the A84 from Callander (signposted to Crianlarich). The road ends in the glen, so you will have to turn back and rejoin the A84 to continue your journey— but it's certainly worth the diversion.

EXPLORING

Grave of Rob Roy MacGregor. The area around Balquhidder Glen is known as the Braes (Slopes) of Balquhidder and was the home of the MacLarens and the MacGregors. The grave of Rob Roy MacGregor, the 18th-century Scottish outlaw hero and subject of Sir Walter Scott's novel *Rob*

Roy, is signposted beside Balquhidder village. The site of his house, now a private farm, is beyond the parking lot at the end of the road up the glen. The glen has no through road, though there is a right-of-way (on foot) from the churchyard where Rob Roy is buried, through Kirkton Glen and on to open grasslands and a lake.

WHERE TO STAY

For expanded hotel reviews, visit Fodors.com.

$$$
Fodor's Choice
★

Monachyle Mhor. Set on 2,000 acres of forests and moorland, this beautifully converted farmhouse sits in splendid isolation against a backdrop of mountains and views over Lochs Voil and Doine. **Pros:** stunning scenery; delicious food; complimentary salmon and trout fishing. **Cons:** you're pretty isolated; rooms are on the small side. ⊠ *Off A84, Balquhidder* ☎ *01877/384622* ⊕ *www.mhor.net* ⇆ *14 rooms* ♿ *In-room: no a/c. In-hotel: restaurant* ⍩*Breakfast.*

THE TROSSACHS

10 mi west of Callander.

With its harmonious scenery of hill, loch, and wooded slopes, the Trossachs has been a popular touring region since the late 18th century, at the dawn of the age of the Romantic poets. Influenced by the writings of Sir Walter Scott, early visitors who strayed into the Highlands from the central belt of Scotland admired this as the first "wild" part of Scotland they encountered. Perhaps because the Trossachs represent the very essence of what the Highlands are supposed to be, the whole of this area, including Loch Lomond, is now protected as a national park. Here you can find birch and pine forests, vistas down lochs where the woods creep right to the water's edge, and, in the background, peaks that rise high enough to be called mountains, though they're not as high as those to the north and west.

GETTING HERE AND AROUND

To reach the Trossachs, take the A84 from Callander through the Pass of Leny, then on to Crianlarich on the A85; from here you can continue down the western shore of Loch Lomond or continue on toward Fort William. Alternately, turn onto the A821 outside Callander and travel past Loch Katrine through the Duke's Pass to Aberfoyle.

EXPLORING

TOP ATTRACTIONS

Ben An. The parking lot by Loch Achray is the place to begin the ascent of steep, heathery Ben An, which affords some of the best Trossachs views. The climb requires a couple of hours and good lungs. The beginning of the path is near Loch Achray. ⊠ *A821.*

★ **Loch Katrine.** At the end of Loch Achray, off the A821 from Callander (9 mi) or Aberfoyle (8 mi), a side road turns right into a narrow pass, leading to Loch Katrine, the heart of the Trossachs. The steamship *Sir Walter Scott* and the motor launch *Lady of the Lake* sail from here several times a day. You can make the round-trip journey around the loch, or head directly across to Stromlachlar and return by bicycle on the loch-side road. Boats depart several times a day between April and October. The loch is owned by the Strathclyde Water Board, since Loch Katrine has supplied Glasgow's drinking water for more than 150 years.

Sir Walter Scott. The steamer *Sir Walter Scott* embarks on cruises of Loch Katrine every day between April and late October. The boat leaves from Trossachs Pier at 10:30, 1:30, and 3. ■ TIP➔ **Do take the cruise if time permits, as the shores of Katrine remain undeveloped and scenic.** ☎ *01877/376316* ☜ *£12 one way, £15.50 round-trip* ✉ *Trossachs Pier, Off A821* ☎ *01877/376316* ⊕ *www.lochkatrine.com* ⊗ *Apr.– late Oct., daily 9–5.*

WORTH NOTING

Brig o' Turk. A few minutes after it passes Loch Venachar, the A821 becomes muffled in woodlands and twists gradually down to the village of Brig o' Turk. (*Turk* is Gaelic for the Scots *tuirc,* meaning wild boar, a species that has been extinct in this region since about the 16th century.) ✉ *A821, Brig o' Turk.*

Loch Achray. Loch Achray, stretching west of the village of Brig o' Turk, dutifully fulfills expectations of what a verdant Trossachs loch should be: small, green, reedy meadows backed by dark plantations, rhododendron thickets, and lumpy hills, thickly covered with heather.

Loch Venachar. The A821 runs west together with the first and gentlest of the Trossachs lochs, Loch Venachar. A sturdy gray-stone building, with a small dam at the Callander end, controls the water that feeds into the River Teith (and, hence, into the Forth).

ABERFOYLE

11 mi south of Loch Katrine, in the Trossachs.

This small tourist town has a somewhat faded air, and several of its souvenir shops seem to have closed their doors. But the surrounding hills (some snowcapped) and the green slopes visible from the town are the reason so many visitors pause here before continuing up to Duke's Pass or on to Inversnaid. Access to nearby Queen Elizabeth Forest Park is another reason to visit.

GETTING HERE AND AROUND

The main route out of Glasgow, the A81, takes you through Aberfoyle and on to Callander and Stirling. There are regular buses from Stirling and Glasgow to Aberfoyle.

> ### SCOTLAND BY BIKE
>
> The region's big attraction for cyclists is the **Lowland/Highland Trail,** which stretches more than 60 mi and passes through Drymen, Aberfoyle, the Trossachs, Callander, Lochearnhead, and Killin. This route runs along former railroad-track beds, as well as private and minor roads, to reach well into the Central Highlands. Another almost completely traffic-free option is the roadway around Loch Katrine. Mountain bikes can tackle many of the forest roads and trails enjoyed by walkers. Avoid main roads, which can be busy with traffic.

ESSENTIALS

Visitor Information Trossachs Discovery Centre ✉ *Main St.* ☎ *08707/200604* ⊕ *www.visitscotland.com.*

EXPLORING

Inchmahome. The tiny island of Inchmahome, on the Lake of Menteith, was a place of refuge in 1547 for the young Mary, Queen of Scots. Between April and September, a ferry takes passengers from the lake's pier to the island. Now owned by the National Trust for Scotland, its ruined **priory** is a lovely place for a picnic. ■ **TIP→ If the boat is not there when you arrive at the pier, turn the board so that the white side faces the island. The boat will come and collect you.** ✉ *Off A81, 4 mi east of Aberfoyle* ☎ *01786/450000* ⛴ *Ferry £5* ⊙ *Apr.–Sept., daily 9:30–5:30.*

☺ **Scottish Wool Centre.** With a vast range of woolen garments and knit-wear, the Scottish Wool Centre also has a small café. Three times a day from April to September it presents an interactive "gathering" when dogs herd sheep and ducks in the large amphitheater, with a little help from the public. Miniature horses watch from a nearby paddock. ✉ *Off Main St.* ☎ *01877/382850* ⛴ *Free* ⊙ *Feb.–Dec., daily 9:30–5:30; Jan., daily 10–4:30.*

6

OFF THE BEATEN PATH

Along the B829. From Aberfoyle you can take a trip to see the more enclosed northern portion of **Loch Lomond.** During the off-season the route has an untamed and windswept air when it extends beyond the shelter of trees. Take the B829 (signposted Inversnaid and Stronach-lachar), which runs west from Aberfoyle and offers outstanding views of Ben Lomond, especially in the vicinity of Loch Ard. The next loch, where the road narrows and bends, is dark **Loch Chon.**

Beyond Loch Chon, the road climbs gently from the plantings to open moor with a breathtaking vista over **Loch Arklet** to the Arrochar Alps, the name given to the high hills west of Loch Lomond. Hidden from sight in a deep trench, Loch Arklet is dammed to feed Loch Katrine. Go left at the road junction (a right will take you to the village of Stronachlachar) and take the open road along Loch Arklet. These deserted green hills were once the rallying grounds of the Clan Gregor. Near the dam on Loch Arklet, on your right, **Garrison Cottage** recalls the days when the government had to billet troops here to keep the MacGregors in order. From Loch Arklet the road zigzags down to **Inversnaid,** with **Loch Lomond** stretching out of sight above and below.

The only return to Aberfoyle is by retracing the same route. Right at the junction is the hamlet of **Stronachlachar,** on Loch Katrine, the outermost landing stage for the SS *Walter Scott*'s trips on the loch. Stop while you are there for lunch or coffee and cakes at the Pier Tea Room.

WHERE TO STAY

For expanded hotel reviews, visit Fodors.com.

$$ 🏨 **Lake of Menteith Hotel.** This restful hotel emphasizes the peaceful air
★ here with its muted colors and simple rooms. **Pros:** elegant, unpretentious bedrooms; beautiful setting. **Cons:** not well signposted; not all

QUEEN ELIZABETH FOREST PARK

Queen Elizabeth Forest Park. For exquisite nature, drive north from Aberfoyle on the A821 and turn right at signposts to Queen Elizabeth Forest Park. Along the way you'll be heading toward higher moorland blanketed with conifers. The conifers hem in the views of Ben Ledi and Ben Venue, which can be seen over the spiky green waves of trees as the road snakes around heathery knolls and hummocks. There's another viewing area, and a small parking lot, at the highest point of the road. Soon the road swoops off the Highland edge and leads downhill. ⊠ *Off A821, 1 mi north of Aberfoyle* ☎ *01877/382383* ⊕ *www. forestry.gov.uk/qefp.*

David Marshall Lodge. At the heart of the Queen Elizabeth Forest Park, the David Marshall Lodge leads to four forest walks, a family-friendly bicycle route, and the 7-mi 3 Lochs Forest Drive, open April to October.

Or you can sit on the terrace of the Bluebell Cafe and scan the forests and hills of the Trossachs. The visitor center has a wildlife-watch room where you can follow the activities of everything from ospreys to water voles. ⊠ *Queen Elizabeth Forest Park, A821, 1 mi north of Aberfoyle* ☎ *01877/382383* ⊕ *www.forestry. gov.uk/qefp* ⊗ *Mar.–Oct. daily 10–6, Nov. and Dec. daily 10–4.*

Go Ape High Wire Forest Adventure. Near the David Marshall Lodge, Go Ape High Wire Forest Adventure is an exhilarating experience for thrill-seekers age 10 and over. After a short orientation course, you can travel 40 feet above the forest via zip lines and rope ladders. ⊠ *Queen Elizabeth Forest Park, A821, 1 mi north of Aberfoyle* ☎ *0845/643–9215* ⊕ *www.goape.com* ⊠ *£30* ⊗ *Apr.–Oct., daily 9–5; Nov., Feb., and Mar., weekends 9–5.*

rooms have lake views. ⊠ *Port of Menteith* ☎ *01877/385258* ⊕ *www. lake-hotel.com* ➦ *17 rooms* ⚬ *In-room: no a/c. In-hotel: restaurant, bar, business center* ⦿ *Breakfast.*

$$$ ⊞ **Macdonald Forest Hills Hotel.** A traditional Scottish country-house theme pervades this hotel, from the rambling white building itself to the wood-paneled lounges, log fires, and numerous sporting activities. **Pros:** stunning views; log fires; good children's programs. **Cons:** restaurant is pricey and food is average; some of the building looks run-down. ⊠ *B829, Kinlochard* ☎ *08448/799057* ⊕ *www.macdonaldhotels. co.uk/foresthills* ➦ *56 rooms* ⚬ *In-room: no a/c. In-hotel: restaurant, pool, tennis court, gym, children's programs, some age restrictions* ⦿ *Breakfast.*

LOCH LOMOND

14 mi west of Aberfoyle.

GETTING HERE AND AROUND

To reach Loch Lomond, take the B837 from Drymen as far as it will take you. (The parking lot that marks the end of the road is also the well-signposted start of the route up Ben Lomond.) From Balloch the A82 hugs the west bank all the way to Crianlarich, where the A85 will take you back to Callander and Stirling. The loch is just a half hour from Glasgow.

You can drive, cycle, or walk along the 32 mi of Loch Lomond along its western shores, and watch the changing face of the loch as you go, or look up towards the shifting slopes of Ben Lomond.

ESSENTIALS

Visitor Information Loch Lomond and the Trossachs National Park Headquarters ☒ *The Old Station, Balloch* ☎ *01389/722600* ⊕ *www. lochlomond-trossachs.org* ☉ *Weekdays 8:30–5.* **Loch Lomond Shores** ☒ *Ben Lomond Way, Balloch* ☎ *01389/751031* ⊕ *www.lochlomondshores.com.*

EXPLORING

★ **Loch Lomond.** Known for its "bonnie, bonnie banks," Loch Lomond is Scotland's largest loch in terms of surface area, and its waters reflect

HIKE THE HIGHLAND WAY

West Highland Way. The long-distance walkers' route, the West Highland Way (⊕ *www.west-highland-way.co.uk*), begins in Glasgow, running 96 mi (154 km) from the lowlands of Central Scotland to the highlands at Fort William. Nearly 50,000 people discover the glens each year, climbing the hills and listening to birds singing in the tree canopy. This is not a difficult walk, but travelers should keep Scotland's ever-changing weather in mind. From Milngavie, in Glasgow, the route follows the banks of Loch Lomond before snaking north into the more demanding hills and ending at Fort William.

the crags that surround it. The song "The Banks of Loch Lomond" is said to have been written by a Jacobite prisoner incarcerated in Carlisle, England. For the most outstanding Loch Lomond view from the south end, take the A831 to Balmaha and climb Conic Hill that rises behind it. Alternatively hire a boat and row (or take a motorboat) around the islands; the nearest is Inchcailloch, where you can tie up your craft and climb the small hill at the island's center. The view in every direction is spectacular. Note how Inchcailloch and the other islands line up with Conic Hill. This geographic line is indicative of the Highland boundary fault, which runs through Loch Lomond and the hill.

Drymen is 3 mi west of the loch via B837, which leads to Loch Lomond's less busy eastern shore. It's a respectable and cozy town in the Lowland fields, with stores, tea shops, and pubs catering to the well-to-do Scots who have moved here from Glasgow.

SPORTS AND THE OUTDOORS

BOAT TOURS **Cruise Loch Lomond.** You can take tours year-round with Cruise Loch Lomond. From April to October boats depart from various ports around the loch, including Tarbet, Luss, Balmaha, and Inversnaid; from November to March boats depart only from Tarbet. ☒ *Boatyard, Tarbet* ☎ *01301/702356.*

Macfarlane and Son. Boats rent for £10 per hour or £30 per day at Macfarlane and Son. The company also runs cruises on the loch. ☒ *Balmaha Boatyard, Balmaha* ☎ *01360/870214.*

WHERE TO EAT

$　✕ **Coach House Coffee Shop.** This lively restaurant and café fits perfectly
BRITISH　into its surroundings with its cheerful, over-the-top Scottishness. Long
wooden tables, a large chimney with an open fire in the winter months,
and a cabinet full of mouthwatering cakes baked by the owner create
the atmosphere. Favorites include rich homemade soups and stokies
(large round rolls filled to overflowing), as well as haggis, served in
king-size quantities. It's worth asking for tea served in ceramic teapots
representing everything from dining rooms to telephone boxes (the pots
are for sale in the shop). ✉ *Church Rd., Luss* ☎ *01436/860341.*

¢　✕ **Drovers Inn.** The portions at this noisy, friendly inn are enormous,
BRITISH　which is just as well since many customers have returned from a day's
walking on the nearby West Highland Way. Scottish staples like sausage and mash, minced beef, and the ubiquitous haggis with mash and
neeps (turnips) jostle for a place beside occasionally more adventurous
dishes. The dining areas are hung with swords and modern copies of old
paintings. This is a genuine traveler's pub, with an appropriate range of
whiskies (hearty rather than elegant). There is traditional music every
weekend, and there are 26 rooms for rent for under £100. The bear at
the door should not put you off (it is stuffed and very old). ✉ *A82, north
of Ardlui, Inverarnan* ☎ *01301/704234* ⊕ *www.thedroversinn.co.uk.*

¢　✕ **Pier Tea Room.** At the historic Stronachlachar Pier, this elegant coffee
shop has a satisfying lunch menu and an expansive deck overlooking
Loch Katrine. Cakes, scones, and soups are made on the premises. Many
people stop here before cycling or walking along the loch road. ✉ *Loch
Katrine, Stronachlachar* ☎ *01877/386374* ⊕ *www.thepiertearoom.com.*

WHERE TO STAY

For expanded hotel reviews, visit Fodors.com.

$　▣ **Balloch House Vintage Inn.** Cute, cozy, and very Scottish, this small
hotel offers tasty breakfasts and hearty pub meals like fish-and-chips
and local smoked salmon for reasonable prices. **Pros:** beautiful building;
recently refurbished; near shopping. **Cons:** noisy pinball machine next to
bar; not all rooms have views. ✉ *Balloch Rd., Balloch* ☎ *01389/752579*
⊕ *www.theinnkeeprslodge.com* ⇆ *11 rooms* ⌂ *In-room: no a/c, Wi-Fi.
In-hotel: restaurant, bar* ¶◎¶ *Breakfast.*

$$$$　▣ **Cameron House.** There is very little that you cannot do at this luxury
resort hotel beside Loch Lomond, including taking to the water in a
motorboat or riding a seaplane above the trees. **Pros:** beautiful grounds;
good dining. **Cons:** prices are high; slightly difficult access from the
A82. ✉ *Loch Lomond, off A82, Alexandria* ☎ *01389/755565* ⊕ *www.
devere.co.uk* ⇆ *96 rooms, 7 suites* ⌂ *In-room: no a/c, Wi-Fi. In-hotel:
restaurant, bar, golf course, pool, tennis court, gym, children's programs*
¶◎¶ *Breakfast.*

$$　▣ **Culcreuch Castle Hotel.** The hand-painted wallpaper in the Chinese
Bird Room dates from 1723, which shows how much the owners of
this authentic castle care about preserving the past. **Pros:** historic build-
ing; expansive and beautiful grounds; good food at reasonable prices.
Cons: a little remote; steep stairways; rather small shower rooms. ✉ *Off
B822, Fintry* ☎ *01360/860555* ⊕ *www.culcreuch.com* ⇆ *14 rooms*

♻ *In-room: no a/c, Wi-Fi. In-hotel: restaurant, bar, business center* 🍽 *Breakfast.*

SHOPPING

Loch Lomond Shores. This lakeside shopping complex contains restaurants, pubs, and a visitor center. ✉ *Ben Lomond Way, Balloch* ✆ *01389/ 751031* ◈ *www.lochlomondshores.com.*

PERTHSHIRE

In some ways, Perthshire is a crossing point between different Scottish landscapes and histories. Perthshire itself is rural, agricultural Scotland, fertile and prosperous. Its woodlands, rivers, and glens (and agreeable climate and strategic position) drew the Romans and later the Celtic missionaries. In fact, the motto of the capital city, Perth, is "the perfect center." If Perthshire's castles invoke memories of past conflicts, the grand houses and spa towns here are testimony to the continued presence of a wealthy, landed gentry. This is also a place for walking, cycling, and water sports.

PERTH

36 mi northeast of Stirling, 43 mi north of Edinburgh, 61 mi northeast of Glasgow.

For many years, Perth was Scotland's capital, and central to its history. One king (James I) was killed here, and the Protestant reformer John Knox preached in St John's Kirk, where his rhetoric moved crowds to burn down several local monasteries. Perth's local whisky trade and the productive agriculture that surrounds the town have sustained it through the centuries. Its grand buildings, especially on the banks of the River Tay, testify to its continued wealth. The open parkland within the city (the Inches) gives the place a restful air, and shops range from small crafts boutiques to department stores. Impressive Scone Palace is nearby.

GETTING HERE AND AROUND

Perth is served by the main railway line to Inverness, and regular and frequent buses run here from Glasgow, Edinburgh, and Stirling. The central artery, the A9, passes through the city en route to Pitlochry and Inverness, while a network of roads opens the way to the glens and hills around Glen Lyon, or the road to Loch Lomond (the A85) via Crianlarich.

ESSENTIALS

Visitor Information Perth Visitor Centre ✉ *Lower City Mills, West Mill St.* ✆ *01738/450600* ◈ *www.visitscotland.co.uk.*

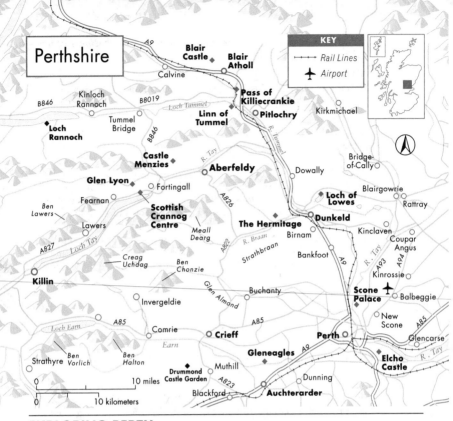

Perthshire

KEY
━┿━ Rail Lines
✈ Airport

Blair Castle
Blair Atholl
Calvine
Kinloch Rannoch
B846
B8019
Loch Tummel
Pass of Killiecrankie
Pitlochry
Kirkmichael
Linn of Tummel
Loch Rannoch
Tummel Bridge
Bridge-of-Cally
Castle Menzies
Glen Lyon
Aberfeldy
Dowally
Blairgowrie
Loch of Lowes
Rattray
Ben Lawers
Fearnan
Fortingall
Scottish Crannog Centre
Meall Dearg
The Hermitage
Dunkeld
Birnam
Kinclaven
Coupar Angus
Lawers
Loch Tay
Creag Uchdag
Ben Chonzie
Strathbraan
Bankfoot
Killin
Invergeldie
Glen Almond
Buchanty
Scone Palace
Balbeggie
Loch Earn
A85
Comrie
Crieff
A85
Perth
New Scone
Glencarse
Ben Vorlich
Ben Halton
Muthill
Gleneagles
Elcho Castle
Strathyre
Drummond Castle Garden
Dunning
Blackford
Auchterarder

0 —— 10 miles
0 —— 10 kilometers

EXPLORING PERTH

TOP ATTRACTIONS

Elcho Castle. From the battlements of Elcho Castle you can see the River Tay stretching east and west. Built around 1560, the castle marks a transition period when these structures began to be built as grand houses rather than fortresses, and it's easy to see that Elcho was built for both comfort and defense. The well conserved but uncluttered rooms let you imagine how life might have been here in the 17th century. The staircases still give access to all floors, and a flashlight is provided for the darker corners. Originally, the castle was accessible only via the river, but today it can be reached by road from Perth. ⊠ *Off A912, close to Rhynd* ☎ *01738/639998* ⊕ *www.historic-scotland.gov.uk/places* 🎫 *£4* ⊙ *Apr.–Sept., daily 9:30–5:30.*

Fodor's Choice
★

Ⓒ **Scone Palace.** About 2 mi from Perth, Scone Palace (pronounced *skoon*) is much more cheerful than the city's other castles, and is the current residence of the Earl of Mansfield but is open to visitors. Although it incorporates various earlier works, the palace today has mainly a 19th-century theme, with mock castellations that were fashionable at the time. There's plenty to see if you're interested in the acquisitions of an aristocratic Scottish family: magnificent porcelain, furniture, ivory, clocks, and 16th-century needlework. A coffee shop, restaurant, gift shop, and play area are on site, and on the extensive grounds is a pine plantation. The palace has its own mausoleum nearby, on the site of a long-gone abbey on **Moot Hill**, the ancient coronation place of the Scottish kings. To be crowned, they sat on the Stone of Scone, which was seized in 1296 by Edward I of England, Scotland's greatest enemy, and placed in the coronation chair at Westminster Abbey, in London. The stone was returned to Scotland in November 1996 and is now on view in Edinburgh Castle. ⊠ *Braemar Rd.* ☎ *01738/552300* ⊕ *www. scone-palace.co.uk* 💷 *£9.60* ⊙ *Apr.–Oct., daily 9:30–5:30, last admission at 5; Nov–Mar., Fri. 10–4.*

WORTH NOTING

Fergusson Gallery. The Round House, with its magnificent and newly restored dome and rotunda, contains this display of selections from a collection of 6,000 works—paintings, drawings, and prints—by the Scottish artist J. D. Fergusson (1874–1961). Fergusson was the longest-lived member of the group called the Scottish Colourists, who took their inspiration from the French Impressionist painters in their use of color and light. ⊠ *Marshall Pl.* ☎ *01738/783425* ⊕ *www.scottishmuseums. org.uk* 💷 *Free* ⊙ *Mon.–Sat. 10–5.*

Perth Art Gallery and Museum. The wide-ranging collection here includes exhibits on natural history, local history, archaeology, and art—including work by the great painter of animals Sir Edwin Landseer and some botanical studies of fungi by Beatrix Potter. ⊠ *78 George St.* ☎ *01738/632488* ⊕ *www.pkc.gov.uk/perthmuseum* 💷 *Free* ⊙ *Mon.– Sat. 10–5.*

Regimental Museum of the Black Watch. Some will tell you the Black Watch was a Scottish regiment whose name is a reference to the color of its tartan. An equally plausible explanation, however, is that the regiment was established to keep an undercover watch on rebellious Jacobites. The Gaelic word for black is *dubh,* meaning, in this case, "hidden" or "covert." A wide range of uniforms, weaponry, and marching banners are displayed. The castle is closed on the last weekend in June. ⊠ *Balhousie Castle, Hay St.* ☎ *01738/638152* ⊕ *www.theblackwatch. co.uk* 💷 *£5* ⊙ *Apr.–Oct., Mon.–Sat. 9:30–5, Sun. 10–4; Nov.–Mar., Mon.–Sat. 9:30–5.*

St. John's Kirk. This cruciform-plan church dates from the 12th century. The interior was divided into three parts at the Reformation, but was restored to something closer to its medieval state by Sir Robert Lorimer in the 1920s. ⊠ *St. John St.* ☎ *01738/638482* ⊕ *www.st-johns-kirk. co.uk* 💷 *£1* ⊙ *Weekdays 10–4, Sun. services at 9:30 and 11.*

WHERE TO EAT AND STAY

For expanded hotel reviews, visit Fodors.com.

$$
✕ Let's Eat. The varied clientele reflects the broad appeal of noted chef

BRITISH
Willie Deans's imaginative menu. Prix-fixe menus combine some surprising dishes (sole with leek mash, broad beans, and bacon) with earthy dishes with a Scottish flavor (roast lamb with cassoulet and Blairgowrie beef fillet). Ingredients are locally sourced. The restaurant is airy and comfortable, merging warm colors and wood. ⊠ *77–79 Kinnoull St.* ☎ *01738/643377* ⊕ *www.letseatperth.co.uk* ⊙ *Closed Sun. and Mon.*

$ ⌂ **Parklands.** This stylish Georgian town house overlooks lush woodland. **Pros:** lovely rooms; superb restaurants. **Cons:** some rooms have better views than others; restaurants closed on Sunday. ✉ *2 St. Leonard's Bank* ☎ *01738/622451* ⊕ *www.theparklandshotel.com* ⬐ *14 rooms* ⚬ *In-room: no a/c. In-hotel: restaurant* ⏀ *Breakfast.*

$ ⌂ **Sunbank House Hotel.** This early Victorian gray stone mansion near
★ Perth's Branklyn Gardens overlooks the River Tay and the city of Perth; unpretentious and comfortable, it offers fine views from its front garden. **Pros:** reasonably priced; friendly staff; delicious local cuisine. **Cons:** some rooms are very small; you can hear traffic from the main road. ✉ *50 Dundee Rd.* ☎ *01738/624882* ✎ *reception@sunbankhouse.com* ⊕ *www.sunbankhouse.com* ⬐ *9 rooms* ⚬ *In-room: no a/c, Wi-Fi. In-hotel: restaurant, bar* ⏀ *Multiple meal plans.*

NIGHTLIFE AND THE ARTS

Perth Repertory Theatre. The Victorian Perth Repertory Theatre stages plays and musicals. ✉ *185 High St.* ☎ *017384/621031* ⊕ *www.horsecross.co.uk.*

Perth Concert Hall. The hall hosts musical performances of all types. ✉ *Mill St.* ☎ *017384/621031* ⊕ *www.horsecross.co.uk.*

SHOPPING

Perthshire Visitor Centre. This is not so much an information center as a shopping complex and restaurant. The complex has a specialist whisky shop, a large delicatessen, a gift shop, and a clothes retail outlet. ✉ *A9, 6 mi from Perth, Bankfoot* ☎ *01738/787696* ⊕ *www.perthshirevisitorcentre.co.uk.*

CERAMICS   Perth is an especially popular hunting ground for china and glass.

Watson of Perth. Watson of Perth has sold exquisite bone china and cut crystal since 1900 and can pack your purchase for shipment overseas. ✉ *163–167 High St.* ☎ *01738/639861* ⊕ *www.watsonsofperth.co.uk.*

CLOTHING   **C & C Proudfoot.** This shop sells a comprehensive selection of sheepskins, leather jackets, rugs, slippers, and handbags. ✉ *104 South St.* ☎ *01738/632483.*

JEWELRY AND   **Cairncross of Perth.** Perth proffers an unusual buy: Scottish freshwater
ANTIQUES   pearls from the River Tay, in delicate settings. The Romans coveted these pearls. If you do, too, then you can make your choice at Cairncross of Perth, where you can also admire a display of some of the more unusual shapes and colors of pearls. Some of the settings take their theme from Scottish flowers. ✉ *18 St. John's St.* ☎ *01738/624367* ⊕ *www.cairncrossofperth.co.uk.*

Timothy Hardie. Antique jewelry and silver, including a few Scottish items, can be found at Timothy Hardie. ✉ *25 St. John's St.* ☎ *01738/633127* ⊕ *www.timothyhardie.co.uk.*

Whispers of the Past. The lovely Whispers of the Past has a collection of jewelry, china, and other gift items. ✉ *15 George St.* ☎ *01738/635472.*

DUNKELD

14 mi north of Perth.

The ruined cathedral above the town of Dunkeld marks its historic beginnings. The present town grew up around the main square, built by the Atholl family in the wake of the 1689 defeat of the Jacobite army (following its earlier victory in the Battle of Killiecrankie). The National Trust for Scotland has helped to maintain the houses with its Little Houses Project; it has a small exhibition above the Dunkeld and Birnam Tourist Information Centre (ask for the Heritage Trail leaflet). Crafts and interior-design shops dominate Atholl Street, which leads down to the River Tay.

GETTING HERE AND AROUND

Dunkeld is on the A9 between Perth and Pitlochry. The town is also on the main train line to Inverness.

ESSENTIALS

Visitor Information Dunkeld and Birnam Tourist Information Centre ⊠ *The Cross* ☎ *01350/727688* ⊕ *www.visitscotland.com.*

EXPLORING

Beatrix Potter Garden. The bridge across the Tay, built by the great engineer Thomas Telford in 1809, connects Dunkeld to the village of Birnam. In the woods on Birnam Hill, some 500 yards from the town center, Macbeth met the three witches who foretold his death. Witty wooden notices lead the visitor to the right tree, a gnarled hollow oak. Less spooky is the Beatrix Potter Garden, which celebrates the life and work of this much-beloved children's writer who, for many years, spent her family holidays in the area. An enchanting garden walk allows you to peep into the homes of Peter Rabbit and Mrs. Tiggy-Winkle, her best-known characters. The visitor center has a well-stocked shop, a small café, and an imaginative exhibition on the writer's life and work (£1.50). ⊠ *Birnam Arts Centre, Station Rd., Birnam* ☎ *01350/727674* ⊕ *www.birnamarts.com* ☉ *Museum daily 10–5.*

★ **Hermitage.** On the outskirts of Dunkeld, the Hermitage is a woodland walk that follows the River Braan. In the 18th century, the dukes of Atholl constructed two follies (a fantasy building) here, **Ossian's Cave** and the awesome **Ossian's Hall,** above a spectacular—and noisy—waterfall. (Ossian was a fictional Celtic poet invented by James MacPherson in the 18th century for an era fascinated by the primitive past.) You'll also be in the presence of Britain's tallest tree, a Douglas fir measuring 214 feet. ⊠ *A9, 1 mi west of Dunkeld.*

Loch of Lowes. At Loch of Lowes, a Scottish Wildlife Trust reserve near Dunkeld, the domestic routines of the osprey, one of Scotland's conservation success stories, can be observed in relative comfort between March and August. There is activity throughout the year, with birds like the great crested grebe at observation and feeding points. ⊠ *Off A923, about 2 mi northeast of Dunkeld* ☎ *01350/727337* ⊕ *www.swt. org.uk* ☐ *£3–£4* ☉ *Apr.–Oct., daily 10–5; Nov.–Mar., daily 10:30–4.*

WHERE TO EAT

¢ ✕ **Taybank Hotel.** This spot overlooking the river is a musical meeting
ECLECTIC   place owned by Scottish singer Dougie MacLean. There is live music
several nights a week. The bar serves good solid Scottish food, including
chicken breast cooked with bacon and kale, and "stovies," an oven-
baked dish of meat, onions, and potatoes. ⊠ *Tay Terr.* ☎ *01350/727340*
⊕ *www.taybank.com.*

SHOPPING

Dunkeld Antiques. Housed in a deconsecrated church facing the river,
Dunkeld Antiques stocks mainly 18th- and 19th-century items, from
large furniture to ornaments, books, and prints. ⊠ *Tay Terr.* ☎ *01350/*
728832 ⊕ *www.dunkeldantiques.co.uk.*

Jeremy Law of Scotland's Highland Horn and Deerskin Centre. At the Jeremy
Law of Scotland's Highland Horn and Deerskin Centre, you can purchase stag antlers and cow horns shaped into walking sticks, cutlery,
and tableware. Deerskin shoes and moccasins and a collection of more
than 200 different whiskys are also for sale. ⊠ *City Hall, Atholl St.*
☎ *01350/727569* ⊕ *www.moccasin.co.uk.*

PITLOCHRY

15 mi north of Dunkeld.

In the late 19th century, Pitlochry was an elegant Victorian spa town,
famous for its mild microclimate and beautiful setting. Today it is a
busy tourist town, with wall-to-wall gift shops, cafés and B&Bs, large
hotels, and a huge golf course. The town itself is oddly nondescript,
but it's a convenient base from which to explore the surrounding hills
and valleys.

GETTING HERE AND AROUND

The main route through central Scotland, the A9, passes through
Pitlochry, as does the main railway line from Glasgow/Edinburgh to
Inverness. From here the B8019 connects to the B846 west to Rannoch
Moor or south to Aberfeldy.

ESSENTIALS

Visitor Information Pitlochry ⊠ *22 Atholl Rd.* ☎ *01796/472215* ⊕ *www.*
visitscotland.com.

EXPLORING

Edradour Distillery. If you have a whisky-tasting bent, visit Edradour
Distillery, which claims to be the smallest single-malt distillery in Scotland (but then, so do others). There's a fun, informative tour of the
distillery where you get to see how the whisky is made; you also get
to savor a free dram at the end of the tour. ⊠ *A924, 2½ mi east of Pit-*
lochry ☎ *01796/472095* ⊕ *www.edradour.co.uk* ✉ *Tours £5* ☉ *Tours*
May–Oct., Mon.–Sat. 10–5, Sun. noon–5; Nov., Dec., Mar., and Apr.,
Mon.–Sat. 10–4, Sun. noon–4; Jan. and Feb., Mon.–Sat. 10–4.

Linn of Tummel. The Linn of Tummel, a series of marked walks along the
river and through tall, mature woodlands, is a little north of Pitlochry.

Above the Linn, the A9 rises on stilts and gives an exciting view of the valley.

Loch Rannoch. With its shoreline of birch trees framed by dark pines, Loch Rannoch is the quintessential Highland loch. Fans of Robert Louis Stevenson (1850–94), especially of *Kidnapped* (1886), will not want to miss the last, lonely section of road. Stevenson describes the setting: "The mist rose and died away, and showed us that country lying as waste as the sea, only the moorfowl and the peewees crying upon it, and far over to the east a herd of deer, moving like dots." Loch Rannoch is off B846, 20 mi west of Pitlochry.

★ **Pass of Killiecrankie.** The Pass of Killiecrankie, set among the oak woods and rocky river just north of the Linn of Tummel, was the site of a famous battle won by the Jacobites in 1689. The spot where a soldier escaped the battle by jumping across the river is now called the Soldier's Leap. The battle was noted for the death of the central Jacobite leader, John Graham of Claverhouse (1649–89), also known as Bonnie Dundee, who was hit by a stray bullet. The rebellion fizzled after Claverhouse's death. ⊠ *B8079, 3 mi north of Pitlochry.*

Killiecrankie Visitor Centre. The National Trust for Scotland's visitor center at Killiekrankie explains the significance of the battle at the Pass of Killiekrankie, which was the first attempt to restore the Stewart monarchy. ⊠ *Off A9, 4 mi north of Pitlochry* ☎ *01796/473233* ⊕ *www.nts.org.uk/Visits* ⊗ *Visitor center Apr.–Oct., daily 10–5:30.*

Pitlochry Dam and Fish Ladder. Most Scottish dams have salmon passes or ladders of some kind, enabling the fish to swim upstream to their spawning grounds. The Pitlochry Dam and Fish Ladder, just behind the main street, leads into a glass-paneled pipe that allows the fish to observe the visitors. ⊠ *Off A9* ☎ *01796/473152* ⊠ *Free* ⊗ *May–Oct., Mon.–Sat. 10–5, Sun. noon–5; Nov. and Dec., Mon.–Sat. 10–4, Sun. noon–4; Jan. and Feb., Mon.–Sat. 10–4.*

WHERE TO EAT AND STAY

For expanded hotel reviews, visit Fodors.com.

¢ ✕ **Moulin Hotel and Brewery.** The Moulin is a traditional pub with dark
BRITISH wooden interiors that serves standard Scottish fare in large quantities. Venison Braveheart, for example, is cooked in the brewery's own beer, and the haggis with neeps and tatties is predictable but good. This is a pleasant place, provided you are not too averse to the stuffed animals along the walls. The home-brewed beer is powerful, and during the afternoon you can visit the adjacent brewery. ⊠ *11–30 Kirkmichael Rd.* ☎ *01796/472196* ⊕ *www.moulinhotel.co.uk.*

$$$ ▥ **Atholl Palace Hotel.** A grand hotel in the best Victorian style, Atholl Palace is a 19th-century vision of a medieval castle. **Pros:** lovely grounds; lots for kids to do; high comfort. **Cons:** old-fashioned feel; long anonymous corridors. ⊠ *A924* ☎ *01796/472400* ⊕ *www.athollpalace.com* ⇨ *106 rooms* ⌂ *In-room: no a/c. In-hotel: restaurant, bar, pool, tennis court, spa* ▯◯▮ *Breakfast.*

$$$$ ▥ **Killiecrankie House Hotel.** This neat oasis is set amid the wooded hills and streams of the Pass of Killiecrankie. **Pros:** lovely location; pleasant rooms. **Cons:** books up fast. ⊠ *B8079, 3 mi north of Pitlochry,*

6

Killiecrankie ☎ *01796/473220* ⊕ *www.killiecrankiehotel.co.uk* ⌁ *10 rooms* ♿ *In-room: no a/c, Wi-Fi. In-hotel: restaurant, bar* ⦿ *Breakfast.*

¢ ▦ **Tir Aluinn Guest House.** Tir Aluinn is a comfortable and friendly B&B that looks down over the town of Pitlochry and the valley beyond. **Pros:** friendly attentive owners; bright decor. **Cons:** slightly outside the town; good but basic furnishings. ⊠ *10 Higher Oakfield* ☎ *01796/ 473811* ⊕ *www.tiraluinn.co.uk* ⌁ *4 rooms* ♿ *In-room: no a/c, Wi-Fi* ⦿ *Breakfast.*

NIGHTLIFE AND THE ARTS

Pitlochry Festival Theatre. The theatre presents six plays each season, hosts Sunday concerts, and holds art exhibitions. It also has a café and restaurant overlooking the River Tummel. ☎ *01796/484626* ⊕ *www. pitlochry.org.uk.*

BLAIR ATHOLL

10 mi north of Pitlochry.

GETTING HERE AND AROUND

Popular Blair Castle is just off the A9 Pitlochry-to-Inverness road, beyond the village of Blair Atholl. The village has a railway station that is on the main Inverness line.

EXPLORING

Fodor's Choice **Blair Castle.** Thanks to its historic contents and war-torn past, Blair
★ Castle is one of Scotland's most highly rated sights. The turreted white castle was home to successive dukes of Atholl and their families, the Murrays, until the death of the 10th duke. One of the castle's fascinating details is a preserved piece of floor still bearing marks of the red-hot shot fired through the roof during the 1745 Jacobite rebellion—the last occasion in Scottish history that a castle was besieged. The castle holds not only military artifacts—historically, the duke was allowed to keep a private army, the Atholl Highlanders—but also a rich collection of furniture, china, and paintings. The Hercules Gardens is a 9-acre Victorian walled garden, and the extensive grounds have woodland and river walks. ⊠ *Off B8079, Blair Atholl* ☎ *01796/481207* ⊕ *www. blair-castle.co.uk* ✎ *Castle and gardens: Apr.–Oct., £9.50, Nov.–Mar., £7.40. Grounds only: Apr.–Oct., £5.25; Nov.–Mar., Free* ☉ *Apr.–Oct., daily 9:30–5:30; Nov.–Mar., weekends 10–4.*

SHOPPING

House of Bruar. An upscale shopping complex, the House of Bruar has a heavy emphasis on traditional tweeds and cashmeres. A large supermarket sells local produce and food, as well as a range of international delicatessen foods. When you're done shopping, take a walk up the path that crosses the Bruar Falls, accessed at the back of the shopping complex. ⊠ *Off A9, Blair Atholl* ☎ *01796/483236.*

John A Lacey. Watch for this house between Killin and Aberfeldy. Its front room is a treasure trove of horn carving, from a full-masted galleon to knives in their sheaths. There are also deerskins for sale. John Lacey has worked here for 30 years; he says the egg spoons are still the most popular items. ⊠ *A827, Aberfeldy* ☎ *01567/820561.*

ABERFELDY

15 mi southwest of Pitlochry, 25 mi southwest of Blair Castle.

The most dramatic thing about Aberfeldy is the high humpbacked bridge into the town, built by William Adam in 1733 and commissioned by General Wade, who marched through Scotland suppressing local resistance after the Jacobite rebellion. The town itself is rather sleepy, but this is a popular base for exploring the region. It's Scotland's first fair-trade town, and a water mill here produces delicious stone-ground oatmeal. There's also a whisky distillery and plenty of local golf courses.

GETTING HERE AND AROUND

You can reach Aberfeldy from Dunkeld via the A9 and the A827. A longer but very pretty route is the A85 from Crieff, then through Killin on the A827. Aberfeldy is served by regular buses from Perth and Pitlochry.

ESSENTIALS

Visitor Information Aberfeldy Tourist Information Centre ✉ *The Square* ☎ *01887/820276* ⊕ *www.visitscotland.com.*

EXPLORING

Dewar's World of Whisky. This established distillery has a whisky museum and a tour that demonstrates how whisky is made (with a tasting at the end, of course). There's also a nature trail on the grounds as well as a café restaurant. ✉ *A827* ☎ *01887/822010* ⊕ *www.dewars.com* 🎫 *£7* ⊙ *Apr.–Oct., weekdays 10–6, Sun. noon–4; Nov.–Mar., Mon.– Sat. 10–4.*

Castle Menzies. A 16th-century fortified tower house, Castle Menzies contains the **Clan Menzies Museum,** which displays many relics of the clan's history. Beside the castle is an old byre that's been converted into a craft shop, winery, and café. The castle stands west of Aberfeldy, on the opposite bank of the River Tay. ✉ *B846, Weem* ☎ *01887/820982* 🎫 *£4* ⊙ *Apr.–Oct., Sun. 2–5, Mon. 10:30–5.*

Glen Lyon. One of central Scotland's most attractive glens, Glen Lyon is one of its longest at 34 mi. It has a rushing river, thick forests, and the typical big house hidden on private grounds. There's a dam at the head of the loch, a reminder that little of Scotland's scenic beauty is unadulterated. The winding road lends itself to an unrushed, leisurely drive, past the visitor center at the access to Ben Lawers, a popular climb, and on to Killin. ✉ *A827, 15 mi north of Aberfeldy.*

OFF THE BEATEN PATH

Scottish Crannog Centre. Here's your chance to travel back 5,000 years to a time when the local inhabitants of this area started building defensive homesteads, known as *crannogs,* on wooden piles standing in lochs. They were approachable only by narrow bridges that could be easily defended. This practice continued until as late as the 17th century. Archaeologists have found many remains of crannogs in lochs throughout Scotland. One of the best preserved was found several feet under the surface of Loch Tay, off the north shore at Fearnan, and it's now possible to visit an accurate replica built on the south shore. An exhibition gives details about crannog construction and the way of life in and around crannogs. The Crannog Centre is just west of Aberfeldy, on the southern shore of Loch Tay. ✉ *Off A827, west of Aberfeldy*

6

☎ *01887/830583* ⊕ *www.crannog.co.uk* 🖃 *£7* ◷ *Apr.–Oct., daily 10–5:30; Dec.–Mar., weekends 10–4; last entry 1 hr before closing.*

SHOPPING

Aberfeldy Water Mill. A bookshop, gallery, and café in the center of town, Aberfeldy Water Mill is considered one of the best independent bookstores in the region. ⊠ *Mill St.* ☎ *01887/822896* ⊕ *www. aberfeldywatermill.com.*

SPORTS AND THE OUTDOORS

Highland Safaris. A full range of off-road activities for cyclists, drivers, and walkers is offered by Highland Safaris. ☎ *01887/820071* ⊕ *www. highlandsafaris.net.*

KILLIN

24 mi southwest of Aberfeldy, 39 mi north of Stirling, 45 mi west of Perth.

Killin's setting near the Breadalbane Mountains at the end of Loch Tay (where the Falls of Dochart rush into the lake) gives the village an almost alpine flavor. You'll find a surprisingly diverse selection of crafts and woolen shops here, as well as a plethora of B&Bs.

GETTING HERE AND AROUND

Killin can be reached from Stirling via the A85 and A827, or from Aberfeldy via the A827, the winding road beside Loch Tay.

ESSENTIALS

Visitor Information Killin Tourist Information Office ☎ *01786/459203.*

EXPLORING

Falls of Dochart. The Falls of Dochart, white-water rapids overlooked by a pine-clad islet, are at the west end of the village of Killin. ⊠ *Off A827.*

Finlarig Castle. Across the River Dochart from Killin sit the ruins of Finlarig Castle, built by Black Duncan of the Cowl, a notorious Campbell laird. The castle grounds can be visited at any time. ⊠ *Off A827.*

BICYCLING

Killin Outdoor Centre and Mountain Shop. If you want to explore the north end of the Glasgow–Killin cycleway, rent a mountain bike from Killin Outdoor Centre and Mountain Shop (£16 for 4 hrs). Also available are canoes, crampons, snowshoes, and ice axes. ⊠ *Main St.* ☎ *01567/820652* ⊕ *www.killinoutdoor.co.uk.*

WHERE TO STAY

For expanded hotel reviews, visit Fodors.com.

$ ⊞ **Bridge of Lochay Hotel.** On the edge of Killin, this small, family-run hotel sits on the banks of the River Tay. **Pros:** good facilities; welcoming atmosphere. **Cons:** basic rooms. ⊠ *Aberfeldy Rd.* ☎ *01567/820272* ⊕ *www.bridgeoflochay.co.uk* 🖚 *10 rooms* ⌂ *In-hotel: restaurant, business center* ⏐◯⏐ *Breakfast.*

¢ ⊞ **Breadalbane House.** This unpretentious but welcoming inn sits in the center of Killin. **Pros:** a lovely location; friendly owners; easy parking.

Cons: no young children allowed; limited public transport. ✉ *Main St.* ☎ *01567/820134* ⊕ *www.breadalbanehouse.com* 🛏 *5 rooms* ♿ *In-hotel: some age restrictions* ℐ◎ℐ *No meals.*

CRIEFF

25 mi southwest of Killin.

A spa and market town in the foothills of the Grampians, Crieff retains the prosperous air of its Victorian heyday. Its central square, where local farmers may once have gathered to trade, is still a lively center. For a very different view of the town, you could climb Knock Hill, which is signposted from the town center.

GETTING HERE AND AROUND

Crieff once prospered because of the arrival of the railway. There is no station here today, but there are regular buses from Stirling and Glasgow. By car, take the A85 from Perth, or the A9, turning onto the A822 after Dunblane.

ESSENTIALS

Visitor Information Crieff ✉ *Town Hall, High St.* ☎ *01764/653418* ⊕ *www. visitscotland.com.*

EXPLORING

Drummond Castle Garden. This large, formal Victorian parterre celebrates family and Scottish heraldry. The flower beds are planted and trimmed in the shapes of various heraldic symbols, such as a lion rampant and a checkerboard, associated with the coat of arms of the family that owns the castle and with the Scottish Royal Coat of Arms. It's regarded as one of the finest of its kind in Europe, and it even made an appearance in the film *Rob Roy.* ✉ *Off A822, 6 mi southwest of Crieff* ☎ *01764/681433* ⊕ *www.drummondcastlegardens.co.uk* 🎫 *£5* ⊙ *May–Oct., daily 1–6; last admission at 5.*

Glenturret Distillery. To discover the delights of whisky distilling, sign up for the "Famous Grouse Experience" at the Glenturret Distillery. Here you learn how whisky is made and why time, water, soil, and air are so important to the taste. A guide takes you through the distillery and to the bar where you can have a glass of Famous Grouse Finest (a blended, not a single-malt whisky) and try your skill at "nosing." You might cap your tour with lunch or dinner at either of the two Scottish restaurants. Signs lead to the distillery on the west side of the town. ✉ *Comrie Rd.* ☎ *01764/656565* ⊕ *www.thefamousgrouseexperience. com* 🎫 *£8.95* ⊙ *Mar.–Dec., daily 9–6, last tour at 4:30; Jan. and Feb., daily 10–4:30, last tour at 3.*

WHERE TO STAY

For expanded hotel reviews, visit Fodors.com.

$$$ ☷ **Crieff Hydro.** One of the great Victorian hydropathy centers scattered across central Scotland, this grand, old-fashioned hotel has been owned and run by the same family for more than a hundred years. **Pros:** fine, extensive grounds; variety of activities; particularly good for children.

Cons: rooms are rather dull; some activities are quite expensive. ⊠ *Off A85* ☎ *01764/655555* ⊕ *www.crieffhydro.com* ⤷ *216 rooms* ♿ *In-room: no a/c, Wi-Fi. In-hotel: golf course, tennis court, gym, spa, children's programs* ¶⊙¶ *Multiple meal plans.*

SHOPPING

Crieff is a center for china and glassware.

Stuart Crystal. The factory shop for Stuart Crystal sells not only its own brand but also Waterford, Dartington, and Wedgwood wares. ⊠ *Muthill Rd.* ☎ *01764/654004* ☼ *June–Sept., daily 10–5:30; Oct.–May, Mon.–Sat. 10–5, Sun. 11–5.*

AUCHTERARDER

11 mi southeast of Crieff.

Famous for the Gleneagles Hotel and nearby golf courses, Auchterarder also has a flock of tiny antiques shops to amuse Gleneagles's golf widows and widowers.

GETTING HERE AND AROUND

Gleneagles Station is on the main Inverness line, while the A9 gives direct access to Gleneagles and Auchterarder via the A823.

ESSENTIALS

Visitor Information Auchterarder ⊠ *90 High St.* ☎ *01764/663450* ⊕ *www.perthshire-scotland.co.uk.*

WHERE TO STAY

For expanded hotel reviews, visit Fodors.com.

$$$$
Fodor's Choice
★

⌂**Gleneagles Hotel.** One of Britain's most famous hotels, Gleneagles is the very essence of modern grandeur. **Pros:** numerous amenities; the three courses are a golfer's paradise. **Cons:** luxury comes at a steep price. ⊠ *Off A823* ☎ *01764/662231* ⊕ *www.gleneagles.com* ⤷ *216 rooms, 13 suites* ♿ *In-room: no a/c, Wi-Fi. In-hotel: restaurant, golf course, tennis court, pool, gym, spa, children's programs* ¶⊙¶ *Breakfast.*

Aberdeen and the Northeast

WORD OF MOUTH

"In Dufftown you will find Glenfiddich distillery. Probably one of the best sellers in the world and almost certainly the best tour. In Aberlour you are in the heart of Speyside on the Whisky Trail. If you have a favorite distillery, ask at a tourist office if they do a tour and just go along."

— Sheila

"Fraser and Drum castles are good for exploring. Fraser is a well-maintained paradigm of a laird's country estate. Drum is a mishmash of styles and expansions from its initial construction in the 1300s. You've already heard that Balmoral is a quick visit because there is little that you can actually access."

— BigRuss

www.fodors.com/community

Updated by
Shona Main

Here, in this granite shoulder of Grampian, are some of Scotland's most enduring travel icons: Royal Deeside, the countryside that Queen Victoria made her own; the Castle Country route, where fortresses stand hard against the hills; and the Malt Whisky Trail, where peaty streams embrace the country's greatest concentration of distilleries. The region's gateway is the city of Aberdeen, constructed of granite and now aglitter with new wealth and new blood drawn together by North Sea oil.

Because of its isolation, Aberdeen has historically been a fairly autonomous place. Even now it's perceived by many U.K. inhabitants as lying almost out of reach in the northeast. In reality, it's a 90-minute flight from London or a little more than two hours by car from Edinburgh. Its magnificent 18th- and early-19th-century city center amply rewards exploration. Yet even if this popular base for travelers vanished from the map, an extensive portion of the northeast would still remain at the top of many travelers' wish lists.

Balmoral, the Scottish baronial–style house built for Queen Victoria as a retreat, is merely the most famous castle in the area, and certainly not the oldest. There are so many others that in one part of the region a Castle Trail has been established, leading you to such fortresses as the ruined medieval Kildrummy Castle, which once controlled the strategic routes through the valley of the River Don. In later structures, such as Castle Fraser, you can trace the changing styles and tastes of each of its owners over the centuries. Grand mansions such as 18th-century Haddo House, with its symmetrical facade and elegant interior, surrender any defensive role entirely.

A trail leading to a more ephemeral kind of pleasure can be found south of Elgin and Banff, where the glens embrace Scotland's greatest concentration of malt-whisky distilleries. With so many in Morayshire, where the distilling is centered in the valley of the River Spey and its tributaries, there's now a Whisky Trail. Follow it, and visit other distilleries as well, to experience a surprising wealth of flavors, considering that whisky is made of three basic ingredients.

The northeast's chief topographical attraction lies in the gradual transition from high mountain plateau—by a series of gentle steps through hill, forest, and farmland—to the Moray Firth and North Sea coast, where the word "unadulterated" is redefined. Here you'll find some of the United Kingdom's most perfect wild shorelines, both sandy and sheer cliff, and breezy fishing villages like Cullen on the Banffshire coat and Stonehaven, south of Aberdeen. The Grampian Mountains, to the west, contain some of the highest ground in the nation, in the area of the Cairngorms. In recognition of this area's very special nature,

TOP REASONS TO GO

Glorious castles: With more than 75 castles, some Victorian and others dating back to the 13th century, this area has everything from ravaged ruins like Dunnottar to opulent Fyvie Castle. They still evoke the power, grandeur, and sometimes the cruelty of Scotland's past.

Fine distilleries: The valley of the River Spey is famous for its single-malt distilleries, including some that are connected by the signposted Malt Whisky Trail. You can choose from bigger operations such as Glen-fiddich to the iconic Strathisla.

Seaside cities and towns: The fishing industry may be in decline, but the big-city port of Abderdeen and the colorful smaller fishing towns

of Stonehaven and Cullen in the northeast are great (and very different) places to soak up the seagoing atmosphere—and some seafood.

Great walking: There are all types of walking for all kinds of walkers, from the bracing but spectacular inclines of the Grampian Hills, to the wooded gardens and grounds of Balmoral and Haddo House, to breath-stealing golden sands near towns such as Cullen.

Superb golf: The northeast has more than 50 golf clubs, some of which have championship courses. Less famous clubs, both inland and by the sea, have some amazing courses as well.

Cairngorms National Park (Scotland's second, after Loch Lomond and the Trossachs National Park) was created in early 2003. The Grampian hills also have shaped the character of the folk who live in the northeast. In earlier times the massif made communication with the south somewhat difficult. As a result, native northeasterners still speak the richest Lowland Scottish.

ORIENTATION AND PLANNING

GETTING ORIENTED

Aberdeen, on the North Sea in the eastern part of the region, is Scotland's third-largest city; many people start a trip here. Once you have spent time in the city, you may be inclined to venture west into rural Deeside, with its royal connections and looming mountain backdrop. To the north of Deeside is Castle Country, with many ancient fortresses. Speyside and the Whisky Trail lie at the western edge of the region, and are equally accessible from Inverness. From Speyside you might travel back east along the pristine coastline at Scotland's northeasternmost tip.

Aberdeen. Family connections or Royal Deeside often take travelers to this part of Scotland, but many are surprised by how grand and rich in history Aberdeen is. The august granite-turreted buildings and rose-lined roads make this a surprisingly pleasant city to explore; don't miss Old Aberdeen in particular.

Royal Deeside and Castle Country. Prince Albert designed Balmoral Castle for Queen Victoria, and so began the Royal family's love affair with Deeside—and Deeside's love affair with it. However, this area has long been the retreat or the fortress of distinguished families, as the clutter of castles throughout the region shows. The majesty of the countryside also guarantees a superlative stop for everyone interested in history and romance.

The Northeast and the Malt Whisky Trail. For lovers of whisky, this is a favored part of Scotland to visit. Unique in their architecture, their ingredients, and the end product, the distilleries of Speyside are keen to share with you their passion for "the water of life." This region also has rolling hills and, to the north, the beautiful, wild coastline of the North Sea.

PLANNING

WHEN TO GO

May and June are probably the loveliest times to visit, but many travelers arrive from late spring to early fall. The National Trust for Scotland tends to close its properties in winter, so many of the northeast's castles are not open for off-season travel, though you can always see them from the outside. The distilleries are open much of the year, but check for the "silent month" when they close down for a holiday. That's often in August, but may vary.

PLANNING YOUR TIME

How you allocate your time may depend on your special interests—castles or whisky, for example. But even if you can manage only a morning or an afternoon, do not miss a walk around the granite streets of Old Aberdeen, and take in Aberdeen Art Gallery, St. Nicholas Kirk, and a pint in the Prince of Wales pub. A trip southward to the fishing town of Stonehaven and the breathtaking cliff-top fortress of Dunnottar makes a rewarding afternoon. Royal Deeside, with a good sprinkling of castles and grandeur, needs a good two days; even this might be tight for those who want to lap up every moment of majesty at Balmoral, Crathes, Fraser, and Fyvie, the best of the bunch. A visit to malt-whisky country should include tours of Glenfiddich, Glenfarclas, Glenlivet, and Glen Grant distilleries, and although it's not technically a maker of malt whisky, Strathisla. Real enthusiasts should allot two days for the distilleries, and they shouldn't pass up a visit to Speyside Cooperage, one of the few remaining cooperages in the Scotland. Cullen and Duff House gallery in Banff, on the coast, can be done in a day before returning to Aberdeen.

GETTING HERE AND AROUND
AIR TRAVEL

Aberdeen Airport is the region's major airport; there's good service to other parts of Britain and to Europe. *For more information, see Getting Here and Around in Aberdeen, below.*

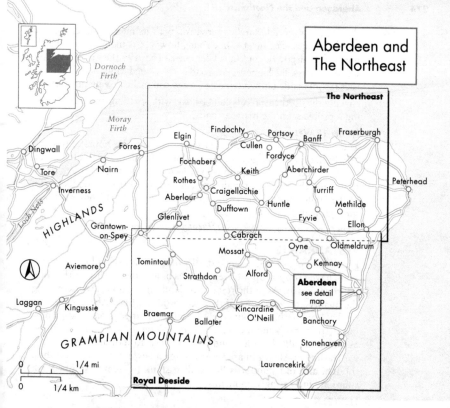

The Northeast

Royal Deeside

BOAT AND FERRY TRAVEL

Northlink Ferries has service between Aberdeen, Lerwick (Shetland), and Kirkwall (Orkney).

Boat and Ferry Contacts Northlink Ferries ✉ *Jamieson's Quay, Aberdeen* ☎ *0845/600–0449* ⊕ *www.northlinkferries.co.uk.*

BUS TRAVEL

Long-distance buses run to Aberdeen from most parts of Scotland, England, and Wales. Contact Megabus, National Express, and Scottish Citylink for bus connections with English and Scottish towns. There's a network of local buses throughout the northeast run by Stagecoach (formerly by Bluebird), but they can take a long time and connections are not always well timed.

Bus Contacts Megabus ☎ *0900/160–0900* ⊕ *www.megabus.com.* **National Express** ☎ *08717/818178* ⊕ *www.nationalexpress.com.* **Scottish Citylink** ☎ *0871/266–3333* ⊕ *www.citylink.co.uk.* **Stagecoach** ☎ *01224/597590* ⊕ *www. stagecoachbus.com/bluebird.*

CAR TRAVEL

A car is the best way to see the northeast. If you are coming from the south, take the A90, continuing on from the M90 (from Edinburgh) or the M9/A9 (from Glasgow), which both stop at Perth. The coastal route, the A92, is a more leisurely alternative, with its interesting resorts and fishing villages. The most scenic route, however, is the A93 from Perth, north to Blairgowrie and into Glen Shee. The A93 then goes over the Cairnwell Pass, the highest main road in the United Kingdom. This route isn't recommended in winter, when snow can make driving difficult.

Around the northeast roads can be busy, with speeding and erratic driving a problem on the main A roads.

TRAIN TRAVEL

You can reach Aberdeen directly from Edinburgh (2½ hours), Inverness (2½ hours), and Glasgow (3 hours). Get a ScotRail timetable for full details. There are also London–Aberdeen routes that go through Edinburgh and the east-coast main line connecting Aberdeen to all corners of the United Kingdom. Sadly, a train no longer runs from Aberdeen through Royal Deeside.

Train Contacts ScotRail ☎ 08457/484950 ⊕ www.scotrail.co.uk.

RESTAURANTS

Partly in response to the demands of workers in the oil industry, restaurants have cropped up all over Aberdeen, and the quality of the food improves yearly. As in the rest of Scotland, this region is rediscovering the quality and versatility of the local produce. Juicy Aberdeen Angus steaks, lean lamb, and humanely reared pork appear on local menus, but despite this being the center of the fishing industry, most seafood available is still of the fish-and-chips variety. Restaurants like the Silver Darling in Aberdeen are spearheading a new interest in fish dishes, though, and old standards like Cullen skink (a creamy smoked-fish soup) are increasingly on menus.

HOTELS

The northeast has some splendid country hotels with log fires and old Victorian furnishings, where you can also be sure of eating well. Many hotels in Aberdeen are in older buildings that have a baronial feel. The trend for serviced apartments has caught on here, with some extremely modish and good-value options for those who want a bit more privacy. This trend is now extending into Deeside, where it's been notoriously difficult to find good accommodations beyond some country-house hotels, even though it's a popular tourist spot.

WHAT IT COSTS IN POUNDS				
	¢	$	$$	$$$	$$$$
RESTAURANTS	under £10	£10–£14	£15–£19	£20–£25	over £25
HOTELS	under £70	£70–£120	£121–£160	£161–£220	over £220

Restaurant prices are for a main course at dinner. Hotel prices are for two people in a standard double room in high season, generally including the 20% V.A.T.

VISITOR INFORMATION

The tourist information center in Aberdeen has a currency exchange, Internet access, and supplies information on all of Scotland's northeast. There are also year-round tourist information offices in Braemar and

Elgin. In summer, also look for tourist information centers in Alford, Ballater, Banchory, Braemar, Dufftown, Elgin, and Stonehaven.

Contacts **Aberdeen** ⊠ *23 Union St., Aberdeen* ☎ *01224/288828* ⊕ *www. aberdeen-grampian.com.*

ABERDEEN

As a gateway to Royal Deeside and the Malt Whisky Trail, Aberdeen attracts visitors, though many are eager to get out into the countryside. Today, though, the city's unique history is finally being recognized as more impressive than many Scots had previously realized, and Aberdeen is being rediscovered. Distinctive architecture, some fine museums, universities, and good restaurants, nightlife, and shopping add to the appeal of Scotland's third-largest city (population 217,000). Union Street is the heart of the city, but take time to explore the university and the pretty streets of Old Aberdeen.

In the 18th century, local granite quarrying produced a durable silver stone that would be used boldly in the glittering blocks, spires, columns, and parapets of Victorian-era Aberdonian structures. The city remains one of the United Kingdom's most distinctive, although some would say it depends on the weather and the brightness of the day. The mica chips embedded in the rock look like a million mirrors in the sunshine. In rain (and there is a fair amount of driving rain from the North Sea) and heavy clouds, however, their sparkle is snuffed out.

The city lies between the Dee and Don rivers, with a working harbor that has access to the sea; it has been a major fishing port and is the main commercial port in northern Scotland. The North Sea has always been important to Aberdeen. In the 1850s the city was famed for its sleek, fast clippers that sailed to India for cargoes of tea. In the late 1960s the course of Aberdeen's history was unequivocally altered when oil and gas were discovered offshore, sparking rapid growth, prosperity, and further industrialization.

GETTING HERE AND AROUND

AIR TRAVEL The city is easy to reach from other parts of the United Kingdom as well as Europe. British Airways, bmi, EasyJet, and Flybe are some of the airlines with service to other parts of Britain. Aberdeen Airport—serving both international and domestic flights—is in Dyce, 7 mi west of the city center on the A96 (Inverness). The drive to the center of Aberdeen is easy via the A96 (which can be busy during rush hour).

Stagecoach Bluebird Jet Service 727 and First Aberdeen Bus 27 operate between the airport terminal and Union Square in the center of Aberdeen. Buses (£2) run frequently at peak times, less often at midday and in the evening; the journey time is approximately 40 minutes. Stagecoach Bluebird Bus 10 stops at Aberdeen Airport, either taking you into the city center or northwest to Elgin.

Dyce is on ScotRail's Inverness–Aberdeen route. The rail station is a short taxi ride from the terminal building. The ride takes 12 minutes, and trains run approximately every two hours.

BUS TRAVEL   First Aberdeen has easy and reliable service within the city of Aberdeen. Timetables are available from the tourist information center in Union Street.

CAR TRAVEL   Aberdeen is a compact city with good signage. Its center is Union Street, the main thoroughfare running east–west, which tends to get crowded with traffic. Anderson Drive is an efficient ring road on the city's west side; be extra careful on its many traffic circles. It's best to leave your car in one of the parking garages (arrive early to get a space) and walk around, or use the convenient park-and-ride stop at the Bridge of Don, north of the city. Street maps are available from the tourist information center, newsdealers, and booksellers.

TAXI TRAVEL   You can find taxi stands throughout the center of Aberdeen: along Union Street, at the railway station at Guild Street, at Back Wynd, and at Regent Quay. The taxis have meters and might be saloon cars (sedans) or black cabs. They are great ways to travel between neighborhoods.

TRAIN TRAVEL   Aberdeen has good ScotRail service. *See Getting Here and Around in Orientation and Planning, above.*

ESSENTIALS

Airport and Transfer Contacts Aberdeen Airport ☎ 0844/481–6666 ⊕ www. aberdeenairport.com. **First Aberdeen** ☎ 01224/650000 ⊕ www.firstaberdeen. co.uk. **ScotRail** ☎ 08457/484950 ⊕ www.scotrail.co.uk.

Bus Contacts First Aberdeen ☎ 01224/650000 ⊕ www.firstaberdeen.co.uk. **Stagecoach** ☎ 01224/597590 ⊕ www.stagecoachbus.com/bluebird.

Visitor and Tour Information Aberdeen ✉ 23 Union St. ☎ 01224/288828 ⊕ www.aberdeen-grampian.com.

AROUND UNION STREET

Aberdeen centers on Union Street, with its many fine survivors of the Victorian and Edwardian streetscape. Marischal College, dating from the late 16th century, has many grand buildings that are worth exploring.

TIMING

You can explore the center of Aberdeen in half a day, but you'll probably want to devote a full day to poking around its interesting old buildings.

TOP ATTRACTIONS

★   **Aberdeen Art Gallery.** Housed in a 19th-century neoclassical building, the museum contains excellent paintings, prints, and drawings, sculpture, porcelain, costumes, and much else—from 18th-century art to major contemporary British works by Lucien Freud and Henry Moore. Scottish artists are well represented in the permanent collection and special exhibits. Local stone has been used in interior walls, pillars, and the central fountain, designed by the acclaimed British sculptor Barbara Hepworth. ■TIP→ **Look for the unique collection of Aberdeen silver on the ground floor.** The museum also has a cake-filled café. ✉ *Schoolhill* ☎ *01224/523700* ⊕ *www.aagm.co.uk* 🎫 *Free* ⊙ *Tues.–Sat. 10–5, Sun. 2–5.*

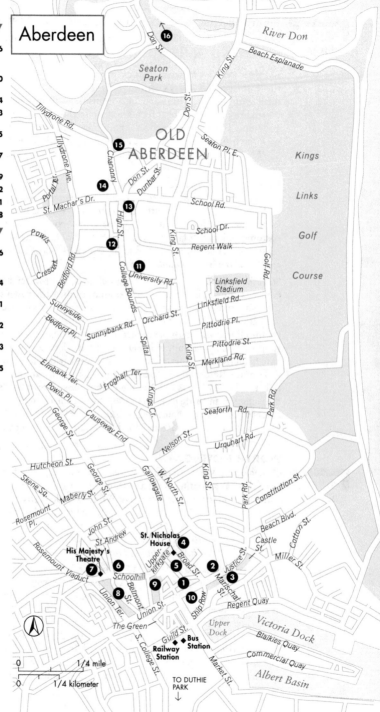

Aberdeen

Around Union Street ▼

Aberdeen Art Gallery **6**

Arberdeen Maritime Museum **10**

Marischal College **4**

Mercat Cross **3**

Provost Skene's House **5**

Rosemount Viaduct **7**

St. Nicholas Kirk **9**

Tolbooth **2**

Union Street **1**

Union Terrace **8**

Old Aberdeen ▼

Brig o'Balgownie **16**

Cruickshank Botanic Gardens **14**

King's College **11**

King's Museum **12**

Old Town House **13**

St. Machar's Cathedral **15**

NEED A
BREAK?

The Beautiful Mountain. This simple, good-natured café is full of life and banter. Stop for a well-filled sandwich and a cup of tea, or perhaps a cake or two. ⊠ *11–13 Belmont St.* ☎ *01224/645353.*

Aberdeen Maritime Museum. This excellent museum, which incorporates the 1593 Provost Ross's House, tells the story of the city's involvement with the sea, from early inshore fisheries to tea clippers and the North Sea oil boom. The information-rich exhibits, fascinating for kids and adults, include ship models, paintings, and equipment associated with the fishing, shipbuilding, and oil and gas industries. ⊠ *Ship Row* ☎ *01224/337700* ⊕ *www.aagm.co.uk* ☜ *Free* ☉ *Tues.–Sat. 10–5, Sun. noon–3.*

Provost Skene's House. Now a museum portraying civic life, the house has restored, furnished period rooms and a painted chapel. Steeply gabled and built from rubble, it dates in part from 1545. The house was originally a mayor's domestic dwelling (*provost* is Scottish for "mayor"). Its costume gallery displays colorful exhibitions of fashions from different centuries. ⊠ *Guestrow, off Broad St.* ☎ *01224/641086* ⊕ *www.aagm. co.uk* ☜ *Free* ☉ *Mon.–Sat. 10–5.*

St. Nicholas Kirk. The original burgh church, the Mither Kirk, as this edifice is known, is not within the bounds of the early town settlement; that was to the east, near the end of present-day Union Street. During the 12th century the port of Aberdeen flourished, and there wasn't room for the church within the settlement. Its earliest features are its pillars—supporting a tower built much later—and its clerestory windows: both date from the 12th century. St. Nicholas was divided into east and west kirks at the Reformation, followed by a substantial amount of renovation from 1741 on. ■TIP➜ In the chapel, look for two books: one lists the victims of an oil-rig disaster in 1989; the second is empty, a reminder of others who have lost their lives. ⊠ *Union St.* ☎ *01224/643494* ⊕ *www. kirk-of-st-nicholas.org.uk* ☜ *Free, but donations welcome* ☉ *Weekdays noon–4.*

WORTH NOTING

OFF THE
BEATEN
PATH

Duthie Park Winter Gardens. A great place to feed the ducks, Duthie Park also has a boating pond and trampolines, carved wooden animals, and playgrounds. In the attractive Winter Gardens (tropical and arid conservatories) are fish in ponds, free-flying birds, and turtles and terrapins among the luxuriant foliage and flowers. The park lies close beside Aberdeen's other river, the Dee. ⊠ *Polmuir Rd., about 1 mi south of city center* ☜ *Free* ☉ *Gardens daily 8 am–1 hr before sunset.*

Marischal College. Founded in 1593 by the Earl Marischal (the earls Marischal held hereditary office as keepers of the king's mares), Marischal College was a Protestant alternative to the Catholic King's College in Old Aberdeen. The two joined to form the University of Aberdeen in 1860. The spectacularly ornate work of the main university building is set off by the gilded flags, and this turn-of-the-20th-century creation is still the world's second-largest granite building. Only El Escorial, outside Madrid, is larger. In 2011, the building's interior was completely rebuilt so it could house the city council. In keeping with the Aberdo-

A GOOD WALK IN DOWNTOWN ABERDEEN

For a lovely stroll downtown, start at the east end of Union Street, east of Marischal Street. Here within the original old town is a square called Castlegate. The actual castle once stood somewhere behind the Salvation Army Citadel (1896), an imposing baronial granite tower whose design was inspired by Balmoral Castle. On the north side of Castle Street stands the 17th-century Tolbooth, a reminder of Aberdeen's earliest days. The impressive Mercat Cross is near King Street. Turn north down Broad Street to reach the main

Marischal College building with its granite frontage.

A survivor from an earlier Aberdeen can be found opposite Marischal College, beyond the concrete supports of St. Nicholas House (which houses the tourist information center): Provost Skene's House was once part of a closely packed area of town houses and is now a museum portraying civic life. Just around the corner on Upperkirkgate, at the lowest point, are two modern shopping malls—the St. Nicholas Centre on the left, the Bon Accord Centre on the right.

nian custom of never throwing anything away, the discarded materials have already been used in buildings around the city. ⊠ *Broad St.*

Mercat Cross. Built in 1686 and restored in 1820, the Mercat Cross (the term stems from "marketplace"), always the symbolic center of a Scottish medieval burgh, stands just beyond King Street. Along its parapet are 12 portrait panels of the Stewart monarchs. ⊠ *Justice and Marischal Sts.*

Rosemount Viaduct. Three silvery, handsome buildings on this bridge are collectively known by all Aberdonians as Education, Salvation, and Damnation. The **Central Library** and **St. Mark's Church** date from the last decade of the 19th century, and **His Majesty's Theatre** (1904–08) has been restored inside to its full Edwardian splendor. If you're taking photographs, you can choose an angle that includes the statue of Scotland's first freedom fighter, Sir William Wallace (1270–1305), in the foreground pointing majestically to Damnation.

Tolbooth. The city was governed from this 17th-century building, which was also the burgh court and jail, for 200 years. Now a museum of crime and punishment, it is as amusing as it is stomach churning—making it a must-see for older kids. ⊠ *Castle St.* ☎ *01224/621167* ⊕ *www. aagm.co.uk* ⊠ *Free* ☉ *Jul.-Sep. Tues.–Sat. 10–4, Sun. 12:30–3:30.*

Union Street. This great thoroughfare is to Aberdeen what Princes Street is to Edinburgh: the central pivot of the city plan and the product of a wave of enthusiasm to rebuild the city in a contemporary style in the early 19th century.

Union Terrace. In the 19th-century development of Union Terrace stands a statue of Robert Burns (1759–96) addressing a daisy. Behind Burns are the **Union Terrace Gardens,** faintly echoing Edinburgh's Princes Street Gardens in that both separate the older part of the city, to the east, from the 19th-century development to the west. Plans are afoot to build above the gardens and the railway lines, a move that will either be to Aberdeen's asthetic benefit or its disgrace, depending on your viewpoint.

OLD ABERDEEN

Very much a separate area of the city, Old Aberdeen is north of the modern center and clustered around St. Machar's Cathedral and the many fine buildings of the University of Aberdeen. Take a stroll on College Bounds; handsome 18th- and 19th-century houses line this cobbled street in the oldest part of the city.

TIMING

The neighborhood is a 20- to 30-minute walk north of the center of town; it's also easily reachable by First Aberdeen bus numbers 1 and 20 from Union Street. The ride takes 5 to 15 minutes. Old Aberdeen is a compact area, and will take you no more than a few hours to explore.

TOP ATTRACTIONS

Cruickshank Botanic Gardens. Built on land bequeathed by Miss Anne Crickshank in memory of her beloved brother Alexander, the small, 11-acre Cruickshank Botanic Garden has a peaceful water garden and lush greens ideal for lounging around on—when the weather allows—and beautifully tended subtropical and alpine collections. Botanical tours are available. ⊠ *St. Machar Dr., at the Chanonry* ☎ *01224/272704* ⊕ *www.abdn.ac.uk/botanic-garden* ✉ *Free* ☉ *May–Sept., weekdays 9–9:30, weekends 2–9:30; Oct.–Apr., weekdays 9–4:30.*

Fodor'sChoice
★
King's College. Founded in 1494, King's College is now part of the University of Aberdeen. Its **chapel**, built around 1500, has an unmistakable flying (or crown) spire. That it has survived at all was because of the zeal of the principal, who defended his church against the destructive fanaticism that swept through Scotland during the Reformation, when the building was less than a century old. Today the renovated chapel plays an important role in university life. ■ **TIP➡ Don't miss the tall oak screen that separates the nave from the choir, the ribbed wooden ceiling, and the stalls, as these constitute the finest medieval wood carvings found anywhere in Scotland.** The **King's College Centre** has more information about the university. ⊠ *High St.* ☎ *01224/272660* ⊕ *www.abdn.ac.uk* ☉ *Weekdays 10–3:30.*

King's Museum. In a modest town house across from the archway leading to King's College Chapel, this museum opened in 2011. With constantly changing exhibitions, it presents some impressive and often strange curiosities from the university's collection, from prehistoric flints to a tiger's penis. ⊠ *17 High St.* ☎ *01224/272000* ⊕ *www.abdn.ac.uk/kingsmuseum* ✉ *Free* ☉ *Weekdays 9:30–4:30, Sat. 11–4.*

NEED A
BREAK?
St. Machar Bar. This small, vibrant pub in the middle of the university campus sells not just pints but also real *stovies* (a hot potato-based stew) made with beef. It's a great place to warm up or pass away the time with a newspaper if the weather is unbecoming. ⊠ *97 High St.* ☎ *01224/483079.*

Old Town House. Owned by Aberdeen University and operating as a gateway to the campus, this plain but handsome Georgian building is a great place to learn about the university before exploring the grounds of this ancient seat of learning. The building was the center of all trading activity in the city before it became a grammar school, a Masonic lodge, and then a library. ☒ *High St.* ☎ *01224/273650* ⊕ *www.abdn. ac.uk/oldtownhouse* ☒ *Free* ⊗ *Mon.–Sat. 9–5.*

St. Machar's Cathedral. Rich in history, this cathedral is worth a look. It's said that St. Machar was sent by St. Columba to build a church on a grassy platform near the sea, where a river flowed in the shape of a shepherd's crook. This spot fit the bill. Although the cathedral was founded in AD 580, most of the existing building dates from the 15th and 16th centuries. (The central tower collapsed in 1688, reducing the building to half its original length.) The nave is thought to have been rebuilt in red sandstone in 1370, but the final renovation was completed in granite by the middle of the 15th century. Along with the nave ceiling, the twin octagonal spires were finished in time to take a battering in the Reformation, when the barons of the Mearns stripped the lead off the roof of St. Machar's and stole the bells. The cathedral suffered further mistreatment until it was fully restored in the 19th century. ☒ *Chanonry* ☎ *01224/485988* ⊕ *www.stmachar.com* ⊗ *Apr.–Oct., daily 9–5; Nov.–Mar., daily 10–4.*

WORTH NOTING

Brig o'Balgownie. Until 1827, the only northern route out of Aberdeen was over the River Don on this single-arch bridge. It dates from 1314 and is thought to have been built by Richard Cementarius, Aberdeen's first provost. ☒ *Seaton Park.*

WHERE TO EAT

¢ ✕**Ashvale.** Ask anyone about this long-established place and the
BRITISH response will probably be overwhelmingly positive. Fish-and-chips are undoubtedly the specialty, and the secret-recipe batter is now the stuff of legend. Attempt the Whale—a gigantic 1-pound fillet of battered cod—and you'll be rewarded with a free dessert. The decor is your basic wood-chairs-and-tables "chippy." ☒ *42–48 Great Western Rd.* ☎ *01224/596981* ⊕ *theashvale.co.uk.*

$ ✕**Café 52.** Right in the historic Grassmarket, this café-restaurant has
BRITISH taken a few years to find its niche but now serves up lovely homemade dishes at pocket-friendly prices. Fat Scottish mussels in a creamy dill sauce and bramble panna cotta are just a few of the quirky options. No matter what you order, local produce makes it tasty and fresh. The handsome restaurant is in a silvery granite building with exposed-stone walls, huge windows, and shiny black tables. ☒ *52 The Green* ☎ *01224/590094* ⊕ *www.cafe52.net* ⊗ *No dinner Sun.*

$$ ✕**Foyer Restaurant and Gallery.** In this splendid restaurant in a former
BRITISH church, curving lines, pale woods, and touches of bright color strike a
★ modern note—a good background for changing art exhibitions. Foyer has a feel-good factor, too: not only are the lunch and dinner offerings exceptional, but all profits support work with the city's unemployed and homeless. Soups, sandwiches, and hot main courses make up lunch; the dinner menu includes seafood chowder and panfried breast of

guinea fowl with a mushroom risotto. Helpings are ample. The three-course fixed-price dinner is a good value at £23. ⊠ *82A Crown St.* ☎ *01224/582277* ⊕ *www.foyerrestaurant.com.*

$$$
SEAFOOD
Fodor's Choice
★

✕ **Silver Darling.** Huge windows overlook the harbor and beach at this quayside favorite in a former customs house, long one of Aberdeen's most acclaimed restaurants. As the name implies, the French-inspired fare focuses on fish: a silver darling is a herring. Try the North Sea crab-and-prawn gateau (cake) for a starter, then move on to wild halibut steamed in seaweed, or fillet of monkfish in black olive oil. The stiff white tablecloths and walls would feel rather too stark if it weren't for the spirited staff. ⊠ *North Pier, Pocra Quay* ☎ *01224/576229* ⊕ *www.silverdarling.co.uk* ♿ *Reservations essential* ⊗ *Closed Sun. No lunch Sat.*

WHERE TO STAY

For expanded hotel reviews, visit Fodors.com.

$$
▦ **Atholl Hotel.** With its many turrets and gables, this granite hotel recalls a bygone era but has modern amenities. **Pros:** clean and friendly; family-run establishment; very pleasant staff. **Cons:** some bedrooms are a little generic. ⊠ *54 Kings Gate* ☎ *01224/323505* ⊕ *www.atholl-aberdeen. com* ⟿ *34 rooms* ♿ *In-room: no a/c, Wi-Fi. In-hotel: restaurant, bar, business center* ▯◎▯ *Breakfast.*

$
▦ **Bauhaus Hotel.** When the owner got his hands on this 1960s-era granite office block, he decided to pay homage to Walter Gropius, the founder of the Bauhaus movement. **Pros:** great design; comfortable rooms; tasty eatery. **Cons:** beware the sharp corners of modern furniture; fake art on the walls—in a city with a great art school. ⊠ *52–60 Langstane Pl.* ☎ *01224/212122* ⟿ *34 rooms, 5 suites* ♿ *In-room: no a/c, Wi-Fi. In-hotel: restaurant, bar, business center* ▯◎▯ *Breakfast.*

$$
▦ **City Wharf.** With one- to four-bedroom apartments in three city-center sites, City Wharf offers fuss-free stays of any length in luxury settings. **Pros:** feels brand-new; all mod cons; guest can use a nearby gym. **Cons:** no porters to help you with your bags; no restaurant. ⊠ *47 Regent Quay* ☎ *01224/589282* ⊕ *www.citywharfapartments.co.uk* ⟿ *22 apartments* ♿ *In-room: no a/c, kitchen, Wi-Fi. In-hotel: laundry facilities* ▯◎▯ *Breakfast.*

$
★
▦ **Craibstone Suites.** On one of Aberdeen's most attractive squares, these modern but comfortable suites come with fully equipped kitchens. **Pros:** great central location; feels more like an apartment than a hotel room. **Cons:** executive suites are small: go for the grand or superior suites if you need elbow room. ⊠ *15 Bon Accord Sq.* ☎ *01224/857950* ⊕ *www. craibstone-suites.co.uk* ⟿ *15 suites* ♿ *In-room: no a/c, kitchen, Wi-Fi* ▯◎▯ *Breakfast.*

$
▦ **The Jays Guest House.** Alice Jennings or her husband George will greet you at the front door of this granite house, a homey bed-and-breakfast. **Pros:** immaculate rooms; expert advice on city's sites; near shops and restaurants. **Cons:** no public areas; incredibly popular, so book in advance. ⊠ *422 King St.* ☎ *01224/638295* ⊕ *www.jaysguesthouse. co.uk* ⟿ *10 rooms* ♿ *In-room: no a/c, Wi-Fi* ▯◎▯ *Breakfast.*

$$$$ 🛏 **Marcliffe Hotel and Spa.** Set on 11 wooded acres, this spacious, elegant country-house hotel combines old and new to impressive effect. **Pros:** lush gardens; well-trained staff; relaxing spa. **Cons:** a little out of town; restaurant prices a bit steep. ⊠ *N. Deeside Rd.* ☎ *01224/861000* ⊕ *www.marcliffe.com* ↩ *35 rooms, 7 suites* ⚷ *In-room: no a/c, Wi-Fi. In-hotel: restaurant, bar, spa* ⏐◎⏐ *Breakfast.*

NIGHTLIFE AND THE ARTS

Aberdeen has a fairly lively nightlife scene revolving around pubs and clubs. Theaters, concert halls, arts centers, and cinemas are also well represented. The principal newspapers—the *Press and Journal* and the *Evening Express*—and *Aberdeen Leopard* magazine can fill you in on what's going on anywhere in the northeast. Aberdeen's tourist information center has a monthly publication with an events calendar.

THE ARTS
Aberdeen is a rich city, both financially and culturally.

Aberdeen International Youth Festival. August sees the world-renowned Aberdeen International Youth Festival, which attracts youth orchestras, choirs, dance troupes, and theater companies from many countries. During the festival some companies take their productions to other venues in the northeast. ⊠ *Custom House, 35 Regent Quay* ☎ *01224/213800* ⊕ *www.aiyf.org.*

ARTS CENTERS **Aberdeen Arts Centre.** The center hosts experimental plays, poetry readings, and exhibitions by local and Scottish artists. ⊠ *33 King St.* ☎ *01224/635208* ⊕ *www.aberdeenartscentre.org.uk.*

Haddo House. About 20 mi north of Aberdeen, Haddo House offers a mixed bag of events, from opera and ballet to Shakespeare, Scots-language plays, and puppetry from spring through fall. ⊠ *Off B999, Tarves* ☎ *0844/4932179* ⊕ *www.nts.org.uk.*

Lemon Tree. The Lemon Tree has an innovative and international program of dance, stand-up comedy, and puppet theater, as well as folk, jazz, and rock-and-roll music. ⊠ *5 W. North St.* ☎ *01224/641122* ⊕ *www.boxofficeaberdeen.com.*

Peacock Visual Arts. Peacock Visual Arts displays photographic, video, and slide exhibits of contemporary art and architecture. ⊠ *21 Castle St.* ☎ *01224/639539* ⊕ *www.peacockvisualarts.com* ⊙ *Tue.–Sat. 9:30–5:30.*

CONCERT **His Majesty's Theatre.** The Edwardian His Majesty's Theatre hosts per-
HALLS formances on par with those in some of the world's biggest cities. It's a regular venue for musicals and operas, as well as classical and modern dance. The restaurant, called 1906, is popular with audiences and cast members alike. ⊠ *Rosemount Viaduct* ☎ *01224/641122* ⊕ *www. boxofficeaberdeen.com.*

Music Hall. The Scottish National Orchestra, the Scottish Chamber Orchestra, and other major groups perform at the Music Hall. Events also include folk concerts, crafts fairs, and exhibitions. ⊠ *Union St.* ☎ *01224/641122* ⊕ *www.boxofficeaberdeen.com.*

7

FILM **The Belmont.** Independent and classic films screen at the Belmont. ⊠ *49 Belmont St.* ☎ *01224/343536* ⊕ *www.picturehouses.co.uk.*

Cineworld. The popular Cineworld shows recent major releases. ⊠ *Queen's Link Leisure Park, Links Rd.* ☎ *0871/200–2000* ⊕ *www. cineworld.co.uk.*

NIGHTLIFE

With a greater club-to-clubber ratio than either Edinburgh or Glasgow, Aberdeen offers plenty of loud music and dancing for a night out. There are also pubs and pool halls for those with two left feet. Pubs close at midnight on weekdays and 1 am on weekends; clubs go until 2 or 3 am.

BARS AND PUBS **Carmelite.** This chic bar serves up champagne and cakes in the afternoon and cocktails and lounge music in the evening. The grill provides tasty modish dishes. ⊠ *Sirling St.* ☎ *01224/589101.*

Illicit Still. The old-fashioned Illicit Still is named after the 18th-century practice of brewing your own beer to avoid the malt tax. A beautifully fitted-out drinking establishment, it also serves up hearty pub grub. ⊠ *Guest Row, Broad St.* ☎ *01224/623123* ⊕ *www.illicit-still.co.uk.*

Old Blackfriars. Drawing a slightly older crowd, the traditional Old Blackfriars enjoys a nice location near the end of Union Street. The lighting is dim, and the big fireplace warms things up on a chilly evening. This cask ale pub has a great selection—Belhaven St. Andrews Ale and Caledonian 80 top the list. ⊠ *52 Castle St.* ☎ *01224/581922* ⊕ *www.old-blackfriars.co.uk.*

Fodor'sChoice ★ **The Prince of Wales.** Dating from 1850, the Prince of Wales has retained its paneled walls and wooden tables. Still regarded as Aberdeen's most traditional pub, it's hardly regal, but good-quality food and reasonable prices draw the regulars back. ⊠ *7 St. Nicholas La.* ☎ *01224/640597.*

Soul. In a converted church, Soul has private booths with stained-glass windows and ecclesiastical furnishings. The eclectic menu includes everything from chicken satay and mussels. It's the most interesting of the Union Street hangouts. ⊠ *333 Union St.* ☎ *01224/211150.*

DANCE CLUBS People tend to dress up a bit to go clubbing, and jeans or sneakers might get you turned away at the door. Clubs are open until 2 am during the week and until 3 am on Friday and Saturday nights.

Club Snafu. This boutique club hosts all manner of specialty nights, from comedy to electronica. ⊠ *1 Union St.* ☎ *01224/596111* ⊕ *www. clubsnafu.com.*

SPORTS AND THE OUTDOORS

GOLF

Northeast Scotland is known for good golf. Despite the continuing outcry from locals and environmentalists, Donald Trump has "stabilized" the dune system that borders the Menie Estate, just north of Aberdeen and the Ythan estuary, to create Trump International Golf Links. It's set to open in summer 2012; www.trumpgolfscotland.com has updates. Just south of Aberdeen, Jack Nicklaus has been lined up to design a championship course at Ury Castle. The financial climate has delayed the project, though.

You can expect to pay £15 to £100 per round at the golf courses in and around Aberdeen. Make reservations at least 24 hours in advance. Some private courses restrict tee times for visiting golfers to certain days or hours during the week, so be sure to check that the course you wish to play is open when you want to play it. *For more courses, including Balgownie, see Chapter 12.*

★ **Murcar.** Sea views and a variety of rugged terrain—from sand dunes to tinkling burns—are the highlights of this course, founded in 1909. It's most famous for breathtaking vistas at the seventh hole, appropriately called the Serpentine. Designer Archibald Simpson considered this course to be one of his finest. ⊠ *Bridge of Don* ☎ *01224/704354* ⊕ *www.murcarlinks.com* ✉ *£75 per round* ⚲ *18 holes, 6,314 yds, SSS 73.*

Royal Aberdeen Golf Club, Balgownie. Founded in 1780, this club is the sixth oldest in the world, and there are fine views of Aberdeen from its fairways. ⊠ *Links Rd., Bridge of Don* ☎ *01224/826591* ✉ *£120 per round* ⚲ *18 holes, 6,900 yds, SSS 73.*

Westhill. This parkland course, founded in 1977, overlooks Royal Deeside. It's the most inexpensive in the area. ⊠ *Westhill Heights, Westhill* ☎ *01224/740159* ⊕ *www.westhillgolfclub.co.uk* ✉ *£20 per round* ⚲ *18 holes, 5,849 yds, SSS 69.*

SHOPPING

You can find most of the large national department stores in the Bon Accord, St. Nicholas, and Trinity shopping malls or along Union Street, but Aberdeen has some good specialty shops as well.

SPECIALTY SHOPS

Aberdeen Art Gallery Shop. The constantly changing crafts and jewelry at the Aberdeen Art Gallery Shop always have something of interest, and there are pretty postcards of the city from times gone by. ⊠ *Schoolhill* ☎ *01224/523695.*

Aberdeen Family History Society Shop. At the Aberdeen Family History Society Shop you can browse through publications related to local history and genealogical research. ■TIP→ **For £10 per hour, the staff will undertake some research on your behalf.** ⊠ *158–164 King St.* ☎ *01224/646323* ⊕ *www.anesfhs.org.uk* ☉ *Weekdays 10–4; Sat. 9–1.*

Aitkins. You can't leave Aberdeen without trying one of its famous *rowies* (or *butteries*), the fortifying morning roll. Aitkins Bakery is considered the finest purveyor of this local speciality. ⊠ *202 Holburn St.* ☎ *01224/582567.*

Alex Scott & Co. For Scottish kilts, tartans, crests, and other traditionally Scottish clothes, a good place to start is Alex Scott & Co. ⊠ *43 Schoolhill* ☎ *01224/643924.*

Books and Beans. This secondhand bookshop has its own little café. You're welcome to browse and sip at the same time. ⊠ *22 Belmont St.* ☎ *01224/646438* ⊕ *www.booksandbeans.co.uk.*

Candle Close Gallery. The shop has some strange and wonderful mirrors, clocks, ceramics, and jewelry that you're unlikely to see elsewhere or ever again. ✉ *123 Gallowgate* ☎ *01224/624940* ⊕ *www. candleclosegallery.co.uk.*

Colin Wood. This shop is the place to go for small antiques, interesting prints, and regional maps. ✉ *25 Rose St.* ☎ *01224/643019.*

ROYAL DEESIDE AND CASTLE COUNTRY

Deeside, the valley running west from Aberdeen down which the River Dee flows, earned its "royal" appellation when discovered by Queen Victoria. To this day, where royalty goes, lesser aristocracy and freshly minted millionaires follow. Many still aspire to own a grand shooting estate in Deeside, and you may appreciate this yearning when you see how the piney hill slope, purple moor, and blue river intermingle tastefully here. As you travel deeper into the Grampian Mountains, Royal Deeside's gradual scenic change adds a growing sense of excitement.

There are castles along the Dee as well as to the north in Castle Country, another region that illustrates the gradual geological change in the northeast: uplands lapped by a tide of farms. All the Donside and Deeside castles are picturesquely sited, with most fitted out with tall slender turrets, winding stairs, and crooked chambers that epitomize Scottish baronial style. All have tales of ghosts and bloodshed, siege and torture. Many were tidied up and "domesticated" during the 19th century. Although best toured by car, much of this area is accessible either by public transportation or on tours from Aberdeen.

STONEHAVEN

15 mi south of Aberdeen.

This historic town near splendid Dunnottar Castle was once a popular holiday destination, with people including Robert Burns enjoying walks along the golden sands. The surrounding red-clay fields were made famous by Lewis Grassic Gibbon (real name James Leslie Mitchell), who attended school in the town and who wrote the seminal Scottish trilogy, *A Scots Quair,* about the people, the land, and the impact of World War I. The decline of the fishing industry emptied the harbor, but the town, being so close to Aberdeen, has begun to thrive again. It's now famous for its Hogmanay (New Year) celebrations, where local men swing huge balls of fire on chains before tossing them into the harbor.

GETTING HERE AND AROUND
Stagecoach Bluebird runs a number of buses to Stonehaven from Aberdeen, but numbers 107 and 109 are the fastest (50 minutes). Most trains heading south from Aberdeen stop at Stonehaven; there's at least one per hour making the 15-minute trip. Drivers should take A90 south and turn off at A957.

ESSENTIALS
Visitor Information Stonehaven ✉ *66 Allardyce St., Stonehaven* ☎ *01569/762806* ⊕ *www.aberdeen-grampian.com* ⊗ *Apr.–Oct.*

EXPLORING

Fodor's Choice **Dunnottar Castle.** It's hard to beat the magnificent cliff-top ruins of Dun-
★ nottar Castle, especially with the panoramic views of the North Sea.
Building began in the 14th century, when Sir William Keith, Marischal
of Scotland (keeper of the king's mares), decided to build a tower house
to demonstrate his power. Subsequent generations added to the structure over the centuries, and important visitors included Mary, Queen
of Scots. The castle is most famous for holding out for eight months
against Oliver Cromwell's army in 1651 and 1652, and thereby saving
the Scottish crown jewels, which had been stored here for safekeeping.
Reach the castle via the A90; take the Stonehaven turnoff and follow the
signs. ■ TIP→ Wear sensible shoes, and allow about two hours. ⊠ Off A92
☎ 01569/762173 ⊕ www.dunnottarcastle.co.uk ⌨ £5 ⊙ Easter–Sept.,
daily 9–6; Nov.–Easter, daily 10–sunset.

☼ **Stonehaven Open-Air Swimming Pool.** They were extremely popular in the
1930s, but the Stonehaven Open-Air Swimming Pool, an aging art-deco
gem, is one of only a few remaining outdoor heated pools in Scotland.
Salty water from the North Sea is pumped in and heated to a toasty
28°C (82°F). Run by a local trust, this place is perfect for families.
■ TIP→ Ask about Wednesday's midnight swims (£5.60), when you can float
under the stars. ⊠ Queen Elizabeth Park, Off A90 ☎ 01569/762134
⊕ www.stonehavenopenairpool.co.uk ⌨ £4.70 ⊙ June and mid-Aug.–
mid-Sept., weekdays 1–7:30, weekends 10–6; July and Aug., weekdays
10–7:30, weekends 10–6.

WHERE TO EAT AND STAY

For expanded hotel reviews, visit Fodors.com.

$ ✕ **Carron Art Deco Restaurant.** For an outstanding meal of classic Scottish
BRITISH dishes served in the most splendid surroundings, try this longtime favorite. Evoking the style and class of the 1930s, it's a must for both lovers of
architecture and food. Look out for the rather risqué figure of a woman
etched onto a mirror between two dazzlingly tiled columns. The cuisine
is not diminished by the surroundings: try the lamb shank braised with
root vegetables or the Aberdeen Angus roast beef with a Drambuie (a
honey-flavored whisky liqueur) gravy. ⊠ Cameron St. ☎ 01569/760460.

$ ▦ **Bayview B&B.** On the beach and down the lane from the town square,
★ this contemporary bed-and-breakfast couldn't be in a more convenient
location—or have better views. **Pros:** spic-and-span rooms; walk to restaurants and shops; eccentric design. **Cons:** standard rooms are smallish; breakfast room is windowless. ⊠ Beachgate La. ☎ 07791/224227
⊕ www.bayviewbandb.co.uk ☞ 3 rooms, 2 suites ⌂ In-room: no a/c,
Wi-Fi. In-hotel: business center � Breakfast.

7

BANCHORY

15 mi west of Stonehaven, 19 mi west of Aberdeen.

Banchory is an immaculate town filled with pinkish granite buildings.
It's usually bustling with ice-cream-eating strollers, out on a day trip
from Aberdeen. Nearby are Crathes and Drum castles.

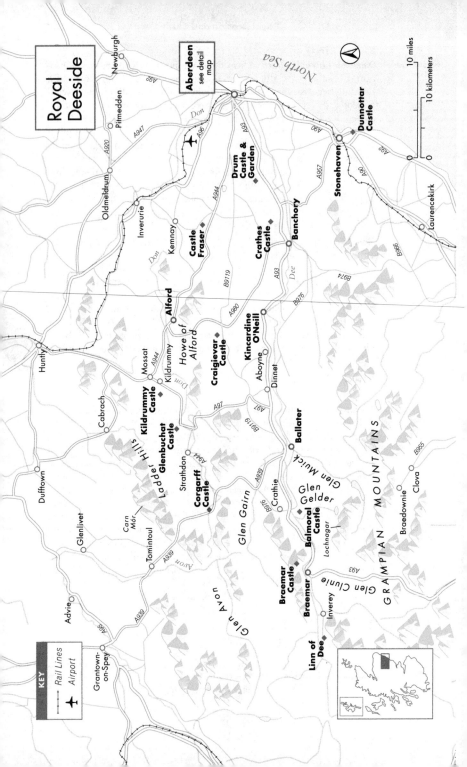

Which Castle Is Right for You?

We admit it—there are almost too many castles in this part of Scotland. Since it's nearly impossible to see all of them, we've noted the prime characteristics of each to help you decide which you'd most like to visit.

■ **Balmoral:** The Queen's home, this is where Queen Victoria and the Royal Family fell in love with Scotland and all things Scottish. Expect baronial largesse and groomed grounds, though you don't see much inside.

■ **Balvenie:** This ruined castle is known for its indomitable bearing and verdant surroundings, right in the midst of the Malt Whisky Trail.

■ **Braemar:** Offering memorable insight into the lives of the Scottish landed gentry, this recently restored castle heaves with memorabilia and mementos of the fascinating Farquharsons, who still hold their clan gathering here.

■ **Corgarff:** You'll find a sober solitude out on the moorland, as well as 18th-century graffiti and the reconstructed barracks used by Jacobite troops in 1746 as they retreated north.

■ **Craigievar:** Highlights of this 17th-century castle are a magical forest, fairy-tale turrets, and the furnishings

and possessions of the Forbes family that fill the house.

■ **Crathes:** Expect tight quarters, notable family portraits, and a network of walled gardens at this well-preserved seat of the Burnett family. Its adventure park keeps the kids occupied.

■ **Drum:** A fusion of architectural styles and some historic roses are notable at this castle, but it's the medieval chapel that stirs the senses.

■ **Dunnottar:** The dramatic, scene-stealing, cliff-top location of Mel Gibson's *Hamlet* (1991), the ruins of this 14th-century tower house by the sea are unbeatable.

■ **Fraser:** Considered the grandest castle in Aberdeenshire, Castle Fraser has opulent period furnishings and woodland walks that make for a rewarding day.

■ **Fyvie:** This 14th-century castle underwent a luxurious Edwardian makeover. Come here for an awesome art collection, rich interiors, and haunting history.

■ **Kildrummy:** This is the place for evocative ruins, some from the 13th century, and tales of a treacherous past. Its austere but poignant chapel is a must-see.

7

GETTING HERE AND AROUND

A car is by far the best way to get around the area; A93 is one of the main roads connecting the towns.

For those reliant on public transport, Stagecoach buses operate a number of services for towns along or just off A93 (Drum Castle, Banchory, Kincardine, Aboyne, Ballater, Balmoral, and Braemar).

ESSENTIALS

Visitor Information Banchory ⊠ *Bridge St.* ☎ *013308/22000* ⊕ *www.aberdeen-grampian.com* ☉ *Apr.–Oct..*

EXPLORING

Brig o'Feuch. If you visit in autumn and have time to spare, drive for a mile along the B974 south of Banchory to the Brig o'Feuch (pronounced *fyooch*, the *ch* as in loch). The area around this bridge is pleasant: salmon leap in season, and the fall colors and foaming waters make for an attractive scene.

Crathes Castle. About 16 mi west of Aberdeen, Crathes Castle was once the home of the Burnett family and is one of the best-preserved castles in Britain. Keepers of the Forest of Drum for generations, the family acquired lands here by marriage and later built a castle, completed in 1596. The National Trust for Scotland cares for the castle, which is furnished with many original pieces and family portraits. Outside are grand gardens with calculated symmetry and clipped yew hedges. Make sure you browse the Horsemill bookshop and sample the tasty home baking in the tearoom. There's an adventure park for kids, and the staff organizes activities that are fun and educational. ⊠ *Off A93* ☎ *0844/493–2166* ⊕ *www.nts.org.uk* ✉ *£11* ☼ *Apr.–Oct., daily 10–4:45; Nov.–Mar., weekends 10:30–3:45; last admission 45 min before closing.*

Drum Castle and Garden. This foursquare tower has an evocative medieval chapel that dates from the 13th century; like many other castles, it also has later additions up to Victorian times. Note the tower's rounded corners, said to make battering-ram attacks more difficult. Nearby, fragments of the ancient Forest of Drum still stand, dating from the days when Scotland was covered by great stands of oak and pine. The Garden of Historic Roses, open from April to October, lays claim to some old-fashioned roses not commonly seen today. Drum Castle is 8 mi east of Banchory and 11 mi west of Aberdeen. ⊠ *Off A93* ☎ *0844/493–2161* ⊕ *www.nts.org.uk* ✉ *Garden £2, castle and garden £9* ☼ *Castle Apr.–June, and Sept., Thurs.–Mon. 11–4:45; June–Aug., daily 11–4:45; last entry 45 mins before closing time. Grounds daily 9:30–sunset.*

OFF THE BEATEN PATH

Kincardine O'Neil. The ruined kirk in this little village 9 mi west of Banchory on A93 was built in 1233 and once sheltered travelers: it was the last hospice before the Mounth, the name given to the massif that shuts off the south side of the Dee Valley. Beyond Banchory (and the B974), no motor roads run south until you reach Braemar (A93), though the Mounth is crossed by a network of tracks once used by Scottish soldiers, invading armies (including the Romans), and cattle drovers. Photography buffs won't want to miss the bridge at Potarch, just to the east.

Queen's View. To reach one of the most spectacular vistas in northeast Scotland—stretching across the Howe of Cromar to Lochnagar—take the B9094 due north from Aboyne, then turn left onto the B9119 for 6 mi.

WHERE TO STAY

For expanded hotel reviews, visit Fodors.com.

$$ 🏨 **Raemoir House Hotel.** Dating from the 16th to 19th centuries, this baronial home 2 mi north of Banchory makes you feel like you're on the set of a period drama. **Pros:** charming old building; extensive grounds; staff is informal and efficient. **Cons:** pricey ⊠ *Off A980, Raemoir* ☎ *01330/824884* ⊕ *www.raemoir.com* ➔ *17 rooms, 3 suites* ⚐ *In-room: no a/c, Wi-Fi. In-hotel: restaurant, bar* ⍟ *Breakfast.*

BALLATER AND BALMORAL CASTLE

22 mi west of Kincardine O'Neill, 43 mi west of Aberdeen.

The handsome holiday resort of Ballater, once noted for the curative properties of its waters, has profited from the proximity of the royals, nearby at Balmoral Castle. You might be amused by the array of "by royal appointment" signs proudly hanging from many of its various shops (even monarchs need bakers and butchers). Take time to stroll around this well-laid-out community. The railway station houses the tourist information center and a display on the glories of the Great North of Scotland branch railway line, closed in the 1960s along with so many others in this country.

The locals have long taken the town's royal connection in stride. To this day, the hundreds who line the road when the queen and her family arrive for services at the family's parish church at Crathie are invariably visitors to Deeside—one of Balmoral's attractions for the monarch has always been the villagers' respect for royal privacy.

GETTING HERE AND AROUND

There's good train service to Aberdeen, but you'll need to catch a bus to get to this and other towns near A93. Stagecoach Bluebird buses numbers 201 and 202 operate hourly to all the main towns, including Ballater. Otherwise, it's an easy car trip.

ESSENTIALS

Visitor Information Ballater ⊠ *Old Royal Station, Station Sq.* ☎ *01339/755306.*

EXPLORING

★ **Balmoral Castle.** The enormous parking lot is indicative of the popularity of Balmoral Castle, one of Queen Elizabeth II's favorite family retreats. Balmoral's visiting hours depend on whether the royals are in residence. In truth, there are more interesting and historic buildings to explore, as the only part of the castle on view is the ballroom, with an exhibition of royal artifacts. The Carriage Hall has displays of commemorative china, carriages, and native wildlife. Thanks to Victoria and Albert, who built the house to Prince Albert's design, stags' heads abounded, the bagpipes wailed incessantly, and the garish Stuart tartan was used for everything from carpets to chair covers. A more somber Duff tartan, black and green to blend with the environment, was later adopted. Queen Elizabeth II follows her predecessors' routine in spending a holiday of about six weeks in Deeside, usually from mid-August to the end of September. During this time Balmoral is closed to visitors, including the grounds. You can take a guided tour in November and December; if the weather is crisp and bright, the estate is at its most dramatic and romantic.

Around and about Balmoral, which is 7 mi west of Ballater, are some notable spots—Cairn O'Mount, Cambus O'May, and the Cairngorms from the Linn of Dee—and some of them may be seen on pony-trekking expeditions, which use Balmoral stalking ponies and go around the grounds and estate.

Tempted by the setting? Balmoral Castle has five cottages (some very large) for rent by the week at certain times. They are atmospheric but can be basic. ⊠ *A93* ☎ *013397/42534* ⊕ *www.balmoralcastle. com* 🖃 *£9* ⊙ *Apr.–July, daily 10–5; last admission 1 hr before closing. Guided tours on certain dates in Nov. and Dec.*

Glen Muick. As long as you have your own car, you can capture the feel of the eastern Highlands yet still be close to town. Start your expedition into Glen Muick (Gaelic for "pig," pronounced mick) by crossing the River Dee and heading west on the B976. When the road forks, you'll take the unnamed single-track road that runs along the River Muick. The native red deer are quite common throughout the Scottish Highlands, but the flat valley floor here is one of the best places to see them. Beyond the lower glen, the prospect opens to reveal fine views of the battlement of cliffs edging the mountain called Lochnagar.

WHERE TO EAT AND STAY
For expanded hotel reviews, visit Fodors.com.

$$$$
BRITISH
★ ✕ **The Green Inn.** A family affair, this restaurant with rooms is run by a couple that takes great pleasure in looking after guests. Their son—trained by the great celebrity chef Raymond Blanc—serves sophisticated food that many consider to be the best in the northeast. The tables are laid with heavy china and polished cutlery, and you can dine in the bright conservatory or the red-walled dining room. A prix-fixe three-course dinner (£42.50) might include seared saddle of roe deer with creamed celeriac and a rhubarb and ginger soufflé. You can extend your stay in one of the three very well-appointed guest rooms. ⊠ *Victoria Rd.* ☎ *01339/55701* ⊕ *www.green-inn.com* ⊙ *No lunch.*

$
🏨 **Auld Kirk.** This strikingly renovated old church makes for an interesting stay. **Pros:** helpful team looks after you; pin-tidy bedrooms and public rooms. **Cons:** bar is popular with locals, so can get noisy; restaurant has reduced hours in the winter. ⊠ *Braemar Rd.* ☎ *01339/755762* ⊕ *www.theauldkirk.com* 🛏 *6 rooms* ⚬ *In-room: no a/c, Wi-Fi. In-hotel: restaurant, bar, business center* ⦿ *Breakfast.*

$
🏨 **Deeside Hotel.** With plenty of period charm, this Victorian-era house offers old-fashioned hospitality and simple, understated comfort. **Pros:** unpretentious feel; good price; forever cheerful staff. **Cons:** a few bedrooms on the small side. ⊠ *45 Braemar Rd.* ☎ *013397/55420* ⊕ *www. deesidehotel.co.uk* 🛏 *9 rooms* ⚬ *In-hotel: restaurant, bar* ⦿ *Breakfast.*

$
★ 🏨 **Schoolhouse B&B.** Just outside the center of town, this solid, dependable B&B offers superior accommodations that, with their Asian touches, are a bit unusual for Aberdeenshire. **Pros:** low-priced luxury; meticulously clean. **Cons:** TV has only four channels. ⊠ *Anderson Rd.* ☎ *01339/756333* ⊕ *www.school-house.eu* 🛏 *4 rooms* ⚬ *In-room: no a/c, Wi-Fi* ⦿ *Breakfast.*

SHOPPING

Byzantium. This boutique and gift shop has an eclectic, fashionable mix of clothing and accessories; even if you don't buy, you will be inspired. ⊠ *1–3 Bridge St.* ☎ *013397/55055.*

Countrywear. At either location of Countrywear, you can find everything you need for Highland country living, including fishing tackle, natty

Balmoral, Queen Victoria's Retreat

Some credit Sir Walter Scott with having opened up Scotland for tourism through his poems and novels. But it was probably Queen Victoria (1819–1901) who gave Scottish tourism its real momentum when, in 1842, she first came to Scotland and when, in 1847—on orders of a doctor, who thought the relatively dry climate of upper Deeside would suit her—she bought Balmoral. The pretty little castle was knocked down to make room for a much grander house in full-blown Scottish baronial style, designed by her husband, Prince Albert (1819–61), in 1855. It had a veritable rash of tartanitis. Before long the entire Deeside and the region north were dotted with country houses and mock-baronial châteaux.

"It seems like a dream to be here in our dear Highland Home again," Queen Victoria wrote. "Every year my heart becomes more fixed in this dear Paradise."

Victoria loved Balmoral more for its setting than its house, so be sure to take in its pleasant gardens. Year by year Victoria and Albert added to the estate, taking over neighboring houses, securing the forest and moorland around it, and developing deer stalking and grouse shooting here.

In consequence, Balmoral is now a large property, with grounds that run 12 mi along the Deeside road. Its privacy is protected by belts of pinewood, and the only view of the castle from the A93 is a partial one, from a point near Inver, 2 mi west of the gates.

There's an excellent bird's-eye view of Balmoral from an old military road, now the A939, which climbs out of Crathie, northbound for Cockbridge and the Don Valley. This view embraces the summit of Lochnagar, in whose *corries* (hollows) the snow lies year-round and whose boulder fields the current Prince of Wales, Charles Windsor, so fondly and so frequently treads.

tweeds, and that flexible garment popular in Scotland between seasons: the body warmer. ✉ *15 and 35 Bridge St.* ☎ *013397/55453.*

Deeside Books. This shop sells old, out-of-print, and hard-to-find books about Scotland, which make splendid gifts for lovers of all things Scots. ✉ *18–20 Bridge St.* ☎ *013397/54080.*

Dee Valley Confectioners. For a low-cost gift you could always see what's being boiled up at Dee Valley Confectioners. ✉ *Station Sq.* ☎ *013397/ 55499.*

McEwan Gallery. The McEwan Gallery, 1 mi west of Ballater, displays fine paintings, watercolors, prints, and books (many with a Scottish or golf theme) in an unusual house built by the Swiss artist Rudolphe Christen in 1902. ✉ *A939* ☎ *013397/55429.*

EN
ROUTE
As you continue west into Highland scenery past Balmoral Castle, further pine-framed glimpses appear of the "steep frowning glories of dark Lochnagar," as it was described by the poet Lord Byron (1788–1824). Lochnagar (3,786 feet) was made known to an audience wider than hill walkers by the current Prince of Wales, who published a children's story, *The Old Man of Lochnagar*.

BRAEMAR

17 mi west of Ballater, 60 mi west of Aberdeen, 51 mi north of Perth via A93.

Synonymous with the British monarchy, due to its closeness to Balmoral, and with the famous Highland Games, this village is popular year-round as a base for walkers and climbers enjoying the Grampian Mountains. There isn't really much else going on in Braemar, although the castle is well worth a couple of hours.

GETTING HERE AND AROUND

The town is on A93; there's bus service here, as to other towns on the road, but the closest train station is Aberdeen.

ESSENTIALS

Visitor Information Braemar ⊠ *The Mews, Mar Rd.* ☎ *013397/41600* ⊕ *www. braemarscotland.co.uk.*

EXPLORING

★ **Braemar Castle.** On the northern outskirts of town, Braemar Castle has been restored by a local trust to show how the Farquharson family would have lived. The castle dates from the 17th century, although its defensive walls, in the shape of a pointed star, came later. At Braemar (the *braes*, or slopes, of the district of Mar), the standard, or rebel flag, was first raised at the start of the unsuccessful Jacobite Rebellion of 1715. Thirty years later, during the last Jacobite rebellion, Braemar Castle was strengthened and garrisoned by government troops. From the early 1800s the castle was the clan seat of the Farquharsons, who hold their clan reunion here every summer. Thanks to the commitment of local volunteers, a remarkable 2008 renovation has restored Braemar back to the home it would have been in the early 20th century, complete with all the necessary comforts and family memorabilia. A dozen rooms are on view, including the Laird's day room with a plush day bed and the kitchen. ⊠ *Off A93* ☎ *013397/41219* ⊕ *www.braemarcastle.co.uk* ☒ *£5* ☉ *Apr.–June, Sept., and Oct., weekends 11–4; July and Aug., Wed. and weekends 11–4.*

Braemar Highland Gathering. The village of Braemar is associated with the Braemar Highland Gathering, held the first Saturday in September. Although there are many such gatherings celebrated throughout Scotland, this one is distinguished by the presence of the royal family. Competitions and events include hammer throwing, caber tossing, and bagpipe playing. If you plan to attend, book accommodations months in advance and be flexible; you may have to travel a good distance. You can get tickets about six months in advance; they do sell out. ⊕ *www. braemargathering.org.*

Braemar Highland Heritage Centre. You can find out more about local lore at the Braemar Highland Heritage Centre, in a converted stable block in the middle of town. The center tells the history of the village with displays and a film. The tourist office and a gift shop are here, too. ⊠ *The Mews, Mar Rd.* ☎ *013397/41944* ☒ *Free* ☉ *Jan.–May, Nov., and Dec., Mon.–Sat. 10:30–1:30 and 2–5, Sun. 1–4; June, Sept., and Oct., daily 9–5; July and Aug., daily 9–6.*

THE HIGHLAND GAMES

They might not all be as royally attended as the Braemar Highland Gathering, but from spring to late summer across a wide swath of northern Scotland, competitors gather to toss, pull, fling, and sing at various Highland events. No two games are the same, but many incorporate agricultural shows, sporting competitions, clan gatherings, or just beer in the sun. VisitScotland (⊕ *www.visitscotland.com*) has a list of them.

Which one to attend? Braemar stands tall on ceremony and tradition, and the chance of seeing royalty up close means it attracts visitors from far and wide. Dufftown Games (⊕ *www.dufftownhighlandgames.org*) is the most competitive, with its race up the nearby Ben Rinnes, while the most picturesque is the Lochcarron Games (⊕ *www.lochcaarrongames.org.uk*), which are played and danced out under the massif of the Torridon hills.

OFF THE BEATEN PATH

Linn of Dee. Although the main A93 slinks off to the south from Braemar, a little unmarked road will take you farther west into the hilly heartland. In fact, even if you do not have your own car, you can still explore this area by catching the post bus that leaves from the Braemar post office once a day. The road offers views over the winding River Dee and the blue hills before passing through the tiny hamlet of Inverey and crossing a bridge at the Linn of Dee. *Linn* is a Scots word meaning "rocky narrows," and the river's gash here is deep and roaring. Park beyond the bridge and walk back to admire the sylvan setting.

WHERE TO EAT AND STAY
For expanded hotel reviews, visit Fodors.com.

$ ✕ **Moorfield House.** While the dining room may be underwhelming and
BRITISH the menu limited, when your plate is set before you, you'll understand why this is considered one of the best eateries in Braemar. The untrained owner-chef—who learned his craft by catering for big groups—offers unpretentious yet superb home-style cooking. Simple main dishes like panfried fish with garden vegetables, followed by a dessert like a seasonal crumble, will satisfy even the most exacting gourmand. ⊠ *Moorfield House Hotel, Chapel Brae* ☎ *013397/41244* ⊕ *www.moorfieldhousehotel.com.*

¢ ✕ **Taste.** It's strangely difficult to eat like a queen in Braemar, but this
CAFÉ chalet-style café serves her subjects well, with the tastiest, freshest soups and sandwiches (Scottish cheddar and homemade meatloaf are two options) and moist cakes. You can get your latte here, too. ⊠ *Auchendryne Sq.* ☎ *01339/741425* ⊟ *No credit cards* ⊗ *No dinner. Closed Sun.*

$ ⊞ **Clunie Lodge.** This handsome but homey Victorian manse situated in wooded grounds is not particularly posh or spacious, but everything from the well-polished dressing tables and ironed sheets in the bedrooms to the creamy porridge "stirred clockwise" in the mornings (or bacon and eggs, if you prefer) is done just right. **Pros:** beautiful location; thoughtful hosts who know everything about the area. **Cons:** some rooms are small, and some bathrooms are tiny. ⊠ *Cluniebank Rd.*

7

☎ *013397/41330* ⊕ *www.clunielodge.com* ⇨ *5 rooms* ♿ *In-room: no a/c. In-hotel: laundry facilities, parking* ⊚ *Breakfast.*

GOLF

Braemar Golf Course. The tricky 18-hole Braemar Golf Course, founded in 1902, is laden with foaming waters. Erratic duffers take note: the compassionate course managers have installed, near the water, poles with little nets on the end for those occasional shots that may go awry. The cost for a round is £25. ⊠ *Cluny Bank Rd.* ☎ *013397/41618* ⊕ *www.braemargolfclub.co.uk* 🏌 *18 holes, 4,935 yds, SSS 64.*

CORGARFF CASTLE

23 mi northeast of Braemar, 14 mi northwest of Ballater.

GETTING HERE AND AROUND

By car, take A939 and then follow signs. From May to September, the Heather Hopper Bus runs twice daily from Ballater; it stops at Strathdon and Corgarff.

Contacts Heather Hopper ☎ *01224/664584* ⊕ *www.royal-deeside.org.uk.*

EXPLORING

Corgarff Castle. Eighteenth-century soldiers paved a military highway, now the A939, north from Ballater to Corgarff Castle, an isolated tower house on the moorland with a star-shape defensive wall—a curious replica of Braemar Castle. Corgarff was built as a hunting lodge for the earls of Mar in the 16th century. After an eventful history that included the wife of a later laird being burned alive in a family dispute, the castle ended its career as a garrison for Hanoverian troops. The troops were responsible for preventing illegal whisky distilling. Reconstructed barracks show what the castle must have been like when the redcoats arrived in 1746. ⊠ *Off A939, Corgarff* ☎ *01975/651460* ⊕ *www.historic-scotland.gov.uk* ⊠ *£5* ☉ *Apr.–Sept., daily 9:30–6:30; Oct., daily 9:30–4:30; Nov.–Mar., weekends 9:30–4:30; last admission 30 mins before closing.*

EN ROUTE

Castle Trail. If you return east from Corgarff Castle to the A939/A944 junction and make a left onto the A944, the thorough castle signposting indicates you're on the Castle Trail. The A944 meanders along the River Don to the village of Strathdon, where a great mound by the roadside—on the left—turns out to be a *motte*, or the base of a wooden castle, built in the late 12th century. Although it takes considerable imagination to become enthusiastic about a great grass-covered heap, surviving mottes have contributed greatly to the understanding of the history of Scottish castles. The A944 then joins the A97 (go left), and a few minutes later a sign points to **Glenbuchat Castle**, a plain Z-plan tower house. ⊕ *www.aberdeen-grampian.com*

Language and the Scots

"Much," said Doctor Johnson, "may be made of a Scotchman if he be caught young." This quote sums up, even today, the attitude of some English people—confident in their English, the language of parliament and much of the media—toward the Scots language. The Scots have long been made to feel uncomfortable about their mother tongue, and until the 1970s (and in some private schools, even today) they were encouraged to mimic the dialect of the Thames Valley ("standard English") in order to "get on" in life.

LOWLAND SCOTS

The Scots language (that is, Lowland Scots, not Gaelic) was a northern form of Middle English and in its day was the language used in the court and in literature. It borrowed from Scandinavian, Dutch, French, and Gaelic. After a series of historical blows—such as the decamping of the Scottish court to England after 1603 and the printing of the King James Bible in English but not in Scots—it declined as a literary or official language. It survives in various forms but is virtually an underground language, spoken among ordinary folk, especially in its heartland, in the northeast.

You may even find yourself exporting a few useful words, such as *dreich* (gloomy), *glaikit* (acting and looking foolish), or *dinna fash* (don't worry), all of which are much more expressive than their English equivalents.

Some Scottish words are used and understood across the entire country (and world), such as *wee* (small), *aye* (yes), *lassie* (girl), and *bonny* (pretty). Regional variations are evident even in the simplest of greetings. When you meet someone in the Borders, *Whit*

fettle? (What state are you in?) or *Hou ye lestin?* (How are you lasting?) may throw you for a loop; elsewhere you could hear *Hou's yer dous?* (How are your pigeons?). If a group of Scots takes a fancy to you at the pub, you may be asked to *Come intil the body o the kirk,* and if all goes well, your departure may be met with a jovial farewell, *haste ye back* (return soon).

GAELIC

Scottish Gaelic, an entirely different language, is still spoken across the Highlands and Hebrides. There's also a large Gaelic-speaking population in Glasgow as a result of the Celtic diaspora—islanders migrating to Glasgow in search of jobs in the 19th century. Speakers of Gaelic in Scotland were once persecuted, after the failure of the 18th-century Jacobite rebellions. Official persecution has now turned to guilt-tinged support, as the promoters of Gaelic lobby for substantial public funds to underwrite television programming and language classes for new learners.

One of the joys of Scottish television is watching Gaelic news programs to see how the ancient language copes with such topics as nuclear energy, the Internet, and the latest band to hit the charts. A number of Gaelic words have been absorbed into English: *banshee* (a wailing female spirit), *galore* (plenty), *slob* (a slovenly person), and *brat* (a spoiled or unruly child).

To experience Gaelic language and culture in all its glory, you can attend the Royal National Mod—a competition-based festival with speeches, drama, and music, all in Gaelic—held in a different location every year.

7

KILDRUMMY CASTLE

18 mi northeast of Corgarff, 23 mi north of Ballater, 22 mi north of Aboyne.

GETTING HERE AND AROUND

By car, take A97 off A93 (or the A980 if you're coming direct from Banchory). Be wary of the sign for Kildrummy Castle Garden and Hotel. You want the turn after this for Kildrummy Castle itself.

EXPLORING

Kildrummy Castle. Although in ruins, Kildrummy Castle is significant because it dates to the 13th century and has ties to the mainstream medieval traditions of European castle building. It shares features with Harlech and Caernarfon, in Wales, as well as with Château de Coucy, near Laon, France. Kildrummy underwent several expansions at the hands of England's King Edward I (1239–1307); the castle was back in Scottish hands in 1306, when it was besieged by King Edward I's son. The defenders were betrayed by Osbarn the Smith, who was promised a large amount of gold by the English forces. They gave it to him after the castle fell, pouring it molten down his throat, or so the ghoulish story goes. Kildrummy's prominence ended after the collapse of the 1715 Jacobite uprising. It had been the rebel headquarters and was consequently dismantled. Although the castle is almost completely ruined, its unadorned yet strangely moving chapel remains intact. ⊠ *A97* ☎ *019755/71331* ⊕ *www.historic-scotland.gov.uk* 🗁 *£4* ⏱ *Apr.–Sept., daily 9–5.*

Kildrummy Castle Gardens. The Kildrummy Castle Gardens, behind the castle and with a separate entrance from the main road, are built in what was the original quarry for the castle. This sheltered bowl within the woodlands has a broad range of shrubs and alpine plants and a notable water garden. ⊠ *A97* ☎ *019755/71203* ⊕ *www.kildrummy-castle-gardens.co.uk* 🗁 *£4.50* ⏱ *Apr.–Oct., daily noon–5.*

ALFORD

9 mi east of Kildrummy, 28 mi west of Aberdeen.

A plain and sturdy settlement in the Howe (Hollow) of Alford, this town gives those who have grown somewhat weary of castle-hopping a break: it has a museum instead. Craigievar Castle and Castle Fraser are nearby, though.

GETTING HERE AND AROUND

The town is on A944.

ESSENTIALS

Visitor Information Alford ⊠ *Old Station Yard, Main St.* ☎ *019755/62052* ⊕ *www.aberdeen-grampian.com* ⏱ *Apr.–Sept.*

EXPLORING

Castle Fraser. About 8 mi southeast of Alford, the massive Castle Fraser is the ancestral home of the Frasers and one of the largest of the castles of Mar; it's certainly a contender as one of the grandest castles in the northeast. Although the well-furnished building shows a variety of styles reflecting the taste of its owners from the 15th through the 19th centuries, its design is typical of the cavalcade of castles in the region, and for good reason. This—along with many others, including Midmar, Craigievar, Crathes, and Glenbuchat—was designed by a family of master masons called Bell. There are plenty of family items, but don't miss the two Turret Rooms—one of which is the trophy room—and Major Smiley's Room. He married into the family but is famous for having been one of the escapees from Colditz (a high-security prisoner of war camp) during World War II. The walled garden includes a 19th-century knot garden, with colorful flowerbeds, box hedging, gravel paths, and splendid herbaceous borders. Have lunch in the tearoom or the picnic area. ⊠ *Off A944* ☎ *0844/493–2164* ⊕ *www.nts.org.uk* ⌨ *£9* ◷ *Apr.– June, Sept., and Oct., Wed.–Sat. noon–5; July and Aug., daily 11–5; last admission 45 min before closing.*

Craigievar Castle. Much as the stonemasons left it in 1626, Craigievar Castle has pepper-pot turrets that make it an outstanding example of a tower house. Striking and well preserved, it has many family furnishings, and the lovely grounds are worth exploring, too. Craigievar was built in relatively peaceful times by William Forbes, a successful merchant in trade with the Baltic Sea ports (he was also known as Danzig Willie). ⊠ *A980, 5 mi south of Alford* ☎ *0844/493–2174* ⊕ *www.nts. org.uk.* ⌨ *11* ◷ *May, June, and Sept., Fri.–Tues. 11–5; July and Aug., daily 11–5.*

🔄 ★ **Grampian Transport Museum.** The entertaining and enthusiastically run Grampian Transport Museum specializes in road-based means of locomotion, backed up by an archive and library. Its collection of buses is second to none, but the Craigievar Express, a steam-driven creation invented by the local postman to deliver mail more efficiently, is the most unusual. There's a small café that offers tea, baked goods, and ice cream. ⊠ *Montgarrie Rd.* ☎ *019755/62292* ⊕ *www.gtm.org.uk* ⌨ *£6* ◷ *Apr.–Sept., daily 10–5; Oct., daily 10–4.*

THE NORTHEAST AND THE MALT WHISKY TRAIL

North of Deeside another popular area of this region lies inland, toward Speyside—the valley, or strath, of the River Spey—famed for its whisky distilleries, some of which it promotes in another signposted trail. Distilling scotch is not an intrinsically spectacular process. It involves pure water, malted barley, and sometimes peat smoke, then a lot of bubbling and fermentation, all of which cause a number of odd smells. The result is a prestigious product with a fascinating range of flavors that you may either enjoy immensely or not at all.

Instead of closely following the Malt Whisky Trail, dip into it and blend visits to distilleries with some other aspects of the county of Moray, particularly its coastline. Whisky notwithstanding, Moray's scenic qualities, low rainfall, and other reassuring weather statistics are worth remembering. You can also sample the northeastern seaboard, including some of the best but least-known coastal scenery in Scotland.

DUFFTOWN

54 mi west of Aberdeen.

On one of the Spey tributaries, Dufftown was planned in 1817 by the Earl of Fife. Its simple cross layout with a square and a large clock tower (originally from Banff and now the site of the visitor center) is typical of a small Scottish town built in the 19th century. Its simplicity is made all the more stark by the brooding, heather-clad hills that rise around it. Dufftown is convenient to a number of distilleries.

GETTING HERE AND AROUND
To get here from Aberdeen, drive west on A96 and A920; then turn west at Huntly. It's not easy or quick, but you can take the train to Elgin or Keith and then the bus to Dufftown.

ESSENTIALS
Visitor Information **Dufftown** ✉ *The Square* ☎ *01340/820501* ⊙ *Apr.–Oct.*

EXPLORING
TOP ATTRACTIONS

Fodor'sChoice **Balvenie Distillery.** Offering just a handful of tours each week, you'd
★ think that Balvenie Distillery didn't want visitors. Yet as soon as you step into the old manager's office—now gently restored and fitted with knotted-elm furniture—you realize Balvenie just wants to make sure that all visitors get to see, smell, and feel the magic of the making of this malt. Balvenie is unusual because it has its own cooperage with six coopers hard at work turning the barrels. During the three-hour tour you'll see the mashing, fermentation, and distillation process, culminating in a five-malt tasting session. ✉ *Balvenie St.* ☎ *01340/822062* ⊕ *www.thebalvenie.com* ☐ *£25* ⊙ *Tours Mon.–Thurs. at 10 and 2, Fri. at 10.*

Glenfiddich Distillery. Many make Glenfiddich Distillery, ½ mi north of Dufftown, their first stop on the Malt Whisky Trail. The independent company of William Grant and Sons Limited was the first to realize the tourist potential of the distilling process. The company began offering tours around the typical pagoda-roof malting buildings and subsequently built an entertaining visitor center. Besides a free 20-minute tour of the distillery there's a two-hour in-depth Connoisseurs' Tour (£20; reserve ahead in summer) that includes a special nosing and tasting session. Check out the Glenfiddich Distillery Art Gallery, showing the work of international artists. ✉ *A941* ☎ *01340/820373* ⊕ *www.glenfiddich.com* ☐ *Free, Connoisseurs' Tour £20* ⊙ *Easter–mid-Oct., daily 9:30–4:30; mid-Oct.–Easter, weekends 9:30–4:30.*

★ **Strathisla Distillery.** Whisky lovers should take the B9014 11 mi northeast from Dufftown—or alternatively, ride the Keith Dufftown Railway—to see one of Scotland's most iconic distilleries, the Strathisla Distillery, with its cobblestone courtyard and famous double pagoda roofs. Stretching over the picturesque River Isla, the Strathisla Distillery was built in 1786 and now produces the main component of the Chivas Regal blend. Guided tours take you to the mash house, tun room, and still house—all pretty much the same as they were when production

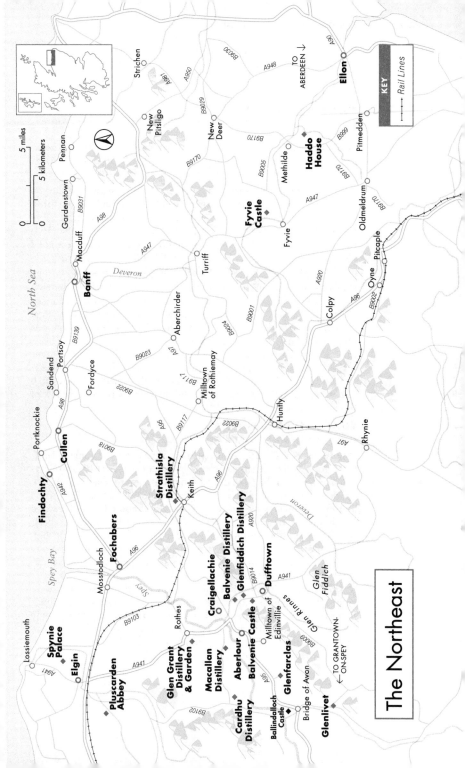

The Northeast

KEY
→ Rail Lines

5 miles
5 kilometers

North Sea

Spey Bay

Lossiemouth
Spynie Palace
Elgin
Pluscarden Abbey

Portknockie
Findochty
Cullen
Sandend
Portsoy
Fordyce
Macduff
Banff
Pennan
Gardenstown

Deveron

Mosstodloch
Fochabers
Rothes
Keith
Strathisla Distillery

Glen Grant Distillery & Garden
Macallan Distillery
Cardhu Distillery
Aberlour
Balvenie Castle
Craigellachie
Balvenie Distillery
Glenfiddich Distillery
Dufftown
Milltown of Edinvillie
Glenfarclas
Ballindalloch Castle
Bridge of Avon
Glenlivet
TO GRANTOWN-ON-SPEY

Glen Fiddich
Glen Rinnes

Aberchirder
Turriff
Millton of Rothiemay
Huntly
Rhynie

New Pitsligo
Strichen
New Deer
Fyvie Castle
Fyvie
Methlide
Haddo House
Pitmedden
Oldmeldrum
Pitcaple
Oyne
Colpy

TO ABERDEEN →
Ellon

began. The tour ends with a tasting session. ✉ *Seafield Ave., Keith* ☎ *01542/783044* ⊕ *www.chivas.com* 🎫*£6* ⊙ *Apr.–Oct., Mon.–Sat. 9:30–4, Sun. noon–4.*

WORTH NOTING

Balvenie. On a mound just above the Glenfiddich Distillery is a grim, gray, and squat curtain-walled castle, Balvenie. This ruined fortress, which dates from the 13th century, once commanded the glens and passes toward Speyside and Elgin. ✉ *A941* ☎ *01340/820121* ⊕ *www. historic-scotland.gov.uk* 🎫 *£4* ⊙ *Apr.–Sept., daily 9:30–5:30; last entry ½ hr before closing.*

Keith and Dufftown Railway. Leaving from Dufftown twice a day on weekends, this restored locomotive chugs 11 mi around forests, fields, and rivers. It passes Drummuir Castle on its way to Keith, home of the Strathisla Distillery. The Buffer Stop restaurant car at the Dufftown Station serves snacks, scones, and tea. Reservations are a good idea. ✉ *Dufftown Station, Station Rd.* ☎ *01340/821181* ⊕ *www.keith-dufftown-railway.co.uk* 🎫 *£6* ⊙ *Easter–Sept., weekends.*

Mortlach Church. Set in a hollow by the Dullan Water, Mortlach Church is thought to be one of Scotland's oldest Christian sites, perhaps founded by St. Luag, a contemporary of St. Columba, as early as AD 566. Note the weathered Pictish cross in the churchyard and the even older stone under cover in the vestibule, with a strange Pictish elephantlike beast carved on it. Though much of the church was rebuilt after 1876, some early work survives, including three lancet windows from the 13th century and a leper's squint (a hole extended to the outside of the church so that lepers could hear the service but be kept away from the rest of the congregation). ✉ *Church St.*

WHERE TO EAT AND STAY

For expanded hotel reviews, visit Fodors.com.

$$$
FRENCH
Fodor's Choice
★

✕ **La Faisanderie.** Gourmands from around the northeast come to Dufftown for a truly French gastronomic experience. A large, distillery-inspired fresco in the plain dining room adds some panache to the tall windows, creaky wood floors, and crisp white tablecloths. The French and English owners use fine cuts of local beef and game and seafood caught on the coast to create classic dishes with not-too-heavy sauces. Worth trying is the Strathdon blue (a fine Scottish cheese) soufflé and, to end your meal, an iced whisky with chestnut puree: the ultimate way for a sweet-toothed whisky lover to enjoy a tipple. ✉ *2 Balvenie St.* ☎ *01340/821273* ⊙ *Closed Tues. and Wed. in Oct.–Mar.*

¢

🏨 **Tannochbrae.** This townhouse B&B has six bedrooms upstairs, individual in style but all with simple color schemes and silky-soft throws. **Pros:** beautiful location; cozy bar. **Cons:** town can be surprisingly noisy on a weekend night. ✉ *22 Fife St.* ☎ *01340/820541* ⊕ *www. tannochbrae.co.uk* 🛏 *6 rooms* ⌂ *In-room: no a/c. In-hotel: restaurant, bar* ⏐⊙⏐ *Breakfast.*

CLOSE UP

Whisky, the Water of Life

Conjured from an innocuous mix of malted barley, water, and yeast, malt whisky is for many synonymous with Scotland. Clans produced whisky for hundreds of years before it emerged as Scotland's national drink and major export. Today those centuries of expertise result in a sublimely subtle drink with many different layers of flavor. Each distillery produces a malt with—to the expert—instantly identifiable, predominant notes peculiarly its own.

WHISKY TYPES AND STYLES
There are two types of whisky: malt and grain. Malt whisky, generally acknowledged to have a more sophisticated bouquet and flavor, is made with malted barley—barley that is soaked in water until the grains germinate and then is dried to halt the germination, all of which adds extra flavor and a touch of sweetness to the brew. Grain whisky also contains malted barley, but with the addition of unmalted barley and maize.

Blended whiskies, which make up many of the leading brands, usually balance malt- and grain-whisky distillations; deluxe blends contain a higher percentage of malts. Blends that contain several malt whiskies are called "vatted malts." Whisky connoisseurs often prefer to taste the single malts:

the unblended whisky from a single distillery.

In simple terms, malt whiskies may be classified into "eastern" and "western" in style, with the whisky made in the east of Scotland, for example in Speyside, being lighter and sweeter than the products of the western isles, which often have a taste of peat smoke or even iodine.

The production process is, by comparison, relatively straightforward: just malt your barley, mash it, ferment it and distill it, then mature to perfection. To find out the details, join a distillery tour, and be rewarded with a dram. Check out ⊕ www.scotlandwhisky.com for more information.

TASTING WHISKY
When tasting whisky, follow these simple steps. First, pour a dram. Turn and tilt the glass to coat the sides. Smell the whisky, "nosing" to inhale the heady aromas. If you want, you can add a little water and turn the glass gently to watch it "marry" with the whisky, nosing as you go. Take a wee sip and swirl it over your tongue and sense what connoisseurs call the "mouthfeel." Swallow and admire the finish. Repeat until convinced it's a good malt!

7

SHOPPING
Collector's Cabin. Two adjoining shops—one with Scottish silver, fossils, and book illustrations, the other with kilts, ceramics, and other curiosities—are filled with conversation starters. This is truly a trove worth delving into. ✉ *22 and 24 Balvenie St., Dufftown AB55 4AB* ☎ *01340/821393.*

CRAIGELLACHIE

4 mi northwest of Dufftown via A941.

Renowned as an angling resort, Craigellachie, like so many settlements on the River Spey, is sometimes enveloped in the malty reek of the local industry. Glen Grant is one of the distilleries nearby. The Spey itself is crossed by a handsome suspension bridge, designed by noted engineer Thomas Telford (1757–1834) in 1814 and now bypassed by the modern road.

GETTING HERE AND AROUND

The town is on A491; it's best to drive here, as public transportation is infrequent and complicated.

EXPLORING

★ **Glen Grant Distillery & Garden.** James Grant founded a distillery in 1840 when he was only 25, and it was the first in the country to be electrically powered. This place will come as a welcome relief to companions of dedicated Malt Whisky Trail followers, because in addition to the distillery there's a large and beautiful garden. It's planted and tended as Grant envisioned, with orchards and woodland walks, log bridges over waterfalls, a magnificent lily pond, and azaleas and rhododendrons in profusion. Glen Grant produces a distinctive pale-gold, clear whisky, with an almost floral or fruity finish, using peculiarly tall stills and special purifiers that follow a design introduced over a century ago. You'll see these on your tour. ⊠ *A941, Rothes* ☎ *01340/832118* ⊕ *www.glengrant.com* 🖃 *£3.50* ⊗ *May–Oct., daily 9:30–4; Nov.–Apr., Mon.–Sat. 9:30–4, Sun. noon–5.*

Macallan Distillery. On the sprawling Easter Elchies Estate, Macallan Distillery offers unique whisky matured in sherry casks and, more recently, in oak bourbon casks. The Experience Tour lasts almost 90 minutes and takes you from the still house to the warehouse where maturation takes place, finishing off with a wee dram. The Precious Tour lasts an hour longer and gives a more in-depth look at the process before an extended nosing and tasting session. Booking is essential. ⊠ *Off B9102* ☎ *01304/872280* ⊕ *www.themacallan.com* 🖃 *Experience Tour £10, Precious Tour £20* ⊗ *Easter–June and Aug., Mon.–Sat. 9:30–4:30; Sept. and Oct., weekdays 9:30–4:30; Nov.–Easter, weekdays 11–3.*

★ **Speyside Cooperage and Visitor Centre.** A major stop on the Malt Whisky Trail, the huge Speyside Cooperage and Visitor Centre is a must for all whisky fans. Retired coopers will talk you through the making of the casks, a surprisingly physical and dramatic process that uses the same tools and skills employed for hundreds of years. Inside you can watch highly skilled craftspeople make and repair oak barrels used in the local whisky industry. The Acorn to Cask exhibit tells all about the ancient craft of coopering. There's a cottage café with huge cakes and sandwiches for those in need of fortification. ⊠ *Dufftown Rd.* ☎ *01340/871108* ⊕ *www.speysidecooperage.co.uk* 🖃 *£3.30* ⊗ *Weekdays 9–4.*

CHOOSING A DISTILLERY TOUR

Like whiskies, distillery tours are not the same, though you'll usually spend about an hour or two at each place. The company's history, size, and commercial savvy create different experiences. You should also investigate any special in-depth tours if you're willing to pay extra and spend more time. Here's a cheat sheet to help you choose a tour or two to suit your taste.

Balvenie: This distillery's tour is for those who want to understand and celebrate the details of distilling. No other distillery lets you see and smell the malting floor before watching the coopers turn their barrels.

Cardhu: Architecturally, the stocky buildings and proud towers of Cardhu, formerly an illicit still, seem to have a grim defiance. The tour gives you a great understanding of whisky's simple ingredients, including locally sourced springwater, and the process it undergoes.

Glen Grant: The distillery tour is good, but the gardens of Major Grant are sublime. He traveled the world collecting species and created a Victorian garden that has been gloriously restored.

Glenfarclas: This proud family-owned still may not provide the slickness of the Glenfiddich tour, but the quiet passion of the still workers and their belief in their whisky is more powerful than a dram of the stuff.

Glenfiddich: Owned by the same family since day one, this distillery offers both entry-level and enthusiasts' tours that cover the older, more atmospheric buildings and the swankier visitor center.

Glenlivet: It's a beautiful drive to this, the first licensed distillery in the Highlands. You'll learn the fascinating story of Glenlivet's founder, George Smith.

Macallan: Situated on the green and pleasant Easter Elchies Estate, this vast distillery is dominated by a warehouse with row upon row of sherry casks imbuing this whisky with its sweetness.

Speyside Cooperage: Although this isn't a distillery, real whisky enthusiasts shouldn't miss a visit to one of the few remaining cooperages in Scotland. Watch the coopers at work and see just how much craft goes into making and treating these precious barrels.

Strathisla: Home of Chivas, not a malt but a fine blended whisky, this is perhaps one of the prettiest and most compact distilleries in the northeast and is delightfully situated on the River Isla.

WHERE TO STAY

For expanded hotel reviews, visit Fodors.com.

$ 🏨 **Highlander Inn.** Don't be fooled by the rather Alpine exterior: this very Scottish hotel prides itself on its whisky bar and its friendliness. **Pros:** simple accommodations; a warm welcome. **Cons:** bar meals could be more exciting. ⊠ *Victoria St.* 🕾 *01340/881446* ⊕ *www.whiskyinn. com* 🛏 *5 rooms* ⚛ *In-room: no a/c, Wi-Fi. In-hotel: restaurant, bar* 🍽 *Breakfast.*

ABERLOUR

2 mi southwest of Craigellachie.

Aberlour, often listed as Charlestown of Aberlour on maps, is a handsome little burgh, essentially Victorian in style, though actually founded in 1812 by the local landowner. The names of the noted local whisky stills are Cragganmore, Aberlour, and Glenfarclas; Glenlivet and Cardhu are also nearby. Also in Aberlour is Walkers, famous for producing shortbread, tins of buttery, crumbly goodness, since 1898.

GETTING HERE AND AROUND

Aberlour is on A95; public transportation here is infrequent.

EXPLORING

Cardhu Distillery. The striking outline of Cardhu Distillery, whose main product lies at the heart of Johnnie Walker Blends, is set among the heather-clad Mannoch hills. Established by John and Helen Cumming in 1811, it was officially founded in 1824, after distilling was made legal by the Excise Act of 1823. Today Cardhu is owned by the superbrewer Diageo (who tried to rename it Cardow, although the single malt is still known as Cardhu). Guided tours take you to the mashing, fermenting, and distilling halls, and they explain the malting process that now takes place at Burghead on the coast. Take time to walk around the attractive grounds or picnic there. Cardhu is 10 mi north of Glenlivet via B9008, A95, and B9102; it's 7 mi west of Aberlour. ✉ *B1902, Knockando* ☎ *01340/875635* ⊕ *www.scotlandwhisky.com* 🎫 *£4* ⊗ *Oct.–Apr., weekdays 11–3; May–June, weekdays 10–5; July–Sept., Mon.–Sat. 10–5, Sun. 11–4; last tour 1 hr before closing.*

Glenfarclas. In an age when most small distilleries have been taken over by multinationals, Glenfarclas remains family owned, passed down from father to son since 1865. That link to the past is most visible among its low buildings, where the retired still sits outside: if you didn't know what it was, you could mistake it for part of a submarine. The tours end with tastings in the superlative Ship Room, the intact lounge of an ocean liner called the *Empress of Australia*. An in-depth Ambassador's Tour and tasting is available for £15. ✉ *Off A95, Ballindalloch* ☎ *01807/500345* ⊕ *www.glenfarclas.co.uk* 🎫 *£3.50* ⊗ *Apr.–June, weekdays 10–5; July–Sept., weekdays 10–5, Sun. 10–4; Oct.–Mar., weekdays 10–4.*

Glenlivet. The famous Glenlivet was the first licensed distillery in the Highlands, founded in 1824 by George Smith. Today it produces one of the best-known 12-year-old single malts in the world. Take the free distillery tour for a chance to see inside the huge bonded warehouse where the whisky steeps in oak casks. The tour has two aspects: the Spirit of the Glen examines how unique factors come together to make this nectar, and the Glenlivet Legacy looks at the dream of the distillery's founder. There's a coffee shop with home baking and, of course, a whisky shop. Glenlivet is 10 mi southwest of Aberlour via A95 and B9008. ✉ *Off B9008, Ballindalloch* ☎ *01340/821720* ⊕ *www.glenlivet. com* 🎫 *Free* ⊗ *Apr.–Oct., Mon.–Sat. 10–4, Sun. 12:30–4.*

WHERE TO EAT AND STAY

For expanded hotel reviews, visit Fodors.com.

¢ ✕ **Old Pantry.** This pleasantly rus-
BRITISH tic corner restaurant and gift shop overlooks Aberlour's tree-shaded central square. The kitchen serves–albeit sometimes slowly–everything from a cup of coffee with a sticky cake at teatime to a three-course spread of soup, roast meat, and traditional pudding. ✉ *The Square* ☎ *01340/871617* ⊘ *No dinner Oct.–May.*

$ 🏠 **Cardhu Country House.** After a top-to-bottom renovation in 2009, this once-abandoned manse (minister's house) looks as if it has always been loved and lived in. **Pros:** period charm and modern comforts; tasty meals. **Cons:** you need a car to get here. ✉ *Off B9102, Knockando* ☎ *01340/810895* ⊕ *www.cardhucountryhouse.co.uk* ⤢ *6 rooms* ♿ *In-room: no a/c, Wi-Fi* ⦿ *Breakfast.*

$ 🏠 **Mash Tun.** Curvy yet sturdy, this former station hotel harks back to
★ a time when Aberlour was a busy holiday destination on the Aberdeen to Aviemore train line; now a smart B&B and popular restaurant, it is once again the heart of the village. **Pros:** superb accommodation; great atmosphere in the restaurant and bar. **Cons:** book well ahead in summer. ✉ *8 Broomfield Sq.* ☎ *01340/88171* ⊕ *www.mashtun-aberlour. com* ⤢ *4 rooms, 1 suite* ♿ *In-room: no a/c, Wi-Fi. In-hotel: restaurant, bar* ⦿ *Breakfast.*

SHOPPING

Speyside Pottery. A couple of miles west of Aberlour, look for Speyside Pottery, where Thomas and Anne Gough produce domestic stoneware in satisfying, sturdy traditional shapes. Call ahead November through March, as hours are limited. ✉ *A95, Ballindalloch* ☎ *01807/500338.*

ELGIN

15 mi north of Craigellachie, 69 mi northwest of Aberdeen, 41 mi east of Inverness.

As the center of the fertile Laigh (low-lying lands) of Moray, Elgin has been of local importance for centuries. Sheltered by great hills to the south, the city lies between two major rivers, the Spey and the Findhorn. Beginning in the 13th century, Elgin became an important religious center, a cathedral city with a walled town growing up around the cathedral and adjacent to the original settlement.

Elgin prospered, and by the early 18th century it became a mini-Edinburgh of the north and a place where country gentlemen spent their winters. It even echoed Edinburgh in carrying out wide-scale reconstruction in the 18th century. Many fine neoclassical buildings survive today despite much misguided demolition in the late 20th century for better traffic flow. However, the central main-street plan and some of the older little streets and *wynds* (alleyways) remain. You can also see Elgin's past in the arcaded shop fronts—some of which date from the late 17th century—on the main shopping street.

GETTING HERE AND AROUND

Elgin is on the A96 road from Aberdeen to Inverness. The A941 runs north from the distillery area to the city. There's a train stop here on the line that links Aberdeen and Inverness: Aberdeen is 90 minutes away.

ESSENTIALS

Visitor Information **Elgin** ⊠ *Cooper Park* ☎ *01343/562616* ⊘ *Mon.–Sat. 10–4.*

EXPLORING

Elgin Cathedral. Cooper Park contains a magnificent ruin, the Elgin Cathedral, consecrated in 1224. Its eventful story included devastation by fire: a 1390 act of retaliation by Alexander Stewart (circa 1343–1405), the Wolf of Badenoch. The illegitimate-son-turned-bandit of King David II (1324–71) had sought revenge for his excommunication by the bishop of Moray. The cathedral was rebuilt but finally fell into disuse after the Reformation in 1560. By 1567 the highest authority in the land, the regent earl of Moray, had stripped the lead from the roof to pay for his army. Thus ended the career of the religious seat known as the Lamp of the North. Some traces of the cathedral settlement survive—the gateway Pann's Port and the Bishop's Palace—although they've been drastically altered. ⊠ *Cooper Park* ☎ *01343/547171* ⊕ *www.historic-scotland.gov. uk* 🔊 *£5; £6.70 with Spynie Palace* ⊘ *Apr.–Sept., daily 9:30–5:30; Oct., daily 9:30–4:30; Nov.–Mar., Sat.–Wed. 9:30–4:30; last admission ½ hr before closing.*

St. Giles Church. At the center of Elgin, the most conspicuous structure is St. Giles Church, which divides High Street. The grand foursquare building, constructed in 1828, exhibits the Greek Revival style: note the columns, the pilasters, and the top of the spire, surmounted by a representation of the Lysicrates Monument. ⊠ *High St..*

OFF THE BEATEN PATH

Pluscarden Abbey. Given the general destruction caused by the 16th-century upheaval of the Reformation, abbeys in Scotland tend to be ruinous and deserted, but at Pluscarden Abbey the monks' way of life continues. Originally a 13th-century structure, the abbey was abandoned by the religious community after the Reformation. Monks from Prinknash Abbey near Gloucester, England, returned here in 1948, and the abbey is now a Benedictine community. It's 6 mi southwest of Elgin. ⊠ *Off B9010* ⊕ *www.pluscardenabbey.org* 🔊 *Free* ⊘ *Daily 9–5.*

Spynie Palace. Just north of Elgin sits Spynie Palace, the impressive 15th-century former headquarters of the bishops of Moray. It has now fallen into ruin, though the top of the tower has good views over the Laigh of Moray. Find it by turning right off the Elgin–Lossiemouth road. ⊠ *Off A941* ☎ *01343/546358* ⊕ *www.historic-scotland.gov.uk* 🔊 *£4; £6.70 with Elgin Cathedral* ⊘ *Apr.–Sept., daily 9:30–6:30; Oct., daily 9:30–4:30; Nov.–Mar., weekends 9:30–4:30; last admission ½ hr before closing.*

SHOPPING

Gordon and MacPhail. An outstanding delicatessen and wine merchant, Gordon and MacPhail also stocks rare malt whiskies. This is a good place to shop for gifts for those foodies among your friends. ✉ *58–60 South St.* ☎ *01343/545110* ⊕ *www.gordonandmacphail.com.*

Johnstons of Elgin. This woolen mill has a worldwide reputation for its luxury fabrics, especially cashmere. The large shop stocks not only the firm's own products but also top-quality Scottish crafts and giftware. There's a coffee shop on the premises. Free tours are available for the mill but you must prebook. ✉ *Newmill Rd.* ☎ *01343/554099* ⊕ *www. johnstonscashmere.com.*

FOCHABERS

9 mi east of Elgin.

With its hanging baskets of fuchsia in summer and its perfectly mowed village square, Fochabers has a cared-for charm that makes you want to stop here, even just to stretch your legs. Lying just to the south of the River Spey, the former market town was founded in 1776 by the Duke of Gordon. The duke moved the village from its original site because it was too close to Gordon Castle. Famous today for being home to the Baxters brand of soups and jams, Fochabers is near some of the best berry fields: come and pick your own in the summer months.

GETTING HERE AND AROUND

Fochabers is not on the Inverness-to-Aberdeen train line, but there is an hourly bus service (Stagecoach Bluebird number 10) from Fochabers to Elgin. It's near the junction of A98 and A96.

EXPLORING

Baxters Highland Village. Just a mile west of the center of Fochabers, you can see the works of a major local employer, Baxters of Fochabers. From Tokyo to New York, upmarket stores stock the company's soups, jams, chutneys, and other gourmet products—all of which are made here, close to the River Spey. Take home a can of Royal Game Soup, a favorite of the late Queen Mum. The Baxters Highland Village presents a video about the history of the business, plus interactive exhibits and cooking demonstrations. You can have a look at a re-creation of the Baxters' first grocery shop, and browse around the Best of Scotland, specializing in all kinds of Scottish products. A restaurant serves up an assortment of delectables. ✉ *A96* ☎ *01343/820666* ⊕ *www.baxters. com* 🖾 *Free* ⊙ *Daily 10–5.*

Fochabers Folk Museum. Once over the Spey Bridge and past the cricket ground (a very unusual sight in Scotland), you can find the symmetrical, 18th-century Fochabers village square lined with antiques dealers. Through one of these shops, Pringle Antiques, you can enter the Fochabers Folk Museum, a converted church with a fine collection of items relating to past life in the village and surrounding area. Exhibits include carts and carriages, farm implements, and Victorian toys. ✉ *High St.* ☎ *01343/821204* ⊕ *www.fochabers-heritage.org.uk* 🖾 *Free* ⊙ *Easter– Oct., Tues.–Fri. 11–4, weekends 2–4.*

7

Gordon Chapel. One of the village's lesser-known treasures is the Gordon Chapel, which has an exceptional set of stained-glass windows by Pre-Raphaelite artist Sir Edward Burne-Jones. ✉ *Castle St., just off The Square.*

SHOPPING

Just Art. If you're interested in works by local artists, head to Just Art, a fine gallery with high-quality contemporary ceramics and paintings. ✉ *64 High St.* ☎ *01343/820500.*

The Quaich. At The Quaich you can stock up on cards and small gifts, then sit with a cup of tea and a home-baked snack. ✉ *85 High St.* ☎ *01343/820981.*

Watts Antiques. Watts Antiques has small collectibles, jewelry, ornaments, and china. ✉ *45 High St.* ☎ *01343/820077.*

CULLEN

★   *13 mi east of Fochabers, 3 mi east of Findochty.*

Look for some wonderfully painted homes at Cullen, in the old fishing town below the railway viaduct. The real attractions of this charming little seaside resort, however, are its white-sand beach (the water is quite cold, though) and the fine view west toward the aptly named Bowfiddle Rock. In summer Cullen bustles with families carrying buckets and spades and eating ice cream and chips.

A stroll past the small but once busy harbor reveals numerous fishers' cottages, huddled together with small yards where they dried their nets. Beyond these, the vast stretch of beach curves gently round the bay. Above is the disused Victorian viaduct—formerly the Peterhead train line—and the 18th-century town.

GETTING HERE AND AROUND
Cullen is on A98, on Cullen Bay.

EXPLORING

Seafield Street. The town has a fine mercat (market) cross and one main street—Seafield Street—that splits the town. It holds numerous specialty shops—antiques and gift stores, an ironmonger, a baker, a pharmacy, and a locally famous ice-cream shop among them—as well as several cafés.

Ice Cream Shop. In summer it can seem as if everyone you see in Cullen is licking a cone from the Ice Cream Shop. It sells just a handful of flavors but they are all made on-site. ✉ *40 Seafield St.* ☎ *01542/840484.*

NEED A BREAK?

Linda's Fish & Chips. This place serves the freshest fish, caught in nearby Buckie and cooked to crispy perfection. There's a seating area inside, but walk down the hill and head toward the harbor for some benches with sweeping views. ✉ *54 Seafield St.* ☎ *01542/840202.*

WHERE TO EAT AND STAY
For expanded hotel reviews, visit Fodors.com.

¢   ✕ **Puddleduck Patch.** The name suggests something child or duck related,
CAFÉ   but this cheery café serves uncomplicated and fresh lunches, including chunky sandwiches oozing tasty fillings and Cullen skink (a popular

soup made from smoked fish). There's also a mountain of cakes from which to choose. ⊠ *Seafield St.* ☎ *01542/841888.*

$ ⚑ **Academy House.** About 10 minutes from the seaside town of Cullen,
★ this bed-and-breakfast in a handsome Victorian house was once the headmaster's house for the local secondary school. **Pros:** good home cooking; delightful setting. **Cons:** rooms book up fast; there's little to do in Fordyce. ⊠ *School Rd., Fordyce* ☎ *01261/842743* ⊕ *www. fordyceaccommodation.com* ⤳ *2 rooms* ⚭ *In-room: no a/c, Wi-Fi. In-hotel: some pets allowed* ⊟ *No credit cards* ❚❂❚ *Breakfast.*

SHOPPING

Abra Antiques. With surprisingly pleasing prices, Abra Antiques over-flows with all kinds of trinkets, Victoriana, antiquarian books, and Scottish miscellany. ⊠ *6 Seafield St.* ☎ *01542/840605.*

BANFF

36 mi east of Elgin, 47 mi north of Aberdeen.

Midway along the northeast coast, overlooking Moray Firth and the estuary of the River Deveron, Banff is a fishing town of considerable elegance that feels as though it's a million miles from tartan-clad Scot-land. Part Georgian, like Edinburgh's New Town, and part 16th-century small burgh, like Culross, Banff is an exemplary east-coast salty town, with a tiny harbor and fine architecture. It's also within easy reach of plenty of unspoiled coastline—cliff and rock to the east, at Gardens-town (known as Gamrie) and Pennan, or beautiful little sandy beaches westward toward Sandend and Cullen.

GETTING HERE AND AROUND

Banff is on the A98 coastal road and at the end of the tree-lined A947 to Aberdeen. If you are relying on public transportation, Bus 325 from Aberdeen Bus Station takes two hours and gets you into Low Street, just five minutes from Duff House.

ESSENTIALS

Visitor Information Banff ⊠ *Collie Lodge, Low St.* ☎ *01261/812419* ⊗ *Apr.–Sept.*

EXPLORING

★ **Duff House.** The jewel in Banff's crown is the grand mansion of Duff House, a splendid William Adam–designed (1689–1748) Georgian mansion. Restored as an outstation of the National Galleries of Scot-land, it exhibits many fine paintings, including works by El Greco, Sir Henry Raeburn, and Thomas Gainsborough, in rooms furnished to reflect the days when the dukes of Fife occupied the house. A good tea-room and a shop are on the ground floor. ⊠ *Off A98* ☎ *01261/818181* ⊕ *www.duffhouse.org.uk* ⤳ *£6.85* ⊗ *Apr.–Oct., daily 11–5; Nov.–Mar., Thurs.–Sun. 11–4.*

⚉ **Macduff Marine Aquarium.** Across the river in Banff's twin town, Macduff, on the shore east of the harbor, stands the conical Macduff Marine Aquarium. A 250,000-gallon central tank and many smaller display areas and touch pools show the sea life of the Moray Firth and North Atlantic. There's always some creature being fed around 2, as well as divers handfeeding the fish and rock pool displays. ✉ *11 High Shore* ☎ *01261/833369* ⊕ *www.macduff-aquarium.org.uk* 🎫 *£5.90* 🕙 *April.– Oct., weekdays 10–4, weekends 10–5; Nov.–Mar., Sat.–Wed. 11–4.*

FYVIE CASTLE

18 mi south of Banff, 18 mi northwest of Ellon.

GETTING HERE AND AROUND

If you're driving from Banff, take the A947 south for 20 minutes or so until you see the turnoff.

EXPLORING

Fyvie Castle. In an area rich with castles, Fyvie Castle stands out as the most complex. Five great towers built by five successive powerful families turned a 13th-century foursquare castle into an opulent Edwardian statement of wealth. Some superb paintings are on view, including 12 works by Sir Henry Raeburn, and there are myriad sumptuous interiors; you can also explore many walks on the castle grounds. A former lady of the house, Lillia Drummond, was apparently starved to death by her husband, who entombed her body inside the walls of a secret room. In the 1920s, when the bones were disrupted during renovations, a string of such terrible misfortunes followed that they were quickly returned and the room sealed off. Her name is carved into the windowsill of the Drummond Room. ✉ *Off A947, Turriff* ☎ *0844/493–2182* ⊕ *www. nts.org.uk* 🎫 *£11* 🕙 *Apr.–June and Sept., Sat.–Wed. noon–5; July and Aug., daily 11–5; last admission 45 mins before closing.*

ELLON

32 mi southwest of Banff, 14 mi north of Aberdeen.

Formerly a market center on what was then the lowest bridging point of the River Ythan, Ellon, a bedroom suburb of Aberdeen, is a small town at the center of a rural hinterland. It's also well placed for visiting Fyvie Castle and Haddo House.

GETTING HERE AND AROUND

To get to Ellon, take the A947 from Banff or the A90 from Aberdeen; both routes take half an hour.

EXPLORING

Fodor's Choice **Haddo House.** Built in 1732, this elegant mansion has a light and grace-
★ ful Georgian design, with curving wings on either side of a harmonious, symmetrical facade. The interior is late-Victorian ornate, filled with magnificent paintings (including works by Pompeo Batoni and Sir Thomas Lawrence) and plenty of objets d'art. Pre-Raphaelite stained-glass windows by Sir Edward Burne-Jones grace the chapel. Outside is a terrace garden with a fountain, and few yards farther is Haddo Country Park, which has walking trails leading to memorials about the Gordon family. Visits are by prebooked tour only. The house is 8 mi northwest of Ellon. ✉ *Off B999* ☎ *0844/493–2179* ⊕ *www.nts.org.uk* 🎫 *£9* 🕙 *Easter–June. and Sept.–Oct., Fri.–Mon., tours at 11:30, 1:30, and 3:30; July and Aug., daily, guided tours at 11:30, 1:30, and 3:30.*

Argyll and the Isles

WORD OF MOUTH

"Just to add to the recommendation for Arran, it is referred to as Scotland in miniature. It's easy to get there via ferry and there's plenty to do on the island with two castles (one a ruin, the other intact), stone circles, and the Heritage Museum. Also plenty of wonderful walks and villages."

—historytraveler

"If whisky is the important part, by all means choose Islay. It is an interesting island with plenty of beauty spots, historic sites, and Highland cows. For wildlife you can always make the short ferry ride to Jura, where the deer far outnumber people. BTW they also make a very nice whisky on Jura."

—HollydaleK

Updated
by Mike
Gonzalez

Argyll's rocky seaboard looks out onto islands that were once part of a single prehistoric landmass. Here narrow roads wind around natural obstacles, slowing travel but forcing you to see and admire the lochs, the woods, and the ruins that hint at the region's dramatic past. Highlights include everything from grand houses such as Brodick Castle and gardens such as Crarae to the excellent walks on the small western isles. This is whisky country, too: the distilleries on Islay should not be missed. Distances are relatively small, as the area is within three hours of Glasgow.

Divided in two by the long peninsula of Kintyre, western Scotland has a complicated, splintered coastline. Looking out onto the islands and the Atlantic Ocean beyond, it is breathtakingly beautiful, though it often catches extremely wet ocean weather. Locals say that you can experience four seasons in a single day, and cliffs and woods can suddenly and dramatically disappear and re-emerge from sea mist. Oak woods and bracken-covered hillsides dot the region, and the everywhere you'll encounter the bright interplay of sea, loch, and rugged green peninsula.

Ruined ancient castles like Dunstaffnage, Kilchurn, and the towers on the islands of Loch Awe give testimony to the region's past importance. The stone circles, carved stones, and Bronze and Iron Age burial mounds around Kilmartin and on Islay are reminders of even earlier periods, when prehistoric peoples left their mark here. More recent grand houses, like Inveraray Castle and Brodick Castle on the island of Arran, guard their own historic interiors, filled with art and antique furniture. Their grounds, nourished by the temperate west coast climate, hold great gardens that are the pride of Argyll. Crarae, south of Inveraray, has winding paths through plantings of magnolias and azaleas, and Ardkinglas Woodland Garden holds an outstanding conifer collection. The gardens of the isle of Gigha display surprising tropical plants that have benefited from the protected climate of the island.

The working people of Glasgow traditionally spent their family holidays on the Clyde estuary, taking day trips to Dunoon or Rothesay on the Isle of Bute. Carrick Castle and Benmore Garden are a short trip from Dunoon. From Ardrossan, further down the coast, ferries cruise to the prosperous and varied Isle of Arran.

Western Scotland's small islands have jagged cliffs or tongues of rock, long white-sand beaches, fertile pastures where sheep and cattle graze, fortresses, and shared memories of clan wars and mysterious beasts. Their cliff paths and loch-side byways are a paradise for walkers and cyclists, and their whisky the ideal reward after a long day outside. While the islands' western coasts are dramatic, their more sheltered

TOP REASONS TO GO

Whisky, whisky, whisky: Take the "whisky trail" in Port Ellen on the Isle of Islay; it's a leisurely 3-mi stroll passing Ardbeg, Laphroaig, and Lagavulin distilleries, whose whiskies share the distinct flavors of peat, seaweed, and iodine. Arran, Oban, and Jura have their own unique distilleries. All have plenty of local character and provide an intimate visiting experience.

Seaside biking: Oban and Arran are two great cycling destinations. Biking along the coast provides breathtaking scenery; just keep in mind that it rains a lot in this part of the country, so bring rain gear.

Iona and its abbey: Maybe it's the remoteness—especially if you explore beyond the abbey—that adds to the almost mystical sense of history here, but a visit to this early center of Scottish Christianity is a magical experience. This was also the burial place of Scottish kings until the 11th century.

Fantastic fishing and golf: The largest skate in Britain are found in the waters off the Isle of Mull. There are 20 coastal settlements suited to sea angling where charter-boat companies offer trips. If it's loch and river sites you're after, there are 50 for game fishing that yield salmon, trout, and other fish. Prefer to tee off? Western Scotland has about two dozen golf courses, notably some fine coastal links. Machrihanish, near Campbeltown, is the best known.

Glorious gardens: Plants flourish in the mild Gulf Steam that brushes against this broken, western coastline. For vivid flowers, trees, birds, and butterflies, visit Crarae Garden, southwest of Inveraray. The Achamore House Gardens on the Isle of Gigha are another colorful extravaganza.

8

eastern seaboards are the location for the pretty harbor towns like the brightly painted Tobermory on Mull, or Port Ellen, with its neat rows of low whitewashed houses, on Islay. Arran is often said to be Scotland in miniature, the rich green fields of the southern part of the island giving way to the challenging Goatfell in the north.

ORIENTATION AND PLANNING

GETTING ORIENTED

With long sea lochs carved into its hilly, wooded interior, Argyll is a beguiling interweaving of water and land. The Kintyre Peninsula stretches between the islands of the Firth of Clyde (including Arran) and the islands of the Inner Hebrides. Ferry services allow all kinds of interisland tours and can shorten mainland trips as well.

On land, you can take the A85 to Oban (convenient for the ferry to Mull) past barren hills and into the forest of Argyll after Loch Lomond (and the A82) ends. The roads grow narrower as they wind around the banks of Loch Awe and Loch Etive. Alternatively, you can turn off the A82 at Arrochar and trace the longer route around Loch Fyne, once an active fishing center, to Inveraray and down to Campbeltown. Along the way you'll pass Kennacraig, where ferries sail to Isay and Jura.

Arran. Touring this island will give you a glimpse of the whole of Scotland in a day or two. In the north, the forbidding Goatfell is a challenge that draws walkers and climbers. The island's wilder west coast attracts bird-watchers and naturalists, while the fertile south of the island contains nine lovely golf courses, leisurely walks, and Brodick Castle.

Islay and Jura. The smell of peat that hangs in the air on Islay is bottled in its famous whiskies. Aside from distilleries, the island's historical sites evoke a past in which these islands were far less remote. The whitewashed cottages along its coast line clean and beautiful beaches, many of them visited by a variety of wildlife.

Iona and the Isle of Mull. The pretty harbor of Tobermory, with its painted houses, is a relaxing base from which to explore the varied and beautiful island of Mull. Along Mull's west coast, spectacular cliffs and rocky beaches look out on to the Atlantic. From Craignure, the road crosses the sweeping green valleys of the Ross of Mull to Fionnphort and the ferry to the meditative island of Iona.

Argyll. The twin peninsulas of Kintyre are thickly wooded areas broken up by long, pretty lochs. From Inverarary at the head of Loch Fyne, you can take in Auchindrain's re-created fishing village on the way to the Arran ferry. Or turn west toward Crinan and the prehistoric sites around Kilmartin, then travel northward toward Loch Awe and its intriguing island ruins. A short drive away is Oban, the busy resort where you catch the island ferries.

The Smaller Islands. These islands seem closer to the remoter Outer Hebrides than to the greener pastures of Mull or Arran. Abandoned by many of their original inhabitants, they are havens for birdlife, particularly Coll's giant dunes or the cliffs of Tiree. Colonsay's Kiloran Bay is open to the Atlantic's breakers, while Tiree's waves draw surfers from around the world.

PLANNING

WHEN TO GO

This part of the mainland is close enough to Glasgow that it's convenient to reach year-round. Oban is just over two hours from the city by car (three hours by bus), but getting to the isles via ferries takes longer. You can take advantage of quiet roads and plentiful accommodations in early spring and late autumn. The summer months of July and August can get very busy indeed; book accommodations and restaurants in advance during high season, or you'll miss out. In winter, short daylight hours and winds can make island stays rather bleak.

This is a coastal region, buffeted by Atlantic winds and rains. The climate is erratic, and locals take a curious pride in the fact that the area often experiences several seasons in a single day. Come prepared with adequate clothing for the changing weather, including good walking shoes, waterproof outerwear, and sunscreen.

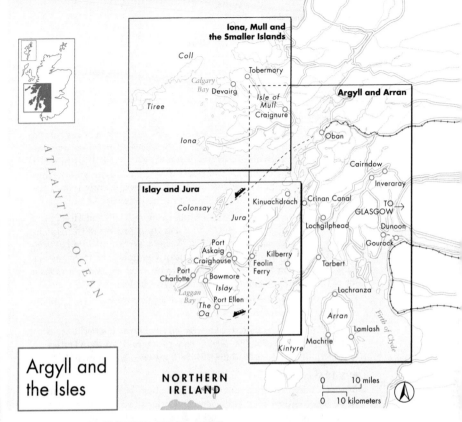

Argyll and
the Isles

PLANNING YOUR TIME

You could easily spend a week exploring the islands alone, so consider spending at least a few nights in this region. Argyll and some island excursions make pleasant and easy side trips from Glasgow and Loch Lomond. Driving anywhere here takes a little longer than you'd think, so allow ample travel time. A leisurely day will take you to Inveraray, its castle, and the surrounding gardens (don't miss the folk museum at Auchindrain). From there you can drive on to Ardrossan and take the ferry to Arran. Spend the night and see the gardens and Brodick Castle before returning to Kennacraig to take the ferry for Islay and Jura. Two or three days here will give you a sense of the history and varied landscapes of these stunning islands—and time for a distillery or two. If time is a constraint, begin in Oban and sail to Mull, returning the same day or the next to take in the Scottish Sealife Sanctuary. And if you can, drive around Loch Awe on your way back to Glasgow.

Plan ahead: ferries fill up in the summer months, and some of the smaller islands are served only once or twice a week. Bear in mind that it is not easy to find places to eat after 9 pm at any time of year—though you can usually find a place that will sell you a whisky.

GETTING HERE AND AROUND

AIR TRAVEL

Flybe operates flights from Glasgow to Campbeltown, Islay, Tiree, and Mull.

Air Travel Contacts Flybe ☎ 08717/002000 ⊕ www.flybe.com.

BOAT AND FERRY TRAVEL

Caledonian MacBrayne (CalMac) operates car-ferry services to and from the main islands; timetables can be accessed from its website. It is important to plan ahead when traveling to the islands in order to coordinate the connecting ferries; CalMac can advise you on this. Multiple-island tickets are available and can significantly reduce the cost of island-hopping, and give you a memorable trip.

CalMac ferries run from Oban to Mull, Lismore, Coll, and Tiree; from Kennacraig to Islay, Jura, and Gigha; and from Ardrossan to Arran as well as a number of shorter routes. Western Ferries operate between Dunoon, in Argyll, and Gourock, west of Glasgow. The ferry passage between Dunoon and Gourock is one frequented by locals; it saves a lot of time, and you can take your car across as well.

Ferry reservations are needed if you have a car; passengers traveling by foot do not need to make reservations.

Boat and Ferry Travel Contacts Caledonian MacBrayne (*CalMac*). ✉ *Ferry terminal, Gourock* ☎ 0800/066–5000 ⊕ www.calmac.co.uk. **Western Ferries** ✉ *Hunter's Quay, Dunoon* ☎ 01369/704452 ⊕ www.western-ferries.co.uk.

BUS TRAVEL

You can travel throughout the region by bus, but service here tends to be less frequent than elsewhere in Scotland. Scottish Citylink runs daily service from Glasgow's Buchanan Street Station to the mid-Argyll region and Kintyre; the trip to Oban takes about three hours. Several other companies provide local service within the region.

Bus Contacts B. Mundell Ltd ☎ 01496/840273. **Bowman's Tours** ☎ 01631/566809 ⊕ www.bowmanscoaches.co.uk. **Islay Coaches** ☎ 01496/840273. **Jura Bus** ☎ 01496/820314. **Royal Mail** ☎ 08457/740740. **Scottish Citylink** ☎ 0871/266–3333 ⊕ www.citylink.co.uk. **Stagecoach West Scotland** ☎ 01292/613502 ⊕ www.stagecoachbus.com. **West Coast Motors** ☎ 01586/552319 ⊕ www.westcoastmotors.co.uk.

CAR TRAVEL

Negotiating this area is easy except in July and August, when the roads around Oban may be congested. There are some single-lane roads, especially on the east side of the Kintyre Peninsula and on the islands. You'll probably have to board a ferry at some point during your trip; nearly all ferries take cars as well as pedestrians.

From Glasgow, you can take the A85 to Oban, the main ferry terminal for Mull (about 2½ hours by car). The A83 rounds Loch Fyne to Inveraray; from there you can take the A819 from Inveraray around Loch Awe and rejoin the Glasgow–Oban road. Alternatively, you can stay on the A83 and head down Kintyre to Kennacraig, the ferry terminal for Islay. Farther down the A83 is Tayinloan, the ferry port for

Gigha. You can reach Brodick on Arran by ferry from Ardrossan, on the Clyde coast (M8/A78 from Glasgow); in summer, you can travel to Lochranza from Claonaig on the Kintyre Peninsula.

TRAIN TRAVEL

Oban and Ardrossan are the main rail stations; it's a three-hour trip from Glasgow to Oban. For information call ScotRail. All trains connect with ferries.

Trail Contacts **ScotRail** ☎ *0845/601–5929* ⊕ *www.scotrail.co.uk.*

RESTAURANTS

Until recently this part of Scotland had few restaurants of distinction. Today, though, more and more quality restaurants are opening and using the excellent local produce—fine fish and shellfish, lamb, and excellent venison, as well as game of many kinds. Most hotels and many guesthouses offer evening meals, though the quality can vary. Bear in mind that most restaurants and pubs stop serving food by nine in the evening; lunch usually ends at 2:30.

HOTELS

Accommodations in Argyll and on the isles range from country-house hotels—once home to landowning families—to homes and farms offering a bed and breakfast. Most small, traditional, provincial hotels in coastal resorts have updated and modernized (while still retaining personalized service). And though hotels often have a restaurant offering evening meals, the norm for bed-and-breakfasts is to offer breakfast only.

WHAT IT COSTS IN POUNDS				
¢	$	$$	$$$	$$$$
RESTAURANTS under £10	£10–£14	£15–£19	£20–£25	over £25
HOTELS under £70	£70–£120	£121–£160	£161–£220	over £220

Restaurant prices are for a main course at dinner. Hotel prices are for two people in a standard double room in high season, generally including the 20% V.A.T.

TOURS

BOAT TOURS

Getting out on the water is a wonderful way to see the landscape of the islands and also sea life.

Gordon Grant Tours leads an excursion from Oban to Mull, Iona, and Staffa and leaves Mull on other trips to Treshnish Isles and Staffa. From Taynuilt, near Oban, boat trips are available from Loch Etive Cruises Easter through October. Sea Life Surveys offers four- and six-hour whale-watching and wildlife day trips from Tobermory, on the Isle of Mull.

Turas-Mara runs daily excursions in summer from Oban and Mull to Staffa, Iona, and the Treshnish Isles and specializes in wildlife tours. On a daylong trip to the Treshnish islands, you might see puffins, seals, otters, and, at certain times of year, dolphins and the occasional whale. Staffa is the site of Fingal's Cave, immortalized by Mendelssohn's overture.

Boat Tour Contacts **Gordon Grant Tours** ⊠ *Railway Pier, Achavaich, Isle of Iona* ☎ *01681/700338* ⊕ *www.staffatours.com.* **Loch Etive Cruises** ⊠ *Kelly's Pier, Etive View, Taynuilt* ☎ *01866/822430.* **Sea Life Surveys** ⊠ *Taigh Solais, Ledaig, Tobermory* ☎ *01688/302916* ⊕ *www.sealifesurveys.com.* **Turas-Mara** ⊠ *Penmore Mill, Dervaig* ☎☎ *01688/400242* ⊕ *www.turasmara.com.*

BUS TOURS

Many of the bus companies in the area also arrange sightseeing tours, so check with them (see Getting Here and Around, above). Bowman's Tours runs trips from Oban.

Bus Tour Contacts **Bowman's Tours** ⊠ *Waterfront, Railway Pier, Oban* ☎ *01631/563221* ⊕ *www.bowmanstours.co.uk.*

VISITOR INFORMATION

The tourist offices in Lochgilphead, Tarbert, and Tobermory (Mull) are open April through October only; other offices are open year-round.

Contacts **Visit Scottish Heartlands** ⊕ *www.visitscottishheartlands.com.*

AROUND ARGYLL

Topographical grandeur and rocky shores are what make Argyll special. Try to take to the water at least once, even if your time is limited. The sea and the sea lochs have played a vital role in the history of western Scotland since the time of the war galleys of the clans. Oban is the major ferry gateway and transport hub, with a main road leading south into the Kintyre Peninsula.

OBAN

96 mi northwest of Glasgow, 125 mi northwest of Edinburgh, 50 mi south of Fort William, 118 mi southwest of Inverness.

It's almost impossible to avoid Oban when touring the west. Its waterfront has some character, but the town's main role is as a launch point for excursions into Argyll and for ferry trips to the islands. A traditional Scottish resort town, Oban has many music festivals, *ceilidhs* with Highland dancing, as well as all the usual tartan kitsch and late-night revelry in pubs and hotel bars. The Oban Distillery is on Stafford Street in town, offering tours and a shop. Still, there are more exciting destinations just over the horizon, on the islands and down Kintyre.

GETTING HERE AND AROUND

From Glasgow, the A82 along Loch Lomond meets the A85 at Crianlarich. Turn left and continue to Oban. In summer the center of Oban can become gridlocked with ferry traffic, so leave yourself time for the wait. Alternatively, the A816 from Lochgilphead enters Oban from the less crowded south. Train services run from Glasgow to Oban (ScotRail); bus services from Glasgow to Oban by Scottish Citylink run several times a day.

ESSENTIALS

Visitor Information **Oban** ⊠ *Argyll Sq.* ☎ *08707/200630* ⊕ *www.visitscotland.com.*

EXPLORING

Dunstaffnage Castle. Four miles north of Oban stands Dunstaffnage Castle, an important stronghold of the MacDougall clan in the 13th century. From the ramparts you have outstanding views across the **Sound of Mull** and the **Firth of Lorne,** a nautical crossroads of sorts, once watched over by Dunstaffnage Castle and commanded by the galleys (*birlinn* in Gaelic) of the Lords of the Isles. ⊠ *Off A85* ☎ *01631/562465* ⊕ *www.historic-scotland.gov.uk/places* ◩ *£4* ☉ *Apr.–Sept., daily 9:30–5:30; Oct., daily 9:30–4:30; Nov.–Mar., Mon.–Wed. and weekends 9:30–4:30.*

♻ **Scottish Sealife Sanctuary.** At the sanctuary kids and adults love the outstanding display of marine life, including shoals of herring, sharks, rays, catfish, otters, and seals. Many of the animals have been rescued, and this is where they receive rehabilitation before being released into the wild. There is also a beautiful aquarium, and kids will appreciate the adventure playground and gift shop. The restaurant serves morning coffee, plus a full lunch menu and afternoon tea. To get here, drive north from Oban for 10 mi on the A828; West Coast Motors also provides a regular bus service. ⊠ *Barcaldine, off A828, Connel* ☎ *01631/720386* ⊕ *www.sealsanctuary.co.uk* ◩ *£12.50* ☉ *Jan.–mid-Feb., weekends 10–3; Mar.–Oct., daily 10–5; Nov.–Dec., daily 10–4. Last admission 1 hr before closing.*

WHERE TO EAT

$$
SEAFOOD
✗ **Ee-usk.** This clean-lined, modern restaurant's name means "fish" in Gaelic, and it has earned quite a reputation for serving excellent seafood dishes made with the freshest fish and shellfish delivered directly from Oban's harbor. The signature creations use plain sauces; try oven-baked wild halibut with creamed leeks or the full-scale seafood platter. Good-value options are fixed-price menus for lunch (£11.50 for two courses) and dinner (£15.95 or £17.95 for two or three courses). On clear days, there are nice views of the islands through the large glass windows. ⊠ *North Pier* ☎ *01631/565666* ⊕ *www.eeusk.com* ☉ *Closed Sun.*

¢
CAFÉ
✗ **Kitchen Garden.** Directly across the road from the ferry port, this delicatessen serves good homemade soups, panini, and sandwiches as well as fresh cakes. Service is sometimes a little slow; prices are reasonable and the location is quite convenient. ⊠ *14 George St., North Pier* ☎ *01631/566332* ☉ *No dinner.*

WHERE TO STAY

For expanded hotel reviews, visit Fodors.com.

$
🏨 **Glenburnie House.** At this typical seafront guesthouse in a Victorian house with fine views over Oban Bay, most rooms are spacious and comfortable, if slightly overdecorated in traditional style. **Pros:** centrally located; good sea views. **Cons:** too many flowery fabrics for some tastes; slightly expensive for what you get; no elevator. ⊠ *Esplanade* ☎ *01631/562089* ⊕ *www.glenburnie.co.uk* ⇖ *12 rooms* ☉ *Closed mid-Nov.–Feb.* ⊠ *Breakfast.*

$
🏨 **Kilchrenan House.** Just a few minutes' walk from the town center, this Victorian-era stone house has been fully refurbished and transformed into a lovely bed-and-breakfast. **Pros:** great sea views; tasteful

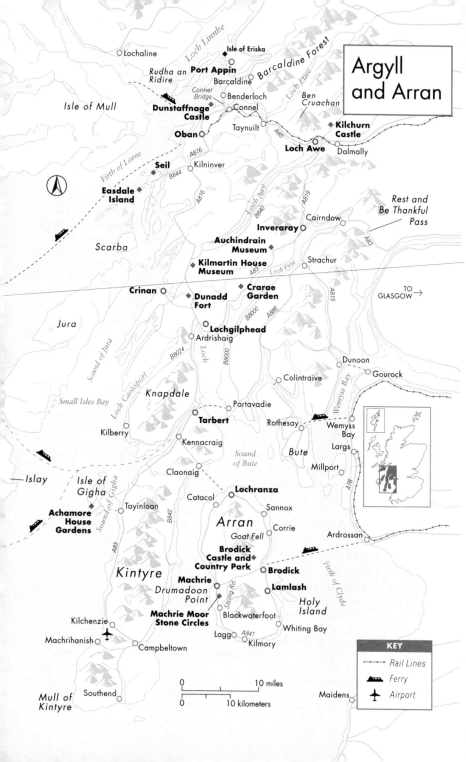

attention to detail. **Cons:** some bedrooms may be too colorfully deco-rated for some tastes; attic rooms on the top floor have a slanting roof that can be irritating. ⊠ *Corran Esplanade* ☎ *01631/562663* ⊕ *www.kilchrenanhouse.co.uk* ⟿ *10 rooms* ♿ *In-room: no a/c. In-hotel: bar* ☉ *Closed Dec. and Jan.* ✝⊙✝ *Breakfast.*

$$$ 🏠 **Manor House Hotel.** On the coast near Oban, this 1780 stone house—once the home of the duke of Argyll—has wonderful sea views; public areas are furnished with antiques, and the bedrooms are filled with lovely reproductions. **Pros:** excellent restaurant; location near all nec-essary amenities. **Cons:** smallish bedrooms, only five with a view; no children under 12. ⊠ *Gallanach Rd.* ☎ *01631/562087* ⊕ *www.manorhouseoban.com* ⟿ *11 rooms* ♿ *In-room: no a/c, Internet, Wi-Fi. In-hotel: restaurant, bar, some age restrictions* ✝⊙✝ *Breakfast.*

$ 🏠 **Ronebhal Guest House.** You can see Loch Etive and the mountains beyond from this stone house 5 mi east of Oban (in Connel), set back within its own lovely grounds; rooms are light and modern, and some have expansive bay windows. **Pros:** nice library; good breakfast. **Cons:** some slightly worn decor; several rooms don't have a private bathroom; no children under seven. ⊠ *A85, Connel* ☎ *01631/710310* ⊕ *www.ronebhal.co.uk* ⟿ *6 rooms, 4 with bath* ♿ *In-room: no a/c, Wi-Fi. In-hotel: bar, some age restrictions* ☉ *Closed Dec. and Jan.* ✝⊙✝ *Breakfast.*

SPORTS AND THE OUTDOORS

BICYCLING **Oban Cycles.** You can rent bicycles from Oban Cycles, whose shopkeep-ers will give you advice on waterside routes as far out as Ganavan Bay and Dunstaffnage Castle. ⊠ *29 Lochside St.* ☎ *01631/566996.*

FISHING **Gannet.** This charter-fishing company run by Adrian Lauder offers full-day sea-angling trips for £500 for 6 hours or £800 for 10 hours; a light lunch is included. Fishing parties are limited to 10 people (8 for skate fishing); the cost is divided among the number of people who book the trip. ⊠ *3 Kiel Croft, Benderloch* ☎ *01631/720262* ⊕ *www.obanfishing.co.uk.*

8

APPIN

The little peninsula of Appin, some 20-minutes' drive from Oban, is a charming, well-kept secret. Just 2 mi along a narrow road from the main Fort William route (A828), the bay opens to Lismore and the sea. Castle Stalker, a privately owned castle on the water, sits magnificently in the center of the picture, a symbol of ancient coastal Scotland. This is an excellent, uncrowded base for walking, fishing, water sports, and cycling. The Appin Rocks, on the headland, are frequently visited by seals.

GETTING HERE AND AROUND

From Oban, follow the A828 around Loch Creran and take the left turn to Port Appin just beyond Tynribbie. Continue for just over 2 mi to the old pier. From the port, the passenger ferry runs to the island of Lismore throughout the year; steamers once plied the waters of Loch Linnhe, but today the largest boats here are those taking workers to the quarries of Kingairloch.

WHERE TO STAY

For expanded hotel reviews, visit Fodors.com.

$$$$ ⭐ 🏨 **Airds Hotel and Restaurant.** The old ferry inn for travelers visiting Lismore now houses this luxurious small hotel; rooms are stylish and restrained, with superb views either toward the sea or the woods behind. **Pros:** fabulous views from the breakfast room; spare boots for the unprepared; beautiful location. **Cons:** an expensive option; dinner being included in the cost might not appeal to all. ✉ *A828, Port Appin* ☎ *01631/730236* ⊕ *www.airds-hotel.com* ⮌ *9 rooms, 2 suites, 1 cottage* ⚅ *In-room: Wi-Fi. In-hotel: restaurant, bar, some pets allowed* �’⊙ *Some meals.*

$$$$ 🏨 **Isle of Eriska.** A severe, baronial-style granite facade belies the sense of welcome within this hotel, set on its own island 10 mi north of Oban and accessible by a bridge from the mainland; the rooms are individual and luxurious in their detail, and a range of outdoor activities is available, as are a spa, pools, and gyms—all on the island. **Pros:** exceptional food; good service; peace and quiet. **Cons:** you're in the middle of nowhere, so you don't have a lot of choice when it comes to dining out. ✉ *Off A828, Eriska* ☎ *01631/720371* ⊕ *www.eriska-hotel. co.uk* ⮌ *25 rooms* ⚅ *In-room: no a/c. In-hotel: restaurant, golf course, pool, tennis court, gym, spa* �’⊙ *Multiple meal plans.*

$$ 🏨 **Pierhouse Hotel.** The twin round towers of the old pier mark the entrance to this hotel and restaurant, appealingly situated on the water's edge beside the Port Appin jetty; rooms are quite small, but clean and comfortable. **Pros:** breathtaking view across the loch; lively, warm atmosphere; good restaurant. **Cons:** rooms are a little small; not all rooms have views over the water. ✉ *Port Appin* ☎ *01631/730302* ⊕ *www.pierhousehotel.co.uk* ⮌ *12 rooms* ⚅ *In-room: no a/c, Wi-Fi. In-hotel: restaurant, bar, parking, some pets allowed* �’⊙ *Multiple meal plans.*

LOCH AWE

18 mi east of Oban.

At more than 25 mi long, Loch Awe is Scotland's longest stretch of fresh water. Its northwest shore is quiet; forest walks crisscross the Inverliever Forest here. At the loch's northern end tiny islands, many with ruins, pepper the water. One, Inishail, is home to a 13th-century chapel.

GETTING HERE AND AROUND

From Oban the A85 will bring you to the head of Loch Awe and the small town of the same name. Turn onto the B845 at Taynuilt to reach the loch's northern shore, or continue through the forbidding Pass of Brander and turn onto the A819 to get to the southern shore. From here you can continue on to Inveraray, or drive along the loch on the B840.

EXPLORING

Duncan Ban Macintyre Monument. The monument was erected in honor of this Gaelic poet (1724–1812), sometimes referred to as the Robert Burns of the Highlands. ■ **TIP→ The view from here is one of the finest in Argyll, taking in Ben Cruachan and the other peaks nearby, as well as Loch Awe and its scattering of islands.** To find the monument from Dalmally, just east of Loch Awe, follow an old road running southwest toward the banks of the loch. You can see the round, granite structure from the road's highest point, often called Monument Hill.

★ **Kilchurn Castle.** A striking ruined fortress at the northeastern end of Loch Awe, the castle was built in the 15th century by Sir Colin Campbell (d. 1493) of Glenorchy, and rebuilt in the 17th century. Airy vantage points amid the towers have fine panoramas of the surrounding highlands and loch. It is accessible on foot along an old railway line near A85. ✉ *Off A85, 2.5 mi west of Dalmally* ☎ *01866/833333* ⊕ *www. historic-scotland.gov.uk/places* ✆ *Free* ☼ *Apr.–Sept, daily.*

WHERE TO STAY

For expanded hotel reviews, visit Fodors.com.

$$ 🏨 **Taychreggan Hotel.** Once a drover's inn, this beautiful country-house hotel on the shores of Loch Awe, near Taynuilt, has spectacular views; it's a good base for walking or simply relaxing. **Pros:** lovely setting; high level of comfort. **Cons:** slightly fussy decor; a little isolated. ✉ *Off B845, Kilchrenan* ☎ *01866/833211* ⊕ *www.taychregganhotel.co.uk* ⇦ *18 rooms* ♿ *In-room: no a/c, Wi-Fi. In-hotel: restaurant, bar, parking, some pets allowed* �🍴 *Breakfast.*

EN ROUTE The A819 south to Inveraray initially runs alongside Loch Awe, but soon leaves these pleasant banks to turn east and join the A83, which carries traffic from Glasgow and Loch Lomond by way of the high **Rest and Be Thankful** pass. This quasi-alpine pass, set among high green slopes and gray rocks, is one of the most scenic points along the road.

INVERARAY

8

★ *21 mi south of Loch Awe, 61 mi north of Glasgow, 29 mi west of Loch Lomond.*

The town is a sparkling fishing village with cute shops, attractions, and the haunted Campbell Castle all within walking distance. There are lovely views of the water and plenty of fishing boats to watch; several worthwhile gardens and museums are nearby, too. On the approaches to Inveraray, note the ornate 18th-century bridgework that carries the road along the loch side. This is your first sign that Inveraray is not just a jumble of houses; in fact, much of it was designed as a planned town for the third duke of Argyll in the mid-18th century.

GETTING HERE AND AROUND

If you're driving from Oban, take the A85 and the A819 beyond Loch Awe (the village). From Glasgow, take the A82, turn on to the A83 at Arrochar, and make the long drive around Loch Fyne.

ESSENTIALS

Visitor Information Inveraray ✉ *Front St.* ☎ *01499/302063* ⊕ *www. visitscotland.com.*

EXPLORING
TOP ATTRACTIONS

Ardkinglas Woodland Garden. One of Britain's finest collections of conifers is set off by rhododendron blossoms in early summer. You'll find the garden around the head of Loch Fyne, about 10 mi east of Inveraray. The house is usually not open to visitors, though you can take a tour the second-to-last Friday of each month between April and October. ✉ *A83, Cairndow* ☎ *01499/600261* ⊕ *www.ardkinglas.com* 💰 *£4.50* ⊙ *Daily sunrise–sunset.*

★ **Auchindrain Museum.** Step a few centuries back in time at this open-air museum, a rare surviving example of an 18th-century communal tenancy farm. Its old bracken-thatch and iron-roof buildings, about 20 in all, give you a feel for early farming life in the Highland communities, and the interpretation center explains it all. Among the furnished buildings are cottages, longhouses, and barns. The museum is 6 mi south of Inveraray. ✉ *Off A83* ☎ *01499/500235* ⊕ *www.auchindrain-museum.org.uk* 💰 *£5.95* ⊙ *Apr.–Oct., daily 10–5; last admission 4.*

★ **Crarae Garden.** Well worth a visit for plant lovers is this 100-acre garden, where magnolias, azaleas, and rhododendrons flourish in the moist, lush environment around Crarae Burn (a burn is a small stream). A rocky gorge and waterfalls add appeal, and the flowers and trees attract several different species of birds and butterflies. The gardens are 10 mi southwest of Inveraray. ✉ *Off A83* ☎ *01546/886614* ⊕ *www.nts.org.uk/Visits* 💰 *£6* ⊙ *Garden daily 9:30–sunset. Visitor center Apr.–Oct., daily 10–5:45; last admission at 5.*

Inveraray Castle. The current seat of the Campbell duke is a smart, grayish-green turreted stone house with a self-satisfied air, visible through trees from the town itself. Spires on the four corner turrets give it a vaguely French look. Like the town, the castle was begun around 1743. Tours of the interior convey the history of the powerful Campbell family. There is a tearoom for snacks and light lunches. You can hike around the extensive estate grounds, but wear sturdy footwear. ✉ *Off A83* ☎ *01499/302203* ⊕ *www.inveraray-castle.com* 💰 *£10* ⊙ *Apr.–Oct., daily 10–5:45, last admission at 5.*

WORTH NOTING

⟳ **Inveraray Jail.** In this old jail, realistic courtroom scenes, carefully recreated cells, and other paraphernalia give you a glimpse of life behind bars in Victorian times—and today. The site includes a Scottish crafts shop. ✉ *Off Main St.* W ☎ *01499/302381* ⊕ *www.inverarayjail.co.uk* 💰 *£8.95* ⊙ *Apr.–Oct., daily 9:30–6; Nov.–Mar., daily 10–5; last admission 1 hr before closing.*

Loch Fyne Oysters Shop. About 10 mi northeast of Inveraray on the main A83, you can stop at the shop here to purchase delicious oysters to go, or order them to be shipped. The shop sells a wide range of other seafood too. You can also consume a dozen with a glass of wine at Loch Fyne Oysters restaurant, to which the shop is attached. ✉ *Clachan Farm, A83, Cairndow* ☎ *01499/600236* ⊕ *www.lochfyne.com* ⊙ *Daily 9–7.*

WHERE TO EAT AND STAY

For expanded hotel reviews, visit Fodors.com.

$$ ✕**Loch Fyne Oyster Bar and Restaurant.** The original restaurant in a Brit-
SEAFOOD ish chain, this well-regarded seafood spot 10 mi northeast of Inverary
sits surrounded by hills at the head of Loch Fyne, with beautiful views
in both directions. Polished wood, and paintings and sketches with
references to the sea and fishing help set the mood. Dishes are gener-
ally simple and unpretentious; try the seafood risotto or the scallops
with pea puree and pancetta, and don't miss the oysters. Note that the
restaurant closes at 7:30 in summer. ⊠ *A83, Clachan Farm, Cairndow*
☎ *01499/600482* ⊕ *www.lochfyne.com* ⚑ *Reservations essential* ☺ *No
dinner Nov.–Mar.*

$ ⊡ **The George Hotel.** The Clark family has run this 18th-century for-
Fodor'sChoice mer coaching inn at the heart of Inveraray town for six generations,
★ and the warmth of the welcome reflects the benefit of continuity: roar-
ing log fires invite repose in the common rooms, and antiques and oil
paintings in the individually decorated rooms make you feel as though
you were in a slower-paced era. **Pros:** excellent restaurant; atmospheric
stone-floored bars; hotel Scottish in every way. **Cons:** too much tartan
for some; unattractive reception area; some old mattresses. ⊠ *Main St.
E* ☎ *01499/302111* ⊕ *www.thegeorgehotel.co.uk* ⤵ *17 rooms* ⚘ *In-
room: no a/c. In-hotel: restaurant, bar* ⊙ *Breakfast.*

LOCHGILPHEAD

26 mi south of Inveraray.

Lochgilphead, the largest town in this region, looks best when the tide
is in, as Loch Gilp (really a bite out of Loch Fyne) reveals a muddy
shoreline at low tide. With a series of well-kept, colorful buildings along
its main street, this neat little town is worth a look.

GETTING HERE AND AROUND

From Inveraray continue south for 24 mi along the A83, which follows
the bank of the Loch Fyne.

SHOPPING

Highbank Collection. The factory shop here sells hand-painted pottery and
glassware, colorful ceramics, and model wooden boats. ⊠ *Highbank
Industrial Estate* ☎ *01546/602044.*

CRINAN

10 mi northwest of Lochgilphead.

Crinan is synonymous with its canal, the reason for this tiny commu-
nity's existence and its mainstay. The narrow road beside the Crinan
Hotel bustles with yachting types waiting to pass through the locks,
bringing a surprisingly cosmopolitan feel to such an out-of-the-way cor-
ner of Scotland. Also accessible from Crinan is the worthwhile Kilmar-
tin House Museum.

8

GETTING HERE AND AROUND

To reach Crinan, take the A816 Oban road north from Lochgilphead for about a mile, then turn left at Cairnbaan.

EXPLORING

Crinan Canal. The canal, a reminder of the industrial past, opened in 1801 to let fishing vessels reach Hebridean fishing grounds without making the long haul south around the Kintyre Peninsula. At its western end the canal drops to the sea in a series of locks, the last of which is beside the Crinan Hotel. Today it's popular with pleasure boats traveling to the west coast.

★ **Kilmartin House Museum.** For an exceptional encounter with early Scottish history, start at this museum 8 mi north of Crinan and then explore some of the more than 300 ancient monuments within a 6-mi radius of Kilmartin village. Exhibits provide information about the stone circles and avenues, burial mounds, and carved stones dating from the Bronze Age and earlier that are scattered thickly nearby; an audiovisual presentation helps set you on your way. Although the museum is closed in January and February, it holds some events during those months. Nearby **Dunadd Fort**, a rocky hump rising out of the level ground between Crinan and Kilmartin, was once the capital of the early kingdom of Dalriada, founded by the first wave of Scots who migrated from Ireland around AD 500. Clamber up the rock to see a basin, a footprint, and an outline of a boar carved on the smooth upper face of the knoll. ⊠ *A816, Kilmartin* ☎ *01546/510278* ⊕ *www.kilmartin.org* ⊡ *£5* ⊙ *Mar.–Oct., daily 10–5:30; Nov. and Dec., daily 11–4.*

WHERE TO STAY

For expanded hotel reviews, visit Fodors.com.

$ ⊞ **Allt-Na-Craig.** A location on the edge of the village and overlook-
★ ing Loch Fyne distinguishes this large, stone, Victorian house set in lovely gardens; rooms are traditional in style. **Pros:** atmospheric; good food and views. **Cons:** you're pretty isolated, so it helps to have a car. ⊠ *Tarbert Rd., Ardrishaig* ☎ *01546/603245* ⊕ *www.allt-na-craig.co.uk* ⊅ *5 rooms, 1 cottage* ⎐ *In-room: no a/c, Wi-Fi. In-hotel: restaurant* ‖⊙‖ *Breakfast.*

$$$ ⊞ **Crinan Hotel.** One of a group of houses around the last loch of the Crinan Canal, the hotel has a dramatic setting overlooking the Sound of Jura and Craignish Point; it echoes the style of the boats on the canal in its use of wood, and has references to fishing and the sea on its walls. **Pros:** elevator for rooms on three floors; good restaurants. **Cons:** Wi-Fi in public areas but not in rooms. ⊠ *Off B841* ☎ *01546/830261* ⊕ *www.crinanhotel.com* ⊅ *20 rooms* ⎐ *In-hotel: restaurant, bar* ‖⊙‖ *Breakfast.*

KINTYRE PENINSULA

52 mi south of Lochgilphead (to Campbeltown).

Rivers and streams crisscross this long, narrow strip of green pasture-lands and hills stretching south from Lochgilphead.

GETTING HERE AND AROUND

Continue south on the A83 (the road to Campbeltown) to Tarbert. Some 4 mi farther along the A83, just beyond Kennacraig, is the pier at Tayinloan; CalMac ferries run from here to the Isle of Gigha.

ESSENTIALS

Air Travel Contacts Campbeltown Airport ☎ *01586/553797* ⊕ *www.hial. co.uk.*

Visitor Information Campbeltown ⊠ *Mackinnon House, The Pier, Campbeltown* ☎ *01586/552056* ⊕ *www.visitscotland.com.* **Tarbert, Loch Fyne** ⊠ *Harbour St., Tarbert* ☎ *01880/820429* ⊕ *www.visitscotland.com.*

EXPLORING

Achamore House Gardens. One relic of the Isle of Gigha's aristocratic legacy is the Achamore House Gardens, which produce lush shrubberies with spectacular azalea displays in late spring. For a nimble day trip, take the 20-minute ferry to Gigha from Tayinloan and walk right over to the gardens. You may not want to take your car, as the walk is fairly easy. ⊠ *Isle of Gigha* ☎ *01583/505392* ⊕ *www.isle-of-gigha.co.uk* ⊠ *Gardens £2, ferry £5.90 per person plus £20.50 per car* ☉ *Gardens daily sunrise–sunset. Ferry Mon.–Sat. 9–5, Sun. at 11, 2, and 3.*

Isle of Gigha. Barely 7 mi long, Gigha is sheltered in a frost-free, sea-warmed climate between Kintyre and Islay, and has sandy beaches and rich wildlife. The island was long favored by British aristocrats as a summer destination. In 2002, the community purchased the island and now runs it, and the official Web site provides comprehensive information, including places to stay. ⊠ *Isle of Gigha* ☎ *01583/505392* ⊕ *www. gigha.org.uk.*

Tarbert. A name that appears throughout the Highlands, Tarbert is the Gaelic word for "place of portage," and a glance at the map tells you why it was given to this little town with a workaday waterfront: Tarbert sits on the narrow neck of land between East and West Loch Tarbert, where long ago boats were actually carried across the land to avoid looping all the way around the peninsula. The town's visitor center is on Harbour Street. ⊕ *www.visitscotland.com.*

GOLF

Machrihanish Golf Club. Gulf Stream breezes warm the club's perfectly manicured 18 holes. U.S. Navy SEAL teams-in-training have been known to drop from the air into a chilly nearby loch. ⊠ *Front Row, off A83, Campbeltown* ☎ *01586/810213* ⊕ *www.machgolf.com* ⊠ *£62 per round* ⚑ *18 holes, 6,228 yds, par 70.*

ARRAN

Approaching Arran by sea, you'll first see the forbidding Goatfell (2,868 feet) in the north, then the green fields of the south. It is this contrast and varied geography that has led visitors to describe Arran as "Scotland in Miniature." The island's temperate climate allows tropical plants to grow, and this relative warmth probably attracted the ancient cultures whose stone circles still stand on the island. This weather also explains why it has long been a favorite resort getaway for Glasgow's residents, who come here to walk, climb Goatfell, play golf on Arran's nine courses, observe the rich birdlife, and simply enjoy the sea.

GETTING HERE AND AROUND

Caledonian MacBrayne runs regular car and passenger ferries cross the Firth of Clyde from Ardrossan (near Saltcoats) to Brodick throughout the year (crossing takes just under an hour). There is also a small ferry from Claonaig on the Kintyre Peninsula to Lochranza during the summer months.

Connecting trains run to the ferry at Ardrossan from Glasgow's Queen Street station. Stagecoach runs regular local bus services around the island. Exploring the island by car is easy, as the A841 road circles it.

BRODICK

1 hr by ferry from Ardrossan.

Arran's largest village, Brodick, has a main street that is set back from the promenade and the lovely bay beyond. Other than its accommodation, there is little to keep the visitor here before exploring the island.

GETTING HERE AND AROUND

You can reach Brodick from Ardrossan by ferry. From Brodick the A841 circles the island; head south to reach Lamlash, north to reach Lochranza. The String Road crosses the island between Brodick and Machrie.

ESSENTIALS

Visitor Information Brodick, Arran ⊠ *The Pier* ☎ *01770/303774* ⊕ *www.visitscotland.com.*

EXPLORING

★ **Brodick Castle and Country Park.** Arran's biggest cultural draw is Brodick Castle, on the north side of Brodick Bay. This red-sandstone structure— parts of which date back to the 13th century—is surrounded by lush woods and parkland. Several rooms are open to the public, both in the original 16th-century section and in the Victorian additions (which illustrate the Hamilton family's opulent lifestyle). The large downstairs kitchen gives a contrasting impression—showing how servants lived— and the 87 stag heads on the stairs are a slightly disturbing reminder of how the aristocracy spent their leisure time. There is a guide in each room with all the information you need. The vast gardens, open all year, are filled with rhododendrons and azaleas. A café in the Servants' Hall serves morning coffee and homemade cakes as well as a light lunch menu.

The country park here includes **Goatfell,** at 2,867 feet the highest peak in Arran; its outline defines the island. The beautiful upland landscape is more challenging to explore than it seems, but the views from the peak merit the effort to get there. Access (all year) is from the country park or from Cladach on the A841. ⊠ *Off A841, 1 mi north of Brodick Pier* ☎ *01770/302202* ⊕ *www.nts.org.uk* ⊠ *Castle and gardens £11; gardens and country park £6* ☉ *Castle and restaurant Easter–Oct.,* *daily 11–4:30. Reception center, shop, and walled garden Easter–Oct., daily 10–4:30, Nov. and Dec., Fri.–Sun. 10–3:30. Country park daily 9:30–sunset.*

Glen Rosa. Here you can stroll through a long glen glimpsing the wild ridges that beckon so many outdoors enthusiasts. To get here from Brodick, pass the Isle of Arran Heritage Museum and find the junction where the String Road cuts across the island. Drive a short way up the String Road and turn right at the signpost into the glen. The road soon becomes undrivable; park the car and wander on foot. ✉ *Off String Rd.*

Isle of Arran Heritage Museum. The museum documents life on the island from ancient times to the present. Several buildings, including a cottage and *smiddy* (smithy), have period furnishings as well as displays on prehistoric life, farming, fishing, and other aspects of the island's social history. ✉ *Rosaburn* ☎ *01770/302636* 🌐 *www.arranmuseum.co.uk* 🎫 *£3* ⏲ *Apr.–Oct., daily 10:30–4:30.*

WHERE TO EAT AND STAY

For expanded hotel reviews, visit Fodors.com.

$ ITALIAN ✕ **Eilean-Mor Bar Bistro.** Painted bright red, this small unpretentious Italian style bar-bistro has friendly and attentive staff. The pastas, pizzas, and burgers are substantial and well made—even the haggis ravioli in whisky sauce is startlingly tasty. ✉ *Shore Rd.* ☎ *01770/302579.*

$ 🏨 **Glencloy Farmhouse.** Surrounded by colorful gardens, this 19th-century sandstone house nestles in a peaceful valley; Brodick and views of the hills and sea are a few minutes' walk away. **Pros:** outstanding breakfast; lovely location. **Cons:** plenty of the owners' personal decorations all around; access road has many potholes; some rooms share baths. ☎ *01770/302251* *5 rooms, 2 with bath* *In-room: no a/c* ⏲ *Closed Nov.–Feb.* *Breakfast.*

OUTDOOR ACTIVITIES AND SPORTS

Arran Adventure Centre. The services of this multisport company include mountain bike rentals and gorge walking and sea kayaking. ✉ *Auchranie Rd.* ☎ *01770/302244* 🌐 *www.arranadventure.com.*

SHOPPING

Arran's shops are well stocked with locally produced goods. The Home Farm is a popular shopping area with several shops and a small restaurant.

Creelers Smokery and Restaurant. The smokehouse sells delicious fish, smoked and otherwise; it also has a restaurant that offers a fixed-price lunch at £10 and dinner at £15 to £25 based on the number of courses. ✉ *The Home Farm, off A841* ☎ *01770/302810* 🌐 *www.creelers.co.uk.*

Duchess Court Shops. The shops here include Bear Necessities, with everything bear-themed; the Nature Shop, with nature-oriented books and gifts; and Arran Aromatics, one of Scotland's top makers of toiletries (lovely lavender-scented soaps and lotions, and more). ✉ *The Home Farm* ☎ *01770/302831.*

Island Cheese Company. Stop here to buy Arran blue cheese among other handmade Scottish cheeses. ✉ *The Home Farm* ☎ *01770/302788.*

LAMLASH

4 mi south of Brodick.

With views offshore to Holy Island, which is now a Buddhist retreat, Lamlash has a breezy seaside-holiday atmosphere. To reach the highest point accessible by car, go through the village and turn right beside the bridge onto Ross Road, which climbs steeply from a thickly planted valley, **Glen Scorrodale,** and yields fine views of Lamlash Bay. From Lamlash you can explore the southern part of Arran: 4 mi to the southwest, **Whiting Bay** has a pleasant well-kept waterfront and a range of hotels and guesthouses. If you travel another 6 mi, you'll reach the little community of **Lagg,** which sits peacefully by the banks of the Kilmory Water.

GETTING HERE AND AROUND

You can reach Lamlash by driving south from Brodick on the A841. The town is also served by Stagecoach buses.

WHERE TO STAY

For expanded hotel reviews, visit Fodors.com.

$ ★ 🏨 **Lagg Hotel.** Arran's oldest inn is an 18th-century lodge with fireplaces in the common rooms and 11 acres of gardens and grounds that meander down to the river. **Pros:** beautiful gardens; warming fireplaces; good-size rooms. **Cons:** floral designs everywhere. ⊠ *Kilmory, Isle of Arran* 🕾 *01770/870255* ⊕ *www.lagghotel.com* ⇆ *13 rooms* ♢ *In-room: no a/c. In-hotel: restaurant, bar* ◯│ *Breakfast.*

SHOPPING

Patterson Arran. The store is famous for its preserves and marmalades, as well as its mustards. ⊠ *The Old Mill* 🕾 *01770/600606.*

MACHRIE

10 mi west of Brodick, 11 mi north of Lagg.

The area surrounding Machrie, home to a popular beach, is littered with prehistoric sites: chambered cairns, hut circles, and standing stones dating from the Bronze Age.

GETTING HERE AND AROUND

The quick route to Machrie is via the String Road (B880) from Brodick; turn off onto the Machrie Road 5 mi outside Brodick. A much longer but stunning journey will take you from Brodick, north to Lochranza, around the island to Machrie, and down the island's dramatic west coast, a distance of some 28 mi.

EXPLORING

★ **Machrie Moor Stone Circles.** From Machrie, a well-surfaced track takes you to a grassy moor by a ruined farm, where you can see the Machrie Moor Stone Circles: small, rounded granite-boulder circles and much taller, eerie red-sandstone monoliths. Out on the bare moor, the lost and lonely stones are very evocative, well worth a walk to see if you like the feeling of solitude. The stones are about 1 mi outside of Machrie; just follow the "Historic Scotland" sign pointing the way. ⊕ *www.historic-scotland.gov.uk.*

HORSEBACK RIDING

Cairnhouse Riding Centre. Even novices can enjoy a guided ride on a mount from the center. ⊠ *A84, 2 mi south of Machrie, Blackwaterfoot* ☎ *01770/860466* ⊕ *www.cairnhousestables.com.*

SHOPPING

Old Byre Showroom. This shop sells sheepskin goods, hand-knit sweaters, designer knitwear, leather goods, and rugs. The store is at Auchencar Farm. ⊠ *A841, 2 mi north of Machrie, Auchencar* ☎ *01770/840227* ⊕ *www.oldbyre.co.uk.*

EN ROUTE Continuing south to Blackwaterfoot, you can return to Brodick via the String Road: from the Kinloch Hotel, head up the hill. As you drive, there are more fine views of the granite complexities of Arran's hills: gray-notched ridges beyond brown moors and, past the watershed, a vista of Brodick Bay.

LOCHRANZA

11 mi north of Brodick.

The road from Blackwaterfoot to Lochranza exposes another face of Arran: muddy, rocky beaches line one side, while the other has views of the sweeping slopes up to Goatfell and Caisteal Abhail (2,735 feet), whose stark granite peaks dominate the skyline of the north of the island. The variety of birdlife here is striking, which is why ornithologists flock to Arran in the off-season.

Arran's only distillery, the sparkling Isle of Arran Distillery, is in Lochranza, nestled in the hills overlooking Lochranza Bay.

8

GETTING HERE AND AROUND
Lochranza is 11 mi north of Brodick via the A841.

EXPLORING
Lochranza Castle. Set on a low sand spit on the mud flats of the bay, this ruined castle is quite picturesque, and you'll often see deer grazing nearby, and sometimes seals in the bay. The castle's ground-floor rooms and some upstairs can be visited during the summer months. This is said to have been the landing place of Robert the Bruce when he returned from Rathlin Island in 1307 to start the campaign that won Scotland's independence. A sign indicates where you can pick up the key to get in. ⊠ *Off A841* ☎ *0131/668–8800* ⊕ *www.historic-scotland.gov.uk* 🖾 *Free* ☉ *Apr.–Sept., daily 9:30–5:30.*

WHERE TO STAY
For expanded hotel reviews, visit Fodors.com.

$ 🏨 **Apple Lodge.** A charming whitewashed house that was once the manse (or pastor's house), Apple Lodge sits beneath the hills at the edge of Lochranza, close to the brewery; it has elegant landscaped gardens and a reputation for good home cooking. **Pros:** lovely setting; charming gardens. **Cons:** on the outskirts of Lochranza; dinner not always available; no children under 12. ⊠ *Lochranza* ☎ *01770/830229* 🛏 *4 rooms* ⚘ *In-room: no a/c, Wi-Fi. In-hotel: restaurant, some age restrictions* 🍽 *No credit cards* ⎮○⎮ *Breakfast.*

ISLAY AND JURA

Islay has a character distinct from that of the rest of the islands that make up the Hebrides. In contrast to areas where most residents live on crofts (small plots generally worked by people in their spare time), Islay's western half in particular has large, self-sustaining farms. Many of the island's wildlife preserves, historical sites, and beautiful beaches are also on the western side of the island. It's dangerous to swim at the coastal beaches, but the white-sand beaches around Loch Indaal are safe and clean. The southeast, by contrast, is mainly an extension of the island of Jura's inhospitable quartzite hills. Islay is particularly known for its birds, including the rare chough (a crow with red legs and beak) and, in winter, its barnacle geese. Several distilleries produce Islay's characteristically peaty malt whiskies, and most welcome visitors. Some charge a small fee for a tour, which you can usually credit toward any whisky purchases.

> **THE WHISKY COAST**
>
> Scotland likes trails for travelers, whether castles or whiskies are being pursued. The country's dramatic west coast, from the Isle of Skye in the north to Islay and Arran in the south, has plenty of distinguished distilleries. The **Whisky Coast** (⊕ www.whiskycoast.co.uk) is a consortium of distilleries, hotels, restaurants, golf courses, and tour operators created to make planning a trip around the area easier. The website is one starting point if you're dreaming of touring this part of the country in search of the perfect dram.

Although it's possible to meet an Islay native in a local pub, such an event is less likely on Jura, given the island's one road, one distillery, one hotel, and six sporting estates. In fact, you have a better chance of bumping into one of the island's red deer, which outnumber the human population by at least 20 to 1. The island is more rugged than Islay, with its profiles of the Paps of Jura, a hill range at its most impressive when basking in the rays of a west-coast sunset.

BOWMORE

On Islay: 11 mi north of Port Ellen.

Compact Bowmore, on Islay, is about the same size (population 1,000) as another island town, Port Ellen; but it works slightly better as a base for touring because it's central to Islay's main routes. Sharing a name with the whisky made in the distillery by the shore, Bowmore is a tidy town, its grid pattern having been laid out in 1768 by the local landowner Daniel Campbell, of Shawfield. Main Street stretches from the pier head to the commanding parish church, built in 1767 in an unusual circular design—so the devil could not hide in a corner.

GETTING HERE AND AROUND

Flybe flights from Glasgow to Islay take 40 minutes; the airport is 5 mi north of Port Ellen. The trip by CalMac ferry from Kennacraig to Port Ellen takes about two-and-a-half hours; ferries also travel less frequently to Port Askaig. From Port Ellen, you'll need to travel 10 mi on the A846 to reach Bowmore; drivers should use caution during the first mile out of Port Ellen, as the road is filled with sharp turns. The rest of the route is straight but bumpy, since the road is laid across peat bog. The ferry to Feolin on Jura departs from Port Askaig; the crossing takes five minutes.

Bus service is available on the island through Islay Coaches and Royal Mail; comprehensive timetables are available from the tourist information center.

ESSENTIALS

Air Travel Contacts Glenegedale Airport, Islay ☎ 01496/302361 ⊕ www. hial.co.uk.

Visitor Information Bowmore, Islay ✉ The Square ☎ 08707/200617 ⊕ www. visitscotland.com.

EXPLORING

Bowmore Distillery. You can purchase whisky and take a tour (year-round) of the distillery, founded in 1779, which sits near the water's edge. The more expensive Craftsman's Tour, costing £40 per person, is best for the whisky expert. Tours must be booked in advance. ✉ School St. ☎ 01496/810671 ⊕ www.bowmore.com 🎟 £6 tour ☉ Distillery tours: Easter–Aug., Mon.–Sat. at 10, 11, 2, and 3; Sept.–Easter, weekdays at 10:30 and 3; Sat. at 10. Visitor center: Easter–June, Mon.–Sat. 9–5; July–Sept., Mon.–Sat. 9–5, Sun. noon–4; Oct.–Easter, Mon.–Sat. 9–noon.

★ **Islay Woollen Mill.** The mill, in a wooded hollow by the river, has a fascinating array of working machinery; proud owner Gordon will take you on a personal tour. A shop sells high-quality products that were woven on-site. Beyond the usual tweed there's a distinctive selection of hats, caps, and clothing made from the mill's own cloth. All the tartans and tweeds worn in the film *Braveheart* were woven here. The mill is on the A846 between Bridgend and Port Askaig, 3 mi outside Bridgend. ✉ A846 ☎ 01496/810563 ⊕ www.islaywoollenmill.co.uk 🎟 Free ☉ Mon.–Sat. 10–5.

WHERE TO STAY

For expanded hotel reviews, visit Fodors.com.

$$ 🏨 **Harbour Inn.** The cheerfully noisy bar of this harborside inn is frequented by off-duty distillery workers who are happy to rub elbows with travelers and exchange island gossip; the superb restaurant has expansive views over the water and serves morning coffee, lunch, and dinner. **Pros:** great location; excellent food. **Cons:** restaurant service can be slow; bedroom linens could be a bit nicer for the price; no children under 10. ✉ The Square ☎ 01496/810330 ⊕ www.harbour-inn.com 🛏 7 rooms ♿ In-room: no a/c. In-hotel: restaurant, bar 🍴 Breakfast.

8

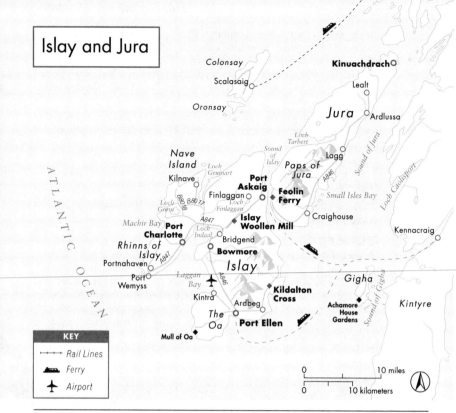

Islay and Jura

Colonsay

Scalasaig

Oronsay

Kinuachdrach

Lealt

Jura

Ardlussa

Loch Tarbert

Nave Island

Sound of Islay

Paps of Jura

Lagg

Loch Gruinart

Kilnave

Port Askaig

Feolin Ferry

Small Isles Bay

Finlaggan

Loch Finlaggan

Loch Gorm

B8018

Islay Woollen Mill

Craighouse

Machir Bay

Port Charlotte

A847

Loch Indaal

Bridgend

Kennacraig

Rhinns of Islay

Bowmore

Portnahaven

A847

Islay

Port Wemyss

Laggan Bay

A846

Gigha

Kintra

Kildalton Cross

Kintyre

Ardbeg

Achamore House Gardens

The Oa

Port Ellen

Mull of Oa

ATLANTIC OCEAN

Sound of Jura

Loch Caolisport

Sound of Gigha

KEY

Rail Lines

Ferry

Airport

0   10 miles

0   10 kilometers

PORT CHARLOTTE

On Islay: 11 mi west of Bowmore.

A delightful conservation village (meaning an area of architectural or historical interest) at the head of Loch Indaal on Islay, Port Charlotte is home to the Museum of Islay Life, the lovely Natural History Trust, and safe, sandy beaches.

GETTING HERE AND AROUND

To reach Port Charlotte from Bowmore, take the A846 via Bridgend and then the A847, Portnahaven Road. Islay Coaches and Royal Mail buses also travel here from Bowmore.

EXPLORING

Museum of Islay Life. Above the road on the north side in a converted kirk (church) is this local museum, a haphazard but authentic collection of local artifacts, photographs, and memorabilia. ✉ *A847* ☎ *01496/850358* ⊕ *www.islaymuseum.org* 🎫 *£3* ✆ *Apr.–Oct., Mon.–Sat. 10–5.*

Natural History Visitor Centre. The center has a comprehensive exhibition of Islay wildlife, with lots of hands-on activities for children. It's a great stop on rainy days. ✉ *Main St.* ☎ *01496/850288* ⊕ *www.islaynaturalhistory.org* 🎫 *£3* ✆ *May–Oct., daily 10–4.*

Rhinns of Islay. South of Port Charlotte, the A847 continues along the wild landscape of the Rhinns of Islay. The road ends at **Portnahaven** and its twin, **Port Wemyss**, where pretty white cottages built in a crescent around the headland belie the harsh lives of the fisher families who live and work here. Return to Port Charlotte via the bleak, unclassified road that loops north and east, passing by the recumbent stone circle at Coultoon and the ruined chapel at Kilchiaran along the way. The strange whooping sound you may hear as you turn away from Portnahaven comes from Scotland's first wave-powered generator, sucking and blowing as it supplies electricity for both villages. It's well worth the climb down to the shore to see it in action.

WHERE TO STAY

For expanded hotel reviews, visit Fodors.com.

$$$ 🏨 **Port Charlotte Hotel.** A whitewashed building, once a row of fishermen's cottages and with views over a sandy beach, this restored Victorian hotel with simple rooms is warm and bright, its walls decorated with the owners' interesting contemporary art collection. **Pros:** beautiful location in a conservation village. **Cons:** slightly expensive; rooms are quite small; can be a little noisy from the bar. ⊠ *Main St.* ☎ *01496/850360* ⊕ *www.portcharlottehotel.co.uk* ➫ *10 rooms* ⌂ *In-room: no a/c, Wi-Fi. In-hotel: restaurant, bar, parking, some pets allowed* ⦿ *Breakfast.*

PORT ELLEN

On Islay: 11 mi south of Bowmore.

Islay's sturdy community of Port Ellen was founded in the 1820s, and much of its architecture dates from the following decades. It has a harbor (ferries stop here), a few shops, and a handful of inns. The road traveling east from Port Ellen (the A846 to Ardbeg) passes three top distilleries and makes a pleasant afternoon's "whisky walk." Tours are free at all three distilleries, but you must call ahead for an appointment; there may be no tours on weekends at times.

GETTING HERE AND AROUND

It is likely that Port Ellen will be your port of arrival on Islay. From here you can travel north to Bowmore, along the A846 before turning northwest towards Bridgend and Port Askaig.

EXPLORING

Ardbeg Distillery. It's best to make tour reservations in advance for the distillery farthest from Port Ellen. ⊠ *Off Port Ellen Rd.* ☎ *01496/302244* ⊕ *www.ardbeg.com* ☉ *Oct.–Apr., weekdays 9:30–5; May and Sept., Mon.–Sat. 9:30–5; June–Aug., daily 9:30–5.*

★ **Kildalton Cross.** About 8 mi northeast of Port Ellen is one of the highlights of Scotland's Celtic heritage. After passing through a pleasantly rolling, partly wooded landscape, take a narrow road (it's signposted "Kildalton Cross") from Ardbeg. This leads to a ruined chapel with surrounding kirkyard, in which stands the finest carved cross anywhere in Scotland: the 8th-century Kildalton Cross. Carved from a single slab of epidiorite rock, the ringed cross is encrusted on both sides with elaborate designs in the style of the Iona school. The surrounding grave slabs date as far back as the 12th and 13th centuries. ⊕ *www.historic-scotland.gov.uk.*

Lagavulin Distillery. The whisky produced here has the strongest iodine scent of all the island malts. Twice a week (Tuesday and Thursday at 10:30) there are special warehouse tours; call to reserve this and other tours. ⊠ *A846* ☎ *01496/302749* ⊕ *www.malts.com* ✉ *£6; warehouse tours £15* ☾ *Jan.–Apr., Nov., and Dec., weekdays 9–12:30; May, June, Sept., and Oct., weekdays 9–5, Sat. 9–12:30; July and Aug., weekdays 9–7, Sat. 9–5, Sun. 12:30–4:30.*

Laphroaig Distillery. Whisky produced here is one of the most distinctive in the Western Isles, with a tangy, peaty, seaweed-and-iodine flavor. The distillery is a little less than 1 mi from Port Ellen toward Ardbeg. Its visitor center is free, and there's a basic tour for £4.80 along with some other, more expensive options. Call to prebook tours. ⊠ *A846* ☎ *01496/302418* ⊕ *www.laphroaig.com* ✉ *Free* ☾ *Mar.–Oct., weekdays 9:30–5:30, weekends 10–4; Nov. and Dec., daily 10–4; Jan. and Feb., weekdays 10–4.*

Oa Peninsula. The southern Oa Peninsula, west of Port Ellen, is a region of caves that's rich in smuggling lore. At its tip, the Mull of Oa, is a monument recalling the 650 men who lost their lives in 1918 when the British ships *Tuscania* and *Otranto* sank nearby. Bring good, strong walking shoes.

SPORTS AND THE OUTDOORS

GOLF **Machrie Golf Links.** This course would be a lot more crowded if it were a little more accessible. It was designed in 1891, and except for minor changes in the 1970s, has changed little. Watch out for the sand dunes! ⊠ *Off A846, 4 mi from Port Ellen* ☎ *01496/302310* ⊕ *www.machrie. net* ✉ *£60 per round* ⚐ *18 holes, 5,894 yds, par 71.*

HORSEBACK RIDING **Ballivicar Pony Trekking.** The company leads trips on nearby beaches and into the surrounding countryside. ⊠ *Ballivicar Farm* ☎ *01496/302251.*

PORT ASKAIG

On Islay: 11 mi northeast of Bowmore.

Serving as the ferry port for Jura and receiving ferries from Kennacraig, Port Askaig is a mere cluster of cottages. Uphill, just outside the village, a side road travels along the coast, giving impressive views of Jura on the way. There are distilleries near here, too; make appointments for tours.

GETTING HERE AND AROUND

Traveling from Bowmore, you can reach Port Askaig (where the road ends) via A846. The village is also served by local buses.

EXPLORING

Bunnahabhain Distillery. At road's end, the Bunnahabhain Distillery sits on the shore, with great water views; it was established in 1881. This is one of the milder single malts on Islay. You can upgrade to a more elaborate tour if you prebook. ⊠ *A846* ☎ *01496/840646* ⊕ *www.bunnahabhain. com* 🖰 *£4 standard tour* ☉ *Mar.–Oct., weekdays 10–4:15; tours at 10:30, 1:30, and 3:15.*

JURA

5 mins by ferry from Port Askaig.

The rugged, mountainous landscape of the island of Jura—home to only about 200 people—looms immediately east of Port Askaig, across the Sound of Islay. Jura has only one single-track road (the A846), which begins at Feolin, the ferry pier. It climbs across moorland, providing scenic views of the island's most striking feature, the Paps of Jura, three beastlike rounded peaks. The ruined Claig Castle, on an island just offshore, was built by the Lords of the Isles to control the Sound.

Jura House lies between Feolin and Craighouse, the island's only village, some 8 mi away (its walled gardens are open to the public for part of the year). Jura's solitude attracted George Orwell to the remote farmhouse at Barnhill, where he completed his famous novel *1984*.

GETTING HERE AND AROUND
The Port Askaig–Feolin car ferry takes five minutes to cross the Sound of Islay. Bus service is also available from Craighouse and Inverlussa.

EXPLORING
Isle of Jura Distillery. The community of Craighouse has the island's only distillery, producing malt whisky since 1810. Phone ahead to reserve your place on a tour. ⊠ *A846* ☎ *01496/820385* ⊕ *www.isleofjura.com* ☉ *Apr.–Sept, weekdays10–4, Sat. 10–2; tours weekdays at 11 and 2. Oct.–Mar., weekdays 11–2; tour at 11.*

Kinuachdrach. The settlement of Kinuachdrach once served as a crossing point to Scarba and the mainland. To get to Kinuachdrach after crossing the river at Lealt, follow the track beyond the surface road for 5 mi. The coastal footpath to Corryvreckan lies beyond, over the bare moors. This area has two enticements: the first is the house at **Barnhill** (not open to the public) where George Orwell wrote *1984*; the second, for wilderness enthusiasts, is the whirlpool of the **Gulf of Corryvreckan,** where Orwell nearly died, and the unspoiled coastal scenery.

WHERE TO STAY
For expanded hotel reviews, visit Fodors.com.

$ 🛏 **Jura Hotel.** In spite of its monopoly on Jura, this hotel surrounded by pleasant gardens can be relied on for adequate accommodations; rooms are simple and a bit old-fashioned. **Pros:** good views across the bay; spacious rooms; next door to distillery. **Cons:** room decor is tired, to say the least; you may have to share a bathroom. ⊠ *A846, Craighouse* ☎ *01496/820243* ⊕ *www.jurahotel.co.uk* 🛏 *17 rooms, 11 with bath* 🛆 *In-room: no a/c, no TV, Wi-Fi. In-hotel: restaurant, bar* ❧ *Breakfast.*

ISLE OF MULL AND IONA

Though its economy has historically been built on agriculture, fishing, and whisky distilling, today the Isle of Mull relies on tourism dollars—which makes sense, since there are many wonderful things to see here. The landscapes range from the pretty harbor of Tobermory and the gentle slopes around Dervaig to the dramatic Atlantic beaches on the west. In the south, the long road past the sweeping green slopes of the Ross of Mull leads to Iona, a year-round attraction.

GETTING HERE AND AROUND

Ferries to Mull are run by the ubiquitous Caledonian MacBrayne. Its most frequent car-ferry route to Mull is from Oban to Craignure (45 minutes). Two shorter routes are from Lochaline on the Morvern Peninsula to Fishnish (15 minutes), or Kilchoan (on the Adrnamurchan Peninsula) to Tobermory (15 minutes). The ferries do not accept reservations, and the Lochaline ferry does not run on Sunday. Bowman's Coaches serves the east coast, running between Tobermory, Craignure, and Fionnphort (for the ferry to Iona).

CRAIGNURE

On Mull: 40-min ferry crossing from Oban, 15-min ferry crossing to Fishnish (5 mi northwest of Craignure) from Lochaline.

Craignure, little more than a pier and some houses, is close to well-known Duart Castle. Reservations for the year-round ferries that travel from Oban to Craignure are advisable in summer. The ferry from Lochaline to Fishnish, just northwest of Craignure, does not accept reservations and does not run on Sunday.

GETTING HERE AND AROUND

The arrival point for the 40-minute ferry crossing from Oban, Craignure is the starting point for further travel on Mull northwest toward Salen and Tobermory, or toward Fionnphort and the Iona ferry to the southwest.

ESSENTIALS

Visitor Information Craignure, Mull ⊠ *The Pierhead* ☎ *01680/812377* ⊕ *www.visitscotland.com.*

EXPLORING

Duart Castle. The 13th-century Duart Castle, ancient seat of the Macleans, was ruined by the Campbells in 1691 but purchased and restored by Sir Fitzroy Maclean in 1911. It stands dramatically on a cliff top overlooking the Sound of Mull. Inside, one display depicts the wreck of the *Swan,* a Cromwellian vessel sunk offshore in 1653 and excavated in the 1990s by marine archaeologists. Outside you can visit nearby **Millennium Wood,** planted with groups of Mull's indigenous trees. To reach Duart by car, take the A849 and turn left around the shore of Duart Bay. For buses to the castle from Craignure, call the castle in advance. From Craignure ferry port, there is a direct bus (10 mins) to the castle. ⊠ *Off A849, 3 mi southeast of Craignure* ☎ *01680/812309* ⊕ *www.*

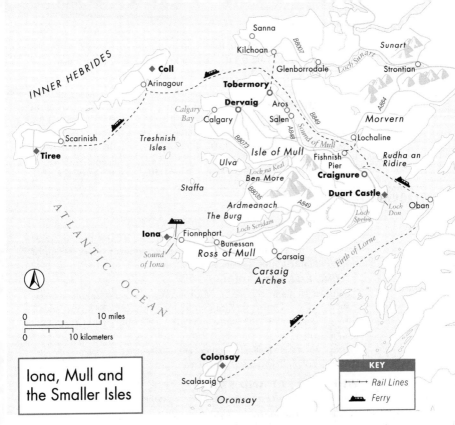

Iona, Mull and the Smaller Isles

KEY
+——+ Rail Lines
🛳 Ferry

duartcastle.com 🖼 *£5.50* ⏱ *Apr., Sun.–Thurs. 11–4; May–mid-Oct., daily 10:30–5:30.*

WHERE TO STAY
For expanded hotel reviews, visit Fodors.com.

$ 🏨 **Craignure Inn.** This 18th-century, whitewashed, drovers inn, a short walk from the ferry pier, has a lively bar that often hosts local musicians; guest rooms are warm and snug, with polished-wood furniture, exposed beams, and views of the Sound of Mull. **Pros:** lively bar scene; hearty local food. **Cons:** live music can get loud. ⊠ *Near the ferry pier* ☎ *01680/812305* ⊕ *www.craignure-inn.co.uk* 🛏 *3 rooms* 🛏 *In-room: no a/c. In-hotel: restaurant, bar* 🍴 *Breakfast.*

DERVAIG

On Mull: 27 mi northwest of Craignure, 60 mi north of Fionnphort.

A pretty riverside village, Dervaig has a circular, pointed church tower that is reminiscent of the Irish-Celtic style of the 8th and 9th centuries. The Bellart is a good trout- and salmon-fishing river, and Calgary Bay, 5 mi away, has one of the best beaches on Mull.

GETTING HERE AND AROUND

You can reach Dervaig from Craignure via the A849. From Salen, take the B8073, and from Tobermory, take the B8073.

EXPLORING

Old Byre Heritage Centre. At this museum, an audiovisual presentation on the history of the region plays hourly. The tearoom's wholesome fare, particularly the homemade soup, is a boon to travelers. There's also a craft shop here. You'll see signs for the center on the B8073, just before Dervaig. ⊠ *Off B8073* ☎ *01688/400229* ⊕ *www.old-byre.co.uk* ⊠ *£4* ☉ *Easter–Oct., Wed.–Sun. 10:30–6:30; last admission at 5:30.*

TOBERMORY

5 mi northeast of Dervaig, 21 mi north of Craignure.

Founded as a fishing station, Tobermory is now a lively tourist center and a base for exploring Mull. The town is famous for its crescent of brightly painted houses around the harbor.

GETTING HERE AND AROUND

The most frequent service to Mull is via the Oban-Craignure ferry. Tobermory is 21 mi from Craignure along the A849/848 (via Salen). Bowman's Coaches runs services between Tobermory and Craignure.

ESSENTIALS

Visitor Information Mull Information Centre ⊠ *Pierhead, Craignure* ☎ *01680/812377* ⊕ *www.visitscotland.com.*

WHERE TO EAT AND STAY

For expanded hotel reviews, visit Fodors.com.

$$ ✕ **Café Fish.** The location of this restaurant has certainly contributed
SEAFOOD to its success. Perched on the pier at the end of Tobermory and overlooking the bay beyond, Café Fish prides itself on the freshness of its fish; the owners have their own boat and land their own shellfish daily. Fish is served simply, grilled with a slice of lemon, to let the natural flavors speak for themselves. Diver-harvested scallops are served with vermouth and orange juice over rice. Other popular dishes include fish stew and the langoustines and squat lobster (not really a lobster—it's related to crab). ⊠ *The Pier* ☎ *01688/301253* ⊕ *www.thecafefish.com* ☉ *Closed Jan.–mid-Mar.*

$$ ᛁ **Highland Cottage.** Set on the hill above the harbor, this elegant family-run hotel prides itself on the detail of its rooms and its fine dining; the upstairs rooms have sea views. **Pros:** comfortable hotel with attentive owners; high-quality dining. **Cons:** rooms are a bit small; no children under 10. ⊠ *Breadalbane St.* ☎ *01688/302030* ⊕ *www.highlandcottage. co.uk* ⇆ *6 rooms* ♿ *In-room: no a/c, Wi-Fi. In-hotel: restaurant, parking, some pets allowed, some age restrictions* ⊧◉⊦ *Breakfast.*

$ ᛁ **Tobermory Hotel.** Made up of five former fishermen's cottages, this lodging on Tobermory's waterfront has a warm, intimate feel. **Pros:** adorable cottage setting with fireplace; toys for children. **Cons:** small rooms; small bathrooms. ⊠ *Main St.* ☎ *01688/302091* ⊕ *www. thetobermoryhotel.com* ⇆ *18 rooms* ♿ *In-room: no a/c, Wi-Fi. In-hotel: restaurant, bar* ☉ *Closed Jan.* ⊧◉⊦ *Breakfast.*

$ ⛆ **Western Isles Hotel.** Like an elderly dowager, this grand hotel from the Victorian era looks down on Tobermory from its wonderful location overlooking the Sound of Mull; it suffered a period of neglect but is now being refurbished and restored to its former state. **Pros:** the view; spacious public rooms; great food. **Cons:** outmoded plumbing; occasional lack of hot water; still being renovated. ⊠ *Off B882* ☎ *01688/302012* ⊕ *www.westernisleshotel.co.uk* ⇗ *26 rooms* ⚭ *In-room: no a/c. In-hotel: restaurant, bar* ⧄ *Breakfast.*

THE ARTS
Mull Theatre. The renowned Mull Theatre, founded in 1966, once prided itself on being the smallest theater in the United Kingdom. Its premises at the Druimfin Centre are too large to maintain the claim, but its productions still tour the islands; consult the website and book ahead. ⊠ *Druimfin, on the Salen Rd.* ☎ *01688/302828* ⊕ *www.mulltheatre. com.*

EN ROUTE Between Craignure and Fionnphort at the end of the Ross of Mull, the double-lane road narrows as it heads southwest, touched by sea inlets at Lochs Don and Spelve. Inland, vivid grass and high rock faces in Glen More make gray and green the prevalent hues. These stepped-rock faces reach their highest point in Ben More, the only island *munro* (a Scottish mountain more than 3,000 feet high) outside Skye. Stay on the A849 for a pleasant drive the length of the Ross of Mull, a wide promontory with scattered settlements. The National Trust for Scotland cares for the rugged stretch of coast, known as the Burg. The A849 eventually ends in a long parking lot opposite the houses of Fionnphort.

8

IONA

5 mins by ferry from Fionnphort (Mull), which is 36 mi west of Craignure.

The ruined abbey on Iona gives little hint that this was once one of the most important Christian religious centers in the land. The priceless Book of Kells (now in Dublin) was illustrated here, and it was the monks of Iona who spread Christian ideas across Scotland and the north. The abbey was founded in the year 563 by the fiery and argumentative Columba (circa 521–97) after his expulsion from Ireland. Until the 11th century, many of Scotland's kings and rulers were buried here, their tombstones still visible inside the abbey. While few visitors venture beyond the pier and the abbey, there are several tranquil paths.

GETTING HERE AND AROUND
Caledonian MacBrayne's ferry from Fionnphort departs at regular intervals throughout the year (£4.50 round-trip). Timetables are available on the Caledonian MacBrayne website. Note that cars are not permitted; there's a parking lot by the ferry at Fionnphort.

EXPLORING
Iona Abbey. The abbey, an important religious center dating back to the 6th century, survived repeated Norse sackings but finally fell into disuse around the time of the Reformation. Restoration work began at the turn of the 20th century. Today the restored buildings, including the

abbey, serve as a spiritual center under the jurisdiction of the Church of Scotland. Guided tours, run by the Iona Community, are every half hour in summer and on demand in winter. ✉ *Isle of Iona* ☎ *01681/700793* 🌐 *www.iona.org.uk* 🎟 *£5.50* ⏲ *Apr.–Sept., daily 9:30–5:30; Oct.–Mar., daily 9:30–4:30.*

Iona Community. In 1938 the Iona Community, an ecumenical religious group, was founded by George MacLeod. Originally a Gaelic-speaking community dedicated to rebuilding the abbey, it was transformed over time into a more open and wide-ranging ecumenical community. It now offers programs, retreats, and activities across the island, and can be contacted through the Community Shop. ☎ *01681/700404* 🌐 *www.iona.org.uk.*

WHERE TO STAY

For expanded hotel reviews, visit Fodors.com.

$ **St. Columba Hotel.** Rooms in this 1846 former manse are very simple, but all front rooms have glorious views across the Sound of Iona to Mull. **Pros:** eco-minded; this place is all about what's good for the earth and soul; nice log fires. **Cons:** no TV in hotel; rooms minimal in style; sea-view rooms cost a little more. ✉ *Next to cathedral, about ¼ mi from the ferry pier* ☎ *01681/700304* 🌐 *www.stcolumba-hotel.co.uk* *27 rooms* *In-room: no a/c, no TV. In-hotel: restaurant, bar* ⏲ *Closed mid-Oct.–Easter* *Breakfast.*

SHOPPING

Old Printing Press Bookshop. Iona has a few pleasant surprises for shoppers, the biggest of which is the Old Printing Press Bookshop, an excellent antiquarian bookstore. ✉ *Beside St. Columba Hotel* ☎ *01681/700699.*

Iona Community Shop. The shop carries Celtic-inspired gift items, as well as sheet music and songbooks, and CDs and tapes. ✉ *Across from Iona Abbey* ☎ *01681/700404* 🌐 *www.iona.org.uk.*

THE SMALLER ISLANDS

The smaller islands, sometimes known as the Southern Hebrides, may seem quite remote but were once important centers of power and production. Successively depopulated by force or by emigration to Glasgow's industries or the promise of the Americas, the islands still survive on fishing, cattle and sheep raising, and, of course, whisky production. Their Gaelic language is vibrant once again, but their populations remain small. For the visitor, the experience is one of open, often barely populated landscapes and a slightly brooding sense of history.

TIREE

4-hr sail from Oban, via Coll.

GETTING HERE AND AROUND

Caledonian MacBrayne runs ferries to Tiree via Coll, four times a week (Tuesday, Thursday, Saturday, and Sunday). You can also fly here from Glasgow on Flybe or from Oban on Highland Airways. On Tiree, the Royal Mail postbus (which carries mail and passengers) runs an infrequent service around the island; there is a shared taxi service (☎ *01879/220311*), which you should book ahead of your arrival. An alternative is to rent a bike from **Skerryvore House** (☎ *01879/220268*).

ESSENTIALS

Air Travel Contacts Tiree Airport ☎ *01879/220456* ⊕ *www.hial.co.uk.*

EXPLORING

Tiree. A fertile, low-lying island with its own microclimate, Tiree is windswept, but has more hours of sunshine per year than any other part of the British Isles. Long, rolling Atlantic swells attract surfers, and summer visitors can raise the population to the nearly 4,500 it supported in the 1830s. Among Tiree's several archaeological sites are a large boulder near Vaul covered with more than 50 Bronze Age cup marks, and an excavated *broch* (stone tower) at Dun Mor Vaul. ☎ ⊕ *www.isleoftiree.com.*

COLL

3-hr sail from Oban.

GETTING HERE AND AROUND

Caledonian MacBrayne runs ferries to Coll on Tuesday, Thursday, Saturday, and Sunday. You can also fly here from Oban on Highland Airways. There is no public transportation on Coll, but you can rent a bike (☎ *01879/230333*) or use the island's one taxi (☎ *01879/230402*).

EXPLORING

Coll. Unlike their neighbors in nearby Tiree, Coll's residents were not forced to leave the island in the 19th century. Today half of the island's sparse population lives in its only village, Arinagour. Its coasts offer extraordinarily rich birdlife, particularly along the beautiful sandy beaches of its southwest. Coll is even lower lying than Tiree but also rockier and less fertile.

The island is rich in archaeology, with standing stones at Totronald, a cairn at Annagour, and the remains of several Iron Age forts. The keep of Breachacha Castle, on the south end of Coll, dates to 1450. A former stronghold of the Maclean clan, the castle is privately owned today, but you may view it from the road near Uig.

COLONSAY

2½-hr sail from Oban.

Less bleak than Coll and Tiree, Colonsay is one of Scotland's quietest, most unspoiled, and least populated islands. It is partly wooded, with a fine quasi-tropical garden at Colonsay House and a great variety of wildlife.

GETTING HERE AND AROUND

Caledonian MacBrayne ferries run to Colonsay on Monday, Wednesday, Friday, and Sunday. The island of Oronsay lies half a mile away and can be reached at certain times across a natural causeway. There is a limited postbus service on Colonsay; bikes can be rented from **A. McConnel** (☎ *01951/200355*).

EXPLORING

Colonsay. Colonsay is one of Scotland's quietest, most unspoiled, and least populous islands. The beautiful beach at Kiloran Bay is an utterly peaceful place even at the height of summer. The standing stones at Kilchattan Farm are known as Fingal's Limpet Hammers. Fingal, or Finn, MacCoul is a warrior of massive size and strength in Celtic mythology. Standing before the stones, you can imagine Fingal wielding them like hammers to cull equally large limpets from Scotland's rocky coast. The island's social life revolves around the bar at the 19th-century Colonsay Hotel, 100 yards from the ferry pier. The adjacent island of Oronsay with its ruined cloister can be reached at low tide via a 1½-mi wade across a sandy sound.

Oronsay. The island of Oronsay, beside Colonsay, can be reached at low tide, at the expense of wet legs, in a 1½-mi wade across a sandy sound separating the two islands (after which an intake of reviving malt whisky never tastes better). Mesolithic shell mounds show the island was populated from before 4000 BC, though only a handful of people live here now. The cloister ruins of a formerly rich and influential 14th-century Augustinian priory, including a stone cross, are well worth the paddle.

Around the
Great Glen

WORD OF MOUTH

"We drove along Loch Ness and the entire drive (including out of Inverness) was gorgeous. It was a great way to enjoy seeing much of the country in the warm comfort of our car. We didn't get road fatigue because it's so different from going from point A to point B in the U.S."

—junkgalore

"If you are driving to Mallaig, as you get closer to the town do get off the main road and take the coast roads. The beaches along this short stretch have the most lovely white sand and were quite empty of other people. These beaches were one of the many highlights of our trip and could so easily be missed by just staying on the main road."

—tjhome1

Updated by
Elizabeth
Reeder

Defined by a striking geological feature, the Great Glen brings together mountains and myths, battles and whisky— and there's a great view around nearly every bend in the road. The city of Inverness sits at the northern end of the glen, and Loch Ness, home to the elusive Loch Ness Monster, stretches south. Daunting mountain ranges and expansive coasts flank the Great Glen and make for scenic traveling. There's also plenty here for history buffs, as the area was the site of the massacre at Glencoe in 1692 and the defeat of the Jacobites at Culloden in 1746.

The Great Glen Fault runs diagonally through the highlands of Scotland and was formed when two tectonic plates collided, shoving masses of the crust southwest toward the Atlantic Ocean. Over time the rift broadened into a glen, and a thin line of lochs now lies along its seam.

Inverness has a growing reputation for excellent restaurants, and from here nearly everything in the Great Glen is an easy day trip. Just south of the city, the iconic 13th-century ruined Urquhart Castle sits on the shores of the deep, murky Loch Ness. In Fort Augustus, located 17 mi south of the castle, the Caledonian Canal joins Inverness in the north to Fort William in the west via a series of 29 locks. At the western end of the canal, Ben Nevis, Britain's highest mountain, rises sharply. The Nevis Range, like Cairngorm National Park to the east, is ideal for outdoor activities; the landscape can best be appreciated by walking, climbing, and mountain biking through the hills and glens.

Fort William makes a good base for exploring Glencoe, the scene of the 1692 massacre of the MacDonald clan. It's an area where history seems to be imprinted on the landscape, and it remains desolate, with some of the steepest, most atmospheric hills of any drive in Scotland.

Just north of Fort William, the Road to the Isles offers impressive coastal views. By car or train, the coast is stunning, with the small isles of Rum and Eigg creating a low rocky skyline across the water. Near the start of this road lies Glenfinnan, where in 1745 Bonnie Prince Charlie rallied his Jacobite troops. It's 84 mi back along the Great Glen to Culloden Moor, which is east of Inverness: this was the scene of the Jacobites' final defeat in 1746. At the battlefield, a new visitor center helps bring history to life.

The surrounding Morayshire coast is home to a more pastoral landscape, and 14th-century Cawdor Castle and its gardens have an opulent air. Nearby Brodie Castle has an awe-inspiring library and art collection. Impressive long, sandy beaches stretch out along the coast from the towns of Nairn and Findhorn, and the eco-village at Findhorn suggests possibilities for greener living. The Malt Whisky Trail begins in

TOP REASONS TO GO

Castles, fortresses, and battle- fields: Hear stories of the Highland people and famous figures like Bon- nie Prince Charlie, and absorb the atmosphere of castles and battle- fields, at Culloden Moor, Cawdor and Brodie castles, Fort George, and Glencoe.

Hill walking and outdoor activi- ties: The Great Glen is renowned for its hill walking. Some of the best routes are around Glen Nevis, Glencoe, and on Ben Nevis, the highest mountain in Britain. It's not just hiking: Glenmore Lodge in the Cairngorms offers everything from kayaking to mountain biking to ice climbing.

Wild landscapes and rare wildlife: Spot rare plants and beasts including tiny least willow trees and golden eagles in the near-arctic tundra of Cairngorms National Park.

Whisky Trail: The two westernmost distilleries on the Malt Whisky Trail are in Forres. Benromach is the smallest distillery in Moray and has excellent tours; Dallas Dhu is pre- served as a museum. You can strike out from here to nearby distilleries in Speyside *(see Chapter 7).*

Stunning beaches: The west coast may not have tropical temperatures, but it has untouched white-sand beaches with clear waters. The coastline between Morar and Arisaig is lined with miles upon miles of them.

Boat trips: There are many ferries to the small isles (or to Skye) from Arisaig and Mallaig. You can also go Nessie-watching on Loch Ness or hire a small boat and travel the Caledonian Canal.

Forres and follows the wide, fast River Spey south until it butts against the Cairngorm Mountains and the old Caledonian forests, with their diverse and rare wildlife.

9

ORIENTATION AND PLANNING

GETTING ORIENTED

If Inverness is the center point of a compass, the Great Glen spreads out to the east, south and west. To the east stretches the Morayshire coast, populated with castles, distilleries, beaches. Head southeast and you hit the Cairngorm National Park and other nature preserves. The A82 heads south from Inverness, hugging the west side of Loch Ness. Nearby are the contemplative ruins at Urquhart Castle and the inter- esting locks of the Caledonian Canal. Farther southwest, Fort William can be a good base for day trips to the foreboding and steep mountain pass of Glencoe.

Inverness and Environs. From the small city of Inverness, just about anywhere in the Great Glen is a day trip. Spend your days exploring Culloden Moor, Brodie Castle, or Cawdor Castle. There are long, walk- able beaches at Nairn and Findhorn.

Speyside and the Cairngorms. Speyside is best known for its whisky distilleries, and those who enjoy a good dram often follow the Whisky Trail. In and around the Cairngorms there are mountains, lochs, rivers, and dozens of cycling and walking paths that make it tailor-made for outdoors enthusiasts.

Loch Ness and Toward the Small Isles. Have a go trying to spot Nessie from the banks of Loch Ness. For something wilder, base yourself at Fort William and take in the spectacular scenery of Glencoe and Glen Nevis. If you dare, climb Britain's highest peak, Ben Nevis. The Road to the Small Isles, known for larger-than-life figures both old (the Bonnie Prince) and new (Harry Potter), has classic views across water to rocky islands perched on blue seas.

PLANNING

WHEN TO GO

Late spring to early autumn is the best time to visit the Great Glen. If you catch good weather in summer, the days can be glorious. Summer is also when you might encounter midges (biting insects: keep walking, as they can't move very fast). Winter can bring a damp chill, gusty winds, and snow-blocked roads, although many Scots value the open fires and the warming whisky that make the off-season so appealing.

PLANNING YOUR TIME

The Great Glen is an enormous area that can easily be broken into two separate trips. The first would be based in or near Inverness, allowing an exploration of Speyside, the Cairngorms, Cawdor and Brodie castles, and perhaps a few whisky distillery tours. The second, based in Fort William, moves through the cloud-laden Glencoe and down through the moody Rannoch Moor, or toward the Road to the Isles.

For those with more time, a trip around the Great Glen could be combined with forays north into the Northern Highlands, east toward Aberdeen and the rest of the Malt Whisky Trail, southeastward to the Central Highlands, or south to Argyll.

GETTING HERE AND AROUND

AIR TRAVEL

Inverness Airport has flights from London, Edinburgh, and Glasgow. Domestic flights covering the Highlands and islands are operated by British Airways, Servisair, easyJet, and Eastern Airways. Fort William has bus and train connections with Glasgow, so Glasgow Airport can be a good access point.

BUS TRAVEL

A long-distance Scottish Citylink service connects Glasgow and Fort William. Inverness is also well served from the central belt of Scotland. Discount carrier Megabus (book online to avoid phone charges) has service to Inverness from various cities.

There's limited service available within the Great Glen area and some local service running from Fort William. Stagecoach Highland serves the Great Glen and around Fort William. A number of post-bus services

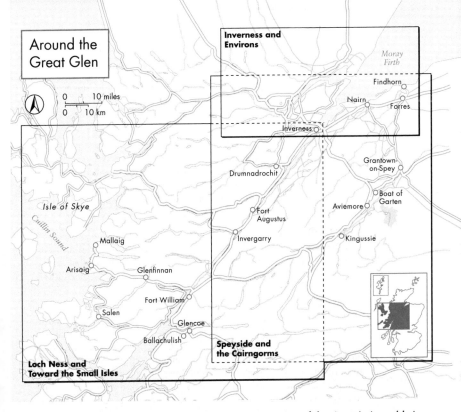

Around the
Great Glen

0   10 miles
0   10 km

Inverness and
Environs

Moray
Firth

Findhorn

Nairn

Forres

Inverness

Isle of Skye

Cuillin Sound

Mallaig

Arisaig

Glenfinnan

Fort William

Salen

Glencoe

Ballachulish

Drumnadrochit

Fort
Augustus

Invergarry

Grantown-
on-Spey

Boat of
Garten

Aviemore

Kingussie

Speyside and
the Cairngorms

Loch Ness and
Toward the Small Isles

will help get you to the more remote corners of the area. A timetable is available from Royal Mail Post Buses.

Bus Contacts Stagecoach Highlands ☎ *0871/2663333* ⊕ *www. stagecoachbus.com.* **Megabus** ☎ *08705/505050* ⊕ *www.megabus.com.* **Royal Mail Post Buses** ☎ *0845/7740740* ⊕ *www.royalmail.com.* **Scottish Citylink** ☎ *0871/2663333* ⊕ *www.citylink.co.uk.*

CAR TRAVEL

As in all areas of rural Scotland, a car is a great asset for exploring the Great Glen, especially since the best of the area is away from the main roads. You can use the main A82 from Inverness to Fort William, or use the smaller B862/B852 roads to explore the much quieter east side of Loch Ness. Mallaig, west of Fort William, is reached via a new road, but there are still a few narrow and winding single-lane roads, which require slower speeds and concentration.

In the Great Glen, the best sights are often hidden from the main road, which is an excellent reason to favor peaceful rural byways and to avoid as much as possible the busy A96 and A9, which carry much of the traffic in the area.

TRAIN TRAVEL

ScotRail has connections from London to Inverness and Fort William (including overnight sleeper service), as well as reliable links from Glasgow and Edinburgh. There's train service between Glasgow (Queen Street) and Inverness, via Aviemore, which gives access to the heart of Speyside.

Although there's no rail connection among towns within the Great Glen, this area has the West Highland Line, which links Fort William to Mallaig. This train, run by ScotRail, remains the most enjoyable way to experience the rugged hills and loch scenery between these two places. The Jacobite Steam Train is an exciting summer (mid-May–mid-October) option on the same route.

Train Contacts Jacobite Steam Train ☎ 0845/128–4681 ⊕ www.westcoastrailways.co.uk. **ScotRail** ☎ 08457/550033 ⊕ www.scotrail.co.uk.

RESTAURANTS

Inverness, Aviemore, and Fort William have plenty of cafés and restaurants in all price ranges. Inverness has particularly diverse dining options. Outside of the towns, there are many country-house hotels serving superb meals.

HOTELS

In the Great Glen, towns have a range of accommodations ranging from cozy inns to expansive hotels; in more remote areas your choice will usually be limited to smaller establishments. Because this is an established vacation area, you should have no trouble finding a room for a night; however, the area is quite busy in the peak season and the best places book up early. In Inverness, you may find it more appealing to stay outside the city center or in the nearby, very pretty countryside.

WHAT IT COSTS IN POUNDS					
	¢	$	$$	$$$	$$$$
RESTAURANTS	under £10	£10–£14	£15–£19	£20–£25	over £25
HOTELS	under £70	£70–£120	£121–£160	£161–£220	over £220

Restaurant prices are for a main course at dinner. Hotel prices are for two people in a standard double room in high season, generally including the 20% V.A.T.

TOURS

Inverness Tours runs the occasional boat cruise but is mainly known for tours around the Highlands in well-equipped vehicles, which are led by expert guides and heritage enthusiasts. James Johnstone, a personal guide, is based in Inverness but will drive you anywhere; he has a particularly good knowledge of the Highlands and islands, including the Outer Isles.

Tour Contacts Inverness Tours ☎ 01456/450168 ⊕ www.invernesstours.com. **James Johnstone** ☎ 01463/798372 ⊕ www.jajcd.com.

VISITOR INFORMATION

Aviemore, Fort William, and Inverness have year-round tourist offices. Other tourist centers, open seasonally, include those at Fort Augustus, Grantown-on-Spey, Kingussie, Mallaig, and Nairn.

Visitor Information **Visit Highlands** ⊕ *www.visithighlands.com.*

INVERNESS AND ENVIRONS

Because Jacobite tales are interwoven with landmarks throughout this entire area, you should first learn something about this thorny but colorful period of Scottish history in which the Jacobites tried to restore the exiled Stuarts to the British monarchy. The infamous Culloden Moor still looks desolate on most days, and you can easily imagine the fierce, brief, and bloody battle that took place here in 1746 that ended in final, catastrophic defeat for the Jacobites.

The Morayshire coast boasts many long beaches and some refined castles (Cawdor and Brodie) that are definitely worth a visit. Moving east along the inner Moray Firth, you might be tempted by Benromach distillery in Forres, a taste of what you can find further south if you follow the Malt Whisky Trail.

At the center of this region is Inverness, a small city that makes a perfect gateway to the Great Glen. It has a good range of restaurants and accommodations, but its cultural offerings remain more or less limited to what is happening at Eden Court and the live music at a few good pubs.

INVERNESS

176 mi north of Glasgow, 109 mi northwest of Aberdeen, 161 mi northwest of Edinburgh.

9

The city makes a great base for exploring the region, and you can fan out in almost any direction from Inverness for interesting day trips: east to Moray and the distilleries near Forres, southeast to the Cairngorms, and south to Loch Ness. Compared with other Scottish towns, though, Inverness has less to offer visitors with a keen interest in Scottish history. Throughout its past the town was burned and ravaged by Highland clans competing for dominance.

GETTING HERE AND AROUND

You can easily fly into Inverness Airport, as there are daily flights from London, Edinburgh, and Glasgow. However, there are also easy train and bus connections from Glasgow Airport. Scottish Citylink has service here, and Megabus has long-distance bus service from Edinburgh and Glasgow. ScotRail runs trains here from London, Edinburgh, Glasgow, and other cities.

Once you're here, you can explore much of the city by foot. A rental car makes exploring the surrounding area much easier. But if you don't have a car, there are bus and boat tours from the city center to a number of places in the Great Glen.

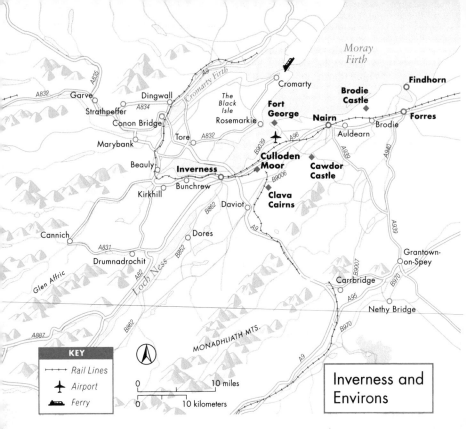

Inverness and Environs

KEY
⊢•••••⊣ Rail Lines
✈ Airport
⛴ Ferry

0 — 10 miles
0 — 10 kilometers

ESSENTIALS

Airport Contacts Inverness Airport ✉ *Dalcross* ☎ *01667/464000* ⊕ *www.hial. co.uk/inverness-airport.*

Bus Contacts Inverness Coach Station ✉ *Margaret St* ☎ *01463/233371.*

Visitor Information Inverness ✉ *Castle Wynd* ☎ *01463/234353* ⊕ *www. inverness-scotland.com.*

EXPLORING

★ **Fort George.** As a direct result of the battle at Culloden, the nervous government in London ordered the construction of a large fort on a promontory reaching into the Moray Firth: Fort George was started in 1748 and completed some 20 years later. It's perhaps the best-preserved 18th-century military fortification in Europe. A visitor center and tableaux at the fort portray the 18th-century Scottish soldier's way of life. The fort is 14 mi northeast of Inverness. ✉ *off B9006, Ardersier* ☎ *01667/460232* ⊕ *www.historic-scotland.gov.uk* 🎟 *£6.90* ☉ *Apr.– Sept., daily 9:30–5; Oct.–Mar., daily 10–4; last admission 45 mins before closing.*

Highlanders Museum. The on-site Highlanders Museum at Fort George gives you a glimpse of the fort's history. Note: the museum is closed until fall 2012; check in advance. ☎ *0131/310–8701* ✉ *Free* ⊙ *Apr.–Sept., daily 9:30–5:15; Oct.–Mar., weekdays 10–4*

Inverness Castle. One of Inverness's few historic landmarks is reddish sandstone Inverness Castle (now the local Sheriff Court), nestled above the river off Castle Road on Castle Hill. The current structure is Victorian, built after a former fort was blown up by the Jacobites in the 1745 campaign.

Inverness Museum and Art Gallery. The excellent, although small, Inverness Museum and Art Gallery covers archaeology, art, local history, and the natural environment in its lively displays. ⊠ *Castle Wynd* ☎ *01463/237114* ⊕ *www.invernessmuseum.com* ✉ *Free* ⊙ *Tues.–Sat. 10–5.*

Inverness Dolphin Cruises. With trips by boat from Inverness harbor into the Moray Firth, Inverness Dolphin Cruises offers you the chance to see dolphins in their breeding areas. ☎ *01463/717900* ⊕ *www.inverness-dolphin-cruises.co.uk.*

John o'Groats Ferries. An unusual option from Inverness is a day trip to Orkney. John o'Groats Ferries runs day tours from Inverness to Orkney, daily from May through August. ☎ *01955/611353* ⊕ *www.jogferry.co.uk.*

WHERE TO EAT

$$
MODERN BRITISH
✕ **Cafe 1.** Locals recommend this restaurant before any other, so it's no surprise that a well-dressed and diverse crowd fills the dining room daily. The decor is refined, with thin-legged metal chairs, laquered wood-topped tables, and Celtic knot mirrors. Dishes like Angus rump steak with a balsamic reduction or sticky pork belly with wok-seared vegetables are served with a welcome calm. The tiny bar at the front is slick and dark and has a great view of the castle. ⊠ *75 Castle St.* ☎ *01463/226200* ⊕ *www.cafe1.net.*

¢
BRITISH
✕ **Dores Inn.** In a low-slung, classic white-stone building on the eastern shore of Loch Ness, this eatery serves tasty and traditional pub food. Just 8 mi south of Inverness, it sits off a pretty, quiet country road and is a good place to stop for lunch or dinner. Stick with favorites like the fish-and-chips, which are good and reasonably priced. The fancier dishes are sometimes expensive for what you get. It's busy during the summer and on weekends, so book ahead. ⊠ *Off B862, Dores* ☎ *01463/751203* ⊕ *www.thedoresinn.co.uk.*

$$
ITALIAN
✕ **Riva.** Facing Inverness Castle, Riva has views over the River Ness from its window seats. The dining room has subtly lighted deep-red walls lined with black-and-white photographs of Italian cityscapes. Tasty Italian dishes include pasta carbonara (with eggs, cream, and bacon), as well as more unusual concoctions like ravioli *alla granchio* (crab-and–tiger prawn ravioli on arugula). The service can be inconsistent. ⊠ *4–6 Ness Walk* ☎ *01463/237377* ⊙ *No lunch Sun.*

$$
BRASSERIE
✕ **Rocpool Restaurant.** Highly recommended by locals, the Rocpool has a calming mix of dark and light woods and cream and pale mint furnishings. The frequently changing menu may include such favorites as sweet-pea-and-spinach risotto for lunch and loin of venison with

9

creamed parsnips and wild mush-rooms for dinner. ☒ *1 Ness Walk* ☎ *01463/717274* ◎ *Closed Sun.*

WHERE TO STAY

There are many places to stay in Inverness, but if your goal is to explore the countryside, a hotel outside the center may be a good choice.

For expanded hotel reviews, visit Fodors.com.

¢ 🖭 **Avalon.** A 20-minute walk from the city center, this neat and modern B&B is a rare find. **Pros:** well-run establishment; good-sized rooms; ample parking. **Cons:** slightly far outside the city. ☒ *79 Glenurqu-hart Rd* ☎ *01463/239075* ⊕ *www.*

inverness-loch-ness.co.uk ☞ *6 rooms* ⚹ *In-room: Wi-Fi* ¶◎¶ *Breakfast.*

$ 🖭 **Bluebell House.** Each room at Bluebell House has sturdy oak furni-ture, including a downstairs bedroom boasting a full-curtained four-poster bed and a curved chaise lounge. **Pros:** large rooms; decadent furnishing; great hosts. **Cons:** smallish bathrooms. ☒ *31 Kenneth St.* ☎ *01463/238201* ⊕ *www.bluebell-house.com* ☞ *4 rooms* ⚹ *In-room: Wi-Fi* ¶◎¶ *Breakfast.*

$$$ 🖭 **Glenmoriston Town House.** Great food and excellent fishing distinguish ★ this stylish hotel with exclusive rights to a stretch of the River Nairn. **Pros:** fabulous restaurant; comfortable beds. **Cons:** cramped rooms; lacks decent soundproofing. ☒ *20 Ness Bank* ☎ *01463/223777* ⊕ *www.glenmoristontownhouse.com* ☞ *30 rooms* ⚹ *In-room: no a/c, Wi-Fi. In-hotel: restaurant, bar* ¶◎¶ *Breakfast.*

$ 🖭 **Moyness House.** Scottish author Neil M. Gunn (1891–1973), known for short stories and novels that evoke images of the Highlands, such as *Morning Tide, Highland River,* and *Butcher's Broom,* once lived in this lovely Victorian villa. **Pros:** relaxing interiors; lovely garden; great loca-tion near the river. **Cons:** public rooms a bit fussy for some; books up quickly. ☒ *6 Bruce Gardens* ☎ *01463/233836* ⊕ *www.moyness.co.uk* ☞ *6 rooms* ⚹ *In-room: no a/c, Wi-Fi* ¶◎¶ *Breakfast.*

$ 🖭 **Pottery House.** This well-run modern lodging, about 8 mi south of Inverness, provides lovely extras like having jugs of ice water and fresh milk for tea or coffee in the refrigerator. **Pros:** great location; spa-cious rooms; delicious breakfasts. **Cons:** some decor could use updat-ing; no public rooms. ☒ *Off B862, Dores* ☎ *01463/751267* ⊕ *www.potteryhouse.co.uk* ☞ *3 rooms* ⚹ *In-room: Wi-Fi* ¶◎¶ *Breakfast.*

$ 🖭 **Strathness House.** Standing on the banks of the River Ness, this 12-room guest house is a quick walk from the well-regarded Eden Court Theatre and the rest of the attractions of the city center. **Pros:** overlooks the river; close to the city center. **Cons:** parking can be dif-

ficult. ⊠ *4 Adross Terr.* ☏ *01463/232765* ⊕ *www.strathnesshouse.com*
🛏 *12 rooms* ⚲ *In-room: Wi-Fi* ⍾ *Breakfast.*

$ ⊞ **Trafford Bank.** A 15-minute walk from downtown Inverness, this for-
mer manse is the perfect place to base yourself. **Pros:** welcoming atmosphere; stylish rooms; relaxing vibe. **Cons:** rooms on the small side.
⊠ *96 Fairfield Rd.* ☏ *01463/241414* ⊕ *www.traffordbankguesthouse.*
co.uk 🛏 *5 rooms* ⚲ *In-room: no a/c, Wi-Fi* ⍾ *Breakfast.*

NIGHTLIFE AND THE ARTS

BARS AND **Blackfriars Pub.** This pub prides itself on its cask-conditioned ales. You
LOUNGES can enjoy one to the accompaniment of regular live entertainment
including jazz nights and *ceilidhs* (a mix of country dancing, music, and
song; pronounced *kay*-lees). ⊠ *93–95 Academy St.* ☏ *01463/233881*

Hootenany. Hootenany is an odd combination of Scottish pub, concert
hall, and Thai restaurant. The excellent pub has a warm atmosphere
and serves food that is highly recommended by locals. ⊠ *67 Church*
St. ☏ *01463/233651.*

THEATER **Eden Court Theatre.** There's plenty of drama at the Eden Court Theatre,
★ and the varied program includes movies, music, comedy, ballet, and
even pantomime. Check out the art gallery and the bright café, and
take a walk around the magnificent Bishop's Palace. ⊠ *Bishops Rd.*
☏ *01463/234234* ⊕ *www.eden-court.co.uk.*

GOLF

Inverness Golf Club. Established in 1883, Inverness Golf Club welcomes
visitors to its parkland course 1 mi from downtown. ⊠ *Culcabock Rd.*
☏ *01463/239882* ⊕ *www.invernessgolfclub.co.uk* 🏌 *18 holes, 6,256*
yds, par 69.

Torvean Golf Course. This municipal course has one of the longest
par-5 holes (565 yards) in the north of Scotland. ⊠ *Glenurquhart Rd.*
☏ *01463/225651* ⊕ *www.torveangolfclub.co.uk* 🏌 *18 holes, 5,784 yds,*
par 68.

SHOPPING

Although Inverness has the usual indoor shopping malls and department stores—including Marks and Spencer—the most interesting goods
are in the specialty outlets in and around town.

Victorian Market. Don't miss the atmospheric indoor Victorian Market,
built in 1870. It houses more than 40 privately owned specialty shops.
⊠ *Academy St..*

BOOKSTORES **Leakey's Secondhand Bookshop.** This shop claims to be the biggest secondhand bookstore in Scotland. When you get tired of leafing through
the 100,000 or so titles, climb to the mezzanine café and study the
cavernous church interior. Antique prints and maps are housed on the
balcony. ⊠ *Greyfriars Hall, Church St.* ☏ *01463/239947.*

CLOTHING **Duncan Chisholm and Sons.** This shop specializes in Highland dress and
tartans. Mail-order and made-to-measure services are available. ⊠ *47–*
51 Castle St. ☏ *01463/234599.*

9

GALLERIES **Castle Gallery.** The gallery sells contemporary paintings, sculpture, prints, and crafts. It occasionally hosts exhibitions by up-and-coming artists. ✉ *43 Castle St.* ☎ *01463/729512.*

★ **Riverside Gallery.** The Riverside Gallery sells paintings, etchings, and prints of Highland landscapes, as well as abstract and representational contemporary work by Highland artists. ✉ *11 Bank St.* ☎ *01463/ 224781* ⊕ *www.riverside-gallery.co.uk.*

LOCAL **Maya Belgian Chocolates.** Offering an exquisite range of chocolates and
SPECIALTIES truffles, this small, glass-fronted shop is said to have the best sweets in Scotland. The chocolates are made by Fabienne de Mulder, who was classically trained in Belgium. ✉ *5 Strothers Ln.* ☎ *01463/419201* ⊕ *www.mayachocolates.co.uk.*

★ **Moniack Castle.** At Moniack Castle you can buy wines made with Scottish ingredients, such as birch sap. The company also makes jams, marmalade, and other preserves. ✉ *A862, 7 mi west of Inverness toward Beauly, Kirkhill* ☎ *01463/831283.*

CULLODEN MOOR

8 mi east of Inverness.

GETTING HERE AND AROUND

Driving along the B9006 from Inverness is the easiest way to Culloden Moor, and there's a generous car park to handle many visitors. Local buses also run from Inverness to the battlefield.

EXPLORING

Clava Cairns. Not far from Culloden, on a narrow road southeast of the battlefield, are the Clava Cairns, dating from the Bronze Age. In a cluster among the trees, these stones and monuments form a large ring with passage graves, which consist of a central chamber below a cairn, reached via a tunnel. Placards explain the graves' significance. ✉ *B851, Culloden.*

★ **Culloden Moor.** Culloden was the scene of the last major battle fought on British soil—to this day considered one of the most infamous and tragic of all. Here, on a cold April day in 1746, the outnumbered, fatigued Jacobite forces of Bonnie Prince Charlie were destroyed by the superior firepower of George II's army. The victorious commander, the duke of Cumberland (George II's son), earned the name of the "Butcher" of Cumberland for the bloody reprisals carried out by his men on Highland families, Jacobite or not, caught in the vicinity. In the battle itself, the duke's army—greatly outnumbering the Scots—killed more than 1,000 soldiers. The National Trust for Scotland has re-created a slightly eerie version of the battlefield as it looked in 1746 that you can explore with a guided audio tour. An innovative visitor center enables you to get closer to the sights and sounds of the battle and to interact with the characters involved. Academic research and technology have helped re-create the Gaelic dialect, song, and music of the time. The excellent on-site café serves homemade soups, sandwiches,

Bonnie Prince Charlie

His life became the stuff of legends. Charles Edward Louis John Casimir Silvester Maria Stuart, better known as Bonnie Prince Charlie or the Young Pretender, was born in Rome in 1720. The grandson of ousted King James II of England, Scotland, and Ireland (King James VII of Scotland) and son of James Stuart, the Old Pretender, he was the focus of Jacobite hopes to reclaim the throne of Scotland. Charles was charming and attractive, and he enjoyed more than the occasional drink.

In 1745 Charles led a Scottish uprising to restore his father to the throne. He sailed to the Outer Hebrides with only a few men but with promised support from France. When that support failed to arrive, he sought help from the Jacobite supporters, many from the Highland clans, who were faithful to his family. With 6,000 men behind him, Charles saw victory in Prestonpans and Falkirk, but the tide turned when he lied to his men about additional Jacobite troops waiting south of the border. When these fictitious troops did not materialize, his army retreated to Culloden where, on the April 16, 1746, they were massacred.

Charles escaped to the Isle of Benbecula where he met and is rumored to have fallen in love with Flora MacDonald. After he had hidden there for a week, Flora dressed him as her maid and brought him to sympathizers on the Isle of Skye. They helped him escape to France.

Scotland endured harsh reprisals from the government after the rebellion. As for Charles, he spent the rest of his life in drunken exile, taking the title count of Albany. In 1772 he married Princess Louise of Stolberg-Gedern, only to separate from her eight years later. He died a broken man in Rome in 1788.

—by Fiona G. Parrott

and cakes. ⊠ *B9006, Culloden* ☎ *0844/493–2159* ⊕ *www.nts.org.uk/ Culloden* ⊡ *£10* ⊗ *Nov.–Mar., daily 10–4; Apr.–Oct., daily 9–6; last entry half hr before closing.*

NAIRN

12 mi east of Culloden Moor, 17 mi east of Inverness, 92 mi west of Aberdeen.

This once-prosperous fishing village has something of a split personality. King James VI (1566–1625) once boasted of a town so large the residents at either end spoke different languages. This was a reference to Nairn, whose fisherfolk, living by the sea, spoke Lowland Scots, whereas its uptown farmers and crofters spoke Gaelic. Nearby is Nairn Castle, loaded with history. East of Nairn pier is a long beach, great for a stroll.

GETTING HERE AND AROUND

A car gives you the most flexibility, but Nairn is close to Inverness (via B9006/B9091), and regular local buses service the town.

EXPLORING

Cawdor Castle. Shakespeare's Macbeth was Thane of Cawdor, but the sense of history that exists within the turreted walls of Cawdor Castle is more than fictional. Cawdor is a lived-in castle, not an abandoned, decaying structure. The earliest part of the castle is the 14th-century central tower; the rooms contain family portraits, tapestries, fine furniture, and paraphernalia reflecting 600 years of history. Outside the castle walls are sheltered gardens and woodland walks. Children will have a ball exploring the lush and mysterious Big Wood, with its wildflowers and varied wildlife. There are lots of creepy stories and fantastic tales amid the dank dungeons and drawbridges. If you like it here, the estate has cottages to rent. ⊠ *B9090, 5 mi southwest of Nairn, Cawdor* ☎ *01667/404401* ⊕ *www.cawdorcastle.com* ⊠ *Grounds £5.50; castle £9.50* ⊙ *May–mid-Oct., daily 10–5.*

Fodor's Choice ★

Nairn Museum. The fishing boats have moved to larger ports, but Nairn's historic flavor has been preserved at the Nairn Museum, in a handsome Georgian building in the center of town. Exhibits emphasize artifacts, photographs, and model boats relating to the town's fishing past. A genealogy service is also offered, and there are occasional craft demonstrations. A library in the same building has a strong local history section. ⊠ *Viewfield House, Viewfield Dr.* ☎ *01667/456791* ⊕ *www.nairnmuseum.co.uk* ⊠ *£3* ⊙ *Apr.–Oct., weekdays 10–4:30, Sat. 10–1.*

WHERE TO STAY

For expanded hotel reviews, visit Fodors.com.

$$$$ **Boath House.** An elegant Regency survivor, this stunning 1820s manor house is surrounded by 20 acres of lovingly nurtured gardens. **Pros:** excellent dining; well-kept grounds; relaxed atmosphere. **Cons:** expensive rates; airplane noise can puncture the silence. ⊠ *A96, Auldearn* ☎ *01667/454896* ⊕ *www.boath-house.com* ↩ *8 rooms* ⌂ *In-room: no a/c. In-hotel: restaurant, spa* ⦿| *Breakfast.*

GOLF

Nairn's courses are highly regarded by golfers and are very popular, so book far in advance.

Nairn Dunbar Golf Club. Founded in 1899, Nairn Dunbar Golf Club is a difficult course with gorse-lined fairways and lovely sea views. ⊠ *Lochloy Rd.* ☎ *01667/452741* ⊕ *www.nairngolfclub.co.uk* ⚑ *18 holes, 6,765 yds, par 72.*

★ **Nairn Golf Club.** Nairn Golf Club, founded in 1887, hosted the 1999 Walker Cup on its Championship Course, a traditional Scottish coastal golf links with what are claimed to be the finest greens in Scotland. ⊠ *Seabank Rd.* ☎ *01667/453208* ⊕ *www.nairngolfclub.co.uk* ⚑ *18 holes, 6,721 yds, par 72.*

SHOPPING

Auldearn Antiques. At Auldearn Antiques, 3 mi east of Nairn, it's easy to spend an hour wandering around the old church filled with furniture, fireplaces, architectural antiques, and linens, and the converted farmsteads, with their tempting antique (or just old) chinaware and textiles. ⊠ *Dalmore Manse, Lethen Rd., Auldearn* ☎ *01667/453087.*

Brodie Countryfare. Visit Brodie Countryfare, 6 mi east of Nairn, only if you're feeling flush: you may covet the unusual knitwear, quality designer clothing and shoes, gifts, and toys, but they are *not* cheap. The excellent restaurant, on the other hand, is quite inexpensive. ⊠ *A96, Brodie* ☎ *01309/641555* ⊕ *www.brodiecountryfare.com.*

FORRES

10 mi east of Nairn.

The burgh of Forres is everything a Scottish medieval town should be, with a handsome tolbooth (the former courthouse and prison) and impressive gardens as its centerpiece. It's remarkable how well the old buildings have adapted to their modern retail uses. With two distilleries—one still operating, the other preserved as a museum—Forres is a key point on the Malt Whisky Trail. Brodie Castle is also nearby. Just 6 mi north you'll find Findhorn Ecovillage and a sandy beach stretches along the edge of the semi-enclosed Findhorn Bay, which is excellent bird-watching territory.

GETTING HERE AND AROUND

Forres is easy to reach by car from Inverness on the A96. Daily ScotRail trains run here from Inverness and Aberdeen.

EXPLORING

Benromach Distillery. The smallest distillery in Moray, Benromach Distiller was founded in 1898. It's now owned by whisky specialist Gordon and MacPhail, who stocks a vast range of malts. An informative hourly tour ends with a tutored nosing and tasting. ⊠ *Invererne Rd.* ☎ *01309/675968* ⊕ *www.benromach.com* ⊡ *£5* ⊘ *Oct.–Apr., weekdays 10–4; May and Sept., Mon.–Sat. 9:30–5; June–Aug., Mon.–Sat. 9:30–5, Sun. noon–4.*

Brodie Castle. About 2 mi west of Forres, this original medieval castle was rebuilt and extended in the 17th and 19th centuries. Fine examples of late-17th-century plasterwork are preserved in the Dining Room and Blue Sitting Room; an impressive library and a superb collection of pictures extend into the 20th century. Brodie Castle is in the care of the National Trust for Scotland. ⊠ *A96, Brodie* ☎ *0844/493–2156* ⊕ *www.nts.org.uk* ⊡ *Grounds free, castle £8.50* ⊘ *Grounds daily 10:30–sunset. Castle Apr., July, and Aug., daily 10:30–4:30; May and Sept.–Oct., Sun.–Wed. 10:30–4:30.*

Dallas Dhu Historic Distillery. The final port of call on the Malt Whisky Trail, the Dallas Dhu Historic Distillery was the last distillery built in the 19th century. No longer a working distillery, the entire structure is open to visitors. An audiovisual presentation tells the story of Scotch whisky. ⊠ *Mannachie Rd.* ☎ *01309/676548* ⊕ *www.dallasdhu.com* ⊡ *£5.50* ⊘ *Apr.–Sept., daily 9:30–5:30; Oct., daily 9:30–4:30; Nov.–Mar., Sat.–Wed. 9:30-4:30.*

Findhorn Ecovillage. About 6 mi from Forres, the Findhorn Ecovillage is an education center dedicated to developing "new ways of living infused with spiritual values." Drawing power from their own wind turbines, village inhabitants farm and garden to sustain themselves.

9

A £5 tour—check in at visitor reception for information—affords a thought-provoking glimpse into the lives of the ultra-independent villagers. See homes made out of whisky barrels, and the Universal Hall, made of wood and beautiful engraved glass. The Phoenix Shop sells organic foodstuffs and handmade crafts, and the Blue Angel Café serves organic and vegetarian fare. ⊠ *The Park, Off B9011, Findhorn* 🕾 *01309/690311* ⊕ *www.findhorn.org* ✉ *Free* ☉ *Mar., Apr., Oct., and Nov., weekdays 10–5, Sat. 1–4; May–Sept., weekdays 10–5, weekends 1–4; Dec.–Feb., weekdays 10–5.*

Sueno's Stone. At the eastern end of town, don't miss Sueno's Stone, a soaring pillar of stone carved with ranks of cavalry, foot soldiers, and dying victims. The stone is said to commemorate a 10th-century victory.

SPORTS AND THE OUTDOORS

Findhorn Bay. Along the edge of Findhorn Bay you'll find a long stretch of beach, great for an afternoon by the sea. You can reach the beach through the dunes from the northern end of the Findhorn Ecovillage, or park at the edge of the village of Findhorn for a shorter stroll. There are public restrooms but few other amenities. ⊠ *Off B89011, Findhorn.*

SPEYSIDE AND THE CAIRNGORMS

The Spey is a long river, running from Fort Augustus to the Moray Firth, and its fast-moving waters make for excellent fishing at many points along its way. They also give Speyside malt whiskies a softer flavor than those made with peaty island water. The area's native and planted pine forests draw many birds each spring and summer, and people come for miles to see the capercaillies and ospreys.

Defining the eastern edge of the Great Glen, Cairngorms National Park provides sporty types with all the adventure they could ask for, including walking, kayaking, rock climbing, and even skiing, if the winter is cold enough. The park has everything but the sea: craggy mountains, calm lochs, and swift rivers. While the unremarkable town of Aviemore may put off some travelers, the Cairngorms are truly remarkable.

GRANTOWN-ON-SPEY

24 mi south of Forres, 14 mi northeast of Aviemore.

The sturdy settlement of Grantown-on-Spey, set amid tall pines that flank the River Spey, is a classic Scottish planned town. The community was laid out by the local landowner, in this case Sir James Grant, in 1776. It has handsome buildings in silver granite and some good shopping for locally made crafts.

GETTING HERE AND AROUND

If you don't have a car, the easiest way to get to Grantown-on-Spey is taking the train to Carrbridge and connecting via a local bus. By car, take the A940 and A939 from Forres or the A9 and A95 from Aviemore.

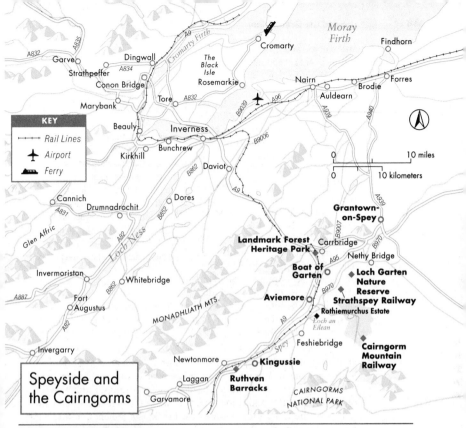

BOAT OF GARTEN

11 mi southwest of Grantown-on-Spey; 6 mi northeast of Aviemore.

In the peaceful village of Boat of Garten, the scent of pine trees mingles with an equally evocative smell—that of steam trains. You can take a nostalgic steam train trip on the Strathspey Steam Railway between Aviemore and Boat of Garden. Close to Cairngorms National Park, Boat of Garten is building a reputation as a great place to stay while exploring the region.

GETTING HERE AND AROUND

This charming town is an easy drive from Inverness or Aviemore via the A9 and the A95 and from Grantown via the B970. It's also serviced by local buses, and some people travel here on the Strathspey Steam Train.

EXPLORING

Landmark Forest Theme Park. About 4 mi northwest of Boat of Garten, Landmark Forest Theme Park has entertainments such as a Timber Trail with a fire tower you can climb, a steam-powered sawmill, and a Clydesdale horse that hauls the logs. At the forestry workshop, you can try out the crosscut saw. Kids will want to check out the forest maze, terrifyingly steep waterslides, a climbing wall, miniature cars and trucks, and an adventure play-ground. ■TIP→ **Plan on spending about three to five hours here.** To get to Carrbridge, take the quiet B9153 rather than the crowded A9. ⊠ *B9153, Carrbridge* ☎ *0800/731–3446* ⊕ *www.landmarkpark.co.uk* ▣ *£12.60* ☉ *Apr.–mid-July, daily 10–6; mid-July and Aug., daily 10–7; Sept.–Mar., daily 10–5; last admission 1 hr before closing.*

Loch Garten Nature Reserve. Set in the heart of Abernethy Forest, the Loch Garten Nature Reserve offers a glimpse of the osprey, a large fishing bird that come here to breed. The reserve, one of the last stands of ancient Scots pines in Scotland, attracts a host of birds, including the bright crossbill and the crested tit. You might also spot the rarely seen red squirrel. The sanctuary is administered by the Royal Society for the Protection of Birds. ⊠ *Off B970, 1 mi east of Boat of Garten, B970* ☎ *01479/831476* ⊕ *www.rspb.org.uk* ▣ *£3* ☉ *Apr.–Aug., daily 10–6.*

☾ **Strathspey Steam Railway.** In Boat of Garten you can hop aboard the Strathspey Steam Railway. The oily scent of smoke and steam hangs faintly in the air near the authentically preserved train station. Travel in old-fashioned style and enjoy superb views of the high and often white domes of the Cairngorm Mountains. Breakfasts, lunches, and special dinners are served on board from March to mid-September. ⊠ *Boat of Garten Station, Spey Ave.* ☎ *01479/810725* ⊕ *www.strathspeyrailway.co.uk.*

WHERE TO STAY

For expanded hotel reviews, visit Fodors.com.

$ 🖳 **Mountview Hotel.** An old hunting lodge perched in the hills of Nethybridge, this hotel boasts great views out over the valley. **Pros:** quiet setting; stunning views; great restaurant. **Cons:** older carpets in some areas. ⊠ *B970, Nethybridge* ☎ *01479/821515* ⊕ *www.mountviewhotel.co.uk* ⇔ *12 rooms* ⚷ *In-room: Wi-Fi* |○| *Breakfast.*

SHOPPING

Boat of Garten Post Office. Expertly run by Beth and David Woolsey, this local post office and gift shop more than pulls its weight. With fruit, chocolate, cheese, freshly baked breads, and hot pies, it's a great place to stock up for a day hiking in the hills. The small shop at the front is excellent for postcards and souvenirs to take home. ⊠ *Dershar Rd.* ☎ *01479/831527* ⊕ *www.boatofgartenpostoffice.co.uk.*

SPORTS AND THE OUTDOORS

Cairngorm Bike & Hike. This small, well-stocked outdoor shop rents well-maintained bikes, offers a good selection of lightweight backpacks, and has all sorts of outdoor gear—everything you'll need for your biking excursions around the Cairngorms. ⊠ *Boat of Garten Station, Spey Ave.* ☎ *01479/831745.*

AVIEMORE

6 mi southwest of Boat of Garten, 30 mi south of Inverness.

At the foot of the Cairngorms, the once-quiet Aviemore now has all the brashness and boxiness of a year-round holiday resort. In the summer months it's filled with walkers, cyclists, and rock-climbers, so it's a great place for stocking up on supplies. Many of the smaller villages nearby are quieter places to stay.

■ TIP➡ Be forewarned: this region can get very cold above 3,000 feet, and weather conditions can change rapidly, even in the middle of summer.

GETTING HERE AND AROUND

The A9, Scotland's major north–south artery, runs past Aviemore. From Boat of Garten, take the B970. The town is serviced by regular trains and buses from Inverness.

ESSENTIALS

Visitor Information Aviemore ⊠ *Grampian Rd.* ☎ *01479/810930* ⊕ *www.visitcairngorms.com.*

EXPLORING

CairnGorm Mountain Railway. A funicular railway to the top of Cairn Gorm (the mountain that gives its name to the region), the CairnGorm Mountain Railway operates both during and after the ski season and affords extensive views across the Cairngorms and the broad valley of the Spey. At the top is a visitor center and restaurant. Prebooking is recommended. ⊠ *B970* ☎ *01479/861261* ⊕ *www.cairngormmountain.co.uk* ⤴ *£9.95* ⊙ *Daily 10–4:30.*

★ **Cairngorms National Park.** A rugged wilderness of mountains, moorlands, glens, and lochs, Cairngorms National Park is the country's second-oldest national park. Past Loch Morlich at the high parking lot on the exposed shoulders of the Cairngorm Mountains are dozens of trails for hiking and cycling. The park is especially popular with birding enthusiasts, as it's the best place to see the Scottish crossbill, the only bird unique to Britain. Weather conditions in the park change abruptly, so be sure to have the proper gear or seek out many of the guided options. This is a massive park, but a good place to start exploring is the visitor center in Aviemore. ☎ *01479/873535* ⊕ *www.cairngorms.co.uk.*

⟳ **Cairngorm Reindeer Centre.** On the high slopes of the Cairngorms, you may see the reindeer herd that was introduced here in the 1950s. Inquire at the Cairngorm Reindeer Centre about accompanying the herders on their daily rounds. Daily visits from May to September depart at 11 and 2:30. The reindeer are docile creatures and seem to enjoy human company. Be sure to wear waterproof gear, as conditions can be wet

9

Cairngorms National Park

Britain's newest national park is also its largest, covering nearly 1,400 square mi of countryside. At its heart is a wild arctic landscape that sits on a granite plateau. Five of Scotland's nine 4,000-feet-high mountains are found in this range, and there are 13 more over 3,000 feet. These rounded mountains, including Cairn Gorm (meaning "blue hill" in Gaelic) and Ben Macdui, the second highest in Britain at 4,295 feet, were formed at the end of the last ice age. The Larig Ghru Pass, a stunning U-shape glen, was formed by the retreating glacier.

Hikers, underestimate this landscape at your peril: the fierce conditions often found on the Cairngorms plateau have claimed many lives. If you venture out into it, make sure you are well prepared and have informed someone of your planned route and estimated return time.

The environment supports rare arctic-alpine and tundra plant and animal species (a quarter of Britain's threatened species) including flora such as the least willow and alpine blue-sow thistle, and birds such as the ptarmigan, Scottish crossbill, and dotterel. Lower down the slopes, terrain that was once filled with woodland is now characterized by heather, cotton grass, and sphagnum moss. This open expanse allows visitors to glimpse wild animals such as the golden eagle, roe deer, or red deer.

Fragments of the ancient Caledonian forest (largely Scots pine, birch, and rowan) remain and are home to pine martins, red squirrels, and capercaillie (a large grouse). Studding these forests are dramatic glens and the rivers Spey, Don, and Dee, which are home to Atlantic salmon, otters, and freshwater pearl mussels.

and muddy. ⌂ *Glenmore Forest Park, B970, 6 mi east of Aviemore* ☎ *01479/861228* ⊕ *www.cairngormreindeer.co.uk* ☑ *£10* ⊗ *Feb.–Dec., daily 10–5.*

★ **Loch an Eilean.** The place that best sums up Speyside's piney ambience is probably a nature reserve called Loch an Eilean. There are great low-level paths around the tree-rimmed loch (perfect for bikes) or longer trails to Glen Einich. A converted cottage beside Loch an Eilean serves as a visitor center.

Rothiemurchus Estate. Loch an Eilein is on the Rothiemurchus Estate, which offers several diversions, including hiking, biking, fly-fishing for salmon and trout, dogsledding, clay-pigeon shooting, and farm-shop tastings of estate-produced beef, venison, and trout. ⌂ *B970* ☎ *01479/812345* ⊕ *www.rothiemurchus.net* ☑ *Free* ⊗ *Daily 9:30–4:30.*

WHERE TO EAT

¢ ✕ **Mountain Cafe.** On the main street in Aviemore, the Mountain Café
CAFÉ is a down-to-earth find in this touristy town. It's known for hearty all-day breakfasts, well-seasoned sandwiches and burgers, and rich coffee. Leave room for the cakes, which are made on the premises. The service can be slow at peak times, meaning you may have to wait for a table.

There are great views of the Cairngorms from the dining room. ⊠ *111 Grampian Rd.* ☎ *01479/812473* ⊕ *www.mountaincafe-aviemore.co.uk* ☺ *No dinner.*

$$ ✕ **Old Bridge Inn.** Across a pedestrian bridge from Aviemore Station, this
MODERN BRITISH old-style bar and conservatory restaurant serves what locals call the best pub food in Aviemore. The simple fare includes local favorites like Morayshire cod or black-faced lamb, and the garlic roasted potatoes are recommended as a side for any main dish. The bar serves a wide selection of local brews, and there's often live music playing. Roaring fires are very welcome in a place that can have cool nights anytime of year. ⊠ *Dalfaber Rd.* ☎ *01479/811137* ⊕ *www.oldbridgeinn.co.uk* ⚠ *Reservations essential.*

SPORTS AND THE OUTDOORS

G2 Outdoor. The wide range of adventures at G2 Outdoor includes white-water rafting, gorge walking, and rock climbing. The company offers a family float trip on the River Spey in summer, and in winter runs ski courses. ⊠ *Dalfaber Industrial Estate, off Dalfaber Dr.* ☎ *01479/811008.*

★ **Glenmore Lodge.** About 6 mi east of Aviemore in Cairngorms National Park, Glenmore Lodge is your best bet for trying a new activity or enhancing your outdoor skills. Take your pick from the impressive courses on rock and ice climbing, hiking, kayaking, ski touring, mountain biking, and more. Some classes are for kids over 14. There are superb facilities, such as an indoor climbing wall. ⊠ *B970* ☎ *01479/861256* ⊕ *www.glenmorelodge.org.uk.*

Mikes Bikes. This small bike shop stocks all the gear you might need to take advantage of the many paths around Aviemore. It also rents and repairs bikes. The place is somewhat hard to find, tucked down some stairs below the street. ⊠ *Myrtlefield Shopping Centre, Grampian Rd.* ☎ *01479/810478* ⊕ *www.aviemorebikes.co.uk.*

9

KINGUSSIE

13 mi southwest of Aviemore.

Set in a wide glen, Kingussie is a pretty town east of the Monadhliadh Mountains. With great distant views of the Cairngorms, it's perfect for those who would prefer to avoid the far more hectic town of Aviemore.

GETTING HERE AND AROUND

From Aviemore, Kingussie is easy to reach by car via the A9 and the A86.

EXPLORING

☾ **Highland Folk Museum.** In Newtonmore, the Highland Folk Museum allows you to explore reconstructed Highland buildings, including a Victorian-era schoolhouse, and watch tailors, clockmakers, and joiners demonstrating their trades. Walking paths (or old-fashioned buses) take you to an 18th-century township that includes a feal house (made of turf) and a weaver's house. Throughout the museum there are hands-on exhibitions like a working quern stone for grinding grain, making this a great outing for kids. ⊠ *Kingussie Rd., Newtonmore* ☎ *01540/673551*

⊕ *www.highlandfolk.com* ✉ *Free* ⊙ *Apr.–Aug., daily 10:30–5:30; Sept.–Oct., daily 11–4:30.*

Ruthven Barracks. Looking like a ruined castle on a mound, Ruthven Barracks is redolent with tales of "the '45" (as the last Jacobite rebellion is often called). The defeated Jacobite forces rallied here after the battle at Culloden, but then abandoned and blew up the government outpost they had earlier captured. You'll see its crumbling yet imposing stone outline as you approach Kingussie. ⊠ *B970, ½ mi south of Kingussie* ☎ *01667/460232* ⊕ *www.historic-scotland.gov.uk* ✉ *Free* ⊙ *Daily 24 hrs.*

WHERE TO EAT AND STAY

For expanded hotel reviews, visit Fodors.com.

BIKING THE GLEN

A dedicated bicycle path, created by Scotland's National Cycle Networks, runs from Glasgow to Inverness, passing through Fort William and Kingussie. Additionally, a good network of back roads snakes around Inverness and toward Nairn. The B862/B852, which runs by the southeast side of Loch Ness, has little traffic and is a good bet for cyclists. Stay off the A9, however, as it's busy with vehicular traffic on both sides of Aviemore. The very busy A82 main road, along the northwest bank of Loch Ness via Drumnadrochit, is for the same reason not recommended for cyclists.

¢ ✕ **The Potting Shed.** Seasonal fruits and smooth cream top many of the
CAFÉ delectable desserts at this cake shop on Main Street in Kinguissie. Taught by his Norwegian mother, John Borrowman makes sponges that are rich and light and contain no butter or fat (although you can't say the same thing about the rich cream they're topped with). The shop also offers gluten-free options that use almonds in the place of flour, and these are by no means lacking in richness or flavor. There's a chocolate cake with a description that simply reads "lots of chocolate." An accompanying wide selection of coffees and teas makes this an excellent place to stop and plan your next activity. ⊠ *Main St.* ☎ *01540/651287* ⊕ *www.inshriachnursery.co.uk.*

$ ✕ **Sili Restaurant.** In the Silverfjord Hotel, this glass-walled, crisply dec-
BRITISH orated restaurant is like a beacon when seen from the outside. The kitchen serves well-made standards like Scottish rib-eye steak. You can't go wrong ordering from the excellent specials board, which might include pan-seared duck breast or smoked salmon. The bar often serves the same food, only slightly cheaper. The hotel's rooms are inexpensive, but not as bright and pleasing as the restaurant. ⊠ *Silverfjord Hotel, Ruthven Rd.* ☎ *01540/661292* ⊕ *www.silverfjordhotel.co.uk.*

$$$$ ✕ **The Cross.** This former tweed mill, with a burn (a narrow river) run-
BRITISH ning alongside its stone walls, is set in 4 acres of woodlands. The inti-
★ mate dining room, where the stone walls have been painted a creamy white, is warmed by a crackling fireplace. The food here is smart and bold, with dishes such as baked Scrabster brill, slow-roasted Ayrshire pork, and honey-baked apricots. Each dish reveals an intimate knowledge of textures and flavors. If you like it here so much you don't want to leave, you'll be glad to know that there are also rooms available.

✉ *Tweed Mill Brae, Ardbroilach Rd.* ☎ *01540/661166* ⊕ *www.thecross. co.uk* ⊘ *Closed Jan. No dinner Sun. and Mon.*

$ 🏨 **Coig Na Shee.** This century-old Highland lodge has a warm and cozy atmosphere. **Pros:** excellent rooms; quiet location; great walks from house. **Cons:** a bit out of the way. ✉ *Laggan Rd., Newtonmore* ☎ *01540/670109* ⊕ *www.coignashee.co.uk* ⤴ *5 rooms* ♿ *In-room: no a/c, Wi-Fi* ♎ *Breakfast.*

LOCH NESS AND TOWARD THE SMALL ISLES

Compared with other lochs, Loch Ness is by no means known for its beauty, but it draws attention for its famous monster. Heading south from Inverness, you can travel along the loch's quiet east side or the more touristy west side. A pleasant morning can be spent at Urquhart Castle, in the monster-gazing town of Drumnadrochit, or a bit farther south in the pretty town of Fort Augustus, where the Caledonian Canal meets Loch Ness. As you travel south and west, the landscape opens up and the Nevis Range comes into view.

From Fort William you can visit the dark, cloud-laden mountains of Glencoe and the desolate stretch of moors and lochans at Rannoch Moor. Travelers drive through this region to experience the landscape, which changes at nearly every turn. It's a brooding, haunting area that's worth a visit in any season.

The Road to the Isles, less romantically known as the A830, leads from Fort William to the coastal towns of Arisaig, Morar and Mallaig, with access to the small isles of Rum, Eigg, Canna, and Muck. From here you can also visit the Isle of Skye *(see Chapter 10)* via the ferry at Mallaig.

DRUMNADROCHIT

14 mi south of Inverness.

A tourist hub at the curve of the road, Drumnadrochit is not known for its style or culture, but it does seem to attract people interested in mythical monsters. There aren't many good restaurants, but there are some solid hotels.

GETTING HERE AND AROUND

It's easy to get here from Fort Augustus or Inverness via the A82, either by car or by local bus.

EXPLORING

Jacobite Cruises. Jacobite Cruises runs morning and afternoon cruises on Loch Ness to Urquhart Castle and other destinations throughout the region. The harbor is 5 mi northeast of Drumnadochit via the A82. ✉ *Clansman Harbour, A82* ☎ *01463/233999* ⊕ *www.jacobite.co.uk.*

Loch Ness. From the A82 you get many views of the formidable and famous Loch Ness, which has a greater volume of water than any other Scottish loch, a maximum depth of more than 800 feet, and its own monster—at least according to popular myth. Early travelers who passed this way included English lexicographer Dr. Samuel Johnson (1709–84) and his guide and biographer, James Boswell (1740–95),

9

who were on their way to the Hebrides in 1783. They remarked at the time about the poor condition of the population and the squalor of their homes. Another early travel writer and naturalist, Thomas Pennant (1726–98), noted that the loch kept the locality frost-free in winter. Even General Wade came here, his troops blasting and digging a road up much of the eastern shore. None of these observant early travelers ever made mention of a monster. Clearly, they had not read the local guidebooks.

🕓 **Loch Ness Centre & Exhibition.** If you're in search of the infamous beast Nessie, head to this exhibition, which explores the facts and the fakes, the photographs, the unexplained sonar contacts, and the sincere testimony of eyewitnesses. You'll have to make up your own mind on Nessie. All that's really known is that Loch Ness's huge volume of water has a warming effect on the local weather, making the loch conducive to mirages in still, warm conditions. Whether or not the *bestia aquatilis* lurks in the depths is more than ever in doubt since 1994, when the man who took one of the most convincing photos of Nessie confessed on his deathbed that it was a fake. You can take a cruise of the loch from the center, too. ✉ *A82* ☎ *01456/450573* ⊕ *www.lochness.com* 💷 *£6.50* 🕓 *Easter–May, Sept., and Oct., daily 9:30–5; June, 9–5:30; July and Aug., daily 9–6; Nov.–Easter, daily 10–3:30; last admission ½ hr before closing.*

Urquhart Castle. About 2 mi southeast of Drumnadrochit, Urquhart Castle is a favorite Loch Ness monster–watching spot. This broken-down fortress stands on a promontory overlooking the loch, as it has since the Middle Ages. Because of its central and strategic position in the Great Glen line of communication, the castle has a complex history involving military offense and defense, as well as its own destruction and renovation. The castle was begun in the 13th century and was destroyed before the end of the 17th century to prevent its use by the Jacobites. The ruins of what was one of the largest castles in Scotland were then plundered for building material. A visitor center relates these events and gives an idea of what life was like here in medieval times. ✉ *A82* ☎ *01456/450551* ⊕ *www.historic-scotland.gov.uk/places* 💷 *£7.20* 🕓 *Apr.–Sept., daily 9:30–6; Oct., 9:30–5; Nov.–Mar., daily 9:30–4:30; last admission 45 mins before closing.*

WHERE TO STAY

For expanded hotel reviews, visit Fodors.com.

$$$$ 🏨 **Loch Ness Lodge.** Run by siblings Scott and Iona Sutherland, Loch Ness Lodge is an exquisite place: opulent, classy, and welcoming. **Pros:** excellent staff; superb views; near Inverness. **Cons:** pricey rates; near a busy road. ✉ *A82, Brachla* ☎ *01456/459469* ⊕ *www.loch-ness-lodge. com* 🛏 *7 rooms* ♿ *In-room: no a/c, Wi-Fi. In-hotel: restaurant, spa* 🍴 *Some meals.*

EN ROUTE A more leisurely alternative to the fast-moving traffic on the busy A82, and one that combines monster-watching with peaceful road touring, is to take the **B862** south from Inverness and follow the east bank of Loch Ness. Take the opportunity to view the waterfalls at Foyers and the peaceful, reedy Loch Tarff. Descend through forests and moorland

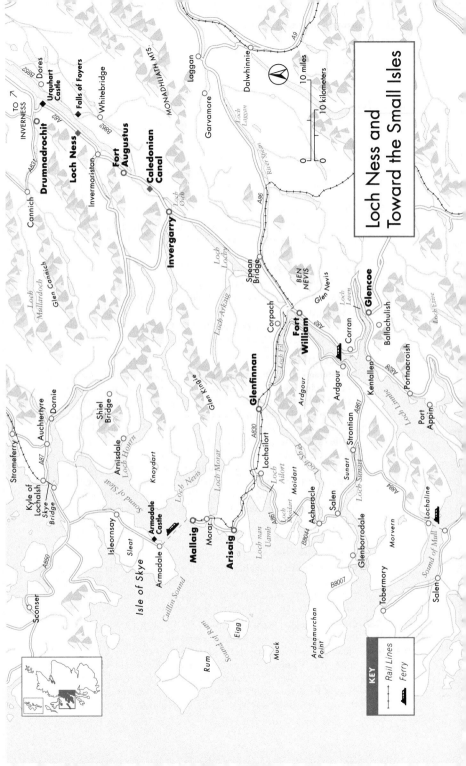

Loch Ness and Toward the Small Isles

until the road runs around the southern tip of Loch Ness. The half-hidden track beside the road is a remnant of the military road built by General Wade.

FORT AUGUSTUS

19 mi south of Drumnadrochit, 33 mi south of Inverness, 31 mi northeast of Fort William.

The best place to see the locks of the Caledonian Canal is at Fort Augustus, at the southern tip of Loch Ness. This bustling small town is a great place to begin walking and cycling excursions, or to sit by the canal watching the locks fill and empty as boats sail between Loch Ness to Loch Laggan.

Fort Augustus itself was captured by the Jacobite clans during the 1745 Rebellion. Later the fort was rebuilt as a Benedictine abbey, but the monks no longer live here.

GETTING HERE AND AROUND

Fort Augustus is an easy drive from Inverness or Invergarry on the A82. Buses run frequently, as this is a busy tourist destination.

ESSENTIALS

Visitor Information Caledonian Canal Visitor Centre ⊠ *Ardchattan House, Canalside* ☎ *01463/725500* ⊕ *www.scottishcanals.co.uk.*

EXPLORING

Caledonian Canal. The canal, which links the lochs of the Great Glen—Loch Lochy, Loch Oich, and Loch Ness—owes its origins to a combination of military as well as political pressures that emerged at the time of the Napoleonic Wars with France: for the most part, the British needed a better and faster way to get naval vessels from one side of Scotland to the other. The great Scottish engineer Thomas Telford (1757–1834) surveyed the route in 1803. The canal, which took 19 years to complete, has 29 locks and 42 gates. Telford ingeniously took advantage of the three lochs that lie in the Great Glen, which have a combined length of 45 mi, so that only 22 mi of canal had to be constructed to connect the lochs and complete the waterway from coast to coast.

Along and near the canal there are often stunning vistas of mountains and lochs and glens, and as you head south you can see the impressive profile of Ben Nevis.

Clansman Centre. In a handsome Victorian building, the Clansman Centre tells some stirring tales about life in this region. The gift shop sells Celtic jewelry, traditional Highland garb, and ceremonial armor. ⊠ *Canalside* ☎ *01320/366444* ⊕ *www.scottish-swords.com.*

OFF THE BEATEN PATH

Creag Meagaidh Nature Reserve. A stretch of the A86, quite narrow in some places, hugs the western shore of Loch Laggan. It has superb views of the mountainous heartlands to the north, and, over the silvery spine of hills known as the Grey Corries, culminates with views of Ben Nevis to the south. Halfway along the loch is the Creag Meagaidh Nature Reserve, a sublime picnic spot and a good base for walks into the restored woodland below the spectacular ice-carved crags of Coire

Ardair. ⊠ *Off A86, Kinloch Laggan* ☎ *01528/544265* ⊕ *www.nnr-scotland.org.uk.*

WHERE TO STAY

For expanded hotel reviews, visit Fodors.com.

$ ☒ **Glengarry Castle Hotel.** This rambling Victorian baronial mansion,
HOTEL tucked away in Invergarry, makes a good base for touring the area; the
★ village is just south of Loch Ness and within easy reach of the Great
Glen's most popular sights. **Pros:** atmospheric building and gardens;
good-value takeout lunches; family rooms available. **Cons:** showers
not always piping hot; steps to climb. ⊠ *A82, Laggan* ☎ *01809/501254*
⊕ *www.glengarry.net* ↪ *26 rooms* ⌂ *In-room: no a/c, Wi-Fi. In-hotel:
restaurant, tennis court, water sports* ⊗ *Closed mid-Nov.–mid-Mar.*
⊠| *Breakfast.*

FORT WILLIAM

16 mi north of Glencoe, 69 mi southwest of Inverness, 108 mi north-west of Glasgow, 138 mi northwest of Edinburgh.

As its name suggests, Fort William originated as a military outpost, first
established by Oliver Cromwell's General Monk in 1655 and refortified
by George I (1660–1727) in 1715 to help combat an uprising by the
turbulent Jacobite clans. It remains the southern gateway to the Great
Glen and the far west, and it's a busy, commercial, tourist-oriented place
with plenty of places to stay and shop.

GETTING HERE AND AROUND

From Glasgow (to the south) and Inverness (to the north), the A82
takes you the entire way. From Edinburgh, take the M9 to the A84.
This empties into the A85, which connects to the A82 that takes you
to Fort William. Roads around Fort William are well maintained, but
mostly one lane in each direction. They can be very busy in summer.

A long-distance Scottish Citylink bus connects Glasgow and Fort William. ScotRail has trains from London, as well as connections from
Glasgow and Edinburgh. It also operates a diesel train on the line
between Fort William and Mallaig. Many travelers use it to shuttle
back and forth between these towns.

ESSENTIALS

Visitor Information Fort William ⊠ *15 High St.* ☎ *01397/701801* ⊕ *www.
visitscotland.com.*

EXPLORING

Ben Nevis. Great Britain's highest mountain, the 4,406-foot Ben Nevis,
looms over Fort William, less than 4 mi from Loch Linnhe. A trek to
its summit is a rewarding experience, but you should be fit and well
prepared—food and water, map and compass, first-aid kit, whistle, hat,
gloves, and warm clothing (yes, even in summer) for starters—as the
unpredictable weather can make it a hazardous hike. Ask for advice at
the local tourist office before you begin.

★ **Jacobite Steam Train.** The most relaxing way to take in the landscape
of birch- and bracken-covered wild slopes is by rail. The best ride is

on the Jacobite Steam Train, a famously scenic 84-mi round-trip that runs between Fort William and Mallaig from mid-May through mid-October; cost is £32. You'll see mountains, lochs, beaches, and islands along the way. ☎ 0845/1284681 ⊕ *www.westcoastrailways.co.uk* ⊘ *Mid-May–Oct., weekdays; July–Aug., daily.*

West Highland Museum. In the town center, the West Highland Museum explores the history of Prince Charles Edward Stuart and the 1745 Rebellion. Included in the museum's folk exhibits are a costume and tartan display and a famous collection of Jacobite relics. ✉ *Cameron Sq.* ☎ 01397/702169 ⊕ *www.westhighlandmuseum.org.uk* ⊠ *Free* ⊘ *June–Sept., Mon.–Sat. 10–5; Aug., and Oct.–May, Mon.–Sat. 10–4.*

WHERE TO EAT AND STAY

For expanded hotel reviews, visit Fodors.com.

$$$ ╳ **Crannog Seafood Restaurant.** With its reputation for quality and simSEAFOOD plicity, this restaurant on the town pier offers tasty seafood on the water.
★ The sight of a fishing boat drawing up on the shores of Loch Linnhe to take its catch straight to the kitchen says it all about the freshness of the fish. The chef's capable touch ensures the fresh flavors are not overwhelmed. From the window seats you can watch the sun setting on the far side of the loch. The eatery runs four daily cruises between March and October. A good choice in a town with limited options. ✉ *The Pier* ☎ 01397/705589.

$ ▦ **The Grange.** This meticulously renovated Victorian villa stands in
Fodor's Choice pretty gardens a 10-minute walk from downtown. **Pros:** lots of little
★ extras; great attention to detail; elegant lounge with plenty of books. **Cons:** not suitable for families with younger children. ✉ *Grange Rd.* ☎ 01397/705516 ⊕ *www.thegrange-scotland.co.uk* ➴ *3 rooms* ⚭ *In-room: Wi-Fi. In-hotel: some age restrictions* ⊘ *Closed Oct.–Mar.* ⦿ *Breakfast.*

$$$$ ▦ **Inverlochy Castle Hotel.** A red-granite Victorian mansion, Inverlochy Castle stands on 50 acres of woodlands in the shadow of Ben Nevis, with striking Highland landscape visible on every side. **Pros:** relaxing public rooms; sublime views. **Cons:** pricey rates; bland bathrooms. ✉ *A82* ☎ 01397/702177 ⊕ *www.inverlochycastlehotel.com* ➴ *14 rooms, 3 suites* ⚭ *In-room: no a/c, Wi-Fi. In-hotel: restaurant, tennis court* ⊘ *Closed Jan. and Feb.* ⦿ *Breakfast.*

SPORTS AND THE OUTDOORS

BICYCLING **Nevis Range Mountain Bike Track.** For a thrilling ride down Ben Nevis, take the gondola up to the beginning of the Nevis Range Mountain Bike Track and then shoot off on a 2,000-foot descent. The lift costs £11.50. It's open May to September, weather permitting. Bike rentals are available near the gondola. ✉ *A82* ☎ 01397/705825 ⊕⊕⊕⊕ *bike.nevisrange.co.uk.*

GOLF **Fort William Golf Club.** The Fort William Golf Club has spectacular views of Ben Nevis and welcomes visitors. ✉ *Torlundy* ☎ 01397/704464 ⅂ *18 holes, 6,217 yds, par 70.*

HIKING This area—especially around Glen Nevis, Glencoe, and Ben Nevis—is popular with hikers; however, routes are not well marked, so contact the Fort William tourist information center before you go. The center will provide you with route advice based on your interests, level of fitness, and hiking experience.

Ben Nevis. This is a large and dangerous mountain, where snow can fall on the summit plateau any time of the year. Several excellent guides are available locally; they should be consulted for high-altitude routes.

Glen Nevis. For a walk in Glen Nevis, drive north from Fort William on the A82 toward Fort Augustus. On the outskirts of town, just before the bridge over the River Nevis, turn right up the unclassified road signposted Glen Nevis. Drive about 6 mi, crossing the River Nevis over the bridge at Achriabhach (Lower Falls). Park at a parking lot about 2½ mi from the bridge. Starting here, a footpath leads to waterfalls and a steel-cable bridge (1 mi), and then to Steall, a ruined croft beside a boulder-strewn stream (a good picnic place). You can continue up the glen for some distance without danger of becoming lost, so long as you stay on the path and keep the river to your right. Watch your step going through the tree-lined gorge. The return route is back the way you came.

SKIING **Nevis Range.** About 7 mi north of Fort William, Nevis Range is a modern development on the flanks of Aonach Mor. It has good and varied skiing, as well as views of Ben Nevis. There's a gondola system and runs for all skill levels. Skiing gets under way, adequate snowfall permitting, at the end of December. The season normally continues until early April. Daily ski passes are £29. ☎ *01397/705825* ⊕ *snowsports. nevisrange.co.uk.*

SHOPPING
The majority of shops here are along High Street, which in summer attracts bustling crowds intent on stocking up for excursions to the west.

Ellis Brigham Mountain Sports. This shop can help you get kitted out for your outdoor adventures. ⊠ *St. Marys Hall, Belford Rd.* ☎ *01397/706220* ⊕ *www.ellis-brigham.com.*

★ **Nevisport.** Nevisport has been selling outdoor supplies, maps, and travel books for more than 30 years from its flagship store. ⊠ *High St.* ☎ *01397/704921* ⊕ *www.nevisport.com.*

GLENCOE

Fodor's Choice ★ *16 mi south of Fort William, 92 mi north of Glasgow, 44 mi northwest of Edinburgh.*

Glencoe is both a small town and a region of awesome beauty, with high peaks and secluded glens. The area, where wild, craggy buttresses loom darkly over the road, has a special place in the folk memory of Scotland: the glen was the site of an infamous massacre in 1692, still remembered in the Highlands for the treachery with which soldiers of the Campbell clan, acting as a government militia, treated their hosts, the MacDonalds. According to Highland code, in his own home a clansman should give shelter even to his sworn enemy. In the face of bitter weather, the Campbells were accepted as guests by the MacDonalds. Apparently acting on orders from the British government, the Campbells turned on their hosts.

GETTING HERE AND AROUND

Glencoe is easily accessed by car via the A82. ScotRail trains and regional buses arrive from most of Scotland's major cities.

EXPLORING

Visitor Center at Glencoe. The National Trust for Scotland's Visitor Center at Glencoe (1 mile south of Glencoe Village) tells the story of the MacDonald massacre and has an excellent display on mountaineering. You can also get advice about walking. ⊠ *Off A82* ☎ *01855/811307* ⊕ *www.glencoe-nts.org.uk* ☒ *Exhibition £5.50* ⊙ *Nov.–Mar., Thurs.– Sun. 10–4; Apr.–Aug., daily 9:30–5:30; Sept.–Oct., daily 10–5.*

GLENFINNAN

10 mi west of Fort William, 26 mi southeast of Mallaig.

Perhaps the most visitor-oriented stop on the route between Fort William and Mallaig, Glenfinnan has much to offer if you're interested in Scottish history. Here the National Trust for Scotland has capitalized on the romance surrounding the story of the Jacobites and their intention of returning a Stuart monarch and the Roman Catholic religion to a country that had become staunchly Protestant. It was at Glenfinnan that the rash adventurer Prince Charles Edward Stuart gathered his meager forces for the final Jacobite Rebellion of 1745–46.

GETTING HERE AND AROUND

If you're driving from Fort William, travel via the A830. For great views, take a ride in the Jacobite Steam Train, which you can catch in Fort William.

EXPLORING

Glenfinnan Monument. The raising of the prince's standard is commemorated by the Glenfinnan Monument, an unusual tower on the banks of Loch Shiel; the story of his campaign is told in the nearby visitor center. Note that the figure at the top of the monument is of a Highlander, not the prince. ■ TIP→ The view down Loch Shiel from the Glenfinnan Monument is one of the most photographed in Scotland. ⊠ *A830* ☎ *08444/932221* ⊕ *www.nts.org.uk* ☒ *£3.50* ⊙ *Visitor center Apr.– June, Sept., and Oct., daily 10–5; July and Aug., daily 9:30–5:30.*

Glenfinnan Viaduct. The impressive Glenfinnan Viaduct, 1,248 feet long, was in its time the wonder of the Highlands. The railway's contractor, Robert MacAlpine, known as Concrete Bob by the locals, pioneered the use of concrete for bridges when his company built the Mallaig extension, which opened in 1901. The viaduct is famous again, this time for its appearance in the Harry Potter films.

WHERE TO STAY

For expanded hotel reviews, visit Fodors.com.

$$ ☒ **Glenfinnan House.** This high-ceilinged hotel was built in the 18th century as the home of Alexander MacDonald VII of Glenaladale, who was
★ wounded fighting for Bonnie Prince Charlie, and was transformed into an even grander mansion in the mid-19th century. **Pros:** fabulous setting; atmospheric dining experience. **Cons:** driveway not well maintained;

some guest rooms look a little tired. ⊠ *A830* ☎ *01397/722235* ⊕ *www. glenfinnanhouse.com* ↩ *14 rooms* ⌂ *In-room: no a/c, no TV. In-hotel: restaurant, bar* ☉ *Closed mid-Nov.–mid-Mar.* ⦿ *Breakfast.*

**EN
ROUTE**
As you get closer to **Arisaig** along A830, you'll be able to spot Eigg, a low island marked by the dramatic black peak of An Sgurr. Beyond Eigg is the larger Rum, with its range of hills and the Norse-named, cloud-capped Rum Coullin looming over the island. The breathtaking seaward views should continue to distract you from the road beside Loch nan Uamh (from Gaelic, meaning "cave" and pronounced *oo*-am). This loch is associated with Prince Charles Edward Stuart's nine-month stay on the mainland, during which he gathered a small army, marched as far south as Derby in England, alarmed the king, retreated to unavoidable defeat at Culloden in the spring, and then spent a few months as a fugitive in the Highlands. A cairn by the shore marks the spot where the prince was picked up by a French ship; he never returned to Scotland.

ARISAIG

15 mi west of Glenfinnan.

Considering its small size, Arisaig, gateway to the **Small Isles,** offers a surprising choice of high-quality options for dining and lodging. To the north of Arisaig, the road cuts across a headland to reach a stretch of coastline where silver sands glitter with the mica in the local rock; clear water, blue sky, and white sand lend a tropical flavor to the beaches—when the sun is shining.

From Arisaig try to visit a couple of the Small Isles: **Rum, Eigg, Muck,** and **Canna,** each tiny and with few or no inhabitants. Rum serves as a wildlife reserve, while Eigg has the world's first solely wind-, wave-, and solar-powered electricity grid.

GETTING HERE AND AROUND
From Glenfinnan, you reach Arisaig on the A830, the only road leading west. The Fort William–Mallaig train also stops here.

EXPLORING
Arisaig Marine. Along with whale-, seal-, and bird-watching excursions, Arisaig Marine runs a boat service from the harbor at Arisaig to the islands at Easter and from May to September. Trips depart daily at 11. The MV *Shearwater* delivers supplies and sometimes visitors to the tiny island communities. Available for charter is a fast twin-engine motor yacht, which can take up to 12 passengers around the Small Isles and farther afield. ⊠ *Arisaig Harbour* ☎ *01687/450224* ⊕ *www. arisaig.co.uk.*

WHERE TO EAT AND STAY
For expanded hotel reviews, visit Fodors.com.

$$$
FRENCH
✕ **Old Library.** On the waterfront, this 1722 barn has been converted into a fine, reasonably priced restaurant. Local fish and other fare is prepared in a French-bistro style and served in the whitewashed, airy dining room. Six cozy rooms with contemporary furnishings are available as well. ⊠ *A30* ☎ *01687/450651.*

9

$ 🖼 **Arisaig Hotel.** A 1720 former coaching inn, this hotel is close to the water and has magnificent views of the Small Isles. **Pros:** good-value restaurant; lots of life and music in the bar. **Cons:** dated furnishings; the main bar may be noisy for some. ⊠ *A830* ☎ *01687/450210* ⊕ *www. arisaighotel.co.uk* 📑 *13 rooms* ♿ *In-room: no a/c, Wi-Fi. In-hotel: restaurant, bar* 🍽 *Breakfast.*

MALLAIG

8 mi north of Arisaig, 44 mi northwest of Fort William.

After the approach along the coast, the workaday fishing port of Mallaig itself is anticlimactic. It has a few shops, and there's some bustle by the quayside when fishing boats unload or the Skye ferry departs: this is the departure point for the southern ferry connection to the Isle of Skye, the largest island of the Inner Hebrides *(see Chapter 10)*.

Mallaig is also the starting point for day cruises up the Sound of Sleat, which separates Skye from the mainland. The sound offers views into the rugged Knoydart region and its long, fjordlike sea lochs: Lochs Nevis and Hourn. The area to the immediate north and west beyond Loch Nevis, one of the most remote in Scotland, is often referred to as the Rough Bounds of Knoydart.

GETTING HERE AND AROUND

The Fort William–Mallaig train is by far the best way to travel to Mallaig, because you can relax and enjoy the stunning views. But road improvements on the A830 beyond Fort William makes the drive far less taxing and time-consuming than it used to be.

EXPLORING

★ **Bruce Watt Sea Cruises.** For year-round cruises to Loch Nevis, Inverie, and Tarbet, contact Bruce Watt Sea Cruises. ☎ *01687/462320* ⊕ *www. knoydart-ferry.co.uk.*

Caledonian MacBrayne. Caledonian MacBrayne runs scheduled service and cruises from Mallaig to Skye, the Small Isles, and Mull. ☎ *0800/066–5000* ⊕ *www.calmac.co.uk.*

Loch Morar. A small, unnamed side road just south of Mallaig leads east to an even smaller road that will bring you to Loch Morar, the deepest of all the Scottish lochs (more than 1,000 feet). The next deepest point is miles out into the Atlantic, beyond the continental shelf. The loch is said to have a resident monster, Morag, which undoubtedly gets less recognition than its famous cousin Nessie.

The Northern Highlands and the Western Isles

WORD OF MOUTH

"North Uist: It's lovely, and has eagles. And corncrakes (well, so do the others have corncrakes, but not such good corncrakes). Lots of nice things to see and do. At the pierhead at Lochmaddy you will find the Taigh Chearsabghagh museum and arts center, which is well worth a visit and is a great place to get a bowl of soup if you're freezing cold."

—sheila

Updated by
Elizabeth
Reeder

Wild and remote, the Northern Highlands and the Western Isles of Scotland have a timeless grandeur. Dramatic cliffs, long beaches, and craggy mountains jutting up from moorland heighten the romance and mystery of places like the well-preserved Eilean Donan Castle and the Isle of Skye, the latter famous for the misty and stark Cuillin Mountains and forever associated with Bonnie Prince Charlie. History can be seen everywhere as you pass crumbling castles, prehistoric ruins, and abandoned crofts.

In Sutherland and Caithness in northern Scotland, the roads hug the coast, dipping down toward beaches and up again to give stunning views over the ocean or across rippled, desolate stretches of heather moorland toward the impressive and singular profiles of mountains like Ben Hope and Suilven. These twisted, undulating roads demand you shift down a gear, pause to let others pass, and take the time to do less and see more of the rough-hewn beauty. If you're lucky, you may see an otter fishing along the coast, an eagle soaring overhead, or catch sight of deer with their antlers jutting above the horizon.

Sutherland was once the southernmost land belonging to the Vikings, and some names reflect this. Cape Wrath got its name from the Viking word *hvarth*, meaning "turning point," and Suilven translates as "pillar." The Isle of Skye and the Outer Hebrides are referred to as the Western Isles, and remain the stronghold of the Gaelic language. Skye is often called Scotland in miniature because the terrain shifts from lush valleys in the south, to the rugged girdle of the Cuillin Mountains, and then to the steep cliffs that define the northern coast. A short ferry journey away, moody Harris lays claim to the brilliant golden sands of Luskentyre. To the north, Lewis boasts incredible prehistoric sites, including the lunar-aligned Calanais Standing Stones and Dun Carloway (an Iron Age circular tower), and a lighthouse that looks ready to tip into the Atlantic.

Depending on the weather, a trip to the Northern Highlands and the Western Isles can feel like a tropical getaway or a blustery, rain-drenched holiday where this much-touted phrase makes sense: "There's no such thing as bad weather, just inappropriate clothing."

TOP REASONS TO GO

Explore Skye, the misty island:
The landscape ranges from the lush, undulating hills and coastal tracks of Sleat in the Garden of Skye to the deep glens that cut into the saw-toothed peaks of the Cuillin Mountains. Farther north are stunning geological features like the Old Man of Storr and Kilt Rock.

Tuck into the local harvest:
Sample fresh seafood like Bracadale crab, Dunvegan Bay langoustines, and Sconser king scallops, as well as the local smoked salmon, lobster, and oysters. Finish with cranachan, a dessert made with locally grown raspberries atop whisky cream and toasted oatmeal.

Walk the coast in the Outer Hebrides: There are no wilder places in Britain to enjoy an invigorating coastal walk than on the islands of Lewis, Harris, and the Uists.

Expect vast swaths of golden sand set against blue bays, or—when the weather is rough—giant waves crashing against the rocks.

Get close to nature: Seals, deer, otters, as well as an abundance of birdlife can be seen throughout the Northern Highlands and Western Isles. Don't miss a boating foray to the Handa Island bird reserve, off Scourie.

Drive a single-track road: In the Northern Highlands, take a drive on single-track roads like Destitution Road, north of Gairloch, which lead through the most dramatic scenery in Britain. The area is a primeval landscape where strange craggy mountains, with Gaelic and Nordic names like An Teallach, Suilven, and Stac Pollaidh, jut out of vast, desolate moorlands dotted with lochans.

ORIENTATION AND PLANNING

GETTING ORIENTED

Moving north and west from Inverness toward land's end at John o'Groats, this rugged land includes the old counties of Ross and Cromarty (sometimes called Easter and Wester Ross), Sutherland, and Caithness; together they constitute the most northern portion of mainland Scotland. To the west, to get to Skye, you can travel from Kyle of Lochalsh across the Skye Bridge or take a short summer ferry ride from Mallaig to Armadale. From Skye you can hop from island to island, taking in the Isles of Lewis, Harris, and the Uists.

10

The Northern Landscapes. North of Inverness, northwest Scotland is known for its dramatic coastlines and desolate landscapes. It's no wonder that this part of the country has been designated as Scotland's first UNESCO Geopark. You'll want to explore Stoer Point Lighthouse, the beaches north of Lochinver, and islandlike hills such as Suilven.

Torridon. A few hours' drive west of Inverness, Torridon has cool glens, mirrorlike lochs, impressive mountains, and tantalizing glimpses across to the Isle of Skye. Single-track roads lead to lighthouses on promontories battered by the sea. Glen Torridon is worth a visit.

Isle of Skye. Scotland's most famous island is home to the Cuillin Mountains, the quiet gardens of Sleat, and the dramatic peninsulas of Waternish and Trotternish. You can take a day trip to Skye, but it's worth spending a few days exploring its shores.

The Outer Hebrides. Extending about 130 mi from north to south, this archipelago is reached by ferry from the mainland and from the Isle of Skye. Lewis has wonderful historic attractions, such as the Calanais Standing Stones, sandy beaches, and traditional "black houses." The Uists are dotted with old cairns and ruined forts and chapels. Barra is so small you can easily walk from one end to the other.

PLANNING

WHEN TO GO

The Northern Highlands and islands are best seen from May to September. The earlier in the spring or later in the autumn you go, the greater the chances of your encountering the elements in their extreme form, and the fewer attractions and accommodations you will find open. Even tourist-friendly Skye closes down almost completely by the end of October. As a final deciding factor, you may not want to take a western sea passage in a gale, a frequent occurrence in the winter months.

PLANNING YOUR TIME

The rough landscape of the Highlands and Islands, as this region is sometimes called, means that this is not a place you can rush through. Single-track roadways, undulating landscapes, and eye-popping views will slow you down. You can base yourself in a town like Ullapool or Portree, or choose a B&B or hotel tucked into the hills or sitting at the edge of a sea loch. If you have limited time, head directly to the Isle of Skye and the other islands off the coast. They attract hordes of tourists, and for good reason, yet you don't have to walk far to find yourself in wild places, often in solitude.

You could easily combine a trip to the Northern Highlands with forays into the Great Glen (including Inverness and Loch Ness) or up to Orkney and the Shetland Islands.

GETTING HERE AND AROUND

AIR TRAVEL

On a map, this area may seem far from major urban centers, but it's easy to reach. Inverness has an airport with direct links to London, Edinburgh, Glasgow, and Amsterdam.

The main airports for the Northern Highlands are Inverness and Wick (both on the mainland). Loganair has direct air service from Edinburgh and Glasgow to Inverness and from Edinburgh to Wick. You can fly from London Gatwick, Luton Airport (near London), or Bristol to Inverness on one of the daily easyJet flights. British Airways also has a service from Gatwick. Loganair operates flights among the islands of Barra, Benbecula, and Lewis in the Outer Hebrides (weekdays only).

Airport Contacts Inverness Airport ☎ *01667/464000* ⊕ *www.hial.co.uk/inverness-airport.html.*

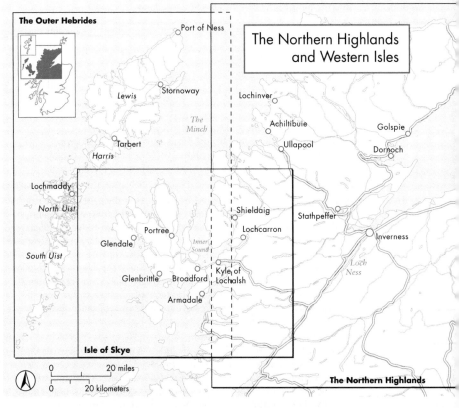

The Northern Highlands
and Western Isles

Port of Ness

Lewis   Stornoway   Lochinver

The Minch   Achiltibuie   Golspie

Tarbert   Ullapool   Dornoch
Harris

Lochmaddy

North Uist   Shieldaig   Stathpeffer

Portree   Lochcarron   Inverness
Glendale   *Inner Sound*

South Uist   *Loch Ness*

Glenbrittle   Broadford   Kyle of Lochalsh

Armadale

Isle of Skye

The Northern Highlands

0 — 20 miles
0 — 20 kilometers

BOAT AND FERRY TRAVEL

Ferry services are generally reliable, weather permitting. Car and passenger ferries run from Ullapool to Stornoway, from Oban to Castlebay
and Lochboisdale, and from Uig (on the Isle of Skye) to Tarbert and
Lochmaddy. Causeways link North Uist, Benbecula, and South Uist.
The Island Hopscotch planned-route ticket and the Island Rover pass,
both offered by Caledonian MacBrayne (called CalMac) give considerable reductions on interisland ferry fares. Various tickets are available,
including the Hopscotch 12 (connecting Skye, Harris, Lewis, and the
Uists), which costs £25 per person.

Boat and Ferry Contacts Caledonian MacBrayne ☎ *08000/665000* ⊕ *www.
calmac.co.uk.*

BUS TRAVEL

Scottish Citylink and National Express run buses to Inverness, Ullapool,
Thurso, Scrabster, and Wick. There are also coach connections between
the ferry ports of Tarbert and Stornoway; consult the local tourist information center for details. Buses can be a good way to see this region,
but they don't run frequently.

Stagecoach Highlands provides a bus service in the region. On the Outer
Hebrides several small operators run regular routes to most towns and
villages. The post-bus service—which also delivers mail—becomes

increasingly important in remote areas. It supplements the regular bus service, which runs only a few times per week. A full timetable of services for the Northern Highlands (and the rest of Scotland) is available from the Royal Mail. Traveline Scotland, a handy website, provides timetables and a journey planner to help you navigate around Scotland. There's an app too.

Bus Contacts Stagecoach Highlands ☎ *01463/233371* ⊕ *www. stagecoachbus.com.* **National Express** ☎ *08705/808080* ⊕ *www. nationalexpress.co.uk.* **Royal Mail Post Buses** ☎ *0845/7740740* ⊕ *www. royalmail.com/postbus.* **Scottish Citylink** ☎ *0871/2663333* ⊕ *www.citylink. co.uk.* **Traveline Scotland** ☎ *08706/082608* ⊕ *www.travelinescotland.com.*

CAR TRAVEL

Because of the infrequent bus services and sparse railway stations, a car is definitely the best way to explore this region. The twisting, winding, single-lane roads demand a degree of driving dexterity, however. Local rules of the road require that when two cars meet, whichever driver reaches a passing place first must stop and allow the oncoming car to continue (this may entail a bit of backing up). Small cars tend to yield to large commercial vehicles. Never park in passing places, and remember that these sections of the road can also be used to allow traffic behind you to pass. Note that in this sparsely populated area, distances between gas stations can be considerable.

TRAIN TRAVEL

Main railway stations in the area include Oban (for ferries to Barra and the Uists) and Kyle of Lochalsh (for Skye), on the west coast, or Inverness (for points north to Thurso and Wick). There's direct service from London to Inverness and connecting service from Edinburgh and Glasgow. For information contact National Rail or ScotRail.

Train Contacts National Rail ☎ *08457/484950, 4420/72785240 from abroad* ⊕ *www.nationalrail.co.uk.* **ScotRail** ☎ *08457/550033* ⊕ *www.scotrail.co.uk.*

TOURS

J.A. Johnstone Chauffeur Drive will escort you anywhere and gives a lot of information about the Highlands and islands, including the Outer Hebrides. Raasay Outdoor Centre organizes courses in kayaking, sailing, windsurfing, climbing, rappelling, archery, walking, and navigation skills.

Tour Contacts J.A. Johnstone Chauffeur Drive ☎ *01463/798372.* **Raasay Outdoor Centre** ☎ *01478/660266* ⊕ *www.raasay-house.co.uk.*

RESTAURANTS

Northern Scotland has many excellent restaurants where talented chefs use locally grown produce. Most country-house inns (a good choice if you're looking for a restaurant) and pubs serve reliable, hearty seafood and meat-and-potatoes meals. The Isle of Skye has the most, and the most expensive, restaurants, many of them quite good. But you can find good meals almost everywhere, which wasn't the case a few years ago. In the more remote regions you may have to drive some distance to find them, however.

HOTELS

Charming, earthy, inexpensive inns and a few excellent luxury hotels will welcome you after a day of touring the Highlands. Check out hotel restaurants in this area, as they can be a fine option.

In the more remote parts of Scotland, your best lodging option may be to rent a cottage or house. Besides allowing you to make your own meals and to come and go as you please, it can also be less expensive. Visit Scotland (⊕ *www.visitscotland.com*), the official tourism agency, lists many cottages and even rates them with stars, just like hotels.

WHAT IT COSTS IN POUNDS					
	¢	$	$$	$$$	$$$$
RESTAURANTS	under £10	£10–£14	£15–£19	£20–£25	over £25
HOTELS	under £70	£70–£120	£121–£160	£161–£220	over £220

Restaurant prices are for a main course at dinner. Hotel prices are for two people in a standard double room in high season, generally including the 20% V.A.T.

VISITOR INFORMATION

The tourist information centers at Dornoch, Dunvegan, Durness, Portree, Stornoway, Tarbert, and Ullapool are open year-round, with limited winter hours at Dunvegan, Durness, and Ullapool.

Seasonal tourist information centers are at Bettyhill, Broadford (Skye), Castlebay (Barra, Outer Hebrides), Gairloch, Helmsdale, John o'Groats, Kyle of Lochalsh, Lairg, Lochboisdale (South Uist, Outer Hebrides), Lochcarron, Lochinver, Lochmaddy (North Uist, Outer Hebrides), North Kessock, Shiel Bridge, Thurso, and Uig.

Information Highlands of Scotland Tourist Board ☎ *08452/255121* ⊕ *www. visithighlands.com.*

THE NORTHERN LANDSCAPES

Wester Ross and Sutherland, the northernmost part of Scotland, have some of the most distinctive mountain profiles and coastal stretches in all of Scotland. The rim roads around the wilds of Durness overlook rocky shores and the long beaches are as dramatic as the awe-inspiring and desolate cross-country routes like Destitution Road in Wester Ross.

10

ULLAPOOL

238 mi north of Glasgow.

By the shores of salty Loch Broom, Ullapool was founded in 1788 as a fishing station to exploit the local herring stocks. There's still a smattering of fishing vessels, as well as visiting yachts and foreign ships. When their crews fill the pubs, the town has a cosmopolitan feel. The harbor area comes to life when the Lewis ferry arrives and departs. Ullapool is an ideal base for hiking throughout Sutherland and taking wildlife and nature cruises, especially to the Summer Isles.

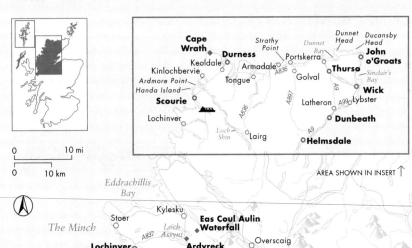

Cape Wrath
Durness
Keoldale
Kinlochbervie
Ardmore Point
Handa Island
Scourie
Lochinver
Strathy Point
Dunnet Bay
Armadale
Tongue
A836
Golval
A836
A897
Dunnet Head
Portskerra
Ducansby Head
John o'Groats
Thurso
Sinclair's Bay
Wick
A9
Latheron
Lybster
A99
Dunbeath
A9
Loch Shin
Lairg
Helmsdale

AREA SHOWN IN INSERT ↑

0   10 mi
0   10 km

Eddrachillis Bay

The Minch

← TO STORNOWAY

Kylesku
Stoer
Loch Assynt
A837
Eas Coul Aulin Waterfall
Overscaig
Loch Shin
Lochinver
Ardvreck Castle
Suilven
Inverkinkaig
Loch Sionascaig
Ledmore
Rhian
Achiltibuie
Stac Pollaidh
Knockan Crags
A835
A837
Lairg
A839
Beinn a Bragaidh
Brora
Golspie
Dunrobin Castle
Ullapool
Invercassley
Inveran
Bonar Bridge
Ardgay
Spinningdale
Dornoch
Dundonnell
Loch Broom
Inverewe Gardens
An Teallach
A832
Corrieshalloch Gorge
A835
Loch Glascarnoch
Dornoch Firth
Tain
Wilkhaven
Gairloch
A832
Loch Maree
A832
Nigg
Badachro
Loch Fannich
Invergordon
Cromarty Firth
Cromarty
Lower Diabaig
Kinlochewe
Garve
Loch Garve
Evanton
Alness
A9
A832
Moray Firth
Inveralligin
Glen Torridon
Achnasheen
Dingwall
Maryburgh
Rosemarkie
Fortrose
A832
Nairn
Torridon Visitor Center
A890
Strathpeffer
A834
A835
Tore
A9
B9161
A96
Shieldaig
Annat
Marybank
A896
Loch Shieldag
Applecross
Beauly
Beauly Firth
Loch Kishorn
Lochcarron
A896
Inverness
Kyle of Lochalsh
Dornie
Loch Carron
Daviot
Skye Bridge
Glenelg
Eilean Donan Castle
Loch Mullardoch
Glen Cannich
Cannich
Dores
Drumnadrochit
Carrbridge
Glen Affric
Loch Ness
A9
A87
Invermoriston
A87
Monadhliath Mountains
Fort Augustus

The Northern Highlands

KEY
⊢•⊣ Rail Lines
🚢 Ferry
✈ Airport

GETTING HERE AND AROUND

A desolate but well-maintained stretch of the A835 takes you from Inverness to Ullapool.

ESSENTIALS

Visitor Information Ullapool ⊠ *Argyll St.* ☎ *01854/612486* ⊕ *www. visithighlands.com.*

EXPLORING

Ceilidh Place. Ullapool's cultural focal point is Ceilidh Place, an excellent venue for music and literary events throughout the year. It started out as a small café, and over the years has added space for performers, an excellent bookshop, and a handful of rooms for those who want to spend the night. It's a great place for afternoon coffee or a wee dram in the evening. ⊠ *14 W. Argyle St.* ☎ *01854/612103* ⊕ *www. theceilidhplace.com.*

★ **Corrieshalloch Gorge.** For a thrilling touch of vertigo, don't miss Corrieshalloch Gorge, 12 mi south of Ullapool, just off the A835. Draining the high moors, the Falls of Measach plunge 150 feet into a 200-foot-deep, thickly wooded gorge. There's a suspension-bridge viewpoint and a heady atmosphere of romantic grandeur, like an old Scottish print come to life. A short walk leads from a parking area to the viewpoint.

Falls of Rogie. Just north of Contin (about 35 mi south of Ullapool), you will find the Falls of Rogie, where an interestingly bouncy suspension bridge presents you with a fine view of the waters below. ⊠ *A835, Contin.*

Ullapool Museum. In the Ullapool Museum, films, photographs, and audiovisual displays tell the story of the area from the ice age to modern times. There's an ongoing exhibition on weather, climate change, and the environment. ⊠ *7–8 W. Argyle St.* ☎ *01854/612987* ⊕ *www. ullapoolmuseum.co.uk* 🎫 *£3* ⊙ *Apr.–Oct., Mon.–Sat. 10–5.*

WHERE TO STAY

For expanded hotel reviews, visit Fodors.com.

$ ★ **The Royal Hotel.** In a beautiful town that is struggling to provide consistent accommodation, the Royal Hotel does the job well. **Pros:** a short walk to Ullapool; good breakfasts. **Cons:** restaurant is uneven; some rooms have older mattresses; uninspired interiors. ⊠ *Garve Rd.* ☎ *01854/612181* ⊕ *www.ullapoolhotel.com* 🛏 *52 rooms* ♿ *In-room: no a/c. In-hotel: restaurant, bar* ⦿ *Breakfast.*

EN ROUTE

Coigach and Assynt. Drive north of Ullapool on the A835 into Coigach and Assynt and you enter a different kind of landscape. Here you won't find the broad, steep flanks of great hills that hem you in, as you would in the Great Glen or Glencoe. Instead, in Wester Ross the mountains punch out of the heathered terrain and seem to shift their position, hiding behind one another. Even their names seem different from those of the *bens* (mountain peaks or high hills) elsewhere: Cul Mor, Cul Beag, Stac Pollaidh, Canisp, Suilven. Some owe their origins to Norse words rather than to Gaelic—a reminder that Vikings used to sail this northern seaboard. Much of this area lies within the Inverpolly National Nature Reserve, now encompassed within the North West Highlands Geopark.

10

ACHILTIBUIE

25 mi northwest of Ullapool.

Off the beaten track, Achiltibuie is a small coastal community set at the foot of magnificent mountains. It looks out over the Summer Isles, whose history dates back to Viking raids. Cruises leave from a small jetty just west of Achiltibuie and take you to the largest and only inhabited island, Tanera Mhor, where you can buy special Summer Isle stamps—Tanera Mhor is the only Scottish island to have a private postal service.

GETTING HERE AND AROUND

Achiltibuie is a two-hour drive from Inverness, much of it on the quick A835, with the last 15 mi on an occasionally daunting single-track road.

> ### GET HOOKED IN THE HIGHLANDS
>
> The possibilities for fishing are endless in Sutherland, as a glance at the loch-covered map suggests. Brown trout and salmon are abundant. You can fish from the banks of Loch Garve, 35 mi south of Ullapool, or Loch Assynt, 5 mi east of Lochinver, from March to October. Boat fishing is popular on Loch Maree, southeast of Gairloch and north of Poolewe, from May to October. Fishing permits are available at local post offices, shops, and hotels.

EXPLORING

Achiltibuie Smokehouse. At the Achiltibuie Smokehouse, Summer Isles Foods deliciously smokes all sorts of fish—salmon, haddock, eel, and trout—which can be purchased in the small shop. ⊠ *Altandhu* ☎ *01854/622353* ⊕ *www.summerislesfoods.com* ☉ *Easter–Oct., daily 9:30–5.*

WHERE TO STAY

For expanded hotel reviews, visit Fodors.com.

$$ ⬚ **Summer Isles Hotel.** Halfway along a road that ends at the sea, this well-kept hotel is built into a small hill and contemplates the mystical Summer Isles. **Pros:** stunning views; remote location; good food. **Cons:** not much to do nearby; quality fell for a year or two but seems to be back on track. ⊠ *Achiltibuie Rd.* ☎ *01854/622282* ⊕ *www.summerisleshotel. com* ➟ *6 rooms* ♿ *In-hotel: restaurant, bar* ☉ *Closed Nov.–Mar.*

SPORTS AND THE OUTDOORS

Stach Pollaidh. For a great afternoon of walking, ascend the dramatic hill of Stach Pollaidh (pronounced "stack Polly"), about 16 km east of Achiltibuie. The clearly marked path climbs for a bit and then curves around to the right and takes you on a loop with incredible views over Sutherland, north to Suilven, and west to the Summer Isles. About halfway around the hill, a steeper path takes you to the start of the ridge. Only very experienced rock climbers should continue from here, as the route requires rock climbing in very exposed conditions. But not to worry, because from the west side of the looped path you can see the pinnacled pitch of Stach Pollaidh. Start your walk from a car park about 5 mi from A835. ⊠ *Off A835, Dornie.*

EN ROUTE A single-lane unclassified road winds north from Achiltibuie through a wild though harmonious landscape of bracken and birch trees, heather and hills, with outstanding sea views on the second half of the route. Don't fall victim to the breathtaking landscape views, however; the road has several blind curves that demand extreme care.

LOCHINVER

18 mi north of Achiltibuie, 38 mi north of Ullapool.

Lochinver is a quiet shoreside community of whitewashed cottages, with a harbor used by the west coast fishing fleet, and a couple of good dining and lodging options. Behind the town the mountain Suilven rises abruptly. Take the cul-de-sac, **Baddidarroch Road,** for a great photo opportunity. Lochinver is a perfect base for exploring Sutherland.

GETTING HERE AND AROUND
To get to Lochinver, take A835/A837 north from Ullapool.

ESSENTIALS
Visitor Information Assynt Visitor Centre ⊠ *Main St.* ☎ *01571/844654* ⊕ *www.highland.gov.uk.*

EXPLORING

OFF THE BEATEN PATH **Ardvreck Castle.** Beside Loch Assynt on the A837 stand the ruins of Ardvreck Castle, a Clan MacLeod stronghold, built in the 15th century. ⊠ *A837, 11 mi east of Lochniver* ☎ *No phone* 🎫 *Free.*

Drumbeg Loop. Bold souls spending time at Lochinver may enjoy the interesting single-track B869 Drumbeg Loop to the north of Lochinver—it has several challenging hairpin turns along with breathtaking views. (The junction is on the north side of the River Inver bridge on the outskirts of the village, signposted as "stoer" and "clashnessie".) Just beyond the scattered community of Stoer, a road leads west to **Stoer Point Lighthouse.** If you're an energetic walker, you can hike across the short turf and heather along the cliff top for fine views west over toward the Isle of Skye. There's also a red-sandstone sea stack: the **Old Man of Stoer.** This makes a pleasant excursion on a long summer evening.

Eas Coul Aulin Waterfall. With a drop of 685 feet, this is the longest waterfall in the United Kingdom. A rugged hike leads to the falls, which are at the head of Loch Glencoul. Consult local maps, be prepared, dress properly, and start from car park off A894, approximately 17 mi east and north from Lochinver. In summer, cruises from Kylesku

---

DRIVING TIPS

In the Northern Highlands you'll encounter plenty of single-track roads wide enough only for just one car. When you meet an oncoming vehicle, or when a faster one wants to pass, pull into a passing place (always pull to the left, into the passing place or into the space on the road beside it). Drivers always wave, as a courtesy and as a genuine greeting. On bad days, you encounter trucks at the most awkward of spots. On good days, single-track driving can be relaxing, with a lovely pace of stopping, waving, moving on.

10

Old Ferry Pier offer a less taxing alternative. ⊠ *A894, 3 mi southeast of Kylesku Bridge.*

WHERE TO EAT

¢   ✕ **Lochinver Mission.** An abandoned fishermen's mission (a place where
BRITISH fishermen stayed while in port), houses this cafeteria-style restaurant with top-notch local fare. The restaurant starts the day by serving a hot breakfast, and for lunch and dinner offers expertly prepared langoustines and other local seafood, as well as soups and burgers. In a very short time it's become a local favorite and draws considerable crowds on weekends. The building also contains the local archives, a marine center, and three guest rooms. ⊠ *Culag Park* ☎ *01571/844324* ⊕ *www.lochinvermission.org.uk.*

WHERE TO STAY

For expanded hotel reviews, visit Fodors.com.

$$$ 🛏 **Inver Lodge Hotel.** On a hillside above Lochinver, this modern hotel has stunning views of the sea. **Pros:** cozy public room with a fireplace; refreshing sauna; great fishing nearby. **Cons:** drab exterior; not good for families with children. ⊠ *Iolaire Rd.* ☎ *01571/844496* ⊕ *www.inverlodge.com* ➘ *20 rooms* ⚬ *In-room: no a/c, Wi-Fi. In-hotel: restaurant, some age restrictions* ❡❍❘ *Breakfast.*

¢   🛏 **Tigh Na Sith.** Set just above the bay at Lochinver, this newly built B&B wins rave reviews for its warm welcome; owners Nick and Patrycja Matthews pack lunches for your day excursions and provide binoculars so you can get the most of the views down to the loch and over the hills. **Pros:** great hosts; fantastic views. **Cons:** room at back doesn't have a view; shared dining table for breakfast may not suit everyone. ⊠ *A837* ☎ *01571/844352* ⊕ *www.tighnasith.com* ➘ *3 rooms* ⚬ *In-room: Wi-Fi* ❡❍❘ *Breakfast.*

SHOPPING

Achins Book & Craft Shop. Reached via the Lochinver-Achiltibuie single-track road is must-see Inverkirkaig's Achins Book & Craft Shop. It's a great place to find Scottish books on natural history, hill walking, and trout fishing. It also sells craft items—knitwear, tweeds, and pottery—along with works by local artists and recordings of traditional music. The shop and pleasant café are open daily from 10 to 5 (except for Sunday from October to March). ⊠ *Off B869, Inverkirkaig* ☎ *01571/844262.*

Highland Stoneware. In its showroom, Highland Stoneware displays tableware and decorative items with hand-painted designs of wildflowers, animals, and landscapes. It's open weekdays from 9 to 6 (also 9 to 5 on Saturday from Easter to October). ⊠ *Baddidarroch* ☎ *01571/844376* ⊕ *www.highlandstoneware.com.*

SCOURIE

28 mi north of Lochinver.

Scourie is a small settlement catering to visitors—fisherfolk especially—with a range of accommodations. The bay-side town makes a good base for a trip to the bird sanctuary on Handa Island.

GETTING HERE AND AROUND

From Lochinver, take the A837, which becomes the A894 as you turn north.

EXPLORING

★ **Handa Island.** Just off the coast of Scourie is Handa Island, a bird sanctuary that shelters huge seabird colonies, especially impressive at nesting time in spring and early summer. Visitors can gaze on more than 200,000 birds nesting on spectacular cliffs, including guillemots, razorbills, great skuas, kittiwakes, and even the odd puffin from the towering sandstone vantage point of Stack an Seabhaig (Hawk's Stack). This remarkable reserve, administered by the Scottish Wildlife Trust, is open only in spring and summer. It can be reached by a small open boat from Tarbet; contact the tourist information center in Lochinver or Durness for details. ■ **TIP→ Sturdy boots, a waterproof jacket, and a degree of fitness are needed to walk the path around the island.**

WHERE TO STAY

For expanded hotel reviews, visit Fodors.com.

$ 🏨 **Eddrachilles Hotel.** This longtime favorite has one of the best views of any lodging in Scotland—toward the tiny islands of Badcall Bay. **Pros:** attractive garden; stunning shoreline nearby; close to bird sanctuary. **Cons:** restaurant's quality can vary; service sometimes disappoints. ✉ *Badcall Bay, off A894* ☎ *01971/502080* ⊕ *www.eddrachilles.com* 🛏 *11 rooms* ⚄ *In-room: no a/c. In-hotel: restaurant, bar* ☉ *Closed early Oct.–late Mar.* ¶⊙¶ *Breakfast.*

$ 🏨 **Kylesku Hotel.** This charming hotel looks out over Loch Glendhu and toward Eas Coul Aulin, Scotland's highest waterfall. **Pros:** stunning views; great staff; delicious food. **Cons:** some old-building quirks; two attic rooms are small (but cheaper). ✉ *Off A894, Kylesku* ☎ *01971/ 502231* 🛏 *8 rooms* ⚄ *In-hotel: restaurant* ¶⊙¶ *Breakfast.*

10

DURNESS

27 mi north of Scourie, 55 mi north of Lochinver.

The sudden patches of green surrounding the village of Durness, on the north coast, are caused by the richer limestone outcrops among the acid moorlands. Here you'll find the country's highest cliff, Clo Mor.

GETTING HERE AND AROUND

Past Scourie, the A894 becomes the A838 as you head north. The road to Durness is often a single lane in each direction.

ESSENTIALS

Visitor Information Durness ✉ *Sango* ☎ *01971/511368* ⊕ *www.durness.org.*

EXPLORING

Cape Wrath. If you've made it this far north, you'll probably want to go all the way to Cape Wrath, a rugged headland at the northwest tip of Scotland. The white-sand beaches, impressive dunes covered in marram grass, and crashing seas of nearby Balnakeil Bay make it an exhilarating place to visit. As this land is owned by the Ministry of Defence, you can't drive your own vehicle. From May through September, a small boat ferries people here from Keoldale, 2 mi outside Durness; once you're across the sea inlet called the Kyle of Durness, a minibus will then take you to the lighthouse. Call ahead or check departure times on the board at the jetty. ☎ *01971/511284* ⊕ *www.capewrath.org.uk.*

Clo Mor. The highest mainland cliffs in Scotland, including 920-foot Clo Mor, lie between the Kyle and Cape Wrath.

Smoo Cave. The spectacular Smoo Cave, hollowed out of the limestone by rushing water, can be reached via a steep cliff path. Also worth exploring are the number of wonderful near white-sand beaches found as you head east toward Tongue, especially the one at Sango Bay. Boat tours around the Kyle of Durness run daily from April through September. ⊕ *www.smoocave.org.*

WHERE TO STAY

For expanded hotel reviews, visit Fodors.com.

$ ⊞ **Tongue Hotel.** With open fireplaces in its public areas and hunting lodge–style rooms, the Tongue Hotel makes a great base for exploring this most northern coast of the Scottish mainland. **Pros:** welcoming atmosphere; stunning views; relaxing public rooms. **Cons:** you'll need a car to make the most of this area. ⊠ *On A838, near Lairg, Tongue* ☎ *01847/611206* ⊕ *www.tonguehotel.co.uk* ⇦ *18 rooms* ⌂ *In-room: Wi-Fi* ⎟◎⎟ *Breakfast.*

SHOPPING

★   **Balnakeil Craft Village.** Artisans sell pottery, leather, weavings, paintings, and more from their studios at Balnakeil Craft Village. On an unnamed road running northwest from Durness, Balnakeil is located in old military buildings and is open April through October. Hours at the studios vary, but most are open daily from 10 to 5, and even later on summer evenings. Cocoa Mountain is a must for those with a sweet tooth; its "chocolate bar" serves up world-class truffles and stunningly rich hot chocolate. ☎ *01971/511777.*

EN ROUTE The north-coast road along the top of Scotland is both attractive and severe. It runs, for example, around the head of Loch Eriboll, which was a World War II convoy assembly point and was usually referred to as "Loch 'orrible" by the crews. Yet it has its own desolate charm. There are lots of landmarks, including croft dwellings, crumbling lime kilns, and a pebbly beach that reaches out to a mound of land, Ard Neakie.

THURSO

74 mi east of Durness.

The town of Thurso is quite substantial for a community so far north. In town are the Thurso Heritage Museum and Old St. Peter's Kirk, which dates back to the 12th century. There are also fine beaches, particularly at Dunnet Bay, and great seabird watching at Dunnet Head.

GETTING HERE AND AROUND

A car remains the best way to see this region, although local buses and the post bus run on most days. At Tongue, the A838 becomes the A836.

ESSENTIALS

Visitor Information Thurso ⊠ *Riverside Rd.* ☎ *01847/893155* ⊕ *www. visithighlands.com.*

EXPLORING

Dunnet Head. Many people make the trip to the northernmost point of mainland Britain, which is at Dunnet Head, with its fine views over the sea to Orkney. Dunnet Head Lighthouse, built in 1831, still stands here.

WHERE TO STAY

For expanded hotel reviews, visit Fodors.com.

$$ ⊞ **Forss Country House Hotel.** Don't be fooled by the stark exterior, as this house dating from 1810 is a charming place to stay. **Pros:** large guest rooms; lots of outdoor activities; hearty meals. **Cons:** heavy old doors make a racket. ⊠ *A836* ☎ *01847/861201* ⊕ *www.forsshousehotel.co.uk* ↪ *14 rooms* ♿ *In-room: no a/c. In-hotel: restaurant, bar* ⎛⎝*Breakfast.*

BICYCLING

Wheels Cycle Shop. At the Wheels Cycle Shop, the staff rents bikes and gives advice on the best routes. ⊠ *35 High St.* ☎ *01847/896124.*

JOHN O'GROATS

21 mi east of Thurso.

The windswept little outpost of John o'Groats is usually taken to be the most northern community on the Scottish mainland, though that is not strictly accurate, as an exploration of the network of roads between Dunnet Head and John o'Groats will confirm. A crafts center has a few high-quality shops selling knitwear, candles, and gifts.

GETTING HERE AND AROUND

Traveling east from Thurso, take the coast-hugging A836.

EXPLORING

Duncansby Head. Head east to Duncansby Head for spectacular views of cliffs and sea stacks by the lighthouse—and puffins, too.

John o'Groats Ferries. The company operates wildlife cruises from John o'Groats Harbor. The 1½-hour trip takes you past spectacular cliff scenery and bird life into the Pentland Firth, to Duncansby Stacks, and to the island of Stroma. Cruises cost £17 and are available daily at 2:30 between June and August. Between May and September the company offers day trips to Orkney for £47 per person. ☎ *01955/611353* ⊕ *www.jogferry.co.uk.*

10

THE ARTS

Lyth Arts Centre. In a Victorian-era school building, the Lyth Arts Centre serves as a cultural hub. From April through November each year, professional touring music and theater companies, as well as exhibitions of contemporary fine art, fill its schedule and the locals fill the seats. It's located between Wick and John o'Groats. ⊠ *Off A9, Lyth* ☎ *01955/641434* ⊕ *www.lytharts.org.uk.*

WICK

17 mi south of John o'Groats, 22 mi southeast of Thurso.

Wick is a substantial town that was built on its fishing industry. The town itself is not very appealing, but it does have the gaunt, bleak ruins of **Castle Sinclair** and **Castle Girnigoe** teetering on a clifftop 3 mi north of the town.

GETTING HERE AND AROUND

From Thurso, the A836 follows the coast to John o'Groats and becomes the A99 as you head south. An alternative route, the A882, cuts away from the coast.

EXPLORING

Wick Heritage Centre. To learn how this town grew, visit the Wick Heritage Centre—the local people who run it are real enthusiasts. The center is the largest museum in the Northern Highlands and has on display a restored fisherman's house, a fish kiln, and a blacksmith's shop, as well as collections of everything from fossils to 19th-century toys. An art gallery and terraced gardens overlooking the town round out the offerings. ⊠ *18–27 Bank Row* ☎ *01955/605393* ⊕ *www.wickheritage. org* ⌨ *£4* ☉ *Easter–Oct., Mon.–Sat. 10–4.*

EN ROUTE

Grey Cairns of Camster. Signposted west off the A9 about 10 mi south of Wick are the extraordinary Grey Cairns of Camster, two Neolithic chambered cairns, dating from 4000 BC to 3000 BC, that are among the best preserved in Britain. **Camster Round Cairn** is 20 yards in diameter and 13 yards high, and **Camster Long Cairn** reaches nearly 77 yards in length. Some 19th-century excavations revealed skeletons, pottery, and flint tools in the round cairn's internal chamber. If you don't mind dirty knees, you can crawl into the chambers in both cairns.

DUNBEATH

21 mi south of Wick.

A tiny coast village, Dunbeath is bordered by moors on one side, the sea on the other. A few interesting museums make it worth a stop.

GETTING HERE AND AROUND

South of Wick, Dunbeath can be reached via the A9. This coast-hugging route, crowded with Orkney ferry traffic, can be quite daunting because of the steep drop-offs when heading south.

EXPLORING

Dunbeath Heritage Centre. The moors of Caithness roll down to the sea at Dunbeath, where you find the Dunbeath Heritage Centre in a former school. Inside are photographs and domestic and crofting artifacts that relay the area's history from the Bronze Age to the oil age. It's particularly helpful to those researching family histories. ✉ *Off A9* ☎ *01593/731233* ⊕ *www.dunbeath-heritage.org.uk* 🎫 *£3* ⊘ *Mar.–Oct., daily 10–5; Nov.–Apr., weekdays 11–3.*

HELMSDALE

15 mi south of Dunbeath.

Helmsdale is a fascinating fishing village with a checkered past. It was a busy Viking settlement and then the scene of an aristocratic poisoning plot before it was transformed into a 19th-century village to house some of the people removed from their land to make way for sheep. These "clearances," perpetrated by the Duke of Sutherland, were among the area's most inhumane.

GETTING HERE AND AROUND

Helmsdale is one of the only towns on this part of the coast that has a daily train service from Inverness. However, a car will allow you to see more in the surrounding area. Get here via the coastal A9 or the inland A897.

> ### A BRUTAL DUKE
>
> Traveling south on the A9 from Helmsdale to Golspie, you can see the controversial statue of the first Duke of Sutherland, looking like some Eastern Bloc despot. He's perched on Beinn a Bragaidh (Ben Braggie), the hilltop to the west. Many people want to remove the statue, as the "improvement" policies of the duke were ultimately responsible for the brutality of the Sutherland Clearances of 1810–20, which removed people from their farms so there would be more room for sheep to graze.

EXPLORING

★ **Timespan Heritage Centre.** This thought-provoking mix of displays, artifacts, and audiovisual materials portrays the history of the area from the Stone Age to the 1869 gold rush in the Strath of Kildonan. There's a geology exhibit in the garden and a tour of the Kildonan gold-rush site. The complex also includes a café and an art gallery that often hosts visiting artists and changing exhibitions. ✉ *Dunrobin St.* ☎ *01431/821327* ⊕ *www.timespan.org.uk* 🎫 *£4* ⊘ *April–Oct., Mon.–Sat. 10–5, Sun. noon–5; last admission 1 hr before closing.*

10

GOLSPIE

18 mi south of Helmsdale.

The little coastal town of Golspie is worth a stop if you're heading for Dunrobin Castle. It has a number of shops and accommodations.

GETTING HERE AND AROUND

Golspie can be reached by train from Inverness, and in summer the train also stops at Dunrobin Castle. Drivers should use the A9.

EXPLORING

Dunrobin Castle. The Scottish home of the dukes of Sutherland is flamboyant Dunrobin Castle, an ancient seat developed by the first duke into a 19th-century white-turreted behemoth. As well as lavish interiors, there are falconry demonstrations and Versailles-inspired gardens. Trains so fascinated the duke that he built his own railroad in the park and staffed it with his servants. ⊠ *Off A9* ☎ *01408/633177* ⊕ *www.dunrobincastle.co.uk* 🎫 *£9* ☻ *Apr., May, Sept., and early Oct., daily 10:30–4:30; June–Aug., Mon.–Sat. 10:30–5:30; Sun. noon–4:30; last entry 30 mins before closing.*

SHOPPING

Orcadian Stone Company. The company makes stone products—some crafted from local Caithness slate—such as incised plaques. There's also a geological exhibition. The shop is open from Easter to October and for three weeks before Christmas. ⊠ *Main St.* ☎ *01408/633483* ⊕ *www.orcadianstone.co.uk.*

DORNOCH

10 mi south of Golspie, 40 mi north of Inverness.

A town of sandstone houses, tiny rose-filled gardens, and a 13th-century cathedral with stunning traditional and modern stained-glass windows, Dornoch is well worth a visit. It's noted for golf: you may hear it referred to as the St. Andrews of the North, but because of the town's location so far north, the golf courses here are delightfully uncrowded. Royal Dornoch is the jewel in its crown, praised by the world's top golfers.

GETTING HERE AND AROUND

From Inverness, take the A9 north to Dornoch. Be cautious, as it's often busy with ferry traffic.

ESSENTIALS

Visitor Information Dornoch ⊠ *Sheriff Court House, Castle St.* ☎ *08452/255121* ⊕ *www.visithighlands.com.*

WHERE TO STAY

For expanded hotel reviews, visit Fodors.com.

$$ 🏰 **Dornoch Castle Hotel.** A genuine late-15th-century castle, once sheltering the bishops of Caithness, this hotel blends the quite old and the more modern. **Pros:** grand exterior; lovely gardens; friendly hotel staff. **Cons:** a few rooms still need a lick of paint. ⊠ *Castle St.* ☎ *01862/810216* ⊕ *www.dornochcastlehotel.com* 🛏 *24 rooms* ♿ *In-room: no a/c. In-hotel: restaurant* ⎟○⎟ *Breakfast.*

GOLF

★ **Royal Dornoch.** Were it not for its remote location, Royal Dornoch would undoubtedly be a candidate for the British Open Championship. It's a superb, breezy, challenging links course. ⊠ *Golf Rd.* ☎ *01862/810219* ⊕ *www.royaldornoch.com* 🏌 *18 holes, 6,200 yds, par 70.*

TORRIDON

Located far to the west, Torridon has a grand, rugged, and wild air that feels especially remote, yet it's just a few hours' drive from Inverness before you reach Kinlochewe, near the east end of Glen Torridon. The western side is equally spectacular. Walking trails and mountain panoramas abound. Torridon is a wonderful place to visit if you want to tackle one of the legendary peaks here—Beinn Alligin, Liathach, and Beinn Eighe—or if you enjoy outdoor activities like kayaking, climbing, or mountain biking. The A890, which runs from the A832 into the heart of Torridon, is a single-lane road in some stretches, with plenty of open vistas across the deserted heart of northern Scotland.

LOCHCARRON

66 mi west of Inverness.

Strung along the shore, the village of Lochcarron has some attractive croft buildings, a couple of churches (one an 18th-century ruin set in a graveyard), a golf club, and some handy shops.

GETTING HERE AND AROUND

To drive here from Inverness, take the A9 as it becomes the A835, A832, and then the A890. The single-track road skirts both steep mountains and lochs.

SHOPPING

Lochcarron Weavers. You can observe a weaver producing pure-wool tartans that can be bought here or at the firm's other outlets in the area. There's also a café. ✉ *Mid Strome* ☎ *01520/722212* ⊕ *www. lochcarronweavers.co.uk.*

SHIELDAIG

16 mi northwest of Lochcarron.

Just west of the southern coast of Upper Loch Torridon is Shieldaig, a village that sits in an attractive crescent overlooking a loch of its own, Loch Shieldaig. For an atmospheric evening foray, walk north toward Loch Torridon, at the northern end of the village by the church. The path—fairly well made, though hiking shoes are recommended—leads to exquisite views and tiny rocky beaches.

10

GETTING HERE AND AROUND

Shieldaig is on the A896 between Lochcarron and Kinlochewe.

EXPLORING

**OFF THE
BEATEN
PATH**

Applecross. The tame way to reach this small community facing Skye is by a coastal road from near Shieldaig. The exciting route turns west off the A896 a few miles farther south and then a series of hairpin turns corkscrews up the steep wall at the head of a corrie (a glacier-cut mountain valley), over the **Bealach na Ba** (Pass of the Cattle). There are spectacular views of Skye from the bare plateau on top, and you can brag afterward that you've been on what is probably Scotland's highest drivable road.

★ **Glen Torridon.** The scenic spectacle of Glen Torridon lies east of Shieldaig. Some say that Glen Torridon has the finest mountain scenery in Scotland. It consists mainly of the long gray quartzite flanks of **Beinn Eighe** and **Liathach,** with its distinct ridge profile that looks like the keel of an upturned boat. The National Trust for Scotland operates the Torridon Visitor Center, which explains the ecology and geology of the area. A small deer museum has displays on these quintessentially Scottish beasts. ✉ *A896* ☎ *01445/791221* ⊕ *www.nts.org.uk/property/torridon* 🎟 *£3* ⊙ *Visitor center Easter–Sept., daily 10–6; museum daily 9–5.*

WHERE TO STAY
For expanded hotel reviews, visit Fodors.com.

$ 🖼 **The Torridon and Torridon Inn.** The Victorian Gothic turrets of this former hunting lodge promise atmosphere and grandeur. **Pros:** breathtaking location; center for outdoor activities; bar has more than 300 malts. **Cons:** isolated location; rather pricey for what it is. ✉ *A896, Annat* ☎ *01445/791242* ⊕ *www.thetorridon.com* 📮 *18 rooms* ♿ *In-room: no a/c. In-hotel: restaurant, bar* ⊙ *Breakfast.*

GAIRLOCH

38 mi north of Shieldaig.

Aside from its restaurants and lodgings, peaceful Gairloch has one further advantage: lying just a short way from the mountains of the interior, this small oasis often escapes the rain clouds that can cling to the high summits. You can enjoy a round of golf here and perhaps stay dry, even when the nearby Torridon Hills are deluged.

GETTING HERE AND AROUND
From Ullapool, this coastal town can be reached via A832.

EXPLORING
Gairloch Heritage Museum. In the village is the Gairloch Heritage Museum, with exhibitions covering prehistoric times to the present. It's also a source for genealogical research—by appointment with the curator. ✉ *Junction of A832 and B8031* ☎ *01445/712287* ⊕ *www. gairlochheritagemuseum.org.uk* 🎟 *£4* ⊙ *Apr.–Oct., Mon.–Sat. 10–5.*

★ **Inverewe Gardens.** A highlight of this area is Inverewe Gardens. The main attraction lies in the contrast between the bleak coastal headlands and the lush plantings of the garden behind its dense barrier of trees and shrubs. These are proof of the efficacy of the warm North Atlantic Drift, part of the Gulf Stream, which takes the edge off winter frosts. Inverewe is sometimes described as subtropical, but this inaccuracy irritates the head gardener; do not expect coconuts and palm trees here. Instead, look for rarities like the blue Himalayan poppy. ✉ *A832, 6 mi northeast of Gairloch, Poolewe* ☎ *0844/493225* ⊕ *www.nts.org. uk* 🎟 *£9* ⊙ *Easter–Oct., daily 9:30–9; Jan.–Easter, daily 10:00–3:00.*

Fodor's Choice **Loch Maree.** Southeast of Gairloch stretches one of Scotland's most scenic
★ lochs, Loch Maree. Its harmonious environs, with tall Scots pines and the mountain Slioch looming as a backdrop, witnessed the destruction

EXPLORING

Glen Brittle. You can safely enjoy spectacular mountain scenery in Glen Brittle, with some fine views of the Cuillin Mountains (which are not for the casual walker, as there are many steep and dangerous cliff faces). The drive from Carbost along a single-track road is one of the most dramatic in Scotland and draws outdoorsy types from throughout the world. At the southern end of the glen is a murky-color beach, a campground, and the chance for a gentle stroll amid the foothills. ⊠ *Off A863/B8009.*

THE OUTER HEBRIDES

The Outer Hebrides—the Western Isles in common parlance—stretch about 130 mi from end to end and lie about 50 mi from the Scottish mainland. This splintered archipelago extends from the Butt of Lewis in the north to the 600-foot Barra Head on Berneray in the south, whose lighthouse has the greatest arc of visibility in the world. In the Hebrides, clouds cling to the hills, and rain comes in squalls. Any trip here requires protection from the weather and a conviction that a great holiday does not require the sun.

The Isle of Lewis and Harris is the northernmost and largest of the group. The island's only major town, Stornoway, is on a nearly landlocked harbor on the east coast of Lewis; it's probably the most convenient starting point for a driving tour of the islands if you're approaching the Western Isles from the Northern Highlands. Lewis has some fine historic attractions, including the Calanais Standing Stones—a truly magical place. The Uists are known for their rare, plentiful wildlife.

Just south of the Sound of Harris is the Isle of North Uist, rich in monoliths, chambered cairns, and other reminders of a prehistoric past. Benbecula, sandwiched between North and South Uist, is in fact less bare and neglected-looking than its bigger neighbors to the north. The Isle of South Uist, once a refuge of the old Catholic faith, is dotted with ruined forts and chapels; in summer its wild gardens burst with alpine and rock plants. Eriskay Island and a scattering of islets almost block the 6-mi strait between South Uist and Barra, an isle you can walk across in an hour.

10

Harris tweed is available at many outlets on the islands, including some of the weavers' homes; keep an eye out for signs directing you to weavers' workshops. Sunday on the islands is observed as a day of rest, and nearly all shops and visitor attractions are closed.

STORNOWAY

On Lewis; 2½-hr ferry trip from Ullapool.

The port capital for the Outer Hebrides is Stornoway, the only major town on Lewis. The island's cultural center, it has an increasing number of good restaurants.

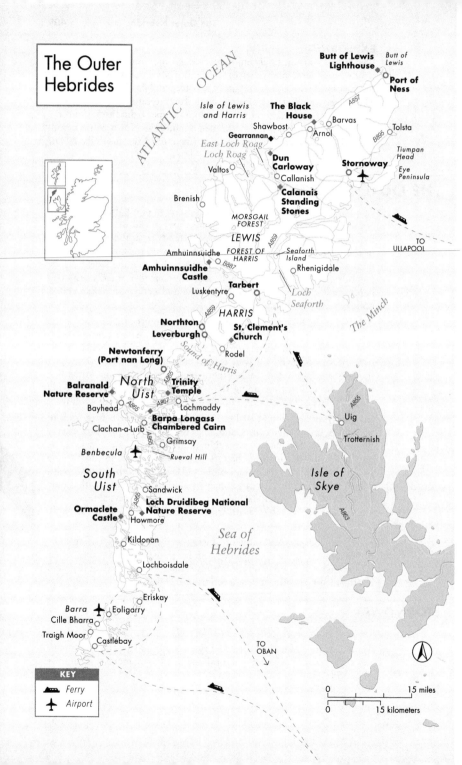

GETTING HERE AND AROUND
The ferry docks at Stornoway, and there's an airport. It's best to have a car to explore the island, but there are also infrequent local buses.

ESSENTIALS
Airport Contact Stornoway Airport ☎ *01851/707400* ⊕ *www.hial.co.uk/ stornoway-airport.html.*

Visitor Information Stornoway ⊠ *26 Cromwell St.* ☎ *01851/703088* ⊕ *www. visithebrides.com.*

EXPLORING
★ **An Lanntair Arts Centre.** The fabulous An Lanntair Arts Centre has exhibitions of contemporary and traditional art, as well as a cinema, a gift shop, and a restaurant serving international and Scottish fare. There are frequent traditional musical and theatrical events in the impressive auditorium. ⊠ *Kenneth St.* ☎ *01851/703307* ⊕ *www.lanntair.com* ⊑ *Free* ☉ *Mon.–Sat. 10 am–8 pm.*

WHERE TO EAT AND STAY
For expanded hotel reviews, visit Fodors.com.

$$ ✕ **Digby Chick.** This local favorite is a great destination on a rainy night.
BRITISH The solid wood floors and white tablecloths brighten the spirits. The seasonal food is hearty even in the middle of summer, with scallops and pea purée, duck breast with citrus syrup, and sweet-toothed desserts like the iced honeycomb meringue tart. ⊠ *5 Bank St.* ☎ *01851/700026* ⊕ *www.digbychick.co.uk.*

$$$ ▦ **Broad Bay House.** It's not in town, but you won't miss the hustle and bustle once you see the great views of the water from Broad Bay House. **Pros:** pure luxury; great coastal walks; fantastic evening meals. **Cons:** no kids; only one room has sea views; you'll need a car to get around. ⊠ *B895* ☎ *01851/820990* ⊕ *www.broadbayhouse.co.uk* ⇆ *4 rooms* △ *In-room: Internet, Wi-Fi. In-hotel: restaurant, beach, laundry facilities, some age restrictions* ❢ *Breakfast.*

SHOPPING
Harris Tweed Artisans Cooperative. The cooperative sells stylish and quirky hand-crafted tweed clothing, hats, accessories, all made by artists belonging to the cooperative. ⊠ *40 Point St.* ☎ *No phone.*

BICYCLING
Alex Dan Cycle Centre. This shop rents bicycles and can give you advice on where to ride, including a route to Tolsta that takes in five stunning beaches before reaching the edge of moorland. ⊠ *67 Kenneth St.* ☎ *01851/704025* ⊕ *www.hebrideancycles.co.uk.*

10

PORT OF NESS

On Lewis; 30 mi north of Stornoway.

The stark, windswept community of Port of Ness cradles a small harbor squeezed in among the rocks.

GETTING HERE AND AROUND
From Stornoway, take the A857 to the Port of Ness.

EXPLORING

Black House. In the small community of Arnol, the Black House is a well-preserved example of an increasingly rare type of traditional Hebridean home. Once common throughout the islands—even into the 1950s—these dwellings were built without mortar and thatched on a timber framework without eaves. Other characteristic features include an open central peat hearth and the absence of a chimney—hence the soot and the designation *black*. On display inside are many of the house's original furnishings. To reach Arnol from Port of Ness, head south on the A857 and pick up the A858 at Barvas. ⊠ *Off A858, 21 mi southwest of Port of Ness, Arnol* ☏ *01851/710395* ⊕ *www. historic-scotland.gov.uk* 🎫 *£2.50* ⊙ *Apr.–Sept., Mon.–Sat. 9:30–5:30; Oct.–Mar., Mon.–Sat. 9:30–4.*

> ### THE BONNIE PRINCE
>
> At the Battle of Culloden, George II's army outnumbered that of Prince Charles Edward Stuart. After the battle, Bonnie Prince Charlie wandered over the Highlands. He escaped to the isles of Harris and South Uist, where he met Flora Macdonald (1722–90), the woman who took him, disguised as her maid, "over the sea to Skye." *Will ye no' come back again . . . Speed, bonnie boat . . . Charlie is my darling . . .* The tunes and lyrics of Lady Nairn, jaunty or mournful, composed long after the events, are as good an epitaph as any adventurer could wish for.

Butt of Lewis Lighthouse. At the northernmost point of Lewis stands the Butt of Lewis Lighthouse, designed by David and Thomas Stevenson (of the prominent engineering family whose best-known member was not an engineer at all, but the novelist Robert Louis Stevenson). The structure was first lighted in 1862. The adjacent cliffs provide a good vantage point for viewing seabirds, whales, and porpoises. The lighthouse is northwest of Port of Ness along the B8014.

SHOPPING

Borgh Pottery. At Borgh Pottery, open from Monday to Saturday 9:30 to 6, you can buy attractive hand-thrown studio pottery made on the premises, including lamps, vases, mugs, and dishes. ⊠ *Fivepenny House, A857, Borve* ☏ *01851/850345* ⊕ *www.borgh-pottery.com.*

EN ROUTE The journey along the A857 takes you past several interesting sights.

Dun Carloway. One of the best-preserved Iron Age *brochs* (circular stone towers) in Scotland, Dun Carloway dominates the scattered community of Carloway. The mysterious tower was probably built around 2,000 years ago as protection against seaborne raiders. The Dun Broch Centre explains more about the broch and its setting. ⊠ *Off A857, Carloway.*

Gearrannan. Up a side road north from Carloway, Gearrannan is an old black-house village that has been brought back to life with a museum screening excellent short films on peat cutting and weaving. For a unique experience, groups can rent the restored houses. ☏ *01851/643416* ⊕ *www.gearrannan.com.*

CALANAIS STANDING STONES

On Lewis; 15 mi west of Stornoway.

GETTING HERE AND AROUND
Take the A858 to reach Calanais.

EXPLORING
★ **Calanais Standing Stones.** These impressive stones are actually part of a cluster of several different archaeological sites in this area. Probably positioned in several stages between 3000 BC and 1500 BC, the grouping consists of an avenue of 19 monoliths extending northward from a circle of 13 stones, with other rows leading south, east, and west. Ruins of a cairn sit within the circle on the east side. Researchers believe they may have been used for astronomical observations, but you can create your own explanations. The visitor center has an exhibit on the stones, a gift shop, and a tearoom. ⊠ *On an unmarked road off A858* ☎ *01851/621422* ⊕ *www.historic-scotland.gov.uk* ☎ *£2.50* ⏱ *Apr., May, Sept., Oct.: Mon.–Sat. 10–6; June–Aug. Mon.–Sat. 10–8; Oct.–Mar., Tues.–Sat. 10–4.*

TARBERT

On Harris; 47 mi south of Calanais.

The main port of Harris, Tarbert has some good shops and a few worthwhile sights. **Traigh Luskentyre,** roughly 5 mi southwest of Tarbert, is a spectacular example of Harris's tidy selection of beaches—2 mi of yellow sands adjacent to **Traigh Seilebost** beach, with superb views northward to the hills of the Forest of Harris.

GETTING HERE AND AROUND
The ferry from Uig arrives at Tarbert once or twice daily. Having a car makes travel on Harris much easier, but with careful planning local buses can make for an excellent trip.

ESSENTIALS
Visitor Information Tarbert ⊠ *Pier Rd.* ☎ *01859/502011* ⊕ *www.visithebrides. com.*

EXPLORING
Amhuinnsuidhe Castle. Turreted Amhuinnsuidhe Castle (pronounced avun-*shooee*) was built in the 1860s by the earls of Dunmore as a base for fishing and hunting in the North Harris deer forest. The castle stands about 10 mi northwest of Tarbert on the B887, and you can view it from the outside only.

Caledonian MacBrayne. This company runs one or two ferries a day beween Tarbert and Uig on the Isle of Skye. ☎ *0800/0665000* ⊕ *www. calmac.co.uk.*

WHERE TO EAT
$$$$ ✕ **Scarista House.** Hearty, well-seasoned food (three courses for £45) is
SEAFOOD what you'll find here, particularly local catches like Sound of Harris langoustine and perfectly pitched desserts like tarte tartin. Stunning views from the dining room extend across a sloping golf course to the

10

sea. An older building, previously a manse, is made cozy with heavy curtains, sturdy sofas and chairs, and an open fire. Rooms and cottages are also for rent. ⊠ *A859, 15 mi south of Tarbert, Sgarasta Gheag* ☎ *01859/550238* ⊕ *www.scaristahouse.com.*

LEVERBURGH

On Harris; 21 mi south of Tarbert.

At Leverburgh you can take the ferry to North Uist. Nearby Northton has several attractions; St. Clement's Church at Rodel is particularly worth a visit.

GETTING HERE AND AROUND
Leverburgh is on the A859 between Tarbert and Rodel.

EXPLORING
MacGillivray Centre. Located in a round building overlooking the bay, the MacGillivray Centre gives insight into the life and work of William MacGillivray (1796–1852), a noted naturalist with strong links to Harris. MacGillivray authored the five-volume *History of British Birds.* This is a great location for a picnic (there are tables for just such a purpose). A walk to a ruined church starts at the parking lot. ⊠ *A859, Northton* 🖺 *Donations accepted* 🕙 *Mon.–Sat. 9–9.*

Seallam! Visitor Centre and Co Leis Thu? Genealogical Research Centre. The center is where you can trace your Western Isles ancestry. Photographs and interpretive signs describe the history of Harris and its people. The owners organize guided walks and cultural evenings weekly between May and September. ⊠ *Off A859, Northton* ☎ *01859/520258* ⊕ *www. seallam.com* 🖺 *£2.50* 🕙 *Mon.–Sat. 10–5.*

St. Clement's Church. At the southernmost point of Harris is the community of Rodel, where you can find St. Clement's Church, a cruciform church standing on a hillock. This is the most impressive pre-Reformation church in the Outer Hebrides; it was built around 1500 and contains the magnificently sculptured tomb (1528) of the church's builder, Alasdair Crotach, MacLeod chief of Dunvegan Castle. Rodel is 3 mi south of Leverburgh and 21 mi south of Tarbert. ⊠ *A859, Rodel.*

NORTH UIST

8 mi south of Rodel via ferry from Leverburgh.

Stunning coastal scenery and ancient ruins are the main draws on the isle of North Uist. Throughout the island you'll find art everywhere: at the end of roads or paths or on the shore, only visible from a boat. Be sure to visit the camera obscura (an old-fashioned projector) just beyond the ferry terminal. Its watery images are evocative and a bit eerie.

GETTING HERE AND AROUND
You can get to North Uist by ferry, either from Harris, the Isle of Skye, or from one of the other islands. Public transport is infrequent, so a car (or a bike) is the most reliable way to travel.

EXPLORING

Balranald Nature Reserve. Administered by the Royal Society for the Protection of Birds, the reserve shelters large numbers of waders and seabirds. It's on the west side of North Uist. ✉ *Off A865, 3 mi northwest of Bayhead* ☎ *01876/560287* ⊕ *www.rspb.org* ✉ *Free* ⊙ *Visitor center Apr.–Aug. 9–6.*

Barpa Langass Chambered Cairn. Dating from the 3rd millennium BC, the Barpa Langass Chambered Cairn is the only chambered cairn in the Western Isles known to have retained its inner chamber fully intact. You can peek inside, but don't venture too far without a light. It sits close to the A867 between Lochmaddy and Clachen.

Dun an Sticar. At Newtonferry (Port nan Long) stands the remains of what was reputed to be the last inhabited broch in North Uist, Dun an Sticar. This defensive tower, reached by a causeway over the loch, was home to Hugh Macdonald, a descendant of Macdonald of Sleat, until 1602.

Taigh Chearsabhagh. Set right on the shore, Taigh Chearsabhagh is a well-run exhibition space, shop, and café. The building has two separate exhibition spaces, a working print shop, and a permanent exhibition in which life on North Uist is brilliantly described. The café serves a selection of cakes and soup, as well as excellent French-press coffee. ✉ *A865, Lochmaddy, North Uist* ⊕ *www.taigh-chearsabhagh. org* ⊙ *Mon.–Sat. 10–5.*

Trinity Temple (Teampull na Trionaid). You can explore the ruins of Trinity Temple (Teampull na Trionaid), a medieval college and monastery said to have been founded in the 13th century by Beathag, daughter of Somerled, the progenitor of the Clan Donald. The ruins stand 8 mi southwest of Lochmaddy, off the A865.

SOUTH UIST

34 mi south of Newtonferry (on North Uist) via Grimsay, Benbecula, and three causeways.

Carpets of wildflowers in spring and early summer, superb deserted beaches, and historical connections to Flora Macdonald and Bonnie Prince Charlie head the list of reasons to visit this island.

GETTING HERE AND AROUND

You can travel the length of South Uist along Route A865, making short treks off this main road on your way to Lochboisdale, on the southeast coast of the island. At Lochboisdale you can catch ferries to

10

Barra, the southernmost principal island of the Outer Hebrides, or to Oban, on the mainland.

EXPLORING

Kildonan Museum and Heritage Centre. The Kildonan Museum and Heritage Centre houses South Uist artifacts collected in the 1950s and 1960s by Father John Morrison, a local priest. On your left when you enter is a simple exhibition with concise and unsentimental descriptions of living on South Uists that reads, "However we interpret it there is nothing surer than history has as much to do with the present as the past." The simple details, like how people filled their mattresses or the names for the tools they used in their houses are what makes this place interesting. ⊠ *A865, Kildonan* ☎ *01878/710343* ⊠ *£2* ☉ *Easter–Oct., Mon.–Sat. 10–5, Sun. 2–5.*

Loch Druidibeg National Nature Reserve. One of only two remaining British native—that is, nonmigrating—populations of greylag geese make their home at Loch Druidibeg National Nature Reserve in a fresh and brackish loch environment. Stop at the warden's office for information about access and nature trails. ⊠ *Off A865* ☎ *01870/620238.*

Our Lady of the Isles. About 5 mi south of the causeway from Grimsay to Benbecula, atop Rueval Hill, stands the 30-foot-high statue of the Madonna and Child known as Our Lady of the Isles. The local Catholic community erected the statue, the work of sculptor Hew Lorimer, in 1957.

WHERE TO STAY

For expanded hotel reviews, visit Fodors.com.

$ ⊡ **Polochar Inn.** With its own standing stone surviving the rough winds off the sea, the Polochar Inn sits at the southern end of South Uist. **Pros:** wild and remote location. **Cons:** some rooms smaller than others. ⊠ *A865, Lochboisdale, South Uist* ☎ *01878/700215* ⊕ *www.polocharinn.com* ⇨ *11 rooms* ⌂ *In-room: no a/c, Wi-Fi. In-hotel: restaurant, bar, beach* ⎮◎⎮ *Breakfast.*

SHOPPING

Hebridean Jewellery. Much of the Celtic-influenced jewelry at Hebridean Jewellery is made in the workshop, which you can tour. A café serves excellent espresso, rich cakes, tasty soups, and panini. ⊠ *Off A865, Iochdar* ☎ *01870/610288* ⊕ *www.hebrideanjewellery.co.uk.*

Orkney and Shetland Islands

WORD OF MOUTH

"On Orkney, we drove around as far as we could and visited the half dozen or so main archaeological sites, St. Magnus Cathedral and the Bishop's and Earl's Palaces in Kirkwall—plus of course the Italian Chapel, which I found extremely moving. The Pier Arts Centre in Stromness is lovely as a building and has contemporary art exhibitions."
—caroline_edinburgh

"A warning about flying to Orkney if your time is limited: the fog came down and I had to give up after the first three flights and return to the mainland by ferry—great experience but disastrous if I had had an international flight to connect with. The Orkneys are absolutely lovely to visit."
—tenaya

Updated by
Shona Main

A Scandinavian heritage gives the 170 islets that make up
Orkney and Shetland a history and an ambience different
from that of any other region of Scotland. Both Orkney and
Shetland are essentially austere and bleak, but they have
awe-inspiring seascapes, fascinating seabirds, remarkable ancient ruins, and genuinely warm, friendly people.
Although a trip requires time and effort, your reward will be
a unique and memorable experience.

An Orcadian has been defined as a farmer with a boat, whereas a Shet-
lander has been called a fisherman with a croft (small farm). Orkney,
the southern archipelago, is greener and is rich with artifacts that testify to the many centuries of continuous settlement here: stone circles,
burial chambers, ancient settlements, and fortifications. UNESCO has
recognized the key remains as a World Heritage Site called the Heart
of Neolithic Orkney.

North of Orkney, Shetland, with its ocean views and sparse landscapes—trees are a rarity because of ever-present wind—seems even
more remote. However, don't let Shetland's desolate countryside fool
you: it has a wealth of historic interest and is far from being a backwater. Oil money from local mineral resources and its position as a crossroads in the northern seas for centuries have helped make Shetland a
busy thriving community that wants for little.

For mainland Scots, visiting these islands is a little like traveling abroad
without having to worry about a different language or currency. Neither
has yet been overrun by tourism, but the people of Orkney and Shetland
will be delighted that you have come so far to see their islands and learn
a little of their extraordinary past.

ORIENTATION AND PLANNING

GETTING ORIENTED

Just 10 mi from Caithness in Scotland, Orkney is made up of 70 islands,
of which 10 are inhabited. A number of ferries travel to ports on the
Mainland, the main island of Orkney, including its administrative center, Kirkwall, where an airport serves Scotland's larger cities. The primary road is essentially a loop that passes near the key historic sites.
The Mainland is linked to the southern island of South Ronaldsay by
way of the Barricades.

About 125 mi north of Orkney lies the spiny outline of Shetland, com-
prising 100 islands. Sumburgh has the main airport, and 25 mi north
is Lerwick, the island's "capital" and a port linking the island to Scotland and Orkney. South Mainland, half an hour from Lerwick, has

TOP REASONS TO GO

Standing stones and ancient sites: Among the many Neolithic treasures in Orkney are the Ring of Brodgar, a 3,000-year old circle of standing stones, and Skara Brae, the remarkable remains of a village uncovered in the grounds of delightful Skaill House. In Shetland, Jarlshof has been the home to different societies since the Bronze Age. Don't miss Mousa Broch and Clickimin Broch in Shetland, two Iron Age towers.

Music and arts festivals: The Shetland Folk Festival in May is a fiddling shindig that attracts musicians and revelers from around the world. Orkney's St. Magnus Festival is less of a pub crawl and more of a highbrow celebration of classical music, poetry, and performance.

Seabirds, seals, and more: These islands have some of the planet's most important colonies of seabirds, with millions clinging to colossal cliffs. You're guaranteed to see seals and may spot dolphins, orcas, or porpoises. In Shetland, Noss and Eshaness nature reserves are prime spots, or you can check out the puffins by Sumburgh Head.

Pure relaxation: There's a much more laid-back approach to life on these islands than on the mainland. Shetlanders are particularly renowned for their hospitality and are often happy to share stories and tips that will enrich your adventure.

Outdoor activities by the coast and ocean: The rugged terrain, beautiful beaches, and unspoiled waters make a perfect backdrop for invigorating strolls, sea fishing, diving, or exploring the coastline and sea lochs by boat.

prehistoric sites. Less than an hour north of Lerwick are dramatic landscapes such as Eshaness. Ferries go beyond the Mainland to Yell and Unst, the latter Britain's most northerly point.

Around Orkney. The towns of Stomness and Kirkwall have sights and museums testifying to Orkney's rich past, including Kirkwall's Norman St. Magnus Cathedral. For many people, though, they're a prelude to impressive Neolithic sites around the Mainland: Maes Howe, Skara Brae, the Ring of Brodgar, and others. Beyond the Mainland, explore sights such as Scapa Flow on Hoy, which reveals the islands' role in two world wars.

Around Shetland. A descent at Sumburgh's airport provides stunning views of a shining white lighthouse, bird-crammed cliffs, and golden bays. Lerwick has the excellent Shetland Museum, and nearby on the South Mainland are the prehistoric sites of Jarlshof, Old Scatness, and Mousa Broch. Worth exploring to the north are the lunarlike Ronas Hill and wave-lashed Eshaness. Unst, the island farthest north, is worth the journey for wide-open ocean views and superb bird-watching at Hermaness National Nature Reserve.

PLANNING

WHEN TO GO

Although shivering, wind-flattened winter visitors braving Orkney and Shetland's winter are not unheard of, the travel season doesn't really start until May, and it runs until September. June is one of the most popular months for both islands. The bird colonies are at their most lively in early summer, which is also when the long northern daylight hours allow you plenty of sightseeing time. Shetland's northerly position means that it has only four or five hours of darkness around the summer solstice, and on a clear night it doesn't seem to get dark at all. Beware the changeable weather even in summer: it could be 75°F one day and then hail the next. Many sights close in September, and by October wilder gales will be mixed with snow flurries one minute and glorious sunshine the next. If you are determined to brave the elements, take into account that there are only six hours of daylight in winter months.

Shetland's festival of fire, Up-Helly-Aa, is held the last Tuesday of each January. The spectacle of Lerwick overrun by Vikings, with torches aflame and a huge Viking longship, has become increasingly popular. Book a year in advance if you want to get a bed for the night.

PLANNING YOUR TIME

Orkney and Shetland require at least a couple of days each if you're to do more than just scratch the surface. Since getting to Shetland isn't easy, you may want to spend three or four days here. The isles generate their own laid-back approach to life, and once here, you may want to take it slowly. A good clutch of the key sites of Mainland Orkney can be seen in a day, if you have a car and are disciplined, but to really get the most out of them, take two days. You can do the Kirkwall sights in a morning before heading to the Italian Chapel on South Ronaldsay in the afternoon. This allows a whole day for Stomness, a town caught in the most poignant of time warps, and the archaeological sites of Maes Howe, the Ring of Brodgar, Skara Brae, and Skaill House and Gurness Broch. To include Birsay, plan your day round the tides.

In Shetland, the sites on the South Mainland—Jarlshof, Scatness, the Crofhouse Museum, St. Ninian's Isle, and Mousa Broch—take the best part of a day, although sailing times for Mousa must be factored in to your schedule. Lerwick and its lanes and spectacular museum is a good day, and can be supplemented with a trip to the Bonhoga Gallery in Weisdale. It's a good idea to take a whole day to explore the north of the islands, including Eshaness and Tangwick Haa, although a car or a guide who drives will be necessary. Ferry times allow for a mad dash round the northern islands of Yell and Unst, but you will see more if you book an overnight stay.

GETTING HERE AND AROUND
AIR TRAVEL

Flybe provides regular service to Sumburgh in Shetland and Kirkwall in Orkney from Edinburgh, Glasgow, Aberdeen, and Inverness. Because of the isolation of Orkney and Shetland, there's also a network of interisland flights, through Directflight in Shetland and Loganair in Orkney.

Airline Contacts **Directflight** ☎ *01595/840246* ⊕ *www.directflight.co.uk.*
Flybe ☎ *01392/268529* ⊕ *www.flybe.com.* **Loganair** ☎ *01856/872494* ⊕ *www.loganair.co.uk.*

BOAT AND FERRY TRAVEL

Northlink operates ferries from Aberdeen to Kirkwall in Orkney and Lerwick in Shetland. These leave Aberdeen harbor each evening (or every second night for Kirkwall), arriving at Kikwall at 11 pm and Lerwick at 7:30 am the next day. These top-notch services have recliner seats for the budget traveler or clean, compact cabins in single, double, or four-berth combinations. There's a shop, a cinema, two bars, and two restaurants (one self-service and one table service) on each boat.

If you're arriving in Aberdeen on Sunday morning and plan on meeting a train, note that the station does not open until 9 am. Northlink allows you to stay in your cabin or the restaurant until 9:30 am.

An alternate way of reaching Orkney is the Northlink ferry from Scrabster to Stromness. There is also a ferry from John o'Groats to Burwick, operated by John o'Groats Ferries, with up to four daily departures May through September. The fastest and smoothest sail is by catamaran from Gills Bay, Caithness, to St. Margaret's Hope on Orkney. Operated by Pentland Ferries, it has three daily departures.

In both Orkney and Shetland, the local council runs the interisland ferry networks (Orkney Ferries and Shetland Island Ferries) to the outer islands. Northlink Ferries has service between Lerwick on Shetland and Kirkwall on Orkney. ■TIP→ **Always book ferry tickets in advance.**

Ferry Contacts **John o'Groats Ferries** ☎ *01955/611353* ⊕ *www.jogferry.co.uk.* **Orkney Ferries** ☎ *01856/872044* ⊕ *www.orkneyferries.co.uk.* **Northlink Ferries** ☎ *0845/600–0449* ⊕ *www.northlinkferries.co.uk.* **Pentland Ferries** ☎ *0800/688–8998* ⊕ *www.pentlandferries.co.uk.* **Shetland Island Ferries** ☎ *01595/743970* ⊕ *www.shetland.gov.uk/ferries.*

BUS TRAVEL

Scottish Citylink and Stagecoach operate buses to Aberdeen where you can get a plane, ferry, or connecting bus to the ferries at John o'Groats, Gills Bay, or Scrabster. John o'Groats Ferries operates the Orkney Bus, a direct express coach from Inverness to Kirkwall (via ferry) that runs daily from June to early September.

The main bus service on Orkney is operated by Stagecoach and on Shetland by ZetTrans (although buses are run by small operators).

Bus Contacts **John o'Groats Ferries** ☎ *01955/611353* ⊕ *www.jogferry.co.uk.* **National Express** ☎ *08705/808080* ⊕ *www.nationalexpress.co.uk.* **Orkney Coaches** ☎ *01856/870555* ⊕ *www.rapsons.co.uk* ☎ *01463/233371.* **Scottish Citylink** ☎ *0871/266–3333* ⊕ *www.citylink.co.uk.* **ZetTrans** ☎ *01595/744868* ⊕ *www.zettrans.org.uk.*

CAR TRAVEL

The most convenient way of getting around these islands is by car, especially if your time is limited. Roads are well maintained and traffic is nearly nonexistent, although speeding cars can be a problem. Orkney has causeways—the Barricades—connecting some of the islands, but in some cases these roads take fairly roundabout routes.

You can transport your rental car from Aberdeen, but for fewer than five days it's usually cheaper to rent a car from one of Shetland and Orkney's agencies. Most are based in Lerwick, Shetland, and Kirkwall, Orkney.

Local Car Rental Contacts **Bolts Car and Minibus Hire** ⊠ *26 North Rd., Lerwick* ☎ *01595/693636* ⊕ *www.boltscarhire.co.uk.* **James D. Peace & Co.** ⊠ *Junction Rd., Kirkwall* ☎ *01856/872866* ⊕ *www.orkneycarhire.co.uk.* **Star Rent-a-Car** ⊠ *22 Commercial Rd., Lerwick* ☎ *01595/692075* ⊕ *www. starrentacar.co.uk.* **W. R. Tullock** ⊠ *Kirkwall Airport, Kirkwall* ☎ *01856/875500* ⊕ *www.orkneycarrental.co.uk.*

TRAIN TRAVEL

There are no trains on Orkney or Shetland, but you can take the train to Aberdeen or Thurso and then take a ferry to the islands.

Train Contacts **ScotRail** ☎ *08457/484950* ⊕ *www.scotrail.co.uk.*

RESTAURANTS

Kirkwall has an increasing number of good cafés and restaurants, as does Lerwick, but both islands now have memorable spots beyond the main towns, from cafés and fish-and-chips spots to some fancier restaurants. Orkney and Shetland have first-class seafood, and in pastoral Orkney the beef is lauded and in Shetland the heather- or seaweed-fed lamb. Orkney is famous for its cheese and its fudge; a glug of its Highland Park malt whisky or some Skull Splitter Ale is also worth trying. Shetlanders are beginning to make much more of their natural edible resources, making ice cream and smoking fish in a variety of ways. Some bakeries create their own version of bannocks—a scone-type baked item you eat with salt beef, mutton, or jam—but Johnson and Wood of Voe (available in shops across the islands) takes the biscuit.

HOTELS

Accommodations in Orkney and Shetland are on par with mainland Scotland, with a growing range of stylish bed-and-breakfasts that might suit some travelers better than the bigger hotels that rely and therefore focus on business customers. Although standards are improving, the islands still do not offer luxury accommodations. To experience a simpler stay, check out the unique "camping böds" in Shetland—old cottages providing inexpensive, basic lodging (log fires, cold water, and sometimes no electricity). For details, contact the Shetland Tourist Information Centre.

WHAT IT COSTS IN POUNDS				
	¢	$	$$	$$$	$$$$
Restaurants	under £10	£10–£14	£15–£19	£20–£25	over £25
Hotels	under £70	£70–£120	£121–£160	£161–£220	over £220

Restaurant prices are for a main course at dinner. Hotel prices are for two people in a double room in high season, generally including the 20% V.A.T.

11

TOURS

Wildabout Orkney runs bus tours combining visits to archaeological sites and information on the folklore, flora, and fauna of the islands. John Leask & Son arranges tours of Shetland and Orkney tailored to your interests.

In Shetland, Island Trails offers excellent tours enriched by the many myths, customs, and folklore of the islanders. To visit the outlying islands of Shetland, such as the mist-capped Foula and the once-inhabited Hildasay, take a Cycharters day or afternoon trip on its boat, the *Cyfish;* the company also offers private charters. Seabirds and Seals tours take you on board the cruiser *Dunter III* to tour Bressay and the island of Noss, a national nature reserve and bird sanctuary, weather permitting.

Tour Contacts **Cycharters** ☎ *01595/696598* ⊕ *www.cycharters.co.uk.* **Island Trails** ☎ *01950/422408* ⊕ *www.island-trails.co.uk.* **J. Leask** ☎ *01595/693162* ⊕ *www.leaskstravel.co.uk.* **Orkney Coaches** ☎ *01856/870555* ⊕ *www.rapsons. co.uk.* **Seabirds and Seals** ☎ *07595/540224* ⊕ *www.seabirds-and-seals.com.* **Wildabout** ☎☏ *01856/877737* ⊕ *www.wildaboutorkney.com.*

VISITOR INFORMATION

The Orkney visitor center in Kirkwall, and the Shetland visitor center, in Lerwick, are open year-round.

Visitor Information **Orkney** ✉ *West Castle St., Kirkwall* ☎ *01856/872856* ⊕ *www.visitorkney.com.* **Shetland** ✉ *Market Cross, Lerwick* ☎ *01595/999440* ⊕ *www.visitshetland.com* ✉ *Sumburgh Airport Terminal, Sumburgh* ☎ *01950/460905.*

AROUND ORKNEY

If you're touring the north of Scotland, the short boat trip to Orkney offers the chance to step outside the Scottish history you've experienced on the mainland. Prehistoric sites such as the Ring of Brodgar, and the remnants of Orkney's Viking-influenced past, are in dramatic contrast to that of the mainland. The Orkney Islands may have a population of just 20,000, but a visit reveals the islands' cultural richness. In addition, Orkney's continued reliance on farming and fishing reminds you how some things can stay the same despite technological advances. At Maes Howe, for example, it becomes evident that graffiti is not solely an expression of today's youths: the Vikings left their marks here way back in the 12th century. ■ TIP→ You can purchase the Historic Scotland joint-entry ticket at the first site you visit; the ticket costs less than paying separately for entry into each site.

STROMNESS AND THE NEOLITHIC SITES

1¾ hrs north of Thurso on Scotland's mainland, via ferry from Scrabster.

On the southwest of the Mainland, on the shore of Hamnavoe, is Stromness, a remarkably attractive fishing town seemingly so unsullied by modernity that it evokes an uncomplicated way of life long gone. Walk past the old-fashioned shops and austere cottages that line the

The Orkney Islands

ATLANTIC OCEAN

Seal Skerry
North Ronaldsay
Hollandstoun

Papa
Westray

Holland

Pierowall

Westray

The North
Sound

North
Ronaldsay
Firth

Northwall
Burness
Kettletoft

Rapness

Sanday

Calfsound

Braeswick

Westray
Firth

Sanday
Sound

Rousay

Wasbister

Eday

Brough of
Birsay

Backaland

Whitehall

Birsay

Brinyan

Aith

Marwick Head
Nature Reserve

Gurness
Broch

Stronsay
Firth

Stronsay

Dounby

Marwick
Bay

Skara Brae

Unstan
Chambered
Tomb

Shapinsay

Mainland

Finstown

Balfour

TO →
SCALLOWAY

Ring of Brodgar

Maes
Howe

Stromness

Stenness

St. Ola

Kirkwall

Orphir
Church

A965

Skaill

Moness

Orphir

Houton

St. Mary's

Scapa
Flow

A961

Copinsay

Rackwick

Italian
Chapel

Scapa Flow
Visitor Centre

Lambholm

Lyness

St. Margaret's
Hope

Hoy

South
Ronaldsay

Pentland Firth

Burwick

Old Head

Pentland
Skerries

Scrabster

Gills

John o'
Groats

A836

Thurso

0   10 miles
0   10 kilometers

KEY
Ferry
Airport

main street and you'll understand why local poet and novelist George Mackay Brown (1921–96) was inspired and moved by its sober beauty.

With its ferry connection to Scrabster in Caithness, Stromness makes a good base for visiting the western parts of Orkney, and the town holds several points of interest. It was once a key trading port for the Hudson Bay company, and the Stromness Museum displays artifacts from those days. Nearby are three spectacular ancient sites, the Ring of Brodgar, Maes Howe, and Skara Brae at Skaill House.

GETTING HERE AND AROUND

Stromness is at the end of the A965 and can be reached by one of the many buses from Kirkwall.

Stagecoach buses 7 and 8 link Kirkwall, the Ring of Brodgar, and Skara Brae and Skaill House with Kirkwall. Altogether there are three bus services there and three back per day, so plan accordingly.

ESSENTIALS

Visitor Information **Stromness** ⊠ *Pier Head* ☎ *01856/850716* ⊕ *www. visitorkney.com* ⊙ *Mar.–Oct., daily 9–5.*

EXPLORING

★ **Maes Howe.** The huge burial mound of Maes Howe, circa 2500 BC, measures 115 feet in diameter and contains an enormous burial chamber. It was raided by Vikings in the 12th century, and Norse crusaders found shelter here, leaving a rich collection of runic inscriptions. Outside you see a large, grassy mound; the stunning interior of the chambered tomb has remarkably sophisticated stonework. This site is 6 mi northeast of Stromness and 1 mi from the Ring of Brodgar. Call early on the day of your visit to reserve a spot on the hourly tours. ⊠ *A965* ☎ *01856/761606 for reservations* ⊕ *www.historic-scotland. gov.uk* 🎟 *£5.50* ⊙ *Apr.–Sept., daily 9:30–5; Oct.–Mar., daily 9:30–4.*

Pier Arts Centre. At the striking Pier Arts Centre, a gallery in a former merchant's house and adjoining buildings, huge sheets of glass offer tranquil harborside views and combine with space-maximizing design to make the best use of every shard of natural light and inch of wall to display the superb permanent collection. The more than 100 20th- and 21st-century paintings and sculptures include works by Barbara Hepworth and Douglas Gordon, and edgy temporary exhibitions showcase international contemporary artists. A chic shop sells design products and art books. ⊠ *28–30 Victoria St.* ☎ *01856/850209* ⊕ *www.pierartscentre.com* 🎟 *Free* ⊙ *Sept.–May, Mon.–Sat. 10:30–5; June–Aug., Mon.–Sat. 10:30–5, Sun. noon–4.*

★ **Ring of Brodgar.** About 5 mi northeast of Stromness, the Ring of Brodgar is a magnificent circle of 36 Neolithic standing stones (originally 60) surrounded by a henge, or deep ditch. When the fog descends over the stones—a frequent occurrence—their looming shapes seem to come alive. The site dates to between 2500 and 2000 BC. Though the original use of the circle is uncertain, it's not hard to imagine strange rituals taking place here in the misty past. The stones stand between Loch of Harray and Loch of Stenness. ⊠ *B9055, Stromness* ☎ *01856/841815* ⊕ *www.historic-scotland.gov.uk* 🎟 *Free* ⊙ *Year-round.*

Fodor's Choice **Skara Brae.** After a fierce storm in 1850, the laird of Breckness, William Graham Watt, discovered this cluster of Neolithic houses at the bottom of his garden. The houses, first occupied around 3000 BC and containing stone beds, fireplaces, dressers, and cupboards, are the most extensive of their kind in northern Europe and provide real insight into this ancient civilization. A reconstruction of one house can be seen in the visitor center, which displays artifacts from the site and hosts an excellent café. Skara Brae stands on the grounds of **Skaill House**, a splendid, intriguing mansion built by the Bishop of Orkney in the 1600s. His descendants, the lairds of Breckness, along with the various ladies of the manor, added to the house and to the eclectic furnishings. These sites offer a joint ticket well worth the price: the juxtaposition of different societies thousands of years apart that shared the same corner of Orkney makes a fascinating visit. ⊠ *B9056, 8 mi north of Stromness, Stromness* ☎ *01856/841815* ⊕ *www.historic-scotland.gov. uk* 🖆 *£5.90 Oct.–Mar. Skara Brae only; £6.90 Apr.–Sept. Skara Brae and Skaill House* ☉ *Skara Brae Apr.–Sept., daily 9:30–5:30; Oct.–Mar., daily 9:30–4:30. Skaill House Apr.–Sept., daily 9:30–5:30.*

☼ **Stromness Museum.** The enchanting Stromness Museum has the feel of **Fodor's Choice** some grand Victorian's private collection but has, in fact, been community owned since it opened in 1837. Its crammed but utterly fascinating exhibits on fishing, shipping, and whaling are full of interesting trinkets from all over the world that found their way to this small Orcadian town because of its connections with the Hudson Bay Shipping Company. The company recruited workers in Stromness between the late 18th and 19th centuries as they were considered more sober and therefore more reliable than other Scots. Also here are model ships and displays on the German fleet that was scuttled on Scapa Flow in 1919. Upstairs, don't miss the beguiling, traditionally presented collection of birds and butterflies that are native to the British Isles. ⊠ *52 Alfred St.* ☎ *01856/850025* 🖆 *£3.50* ☉ *Oct.–Mar., Mon.–Sat. 11–3:30; Apr.–Sept., daily 10–5.*

NEED A BREAK? **Julia's Café Bistro.** Right on the quayside, Julia's Café Bistro serves the kinds of cakes that make you conveniently forget the existence of calories. Expect huge slices of lemon drizzle, coffee layer, raspberry cream, and other cakes, as well as scones and shortbreads. Baked potatoes, quirky salads, and quiches round out the savory side of the menu while real espresso and cappuccino seal the deal. ⊠ *Ferry St.* ☎ *01856/850904.*

WHERE TO STAY
For expanded hotel reviews, visit Fodors.com.

$ 🏠 **Mill of Eyrland.** White-painted stone walls, country antiques, and the rippling sound of a stream running beneath the windows make for a pleasant stay at this bed-and-breakfast in a former mill dating from 1861. **Pros:** the old grinding stones are a stunning focal point in the public lounge; beautiful views out to Scapa Flow. **Cons:** difficult to find; breakfast is served at one big table, so be prepared to socialize. ⊠ *Off A964, Stenness* ☎ *01856/850136* ⊕ *www.millofeyrland.co.uk* 🛏 *4 rooms* ☝ *In-room: no a/c. In-hotel: bar* ⦿ *Breakfast.*

SPORTS AND THE OUTDOORS

DIVING The cool, clear waters of Scapa Flow and eight sunken ships that were part of Germany's fleet during World War I make for an unparalleled diving experience.

Scapa Scuba. Several companies organize trips to Scapa Flow and other nearby dive sites. Dives with Scapa Scuba are from its boat, the *MV Radiant Queen.* ⊠ *Lifeboat House, Dundas St., Stromness* ☎ *01856/ 851218* ⊕ *www.scapascuba.co.uk.*

BIRSAY

12 mi north of Stromness, 25 mi northwest of Kirkwall.

Birsay itself is a small collection of houses, but some interesting historic and natural sites are nearby.

GETTING HERE AND AROUND

The village is on A966; a car is the easiest way to see the nearby sites.

EXPLORING

Broch of Gurness. Gurness Broch, an Iron Age tower built between 500 BC and 200 BC, stands more than 10 feet high and is surrounded by stone huts, indicating that this was a village. The tower's foundations and dimensions suggest that it was one of the biggest brochs in Scotland, and the remains of the surrounding houses are well preserved. The site is along the coast about 8 mi east of Birsay. ⊠ *A966, Aikerness* ☎ *01856/751414* ⊕ *www.historic-scotland.gov.uk* ⊠ *£4.70* ☺ *Apr.–Sept., daily 9:30–5:30.*

Brough of Birsay. A Romanesque church can be seen at the Brough of Birsay, a tidal island with the remains of an early Pictish and then Norse settlement. (*Brough* is another word for burgh.) The collection of roofless stone structures on the tiny island, close to Birsay, is accessible only at low tide by means of a concrete path that winds across the seaweed-strewn bay. The path is slippery, so boots are essential. ■ TIP➔ **To ensure you won't be swept away, check the tides with the tourism office in Kirkwall or Stromness before setting out.** ⊠ *A966* ☎ *01856/841815 (Skara Brae)* ⊕ *www.historic-scotland.gov.uk* ⊠ *£4* ☺ *June–Sept., daily 9:30–5:30.*

Marwick Head Nature Reserve. The Royal Society for the Protection of Birds tends the remote Marwick Head Nature Reserve, where in spring and summer the cliffs are draped in wildflowers like campion and thrift, and resound with thousands of nesting seabirds like cormorants, kittiwakes, and guillemots. The Kitchener Memorial, recalling the 1916 sinking of the cruiser HMS *Hampshire* with Lord Kitchener aboard, sits atop a cliff. Access to the reserve, which is unstaffed, is along a path north from Marwick Bay. ⊠ *Off B9056, 4 mi south of Birsay* ☎ *01856/850176* ⊕ *www.rspb.org.uk* ⊠ *Free* ☺ *Daily 24 hrs.*

KIRKWALL

16 mi east of Stromness.

In bustling Kirkwall, the main town on Orkney, there's plenty to see in the narrow, winding streets extending from the harbor. The cathedral and some museums are highlights.

GETTING HERE AND AROUND

Kirkwall is a ferry port and also near Orkney's main airport. Its sights are all near one another. Visitors to the Highland Park Distillery might want to hop on the T11 Kirkwall Circular or get a taxi (about £5).

ESSENTIALS

Visitor Information Orkney ✉ *West Castle St., Kirkwall* ☎ *01856/872856* ⊕ *www.visitorkney.com.*

EXPLORING

TOP ATTRACTIONS

OFF THE BEATEN PATH

Italian Chapel. During World War II, 550 Italian prisoners of war were captured in North Africa and sent to Orkney to assist with the building of the Churchill Barriers, four causeways that blocked entry into Scapa Flow, Orkney's great natural harbor. Using two corrugated-iron Nissan huts, the prisoners, led by Domenico Chiocchetti, a painter-decorator from the Dolomites, constructed this beautiful and inspiring chapel in memory of their homeland. The elaborate interior frescoes were adorned with whatever came to hand, including bits of metal, colorful stones, and leftover paints. ✉ *A961, 7 mi south of Kirkwall* ⊡ *Free* ⊙ *Apr.–Sept., daily 9 am–10 pm; Oct.–Mar., daily 9–4:30.*

Orkney Museum. With artifacts from the Picts, the Vikings, and other ancient peoples, this museum in Tankerness House (a former residence) has the entire history of Orkney crammed into a rabbit warren of rooms. It's not easily accessible for those with disabilities. The setup may be old-fashioned, but some artifacts—especially those from everyday Orcadian life in the 19th century—are riveting. Lovely gardens around the back provide a spot to recoup after a history lesson. ✉ *Broad St.* ☎ *01856/873191* ⊡ *Free* ⊙ *May–Sept., Mon.–Sat. 10:30–5; Oct.–Apr., Mon.–Sat. 10:30–12:30 and 1:30–5.*

Orkney Wireless Museum. The lifetime collection of Jim MacDonald, a radio operator during World War II, tells the story of wartime communications at Scapa Flow, where thousands of servicemembers were stationed; they used the equipment displayed to protect the Home Fleet. Run by volunteers, the museum also contains many handsome 1930s wireless radios and examples of the handicrafts produced by Italian prisoners of war. ✉ *Kiln Corner, Junction Rd.* ☎ *01856/871400* ⊕ *www.owm.org.uk* ⊡ *£3* ⊙ *Apr.–Sept., Mon.–Sat. 1–4:30, Sun. 2–4.30.*

★ **St. Magnus Cathedral.** Founded by the Norse earl Jarl Rognvald in 1137 and named for his uncle, this grand red and yellow sandstone cathedral was mostly finished by 1200, although more work was carried out during the following 300 years. The cathedral is still in use and contains some fine examples of Norman architecture, although traces of later styles are found here and there. The ornamentation on some of the tombstones in the church is particularly striking. At the far end to the left is the tomb of Dr. John Rae, the Victorian-era Orcadian adventurer who discovered the final section of the Northwest Passage in Canada. ⊠ *Broad St.* ☎ *01856/874894* ⊕ *www.stmagnus.org* ⊙ *Apr.–Sept., Mon.–Sat. 9–6, Sun. 2–6; Oct.–Mar. weekdays 9–1 and 2–5.*

WORTH NOTING

Bishop's Palace. The palace dates to the 12th century when St. Magnus Cathedral was built. In 1253 this was the site of King Hakon IV of Norway's death, marking the end of Norwegian rule over Sudreyjar (the Southern Hebrides). It was rebuilt in the late 15th century, and a round tower was added in the 16th century. ⊠ *Palace Rd.* ☎ *01856/871918* ⊕ *www.historic-scotland.gov.uk* ⊠ *£4.50, includes Earl's Palace* ⊙ *Apr.–Sept., daily 9:30–5:30; Oct., daily 9:30–4:30.*

Earl's Palace. Perhaps the best surviving example of Renaissance architecture in Scotland, this ruined palace was built in 1607 by Patrick Stewart, the much despised (yes, still) Earl of Orkney and Lord of Shetland. There are no tours, so you can explore the palace ruins, including the Great Hall with its large fireplace, at your own pace. ⊠ *Palace Rd.* ☎ *01856/871918* ⊕ *www.historic-scotland.gov.uk* ⊠ *£4.50, includes Bishop's Palace* ⊙ *Apr.–Sept., daily 9:30–5.30; Oct., daily 9:30-4:30.*

Highland Park Distillery. Having come this far, you'll have earned a dram of the local single malt at Scotland's northernmost distillery. It was founded around the turn of the 19th century by Magnus Eunson, a church officer who dabbled in illicit stilling. The tour takes you through the essential aspects of this near-sacred process, from the ingredients, to the hand turning of the malt, the peating in the peat kilns, the mashing, and finally the maturation in oak casks. This smoky but sweet malt can be purchased all over Orkney, as well as from the distillery's austere shop. ⊠ *Holm Rd.* ☎ *01856/874619* ⊕ *www.highlandpark.co.uk* ⊠ *£6* ⊙ *Apr. and Sept., weekdays 10–5; May–Aug., Mon.–Sat. 10–5, Sun. noon–5; Oct.–Mar., weekdays 1–5.*

Unstan Chambered Tomb. This intriguing burial chamber lies within a 5,000-year-old cairn. Access to the tomb can be awkward for those with mobility problems. ⊠ *A964, 7½ mi west of Kirkwall* ☎ *01856/841815* ⊕ *www.historic-scotland.gov.uk* ⊠ *Free* ⊙ *Apr.–Sept., daily 9:30–5:30; Oct.–Mar., daily 9:30–4:30.*

WHERE TO EAT

$$ ✕ **The Creel.** This outstanding "restaurant with rooms" with a glow-
MODERN BRITISH ing reputation sits right on the waterfront of one of Orkney's loveliest
★ harbors at St. Margaret's Hope. On the island of South Ronaldsay, the inn's charm lies partly in the fuss-free approach to hospitality that makes everyone, from the local farmer to a visiting business executive, feel welcome. Imaginative modern Scottish cuisine uses the freshest Orcadian seafood, seaweed-fed lamb, and locally grown vegetables. Three simple guest rooms overlook the bay. ⊠ *Front Rd., 13 mi south of Kirkwall, St. Margaret's Hope* ☎ *01856/831311* ⊕ *www.thecreel. co.uk* ⇨ *Reservations essential* ⊙ *Closed Oct.–Mar.*

¢ ✕ **The Reel.** Orkney's musical tradition is alive and fiddling, but never
CAFÉ more so than at this café and restaurant. As you eat, young Orcadians run up the stairs with their violin cases to the music school, where all

sorts of sprees and shindigs are held in the performance spaces. The eating is cheap and hearty: expect big bowls of soup, doorstop-size sandwiches with inventive fillings, and slices of sponge cake. It becomes more like a pub on a Friday or Saturday night, with locally brewed ales and, of course, live music. ⊠ *3 Castle St.* ☎ *01856/871000.*

WHERE TO STAY

For expanded hotel reviews, visit Fodors.com.

$ 🏨 **Foveran Hotel.** About 34 acres of grounds surround this modern, ranch-style hotel overlooking Scapa Flow, about 3 mi southwest of Kirkwall. **Pros:** friendly, efficient service; food that's cooked to perfection. **Cons:** exterior looks a bit institutional; you must book the popular restaurant ahead. ⊠ *Off A964, St. Ola* ☎ *01856/872389* ⊕ *www.foveranhotel.co.uk* ↘ *8 rooms* ⅓ *In-room: no a/c, Internet. In-hotel: restaurant, bar* ⫶◯⫶ *Breakfast.*

$ 🏨 **Merkister Hotel.** After a long day taking in the sights, the gentle lap of Loch Harray, which the Merkister overlooks, soothes the soul. **Pros:** endless coffee in the lounge and library; notable restaurant. **Cons:** some small rooms; the bedrooms are a bit dated. ⊠ *A965, Harray* ☎ *01856/771366* ⊕ *www.merkister.com* ↘ *16 rooms* ⅓ *In-room: no a/c. In-hotel: restaurant* ⫶◯⫶ *Breakfast.*

¢ 🏨 **Miller's House.** Built by a naval lieutenant, James Miller, Orkney's oldest house dates to before 1660 and now serves as a comfortable bed-and-breakfast. **Pros:** great value for the money; near the ferry. **Cons:** only two rooms; not easy to find; books up well in advance. ⊠ *13 John St.* ☎ *01856/851969* ⊕ *www.millershouseorkney.com* ↘ *2 rooms* ⅓ *In-room: no a/c. In-hotel: laundry facilities* ▭ *No credit cards* ⫶◯⫶ *Breakfast.*

$ 🏨 **The Shore.** Right on the harbor, this friendly hotel above a pub has surprisingly modern bedrooms with small but chic bathrooms. **Pros:** clean and well-maintained rooms; friendly staff. **Cons:** breakfast costs extra; bars have a somewhat cheesy feel; cars tearing up the main road outside may disturb sleep. ⊠ *Shore St.* ☎ *01856/872200* ⊕ *www.theshore. co.uk* ↘ *10 rooms* ⅓ *In-room: no a/c, Wi-Fi. In-hotel: restaurant, bar.*

THE ARTS

St. Magnus Festival. The region's cultural highlight is Kirkwall's St. Magnus Festival, usually held the third week in June. Its impressive program includes distinguished orchestral, operatic, and choral artists. Orkney also hosts an annual folk festival at the end of May. ☎ *01856/871445* ⊕ *www.stmagnusfestival.com.*

SPORTS AND THE OUTDOORS

BICYCLING **Cycle Orkney.** For £15 a day bicycles can be rented from Cycle Orkney, which is open year-round. ⊠ *Tankerness La.* ☎☎ *01856/875777* ⊕ *www.cycleorkney.com.*

FISHING **Merkister Hotel.** The Merkister Hotel, on Loch Harray, arranges fishing packages, with all equipment, including boats, available to rent. ⊠ *A965, Harray* ☎ *01856/771366.*

Island Festivals

11

Islanders know how to celebrate their unique heritage and the performing arts. Joining one of the island festivals can be a memorable part of any trip. Some festivals are very popular, so plan ahead.

Shetland has quite a strong cultural identity, thanks to its Scandinavian heritage. There are, for instance, books of local dialect verse, a whole folklore and identification system for lost fishermen contained in knitting patterns, and a strong tradition of fiddle playing.

In the middle of the long winter, at the end of January, Shetlanders celebrate their Viking culture with the **Up-Helly-Aa Festival,** which—for the men—involves dressing up as Vikings, parading with flaming torches, and then burning a replica of a Viking longship, followed by one or sometimes two nights of carousing. Women play hostess in the halls, feeding and quenching the thirsts of those involved, and dancing with them. The **Shetland Folk Festival,** held in April, and October's **Shetland Accordion and Fiddle Festival** both attract large numbers of visitors.

Orkney's **St. Magnus Festival,** a celebration focusing on classical music, is based in Kirkwall and is usually held the third week in June. Orkney also hosts a jazz festival in April, an annual folk festival at the end of May, the unique Boys' Ploughing Match in mid-August, and The Ba' (ball; street rugby-football played by the Uppies and Doonies residents of Kirkwall) on Christmas and New Year's Day.

On a smaller scale, throughout summer, both islands run mini-festivals and events for lovers of literature, films, food, art, music and, in Shetland, even bannocks! Information about these can be found in the visitor centers.

SHOPPING

Judith Glue. Kirkwall is Orkney's main shopping hub. At Judith Glue you can purchase designer knitwear with traditional patterns, as well as handmade crafts and hampers of local produce. The shop also has a cafe. ✉ *25 Broad St.* ☎ *01856/874225.*

The Longship. Don't miss The Longship, which sells a huge array of Ola Gorrie's original designs in gold and silver jewelry with Celtic and Norse themes. ✉ *11 Broad St.* ☎ *01856/888790.*

Ortak. Selling Celtic-theme jewelry, Ortak also has exhibits and jewelry-making demonstrations. ✉ *Albert St.* ☎ *01856/873536.*

SCAPA FLOW VISITOR CENTRE

On Hoy, 14 mi southwest of Kirkwall, 6 mi south of Stromness.

GETTING HERE AND AROUND

The car ferry from Houton (7 mi east of Stromness) takes 25 minutes to reach Lyness on Hoy and the visitor center. The ferry costs around £22 round-trip for a regular-size car and £7 round-trip per passenger.

ESSENTIALS

Ferry Contacts Orkney Ferries ☎ *01856/872044* ⊕ *www.orkneyferries.co.uk.*

EXPLORING

Scapa Flow Visitor Centre. On the beautiful island of Hoy, Scapa Flow Visitor Centre explores the strategic and dramatic role that this sheltered anchorage played in two world wars. It displays military vehicles and guns, as well as equipment salvaged from the German boats scuttled off the coast. In the plain but poignant graveyard here, British and German personnel both rest in peace. ■ TIP→ **If you want to take your car over to Hoy, book well in advance with Orkney Ferries, as this is a popular route.** The visitor center is a short walk from the ferry terminal. ⊠ *Off B9047* ☎ *01856/791300* 🖃 *Free* ☉ *Mar. and Apr., weekdays 9-4:30; May–Sept., Mon.–Sat. 9–4:30, Sun. 10:30–3:30; Oct., Mon.–Sat. 9–4.*

AROUND SHETLAND

The Shetland coastline is an incredible 900 mi because of the rugged geology and many inlets; there isn't a point on the islands farther than 3 mi from the sea. Lerwick is the primary town, but the population of 22,000 is scattered across the 15 inhabited islands. The oil boom—new wells were recently drilled to the west of the islands—means that communities are well cared for: no one in Shetland lives more than 20 minutes away from a publicly run swimming pool.

In general, the prehistoric treasures such as Jarlshof and Mousa Broch are in the South Mainland. For the geological marvels of the islands, Ronas Hill and Eshaness, visit the North Mainland. The social history of the islands is told most comprehensively in the Shetland Museum and in the lanes of Lerwick. Wherever your interest, you'll see and hear an island that buzzes with music, life, and history.

LERWICK

14 hrs by ferry from Aberdeen.

Founded by Dutch fishermen in the 17th century, Lerwick today is a busy town and administrative center. Handsome stone buildings—known as lodberries—line the harbor; they provided loading bays for goods, some of them illegal. The town's twisting flagstone lanes and harbor once heaved with activity, and Lerwick is still an active port today. This is also where most visitors to Shetland dock, spilling out of cruise ships, allowing passengers to walk around the town.

GETTING HERE AND AROUND

The town center of Lerwick is 1 mi south of Holmsgarth, the terminal for the ferry from Aberdeen. You can take a bus from Holmsgarth to the center or to the bus station for travel to Sumburgh or Scalloway. Car rentals can be arranged to meet you at the ferry terminal. Lerwick is small and compact, and the bus network, overseen by ZetTrans, offers hourly bus service around town.

ESSENTIALS

Transportation Contacts Boddam Cabs ☎ *01950/460111.* **ZetTrans** ☎ *01595/744868* ⊕ *www.zettrans.org.uk.*

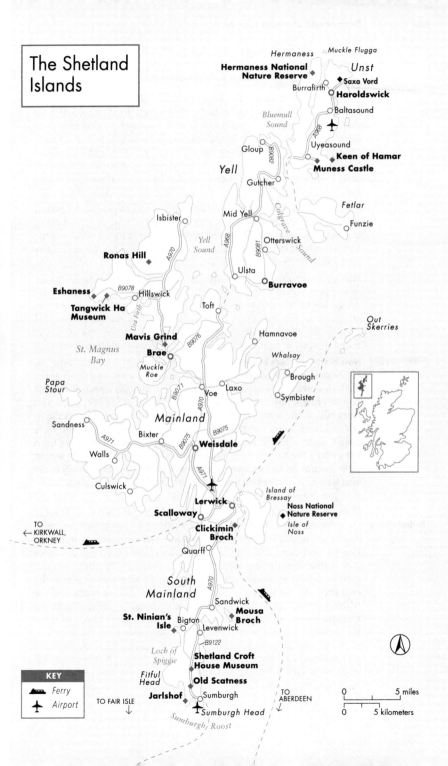

The Shetland Islands

KEY
🛳 Ferry
✈ Airport

Muckle Flugga

Hermaness

Hermaness National Nature Reserve
Unst
Burrafirth
◆ **Saxa Vord**
Haroldswick
Baltasound

Bluemull Sound
A968
Uyeasound

Gloup
B9082
Keen of Hamar
Muness Castle

Yell
Gutcher

Isbister
Mid Yell
Fetlar
Funzie

Ronas Hill
A970
Yell Sound
A968
B9081
Otterswick

Ulsta
Burravoe

Eshaness
B9078
Hillswick
Toft

Tangwick Ha Museum
Una Firth
Hamnavoe
Out Skerries

Mavis Grind
B9076
Whalsay

St. Magnus Bay
Brae
Muckle Roe
●Brough
Symbister

Papa Stour
B9071
Voe
Laxo
A970

Sandness
A971
Bixter
B9075
B9075

Walls
B9075
Weisdale

Culswick

Lerwick
Island of Bressay
Scalloway
Noss National Nature Reserve
Clickimin Broch
Isle of Noss
Quarff

TO
← KIRKWALL,
ORKNEY

South Mainland
A970

Sandwick
Mousa Broch
St. Ninian's Isle
Bigton
Levenwick
B9122

Loch of Spiggie
Shetland Croft House Museum

Fitful Head
Old Scatness

Jarlshof
Sumburgh
TO
ABERDEEN

TO FAIR ISLE
↓
✈ Sumburgh Head
Sumburgh Roost

0   5 miles

0   5 kilometers

Visitor Information Lerwick ⊠ *Market Cross* ☎ *08701/999440* ⊕ *www. visitshetland.com.*

EXPLORING

Clickimin Broch. A stone tower on the site of what was originally an Iron Age fortification, Clickimin Broch makes a good introduction to these mysterious Pictish buildings. It was possibly intended as a place of retreat and protection in the event of attack. South of the broch are vivid views of the cliffs at the south end of the island of Bressay, which shelters Lerwick Harbor. ⊠ *Off A970, 1 mi south of Lerwick* ☎ *01856/841815* ⊕ *www.historic-scotland.gov.uk* ⌧ *Free* ☉ *Daily 24 hrs.*

Fort Charlotte. This artillery fort was built in 1665 to protect the Sound of Bressay from the invading Dutch. They seized it in 1673 and razed the fort to the ground. They were soon chased out of Shetland and the fort was rebuilt in 1781. ⊠ *Market St.* ☎ *01667/460232* ⌧ *Free* ☉ *Apr.– Sept., daily 9:30–6:30; Oct.–Mar., daily 9:30–4:30.*

Mareel. Next to the Shetland Museum, Mareel has a live performance space, two cinemas, and a café and bar. The chunky, shining edifice's design has been controversial, as has its cost. But with the island's creative community bursting at the seams, it will undoubtedly be filled with life the minute its doors are opened. At this writing, the space was slated to open in later 2012. ⊠ *North Ness* ⊕ *www.shetlandarts.org.*

OFF THE BEATEN PATH

Noss National Nature Reserve. The island of Noss (which means "nose" in old Norse) rises to a point called the Noup. The smell and noise of the birds that live on the vertiginous cliffs can assault the senses. Residents nest in orderly fashion: black and white guillemots (45,000 pairs) and razorbills at the bottom; gulls, gannets, cormorants, and kittiwake in the middle; fulmars and puffins at the top. If you get too close to their chicks, some will dive-bomb from above. To get here, take a ferry from Lerwick to Bressay, then an inflatable boat to Noss. ■ TIP→ **Be sure to wear waterproof clothing and sensible shoes; mid-May to mid-July is the best time to view breeding birds.** ⊠ *Noss* ☎ *01595/693345* ⊕ *www.nnr-scotland.org.uk* ⌧ *£3* ☉ *Apr.–Aug. daily 11–5.*

☉ Fodor's Choice ★

Shetland Museum. On the last remaining stretch of the old waterfront at the restored Hay's Dock, the striking Shetland Museum building, with its sail-like tower, is Shetland's cultural hub and a stimulating introduction to local culture. The two-story space is filled with displays about archaeology, textiles, culture, and contemporary art. Standout exhibits include depictions of the minutiae of everyday Shetland life across the centuries, the last remaining *sixareen* (a kind of fishing boat), and the Monk's Stone, a carving depicting the Irish monks who introduced Christianity to the people of Shetland. The museum is also a wonderful place to hang out; look for vintage vessels moored in the dock and seals that pop up to observe everyone checking out the scene from the glass-fronted café-restaurant terrace. ⊠ *Hay's Dock, Commercial Rd.* ☎ *01595/695057* ⊕ *www.shetland-museum.org.uk* ⌧ *Free* ☉ *Mon.– Sat.10–4, Sun. noon–5.*

WHERE TO EAT

$$ ✕ **Hay's Dock.** In the Shetland
BRITISH Museum, this airy, glass-fronted café
★ and restaurant serving reasonably
priced lunches and somewhat pric-
ier dinners has proved very popular.
Chunky wooden tables fitted with
glass panels allow you to see the art-
work featured on top. Good lunch
picks include the seafood chow-
der and salt beef with bannocks (a
savory scone); in the evening, try
tagliatelle with scallops or Shet-
land lamb stew. ⊠ *Hay's Dock, off
Commerical Rd.* ☎ *01595/741569*
⊕ *www.haysdock.co.uk* ⌣ *Reser-
vations essential* ⊗ *No dinner
Sun.–Wed.*

¢ ✕ **The Peerie Shop Cafe.** Who would
CAFÉ believe you could get such good
cappuccino at 60 degrees north? Round the back of the popular Ler-
wick knitwear shop is a modish, consistently good café that sells filled
sponge cakes, lip-smackingly good soups, and, yes, the best coffee
on the islands. It's always busy and Shetlanders do like to talk, so be
prepared to hang around for a table during lunchtime. Alas, the café
closes at 6. ⊠ *Esplanade* ☎ *01595/692816* ⊕ *www.peerieshopcafe.com*
⊗ *Closed Sun. No dinner.*

TROWS AND TALES

The Shetlands have a tradition
of folktales, many with Norse
origins, and it can be easy to
end up believing the place is
teeming with trows, cousins of
Scandinavian trolls. There's a
cavelike dwelling in the Shetland
Museum—the Trowie Knowe—and
a fantastical device—the Trowie
Detector—that may help track
down these elusive characters. To
enter the world of Shetlandic his-
tory and folklore, book a trip or an
evening of storytelling with Island
Trails (☎ *01950/422408* ⊕ *www.
island-trails.co.uk).*

WHERE TO STAY

For expanded hotel reviews, visit Fodors.com.

¢ ⌂ **Alder Lodge Guest House.** Occupying an 1830s-built former bank
building, this guesthouse sits on a quiet street within easy reach of
Lerwick's harbor, shops, pubs, and attractions. **Pros:** comfortable
beds; superb location; child-friendly. **Cons:** booked solid in the sum-
mer months; breakfasts may be too heavy for some. ⊠ *8 Clairmont Pl.*
☎ *01595/695705* ⊕ *www.alder-lodge.co.uk* ⌥ *8 rooms* ⌂ *In-room: no
a/c* ⊟ *No credit cards* ⏀ *Breakfast.*

$$ ⌂ **Kveldsro House Hotel.** If a fussy bed-and-breakfast doesn't suit you, try
the plain but pleasing Kveldsro House, tucked away behind the town's
main thoroughfare. **Pros:** minutes from the city center; cheery bar. **Cons:**
expensive rates for what you get; some walls are a bit thin. ⊠ *Greenfield
Pl., off Commerical St.* ☎ *01595/692195* ⊕ *www.shetlandhotels.com*
⌥ *17* ⌂ *In-hotel: restaurant, bar, parking* ⏀ *Breakfast.*

BICYCLING

Eric Brown Cycles. Open year-round, Eric Brown Cycles rents bikes for
£12.50 a day. ⊠ *Grantfield Garage, North Rd.* ☎ *01595/692709.*

SHOPPING

Anderson & Co. On Commercial Street, Anderson & Co. carries handmade
knitwear and souvenirs. ⊠ *60–62 Commercial St.* ☎ *01595/693714.*

J. G. Rae Limited. J. G. Rae Limited stocks gold and silver jewelry with Norse and Celtic motifs. ✉ *92 Commercial St.* ☎ *01595/693686.*

Ninian. Traditional and funky handmade scarves, clothing, throws and the original Burra Bears (teddy bears made from Fair Isle knits) are found at Ninian. ✉ *80 Commercial St.* ☎ *01595/696655.*

Peerie Shop. The Peerie Shop sells a colorful mix of knitwear, cards, ceramics, and books. ✉ *Esplanade* ☎ *01595/692816.*

Shetland Times. The best bookshop within a radius of about 250 mi, the Shetland Times stocks a good selection of travel guides and local history titles. ✉ *71–79 Commercial St.* ☎ *01595/695531.*

THE SOUTH MAINLAND

14 to 25 mi south of Lerwick via A970.

The narrow 3- or 4-mi-wide stretch of land that reaches south from Lerwick to Sumburgh Head has a number of fascinating ancient sites (and an airport) as well as farmland, wild landscapes, and dramatic ocean views.

GETTING HERE AND AROUND

Arriving in Sumburgh by plane offers stunning views of Sumburgh Head and its golden sands. A fairly regular bus makes the hour-long trip between the airport and Lerwick, and it's also easy to drive here if you're based in Lerwick. You can rent a car from the airport or take a taxi. Jarlshof and Scatness are both within walking distance of the terminal.

ESSENTIALS

Visitor Information **Sumburgh** ✉ *Sumburgh Airport Terminal, A9070, Virkie* ☎ *01950/460905* ⊕ *www.visitshetland.com.*

EXPLORING

Jarlshof. In 1897, a huge storm blew away 4,000 years of sand to expose the extensive remains of Norse buildings, prehistoric wheelhouses, and earth houses that represented thousands of years of continuous settlement. It's a large and complex site, and you can roam the remains freely. The small visitor center is packed with facts and figures, and illustrates Jarlshof's more recent history as a medieval farmstead and home of the 16th-century Earl of Orkney and Shetland, "cruel" Patrick Stewart, who enslaved the men of Scalloway to build Scalloway Castle. ✉ *Sumburgh Head, off A970* ☎ *01950/460112* ⊕ *www. historic-scotland.gov.uk* 🎫 *£5.50* ☉ *Apr.–Sept., daily 9:30–5:30.*

SHETLAND PONIES

The endearingly squat and shaggy Shetland pony has been a common sight for more than 12 centuries. Roaming wild over the hills, the pony evolved its long mane and dense winter coat. The animals stand between 28 and 42 inches tall, which made them ideal for working in cramped coal-mine tunnels in the 1850s, when child labor was restricted. They became a popular pet in the late 19th century; many believe this has helped save the breed. Today a studbook society protects the purity of the stock, and you'll see plenty of ponies at equine events as well as all over the island, chomping the grass.

★ **Mousa Broch.** Sandwick is the departure point for the passenger ferry to the tiny isle of Mousa, where you can see Mousa Broch, a fortified Iron Age stone tower about 40 feet high. The massive walls give a real sense of security, which must have been reassuring for islanders subject to attacks from ship-borne raiders. Exploring this beautifully preserved, curved-stone structure, standing on what feels like an untouched island, makes you feel as if you're back in 100 BC. From April to September, the ferry departs for the island one or twice each afternoon. ⊠ *Ferry terminal, off A970, 14 mi south of Lerwick* ☎ *01950/431367 ferry* ⊕ *www. mousa.co.uk* ☑ *Ferry £13.50 round-trip* ⊗ *Site open daily.*

> ### PUFFINS AND MORE
>
> Every summer more than a million birds alight on the cliff faces in Shetland to nest, feeding on the coastal fish and sand eels. Bird-watchers can spot more than 20 species, from tiny storm petrels to gannets with 6-foot wingspans. Popular with visitors are the puffins, with their short necks, striped beaks, and comical orange feet. Look for them on the cliffs at Sumburgh Head near the lighthouse, 2 mi south of Sumburgh Airport. It's a steep climb to the viewing areas. The visitor center in Lerwick has leaflets about nesting sites.

☺ ★ **Old Scatness.** Ongoing excavations at Old Scatness have uncovered the remains of an Iron Age village, including one building that still has a roof. The digs continue, but enthusiastic and entertaining guides, most in costume, tell stories that breathe life into the stones and the middens. They also show how the former residents made their clothes and cooked their food, including their staple dish: the ghastly seaweed porridge. Call ahead for hours. ⊠ *Off A970* ☎ *01595/694688* ⊕ *www.shetland-heritage.co.uk/amenitytrust* ☑ *£5* ⊗ *June–Sept., hrs vary.*

☺ ★ **Shetland Croft House Museum.** This 19th-century thatched house reveals the way of life of rural Shetlanders, which the traditionally attired attendant will be delighted to discuss with you. The peat fire casts a glow on the box bed, the resting chair, and the wealth of domestic implements, including a hand mill for preparing meal and a straw "keshie" for carrying peat. The upturned boat in the field outside is used for storing and drying fish and mutton. Huts like this inspired the design of the new Scottish Parliament. If you're lucky, the museum's curator may be making bannocks from his homegrown and home-milled flour. ⊠ *East of A970, 7 mi south of Sandwick, South Voe* ☎ *01590/695057* ⊕ *www.shetland-museum.org.uk* ☑ *Donations welcome* ⊗ *Mid-Apr.– Sept., daily 10–1 and 2–5.*

St. Ninian's Isle. It was on St. Ninian's Isle that a schoolboy helping archaeologists excavate the ruins of a 12th-century church discovered the St. Ninian treasure, a collection of 28 silver objects dating from the 8th century. This Celtic silver is housed in the Museum of Scotland in Edinburgh (a point of controversy), but good replicas are in the Shetland Museum in Lerwick. Although you can't see the silver, walking over the causeway of golden sand (called a tombolo) that joins St. Ninian's Isle to the mainland is an unforgettable experience. The island is 8 mi north of Sumburgh via A970 and B9122; then turn left at Skelberry.

WHERE TO STAY

For expanded hotel reviews, visit Fodors.com.

¢ ☒ **Hayhoull B&B.** This restful bed-and-breakfast has rooms that are big and well designed and a dining room and lounge with beautiful views of St. Ninian's Isle and Foula. **Pros:** next to the bus stop for Lerwick; in friendly village next to the magical St Ninian's Isle. **Cons:** 4 mi to the nearest pub or restaurant. ☒ *Off B9122, Bigton* ☎ *01950/422206* ⊕ *www.bedandbreakfastshetland.com* ↩ *3 rooms* ⌂ *In-room: no a/c, Wi-Fi. In-hotel: laundry facilities* ⎰ *Breakfast.*

SCALLOWAY

6 mi west of Lerwick, 21 mi north of St. Ninian's Isle.

On the west coast of Mainland Island is Scalloway, which preceded Lerwick as the capital of the region. During World War II, Scalloway was the port for the "Shetland Bus," a secret fleet of boats that carried British agents to Norway to perform acts of sabotage against the Germans, who were occupying the country. On the return trips, the boats would carry refugees back to Shetland. As you approach the town from the A970, look for the information board, which overlooks the settlement and its castle.

GETTING HERE AND AROUND

The town is just 10 minutes by car from Lerwick, or you can get one of the fairly regular buses or even a taxi (£10).

EXPLORING

Scalloway Castle. On the harbor, Scalloway Castle was built in 1600 by Patrick Stewart, earl of Orkney and Shetland. He was hanged in 1615 for his cruelty and misdeeds, and the castle was never used again. To enter the castle, you must retrieve the key from the shopkeeper at Shetland Woollen Company, or, on Sunday, from the host at the Scalloway Hotel. You may explore the castle ruins to your heart's content. ☒ *A970* ☎ *01856/841815* ⊕ *www.historic-scotland.gov.uk* ☑ *Free* ☉ *Daily.*

SHOPPING

Shetland Woollen Company. Open Monday to Saturday 9:30 to 5, the Shetland Woollen Company sells hand and machine-knitted Shetland knitwear. ☒ *Castle St.* ☎ *01595/880243.*

WEISDALE

9 mi north of Lerwick.

This tiny place is less a village than a group of houses, but it does have a worthwhile gallery.

GETTING HERE AND AROUND

Take A971 from Lerwick. The number 9 bus weekdays runs three times a day; the trip from Lerwick is 20 minutes.

EXPLORING

Bonhoga Gallery. Built in 1855 using stones from the Kergord estate's "cleared" (forcibly evicted) crofts and converted to a museum in 1994, Weisdale Mill is now the Bonhoga Gallery, a contemporary art space

11

showing quirky exhibitions by local, national, and international artists. Other forms of art are represented in programs of films, poetry, and more. Downstairs is a well-appreciated café that looks over the Weisdale burn; try the excellent coffee and snacks. ⊠ *B9075* ☎ *01595/830400* ⊕ *www.shetlandarts.org* ⊗ *Tues.–Sat. 10:30–4:30, Sun. noon–4:30.*

SHOPPING

Shetland Jewellery. The shop sells gold and silver Nordic and Celtic-inspired jewelry made on the on-site workshop. ⊠ *Sound Side* ☎ *01595/ 830275.*

BRAE

15 mi north of Weisdale, 24 mi north of Lerwick.

A thriving community, Brae is where you can see the spoils of Shetland's oil money. The rugged moorland and tranquil *voes* (inlets) of Brae are the home of Busta House, one of the best hotels on the island.

GETTING HERE AND AROUND

There are buses from Lerwick to Brae, but the spread-out sights make it impossible to really see this area without a car. A970 is the main road, and B9078 will take you through Hillswick and to Eshaness.

EXPLORING

Eshaness and Ronas Hill. About 15 mi north of Brae are the rugged, forbidding cliffs around **Eshaness**; drive north and then turn left onto B9078. On the way, look for the striking sandstone stacks or pillars (known as the Drongs) in the bay that resemble a Viking galley under sail. Then return to join the A970 at Hillswick and follow an ancillary road from the head of Ura Firth. This road provides vistas of rounded, bare **Ronas Hill,** the highest hill in Shetland. Though only 1,468 feet high, it's noted for its arctic-alpine flora. If you want to gain a bit of height but haven't the shoes or time to walk, drive up Collafirth Hill, just off A970. It has the remains of an early NATO communications station on the top and a landscape strewn with huge red granite boulders.

OFF THE BEATEN PATH

Tangwick Haa Museum. After viewing the cliffs at Eshaness, call in at Tangwick Haa Museum, the 17th-century home of the Cheynes, now packed full with photographs, household items, and knitting, farming, and fishing equipment from the 18th to early 20th centuries. ⊠ *Off B9078, Tangwick* ☎ *01806/503389* ⊗ *Apr.–Sept., daily 11–5.*

Mavis Grind. North of Brae the A970 meanders past Mavis Grind, a strip of land so narrow you can throw a stone—if you're strong—from the Atlantic, in one inlet, to the North Sea, in another. Keep an eye out for sea otters, which sometimes cross here.

WHERE TO EAT AND STAY

For expanded hotel reviews, visit Fodors.com.

¢ ✕**Braewick Café.** With a stunning position overlooking Eshaness's sea-stacks (columns of rock in the sea), this eatery's famously large portions are popular with visitors and Shetlanders alike. Browse the local knitting and crafts in the shop while waiting for a crispy battered-fish supper, or just sit back in the sofas by the huge picture window and

BRITISH

watch the dramatic sea and sky. Don't pass up the many tempting home-baked desserts like sponges, cheesecakes, and giant scones. ⊠ *Off B9078, Eshaness* ☎ *01806/503345.*

¢ ✕ **Frankie's Fish & Chip Cafe.** Proudly claiming to be the northernmost
BRITISH fish-and-chip shop in Britain, this "chipper" is also the best of its kind
★ on the islands. The combination of super-fresh seafood—skate wings, squid, and crab legs—light and crispy batter, and value for your money means Frankie's is everything a chip shop should be. Try the juicy fresh mussels, too. There's a lovely dining room with views toward Busta Voe, and you can sit on the deck in finer weather. ⊠ *A970* ☎ *01806/522700* ⊘ *No lunch Sun.*

$ 🏠 **Busta House.** Dating from the 16th century, Busta House has a restrained, austere elegance that tells you something of the Gifford family that once lived here—ask the current owners about the Gifford family's ill-starred history. **Pros:** truly haunting atmosphere; atmospheric public rooms; lovely grounds. **Cons:** noisy plumbing; lack of sound-proofing; some dishes in the restaurant come smothered in sauce. ⊠ *Off A970* ☎ *01806/522506* ⊕ *www.bustahouse.com* ⤶ *22 rooms* ⚄ *In-room: no a/c. In-hotel: restaurant, bar, business center* ⫯○⫯ *Breakfast.*

YELL

11 mi northeast of Brae, 31 mi north of Lerwick.

A desolate-looking blanket bog cloaks two-thirds of the island of Yell, creating an atmospheric landscape to pass through on the way to Unst to the north.

GETTING HERE AND AROUND

Although you will see the odd walker or cyclist, a car is needed to explore the northern isles. To get to Yell, take A970 or B9076 and catch the ferry from Toft to Ulsta. On Yell, B9081 runs through Bur-ravoe and up the east side and joins the A968, which leads to Gutcher and the ferry to Unst.

EXPLORING

Old Haa (*hall*). The oldest building on the island, Burravoe's Old Haa is known for its crow-stepped gables (the stepped effect on the ends of the roofs), typical of an early-18th-century Shetland merchant's house. There's an earnest memorial to Bobby Tulloch, the great Shetland natu-ralist (1929–96), and the displays in the upstairs museum tell the story of the wrecking of the German ship, the *Bohus,* in 1924. A copy of the ship's figurehead is displayed outside the building. The Old Haa serves light meals with home-baked buns, cakes, and other goodies and also acts as a kind of unofficial information center. A crafts shop is on the premises, too. ⊠ *Burravoe* ☎ *01957/722339* ⊕ *www.bobbytulloch.com* ⊞ *Free* ⊘ *Apr.–Sept., Tues.–Thurs. and Sat. 10–4, Sun. 2–5.*

UNST

49 mi north of Lerwick.

Unst is the northernmost inhabited island in Scotland, a remote and special place, especially for nature lovers. On a long summer evening, views north to Muckle Flugga, with only the ocean beyond, are incomparable. If you're a bird-watcher, head to the Hermaness and Keen of Hamar nature reserves.

GETTING HERE AND AROUND

A ferry (take the A968 at Mid Yell to Gutcher) crosses the Bluemull Sound to Unst. A car is best for exploring, though there is limited bus service, including from Lerwick; taxis are an option. The island has some B&B and house-rental options if you choose to linger.

EXPLORING

Haroldswick. In the far north of Unst is the town of Haroldswick, with a heritage center and a post office that's proud of its status as the most northerly one in Scotland. Named after King Harold of Norway, it was at this sheltered bay that the Norwegians landed in AD 875 to claim the islands.

Unst Boat Haven. Reflecting Shetland's maritime heritage, Unst Boat Haven displays a collection of traditional small fishing and sailing boats. ⊠ *Beach Rd., Haroldswick* ☎ *01957/711528* ⊕ *www.unst.org* ⊠ *£3* ⊗ *May–Sept., daily 11–5.*

★ **Hermaness National Nature Reserve.** The Hermaness National Nature Reserve, a bleak moorland ending in rocky cliffs, is prime bird-watching territory. About half the world's population (6,000 pairs) of great skuas, called "bonxies" by locals, are found here. ■ TIP→ **These sky pirates attack anything that strays near their nests, including humans, so keep to the paths.** Thousands of other seabirds, including more than 50,000 puffins, nest in spectacular profusion on the cliffs, about an hour's walk from the reserve entrance. Hermaness is not just about birds—gray seals gather in caves at the foot of the cliffs in fall, and offshore, dolphins and occasionally whales (including orcas) can be seen on calm days. The flora include the insect-eating butterwort and sundew, purple field gentians, blue squill, and sea thrift. The visitor center at the lighthouse has leaflets that outline a walk; mid-May to mid-July is the best time to visit. To get here from Haroldswick, follow the B9086 around the head of Burra Firth, a sea inlet. ⊠ *B9086, Burrafirth* ☎ *01957/711278* ⊕ *www.nnr-scotland.org.uk* ⊠ *Free* ⊗ *Mid-Apr.–mid-Sept., daily 9–5.*

Keen of Hamar National Nature Reserve. Just to the north of Muness Castle is the Keen of Hamar National Nature Reserve, off A968, with subarctic flora and arctic terns.

Muckle Flugga. A path in the Hermaness National Nature Reserve meanders across moorland and climbs up a gentle hill, from which you can see, to the north, a series of tilting offshore rocks; the largest of these sea-battered protrusions is Muckle Flugga, meaning "big, steep-sided island," on which stands a lighthouse. The lighthouse was built by engineer Thomas Stevenson, whose son, the great Scottish writer Robert

Louis Stevenson, used the outline of Unst for his map of Treasure Island. Muckle Flugga is the northernmost point in Scotland—the sea rolls out on three sides, and no land lies beyond. ⊠ *Hermaness National Nature Reserve, B9086, Birrafirth*.

Muness Castle. Muness Castle, Scotland's northernmost castle, was built just before the end of the 16th century and has circular corner towers. It is a ruin but has notable architectural details; you can visit when you wish. To get here from the A968, turn right onto the B9084. ⊠ *B9084, Uyeasound* ☎ *No phone* ⊕ *www.historic-scotland.gov.uk* ☞ *Free* ⊙ *Daily 24 hrs*.

WHERE TO EAT

$ ✕ **Saxa Vord.** This restaurant is part of an odd collection of buildings
BRITISH   strewn around the edge of an eye-wateringly—that's the wind—gorgeous peninsula. The tidy, well-run, and informal eatery serves lunches and dinners as fresh and good for you as the Unst air. Try local scallops, Shetland smoked salmon, and lamb hot pot. You can retire to the bar to chat with the locals and sip a tasty real ale such as Auld Wife or Simmer Dim from the local Valhalla brewery. ⊠ *Off A968, Valsgarth* ☎ *01957/711711* ⊕ *www.saxavord.com* ⊙ *Closed Mon. Oct.–Apr.*

A Golfer's Country

WORD OF MOUTH

"Here are a couple of other courses to play. Royal Dornoch is one of the best examples of a links-style course. Might be too far of a drive, but it is a great course! Cruden Bay is another amazing links course. I had a great round here!"

—surfmom

"I definitely agree about Cruden Bay and Royal Dornoch. The folks I've taken on golf trips have enjoyed St. Andrews for the experience and history, but they have without exception *loved* Dornoch."

—janisj

Updated by
Nick Bruno

There are some 550 golf courses in Scotland and only 5.5 million residents, so the country has probably the highest ratio of courses to people anywhere in the world. If you're visiting Scotland, you'll probably want to play the "famous names" sometime in your career.

So, by all means, play the championship courses such as the Old Course at St. Andrews, but remember they *are* championship courses. You may enjoy the game itself much more at a less challenging course. Remember, too, that everyone else wants to play the big names, so booking can be a problem at peak times in summer. Booking three to four months ahead is not too far for the famous courses, although it's possible to get a time up to a month (or even a week) in advance if you are relaxed about your timing. If you're staying in a hotel attached to a course, get it to book for you.

Happily, golf has always had a peculiar classlessness in Scotland. It's a game for everyone, and for centuries Scottish towns and cities have maintained golf courses for the enjoyment of their citizens. Admittedly, a few clubs have always been noted for their exclusive air, and some newer golf courses are losing touch with the game's inclusive origins, but these are exceptions to the tradition of recreation for all. Golf here is usually a democratic game, played by ordinary folk as well as the wealthy.

TIPS ABOUT PLAYING IN SCOTLAND

Golf courses are everywhere in Scotland. Most courses welcome visitors with a minimum of formalities, and some at a surprisingly low cost. Other courses are very expensive, but a lot of great golf can be played for between about £30 to £100 a round. Online booking at many courses has made arranging a golf tour easier, too.

Be aware of the topography of a course. Scotland is where the distinction between "links" and "parkland" courses was first made. Links courses are by the sea and are subject to the attendant sea breezes—some quite bracing—and mists, which can make them trickier to play. The natural topography of sand dunes and long, coarse grasses can add to the challenge of playing, too. Invariably, a parkland course is in a wooded area and its terrain is more obviously landscaped. A "moorland" course is found in an upland area.

Here are three pieces of advice, particularly for North Americans: 1) in Scotland the game is usually played fairly quickly, so don't dawdle if others are waiting; 2) caddy carts are hand-pulled carts for your clubs and driven golf carts are rarely available; and 3) when they say "rough," they really mean "rough."

Unless specified otherwise, course-playing hours are generally sunrise to sundown, which in June can be as late as 10 pm. Note that some courses advertise the SSS, "standard scratch score," instead of par (which may be different). This is the score a scratch golfer could achieve under perfect conditions. Clubs, balls, and other golfing gear are generally for rent from clubhouses, except at the most basic municipal courses. Don't get caught by the dress codes enforced at many golfing establishments: in general, untailored shorts, round-neck shirts, jeans, and sneakers are frowned upon. The prestigious courses may ask for evidence of your golf skills by way of a handicap certificate; check in advance and carry this with you.

Many courses will lower their rates before and after the peak season— at the end of September, for example. It's worth asking about this.

■ TIP➔ Some areas offer regional golf passes that are a great way to save money. Check with the local tourist board.

For a complete list of courses, contact local tourist offices or VisitScotland's official and comprehensive golf website, ⊕ *golf.visitscotland. com.* It has information about the country's golf courses and special golf trails, a course search, links to golf course and regional golf websites, lists of special golfing events and tour operators, and updates on golf passes as well as on accommodations convenient to the courses. Another site, ⊕ *www.uk-golfguide.com*, has a handy feature that allows you to see the courses via Google Earth. *For information about good regional courses, also see individual chapters; see Tours in Travel Smart Scotland for some golf tour operators.*

THE STEWARTRY

At the very southern border, the Stewartry is a delightful part of Scotland set in the rich farmlands around Dumfries, a golfing vacation area since Victorian times. There are also several fine 9-hole courses in the area.

Powfoot Golf Club. A pleasant mix of links and parkland holes and views south over the Solway Firth to distract you make this lesser-known gem designed by James Braid a pleasure to play. ⊠ *Off B724, Cummertrees, Annan* ☎ *01461/204100* ⊕ *www.powfootgolfclub.com* 🖻 *Weekdays £38 per round, £49 per day; weekends £44 per round, £60 per day* 🏌 *18 holes, 6,275 yds, SSS 71* ⊘ *Daily.*

Southerness Golf Club. Mackenzie Ross designed this course, the first built in Scotland after World War II, in 1947. Southerness is a long course, played over extensive links with fine views southward over the Solway Firth. The greens are hard and fast, and the frequent winds make for some testing golf. ⊠ *Southerness St., Southerness, Kirkbean* ☎ *01387/880677* ⊕ *www.southernessgolfclub.com* 🖻 *Weekdays £50 per round, £65 per day; weekends £60 per round, £75 per day* 🖃 *Reservations essential* 🏌 *18 holes, 6,566 yds, par 69* ⊘ *Daily.*

AYRSHIRE AND THE CLYDE COAST

An hour south of Glasgow, Ayrshire and the Clyde Coast have been a holiday area for Glaswegians for generations. Few golfers need an introduction to the names of Turnberry, Royal Troon, Prestwick, or Western Gailes—all challenging links courses along this coast. There are at least 20 other courses in the area within an hour's drive.

Girvan. Opened in 1902, scenic Girvan plays along a narrow coastal strip and a more lush inland section next to the Water of Girvan—a river that provides a testing hazard at the15th, unless you're a big hitter. Like its illustrious neighbor Turnberry, the course has fine views of Ailsa Craig and the Clyde Estuary. ⊠ *40 Golf Course Rd., Girvan* ☎ *01465/714346* ⊕ *www.golfsouthayrshire.com* 🖃 *Weekdays £17 per round, £24 per day; weekends £19 per round, £33 per day* 🏌 *18 holes, 5,064 yds, par 64* ⊙ *Daily.*

Prestwick Golf Club. Tom Morris was involved in designing this challenging Ayrshire coastal links course, which saw the birth of the British Open Championship in 1860. Prestwick has excellent, fast rail links with Glasgow. ⊠ *2 Links Rd., Prestwick* ☎ *01292/477404* ⊕ *www. prestwickgc.co.uk* 🖃 *Weekdays £130 per round, £185 per day; weekends £155 per round.* 🏌 *18 holes, 6,544 yds, par 71* ⊙ *Daily. Limited number of tee times on Sat. afternoons.*

Royal Troon Golf Club. Of the two courses at Royal Troon, it's the Old Course—a traditional links course with superb sea views—that is used for the British Open Championship. Visitor season tee times are limited to certain days from spring through early fall, and change each year according to the tournament program. Advance payment is required, as is a handicap certificate. ⊠ *Craigend Rd., Troon* ☎ *01292/311555* ⊕ *www.royaltroon.com* 🖃 *Old Course: £175 per round (price also includes one round on Portland Course); £130 for round on Old Course in later part of visitors' season.* 🏌 *Old Course: 18 holes, 7,150 yds, SSS 74; Portland Course: 18 holes, 6,289 yds, SSS 70* ⊙ *Mid-Apr.–early Sept. and mid-Sept.–mid-Oct., Mon., Tues., and Thurs. for visitors.*

Fodor's Choice
★ **Turnberry.** The Ailsa Course at Turnberry is one of the most famous links courses in Scotland. Right on the seashore, the course is open to the elements, and the ninth hole requires you to hit the ball over the open sea. The British Open was staged here in 1977, 1986, 1994, and 2009. A second course, the Kintyre, is more compact than the Ailsa, with tricky sloped greens. Five of the holes have sea views; the rest are more inland. ⊠ *Turnberry Resort, Maidens Rd., off A719, Turnberry* ☎ *01655/331000* ⊕ *www.turnberryresort.co.uk* 🖃 *Ailsa Course: £160 per round for hotel guests, £199 per round for nonguests; Kintyre Course: £105 per round for hotel guests, £135 per round for nonguests* 🏌 *Ailsa Course: 18 holes, 7,204 yds, SSS 70; Kintyre Course: 18 holes, 6,853 yds, SSS 72* ⊙ *Daily.*

★ **Western Gailes Golf Club.** Known as the finest natural links course in Scotland, Western Gailes is entirely nature-made, and the greens are kept in truly magnificent condition. This is the final qualifying course when the British Open is held at Royal Troon or Turnberry. Tom Watson lists the par-5 sixth as one of his favorite holes. ⊠ *Gailes Rd., Irvine* ☎ *01294/311649* ⊕ *www.westerngailes.com* 🖃 *Apr.–Sept., Mon., Wed., and Fri. £125 per round, £170 double round (lunch included); Sat. 3:30–4:30 £125 per round; Sun. 2:30–4 £125 per round. Mar. and Oct. £85 (includes two-course lunch); Nov.–Feb. £60 (soup and sandwich included)* 🏌 *18 holes, 6,700 yds, par 71* ⊙ *Mon., Wed., Fri., and weekend afternoons.*

ARGYLL

The lochs and glens of Argyll in the west of Scotland have provided the scenic backdrop for family outings for generations. The string of courses north from the Mull of Kintyre all offer golf in a relaxed environment, with sea, beach, and hills not far away.

Machrihanish Golf Club. Many enthusiasts discuss this course in hushed tones—it's a kind of out-of-the-way golfers' Shangri-la, though developments are now being built around it. It was laid out in 1876 by Tom Morris on the links around the sandy Machrihanish Bay. The drive off the first tee is across the beach to reach the green—an intimidating start to a memorable series of individual holes. Consider flying from Glasgow to nearby Campbeltown if time is short. ⊠ *Off B843, Machrihanish, Campbeltown* ☎ *01586/810277* ⊕ *www.machgolf.com* ⌨ *£62 per round, £93 per day* ⚸ *Reservations essential* ⚐ *18 holes, 6,225 yds, par 70* ☉ *Daily.*

GLASGOW

Most of Glasgow's old golf clubs have moved out to the suburbs—you can tee off from at least 30 different courses less than an hour from the city center. Remember: in addition to these, all the Ayrshire courses are just down the road.

Douglas Park Golf Club. North of the city near Milngavie (pronounced mul-*gai*), Douglas Park is an attractive course set among birch and pine trees where masses of rhododendrons bloom in early summer. The Campsie Fells form a pleasant backdrop. ⊠ *Milngavie Rd., Hillfoot, Bearsden* ☎ *0141/942–0985* ⊕ *www.douglasparkgolfclub.co.uk* ⌨ *£30 per round weekdays, £40 weekends* ⚐ *18 holes, 5,962 yds, par 69* ☉ *On request.*

Gailes Links. The Glasgow Golf Club originally played on Glasgow Green in the heart of the ancient city center, but as the pressure for space grew, the club moved north to the leafy suburb of Bearsden, on the road to Loch Lomond. Killermont, the club's home course, is not open to visitors, but you can play the club's other course at Gailes, near Irvine on the Firth of Clyde. ⊠ *Gailes Rd., Gailes* ✛ *Near Irvine* ☎ *0141/942–2011* ⊕ *www.glasgowgailes-golf.com* ⌨ *Weekdays £75 per round, £90 two rounds (includes a two-course lunch); weekends £80 per round (after 1:30)* ⚐ *18 holes, 6,535 yds, SSS 72* ☉ *Daily.*

EAST LOTHIAN

The sand dunes that stretch eastward from Edinburgh along the southern shore of the Firth of Forth made an ideal location for some of the world's earliest golf courses. Muirfield is perhaps the most famous course in the area, but around it are more than a dozen others. All are links courses, many with views to the islands of the Firth of Forth and northward to Fife. If you weary of the East Lothian courses, try one of the nearly 30 courses within the city boundaries of Edinburgh, 20 mi or so to the west.

Dunbar Golf Club. This ancient golfing site by the sea was founded in 1794 and has a lighthouse at the ninth hole. It's a good choice for experiencing a typical east-coast links course in a seaside town but within easy reach of Edinburgh. There are stunning views of the Firth of Forth

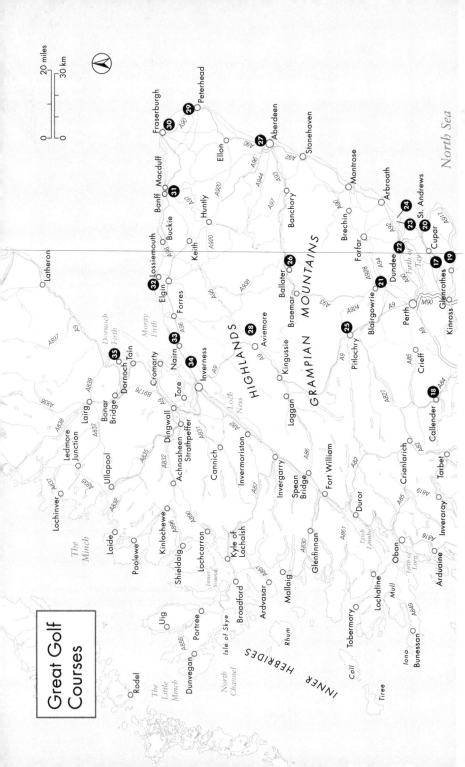

12

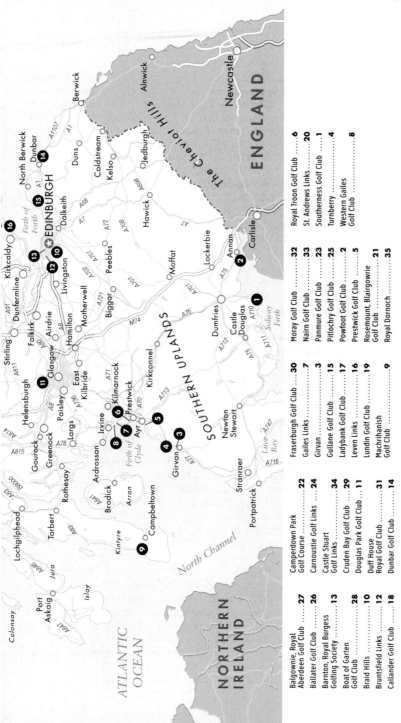

Balgownie, Royal
Aberdeen Golf Club 27

Ballater Golf Club 26

Barnton, Royal Burgess
Golfing Society 13

Boat of Garten
Golf Club 28

Braid Hills 10

Bruntsfield Links 12

Callander Golf Club 18

Camperdown Park
Golf Course 22

Carnoustie Golf Links ... 24

Castle Stuart
Golf Links 34

Cruden Bay Golf Club ... 29

Douglas Park Golf Club .. 11

Duff House
Royal Golf Club 31

Dunbar Golf Club 14

Fraserburgh Golf Club ... **30**

Gailes Links **7**

Girvan **3**

Gullane Golf Club **15**

Ladybank Golf Club **17**

Leven Links **16**

Lundin Golf Club **19**

Machrihanish
Golf Club **9**

Moray Golf Club **32**

Nairn Golf Club **33**

Panmure Golf Club **23**

Pitlochry Golf Club **25**

Powfoot Golf Club **2**

Prestwick Golf Club **5**

Rosemount, Blairgowrie
Golf Club **21**

Royal Dornoch **35**

Royal Troon Golf Club ... **6**

St. Andrews Links **20**

Southerness Golf Club ... **1**

Turnberry **4**

Western Gailes
Golf Club **8**

and May Island. ✉ *East Links, off A1087, Dunbar* ☎ *01368/862086* ⊕ *www.dunbar-golfclub.co.uk* ✉ *Weekdays £60 per round, £80 per day; weekends £95 per round, £105 per day* ♠ *Reservations essential* ⚐ *18 holes, 6,597 yds, par 71* ☺ *Fri.–Wed.*

Gullane Golf Club. Often overshadowed by its more famous neighbor, Muirfield, Gullane provides an equally authentic links experience and a far more effusive welcome than its slightly snooty counterpart just along the road. The three courses here crisscross Gullane hill and all command outstanding views of the Firth of Forth. No. 1 is the toughest test, but No. 2 and No. 3 offer up equally compelling sport. ✉ *West Links Rd., Gullane* ☎ *01620/842123* ⊕ *www.gullanegolfclub.com* ✉ *No. 1. Course: weekdays £93 per round, £128 per day; weekends £108 per round. No. 2. Course: weekdays £47 per round, £57 per day; weekends £52 per round, £72 per day. No. 3. Course: weekdays £36 per day; weekends £46 per day* ♠ *Reservations essential* ⚐ *No. 1. Course: 18 holes, 6,548 yds, par 71; No. 2. Course: 18 holes, 6,385 yds, par 71; No. 3. Course: 18 holes, 5,259 yds, par 68* ☺ *Daily.*

EDINBURGH

Scotland's capital has nearly 30 golf courses within its boundaries. Most are parkland courses, though some of the hillier layouts are more moorland in character. Some are used by private clubs and offer visitors limited access; others that belong to the city are more accessible.

Barnton, Royal Burgess Golfing Society. Dating to 1735, this is one of the world's oldest golf clubs. Its members originally played on Bruntsfield Links; now they and their guests play on manicured parkland in the city's northwestern suburbs. It's a testing course with fine greens. ✉ *181 Whitehouse Rd., Barnton* ☎ *0131/339–2075* ⊕ *www.royalburgess. co.uk* ✉ *Weekdays £60 per round or full day; weekends £80 per day* ♠ *Reservations essential* ⚐ *18 holes, 6,511 yds, par 71* ☺ *Daily.*

Braid Hills. Known to the locals and many others as Braids (no connection with James Braid), this course is beautifully laid out over a rugged range of small hills in the southern suburbs. The views to the south and the Pentland Hills and north over the Edinburgh skyline towards the Firth of Forth are memorable. The city built this course at the turn of the 20th century after development forced golfers out of the city center. The 9-hole Princes Course was completed in 2003. Reservations are recommended for weekend play. ✉ *27 Braids Hill Approach* ☎ *0131/447–6666 for Braids, 0131/666–2210 for Princes* ⊕ *www. edinburghleisuregolf.co.uk* ✉ *Braids: weekdays £20 per round, weekends £24 per round; Princes: weekdays £8 per round, weekends £10 per round* ⚐ *Braids: 18 holes, 5,865 yds, par 71; Princes: 9 holes* ☺ *Daily.*

Bruntsfield Links. The British Seniors and several other championship games are held at this Willie Park–designed 1898 course 3 mi west of the city. The course meanders among 155 acres of mature parkland and has fine views over the Firth of Forth to Fife. Bruntsfield takes its name from one of the oldest (1761) golf links in Scotland, in the center of Edinburgh—now just a 9-hole pitch-and-putt course—where the club used to play. ✉ *32 Barnton Ave., Davidson's Mains* ☎ *0131/336–1479* ⊕ *www.sol.co.uk/b/bruntsfieldlinks* ✉ *Weekdays £65 per round, £85* *per day; weekends £70 per round, £90 per day ⌂ Reservations essential ⌘ 18 holes, 6,446 yds, par 71 ⊙ Daily.*

FIFE

The presence of St. Andrews makes this an important area—a pilgrimage center, even—for fans of the sport, but Fife has other courses, too. Along the north shores of the Firth of Forth is a string of ancient villages, each with its harbor, ancient red-roof buildings, and golf course. In all, there are about 30 courses in the area.

Ladybank Golf Club. Fife is known for its coastal courses, but this one provides an interesting inland contrast. Although Ladybank, designed by Tom Morris in 1876, is laid out on fairly level ground, the fir woods, birches, and heathery rough give it a Highland flavor among the gentle Lowland fields. Qualifying rounds of the British Open are played here when the main championship is played at St. Andrews. ✉ *A92, Annsmuir, Ladybank* ☎ *01337/830814* ⊕ *www.ladybankgolf.co.uk* ✉ *May–Sept., weekdays £53 per round, £79 per day; weekends £60 per round. Oct. and Apr., weekdays £43 per round, £69 per day; weekends £53 per round. Nov.–Mar., weekdays £23 per round; weekends £28 per round ⌂ Reservations essential ⌘ 18 holes, 6,580 yds, par 71 ⊙ Daily; Sun. by appointment.*

Leven Links. A fine Fife course that has been used as a British Open qualifier, these links have a whiff of the more famous St. Andrews, with hummocky terrain and a tang of salt in the air. The 1st and 18th share the same fairway, and the 18th green has a creek running by it. ✉ *The Promenade, Leven* ☎ *01333/428859* ⊕ *www.leven-links.com* ✉ *Weekdays £55 per round, £70 per day; Sun. £60 per round, £75 per day ⌂ Reservations essential ⌘ 18 holes, 6,506 yds, par 71 ⊙ Sun.–Fri.*

Lundin Golf Club. One of a string of fantastic links courses stretching from Leven all the way round the Fife coast to Scotscraig on the Firth of Tay, Lundin Links is a worthy addition to any Scottish golfing itinerary. Designed by the great James Braid, the course is always in prime condition and the greens are a joy to putt on. The pick of the holes is the 14th, a par-3 hole played from an elevated tee back toward the sea. ✉ *Golf Rd., Lundin Links* ☎ *01333/320051* ⊕ *www.lundingolfclub.co.uk* ✉ *Weekdays £57 per round, £77 per day; weekends £65 per round ⌘ 18 holes, 6,371 yards, par 71 ⊙ Daily.*

St. Andrews Links. Few would dispute the claim of St. Andrews to be the home of golf, holding as it does the Royal & Ancient, the organization that governs the sport worldwide. Golf has been played here since the 15th century, and to play in Fife is for most golfers a cherished ambition. St. Andrews Links now has six other 18-hole courses besides the famous 15th-century Old Course, and one 9-hole course. There are also three other courses in the town. *For full details, see St. Andrews in Chapter 5.*

PERTHSHIRE

Perthshire has several attractive country courses developed specifically for visiting golfers. Gleneagles Hotel *(see Chapter 6)* is, with its outstanding facilities, the most famous of these golf resorts. But several

The Evolution of Golf

The matter of who invented golf has been long debated, but there's no doubt that its development into one of the most popular games in the world stems from Scotland. The first written reference to golf, variously spelled as "gowf" or "goff," was in 1457, when James II (1430–60) of Scotland declared that both golf and football (soccer) should be "*utterly cryit doune and nocht usit*" (publicly criticized and prohibited) because they distracted his subjects from archery practice. Mary, Queen of Scots (1542–87), was fond of golf. When in Edinburgh in 1567, she played on Leith Links and on Bruntsfield Links. When in Fife, she played at Falkland and at St. Andrews itself.

GOLF EXPANDS

Golf clubs (i.e., organizations) arose in the middle of the 18th century. The Honourable Company of Edinburgh Golfers, now residing at Muirfield, was founded in 1744. From then on, clubs sprang up all over Scotland: Royal Aberdeen (1780), Crail Golfing Society (1786), Dunbar (1794), and the Royal Perth Golfing Society (1824).

By the early 19th century, clubs had been set up in England, and the game was being carried all over the world by enthusiastic Scots. These golf missionaries spread their knowledge not only of the sport, but also of the courses. Large parts of the Scottish coast are natural golf courses; indeed, the origins of bunkers and the word *links* (courses) are found in the sand dunes of Scotland's shores. Willie Park of Musselburgh, James Braid, and C. K. Hutchison are some of the best known of Scotland's golf-course architects.

CHANGES IN THE GAME

Many of the important changes in the design and construction of balls and clubs were pioneered by the players who lived and worked around the town courses. The original balls, called *featheries*, were leather bags stuffed with boiled feathers and often lasted only one round. In 1848, the gutta-percha ball, called a *guttie*, was introduced. It was in general use until the invention of the rubber-core ball in 1901. Clubs were made of wood with shafts of ash (later hickory), and heads of thorn, apple, or pear. Heads were spliced, then bound to the shaft with twine. Later in the 19th century, manufacturers began to experiment with metal in clubfaces and shafts.

Caddies—the word comes from the French *cadet* (young boy)—carried the players' clubs, usually under the arm. Golf carts didn't come into fashion in Britain until the 1950s, and some people still consider them to be potentially injurious to the national health and moral fiber. The technology of golf continues to change, but its addictive qualities are timeless.

---

courses in the area, set on the edges of beautiful Highland scenery, will delight any golfer.

Callander Golf Club. Designed by Tom Morris in 1890 and extended to 18 holes in 1913 by Willie Fernie, Callander has a scenic upland feel in a town well-prepared for visitors. Pine and birch woods and hilly fairways afford fine views, especially toward Ben Ledi, and the tricky moorland layout demands accurate hitting off the tee. ⊠ *Aveland Rd.,*

Callander ☎ *01877/330090* ⊕ *www.callandergolfclub.co.uk* ✉ *Weekdays £25 per round, £35 per day; weekends £35 per round, £45 per day* ⚐ *18 holes, 5,208 yds, par 66* ☉ *Daily.*

Pitlochry Golf Course. A decent degree of stamina is needed for the first three holes at Pitlochry, where steep climbs are involved. The reward is magnificent Highland scenery. Despite its relatively short length, this beautiful course has more than its fair share of testing surprises. ⊠ *Golf Course Rd., Pitlochry* ☎ *01796/472792* ⊕ *www.pitlochrygolf. co.uk* ✉ *Mar., Apr., Oct., and Nov.: weekdays £27 per round, £37 per day; weekends £37 per round. May, June, and Sept.: weekdays £32 per round, £42 per day; weekends £40 per round, £47 per day. July and Aug: £37 per round, £47 per day; weekends £42 per round, £52 per day* ⚐ *18 holes, 5,681 yds, par 69* ☉ *Daily.*

★ **Rosemount, Blairgowrie Golf Club.** Well-known to native golfers looking for a challenge, Rosemount's 18 (James Braid, 1934) are laid out on rolling land in the pine, birch, and fir woods, which bring a wild air to the scene. There are, however, wide fairways and at least some large greens. If Rosemount is hosting a tournament, you can play on Lansdowne, another 18-hole course, or Wee, a 9-hole course. ⊠ *Golf Course Rd., Blairgowrie* ☎ *01250/872622* ⊕ *www.theblairgowriegolfclub. co.uk* ✉ *Rosemount: £60 per round; Lansdowne: £60 per round; Wee: £25 day ticket. £92 per day (includes 1 round on Rosemount and 1 on Lansdowne)* ⚐ *Rosemount: 18 holes, 6,630 yds, par 72. Lansdowne: 18 holes, 6,886 yds, par 72. Wee: 9 holes, 2,327 yds, par 32* ☉ *Daily.*

ANGUS

East of Perthshire, near the city of Dundee, lies a string of demanding courses along the shores of the North Sea and inland into the foothills of the Grampian Mountains. The most famous course in Angus is probably Carnoustie, one of several British Open Championship venues in Scotland. Golfers who excel in windy conditions particularly enjoy the breezes blowing eastward from the sea. Inland Edzell, Forfar, Brechin, and Kirriemuir all have courses nestling in the Strathmore farmlands.

Camperdown Golf Course. For an alternative to the wild and windy east-coast links courses, try this magnificent municipal parkland golf challenge on the outskirts of Dundee. You can enjoy a game amid tree-lined fairways near the imposing Camperdown House and wildlife park. ⊠ *Camperdown Park, Coupar Angus Rd., Dundee* ☎ *01382/431820* ⊕ *www.dundeecity.gov.uk/golf* ✉ *Weekdays £27 per round, weekends £32 per round* ⚐ *18 holes, 6,588 yards, par 71* ☉ *Daily.*

Fodor's Choice **Carnoustie Golf Links.** The venue for the British Open Championship
★ in 1999 and 2007, the coastal links around Carnoustie have been played since at least 1527. Open winners here have included Armour, Hogan, Cotton, Player, and Watson. There are three courses: the choice Burnside course is full of historical interest and local color, as well as being tough and interesting. The Buddon course, designed by Peter Allis and Dave Thomas, is recommended for links novices. ⊠ *20 Links Parade, Carnoustie* ☎ *01241/802270* ⊕ *www.carnoustiegolflinks. co.uk* ✉ *Championship: Apr.–Oct., £148 per round; Burnside: £38 per round; Buddon: £33 per round; combined ticket for all 3 courses:*

£165 ⌂ Reservations essential ⌇. Championship course: 18 holes, 6,941 yds, par 72; Burnside: 18 holes, 6,028 yds, par 68; Buddon: 18 holes, 5,420 yds, par 66 ☉ Daily.

Panmure Golf Club. Down the road from the famous Carnoustie club, this traditional links course offers an excellent challenge with its seaside climate, undulating greens, and sometimes excruciating—but always entertaining—burrows. The signature sixth is named after British Open Championship winner Ben Hogan, who practiced here prior to his triumphant tournament at Carnoustie in 1953. *⌂ Burnside Rd., off Station Rd., Carnoustie ☎ 01241/855120 ⊕ www.panmuregolfclub. co.uk ✉ £75 per round, £95 per day ⌂ Reservations essential ⌇. 18 holes, 6,551 yds, par 70 ☉ Daily.*

ABERDEENSHIRE

Aberdeen, Scotland's third-largest city, is known for its sparkling granite buildings and amazing displays of roses each summer. Within the city there are six courses, and to the north, as far as Fraserburgh and Peterhead, there are five others, including the popular Cruden Bay.

Balgownie, Royal Aberdeen Golf Club. This old club, founded in 1780, is the archetypal Scottish links course: long and testing over uneven ground, with the frequently added hazard of a sea breeze. Prickly gorse is inclined to close in and form an additional hurdle. The two courses are tucked behind the rough, grassy sand dunes, and there are surprisingly few views of the sea. One historical note: in 1783 this club originated the five-minute-search rule for a lost ball. A handicap certificate and letter of introduction are required. *⌂ Links Rd., Bridge of Don ☎ 01224/702571 ⊕ www.royalaberdeengolf.com ✉ Balgownie: £120 per round, £170 per day (weekdays only). Silverburn: weekdays £60 per round, £85 per day (weekends only). ⌂ Reservations essential ⌇. Balgownie: 18 holes, 6,900 yds, par 71; Silverburn: 18 holes, 4,021 yds, par 64 ☉ Balgownie: tee off weekdays 10–11:30 and 2–3:30, weekends after 3:30; Silverburn: daily.*

Ballater Golf Club. The mountains of Royal Deeside surround this course laid out along the sandy flats of the River Dee. The club, originally opened in 1892, has a holiday atmosphere, and the shops and pleasant walks in nearby Ballater make this a good place for non-golfing partners. *⌂ Victoria Rd., Ballater ☎ 013397/55567 ⊕ www. ballatergolfclub.co.uk ✉ Weekdays £28 per round, £40 per day; weekends £32 per round, £50 per day ⌇. 18 holes, 6,059 yds, par 70 ☉ Daily.*

Cruden Bay Golf Club. An east-coast Lowland course sheltered behind extensive sand hills, Cruden Bay offers a typical Scottish golf experience. Runnels and valleys, among other hazards, on the challenging fairways ensure plenty of excitement. Like Gleneagles and Turnberry, this course owes its origins to an association with the grand railway hotels built in the heyday of steam. Unlike at the other two courses, however, Cruden Bay's railway hotel and the railway itself have gone, but the course remains in fine shape. ■ TIP→ Weekend tee times are extremely limited; book months in advance. *⌂ Aulton Rd., Cruden Bay, Peterhead ☎ 01779/812285 ⊕ www.crudenbaygolfclub.co.uk ✉ Championship: weekdays £70 per day or round; weekends £75 per round. St. Olaf:*

weekdays £20 per day; weekends £30 per day ⬧ Reservations essential ⚐ *Championship: 18 holes, 6,287 yds, par 72; St. Olaf: 9 holes, 2,463 yds, par 32 ⊙ Daily; limited weekend tee times.*

SPEYSIDE

On the main A9 road an hour south of Inverness amid the Cairngorm Mountains, the valley of the River Spey is one of Scotland's most attractive all-year sports centers. The area's main courses are Newtonmore, Grantown-on-Spey, and Boat of Garten, all fine inland courses with wonderful views of the surrounding mountains and challenging golf provided by the springy turf and the heather. Near Inverness is the fabulous Castle Stuart Links, opened in 2009.

Boat of Garten Golf Club. This is possibly one of Scotland's greatest "undiscovered" courses. Boat of Garten, which dates to the late 19th century, was redesigned and extended by James Braid in 1932, and each of its 18 holes is individual: some cut through birch wood and heathery rough; most have long views to the Cairngorms and a strong Highland feel. An unusual feature is the preserved steam railway that runs along part of the course. ✉ *Nethybridge Rd., Boat of Garten* ☎ *01479/831282* ⊕ *www.boatgolf.com* ✉ *Weekdays £37 per round, £49 per day; weekends £42 per round, £54 per day ⬧ Reservations essential* ⚐ *18 holes, 5,876 yds, par 70 ⊙ Daily.*

★ **Castle Stuart Golf Links.** Opened in 2009, this course overlooking the Moray Firth is already considered one of Scotland's finest, hosting the Scottish Open in 2011. Owner Mark Parsinen and golf architect Gil Hanse were also behind the renowned Kingsbarns in Fife. Expect natural-looking, undulating fairways and extensive waste bunkers. The 210-yard 17th provides perilous cliff-top play, and the art deco–inspired clubhouse has stunning views of the firth. ✉ *Balnaglack Farmhouse, Dalcross, B9039, Inverness* ☎ *01463/796111* ⊕ *www.castlestuartgolf. com* ✉ *May–Oct., £170 per round; Apr. and Nov., £130 per round* ⚐ *6,553 yds, par 72 ⊙ Apr.–Nov., daily.*

MORAY COAST

No one can say that the Lowlands have a monopoly on Scotland's fine seaside golf courses. The Moray Coast, stretching eastward from Inverness, has some spectacular sand dunes that have been adapted to create stimulating and exciting links courses. The two courses at Nairn have long been known to golfers.

Duff House Royal Golf Club. Just moments away from the sea, this club combines a coastal course with a parkland setting. It lies only minutes from Banff center, within the grounds of Duff House, a country-house art gallery in a William Adam–designed mansion. Golf records here go back to the 17th century. ✉ *The Barnyards, off A98, Banff* ☎ *01261/812075* ⊕ *www.theduffhouseroyalgolfclub.co.uk* ✉ *Apr.– Sept. weekdays £30 per round, £40 per day; weekends £36 per round, £50 per day. Oct.–Mar. weekdays £15 per round, £20 per day; weekends £18 per round, £25 per day ⬧ Reservations essential* ⚐ *18 holes, 6,007 yds, par 68 ⊙ Daily.*

Fraserburgh Golf Club. The extensive links and dunes around this northeast fishing town have been used for golf since 1613; the club was founded in 1777. Be prepared for a hill climb and a tough finish on James Braid's 1922 redesigned Corbiehill course. The 9-hole Rosehill course provides a challenging warm-up. ✉ *B9033, off A90, Fraserburgh* ✛ *At eastern end of town* ☎ *01346/516616* ⊕ *www.fraserburghgolfclub. org* ✉ *Corbiehill: weekdays £38 per round, weekends £46 per round. Rosehill: £12 per 18 holes, £18 per day* 🏌 *Corbiehill: 18 holes, 6,308 yds, par 70; Rosehill: 9 holes, 4,832 yds, par 66* ⊙ *Daily.*

Moray Golf Club. Discover the relatively mild microclimate of what vacationing Victorians dubbed the Moray Riviera, as Tom Morris did in 1889 when he was inspired by the lay of the natural links. Henry Cotton's New Course (1979) has tighter fairways and smaller greens. A handicap certificate is required for the Old Course. ✉ *Stotfield Rd., Lossiemouth* ☎ *01343/812018* ⊕ *www.moraygolf.co.uk* ✉ *Old Course: weekdays £55 per round, £75 per day; weekends £65 per round, £85 per day. New Course: weekdays £25 per round, £40 per day; weekends £45 per day. Joint ticket (1 round on each course) weekdays £70, weekends £80* 🏌 *Old Course: 18 holes, 6,995 yds, par 71; New Course: 18 holes, 6,008 yds, par 69* ⊙ *Daily.*

★ **Nairn Golf Club.** Well regarded in golfing circles, Nairn dates from 1887 and is the regular home of Scotland's Northern Open. Huge greens, aggressive gorse, a beach hazard for five of the holes, a steady prevailing wind, and distracting views across the Moray Firth to the northern hills make play on the Championship Course unforgettable. The adjoining 9-hole Cameron course is ideal for a warm-up or a fun round for the family. ✉ *Seabank Rd., Nairn* ☎ *01667/453208* ⊕ *www.nairngolfclub. co.uk* ✉ *Championship: £90 per round, £145 for a two-round ticket; Cameron: £15 per round* ⟐ *Reservations essential* 🏌 *Championship: 18 holes, 6,774 yds, par 72; Cameron: 9 holes, 1,634 yds, par 29* ⊙ *Daily.*

DORNOCH FIRTH

The east coast north of Inverness is deeply indented with firths (the word is linked to the Norwegian *fjord*) that border some excellent, relatively unknown golf courses. Knowledgeable golfers have been making the northern pilgrimage to these courses for well over 100 years. There are half a dozen enjoyable links courses around Dornoch and Strathpeffer, an inland Victorian golfing holiday center.

Fodor's Choice **Royal Dornoch Golf Club.** The legendary Championship course, laid out
★ by Tom Morris in 1886 on a sort of coastal shelf, has fast raised greens with views of mountains and white sandy beaches. The springtime yellow blaze of gorse adds to the wild beauty. Dornoch's Struie course, extended in 1999, provides more sea views and challenging golf for the whole family. It's less than an hour's drive north of Inverness Airport. ✉ *Golf Rd., Dornoch* ☎ *01862/810219* ⊕ *www.royaldornoch. com* ✉ *Championship: weekdays £100 per round, weekends £110 per round; Struie: single round £40, day ticket £60. Combined ticket: weekdays £120, weekends £130* ⟐ *Reservations essential* 🏌 *Championship: 18 holes, 6,595 yds, par 70; Struie: 18 holes, 5,192 yds, par 71* ⊙ *Daily.*

UNDERSTANDING SCOTLAND

SCOTLAND AT A GLANCE

BOOKS AND MOVIES

CHRONOLOGY

SCOTLAND AT A GLANCE

FAST FACTS

Capital: Edinburgh

National anthem: "God Save the Queen"

Type of government: Scotland is part of the United Kingdom, which is a constitutional monarchy. It also has its own Parliament, and First Minister Alex Salmond of the Scottish National Party is the head of the government.

Administrative divisions: 32 council areas

Independence: April 6, 1320; the Declaration of Arbroath. Scottish nobles wrote Pope John XXII during the War of Independence and asked him to persuade the English king to stop his hostility toward the Scottish.

Constitution: There is no one document; it's a centuries-old accumulation of statutes as well as common law and practice.

Legal system: Scotland's system is organized separately from that of the rest of the United Kingdom. The two highest courts are the High Court of Justiciary (criminal) and the Court of Session (civil). Appeals to the British House of Lords may be made only from the Court of Session. The sheriff courts deal with less important civil and criminal cases.

Suffrage: 18 years of age

Legislature: Governed as an integral part of the United Kingdom's constitutional monarchy, Scotland is represented by 59 Members of Parliament in the House of Commons in London. On May 6, 1999, Scotland gained its own Parliament, located in Edinburgh, for the first time in nearly 300 years. Parliament has the power to pass Scottish laws; it's responsible for managing agriculture, education, health, and justice, and it can impose certain taxes within Scotland.

Population: 5,494,501. The largest cities are Glasgow (592,820) and Edinburgh (486,120).

Population density: 64 persons per square km (171 persons per square mi)

Median age: male 37, female 39

Life expectancy: male 75, female 80

Literacy: 99%

Language: Predominantly English. Fewer than 1,000 people speak only Gaelic, and fewer than 60,000 speak Gaelic in addition to English, but this is increasing. Scots is now recognized as an official language, too.

Ethnic groups: 98% of the population is Caucasian (88% of this is Scottish and 7.5% other British); Indian, Pakistani, Bangladeshi, and other South Asian groups are the largest ethnic minorities.

Religion: Residents identified their religion as follows: 42.4% Church of Scotland, 27.55% none, 15.88% Roman Catholic, 6.81% other Christian, 0.13% Buddhist, 0.11% Hindu, 0.13% Jewish, 0.84% Muslim, 0.13% Sikh, 0.53% another religion, 5.49% not answered

Discoveries and inventions: Steam engine (1765), postage stamp (1834), telephone (1876), television (1924), penicillin (1928), radar (1935)

We look to Scotland for all our ideas of civilization.

— Voltaire

GEOGRAPHY AND ENVIRONMENT

Land area: 78,722 square km (30,414 square mi)

Coastline: 3,900 km (2,280 mi)

Terrain: Scotland is divided into three distinct regions, roughly from north to south: the Highlands (characterized by mountains with deep ravines, valleys, cliffs, lakes, and sea lochs); the Central Lowlands (mainly hills and rivers); and the Southern Uplands (moorland plateaus, rolling valleys, and mountainous outcrops). Highest mountain, Ben Nevis (4,409 feet). Largest loch, Loch Lomond (56 square km, or 22 square mi)

Islands: 800, of which 130 are inhabited. The largest groups are Shetland and Orkney to the north; and the Hebrides, including Lewis, Harris, Barra, Skye, and Mull, to the west.

Natural resources: Coal, petroleum, natural gas, zinc, iron ore, limestone, clay, silica, gold

Natural hazards: Winter windstorms, floods

Flora: Dominant flora: rowan (tree belonging to the rose family), oak, fir, pine, and larch trees; heather, ferns, mosses, grasses, saxifrage, and mountain willow

Fauna: Principal fauna: deer, hare, rabbit, otter, ermine, pine marten, wildcat, grouse, blackcock, ptarmigan, waterfowl, kite, osprey, golden eagle, salmon, trout, cod, haddock, herring, various types of shellfish

Environmental issues: Climate change, air pollution, wind farms, recycling, nuclear power

There are two seasons in Scotland: June and winter.

—Billy Connolly

ECONOMY

Currency: British pound (GBP)
Exchange rate: £1 = $1.57
GDP: £131 billion ($203 billion)
Per-capita income: £20,086 ($31,105)
Inflation: 1.8% in the United Kingdom
Unemployment: 2.1%
Workforce: 2,475,386 (services 79.1%; agriculture 1.4%; industry 19.5%)
Major industries: Aerospace, chemicals, construction, digital media and creative industries, energy, financial services, food and drink, life sciences, microelectronics and optoelectronics, textiles, and tourism
Agricultural products: Barley, wheat, oats, potatoes, livestock (sheep and cattle)
Exports: £18.8 billion ($29.1 billion)
Major export products: Office machinery, radio/TV/communication equipment, whisky, chemicals, manufactured machinery/equipment and transport equipment
Export partners: United States, Germany, France, Ireland, Spain, Netherlands
Imports: £57 billion ($88.3 billion)

We'll never know the worth of water till the well go dry.

—18th-century Scottish proverb

DID YOU KNOW?

■ Christmas was not celebrated as a festival in Scotland for about 250 years (from the end of the 17th century up to the 1950s) because the Protestant church believed Christmas to be a Catholic holiday and therefore banned it. Many Scots worked over Christmas and their winter solstice holiday took place at New Year or "hogmanay."

■ Kilts are not native to Scotland. They originated in France.

■ The first woman to play golf at St. Andrew's Golf Club was Mary, Queen of Scots, in 1552. She was the club's founder.

■ More redheads are born in Scotland than in any other country: 11% of the population has red hair.

■ Homer Simpson's catchphrase "Doh!" was based on the catchphrase of actor James Finlayson, who was born in Falkirk in 1887 and starred alongside Laurel and Hardy in many of their films.

■ Haggis may not be Scottish after all. In 2009 historian Catherine Brown found literary evidence that placed haggis in England 171 years before it showed up in any Scottish text. The book in question is the *English Hus-Wife* from 1615.

BOOKS AND MOVIES

Books

For the Scot, the "man o' pairts" is the ideal to be aspired to—a person with varied skills and experiences, and a love of knowledge for its own sake. In many ways the great poet Robert Burns (1759–96) was the embodiment of that ideal: a peasant poet, a liver of life, a political thinker, a radical, a man who loved nature and women in equal measure. His poem for the mouse seen in a ploughed field—"that wee sleekit timorous beastie"—is as humane as his wonderful poems proclaiming the equality of all human beings against the rulers and the landowners: "It matters not the guinea's stamp/A man's a man for a' that." Burns is indeed in every sense the national poet.

Scotland has been a place where, for reasons as much religious as cultural, men and women valued education and reading. The powerful Scottish Presbyterian tradition placed great emphasis on the development, moral and intellectual, of the individual.

The literary tradition goes back to the Bothy Ballads, the old rural folk songs of Scotland's northeast, and has grown and expanded until the literary renaissance of the late 20th and early 21st centuries, when Scottish writers have won international recognition. Novelist and artist Alasdair Gray; Irvine Welsh, whose novel *Trainspotting* (1993) traveled the world despite its very local language; Ian Rankin, with his novels about Edinburgh's Inspector Rebus; and the great Glasgow poet laureate Edwin Morgan (1920–2010): all have demonstrated that Scottish writing travels well.

Most of Scotland has its particular voices and its particular accents in the written word. In the 19th century, the fascination of the middle classes with a Scotland made fashionable by Queen Victoria's decision to buy a castle at Balmoral, together with the spread of the railways, brought travelers to the Trossachs and the Highlands. They were seeking the landscapes lovingly portrayed in novels and poems by Sir Walter Scott (1771–1832), who wrote about the Highlands from his beautiful home at Abbotsford, beside the river Tweed. Travelers were also approaching, if gingerly, the wilder parts of the British Isles, the still largely unfamiliar mountains and dark lochs of the Scottish Highlands. Many of them gained their first impressions of this supposedly slightly barbarous place of kilt-wearing warriors from Sir Walter Scott and the poetry of Ossian, a rural poet who turned out to be a fiction created by James Macpherson (1736–96). There was a similar air about James Hogg's (1770–1835) dark ghost story *Confessions of a Justified Sinner* (1824), with its fearsome ending on Arthur's Mount in Edinburgh. Robert Louis Stevenson (1850–94) was an Edinburgh man whose *Kidnapped* evoked the thick woods and lakes in the Central Highlands.

There were other popular novels about Scottish life, such as George Douglas Brown's *The House with Green Shutters* (1901), set in Ayrshire, or Guy McCrone's *Wax Fruit Trilogy* (1947), set in Glasgow. Yet it couldn't be said that there was a vigorous literary life in Scotland, and many of these novels were the only ones their authors published. Lewis Grassic Gibbon (the pseudonym of James Mitchell, 1901–35) produced a trilogy of novels (*A Scots Quair*) set in Scotland's northeast in a rural community on the eve of the World War I. It's much like Howe of Mearns, near Stonehaven, where he was brought up and where his small museum now stands. *Sunset Song*, the first of the three, is a masterpiece; the people in this farming community on the threshold of massive changes still speak in the Doric dialect, the lilting language of the region, which Grassic Gibbon managed to echo in his poetic English.

Scottish writing remained a poor country cousin in Britain. Most publishers were based in London, and those Scottish writers who did win success, like Eric Linklater (1899–1974) or Compton Mackenzie (1883–1972) or, later on, Muriel Spark (1918–2006) and Naomi Mitchison (1897–1999), were not generally recognized as Scottish writers, though each had some writing based in Scotland to their name. Muriel Spark's *The Prime of Miss Jean Brodie* (1969), which portrayed the misplaced idealism of a teacher in a private school in Edinburgh, was one, and Compton Mackenzie's *Whisky Galore!* (1949), the tale of a Hebridean island community suddenly given a gift of a shipload of whisky by the sea, was another. Mackenzie himself was brought up in the beautiful if remote island of Barra, where his house can still be seen.

Even Hugh McDiarmid (1892–1978), the great epic poet of Scotland, emphasized the dilemma of Scottish exclusion by writing in the Scots language of the Lowlands in his glorious evocation of Scottish history called, appropriately perhaps, *A Drunk Man Looks at a Thistle*. The rediscovery of Scotland's culture was reflected in the songs of Ewen McColl (1915–1989) and of Hamish Henderson (1919–2002), who wrote what became a kind of unofficial national anthem called "The Freedom Come All Ye," a song celebrating the life of the Scottish radical leader of the early part of the century, John MacLean.

By the late 1970s Scotland was starting to have a dramatic impact on cultural life beyond its borders, and Scotland itself was becoming aware of its own great cultural and historical traditions beyond Sir Walter Scott and the realist work that came to be called the Kailyard School (which sometimes came perilously close to sentimentality about the lives of the poor).

What made the literary renaissance of the 1970s possible? Theater, and, in particular, the incredible impact of one play produced by the 7:84 Theatre Company:

The Cheviot, the Stag, and the Black Black Oil. It traveled to every corner of the country, with its stage set in a huge pop-up book, to tell the story of Scotland in a new way. After the show was always a *ceilidh,* Scottish traditional dancing to the fiddle and the accordion. Suddenly, in the run-up to the first referendum on devolution (the creation of a separate Scotland) in 1979, a generation of Scottish writers emerged from the mist, particularly poets. Some were new, like Tom Leonard and Liz Lochhead, who wrote in the language of ordinary people. Others had been around, unnoticed, like George Mackay Brown, who wrote about Orkney's prehistoric heritage and its fishing communities in *Fishermen with Ploughs* and *Greenvoe;* or Neil Gunn (1881–1973) with his *The Silver Darlings.* Iain Crichton Smith (1928–98) and Norman McCaig (1910–96) found new audiences for their poetry, and the Gaelic poet Sorley Maclean (1911–96) was heard in his native language for the first time and then translated for a wider public.

By the 1980s the Edinburgh International Festival had become a world-class event, while its Fringe (alternative events scattered around the city) swelled with more than a thousand shows of one kind or another. The city provided the backdrop to new writers of fiction like Iain Banks (*The Wasp Factory*) and Ian Rankin. Rankin's Rebus novels (*Black and Blue* was one) translated detective fiction to the steep streets of Old Edinburgh, launching a tradition of crime writing that found its Glasgow equivalents in William McIlvanney's Laidlaw and the writings of Denise Mina, Louise Welsh, and Val McDermid. Irvine Welsh's *Trainspotting* marked another milestone—an international success despite its setting in the desperately poor Pilton district of Edinburgh and its almost impenetrable local dialect. The Canongate Press, a small publisher that went global in the late 1980s, provided new opportunities for Scottish writers.

And the children were not forgotten: Joan Lingard's teenage novels were set in Northern Ireland and Scotland, while Mairi Heddiwick's Katie Morag stories unfolded on a Hebridean island. Although J. K. Rowling's hugely successful Harry Potter books were set in a world that seemed closer to an English public school, the world learned that they had been written in an Edinburgh café.

Scotland was no longer a literary backwater. Its writers had taken their place in an international culture as the new century began. The *Oxford Literary Guide to the British Isles*, edited by Dorothy Eagle and Hilary Carnell; *A Reader's Guide to Writers' Britain* by Sally Varlow; and *Scotland: A Literary Guide*, by Alan Bold, can direct you to other literary landscapes in addition to those mentioned above. Edinburgh has been named the first UNESCO World City of Literature; Allan Foster's *Literary Traveler in Edinburgh* is an illustrated sightseeing guide to literary hot spots, including writers' homes and the settings for famous works.

Nonfiction

Canadian historian John Prebble (1915–2001) unearthed Scotland's hidden history in the early 1970s. In books such as *Culloden* he used the documents of the time to tell the tragic and heroic story of the final massacre at Culloden, an event that paved the way for English domination of the north. This included the later and terrible experience of the Highland Clearances, when the big landowners drove out their peasant-farmer tenants to make way for sheep, which were much more profitable. The words of the women who fought so hard before they were sent into exile are haunting.

The most complete history is Tom Devine's absorbing *The Scottish Nation*. Neal Ascherson, a highly respected international journalist, returned to his native Scotland as the 1979 referendum approached; his *Native Stones: The Search for Scotland* probably reflects the

rediscovery of his own identity. To the outside world, though, *No Mean City: The Story of a Glasgow Slum*, written by Alexander McArthur and Herbert Kingsley Long in 1935, was probably closer to the Scotland it imagined: a country of mean streets, poverty, and violence. The more recent work of James Robertson and Robert Knight has reopened the debate about the role of Scots in the empire and addressed some uncomfortable truths about slavery and the treatment of indigenous peoples by Scottish settlers and colonists.

For books on Scottish art and architecture, Duncan MacMillan's *Scottish Art in the 20th Century, 1890–2001* is a comprehensive guide to artists from Charles Rennie Mackintosh to Ken Currie. Jude Burkhauser's *Glasgow Girls: Women in Art and Design 1880–1920* is more narrow in scope but equally intriguing. Bella Bathurst's *The Lighthouse Stevensons* uniquely catalogs the engineering revolution of lighthouse building through the work of four generations of writer Robert Louis Stevenson's family. For good background information on castles, look for Damien Noonan's *Castles and Ancient Monuments of Scotland* and John G. Dunbar's *Scottish Royal Palaces*.

Football (soccer) in Scotland is, in many respects, a religion. To find out more on the subject, read David Ross's passionate *The Roar of the Crowd: Following Scottish Football Down the Years*. Another important sport in Scotland is the game invented there: golf. A popular book on the subject, Malcolm Campbell's *Scottish Golf Book*, will not only tell you where to putt but also will give you a thorough background on the game itself. Curtis Gillespie's memoir *Playing Through: A Year of Life and Links Along the Scottish Coast* takes a more personal approach to golf and its past through the year he spent with his family in Gullane, as does Lorne Rubenstein's *A Season in Dornoch: Golf and Life in the Scottish Highlands*.

Travel and landscape books on Scotland are almost as plentiful as the country's native thistle. Although initially published in 1779, the reflections and descriptions in Samuel Johnson and James Boswell's *Journey to the Hebrides* (reprinted in 1996) are just as relevant today. Kathleen Jamie's poetically told *Findings* will whet your taste buds for Scotland's picturesque countryside like no other. Cameron McNeish has written some excellent books; *The Munros: Scotland's Highest Mountains* (out of print but worth seeking out a copy) is a carefully crafted guide to climbing those peaks. Colin Prior's impressive photography collection *Highland Wilderness* gives stunning panoramic views of the wild but wonderful north.

Movies

The Scottish film industry has come of age in recent years. In fact, John Grierson (1898–1972) was the commanding figure in the development of documentary film in Britain in the 1930s. In more recent times, films produced in Scotland have moved some distance from the popular "kilt" movies like *Rob Roy* (1995) with Liam Neeson and Jessica Lange, or the internationally successful film about William Wallace's revolt, *Braveheart* (1995), with Mel Gibson, which convinced people across the world that Scots painted their faces blue. Like Sean Connery's *Highlander* (1986), these films took advantage of the spectacular scenery of Glencoe or Scottish castles from Doune to Eilean Donan to create their atmosphere.

But it was *Trainspotting* (1996) that launched a new kind of Scottish cinema, and with it a new Scottish star in Ewen McGregor, with its powerful yet witty presentation of heroin addicts on an impoverished housing estate. *Shallow Grave* (1994), a sometimes bloody thriller about money and jealousy in an Edinburgh apartment, also starred McGregor. The outstanding director Ken Loach has made several films in Glasgow with his scriptwriter Paul Laverty; *My Name Is Joe* (1998) is a heartbreaking portrayal of an alcoholic wrestling with his problem, and *Sweet Sixteen* (2002) presents a characteristic Loach hero in a young lad trying to survive in a world of poverty and violence. The older *Local Hero* (1983) brings ambitious oilmen to the remote provincial world of the northeast; *Red Road* (2006) is an intense drama in which Kate Dickie becomes obsessed with a man she sees on the CCTV security screens of a Glasgow apartment block.

The makers of *Monty Python and the Holy Grail* (1975) chose lovely Doune Castle for their medieval spoof, and *Mrs. Brown* (1997) looked at the undeclared romantic relationship between Queen Victoria and her "ghillie," or gamekeeper, John Brown (played by Scottish comedian Billy Connolly). The film is set among the hills and woods of the Trossachs, and in the Ardverekie Estate near Dalwhinnie, which stands in for the royal palace at Balmoral.

For more information on movies filmed in Scotland, you can buy *The Pocket Scottish Movie Book* by Brian Pendreigh, or you can visit the Scotland the Movie Guide website (⊕ *www.scotlandthemovie.com*).

CHRONOLOGY

7000 BC Hunter-gatherers move into the north of Scotland after the ice sheets of the last Ice Age recede; these travelers leave arrowheads and bone implements as testimony to their passing.

ca. 6000 BC First settlers arrive, bringing farming methods with them. They leave their mark at Skara Brae in Orkney.

ca. 3000 BC Neolithic migration from Mediterranean: "chambered cairn" people in north (such as the Grey Cairns of Camster). "Beaker people" erect the standing stone circles, like those at Callanish on the Isle of Lewis.

ca. 300 BC Iron Age: arrival of Celtic peoples from the south and from Ireland; "Gallic forts" and "brochs" (towers) built, like the tower at Mousa in Shetland.

AD 43 The Roman conquest of Britain begins.

79–89 Julius Agricola (AD 40–93), Roman governor of Britain, invades Scotland; Scots tribes defeated at the battle of Mons Graupius (thought to be somewhere in the Grampians). Roman forts built at Inchtuthil and Ardoch.

123 Hadrian's Wall is built to mark the northern limit of the Roman Empire.

142 Emperor Antoninus Pius (86–161) orders the defensive Antonine Wall built between the Firths of Forth and Clyde, as the Romans continue their attempt to invade beyond Hadrian's Wall.

185 Antonine Wall abandoned.

392 St. Ninian (ca. 360–432), a Briton and a Christian, sends out a first Christian mission to the Picts from his chapel at Whithorn.

400–500 Tribes of Celtic origin, including the Scotti, emigrate from Ireland to present-day Argyllshire and establish the kingdom of Dalriada. The Pictish kingdom extends as far south as Fife. The Britons, meanwhile, occupy an area between Dumbarton and Carlisle.

400–843 Four kingdoms exist in Scotland: Dalriada (Argyllshire), the kingdom of the Picts (Aberdeenshire down to Fife and the Highlands excepting Argyllshire), Strathclyde (southwest Scotland), and the Lothians (Edinburgh and the Borders).

563 Columba, (ca. 521–97), a Gaelic-speaking Scotti, establishes the monastery at Iona. It will become a major center for the evangelization of Scotland and farther afield.

843 Kenneth MacAlpin, king of Dalriada, unites with the Picts while remaining king. In this way the embryonic Kingdom of Scotland (first called Alba, later Scotia) is born, with its capital at Scone.

780–1065 Scandinavian invasions; the Hebrides remain Norse until 1263, Orkney and Shetland until 1472.

1018 Malcolm II (ca. 953–1034) brings the Lothians into the Kingdom of Scotland and (temporarily) repels the English.

1034 Duncan (d. 1040), king of Strathclyde, ascends the throne of Scotland and unification is complete.

1040 Duncan is slain by his rival, Macbeth (d. 1057), whose wife has a claim to the throne.

1057 Malcolm III (ca. 1031–93), known as Canmore (Big Head), murders Macbeth and assumes the throne. The House of Canmore now assumes the Scottish crown and introduces a feudal landowning system into the country.

1093 Death of Malcolm's English-born queen, St. Margaret (1046–93), who brought Roman Catholicism to Scotland.

1099 Donald III becomes the last king of Scots to be buried on the island of Iona.

1124–53 David I (ca. 1082–1153), *sair sanct* (sore saint), builds the abbeys of Jedburgh (1118), Kelso (1128), Melrose (1136), and Dryburgh (1150) and brings Norman culture to Scotland.

1200 The Royal Burghs, or towns, of Stirling, Edinburgh, and Berwick are established with certain rights and privileges in trade. The Highland clans are largely excluded from power.

1250 Queen Margaret, wife of Malcolm III, is canonized, becoming Scotland's first (and only) royal saint.

1290 Death of Alexander III, great-great-grandson of David I. The heir is his granddaughter, Margaret, Maid of Norway (1283–90). She dies at sea on her way from Norway to claim the Scottish throne and marry the future Edward II (1284–1327), son of Edward I of England (1239–1307). The Scots naively ask Edward I, subsequently known as the Hammer of the Scots, to arbitrate between the remaining 13 claimants to the throne. Edward chooses John Balliol (1249–1315) over his ambitious rival Robert the Bruce.

1295 Under continued threat from England, John Balliol switches allegiance and signs Scotland's first treaty with England's enemy, France. This came to be known as "the Auld Alliance." The wine trade flourishes.

1297 While Robert the Bruce now sides with the English, William Wallace (ca. 1270–1305) leads a rising against the English. His army is made up of peasants and the lower nobility like himself. It is in part a reaction against the extreme cruelty of the English armies under Edward I. The wealthy nobles, for their part, do not resist because many of them have lands in both England and Scotland.

1305 Wallace, betrayed and captured by the English, is executed.

1306–29 Reign of Robert the Bruce (1274–1329), later to become King Robert I, who turns again against the English. He defeats Edward II (1284–1327) at Bannockburn, 1314. The Declaration of Arbroath (1320) affirms Scottish sovereignty, which is eventually recognized by the Treaty of Northampton, 1328.

1329   After the death of Bruce, the nobles fight wars against one another for 50 years. The attempt by the new ruling house, the Stewards, or Stuarts, to control the situation largely fails.

1371   Robert II (1316–90), the first Stewart monarch and son of Robert the Bruce's daughter Marjorie and Walter the Steward, is crowned in 1371, but the struggle between the crown and Scottish barons (later dramatized in several of Sir Walter Scott's novels) continues for another century. Sporadic warfare with the English also continues during this time.

1383   Bishop Wardlaw of Glasgow is the first Scot to be made a cardinal.

1411   University of St. Andrews founded.

1451   University of Glasgow founded.

1488–1513   Reign of James IV (1473–1513). The Renaissance reaches Scotland. The Golden Age of Scots poetry includes Robert Henryson (ca. 1425–1508), William Dunbar (ca. 1460–1530), Gavin Douglas (1474–1522), and the king himself.

1495   University of Aberdeen founded.

1507   Andrew Myllar and Walter Chapman set up first Scots printing press in Edinburgh.

1513   After invading England in support of the French, James IV is slain at Flodden Field.

1542   Henry VIII (1491–1547), king of England, defeats James V (1512–42) at Solway Moss. The dying James, hearing of the birth of his daughter, Mary, declares: "It came with a lass [Marjorie Bruce] and it will pass with a lass."

1542–67   Reign of Mary, Queen of Scots (1542–87). She becomes queen at one year old, and her mother is appointed regent. At six she is married to the heir to the French throne. Romantic, Catholic, and with an excellent claim to the English throne, Mary proved to be no match for her barons, John Knox (1513–72), or her cousin Elizabeth I (1533–1603) of England.

1560   Mary returns to Scotland from France after the death of her husband, Francis II of France, at the same time that Catholicism is abolished in favor of Protestantism. She finds a Scotland dominated by a Protestantism influenced by the fiery John Knox.

1565   Mary marries Lord Darnley (1545–67), a Catholic but a self-indulgent consort.

1567   Darnley is murdered at Kirk o' Field and Mary marries one of the conspirators, the Earl of Bothwell (ca. 1535–78). Driven from Scotland, she appeals to Elizabeth, who imprisons her. Mary's son, James (1566–1625), is crowned James VI of Scotland.

1582   University of Edinburgh is founded.

1587   Elizabeth orders the execution of Mary.

1600   Charles I is born in Scotland.

1603   Elizabeth dies without issue; James VI is crowned James I of England, uniting the two crowns. But the Parliaments remain separate for another century.

1638   National Covenant challenges Charles I's personal rule.

1639–41 Crisis. The Scots and then the English parliaments revolt against Charles I (1600–49).

1643   Solemn League and Covenant establishes Presbyterianism as the Church of Scotland (the Kirk). In England, Parliament rises against Charles I, who had summoned it after 11 years in the hope it would grant him resources for war. Civil War in England.

1649   Charles I beheaded. Oliver Cromwell (1599–1658) made Protector.

1650–52 Cromwell roots out Scots Royalists.

1658   The first Edinburgh–London coach is established. The journey takes two weeks.

1660   Restoration of Charles II (1630–85). Episcopalianism reestablished in Scotland; Covenanters are persecuted and their army attacked by Highland soldiers.

1688   The unpopular James VII of Scotland (and II of England, Scotland, and Ireland) flees to France.

1688–89 Glorious Revolution; James VII and II (1633–1701), a Catholic, deposed in favor of his daughter Mary (1662–94) and her husband, William of Orange (1650–1702). Supporters of James (known as Jacobites) defeated at Killiecrankie. Presbyterianism reestablished.

1692   Highlanders who were late in taking oath to William and Mary massacred at Glencoe.

1695   The first bank in Scotland, the Bank of Scotland, is founded.

1698–1700 Attempted Scottish colony at Darien (on the Isthmus of Panama) fails. Many of the Scottish nobility face bankruptcy, and are therefore open to overtures from an English government anxious to unite the Scottish and English parliaments.

1707   Union of English and Scots parliaments under Queen Anne (1665–1714), the last Stuart monarch; deprived of French wine trade, Scots turn to whisky.

1714   Queen Anne dies; George I (1660–1727) of the House of Hanover, descended from a daughter of James VI and I, is crowned.

1715   First Jacobite Rebellion. James II's son, James Edward Stuart, agrees to undertake an invasion of England. His supporter, the Earl of Mar (1675–1732), the leader of the attempted Rising, is defeated.

1730–90 Scottish Enlightenment. The Edinburgh Medical School is the best in Europe; David Hume (1711–76) and Adam Smith (1723–90) redefine philosophy and economics. In the arts, Allan Ramsay the elder (1686–1758) and Robert Burns (1759–96) refine Scottish poetry; Allan Ramsay the younger (1713–84) and Henry Raeburn (1756–1823) rank among the finest painters of the era. Edinburgh's New Town, developed in the 1770s and including designs by the brothers Adam (Robert, 1728–92; James, 1730–94), provides a fitting setting.

1736   The first public theater in Scotland is opened in Carruber's Close in Edinburgh.

1745–46 Last Jacobite Rebellion. Bonnie Prince Charlie (1720–88), grandson of James II, is defeated at Culloden by the armies of the Duke of Cumberland. He escapes across the water to the Isle of Skye before eventually returning to France. The wearing of the kilt, the use of tartan, and the playing of bagpipes are now banned, and the clans of the north are finally crushed. James Watt (1736–1819), born in Greenock, is granted a patent for his steam engine.

1760   Thomas Braidwood (1715–1806) opens the first school for people who cannot hear or speak in Great Britain, in Edinburgh.

1771   Birth of Walter Scott (1771–1832), Romantic novelist.

1778   First cotton mill, at Rothesay.

1788   Death of Bonnie Prince Charlie in Rome.

1790   Forth and Clyde Canal opened.

1800–50 Highland Clearances: increased rents and the conversion of farms to sheep pasture lead to mass expulsions of the peasants and their forced migration to North America and elsewhere. Meanwhile, the Lowlands industrialize; Catholic Irish immigrate to factories of Glasgow and the southwest.

1807   The first museum in Scotland, the Hunterian Museum, is founded.

1822   Visit of George IV to Scotland, the first British monarch to make such a trip since Charles I. Sir Walter Scott orchestrates the visit, and almost single-handedly invents Scotland's national costume: the formal kilt, tartan plaid, and jacket.

1831   The first passenger rail service in Scotland opens on the line between Glasgow and Garnkirk.

1832   Parliamentary Reform Act expands the franchise, redistributes seats.

1837   Victoria (1819–1901) ascends to the British throne.

1842   Edinburgh–Glasgow railroad opened.

1846   Edinburgh–London railroad opened.

1848   Queen Victoria buys estate at Balmoral as her Scottish residence. Andrew Carnegie emigrates from Dunfermline to Pittsburgh.

1860   The first British Open golf championship is held in Scotland, at Prestwick.

1884–85 Gladstone's Reform Act gives the majority of men over 21 the right to vote. Office of Secretary for Scotland authorized.

1886 Scottish Home Rule Association founded.

1888 Scottish Labour Party founded by Keir Hardie (1856–1915); he later forms the Independent Labour Party (1893)

1890 Forth Rail Bridge opened.

1896 The Glasgow subway opens.

1901 Death of Queen Victoria.

1904–31 One million Scots emigrate to Canada, the United States, New Zealand, Australia, and elsewhere.

1919 Rent strikes across Scotland. Troops are sent to Glasgow as thousands gather in the city's George Square to demand a shorter working week.

1928 Equal Franchise Act gives the vote to women. Scottish Office established as governmental department in Edinburgh. John Logie Baird gives the first demonstration of television. Alexander Fleming, a Scot, discovers penicillin. Death of architect and designer Charles Rennie Mackintosh.

1930 Unemployment in Scotland reaches 25%.

1931 Depression hits industrialized Scotland severely.

1933 The first press stories alleging that there is a monster in Loch Ness. They have continued ever since.

1934 Scottish National Party formed.

1938 The world's largest luxury liner, the *Queen Elizabeth,* is launched on the Clyde.

1939 The first German air raids of World War II on Scotland are made on the Forth Estuary.

1941 The town of Clydebank is bombed by German planes attacking the shipyards: 1,000 people are killed.

1945 Two Scottish Nationalists elected to Parliament.

1947 The Edinburgh International Festival, with events in all the performing arts, is launched.

1950 The Stone of Destiny, on which the kings of Scotland were traditionally crowned, is stolen from Westminster Abbey in London and returned to Scotland. It is found a year later, in Arbroath.

1951 The People's Festival, an alternative to the official Edinburgh Festival, launched. It later becomes the Fringe.

1959 Finnart Oil Terminal, Chapelcross Nuclear Power Station, and Dounreay Fast Breeder Reactor opened.

1964 Forth Road Bridge opened.

1970 British Petroleum strikes oil in the North Sea; revives economy of northeast.

1973 Britain becomes a member of the European Economic Community (formerly known as the Common Market).

1974 Eleven Scottish Nationalists elected as members of Parliament. Old counties reorganized and renamed as new regions and districts.

1975 The first Scottish oil pumped ashore from the North Sea. "It's Scotland's Oil" becomes a slogan used by Nationalists.

1979 Referendum on devolution—the creation of a separate Scotland: 33% in favor, 31% against; 36% don't vote. Britain's Labour government had imposed a minimum vote of 40%.

1981 Europe's largest oil terminal opens at Sullom Voe, Shetland.

1988 Pan Am flight 103 brought down by a terrorist bomb over Lockerbie.

1992 Increasing attention focused on Scotland's dissatisfaction with rule from London. Poll shows 50% of Scots want independence.

1997 The Labour Party wins the general election in May. A referendum in Scotland votes in favor of the establishment of a Scottish parliament (with restricted powers). The first successful cloning of an animal in the world is achieved with the birth of Dolly the Sheep at the Roslin Institute in Edinburgh.

1999 Scotland elects its first parliament in 300 years.

2002 The Millennium Link—the restoration of the canal link between Glasgow and Edinburgh—is completed at a cost of £78 million. It includes the Falkirk Wheel, the world's only rotating boat lift.

2004 The Scottish Parliament Building opens for business in a building whose modern design by Spanish architect Enric Miralles causes controversy.

2007 Alex Salmond, leader of the Scottish National Party, becomes the First Minister of Scotland heading a minority government. Scotland wins its bid for the 2014 Commonwealth Games; Glasgow is the host city.

2009 The country endures recession as part of the international economic upheaval. Scotland invokes compassionate release and sends the convicted ailing Lockerbie bomber back to Libya.

2011 The Scottish National Party under Alex Salmond wins an absolute majority in the Scottish parliamentary elections. In January 2012, he proposes the question for the referendum on Scottish independence that he wants to hold in fall 2014.

Travel Smart Scotland

"Driving conditions are good, but you have to assume that you won't average more than 30 mph in the Highlands because the roads are winding, there are sheep, and you will be stopping often to take pictures. So try to concentrate on one area and don't try to see everything. You also have to assume that there will be a lot of rain and so proper waterproof clothing and boots are mandatory, even if you do only easy hikes."

—mbgg

GETTING HERE AND AROUND

▌ AIR TRAVEL

Scotland's main hubs are Glasgow, Prestwick (near Glasgow), Edinburgh, Inverness, and Aberdeen. Glasgow and Prestwick are the gateways to the west and southwest, Edinburgh the east and southeast, Aberdeen and Inverness the north. All of these cities have excellent bus and train transportation services and well-maintained roads that link them with each other and other cities within Scotland. Taxis are also an efficient and reliable option, but they are three to four times the cost of going by public transport.

Traveling by air is straightforward in Scotland; you shouldn't encounter any surprises. Security is heavy but efficient. You can often breeze through check-in lines by using your airline's online check-in option or bag drop, but confirm this ahead of time.

Flying time to Glasgow (and to Aberdeen) is 6½ hours from New York, 7½ hours from Chicago, 9½ hours from Dallas, 10 hours from Los Angeles, and 21½ hours from Sydney. Flying time to Edinburgh is 7 hours from New York, 8 hours from Chicago, 10 hours from Dallas, 10½ hours from Los Angeles and 22 hours from Sydney. Not all airlines offer direct flights to Scotland; many go via London. For those flights allow an extra four to five hours of travel (two to three for the layover in London plus an addition hour or two for the duration of the flight).

Smoking is prohibited on all flights.

Airline-Security Issues Transportation Security Administration ⊕ www.tsa.gov.

AIRPORTS

The major international gateways to Scotland are Glasgow Airport (GLA), about 7 mi outside Glasgow, and Edinburgh Airport (EDI), 7 mi from the city. Both offer connections for dozens of European cities and regular flights to London's Gatwick (LGW) and Heathrow (LHR) airports. Aberdeen Airport (ABZ) has direct flights to most major European cities. Prestwick (PIK) has direct flights to most major British and European cities at discounted rates. Inverness (INV) offers direct flights in and around the United Kingdom.

Airport tax is included in the price of your ticket. Generally the tax for economy tickets within the United Kingdom from European Union countries is £24. For all other flights it is £60. For first- and club class flights from the United Kingdom and European Union the tax is £24; for all other destinations it can be as much as £60.

All Scottish airports offer typical modern amenities: restaurants, cafés, shopping (from clothes to food to tourist trinkets), sandwich and salad bars, pubs, pharmacies, bookshops, and newsstands; some even have spas and hair salons. Glasgow is the largest, most interesting airport when it comes to a delayed flight. Good food and shopping options abound—try Tartan Plus for Scottish-inspired goods—and if you're in need of some tranquility, head for the Relaxation Station for a clothed massage, no reservation necessary.

There are plenty of hotels near all airports, and all airports also have Internet access.

Airport Information Aberdeen Airport ☎ 0844/481–6666 ⊕ www.aberdeenairport. com. **Edinburgh Airport** ☎ 0844/481–8989 ⊕ www.edinburghairport.com. **Glasgow Airport** ☎ 0844/481–5555 ⊕ www. glasgowairport.com. **Glasgow Prestwick Airport** ☎ 0871/223–0700 ⊕ www. glasgowprestwick.com/. **Inverness Airport** ☎ 01667/464000 ⊕ www.hial.co.uk.

GROUND TRANSPORTATION

The best way to get to and from the airport based on speed and convenience is by taxi. All airport taxi stands are just outside the airport's front doors and are well marked with clear signs; ask one of the airport porters for help if you can't find the stand. Most taxis have a set price when going to and from the airport to the city center but will turn on the meter at your request. Ask the driver to turn on the meter to confirm the flat-rate price.

If you're traveling with a large party, you can request a people carrier to transport everyone, luggage included. Luggage is included in the taxi fare; you should not be charged extra for it. If you're traveling alone, a more economical transfer option is public transportation. Buses travel between city centers and Glasgow, Edinburgh, Aberdeen, and Inverness airports. Trains go direct to Prestwick Airport. All are fast, inexpensive, and reliable. *For more information and specific contacts, refer to the Orientation and Planning sections at the beginning of chapters.*

TRANSFERS BETWEEN AIRPORTS
Scottish airports are relatively close to one another and all are connected by a series of buses and trains. Flights between airports add hours to your journey and are very expensive (between £200 and £400). The best way to travel from one airport to another is by bus, train, car, or taxi. Normally you must take a combination of bus and train, which is easy and—if you travel light—quite enjoyable.

From Edinburgh Airport you can take a bus to the city center (£4.50) and then a train to Glasgow city center (£12.20) and a bus to Glasgow Airport (£4.50). This journey should take you less than two hours. Taxis are fast but costly. The price of a taxi from Edinburgh Airport to Glasgow Airport is around £85, a good choice if you're traveling with a few people. Renting a car would be a good choice if you want to get from Edinburgh to, say, Aberdeen Airport and you're traveling with a few people. Otherwise, take a bus to the city center and then take a train. *For specific information, see the Orientation and Planning section at the start of appropriate chapters.*

FLIGHTS
Scotland has a significant air network for a small country. Contact British Airways or British Airways Express for details on flights from London's Heathrow Airport or from Glasgow, Edinburgh, Aberdeen, and Inverness to the farthest corners of the Scottish mainland and to the islands. *See individual chapters for information on flying to various islands.*

Among the low-cost carriers, bmibaby has service from Heathrow; and easyJet flies from London Luton/Gatwick/Stansted to and between Glasgow, Edinburgh, Aberdeen, and Inverness, plus to and from Belfast. Flybe has services to Aberdeen and Inverness from Bristol, Exeter, Manchester, and Southampton.

Major Airline Contacts British Airways ☎ 800/247–9297 in U.S., 0844/493–0787 in U.K. ⊕ www.britishairways.com. **KLM** ☎ 866/434–0320 in U.S., 0871/231–0000 in U.K. ⊕ www.klm.com. **United Airlines** ☎ 800/864–8331 in U.S., 0845/844–4777 in U.K. ⊕ www.united.com. **US Airways** ☎ 800/428–4322 in U.S., 0845/600–3300 in U.K. ⊕ www.usairways.com. **Virgin Atlantic** ☎ 800/821–5438 in U.S., 0844/209–7770 in U.K. ⊕ www.virgin-atlantic.com.

From London to Edinburgh and Glasgow bmibaby/British Midland ☎ 0905/828–2828 in U.K. ⊕ www.bmibaby.com. **British Airways** ☎ 0870/493–0787 in U.K. ⊕ www.britishairways.com. **easyJet** ⊕ www.easyjet.com. **Ryanair** ☎ 0871/246–0000 in U.K. ⊕ www.ryanair.com.

Within Scotland British Airways ☎ 0870/493–0787 in U.K. ⊕ www.britishairways.com. **easyJet** ☎ 0871/244–2366 in U.K. ⊕ www.easyjet.com. **Flybe** ☎ 011–44–1392–268513 from U.S., 0871/700–2000 from U.K. ⊕ www.flybe.com.

AIRLINE TICKETS
The least expensive airfares to Scotland are often priced for round-trip travel and must usually be purchased in advance. Airlines generally allow you to change

your return date for a fee; most low-fare tickets, however, are nonrefundable.

If you intend to fly to Scotland from London, take advantage of the current fare wars on internal routes—notably among London's four airports and between Glasgow and Edinburgh. Among the cheapest fares are those from easyJet, which offers bargain fares from London Luton/Gatwick/Stansted (all with good rail links from central London) to Glasgow, Edinburgh, Aberdeen, and Inverness. However, British Airways now offers competitive fares on some flights, especially those booked in advance.

AIR PASSES

Oneworld's Visit Europe Pass offers packages based on mileage that allow travel throughout Europe on airlines that include British Airways (which has an extensive network of European flights). You must purchase this pass before you leave home through the Oneworld website. In Britain the best place to search for consolidator tickets, or so-called bucket-shop tickets, is through Cheap Flights, a website that pools all flights available and then directs you to a phone number or site to purchase tickets.

Air Pass Information bmi ☎ 0844/8484–888, 01332/648181 in U.K. ⊕ www.flybmi. com. **Cheap Flights** ☎ no phone number ⊕ www.cheapflights.co.uk. **easyJet** ⊕ www. easyjet.com. **Flightpass by Europe by Air** ☎ 866/478810 in U.S . ⊕ www.europebyair. com. **Oneworld** ⊕ www.oneworld.com.

▌ BIKE TRAVEL

Bicycling in Scotland is variable. The best months for cycling are May, June, and September, when the roads are often quieter and the weather is usually better. Winds are predominantly from the southwest, so plan your route accordingly.

Because Scotland's main roads are continually being upgraded, bicyclists can easily reach the network of quieter rural roads in southern and much of eastern

Scotland, especially Grampian. Still, be careful getting from town centers to rural riding areas; if in doubt, ask a local. In a few areas of the Highlands, notably in northwestern Scotland, the rugged terrain and limited population have resulted in the lack of side roads, making it difficult—sometimes impossible—to plan a minor-road route in these areas.

Several agencies now promote routes for recreational cyclists. These routes are signposted, and agencies have produced maps or leaflets showing where they run. Perhaps best known is the Glasgow–Loch Lomond–Killin Cycleway, which uses former railway track beds, forest trails, quiet rural side roads, and some main roads. VisitScotland has advice on a site dedicated to cycling.

TRANSPORTING BIKES

Although some rural bus services will transport cycles if space is available, don't count on getting your bike on a bus. Be sure to check well in advance with the appropriate bus company.

You can take bicycles on car and passenger ferries in Scotland, and it's not generally necessary to book in advance. Check cycles on car ferries early so that they can be loaded through the car entrance.

ScotRail strongly advises that you make a train reservation for you and your bike at least one month in advance. On several trains reservations are compulsory.

BIKING ORGANIZATIONS

The Cyclists' Touring Club publishes a members' magazine, route maps, and guides. Sustrans Ltd. is a nonprofit organization dedicated to providing environmentally friendly routes for cyclists, notably in and around cities.

Bike Maps and Information Cyclists' Touring Club ☎ 0844/736–8450 ⊕ www.ctc.org.uk. **Sustrans** ☎ 0131/346–1384 ⊕ www.sustrans. org.uk. **VisitScotland** ☎ 0845/225–5121 ⊕ active.visitscotland.com.

▌BOAT AND FERRY TRAVEL

Because Scotland has so many islands, plus the great Firth of Clyde waterway, ferry services are of paramount importance. Most ferries transport vehicles as well as foot passengers, although a few smaller ones are for passengers only.

It's a good idea to make a reservation ahead of time, although reservations are not absolutely necessary. Most travelers show up on the day of departure and buy their tickets from the stations at the ports. Keep in mind that these are working ferries, not tourist boats. Although journeys are scenic, most people use these ferries as their daily means of public transportation to and from their hometowns.

The main operator is Caledonian Mac-Brayne, known generally as CalMac. Services extend from the Firth of Clyde in the south, where there's an extensive network, right up to the northwest of Scotland and all of the Hebrides. CalMac sells an 8-day or 15-day Island Rover runabout ticket, which is ideal for touring holidays in the islands, as well as an island-hopping scheme called Island Hopscotch. Fares can range from £4–£5 for a short trip to almost £50 for a longer trip with several legs.

The Dunoon–Gourock route on the Clyde is served by Western Ferries (for cars) and CalMac (for passengers only).

The Falkirk Wheel in Tamfourhill, about halfway between Glasgow and Edinburgh, is an attraction as much as a form of transportation. The only rotating boat lift in the world, it carries tour boats from the Forth and Clyde Canal over to the Union Canal, and back again.

Northlink Ferries operates a car ferry for Orkney between Scrabster, near Thurso, and Stromness, on the main island of Orkney; and between Aberdeen and Kirkwall, which is also on Mainland, Orkney. Northlink also runs ferries for Shetland between Aberdeen and Lerwick.

For fares and schedules, contact ferry companies directly. Traveler's checks (in pounds), cash, and major credit cards are accepted for payment. *See the Orientation and Planning sections of each chapter for more details about ferry services.*

Information **Caledonian MacBrayne** ☏ *0800/066–5000* ⊕ *www.calmac.co.uk.* **Falkirk Wheel** ✉ *Lime Rd., Tamfourhill* ☏ *08700/500208 reservations* ⊕ *www. thefalkirkwheel.co.uk.* **Northlink Ferries** ☏ *0845/600–0449* ⊕ *www.northlinkferries. co.uk.* **Western Ferries** ☏ *01369/704452* ⊕ *www.western-ferries.co.uk.*

▌BUS TRAVEL

Long-distance buses usually provide the cheapest way to travel between England and Scotland; fares may be as little as a third of the rail fares for comparable trips and are cheaper if you buy in advance. However, the trip is not as comfortable as by train (no dining cart or carriage, smaller bathrooms, less spacious seats), and travel takes longer. Glasgow to London by bus (nonstop) takes 8 hours, 45 minutes; by train it takes about 5 hours, 30 minutes.

Scotland's bus (short-haul) and coach (long-distance) network is extensive. Bus service is comprehensive in cities, less so in country districts. Express service links main cities and towns, connecting, for example, Glasgow and Edinburgh to Inverness, Aberdeen, Perth, Skye, Ayr, Dumfries, and Carlisle; or Inverness with Aberdeen, Wick, Thurso, and Fort William. These express services are very fast, and fares are reasonable. Scottish Citylink, National Express, and Megabus are some of the main operators; there are about 20 in all.

The London terminal is Victoria Coach Station for National Express and the London Victoria Greenline Coach Station for Megabus.

There is one class of service, and all buses are nonsmoking.

To explore really rural areas, consider complementing bus services with the Royal Mail Post Bus, where you and others travel somewhat comfortably with the mail bags. This is a great way to engage with locals. These services run in the Highlands, the Western Isles, Perthshire, and Argyle and Bute.

DISCOUNTS AND DEALS

On Scottish Citylink, the Explorer Passes offer complete freedom of travel on all services throughout Scotland. Three permutations give three days of travel out of a five-day period, five days of travel out of 10, and eight days of travel out of 18. They're available from Scottish Citylink offices, and cost £39 to £79.

National Express offers discounted seats on buses from London to more than 50 cities in the United Kingdom, including Glasgow and Aberdeen. Tickets range from £12 to £25, but only when purchased online. Megabus (order tickets online), a discount service, has similarly competitive prices between major cities throughout Scotland, including Aberdeen, Dundee, Glasgow, Inverness, and Perth.

Travelers ages 16 to 26 are eligible for 30% reductions with the National Express Coachcard (£10).

FARES AND SCHEDULES

Contact Traveline Scotland for information on all public transportation and timetables.

For town, suburban, or short-distance journeys, you buy your ticket on the bus, from a pay box, or from the driver. You need exact change. For longer journeys—for example, Glasgow–Inverness—it's usual (and a good idea; busy routes and times can book up) to reserve a seat and pay at the bus station booking office.

PAYING

Credit cards are accepted at most bus stations.

Bus Information Traveline Scotland ☎ 0871/200–2233 ⊕ www.travelinescotland. com.

Bus Lines Megabus ☎ 0871/266–3333 ⊕ www.megabus.co.uk. **National Express** ☎ 08717/818178 ⊕ www.nationalexpress.com. **Royal Mail Post Bus** ⊕ www.royalmail.com. **Scottish Citylink** ☎ 0871/266–3333 ⊕ www. citylink.co.uk.

∎ CAR TRAVEL

If you plan to stick mostly to the cities, you will not need a car. All cities in Scotland are either so compact that most attractions are within easy walking distance of each other (Aberdeen, Dundee, Edinburgh, Inverness, and Stirling) or are accessible by an excellent local public transport system (Glasgow). And there is often good train and/or bus service from major cities to nearby day-trip destinations. Bus tours are also a good option for a day trip out of town. Once you leave Edinburgh, Glasgow, and the other major cities, a car will make journeys faster and much more enjoyable than trying to work out public-transportation connections to the farther-flung reaches of Scotland (though it is possible, if time consuming, to see much of the country by public transportation). A car allows you to set your own pace and visit off-the-beaten-path towns and sights most easily.

In Scotland your own driver's license is acceptable. International driving permits (IDPs) are available from the American Automobile Association and, in the United Kingdom, from the Automobile Association and Royal Automobile Club. These international permits, valid only in conjunction with your regular driver's license, are universally recognized; having one may save you a problem with local authorities.

GASOLINE

Expect to pay a lot more for gasoline, about £6 a gallon (£1.32 a liter) for unleaded—up to 10p a liter higher in remote rural locations. The British imperial gallon is about 20% more in volume than the U.S. gallon—approximately 4.5 liters. Pumps dispense in liters, not gallons. Most gas stations are self-service and stock unleaded, super unleaded, and LRP (replacing four-star) plus diesel; all accept major credit cards.

PARKING

On-street parking is a bit of a lottery in Scotland. Depending on the location and time of day, the streets can be packed or empty of cars. In the cities, you must pay for your on-street parking by getting a sticker from a parking machine; these machines are clearly marked with a large P. Make sure you have the exact change; it's normally around £2 for four hours but can vary. Put the parking sticker on the inside of your front windshield. Parking lots are scattered throughout urban areas and tend to be more or less the same price as on-street parking. Most parking lots are near shopping malls or busy financial districts.

The local penalty for illegally parked cars is £25, and parking regulations are strictly enforced.

ROAD CONDITIONS

A good network of superhighways, known as motorways, and divided highways, known as dual carriageways, extends throughout Britain. In the remoter areas of Scotland where the motorway hasn't penetrated, travel is noticeably slower. Motorways shown with the prefix M are mainly two or three lanes in each direction, without any right-hand turns. These are the roads to use to cover long distances, though inevitably you'll see less of the countryside. Service areas are at most about an hour apart.

Dual carriageways, usually shown on a map as a thick red line (often with a black line in the center) and the prefix "a" followed by a number perhaps with a bracketed "t" (for example, "a304[t]"), are similar to motorways, except that right turns are sometimes permitted, and you'll find both traffic lights and traffic circles on them. The vast network of other main roads, which typical maps show as either single red A roads, or narrower brown B roads, also numbered, are for the most part the old coach and turnpike roads built originally for horses and carriages. Travel along these roads is slower than on motorways, and passing is more difficult. On the other hand, you'll see much more of Scotland. The A9, Perth to Inverness, is a particularly dangerous road with the worst road accident record in Scotland because its dual carriageway's stopping and starting.

Minor roads (shown as yellow or white on most maps, unlettered and unnumbered) are the ancient lanes and byways of Britain, roads that are not only living history but a superb way of discovering hidden parts of Scotland. You have to drive along them slowly and carefully. On single-track (one-lane) roads, found in the north and west of Scotland, there's no room for two vehicles to pass, and you must use a passing place if you meet an oncoming car or tractor, or if a car behind wishes to overtake you. Never hold up traffic on single-track roads.

For some typical driving times, see the Scotland Planner in Chapter 1.

ROADSIDE EMERGENCIES

For aid if your car breaks down, contact the 24-hour rescue numbers of either the Automobile Association or the Royal Automobile Club. If you're a member of the AAA (American Automobile Association) or another association, check your membership details before you travel; reciprocal agreements may give you free roadside aid.

Emergency Contacts in the U.K. **Automobile Association** (AA). ☎ 0800/887766 ⊕ *www.theaa.co.uk*. **Royal Automobile Club** (RAC). ☎ 0844/774–5942 ⊕ *www.rac.co.uk*.

Emergency Contacts in the U.S. **American Automobile Association** (AAA). ☎ 800/564–6222 ⊕ *www.aaa.com*.

RULES OF THE ROAD

The most noticeable difference for most visitors is that when in Britain, you drive on the left and steer the car on the right.

Give yourself time to adjust to driving on the left—especially if you pick up your car at the airport. One of the most complicated questions facing visitors to Britain is that of speed limits. In urban areas, it's generally 30 mph, but it's 40 mph on some main roads, as indicated by circular red-rimmed signs. In rural areas the official limit is 60 mph on ordinary roads and 70 mph on divided highways and motorways—and traffic police can be hard on speeders, especially in urban areas. Driving while using a cell phone is illegal, and the use of seat belts is mandatory for passengers in front and back seats. Service stations and newsstands sell copies of the Highway Code (£2.50), which lists driving rules and has pictures of signs. It's also available online at ⊕ *www.direct.gov.uk*.

Drunk-driving laws are strictly enforced and penalties are heavy. Avoid alcohol if you're driving.

CAR RENTAL

You can rent any type of car you desire; however, in Scotland cars tend to be on the smaller side. Many roads are narrow, and a smaller car saves money on gas. Common models are the Nissan Micra, Ford Focus, and Vauxhall Corsa. Four-wheel-drive vehicles aren't a necessity. Most cars are manual, not automatic, and come with air-conditioning, although you rarely need it in Scotland. If you want an automatic, reserve ahead. The cars are in very good condition and must pass a series of inspections and tests before they are rented out. When you're returning the car, allow an extra hour to drop it off and sort out any paperwork.

If you're traveling to more than one country, make sure your rental contract permits you to take the car across borders and that the insurance policy covers you in every country you visit. British cars have the steering wheel on the right, so you may want to leave your rented car in Britain and pick up a left-side drive when you cross the Channel.

Rates in Glasgow begin at £25 a day and £120 a week for an economy car with a manual transmission and unlimited mileage. This does not include tax on car rentals, which is 20%. The busiest months are June through August, when rates may go up 30%. During this time, book at least two to four weeks in advance. Online booking is fine.

Companies frequently restrict rentals to people over age 23 and under age 75. If you are over 70, some companies require you to have your own insurance. If you are under 25, a surcharge of £16 per day plus V.A.T. will apply

Child car seats usually cost about £24 extra; you must ask for a car seat when you book, at least 48 hours in advance. The same is true for GPS. Adding one extra driver is usually included in the original rental price.

Local Agencies Arnold Clark ☎ *0141/237-4374* ⊕ *www.arnoldclarkrental.co.uk.*

Major Rental Agencies Avis ☎ *0844/544-6666* ⊕ *www.avis.com.* **Budget** ☎ *0844/544-3439* ⊕ *www.budget.com.* **Hertz** ☎ *0870/844-8844* ⊕ *www.hertz.com.* **National Car Rental** ☎ *0141/531-5220* ⊕ *www.nationalcar.com.*

Wholesalers Auto Europe ☎ *888/223-5555* ⊕ *www.autoeurope.com.* **Europe by Car** ☎ *0800/223-1516 in U.S, 0141/532-5200 in Glasgow* ⊕ *www.europebycar.com.* **Eurovacations** ☎ *877/471-3876 in U.S.* ⊕ *www. eurovacations.com.* **Kemwel** ☎ *877/820-0668 in U.S.* ⊕ *www.kemwel.com.*

▮ TAXI TRAVEL

In Edinburgh, Glasgow, and the larger cities, black hackney taxis—similar to those in London—with their "taxi" sign illuminated can be hailed on the street, or booked by phone (expect to pay an extra 60p charge for this service in Edinburgh). If you call a private-hire taxi from the phone book, expect a regular-looking car to pick you up. The only distinctions are that these private-hire taxis have a special sign attached to their license plate indicating that they have a taxi license and they have a meter stuck on the dashboard, along with an ID card for the driver. Private-hire taxis are cheaper than black hackney taxis and will pick you up only from a specific location. They will not pick you up off the street.

Scottish taxis are reliable, safe, and metered. Meters begin at £2 and should increase in 50p intervals. Beyond the larger cities, most communities of any size have a taxi service; your hotel will be able to supply telephone numbers. Very often you can find an advertisement for the local taxi service in public phone booths, online, or in the phone book.

▌TRAIN TRAVEL

Train service within Scotland is generally run by ScotRail, one of the most efficient of Britain's service providers. Trains are modern, clean, and comfortable. Long-distance services carry buffet and refreshment cars. Scotland's rail network extends all the way to Thurso and Wick, the most northerly stations in the British Isles. Lowland services, most of which originate in Glasgow or Edinburgh, are generally fast and reliable. A shuttle makes the 50-minute trip between Glasgow and Edinburgh every 15 minutes. It's a scenic trip with plenty of rolling fields, livestock, and traditional houses to view along the way. One word of caution: there are very few trains in the Highlands on Sunday and services throughout the country are generally limited on Sunday.

CLASSES

Most trains have first-class and standard-class coaches. First-class coaches are always less crowded; they have wider seats and are often cleaner and less well-worn than standard-class cars, and they're a lot more expensive. However, on weekends you can often upgrade from standard to first class for a fee (often £10 to £20)—ask at the time of booking.

FARES AND SCHEDULES

The best way to find out which train to take, which station to catch it at, and what times trains travel to your destination is to call National Rail Enquiries. It's a helpful, comprehensive, free service that covers all Britain's rail lines. National Rail will help you choose the best train to take, and then connects you with the ticket office for that train company so that you can buy tickets.

Train fares vary according to class of ticket purchased, time (off-peak travel will be much cheaper), and distance traveled. Before you buy your ticket, stop at the Information Office/Travel Centre and request the lowest fare to your destination and information about any special offers. There's sometimes little difference between the cost of a one-way and round-trip ticket, and returns are valid for one month. So if you're planning on departing from and returning to the same destination, buy a round-trip fare upon your departure, rather than purchasing two separate one-way tickets.

It's much cheaper to buy a one-way or round-trip ticket in advance than on the day of your trip (except for commuter services); the closer to the date of travel, the more expensive the ticket will be. Try to purchase tickets at least eight weeks in advance during peak-season summer travel to save money and reserve good seats. You must stick to the train you have booked (penalties can be the full price), and you need to keep the seat reservation ticket, which is part of the valid ticket.

Check train websites, especially ScotRail, for deals. You can also check the trainline, which sells discounted advance-purchase tickets from all train companies to all destinations in Britain. It's worthwhile to compare several sites.

Information **National Rail Enquiries**
☎ *0845/748–4950* ⊕ *www.nationalrail.co.uk.*
ScotRail ☎ *0845/748–4950* ⊕ *www.scotrail. co.uk.* **the trainline** ☎ *0871/244–1545*
⊕ *www.thetrainline.com.*

PAYING

All major credit cards are accepted for train fares paid in person, online, and by phone.

RESERVATIONS

Reserving your ticket in advance is always recommended.

Tickets and rail passes do not guarantee seats on the trains. For that you need a seat reservation (essential for peak travel trains to and from Edinburgh during the summer festivals), which if made at the time of ticket purchase is usually included in the ticket price, or if booked separately, must be paid for at a cost of £1 *per train* on your itinerary. You also need a reservation if you purchase overnight sleeping accommodations.

TRAIN PASSES

To save money, look into rail passes. But be aware that if you don't plan to cover many miles, you may come out ahead by buying individual tickets. If you plan to travel by train in Scotland, consider purchasing a BritRail Pass, which also allows travel in England and Wales. All BritRail passes must be purchased in your home country; they're sold by travel agents as well as ACP, BritRail or Rail Europe. Rail passes do not guarantee seats on the trains, so be sure to reserve ahead. Remember that Eurail Passes aren't honored in Great Britain.

The cost of an unlimited BritRail adult pass for 4 days is $225/$339 (standard/first class); for 8 days, $319/$485; for 15 days, $485/$725; for 22 days, $609/$919; and for a month, $725/$1,085. The Youth Pass, for ages 16 to 25, costs $179/$269 for 4 days, $259/$389 for 8 days, $389/$579 for 15 days, $489/$735 for 22 days, and $579/$869 for one month. The Senior Pass, for passengers over 60, costs $225/$289 for 4 days, $319/$409 for 8 days, $485/$615 for 15 days, $609/$779 for 22 days, and $725/$925 for one month. The Scottish Freedom Pass allows transportation on all Caledonian MacBrayne and Strathclyde ferries

in addition to major bus links and the Glasgow underground. You can travel any 4 days in an 8-day period for $215 or any 8 days in a 15-day period for $285.

Information ACP Rail International ☎ 514/733–9865 ⊕ www.acprail.com. **BritRail Travel** ☎ 866/938–7245 ⊕ www.britrail. com. **Rail Europe** ☎ 800/622–8600 ⊕ www. raileurope.com.

FROM ENGLAND

There are two main rail routes to Scotland from the south of England. The first, the west-coast main line, runs from London Euston to Glasgow Central; it takes 5½ hours to make the 400-mi trip to central Scotland, and service is frequent and reliable. Useful for daytime travel to the Scottish Highlands is the direct train to Stirling and Aviemore, terminating at Inverness. For a restful route to the Scottish Highlands, take the overnight sleeper service, with soundproof sleeping carriages. It runs from London Euston, departing in late evening, to Perth, Stirling, Aviemore, and Inverness, where it arrives the following morning. The east-coast main line from London King's Cross to Edinburgh provides the quickest trip to the Scottish capital. Between 8 am and 6 pm there are 16 trains to Edinburgh, three of them through to Aberdeen. Limited-stop expresses like the Flying Scotsman make the 393-mi London-to-Edinburgh journey in around four hours. Connecting services to most parts of Scotland—particularly the Western Highlands—are often better from Edinburgh than from Glasgow.

Trains from elsewhere in England are good: regular service connects Birmingham, Manchester, Liverpool, and Bristol with Glasgow and Edinburgh. From Harwich (the port of call for ships from Holland, Germany, and Denmark), you can travel to Glasgow via Manchester. But it's faster to change at Peterborough for the east-coast main line to Edinburgh.

SCENIC ROUTES

Although many routes in Scotland run through extremely attractive countryside, several stand out: from Glasgow to Oban via Loch Lomond; to Fort William and Mallaig via Rannoch (ferry connection to Skye); from Edinburgh to Inverness via the Forth Bridge and Perth; from Inverness to Kyle of Lochalsh and to Wick; and from Inverness to Aberdeen.

A private train, the Royal Scotsman, does all-inclusive scenic tours, partly under steam power, with banquets en route. This is a luxury experience: some evenings require formal wear. You can choose itineraries from two nights ($3,760) to seven nights ($11,184) per person.

Train Tours **The Royal Scotsman**
☎ *0845/077–2222 in the U.K., 800/524–2420 in the U.S.* ⊕ *www.royalscotsman.com.*

ESSENTIALS

■ ACCOMMODATIONS

Your choices in Scotland range from small, local B&Bs to large, elegant hotels—some of the chain variety. Bed-and-breakfasts tend to be less expensive than large hotels because many are spare rooms in spacious homes. Proprietors keep costs down and guests get a more personal, Scottish touch. One note: there is a ban on smoking in all indoor public spaces in Scotland, and this includes hotel rooms. Accommodation can seem expensive because the pound has been strong against the dollar, but the economic downturn since 2009 has brought some special deals.

VisitScotland classifies and grades accommodations using a simple star system. The greater the number of stars, the greater the number of facilities and the more luxurious they are.

If you're touring around, you're not likely to be stranded: even in the height of the season—July and August—hotel occupancy runs at about 80%. On the other hand, if you arrive in Edinburgh at festival time or some place where a big Highland Gathering or golf tournament is in progress, you'll have an extremely limited choice of accommodations, and your best bet will be to try for a room in a nearby village.

To secure your first choice, reserve in advance. One option is to reserve through local tourist information centers, making use of their "book-a-bed-ahead" services. Telephone bookings made from home should be confirmed by email or fax. Country hotels expect you to turn up by about 6 pm.

Some hotels, B&Bs and guesthouses offer discounted rates for stays of two nights or longer.

Be sure you understand the hotel's cancellation policy. Some places allow you to cancel without any kind of penalty; others, particularly B&Bs, require you to cancel a week in advance or penalize you.

Most hotels allow children under a certain age to stay in their parents' room at no extra charge, but others charge for them as extra adults; find out the cutoff age for discounts.

The lodgings we list are the cream of the crop in each price category. Properties are assigned price categories based on the price of a standard double room at high season (excluding holidays). Unless otherwise noted, all lodgings listed have a private bathroom, air-conditioning, a room phone, and a television. *Price charts appear at the start of each chapter or, for Edinburgh and Glasgow, in the Where to Stay section.*

We always list the facilities that are available, but we don't specify whether they cost extra; when pricing accommodations, always ask what's included. Many hotels and most guesthouses and B&Bs include a breakfast within the basic room rate. Meal-plan information appears at the end of a review.

CATEGORY	EDINBURGH AND GLASGOW	ELSEWHERE
¢	under £70	under £70
$	£70–£120	£70–£120
$$	£121–£180	£121–£160
$$$	£181–£250	£161–£220
$$$$	over £250	over £220

Prices are for two people in a standard double room in high season, including 20% V.A.T., and are given in pounds.

APARTMENT AND HOUSE RENTALS

Rental houses and flats (apartments) are becoming more popular lodging choices for travelers visiting Scotland, particularly for those staying in one place for more than a few days. Some places may

LOCAL DO'S AND TABOOS

GREETINGS

Although many Scots are fantastic talkers, they're less enthusiastic with greetings on the physical front. If you're in less familiar company, a handshake is more appreciated than a kiss or hug.

SIGHTSEEING

When you are visiting houses of worship, modest attire is appreciated, though you will see shorts and even bared midriffs. Photographs are welcome in churches, outside of services.

Shorts and other close-fitting attire are allowed just about anywhere at any time, weather permitting; these days locals tend not to cover up as much as they used to.

It's the same with food; Scots eat and drink just about anywhere, and much of the time they do it standing up or even walking.

ETIQUETTE

In Scotland it's rude to walk away from conversation, even if it's with someone you don't know. If you're at a pub, keep in mind that it's very important to buy a round of drinks if you're socializing with a group of people. You don't simply buy your own drink; you buy a drink for all of the people you're there with, and those people do the same. It can make for a very foggy evening and public drunkenness, especially on Friday and Saturday nights. Conversational topics that are considered taboo are money matters; the Scots are quite private about their finances. You should give up your seats for elderly people or pregnant women without a second thought. Hold the door open for someone who is leaving or entering the same building as you. Don't let the door go in the person's face or you might have a small riot on your hands. Say please and thank you.

Polite driving etiquette is carefully observed, too; allow people to pass and be courteous. Jaywalking isn't rude or illegal, but it's much safer to cross with the lights, especially if traffic is coming from a direction you might not be used to.

As for waiting in lines and moving through crowds, be courteous. The Scots are very polite and you'll be noticed (and not in a good way) if you're not polite in return.

OUT ON THE TOWN

People may dress up for a special restaurant or for clubbing, but other people will be casual. Some restaurants and clubs frown on jeans and sneakers.

If you're visiting a family home, a simple bouquet of flowers is a welcome gift. If you're invited for a meal, bringing a bottle of wine is appropriate, if you wish, as is some candy for the children. To thank a host for hospitality, either a phone call or thank-you card is always appreciated.

DOING BUSINESS

Punctuality is of prime importance, so call ahead if you anticipate a late arrival. Spouses do not generally attend business dinners, unless specifically invited.

If you invite someone to dine, it's usually assumed that you'll pick up the tab. However, if you're the visitor, your host may insist on paying. Nonetheless, it's always polite to offer to pay.

LANGUAGE

The Lowland Scots language, which borrows from Scandinavian, Dutch, French, and Gaelic, survives in various forms but is virtually an underground language, spoken at home among ordinary folk, especially in its heartland, in northeast Scotland. Gaelic, too, hangs on in spite of the Highlands depopulation.

Otherwise, Scots speak English often with a strong accent (which may be hard for non-native Brits and Americans to understand), but be patient and your ear will soon come to terms with it.

rent only by the week. Prices can work out to be cheaper than a hotel (though perhaps not than a bed-and-breakfast; this will depend on the number in your group), and the space and comfort are much better than what you'd find in a hotel or B&B.

In the country, your chances of finding a small house to rent are good; in the city you're more likely to find a flat (apartment) to let (rent). Either way, your best bet for finding these rentals is online. Individuals and large consortiums can own these properties, so it just depends on what you're looking for. The White House is a good, central place for rentals in Glasgow, and Scottish Apartment is a good source for apartments in Edinburgh. The National Trust for Scotland has many unique properties, from island cottages to castles, for rent.

International Agencies At Home Abroad ☎ 212/421–9165 ⊕ www.athomeabroadinc. com. **Barclay International Group** ☎ 800/845–6636 ⊕ www.barclayweb.com. **Drawbridge to Europe** ☎ 541/482–7778, 888/268–1148 ⊕ www.drawbridgetoeurope. com. **Forgetaway** ⊕ www.forgetaway.com. **Home Away** ☎ ⊕ www.homeaway.com. **Interhome** ☎ 208/877–6370 in the U.S. ⊕ www.interhome.us. **Villas & Apartments Abroad** ☎ 212/213–6435 ⊕ www.vaanyc.com.

Local Contacts National Trust for Scotland ☎ 0131/243–9331, 866/211–7573 in U.S. ⊕ www.nts.org.uk. **Scottish Apartment** ☎ 0131/240–0080 ⊕ www.scottishapartment. com. **White House** ☎ 0141/339–9375 ⊕ www. whitehouse-apartments.com.

BED-AND-BREAKFASTS

B&Bs, common throughout Scotland, are a special British tradition and the backbone of budget travel, with an average price of £40 to £85 per night, depending on the region, time of year, and particular accommodation. They're usually in a family home, occasionally don't have private bathrooms, and usually offer only breakfast. Guest houses are a slightly larger, somewhat more luxurious version. More

upscale B&Bs, along the line of American B&Bs or small inns, can be found in Edinburgh and Glasgow especially, but in other parts of Scotland as well. All provide a glimpse of everyday British life. Note that local tourist offices can book a B&B for you; there may be a small charge for this service.

Reservation Services BedandBreakfast. com ☎ 512/322–2710, 800/462–2632 ⊕ www. bedandbreakfast.com. **UK Bed and Breakfast Accommodation** ⊕ www.bedandbreakfasts. co.uk.

FARMHOUSE AND CROFTING HOLIDAYS

A popular option for families with children is a farmhouse holiday, combining the freedom of B&B accommodations with the hospitality of Scottish family life. You need a car if you're deep in the country, though. Information is available from VisitBritain or VisitScotland, from Scottish Farmhouse Holidays, and from the Farm Stay UK.

Contacts Farm Stay UK ☎ 024/7669–6909 ⊕ www.farmstayuk.co.uk. **Scottish Farmhouse Holidays** ☎ 01334/650233 ⊕ www. scotfarmhols.co.uk.

HOME EXCHANGES

With a direct home exchange you stay in someone else's home while they stay in yours. Some outfits also deal with vacation homes, so you're not actually staying in someone's full-time residence, just their vacant weekend place.

Exchange Clubs HomeExchange.com. Home Exchange.com; $9.95 per month. ☎ 800/877–8723 ⊕ www.homeexchange.com. **HomeLink International.** HomeLink International; $119 for full membership for one year. ☎ 800/638–3841 in U.S., 01962/886882 in U.K. ⊕ www. homelink.org. **Intervac U.S.**; has various online packages ranging from $8.33 per month. ☎ 501/545–5737 ⊕ www.intervacus.com.

HOTELS

Large hotels vary in style and price. Many lean toward Scottish themes when it comes to decoration, but you can expect the same quality and service from a chain hotel wherever you are in the world. Keep in mind that hotel rooms in Scotland are smaller than what you'd find in the United States. Today hotels of all sizes are trying to be greener, and many newer chains are striving for government environmental awards. Discounted rooms are another trend, as are discounts for room upgrades.

In the countryside, some older hotels are former castles or converted, luxurious country homes. These types of hotels are full of character and charm but can be very expensive, and they may not have elevators. Normally they have all the amenities, if not more, of their urban counterparts. Their locations may be so remote that you must eat on the premises, which may be costly.

Some small regional chains operate in Scotland that are not internationally known. Apex (in Edinburgh, Dundee, and London) is modish and has Scandinavian-inspired bedrooms; Malmaison (in Aberdeen, Edinburgh, and Glasgow) is luxury on a budget; Hotel du Vin (Glasgow and Edinburgh), with its chic bistros, sumptuous bedding and original art, may blow the budget.

Hotel Contacts **Apex Hotels** ⊕ *www. apexhotels.co.uk.* **Hotel du Vin** ⊕ *www. hotelduvin.com.* **Malmaison** ⊕ *www. malmaison.com.*

▌ COMMUNICATIONS

INTERNET

Make sure your laptop is dual-voltage; most, but not all, laptops operate equally well on 110 and 220 volts and so require only an adapter. Never plug your computer into any socket without first asking about surge protection: although Scotland is computer-friendly, few hotels and B&Bs outside the major cities have built-in current stabilizers. It's worthwhile to

purchase a surge protector in the United Kingdom that plugs into the socket.

All hotels and many B&Bs have facilities for computer users, such as a dedicated computer room or broadband and Wi-Fi services for Internet access. Cybercafes lists more than 4,000 Internet cafés worldwide.

Contacts **Cybercafes** ⊕ *www.cybercafes.com.*

PHONES

The good news is that you can now make a direct-dial telephone call from virtually any point on earth. The bad news? You can't always do so cheaply. Calling from a hotel is almost always the most expensive option; hotels usually add huge surcharges to all calls, particularly international ones.

When you're calling anywhere in Great Britain from the United States, the country code is 44. When dialing a Scottish or British number from abroad, drop the initial 0 from the local area code. For instance, if you're calling Edinburgh Castle from New York City, dial 011 (the international code), 44 (the Great Britain country code), 131 (the Edinburgh city code), and then 225–9846 (the number proper).

CALLING WITHIN SCOTLAND

Cell phones are ubiquitous, but there are three types of public pay phones: those that accept only coins, those that accept only phone cards, and those that take British Telecom (BT) phone cards and credit cards. For coin-only phones, insert coins *before* dialing (minimum charge is 60p). Sometimes phones have a "press on answer" (POA) button, which you press when the caller answers.

All calls are charged according to the time of day. Standard rate is weekdays 8 am to 6 pm; cheap rate is weekdays 6 pm to 8 am and all day on weekends, when it's even cheaper. A local call made from a landline before 6 pm costs 12p. The minimum charge for a local call from a pay phone is 60p for the first 30 minutes and 10p for each subsequent minute. A daytime call to the United States will cost 19p a minute on a regular phone (weekends are cheaper), 60p on a pay phone.

To call a number with the same area code as the number from which you are dialing, omit the area-code digits when you dial. For long-distance calls within Britain, dial the area code (which usually begins with 01), followed by the telephone number. In provincial areas the dialing codes for nearby towns are often posted in phone booths.

To call the operator, dial 100; directory inquiries (information), 118–500; international directory inquiries, 118–505.

In Scotland cellular-phone numbers, the 0800 toll-free code, and local-rate 0345 numbers do not have a 1 after the initial 0, nor do many premium-rate numbers, for example 0891, and special-rate numbers, for example 08705.

Numbers that start with 0800, 0808, or national information numbers that start with 0845 are free when called from a U.K. landline: they cost anywhere from 10p to 40p a minute when called from a cellular phone. Additionally 0870 numbers are *not* toll-free numbers; in fact, numbers beginning with 0871 or the 0900 prefix are premium-rate numbers, and it costs extra to call them. The amount varies and is usually relatively small when dialed from within the country but can be excessive when dialed from outside the United Kingdom. Many businesses,

especially those offering low-cost services (such as Ryanair or Megabus) communicate with customers via their websites. If they do have a customer services phone number, it's costly to use it.

CALLING OUTSIDE SCOTLAND

The country code for the United States is 1.

To make international calls *from* Scotland, dial 00 + the country code + area code + number. For the international operator, credit card, or collect calls, dial 155.

Access Codes AT&T Direct ☎ *0500/890011 for cable and wireless, 0800/890011 for British Telecom, 0800/0130011 for AT&T/NTL.* **MCI WorldPhone** ☎ *0800/279–5088 In U.K. to call U.S. via MCI.* **Sprint International Access** ☎ *0500/890877 cable and wireless, 0800/890877 British Telecom.*

CALLING CARDS

You can purchase BT (British Telecom) phone cards for use on public phones from shops, post offices, and newsstands. They're ideal for longer calls, are composed of units of 20p, and come in values of £2, £5, £10, and £20. An indicator panel on the phone shows the number of units you've used; at the end of your call the card is returned. Where credit cards are taken, slide the card through, as indicated. Beware of buying cards that require you to dial a free phone number; some of these are not legitimate. It's better to get a BT card.

MOBILE PHONES

If you have a multiband phone (some countries use different frequencies than what's used in the United States) and your service provider uses the world-standard GSM network (as do T-Mobile, Cingular, and Verizon), you can probably use your phone abroad. Roaming fees can be steep, however: 99¢ a minute is considered reasonable. And overseas you normally pay the toll charges for incoming calls. It's almost always cheaper to send a text message than to make a call, since text messages have a very low set fee (often less than 5¢).

If you just want to make local calls, consider buying a new SIM card (note that your provider may have to unlock your phone for you to use a different SIM card) and a prepaid-service plan in the destination. You'll then have a local number and can make local calls at local rates.

Cell phones are getting less and less expensive to buy; so much so that it's now cheaper to buy a new cell phone while abroad than it is to rent one. Rates run from as low as £20 a month for unlimited calls with a pay-as-you-go card.

Contacts Cellular Abroad ☎ *800/287–5072* ⊕ *www.cellularabroad.com.* **Mobal** ☎ *888/888–9162* ⊕ *www.mobalrental.com.*

▌ CUSTOMS AND DUTIES

You're always allowed to bring goods of a certain value back home without having to pay any duty or import tax. But there's a limit on the amount of tobacco and liquor you can bring back duty-free, and some countries have separate limits for perfumes; for exact figures, check with your customs department. The values of so-called "duty-free" goods are included in these amounts. When you shop abroad, save all your receipts, as customs inspectors may ask to see them as well as the items you purchased. If the total value of your goods is more than the duty-free limit, you'll have to pay a tax (most often a flat percentage) on the value of everything beyond that limit.

Check ahead with the Department for Environment, Food and Rural Affairs if you want to bring a pet into Scotland.

Information in Scotland Department for Environment, Food and Rural Affairs ☎ *08459/335577* ⊕ *www.defra.gov.uk.* **HM Revenue & Customs** ☎ *0845/010–9000* ⊕ *www.hmrc.gov.uk.*

U.S. Information U.S. Customs and Border Protection ⊕ *www.cbp.gov.*

▌ EATING OUT

The restaurants we review in this book are the cream of the crop in each price category. Today the traditional Scottish restaurant offers more than fish-and-chips, fried sausage, and black pudding; instead you'll find the freshest of scallops, organic salmon, wild duck, and Aberdeen Angus beef as well as locally grown seasonal vegetables and fruits.

Whether you want to try traditional haggis (ground-up sheep's organs) or black pudding (made from congealed blood) is up to you. Just know that there are other, more tempting Scottish dishes for you to choose from, as well as a wide array of international restaurants: Chinese, French, Greek, Indian, Italian, Japanese, and Mexican (to name but a few) can be truly exceptional. There are a couple of vegetarian options on every menu and most restaurants, particularly pubs that serve food, welcome families with young children.

Places like Glasgow, Edinburgh, and Aberdeen have sophisticated restaurants at various price levels; of these, the more notable tend to open only in the evening. But fabulous restaurants are popping up in the smaller villages as well. Dining in Scotland can be an experience for all the senses but it is rarely cheap, so don't forget your credit card.

Those city Scots who don't dine at their work desk usually take their midday meals in a pub, wine bar, sandwich bar/shop, bistro, or department-store restaurant (which might not serve alcohol). When traveling, Scots generally eat inexpensively and quickly at a country pub or village tearoom.

Note that most pubs do not have any waitstaff, and you're expected to go to the bar and order a beverage and your meal—this can be disconcerting when you're seated in a "restaurant" upstairs but are still expected to go downstairs and get your own drinks and food. You're not expected to tip the bartender, but you are expected to tip restaurant waitstaff, by leaving 10% to 15% of the tab on the table.

Since 2007, smoking has been banned in pubs, clubs, and restaurants throughout Britain.

Properties are assigned price categories based on dinner prices. *Price charts appear at the start of each chapter or, for Edinburgh and Glasgow, in the Where to Eat section.*

CATEGORY	COST
¢	under £10
$	£10–£14
$$	£15–£19
$$$	£20–£25
$$$$	over £25

All prices are per person in pounds for a main course at dinner.

DISCOUNTS AND DEALS
Many city restaurants have very good pre-theater meal deals that last from 5 to 7 pm. Lunch deals can also save you money; some main courses can be nearly half the price of dinner entrées. All supermarkets sell a large variety of high-quality sandwiches, wraps, and salads at reasonable prices. If the weather's dry, opt for a mid-day picnic.

MEALS AND MEALTIMES
To start the day with a full stomach, try a traditional Scottish breakfast of bacon and fried eggs served with sausage, fried mushrooms, and tomatoes, and usually fried bread or potato scones. Most places also serve kippers (smoked herring). All this is in addition to juice, porridge, cereal, toast, and other bread products.

"All-day" meal places are becoming prevalent. The normal lunch period, however, is 12:30 to 2:30. A few places serve high tea—masses of cakes, bread and butter, and jam, served with tea only, around 2:30 to 4:30. Typical dinner times are fairly early, around 5 to 8.

Familiar fast-food chains are often more expensive than a good home-cooked meal in a local café or pub, where large servings of British comfort food—fish-and-chips, stuffed baked potatoes, and sandwiches—are served. In upscale restaurants, cutting costs can be as simple as requesting *tap* water; "water" means a bottle of mineral water that could cost up to £5.

Unless otherwise noted, the restaurants listed in this guide are open daily for lunch and dinner.

PAYING
Some restaurants exclude service charges from the printed menu (which the law obliges them to display outside), then add 10% to 15% to the check, or else stamp "service not included" along the bottom, in which case you should add the 10% to 15% yourself. Just don't pay twice for service—unscrupulous restaurateurs have been known to add service but leave the total on the credit-card slip blank.

Credit cards are widely accepted at most types of restaurants.

For guidelines on tipping, see Tipping below.

PUBS
A common misconception among visitors to Scotland is that pubs are cozy bars. But pubs are also gathering places, conversation zones, even restaurants. Pubs are, generally speaking, where people go to have a drink, meet their friends, and catch up on one another's lives. Traditionally pub hours are 11–12, with last orders called about 20 minutes before closing time, but pubs can choose to stay open until 1 am, or later.

Some pubs are child-friendly, but others have restricted hours for children. If a pub serves food, it will generally allow children in during the day with adults. Some pubs are stricter than others, though, and will not admit anyone younger than 18. Some will allow children in during the day, but only until 6 pm. If you're in doubt, ask the bartender. Family-friendly pubs tend to be packed with kids, parents, and all of their accoutrements.

RESERVATIONS AND DRESS

It's a good idea to make a reservation if you can. We mention them specifically only when reservations are essential (there's no other way you'll ever get a table) or when they are not accepted. For popular restaurants, book as far ahead as you can (often 30 days), and reconfirm as soon as you arrive. (Large parties should always call ahead to check the reservations policy.) We mention dress only when men are required to wear a jacket or a jacket and tie.

Online-reservation services make it easy to book a table before you even leave home. Toptable has listings in many Scottish cities.

Contacts **Toptable** ⊕ *www.toptable.co.uk.*

WINES, BEER, AND SPIRITS

Bars and pubs typically sell two kinds of beer: lager is light in color, very carbonated, and served cold, and ale is dark, semicarbonated, and served just below room temperature. You may also come across a pub serving "real ales," which are hand-drawn, very flavorful beers from smaller breweries. These traditionally produced real ales have a fervent following; check out the Campaign for Real Ale's website, www.camra.org.uk.

You can order Scotland's most famous beverage—whisky (here, most definitely spelled without an *e*)—at any local pub. All pubs serve any number of single-malt and blended whiskies. It's also possible to tour numerous distilleries, where you can sample a dram and purchase a bottle for the trip home. Most distilleries are concentrated in Speyside and Islay.

The legal drinking age in Scotland is 18.

▌ECOTOURISM

Ecotourism is an emerging trend in the United Kingdom. The Shetland Environmental Agency Ltd. runs the Green Tourism Business Scheme (GTBS), a

> ### WORD OF MOUTH
>
> Was the service stellar or not up to snuff? Did the food give you shivers of delight or leave you cold? Did the prices and portions make you happy or sad? Rate restaurants and write your own reviews in "Travel Ratings," or start a discussion about your favorite places in "Travel Talk" on www.fodors.com. Your comments might even appear in our books. Yes, you, too, can be a correspondent!

program that evaluates sites and lodgings in England, Scotland, and Wales and gives them a gold, silver, or bronze rating according to their sustainability. You can find a list of green hotels, B&Bs, apartments, and other properties on the GTBS website. Also check out the VisitBritain and Visit Scotland websites, which have information and tips about green travel in Britain.

Contact **Green Tourism Business Scheme** ☎ *01738/632162* ⊕ *www.green-business.co.uk.*

▌ELECTRICITY

The electrical current in Scotland, as in the rest of Great Britain, is 220–240 volts (in line with the rest of Europe), 50 cycles alternating current (AC); wall outlets take three-pin plugs, and shaver sockets take two round, oversize prongs.

Consider making a small investment in a universal adapter, which has several types of plugs in one lightweight, compact unit. Most laptops and mobile-phone chargers are dual voltage (i.e., they operate equally well on 110 and 220 volts), so require only an adapter. These days the same is true of small appliances such as hair dryers. Always check labels and manufacturer instructions to be sure. Don't use 110-volt outlets marked "for shavers only" for high-wattage appliances such as hair dryers.

▮ EMERGENCIES

If you need to report an emergency, dial 999 for police, fire, or ambulance. Be prepared to give the telephone number you're calling from. You can get 24-hour treatment in Accident and Emergency at British hospitals, but depending on the urgency of your situation, as in any U.S. hospital, you should expect to wait for treatment. Treatment from the National Health Service is free to British citizens; as a foreigner, you will be billed after the fact for your care. (Prices are nowhere near what they are in the United States.)

General Emergency Contacts Ambulance, fire, police ☏ *999.*

U.S. Embassies American Consulate General ✉ *3 Regent Terr., Calton, Edinburgh* ☏ *0131/556–8315* ⊕ *edinburgh. usconsulate.gov.* **U.S. Embassy** ✉ *24 Grosvenor Sq., London, England* ☏ *020/7499–9000* ⊕ *london.usembassy.gov.* **U.S. Passport Unit** ✉ *55 Upper Brook St., London, England* ☏ *020/7499–9000* ⊕ *london.usembassy.gov.*

▮ HEALTH

SPECIFIC ISSUES IN SCOTLAND

If you take prescription drugs, keep a supply in your carry-on luggage and make a list of all your prescriptions to keep on file at home while you are abroad. You will not be able to renew a U.S. prescription at a pharmacy in Britain. Prescriptions are accepted only if issued by a U.K.-registered physician.

If you're traveling in the Highlands and islands in summer, pack some midge repellent and antihistamine cream to reduce swelling: the Highland midge is a force to be reckoned with. Check ⊕ *www. midgeforecast.co.uk* for updates on these biting pests.

OVER-THE-COUNTER REMEDIES

Over-the-counter medications in Scotland are similar to those in the United States, with a few significant differences. Medications are sold in boxes rather than bottles, and are sold in very small amounts—usually no more than 12 pills per package. There are also fewer brands than you're likely to be used to—you can, for example, find aspirin, but usually only one kind in a store. You can buy generic ibuprofen or a popular European brand of ibuprofen, Nurofen, which is sold everywhere. Tylenol is not sold in the United Kingdom, but its main ingredient, acetaminophen, is—although, confusingly, it's called paracetamol.

Drugstores are generally called pharmacies, but sometimes referred to as chemists. The biggest drugstore chain in the country is Boots, which has outlets everywhere, except for the smallest towns. If you're in a rural area, look for shops marked with a sign of a green cross; almost all small drugstores have one of these.

Supermarkets and newsagents all usually have a small supply of cold and headache medicines, often behind the cash register. As in the United States, large supermarkets will have a bigger supply.

MEDICAL INSURANCE AND ASSISTANCE

Consider buying trip insurance with medical-only coverage. Neither Medicare nor some private insurers cover medical expenses anywhere outside of the United States. Medical-only policies typically reimburse you for medical care (excluding that related to pre-existing conditions) and hospitalization abroad, and provide for evacuation. You still have to pay the bills and await reimbursement from the insurer, though.

Another option is to sign up with a medical-evacuation assistance company. A membership in one of these companies gets you doctor referrals, emergency evacuation or repatriation, 24-hour hotlines for medical consultation, and other assistance. International SOS Assistance Emergency and AirMed International provide evacuation services and medical referrals. MedjetAssist offers medical evacuation.

Medical Assistance Companies **AirMed International** ⊕ *www.airmed.com.* **International SOS** ⊕ *www.internationalsos.com.* **MedjetAssist** ⊕ *www.medjetassist.com.*

Medical-Only Insurers **International Medical Group** ☎ *800/628–4664* ⊕ *www.imglobal. com.* **Wallach & Company** ☎ *800/237–6615, 540/687–3166* ⊕ *www.wallach.com.*

SHOTS AND MEDICATIONS

No particular shots are necessary for visiting Scotland from the United States.

Health Warnings **National Centers for Disease Control & Prevention** (*CDC*) ☎ *800/232–4636 international travelers' health line* ⊕ *wwwnc.cdc.gov/travel.* **World Health Organization** (*WHO*) ⊕ *www.who.int.*

▌ HOURS OF OPERATION

Banks are open weekdays 9 to 5. Some banks have extended hours on Thursday evening, and a few are open on Saturday morning. The major airports operate 24-hour banking services seven days a week.

Service stations are at regular intervals on motorways and are usually open 24 hours a day, though stations elsewhere usually close from 9 pm to 7 am; in rural areas many close at 6 pm and Sunday.

Most museums in cities and larger towns are open daily, although some may be closed on Sunday morning. In smaller villages museums are often open when there are visitors around—even late on summer evenings—but closed in poor weather, when visitors are unlikely; there's often a contact phone number on the door. Pharmacies usually open 9 to 5 or 5:30 Monday through Saturday, though most large towns and cities have either a large supermarket open extended hours, with a pharmacy on the premises, or have a rotation system for pharmacists on call (there will be a note displayed in the pharmacy's window with the number to call). In rural areas doctors often dispense medicines themselves. In an emergency the police should be able to locate a pharmacist.

Usual business hours are Monday through Saturday 9 to 5 or 5:30. In small villages many shops close for lunch. Department stores in large cities and many supermarkets even in smaller towns stay open for late-night shopping (usually until 7:30 or 8) one or more days a week. Apart from some newsstands and small food stores, many shops close Sunday except in larger towns and cities, where main shopping malls may open.

HOLIDAYS

The following days are public holidays in Scotland; note that the dates for England and Wales are slightly different. Ne'er Day and a day to recover (January 1–2), Good Friday, May Day (first Monday in May), Spring Bank Holiday (last Monday in May), Summer Bank Holiday (first Monday in August), and Christmas (December 25–26).

▌ MAIL

Stamps may be bought from post offices (open weekdays 9 to 5:30, Saturday 9 to noon), from stamp machines outside post offices, and from news dealers' stores and newsstands; they can also be purchased online. Mailboxes, known as post- or letter boxes, are painted bright red; large tubular ones are set on the edge of sidewalks, and smaller boxes are set into post-office walls. Allow at least four days for a letter or postcard to reach the United States by airmail. Surface mail service can take up to four or five weeks.

Airmail letters to the United States cost 76p (under 10 grams) or £1.10 (under 20 grams); postcards cost 76p. Within the United Kingdom first-class letters cost 46p, second-class letters and postcards 36p. The Royal Mail website is ⊕ *www. royalmail.com.*

If you're uncertain where you'll be staying, you can arrange to have your mail sent to the nearest American Express. The service is free to cardholders; all others pay a small fee. You can also collect letters at any post office by addressing them to *poste restante* at the post office you nominate. In Edinburgh a convenient central office is St. James Centre Post Office, St. James Centre, Edinburgh, EH1 3SR, Scotland.

SHIPPING PACKAGES

Most department stores and retail outlets can arrange to ship your goods home. You should check your insurance for coverage of possible damage. If you want to ship goods yourself, use one of the overnight postal services, such as Federal Express, DHL, or TNT.

To find the nearest branch providing overnight mail services, contact the following agencies.

Express Services DHL ☎ *0844/248–0844* ⊕ *www.dhl.co.uk.* **FedEx** ☎ *08456/070809* ⊕ *www.fedex.com.* **TNT** ☎ *0800/100600* ⊕ *www.tnt.com.*

▌ MEDIA

NEWSPAPERS AND MAGAZINES

Scotland's major newspapers include the *Scotsman*—a conservative sheet that also styles itself as the journal of record—and the moderate Glasgow-based *Herald,* along with the tabloid *Daily Record.* The *Sunday Post,* conservative in bent, is the country's leading Sunday paper; *Scotland on Sunday* competes directly with London's *Sunday Times* for clout north of the border; and the *Sunday Herald,* an offshoot of the *Herald,* is another major title. Scottish newsstands also feature editions of the leading London newspapers, such as the *Times, Telegraph, Independent,* and *Guardian.* Scotland also has many regional publications; the *List,* a twice-monthly magazine with listings, covers the Glasgow and Edinburgh scenes.

For magazines the selection is smaller and its purview is less sophisticated. *Heritage Scotland,* a publication of the National Trust, covers the historic preservation beat. *Scottish Homes and Interiors* is devoted to home design and style, and the *Scottish Field* covers matters dealing with the countryside. For more regional coverage check out the glossy *Scottish Life.*

RADIO AND TELEVISION

The Scotland offshoot of the British Broadcasting Corporation, BBC Scotland, is based in Glasgow and has a wide variety of Scotland-based TV programming. BBC Scotland usually feeds its programs into the various BBC channels, including BBC1, BBC2, BBC3, and BBC4. ITV is used by independent channels, with STV providing the Scottish content. Originating in England, Channel 4 is a mixture of mainstream and off-the-wall programming, whereas Channel 5 has more sports and films.

Satellite TV has brought dozens more channels to Britain.

Radio has seen a similar explosion for every taste, from 24-hour classics on Classic FM (100–102 MHz) to rock (Richard Branson's Virgin at 105.8 MHz). BBC Radio Scotland is a leading radio station, tops for local news and useful as it provides Scottish (rather than English) weather information. Originating from England—and therefore not always received in regions throughout Scotland—the BBC channels include Radio 1 (FM 97.6) for the young and hip; Radio 2 (FM 88) for middle-of-the-roadsters; Radio 3 (FM 90.2) for classics, jazz, and arts; Radio 4 (FM 92.4) for news, current affairs, drama, and documentaries; and 5 Live (MW 693 kHz) for sports and news coverage, with listener phone-ins.

The BBC website is perhaps one of the most comprehensive public service broadcasting websites in the world. You can watch BBC programs online using BBC iplayer, and listen to radio programs for up to a week after broadcast by using its Listen Again facility.

Media Contacts BBC ⊕ *www.bbc.co.uk.*

▌ MONEY

Prices can seem high in Scotland largely because of the exchange rate, though this has improved because of the economic downturn. However, travelers do get some breaks: national museums are free, and staying in a B&B or renting a city apartment brings down lodging costs. *The chart below gives some ideas of the kinds of prices you can pay for day-to-day life.*

ITEM	AVERAGE COST
Cup of Coffee	£1.80
Glass of Wine	£3.90
Pint of Beer	£3.50
Sandwich	£3
One-Mile Taxi Ride Edinburgh	£2.60
Newspaper	60p–£1

Prices throughout this guide are given for adults. Substantially reduced fees are almost always available for children, students, and senior citizens.

▌ **TIP→** Banks never have every foreign currency on hand, and it may take as long as a week to order. If you're planning to exchange funds before leaving home, don't wait until the last minute.

ATMS AND BANKS

ATMs are available throughout Scotland at banks and numerous other locations such as railway stations, gas stations, and department stores. Three banks with many branches are Lloyds, Halifax, and the Royal Bank of Scotland. PINs have four or fewer digits.

Your own bank will probably charge a fee for using ATMs abroad; the foreign bank you use may also charge a fee. Nevertheless, you'll usually get a better rate of exchange at an ATM than you will at a currency-exchange office or even when changing money in a bank. And extracting funds as you need them is a safer option than carrying around a large amount of cash.

▌ TIP→ PINs with more than four digits are not recognized at ATMs in many countries. If yours has five or more, remember to change it before you leave.

ATM Locations Cirrus ☎ *800/424–7787* ⊕ *www.mastercard.com.* **Plus** ☎ *800/843– 7587* ⊕ *www.visa.com.*

CREDIT CARDS

Credit cards are accepted almost everywhere and for everything (except for bus and taxi fares), as are debit cards. You shouldn't experience any problems using your Visa or MasterCard; however, it is a good idea to travel with a picture ID in case you're asked for it. American Express and Diners Club are not as widely accepted.

CURRENCY AND EXCHANGE

Britain's currency is the pound sterling, which is divided into 100 pence (100p). Bills (called notes) are issued in the values of £50, £20, £10, and £5. Coins are issued in the values of £2, £1, 50p, 20p, 10p, 5p, 2p, and 1p. Scottish coins are the same as English ones, but Scottish notes are issued by three banks: the Bank of Scotland, the Royal Bank of Scotland, and the Clydesdale Bank. They have the same face values as English notes, and English notes are interchangeable with them in Scotland.

At this writing, the exchange rate was U.S. $1.57 to the pound. Britain's entry into the European Union's currency—the euro—continues to be debated.

Google does currency conversion. Just type in the amount you want to convert and an explanation of how you want it converted (e.g., "14 Swiss francs in dollars"). Oanda.com also allows you to print out a handy table with the current day's conversion rates. XE.com is another good currency conversion website.

Conversion Sites Google ⊕ *www.google. com.* **Oanda.com** ⊕ *www.oanda.com.* **XE.com** ⊕ *www.xe.com.*

▌ PACKING

Travel light. Porters are more or less extinct these days (and very expensive where you can find them). Also, if you're traveling around the country by car, train, or bus, large, heavy luggage is more of a burden than anything else. Save a little packing space for things you might buy while traveling.

In Scotland casual clothes are the norm, and very few hotels or restaurants insist on jackets and ties for men in the evening. It is, however, handy to have something semi-dressy for going out to dinner or the theater. For summer, lightweight clothing is usually adequate, except in the evening, when you'll need a jacket or sweater. A waterproof coat or parka and an umbrella are essential at any time of year. You can't go wrong with comfortable walking shoes, especially when you're climbing Edinburgh's steep urban hills or visiting Glasgow's massive museums. Drip-dry and wrinkle-resistant fabrics are a good bet since only the most prestigious hotels have speedy laundering or dry-cleaning service. Bring insect repellent if you plan to hike.

Some visitors to Scotland appear to think it necessary to adopt Scottish dress. It's not unless you've been invited to a wedding, and even then it's optional. Scots themselves do not wear tartan ties or Balmoral "bunnets" (caps), and only an enthusiastic minority prefers the kilt for everyday wear.

▌ PASSPORTS AND VISAS

U.S. citizens need only a valid passport to enter Great Britain for stays of up to six months. Travelers should be prepared to show sufficient funds to support and accommodate themselves while in Britain (credit cards will usually suffice for this) and to show a return or onward ticket. If you're within six months of your passport's expiration date, renew it before you leave—nearly extinct passports are not strictly banned, but they make immigration officials anxious, and may cause you problems. Health certificates are not required for travel in Scotland.

If only one parent is traveling with a child under 17 and his or her last name differs from the child's, then he or she will need a signed and notarized letter from the parent with the same last name as the child authorizing permission to travel. Airlines, ferries, and trains have different policies for children traveling alone, so if your child must travel alone, make sure to check with the carrier prior to purchasing your child's ticket.

U.S. Passport Information U.S. Department of State ☎ 877/487–2778 ⊕ *www.travel.state. gov/passport.*

▌ RESTROOMS

Most cities, towns, and villages have public restrooms, indicated by signposts to "wc," "toilets," or "public conveniences." They vary hugely in cleanliness. You'll often have to pay a small amount (usually 30p) to enter public conveniences; a request for payment usually indicates a high standard of cleanliness. Gas stations, called petrol stations, also usually have restrooms (to which the above comments also apply). In towns and cities, department stores, hotels, restaurants, and pubs are usually your best bets for at least reasonable standards of hygiene. The Bathroom Diaries is flush with unsanitized info on restrooms the world over—each one located, reviewed, and rated.

Find a Loo The Bathroom Diaries ⊕ *www. thebathroomdiaries.com.*

▌ SAFETY

Overall, Scotland is a very safe country to travel in, but be a cautious traveler and keep your cash, passport, credit cards, and tickets close to you or in a hotel safe. Don't agree to carry anything for strangers. It's a good idea to distribute your cash, credit cards, IDs, and other valuables between a deep front pocket, an inside jacket or vest pocket, and a hidden money pouch. Don't reach for the money pouch once you're in public. Otherwise, you need not avoid wearing jewelry or be wary of passing cyclists snatching your purse. Use common sense as your guide.

General Information and Warnings Transportation Security Administration (*TSA*). ⊕ *www.tsa.gov.* **U.K. Foreign & Commonwealth Office** ⊕ *www.fco.gov.uk/travel.* **U.S. Department of State** ⊕ *www.travel.state.gov.*

▌ SHOPPING

Tartans, tweeds, and woolens may be a Scottish cliché, but nevertheless the selection and quality of these goods make them a must-have for many visitors, whether a made-to-measure traditional kilt outfit or a classy designer sweater from Skye. Particular bargains can be found in Scottish cashmere sweaters; look for Johnstons of Elgin and Ballantyne, two high-quality labels. Glasgow is great for designer wear, although prices may seem high.

Food items are another popular purchase: whether shortbread, smoked salmon, boiled sweets, *tablet* (a type of hard fudge), marmalade and raspberry jams, Dundee cake, or black bun, it's far too easy to eat your way around Scotland.

Unique jewelry is available all over Scotland but especially in some of the remote regions where get-away-from-it-all craftspeople have set up shop amid the idyllic scenery.

Scottish antique pottery and table silver make unusual, if sometimes pricey, souvenirs: a Wemyss-ware pig for the mantelpiece, perhaps, or Edinburgh silver candelabra for the dining table. Antique Scottish pebble jewelry is a unique style of jewelry popular in Scotland; several specialized antique jewelry shops can be found in Edinburgh and Glasgow. Antiques shops and one- or two-day antiques fairs held in hotels abound all over Scotland. In general, goods are reasonably priced: shops in small communities must deal fairly if they hope for repeat business. Most dealers will drop the price a little if asked "What's your best price?"

▌ SIGHTSEEING PASSES

Discounted sightseeing passes are a great way to save money on visits to castles, gardens, and historic houses. Just check what the pass offers against your itinerary to be sure it's worthwhile.

The Scottish Explorer Ticket, available from any staffed Historic Scotland (HS) property and from many tourist information centers, allows visits to HS properties for 3 days in a 5-day period (£20) or 7 days in a 14-day period (£27.20). The Trust Discovery Ticket, issued by the National Trust for Scotland, is available for 3 days (£27), 7 days (£32), or 14 days (£57) and allows access to all National Trust for Scotland properties. It's available to overseas visitors only and can be purchased from the National Trust for Scotland online and by phone, or at properties and some of the main tourist information centers.

Discount Passes Historic Scotland 🕾 *0131/668–8831* ⊕ *www.historic-scotland. gov.uk/explorer.* **National Trust for Scotland** 🕾 *0844/493–2100* ⊕ *www.nts.org.uk.*

▌ TAXES

An airport departure tax of £50 (£10 for within U.K. and EU countries) per person is included in the price of your ticket.

The British sales tax, V.A.T. (Value-Added Tax), is 20%. It's almost always included in quoted prices in shops, hotels, and restaurants. The most common exception is at high-end hotels, where prices often exclude V.A.T. Be sure to verify whether the quoted room price includes V.A.T.

Further details on how to get a V.A.T. refund and a list of stores offering tax-free shopping are available from VisitBritain.

When making a purchase, ask for a V.A.T.-refund form and find out whether the merchant gives refunds—not all stores do, nor are they required to. Have the form stamped by customs officials when you leave the country or, if you're visiting several European Union countries, when you leave the EU. After you're through passport control, take the form to a refund-service counter for an on-the-spot refund or mail it to the address on the form after you arrive home.

▌ TIME

Great Britain sets its clocks by Greenwich Mean Time, five hours ahead of the U.S. East Coast. British summer time (GMT plus one hour) requires an additional adjustment from about the end of March to the end of October. Timeanddate.com can help you figure out the correct time anywhere.

Time Zones Timeanddate.com ⊕ *www. timeanddate.com/worldclock.*

▌ TIPPING

Tipping is done in Scotland as in the United States, but at a lower level. Some restaurants and hotels add a service charge of 10% to 15% to the bill. In this case you aren't expected to tip. Always check first. Taxi drivers, hairdressers, and barbers should also get 10% to 15%. You're not expected to tip theater- or movie theater ushers, or elevator operators..

TIPPING GUIDELINES FOR SCOTLAND	
Bartender	£1–£5 depending on the size of the round (in the more modern bars). It's common in traditional pubs to buy the bartender a drink as a tip.
Bellhop	£1–£3 per bag
Hotel Concierge	£10 or more, if he or she performs a service for you
Hotel Doorman	£2–£5 if he helps you get a cab
Hotel Maid	£2–£3 a day (either daily or at the end of your stay, in cash)
Hotel Room-Service Waiter	£1 to £2 per delivery, even if a service charge has been added
Porter at Airport or Train Station	£1 per bag
Skycap at Airport	£1 to £2 per bag checked
Taxi Driver	10%–15%, but round up the fare to the next pound amount
Tour Guide	10% of the cost of the tour, but optional
Valet Parking Attendant	£2–£3, but only when you get your car
Waiter	10%–15%, with 15% being the norm at high-end restaurants; nothing additional if a service charge is added to the bill
Other	Restroom attendants in more expensive restaurants expect some small change or £1. Tip coat-check personnel at least £1–£2 per item checked unless there's a fee, then nothing.

■ TOURS

GENERAL-INTEREST TOURS

Many companies offer fully guided tours in Scotland, from basic to luxury. Most of these are full packages including hotels, all food, and transportation costs in one flat fee. Because each tour company has different specialties, do a bit of research—either on your own or through a travel agent—before booking. You'll want to know about the hotels you'll be staying in, how big your group is likely to be, precisely how your days will be structured, and who the other people are likely to be.

CIE Tours offers all-inclusive themed tours of Scotland; moderately priced tours by Globus cover Scotland and Great Britain. Heart of Scotland has a seven-day ultimate tour of Scotland that takes you through the lowlands, highlands, borders, and islands; the company also has many one-day tours that could be appealing for part of a trip.

Another option is Rabbie's Trail Burners, which offers small-group guided tours in and around Scotland, as well as handy day tours from Edinburgh and Glasgow. They have won numerous awards including the Scottish Thistle award for sustainable tourism.

Contacts CIE Tours ☎ 800/243–8687 ⊕ www.cietours.com. **Classic Scotland** ☎ 01866/464–7389 ⊕ www.classic-scotland. com. **Globus** ☎ 866/755–8581 ⊕ www. globusjourneys.com. **Heart of Scotland Tours** ☎ 01828/627799 ⊕ www.heartofscotlandtours. co.uk. **Rabbie's Trail Burners.** Rabbie's Trail Burners ☎ 0131/226–1133 ⊕ www.rabbies. com.

SPECIAL-INTEREST TOURS

You can find tours for many special interests. We recommend Celtic Dream Tours, which specializes in Celtic-inspired and Burns tours, as well as golf and whisky tours. The Wayfarers offers exciting walking tours through the countryside. Classic Scotland offers tours of castles and gardens as well as a literary tour that takes in the homes of Robert Louis Stevenson, Robert Burns, Walter Scott, and J.M Barrie.

Contacts Celtic Dream Tours ☎ 813/317–6039 ⊕ www.celticdreamtours.com. **The Wayfarers** ☎ 800/249–4420 ⊕ www.thewayfarers. com.

GOLF TOURS

Scotland has fabulous golf courses; a tour can help enthusiasts make the most of their time. VisitScotland has a dedicated golf website with a list of tour companies.

Contacts Golf Scotland ☎ 866/875–4653 ⊕ www.golfscotland.com. **Scotland for Golf** ☎ 01334/460762 ⊕ www.scotlandforgolf. co.uk. **Thistle Golf** ☎ 0141/942–4043 ⊕ www. thistlegolf.co.uk.

PRIVATE GUIDES

The Scottish Tourist Guides Association has members throughout Scotland who are fully qualified professional guides able to conduct walking tours in the major cities, half- or full-day tours or extended tours throughout Scotland, driving tours, and special study tours. Many guides speak at least one language in addition to English. Fees are negotiable with individual guides.

Contacts Scottish Tourist Guides Association ☎ 01786/447784 ⊕ www.stga.co.uk.

■ TRIP INSURANCE

Comprehensive trip insurance is valuable if you're booking a very expensive or complicated trip (particularly to an isolated region) or if you're booking far in advance. Comprehensive policies typically cover trip-cancellation and interruption, letting you cancel or cut your trip short because of illness, or, in some cases, acts of terrorism in your destination. Such policies might also cover evacuation and medical care. (For trips abroad you should have at least medical-only coverage. *See Medical Insurance and Assistance under Health.*) Some also cover you for trip delays because of bad weather or mechanical problems as well as for lost or delayed luggage.

Another type of coverage to consider is financial default—that is, when your trip is disrupted because a tour operator, airline, or cruise line goes out of business. Generally you must buy this when you book your trip or shortly thereafter, and it's available to you only if your operator isn't on a list of excluded companies.

Always read the fine print of your policy to make sure that you're covered for the risks that most concern you. Compare several policies to be sure you're getting the best price and range of coverage available.

Insurance Comparison Information
InsureMyTrip.com ☎ *800/487–4722* ⊕ *www. insuremytrip.com.* **Squaremouth.com** ☎ *800/240–0369* ⊕ *www.squaremouth.com.*

Comprehensive Insurers **Access America** ☎ *800/284–8300* ⊕ *www.accessamerica.com.* **CSA Travel Protection** ☎ *800/711–1197* ⊕ *www.csatravelprotection.com.* **Travel Guard** ☎ *800/826–4919* ⊕ *www.travelguard. com.* **Travelex Insurance** ☎ *888/228–9792* ⊕ *www.travelex-insurance.com.* **Travel Insured International** ☎ *800/243–3174* ⊕ *www. travelinsured.com.*

▌ VISITOR INFORMATION

See the Orientation and Planning section at the start of each chapter for regional tourist information offices; look for Essentials sections in towns for local offices.

Contacts in Britain **VisitScotland** ✉ *Ocean Point One, 94 Ocean Dr., Edinburgh* ☎ *0845/859–1006* ⊕ *www.visitscotland.com.* **The Scotland Desk, Britain and London Visitor Centre** ✉ *Drop-in visits, 1 Regent St., Piccadilly Circus, London, England.*

ONLINE RESOURCES

VisitScotland is Scotland's official website and includes a number of special-interest sites on topics from golf to genealogy. VisitBritain, Great Britain's official site, has ample information on Scotland's sights, accommodations, and more.

Historic Scotland cares for the more than 300 historic properties described on its site. The National Trust for Scotland has information about stately homes, gardens, and castles. Both offer sightseeing passes *(see Sightseeing Passes above).*

All About Scotland **VisitScotland** ⊕ *www. visitscotland.com.* **VisitBritain** ⊕ *www. visitbritain.com.*

Historic Sites **Historic Scotland** ⊕ *www. historic-scotland.gov.uk.* **National Trust for Scotland** ⊕ *www.nts.org.uk.*

INDEX

A

Abbey (Paisley), *151*
Abbeys
Aberdeen and the Northeast, 308
Argyll and the Isles, 315, 343–344
Borders and the Southwest, 165, 170, 174, 178–179, 190
Fife and Angus, 224
Glasgow environs, 151
Lothians, 92
Abbotsford House, *177–178*
Aberdeen and the Northeast, *10, 270–312*
arts and nightlife, 283–284
children, attractions for, 278, 279, 287, 298, 311–312
dining, 274, 280, 281–282, 287, 292, 295, 302, 307, 310–311
festivals, 283, 294, 295
lodging, 274, 282–283, 287, 290, 292, 295–296, 302, 305, 307
Northeast and the Malt Whisky Trail, 272, 299–312
price categories, 274
Royal Deeside and Castle Country, 272, 286–299
shopping, 285–286, 292–293, 303, 307, 309, 310, 311
sports and outdoor activities, 284–285, 294, 295, 296, 307
timing the visit, 272
tours, 304, 305
transportation, 272–274
visitor information, 274–275
Aberdeen Art Gallery, *276*
Aberdeen Arts Center, *283*
Aberdeen International Youth Festival, *283*
Aberdeen Maritime Museum, *278*
Aberdeenshire, *454–455*
Aberfeldy, *265–266*
Aberfoyle, *252–254*
Aberlemno, *230*
Aberlour, *306–307*
Academy House ⌂ , *311*
Accommodations, *482, 484–485*
Achamore House Gardens, *329*
Achiltibuie, *388*
Achiltibuie Smokehouse, *388*
Airds Hotel ⌂ , *324*

Airports, *472*
Aitken and Niven (department store), *86*
Alford, *298–299*
Alloway, *155–158*
Allt-Na-Craig ⌂ , *328*
Alva Glen, *90*
Alyth, *231–232*
Alyth Museum, *232*
Amhuinnsuidhe Castle, *413*
An Lanntair Arts Centre, *411*
Andrew Carnegie Birthplace Museum, *92*
Angus. ⇨ *See* Fife and Angus
Angus Folk Museum, *231*
Angus Glens, *228–229*
Anstruther, *213, 215*
Antonine Wall, *245*
Apartment and house rentals, *482, 484*
Appin, *323–324*
Applecross, *397*
Aquariums, *92, 210, 311–312, 321*
Arbroath, *224, 226*
Arbroath Abbey, *224*
Arches (art venue), *142, 144*
Ardbeg Distillery, *337*
Ardkinglas Woodland Garden, *326*
Ardvreck Castle, *389*
Argyll and the Isles, *10, 314–346*
arts and nightlife, 343
children, attractions for, 321, 326
dining, 319, 321, 327, 331, 342
lodging, 319, 321, 323, 324, 325, 327, 328, 331, 332, 333, 335, 337, 339, 341, 342–343, 344
price categories, 319
shopping, 327, 331, 332, 333, 344
sports and outdoor activities, 315, 323, 329, 331, 333, 338, 447
timing the visit, 316
tours, 319–320
transportation, 318–319
visitor information, 320
Argyll's Lodging, *242*
Arisaig, *377*
Arisaig Marine, *377*
Armadale, *402–403*

Armadale Castle Gardens & the Museum of the Isles, *402–403*
Arran, *20, 316, 329–333*
Assembly Rooms, *54*
Assynt, *387*
ATMs, *493*
Auchindrain Museum, *326*
Auchterarder, *268*
Auld Kirk Alloway, *156*
Aviemore, *365–367*
Ayr, *155–158*
Ayrshire, Clyde Coast, and Robert Burns country, *150–151, 153–158, 445–446*

B

Bachelors' Club, *156*
Baddidarach Road, *389*
Bakeries, *17, 22–23*
Balbir's ✕ , *130*
Balgownie, Royal Aberdeen Golf Club, *454*
Ballater, *291–293, 454*
Ballindalloch Castle, *307*
Balmoral Castle, *289, 291–292, 293*
Balmoral Hotel ⌂ , *70*
Balnakeil Craft Village, *392*
Balquhidder Glen, *250–251*
Balranald Nature Reserve, *415*
Balvenie (castle), *289, 302*
Balvenie Distillery, *300, 305*
Banchory, *287, 289–290*
Banff, *311–312*
Banks, *493*
Bannockburn Heritage Centre, *239–240*
Barceló Stirling Highland Hotel ⌂ , *243*
Barnhill, *339*
Barnton, Royal Burgess Golfing Society, *450*
Barpa Langass Chambered Cairn, *415*
Barrie, J.M., birthplace of, *229–230*
Baxters Highland Village, *309*
Bayview B&B ⌂ , *287*
Bealach na Ba, *397*
Beaches, *349, 362, 392, 419*
Beatrix Potter Garden, *261*
Bed-and-breakfasts, *484*
Behavior and etiquette, *483*
Beinn Eighe, *398*
Bella Jane (tour boat), *402*

Ben An, *251*
Ben Nevis, *18, 373*
Benromach Distillery, *361*
Bicycling, *474*
Argyll and the Isles, 315, 323, 331, 345
Borders and the Southwest, 165, 173, 192, 194
Central Highlands, 235, 249, 252, 266
Edinburgh, 82
Fife and Angus, 215
Great Glen, 365, 366, 367, 368, 374
Northern Highlands and the Western Isles, 393, 411
Ornkney and Shetland Islands, 430, 435
Biggar, *161–162*
Biggar Gasworks, *162*
Biggar Puppet Theatre, *162*
Birdwatching, *97, 364, 427, 433, 437, 441*
Birsay, *427*
Bishop's Palace, *429*
Bla Bheinn, *402*
Black House, *412*
Blackness Castle, *90*
Bladnoch Distillery, *198*
Blair Atholl, *264*
Blair Castle, *264*
Blantyre, *159–160*
Blythswood Square ⌂, *135–136*
Boat and ferry travel, *475*
Boat of Garten, *363–365, 455*
Boating, *194, 255, 319–320, 349, 355, 369, 377, 378, 401*
Bonhoga Gallery, *438–439*
Bonnie Prince Charlie, *359, 412*
Books and movies, *460–463*
Bookshop, *198*
Borders and the Southwest, *8, 164–200*
arts and nightlife, 180, 192
children, attractions for, 170, 173, 176, 178, 183, 184
dining, 168, 171, 175, 177, 180, 182, 183, 185–186, 191, 194, 195, 199
Dumfries and Galloway, 165, 186–188, 190–200
festivals, 171, 182, 192, 198
lodging, 168, 173, 175, 177, 180, 182, 184, 186, 191–192, 195–196
price categories, 168

shopping, 173, 175, 180, 181, 183–184, 186, 192, 194, 198
sports and outdoor activities, 165, 173, 192, 193, 194, 196, 199
timing the visit, 166
transportation, 166–168
visitor information, 168, 170
Borders Textile Towerhouse, *183*
Borreraig Park Museum, *407–408*
Borthwick Castle, *94, 96*
Botanic Gardens (Glasgow), *115–116*
Bowhill, *181–182*
Bowmore, *334–335*
Bowmore Distillery, *335*
Brae, *439–440*
Braemar, *294–296*
Braemar Castle, *289, 294*
Braemar Highland Gathering, *294*
Braemar Highland Heritage Centre, *294*
Braid Hills, *450*
Brass Rubbing Centre, *44–45*
Breachacha Castle, *345*
Brechin, *227–228*
Brechin Town House Museum, *227–228*
Brig o'Balgownie, *281*
Brig o'Doon House ✕, *157*
Brig o'Feuch, *290*
Brig o'Turk, *252*
Britannia (ship), *50–51*
British Golf Museum, *207*
Broadford, *401–402*
Broch of Gurness, *427*
Brodick, *330–331*
Brodick Castle and Country Park, *330–331*
Brodie Castle, *361*
Brough of Birsay, *427*
Broughton House, *195*
Broughty Castle, *221*
Bruce Watt Sea Cruises, *378*
Bruce's Stone, *197*
Bruntsfield Links, *450–451*
Bunnahabhain Distillery, *338–339*
Burns, Robert, *53–54, 156, 157, 190*
Burns Cottage, *156*
Burns House, *190*
Burns Monument, *53–54, 156*
Burns National Heritage Park, *156*
Burrell Collection, *120*

Bus travel, *475–476.* ⇨ *See also* Transportation under individual cities and areas
Business hours, *491*
Butt of Lewis Lighthouse, *412*

C

Caerlaverock Castle, *18, 187–188*
Caerlaverock Wildfowl and Wetlands Centre, *188*
Café Royal Circle Bar, *79*
CairnGorm Mountain Railway, *365*
Cairngorm National Park, *18, 350, 362, 365, 366*
Cairngorm Reindeer Centre, *365–366*
Cairns. ⇨ *See* Stone circles and cairns
Calanais Standing Stones, *21, 413*
Caledonian Canal, *372*
Caledonian MacBrayne, *378, 413*
Callander, *248–250, 451–452*
Callendar House, *245*
Camera Obscura (Kirriemuir), *229*
Camera Obscura and World of Illusions (Edinburgh), *45–46*
Camperdown Golf Course, *453*
Camster Long Cairn, *394*
Camster Round Cairn, *394*
Cannonball House, *47*
Canongate, *46*
Canongate Kirk, *46*
Canongate Tolbooth, *46*
Cape Wrath, *392*
Car travel and rentals, *476–478.* ⇨ *See also* Transportation under individual cities and areas
Cardhu Distillery, *305, 306*
Carnoustie Golf Links, *453–454*
Castle Campbell, *91*
Castle Douglas, *193–194*
Castle Fraser, *298–299*
Castle Kennedy Gardens, *199–200*
Castle Menzies, *265*
Castle Stuart Golf Links, *455*
Castle Trail, *18, 296*
Castlehill, *47*
Castles, *18*
Aberdeen and the Northeast, 271, 287, 289, 290, 291–292, 293, 294, 296, 298–299, 312

Argyll and the Isles, 321, 325, 326, 330–331, 333, 340–341, 345

Borders and the Southwest, 165, 170–171, 174, 178, 185, 187–188, 190, 193, 195, 199–200

Central Highlands, 235, 241–242, 247, 258, 264, 265, 266, 267

Edinburgh and the Lothians, 36–37, 41, 89, 90, 91, 94, 96, 97–98

Fife and Angus, 208, 215–216, 217, 221, 231

Glasgow environs, 158

Great Glen, 349, 355, 358, 360, 361, 370

Northern Highlands and the Western Isles, 389, 396, 401, 402–403, 408, 413

Orkney and Shetland Islands, 438, 442

Caverns, *216, 338, 392*

Cawdor Castle, *360*

Ceilidh Place, *387*

Ceilidhs, *80*

Central Highlands, *8, 234–268*
arts and nightlife, 244, 260, 264
children, attractions for, 241, 248, 253, 258–259, 261
dining, 238, 243, 248, 249, 255, 259, 262, 263
lodging, 238, 243–244, 248, 249, 251, 253–254, 256–257, 260, 263–264, 266–267, 268
price categories, 239
shopping, 244–245, 251, 257, 262, 264, 266, 268
sports and outdoor activities, 235, 249, 250, 252, 254, 255, 266
timing the visit, 236
tours, 241, 242, 255, 262, 265, 267
transportation, 237–238, 239
visitor information, 239

Central Library (Aberdeen), *279*

Centre for Architecture, Design, and the City, *113*

Centre for Contemporary Arts, *113–114*

Chapel of the Order of the Thistle, *37, 40*

Chatelherault Country Park, *159–160*

Children, attractions for. ⇨ *See* under individual cities and areas

Chronology, *464–470*

Church of the Holy Rude, *242*

Churches
Aberdeen and the Northeast, 278, 279, 280, 281, 290, 302, 308, 310
Borders and the Southwest, 188, 198–199
Central Highlands, 242, 246–247, 259
Edinburgh and the Lothians, 37, 40, 42, 46, 47, 92, 94, 97
Fife and Angus, 208, 224, 230
Glasgow and environs, 110, 114, 119, 151, 156
Northern Highlands and the Western Isles, 414
Orkney and Shetland Islands, 427, 428–429

CitizenM 🖫 *, 136*

Citizens' Theatre, *142*

City Chambers (Glasgow), *110*

Clan culture, *404*

Clan Menzies Museum, *265*

Clan Tartan Centre, *404*

Clansman Centre, *372*

Clava Cairns, *358*

Clickhimin Broch, *434*

Climate, *12*

Clo Mor, *392*

Clyde Coast. ⇨ *See* Ayrshire, Clyde Coast, and Robert Burns country

Clyde Valley, *158–162*

Co Leis Thu? Genealogical Research Center, *414*

Cocoa Tree Shop & Café, *215*

Coigach, *387*

Coldstream, *175–177*

Coldstream Museum, *176*

Coll, *345*

Colleges and universities
Aberdeen, 278–279, 280
Fife and Angus, 210
Glasgow, 116

Colonsay, *345–346*

Comedy clubs, *80, 145*

Common Ridings, *171, 182*

Communications, *485–487*

Compass Gallery, *148*

Corgarff Castle, *289, 296*

Corinthian Club, The ✕ *, 126*

Corrieshalloch Gorge, *387*

Craibstone Suites 🖫 *, 282*

Craigellachie, *304–305*

Craigievar Castle, *289, 299*

Craignure, *340–341*

Crail, *212–213*

Crail Museum & Heritage Centre, *213*

Crannog Seafood Restaurant ✕ *, 374*

Crarae Gardens, *326*

Crathes Castle, *289, 290*

Creag Meogaidh Nature Reserve, *372–373*

Credit cards, *5, 493*

Creel, The ✕ *, 429*

Creetown Gem Rock Museum, *196*

Crichton Castle, *96*

Cricket, *81–82*

Crieff, *267–268*

Crinan, *327–328*

Crinan Canal, *328*

Cringletie House 🖫 *, 186*

Crofting holidays, *484*

Cross, The ✕ *, 368–369*

Cross Keys ✕ *, 171*

Cruden Bay, *454–455*

Cruickshank Botanic Gardens, *280*

Cruises, *255, 355, 369, 378*

Cuillin Mountains, *408–409*

Cuisine, *22–23*

Cullen, *310–311*

Culloden Moor, *358–359*

Culross, *91*

Culzean Castle and Country Park, *158*

Cupar, *217–218*

Currency, *493*

Customs and duties, *487*

D

Dalbeattie, *192–193*

Dallas Dhu Historic Distillery, *361*

Dalmeny House, *87*

Dance, *74, 141*

David Livingstone Centre, *159*

David Marshall Lodge, *254*

Deep Sea World, *92*

Dervaig, *341–342*

Destitution Road, *399*

Dewar's World of Whisky, *265*

Dining, *5, 13, 487–489.* ⇨ *See also* under individual cities and areas

Dirleton Castle, *97*

Discount passes, *495*

Distilleries
Aberdeen and the Northeast, 271, 300, 302, 303, 304, 305, 306

Argyll and the Isles, 315, 335, 337, 338–339
Borders and the Southwest, 198
Central Highlands, 262, 265, 267
Edinburgh, 49
Great Glen, 361
Orkney and Shetland Islands, 429
Diving, 427
Dollar, 91
Dornoch, 396
Dornoch Firth, 456
Douglas Park, 447
Doune Castle, 247
Drum Castle and Garden, 289, 290
Drumbeg Loop, 389
Drumlanrig Castle, 190
Drummond Castle Garden, 267
Drumnadrochit, 369–370, 372
Dryburgh Abbey, 178–179
Duart Castle, 340–341
Duddingston, 47
Duff House Royal Golf Club, 311, 455
Dufftown, 300, 302–303
Dumfries, 165, 188, 190–192
Dumfries Museum and Camera Obscura, 191
Dun an Sitcar, 415
Dun Carloway, 412
Dunadd Fort, 328
Dunbar, 96, 447, 450
Dunbeath, 394–395
Dunbeath Heritage Centre, 395
Dunblane, 246–248
Dunblane Cathedral, 246–247
Duncan Ban Macintyre Monument, 324–325
Duncansby Head, 393
Dundee, 203, 218–224, 226–232
Dundee Botanic Garden, 220
Dundee Contemporary Arts, 220–221
Dunfermline, 91–92
Dunfermline Abbey and Palace, 92
Dunkeld, 261–262
Dunnet Head, 393
Dunnottar Castle, 287, 289
Dunrobin Castle, 396
Dunskey Castle, 200
Dunstaffnage Castle, 321
Dunvegan Castle, 408
Durness, 391–392
Duthie Park Winter Gardens, 278
Duties, 487

E

Earl's Palace, 429
Eas Coul Aulin Waterfall, 389–390
East Lothian, 93–98, 447, 450
East Neuk Villages, 203, 206–218
Ecotourism, 489
Eden Court Theatre, 357
Edenwater House 🖫 , 175
Edinbane Pottery Workshop and Gallery, 407
Edinburgh and the Lothians, 8, 28–98
arts and nightlife, 74–81
Calton Hill, 53
Castlehill, 47
Charlotte Square, 54
children, attractions for, 36, 42, 44–46, 48, 52, 54, 68, 70, 74–75, 76, 92, 97
dining, 37, 44, 46–47, 48, 55, 56–67, 89
Duddingston, 47
East End, 85–86
excursions, 30, 86–87, 89–94, 96–98
festivals, 74–76, 78
George Street, 54
Grassmarket, 48
Haymarket, 64–65, 71
High Street, 40
Lawnmarket, 48
Leith, 53, 66–67, 73–74, 81, 86
lodging, 67–74, 98
Midlothian and East Lothian, 93–98, 447, 450
Moray Place, 54
Mound, The (street), 55
New Town, 30, 50–56, 60–61, 64, 70–71, 79–81, 84–85
Old Town, 30, 35–37, 40, 42–50, 57–58, 60, 68–69, 78–79, 84
Parliament, 33, 44, 49
passes, 36
price categories, 57, 68
Princes Street, 55
Royal Mile, 40
shopping, 83–86
South Side, 65–66, 72–73, 81, 86
sports and outdoor activities, 81–83, 450
timing the visit, 30
tours, 34
transportation, 30–34, 87, 93
Upper Bow, 47

Victoria Street, 48
visitor information, 34–35, 87
Waterloo Place, 55
West End and Points West, 65, 71–72, 85
West Lothian and the Forth Valley, 87–92
Edinburgh Castle, 14, 18, 36–37
Edinburgh Festival Fringe, 74, 75
Edinburgh International Book Festival, 74–75
Edinburgh International Festival, 19, 75–76
Edinburgh International Film Festival, 76
Edinburgh International Jazz and Blues Festival, 76
Edinburgh International Science Festival, 76
Edinburgh Military Tattoo, 76
Edinburgh Pass, 36
Edinburgh Zoo, 54
Ednam House Hotel 🖫 , 175
Edradour Distillery, 262
Eilean Donan Castle, 18, 401
Elcho Castle, 258
Electricity, 489
Elgin, 307–309
Elgin Cathedral, 308
Elgol, 402
Elie, 216
Ellon, 312
Emergencies, 477, 490
Eshaness, 439
Etiquette and behavior, 483

F

Falkirk, 245–246
Falkirk Wheel, 245–246
Falkland, 216–217
Falkland Palace, 217
Falls of Dochart, 266
Falls of Rogie, 387
Farmhouse and crofting holidays, 484
Fergusson Gallery, 259
Festivals and seasonal events, 19. ⇨ See also under individual cities and areas
Fife and Angus, 8, 202–232
arts and nightlife, 211, 215, 223
beaches, 228
children, attractions for, 208, 210, 215, 218, 219–220, 221–222

dining, 206, 210, 216, 218, 222, 226, 228, 230
Dundee and Angus, 203, 218–224, 226–232
festivals, 208, 210, 216
lodging, 206, 211, 213, 218, 222–223, 226, 229, 232
price categories, 206
St. Andrews & the East Neuk Villages, 203, 206–208, 210–213, 215–218
shopping, 212, 223–224
sports and outdoor activities, 211–212, 215, 451, 453–454
timing the visit, 204
tours, 206, 218
transportation, 204–206
visitor information, 206
Fife Folk Museum, 218
Film, 76, 141–142, 284
Findhorn Bay, 362
Findhorn Ecovillage, 361–362
Fingal MacCoul, 21
Finlarig Castle, 266
Firth of Lorne, 321
Fishing, 307, 315, 323, 341, 356, 366, 388, 430
Flodden Wall, 48
Floors Castle, 15, 18, 174
Fochabers, 309–310
Fochabers Folk Museum, 309
Football, 17, 83, 146
Forfar, 230
Forres, 361–362
Fort Augustus, 372
Fort Charlotte, 434
Fort George, 354
Fort William, 373–375
Forth Bridges, 89
Forth Rail Bridge, 89
Fouter's Bistro ✕, 157
Foyer Restaurant and Gallery ✕, 281–282
Frankie's Fish & Chip Cafe ✕, 440
Fraser Castle, 289
Fraserburgh, 455
Fyvie Castle, 289, 312

G

Gaelic language, 297, 483
Gailes, 447
Gairloch, 398–399
Gairloch Heritage Museum, 398
Galashiels, 181
Galloway, 165, 186–200
Galloway Forest Park, 196

Gardens
Aberdeen and the Northeast, 278, 279–280, 289, 290, 298, 299, 304, 312
Argyll and the Isles, 315, 326, 329
Borders and the Southwest, 179, 193–194, 199–200
Central Highlands, 261, 267
Edinburgh, 52
Fife and Angus, 215–216, 220
Glasgow, 115–115
Northern Highlands and the Western Isles, 398, 402–403
Garrison Cottage, 253
Gasworks (Biggar), 162
Gay and lesbian clubs, 80
Gearrannan, 412
Genealogical research, 55, 56, 414
General Register Office for Scotland, 55
George IV Bridge, 47
George IV, King (statue), 54
George Hotel, The 🏨, 327
Georgian House (Edinburgh), 51, 54
Girvan, 445–446
Gladstone Court Museum, 162
Gladstone's Land (tenement), 47–48
Glamis, 230–231
Glamis Castle, 18, 231
Glasgow, 8, 100–162
Argyle Arcade, 147
Argyle Street, 147
arts and nightlife, 139–145
Barras (market), 107, 110, 147
Buchanan Street, 147
children, attractions for, 111, 112, 115–116, 118–119, 127, 128, 139, 140, 158, 160–161, 162
City Center and Merchant City, 101–102, 112, 122, 126–129, 134–137, 143–144, 147–149
dining, 111, 121–134, 155, 157
excursions, 150–151, 153–162
festivals, 141
George Square, 110
Glasgow Cross, 114
Glasgow Green, 111
history, 113
lodging, 134–139, 153, 154, 155, 161
passes, 112, 114
price categories, 122, 134
Princess Square, 147

shopping, 146, 155, 157–158, 161
South Side, 102, 120–121, 133–134, 139, 150
sports and outdoor activities, 145–146, 155, 447
timing the visit, 102
tours, 106–107
transportation, 103–106, 122, 151, 156, 158
visitor information, 107, 151, 153, 154, 156, 162
West End, 102, 115–116, 118–119, 129–133, 137–139, 144–145, 149–150
West Regent Street, 147
Glasgow Cathedral, 110
Glasgow Gallery of Modern Art, 111
Glasgow Green, 111
Glasgow School of Art, 111
Glasgow Science Centre, 116
Glasgow University, 116
Glasgow's Underground, 119
Glen Brittle, 408–409
Glen Grant Distillery & Garden, 304, 305
Glen Lyon, 265
Glen Muick, 292
Glen Rosa, 331
Glen Torridon, 18, 398
Glen Trool, 197
Glenbuchat Castle, 296
Glencoe, 14, 375–376
Glendale, 407–408
Glendale Toy Museum, 408
Gleneagles Hotel 🏨, 268
Glenfarclas, Distillery, 305, 306
Glenfiddich Distillery, 300, 305
Glenfinnan, 376–377
Glenfinnan House 🏨, 376–377
Glenfinnan Monument, 376
Glenfinnan Viaduct, 376
Glengarry Castle Hotel 🏨, 373
Glenlivet, 305, 306
Glenmore Lodge, 367
Glenmoriston Town House 🏨, 356
Glenturret Distillery, 267
Glenview, The ✕, 406
Globe Inn, 191
Go Ape High Wire Forest Adventure, 254
Goatfell, 330–331
Golf, 19, 444–456
Aberdeen and the Northeast, 271, 284–285, 296
Aberdeenshire, 454–455

Angus, 453–454
Argyll and the Isles, 315, 329, 338, 446–447
Ayrshire, Clyde Coast, and Robert Burns country, 155, 445–446
Borders and the Southwest, 196
Central Highlands, 249, 259
Dornoch Firth, 456
East Lothian, 447, 450
Edinburgh and the Lothians, 82, 450–451
Fife and Angus, 203, 206, 207, 210, 211–212, 451
Glasgow and environs, 145–146, 155, 447
Great Glen, 357, 360, 374
Moray Coast, 455–456
Northern Highlands and the Western Isles, 396, 399
Perthshire, 451–454
Speyside, 455
Stewartry, 445
tours, 206, 497
Golspie, 395–396
Gordon Chapel, 310
Grampian Transport Museum, 299
Grand Central Hotel ☒, 136
Grange, The ☒, 374
Grantown-on-Spey, 362
Grassmarket, 48
Great Glen, 10, 348–378
arts and nightlife, 357
children, attractions for, 355, 360, 363–364, 367–368, 370
dining, 352, 355–356, 366–367, 368–369, 374, 377
lodging, 352, 356–357, 360, 364, 369, 370, 373, 374, 376–377, 378
price categories, 352
shopping, 357–358, 360–361, 364, 375
sports and outdoor activities, 349, 356, 357, 360, 362, 363, 364, 366, 367, 368, 372–373, 374–375
timing the visit, 350
tours, 352, 355, 362, 370, 377
transportation, 350–352
visitor information, 352
Green Inn ☒, 292
Greenhill Covenanters' House, 162
Gretna Green, 187
Grey Cairns of Camster, 394
Grosvenor (theater), 142
Gulf of Corryvreckan, 339

Gullane, 98, 450
Gurness Broch, 427

H

Haddington, 98
Haddo House, 312
Halliwell's House Museum, 182
Hamilton Toy Collection, 248
Handa Island, 391
Harestanes Countryside Visitor Centre, 170
Haroldswick, 441
Hawick, 183–84
Hay's Dock ✕, 435
Health issues, 490–491
Helmsdale, 395
Hermaness National Nature Reserve, 441
Hermitage, 261
Hermitage Castle, 18, 170–171
High Kirk of St. Giles, 37, 40
Highland Folk Museum, 367–368
Highland Games, 295
Highland Park Distillery, 429
Highlanders Museum, 354–355
Hiking, 20, 165, 199, 249, 271, 349, 365, 366, 367, 374–375, 388
Hill of Tarvit House, 218
Hirsel (house), 176
His Majesty's Theatre (Aberdeen), 279, 293
Hoebridge Inn ✕, 180
Hogmanay (New Year's Eve), 78
Holidays, 491
Holmwood House, 120
Home exchanges, 484
Hopetoun House, 89
Horseback riding, 193, 333, 338
Hotel du Vin Bistro ✕, 131
Hotel du Vin Glasgow ☒, 138
Hotel Missoni ☒, 68
Hotels, 5, 485. ⇨ See also Lodging under individual cities and areas
price categories, 5, 68, 134, 168, 206, 239, 274, 319, 352, 385, 422, 482
House for an Art Lover, 120
House of Dun, 227
House of Fraser (department store), 148
House of the Binns, 89
Houses, historic
Aberdeen and the Northeast, 278, 311, 312

Argyll and the Isles, 328, 339
Borders and the Southwest, 165, 170, 174, 176–177, 178, 181–182, 184, 190, 191, 195
Central Highlands, 242, 245, 253
Edinburgh and the Lothians, 40, 41, 44, 46, 47–48, 49–50, 51, 54, 55–56, 87, 89, 92, 93, 98
Fife and Angus, 218, 227
Glasgow and environs, 113, 114, 116, 120, 121, 153, 154, 156, 157, 158, 159–160, 162
Northern Highlands and the Western Isles, 412
Orkney and Shetland Islands, 426, 437, 440
Howard, The ☒, 70–71
Hub, The (cafe), 47
Hunterian Art Gallery, 116
Hunterian Museum, 116, 118

I

Iain Mellis Cheesemonger (shop), 149
Inchmahome, 253
Innerleithen, 184
Insurance, 490–491, 497–498
Internet, 485
Interpretation Centre (Glasgow), 112
Inveraray, 325–327
Inveraray Castle, 326
Inveraray Jail, 326
Inverewe Gardens, 398
Inverness, 349, 353–358
Inverness Castle, 355
Inverness Dolphin Cruises, 355
Inverness Museum and Art Gallery, 355
Inversnaid, 253
Iona, 20, 315, 316, 340–344
Iona Abbey, 315, 343–344
Iona Community, 344
Irvine, 154
Irvine Burns Club, 154
Islay, 20, 316, 334–339
Islay Woollen Mill, 335
Isle of Arran Heritage Museum, 331
Isle of Bute, 20, 153–154
Isle of Gigha, 329
Isle of Jura Distillery, 339
Isle of Mull, 316, 340–344
Isle of Skye, 14–15, 382, 400–409

Italian Chapel, *428*
Itineraries, *24–26*

J

J.M. Barrie's Birthplace,
  229–230
Jacobite Cruises, *369*
Jacobite Steam Train, *373–374*
Jarlshof, *436*
Jedburgh, *169–171, 173*
Jedburgh Abbey, *170*
Jedburgh Castle Jail, *171*
John Knox House, *40*
John Lewis (department store),
  148
John Muir Country Park, *96*
John o'Groats, *393–394*
John o'Groats Ferries, *355,
  393*
John Paul Jones Museum, *191*
Jura, *316, 334–339*
Jute ✕ , *222*

K

Kalpna ✕ , *66*
Kayaking, *331, 367*
Keen of Hamar Nature
  Reserve, *441*
Keith and Dufftown Railway,
  302
Kellie Castle and Garden,
  215–216
Kelso, *173–175*
Kelso Abbey, *174*
Kelvingrove Art Gallery and
  Museum, *14, 118*
Kelvingrove Park, *118*
Kibble Palace, *115–116*
Kilchurn Castle, *325*
Kildalton Cross, *337–338*
Kildonan Museum and Heri-
  tage Centre, *416*
Kildrummy Castle, *289, 298*
Kildrummy Castle Gardens,
  298
Killiecrankie Visitor Centre,
  263
Killin, *266–267*
Kilmartin House Museum, *328*
Kilt Rock, *406*
Kincardine O'Neill, *290*
King's College, *280*
King's Museum, *280*
King's Work, The (pub), *81*
Kingussie, *367–369*
Kintyre Peninsula, *328–329*
Kinuachdrach, *339*
Kirk of the Greyfriars, *40, 42*
Kirkcudbright, *194–196*

Kirkwall, *428–431*
Kirriemuir, *229–230*
Kirriemuir Gateway to the
  Glens Museum, *230*
Kitchin The ✕ , *67*
Kyle of Lochalsh, *401*

L

La Faisanderie ✕ , *302*
Ladybank, *451*
Lagavulin Distillery, *338*
Lagg Hotel ▦ , *332*
Lake of Menteith Hotel ▦ ,
  253–254
Lamlash, *332*
Lanark, *160–161*
Landmark Forest Theme Park,
  363–364
Language, *297, 483*
Laphroaig Distillery, *338*
Law, The, *221*
Lennoxlove House, *98*
Lerwick, *432, 434–436*
Leuchars, *208*
Leuchars Air Show, *208*
Leven, *451*
Leverburgh, *414*
Liathach, *398*
Libraries, *49, 118, 279*
Lighthouse, The, *111*
Linlithgow Palace, *90*
Linn of Dee, *295*
Linn of Tummel, *262–263*
Livingstone, David, *52, 159*
Loch Achray, *18, 252*
Loch an Eilean, *366*
Loch Arklet, *253*
Loch Awe, *324–325*
Loch Bay Seafood Restaurant
  ✕ , *407*
Loch Chon, *253*
Loch Cill Chriosd, *402*
Loch Druidibeg National
  Nature Reserve, *416*
Loch Fyne Oysters, *326*
Loch Garten Nature Reserve,
  364
Loch Katrine, *18, 251–252*
Loch Leven, *18, 217*
Loch Lomond, *15, 18, 235, 236,
  246, 254–257*
Loch Maree, *18, 398–399*
Loch Morar, *378*
Loch Ness, *350, 369–378*
Loch Ness Exhibition Centre,
  370
Loch of Lowes, *261*
Loch Rannoch, *263*
Loch Venachar, *252*

Lochcarron, *397*
Lochcarron of Scotland Cash-
  mere and Wool Centre, *182*
Lochgilphead, *327*
Lochinver, *389–390*
Lochranza, *333*
Lochranza Castle, *333*
Lochs, *18*
Lodging, *5, 13, 482, 484–485.*
  ⇨ *See also* under individual
  cities and areas
Logan Botanic Gardens, *200*
Lothians. ⇨ *See* Edinburgh and
  the Lothians
Lowland Scots (language), *297*
Lundin Links, *451*

M

Macallan Distillery, *304, 305*
MacCallums Oyster Bar ✕ ,
  155
Macduff Marine Aquarium,
  311–312
MacGillivray Centre, *414*
MacGregor, Rob Roy, *250–251*
Machars, *196*
Machrie, *332–333*
Machrie Moor Stone Circles,
  21, 332
Machrihanish, *447*
Mackintosh, Charles Rennie,
  14, 111–112, 116, 117
Mackintosh Interpretation Cen-
  tre, *111–112*
Maclellan's Castle, *195*
Maes Howe (burial mound),
  21, 425
Mail and shipping, *491–492*
Malmaison ▦ , *137*
Mallaig, *378*
Malt Whisky Trail, *15, 299–
  300, 302–312*
Manderston House, *176–177*
Mar Hall ▦ , *153*
Mareel, *434*
Marischal College, *278–279*
Mar's Wark, *242*
Martin Wishart ✕ , *67*
Marwick Head Nature Reserve,
  427
Mary, Queen of Scots House,
  170
Mash Tun ▦ , *307*
Mavis Grind, *439*
McManus Galleries, *221*
Meal plans, *5, 482*
Media, *492*
Meffan Museum and Art Gal-
  lery, *230*

Meigle, *231*
Meigle Sculptured Stone
Museum, *231*
Mellerstain House, *174*
Melrose, *177–180*
Melrose Abbey, *15, 178*
Mercat Cross (Aberdeen), *279*
Mercat Cross (Edinburgh), *40*
Merchants' House, *114*
Midlothian, *93–98*
Mill Glen, *90*
Millennium Wood, *340*
Mills Observatory, *221*
Misty Isle Boat Trips, *401*
Mitchell Library, *118*
Moat Park Heritage Centre,
162
Monachyle Mhor , *251*
Money matters, *13, 493*
Moniack Castle, *358*
Montrose, *226–227*
Montrose Basin Wildlife Cen-
tre, *227*
Montrose Museum, *227*
Moray Golf Club, *456*
Mortlach Church, *302*
Mount Stuart (house), *153*
Mousa Broch, *437*
Movies, *463*
Muckle Flugga, *441–442*
Mull of Galloway, *200*
Muness Castle, *442*
Murcar (golf), *285*
Museum of Childhood, *48*
Museum of Edinburgh, *46, 49*
Museum of Islay Life, *336*
Museum of the University of St.
Andrews, *210*
Museum of Transport, *118–119*
Museums and art galleries
Aberdeen and the Northeast,
*276, 278, 280, 283, 293,
299, 309, 310, 311, 312*
Argyll and the Isles, *326, 328,
331, 336, 342*
Borders and the Southwest,
*170, 174, 176, 177, 180,
181–182, 183, 191, 195,
196, 199*
Central Highlands, *239–240,
241, 242, 244, 245, 248,
259, 263, 264, 265*
Edinburgh and the Lothians,
*36, 42, 43, 46, 48, 49–50,
51, 52, 54, 55, 87, 92, 94*
Fife and Angus, *207, 208, 210,
213, 218, 220–221, 222,
224, 226, 227–228, 229–230,
231, 232*

Glasgow and environs,
*113–114, 116, 118–119, 120,
121, 153, 154, 157, 159,
160, 162*
Great Glen, *354–355, 358,
360, 367–368, 370, 372,
374, 376*
Northern Highlands and the
Western Isles, *387, 393, 394,
395, 398, 402–403, 404,
406, 407–408, 411, 416*
Orkney and Shetland Islands,
*419, 425, 426, 428, 432,
434, 436, 437, 438–439,
440, 441*
Music, *76–77, 140–141, 180,
223, 260, 283*
Mussel Inn ✕, *127*

N

Nairn, *359–361*
Nairn Golf Club, *360, 456*
Nairn Museum, *360*
National Gallery of Scotland,
51
National Library of Scotland,
49
National Monument, *53*
National Museum of Rural
Life, *160*
National Museum of Scotland,
42
National Wallace Monument,
240
Natural History Visitor Centre,
336
Nature reserves
Argyll and the Isles, *321*
Borders and the Southwest,
188, 196–197
Fife and Angus, *217, 218, 227*
Great Glen, *364, 365–366,
372–373*
Northern Highlands and the
Western Isles, *391, 393,
415, 416*
Orkney and Shetland Islands,
427, 434, 441
Necropolis (Glasgow), *112*
Neidpath Castle, *18, 185*
Nelson Monument, *53*
Nevisport (shop), *375*
New Course (golf), *212*
New Lanark, *160–161*
New Observatory, *53*
Newhailes, *93*
Newton Stewart, *196–197*
Newtonferry (Port nan Long),
415

North Berwick, *96–98*
North Carr Lightship, *221–222*
North Uist, *414–415*
Northeast. ⇨ See Aberdeen and
the Northeast
Northern Highlands and the
Western Isles, *10, 380–416*
arts and nightlife, *394, 411*
children, attractions for, *395,
401, 402, 403, 405, 408*
dining, *381, 384, 390, 399,
405, 406, 407, 408, 411,
413–414*
Isle of Skye, *14–15, 382,
400–409*
lodging, *385, 387, 388, 390,
391, 392, 393, 396, 398,
399, 402, 403, 405, 406,
408, 411, 416*
Northern landscapes, *381, 385,
387–396*
Outer Hebrides, *382, 409–416*
price categories, *385*
shopping, *390, 392, 396, 397,
403, 405, 408, 411, 412,
416*
sports and outdoor activities,
381, 388, 393, 396, 399, 411
timing the visit, *382*
Torridon, *381, 397–399*
tours, *384, 401, 407*
transportation, *382–384, 389,
415*
visitor information, *385*
Noss National Nature Reserve,
434
Number One ✕, *61*
Number Sixteen ✕, *132*

O

Oa Peninsula, *338*
Oban, *320–321, 323*
Observatories, *221*
Ochil Hills, *90*
Ochil Hills Woodland Park, *90*
Old Aberdeen, *280–281*
Old Byre Heritage Centre, *342*
Old Course Hotel ✕, *211*
Old Gala House, *181*
Old Haa, *440*
Old Man of Stoer, *389*
Old Man of Storr, *406*
Old Scatness, *437*
Old Town House (Aberdeen),
280–281
Old Town Jail (Stirling), *241*
Opera, *141*
Òran Mór (theater), *142*

Orkney and Shetland Islands, 10, 20, 418–442
arts and nightlife, 419, 430
children, attractions for, 426, 428, 434, 437
dining, 422, 426, 429–430, 435, 439–440, 442
festivals, 419, 430, 431
lodging, 422, 426, 430, 435, 438, 440
price categories, 422
shopping, 430, 435–436, 438, 439
South Mainland, 436–438
sports and outdoor activities, 419, 427, 430, 435
timing the visit, 420
tours, 423
transportation, 420–422
visitor information, 423
Orkney Museum, 428
Orkney Wireless Museum, 428
Oronsay, 346
Our Dynamic Earth, 42
Our Lady of the Isles, 416
Outer Hebrides, 382, 409–416

P

Packing for the trip, 494
Paisley, 151, 153
Paisley Museum & Art Gallery, 153
Palace of Holyroodhouse, 42–44
Palaces
Aberdeen and the Northeast, 308
Central Highlands, 241, 242, 258–259
Edinburgh and the Lothians, 42–44, 90, 92
Fife and Angus, 217
Glasgow, 112, 115–116
Orkney and Shetland Islands, 429
Panmure, 454
Parks, country and forest
Aberdeen and the Northeast, 278
Argyll and the Isles, 330–331
Borders and the Southwest, 196, 197
Central Highlands, 254
Fife and Angus, 208
Glasgow and environs, 111, 115–116, 118, 121, 158, 159–160, 162
Great Glen, 363–364, 365, 366
Lothians, 90, 96

Parliament House, 49
Pass of Killiecrankie, 263
Passports, 494
Paxton House, 177
Peat Inn, The ⬚ , 218
Peebles, 185–187
Peebles War Memorial, 185
People's Palace, 112
Perth, 257–260
Perth Art Gallery and Museum, 259
Perthshire, 236, 257–268, 451–453
Philiphaugh Salmon Centre, 182
Pictavia, 228
Pictish stone carvings, 230
Pier Arts Centre, 425
Pitlochry, 262–264, 453
Pitlochry Dam and Fish Ladder, 263
Pittencrieff House Museum, 92
Pittenweem, 215–216
Pittenweem Arts Festival, 216
Plane travel, 472–474. ⇨ See also Transportation under individual cities and areas
Playwright ✕ , 222
Pluscarden Abbey, 308
Pollok House, 121
Port Askaig, 338–339
Port Charlotte, 336–337
Port Ellen, 337–338
Port of Ness, 411–412
Port Wemyss, 337
Portnahaven, 337
Portpatrick, 200
Portree, 403, 405
Potter, Beatrix, 261
Powfoot, 445
Prestwick, 446
Price categories
Aberdeen and the Northeast, 274
Argyll and the Isles, 319
Borders and the Southwest, 168
Central Highlands, 239
dining, 5, 57, 122, 168, 206, 239, 274, 319, 352, 385, 422, 488
Edinburgh and the Lothians, 57, 68
Fife and Angus, 206
Glasgow environs, 122, 134
Great Glen, 352
lodging, 5, 68, 134, 168, 206, 239, 274, 319, 352, 385, 422, 482

Northern Highlands and the Western Isles, 385
Orkney and Shetland Islands, 422
Prince of Wales (pub), 284
Princes Square (shopping center), 147
Priorwood Gardens, 179
Provand's Lordship (house), 113
Provost Skene's House, 278
Pubs, 16, 48, 78, 79–81, 143–145, 211, 223, 284, 357, 488–489

Q

Queen Elizabeth Forest Park, 254
Queen's Cross Church, 119
Queen's View, 290
Quiraing, 406

R

Ragamuffin (shop), 403
Real Mary King's Close, 44
Regimental Museum of the Black Watch, 259
Regimental Museum of the Royal Highland Fusiliers, 114
Register House, 55
Rest and Be Thankful Pass, 325
Restaurants. ⇨ See also Dining under individual cities and areas
price categories, 5, 57, 122, 206, 239, 274, 319, 352, 385, 422, 488
Restrooms, 494
Rhinns of Islay, 337
Ring of Brogar, 21, 425
Riverside Gallery, 358
Riverside Museum: Scotland's Museum of Transport and Travel, 118–119
Robert Burns Birthplace Museum, 157
Robert Burns Centre, 190
Robert Burns country. ⇨ See Ayrshire, Clyde Coast, and Robert Burns country
Robert Smail's Printing Works, 184
Rogano ✕ , 128
Ronas Hill, 439
Rosemount, Blairgowrie Golf Club, 453
Rosemount Viaduct, 279
Roslin, 94
Rosslyn Chapel, 94
Rothesay, 153

Rothiemurchus Estate, *366*
Round Tower, *228*
Royal & Ancient Golf Club of
  St. Andrews, *210*
Royal Botanic Garden, *52*
Royal Dornoch Golf Club, *396,*
  456
Royal Hotel 🖫 , *387*
Royal Scottish Academy, *55*
Royal Troon, *155, 446*
RSS *Discovery* (research ship),
  219–220
Rufflets Country House Hotel
  🖫 , *211*
Rugby, *82*
Running, *83*
Ruthven Barracks, *368*
Ruthwell, *187–188*
Ruthwell Parish Church, *188*
Rutland Hotel 🖫 , *72*

S
Safety, *494–495*
St. Andrews, *15, 203, 206–208,*
  210–213, 215–218, 451
St. Andrews Aquarium, *210*
St. Andrews Castle, *208*
St. Andrews Cathedral, *208*
St. Clement's Church, *414*
St. Fillan's Cave, *216*
St. Giles Church, *308*
St. John's Kirk, *259*
St. Machar's Cathedral, *281*
St. Magnus Cathedral,
  428–429
St. Mark's Church, *279*
St. Mary's Parish Church, *97*
St. Michael's Churchyard, *190*
St. Mungo Museum of Religious
  Life and Art, *113*
St. Nicholas Kirk, *278*
St. Ninian's Chapel, *198*
St. Ninian's Isle, *437*
St. Rule's Tower, *208*
St. Vincent's Street Church, *114*
Scalloway, *438*
Scalloway Castle, *438*
Scapa Flow Visitor Centre,
  431–432
Schoolhouse B&B 🖫 , *292*
Scone Palace, *258–259*
Scotch Whisky Experience, *49*
Scotia Bar, *144*
Scotland Street School
  Museum, *121*
Scotland's Museum of Trans-
  port and Travel, *118–119*
Scots language, *297, 483*
Scotsman, The 🖫 , *69*

Scott, Sir Walter, *52, 179,*
  251–252
Scott Monument, *52*
Scottish Crannog Centre,
  265–266
Scottish Deer Centre, *218*
Scottish Fisheries Museum, *213*
Scottish Maritime Museum, *154*
Scottish Mining Museum, *94*
Scottish National Gallery of
  Modern Art, *52*
Scottish National Portrait Gal-
  lery, *52*
Scottish Parliament, *44*
Scottish Seabird Centre, *97*
Scottish Sealife Sanctuary, *321*
Scottish Storytelling Centre, *49*
Scottish Wool Centre, *253*
Scott's View, *179*
Scourie, *391*
Seafood Restaurant, The ✕ ,
  210
Seallam! Visitor Centre and
  Co Leis Thu? Genealogical
  Research Centre, *414*
Selkirk, *181–183*
Shetland Croft House Museum,
  437
Shetland Islands. ⇨ *See*
  Orkney and Shetland Islands
Shetland Museum, *434, 435*
Shetland ponies, *436*
Shieldaig, *397–398*
Shopping, *21, 495.* ⇨ *See also*
  under individual cities and
  areas
Sightseeing passes, *495*
Signal Tower Museum, *224,*
  226
Silver Darling ✕ , *282*
Sir Walter Scott (steamer), *252*
Sir Walter Scott's Courtroom,
  182
Skaill House, *426*
Skara Brae, *21, 426*
Skiing, *367, 375*
Skye, *20*
Skye Museum of Island Life,
  406
Skye Serpentarium, *402*
Skye Skyns, *407*
Sloans (pub), *144*
Sma' Shot Cottages, *153*
Smailholm Tower, *174–175*
Small Isles, *350, 369–378*
Smaller Isles, *316, 344–346*
Smith Art Gallery and
  Museum, *242*
Smoo Cave, *392*

Soccer, *17, 83, 146*
Sound of Mull, *321*
South Queensferry, *89*
South Uist, *415–416*
Southern Upland Way, *200*
Southerness, *445*
Southwest. ⇨ *See* Borders and
  the Southwest
Speyside, *350, 362–369, 455*
Speyside Cooperage and Visi-
  tor Centre, *304, 305*
Spoons, The 🖫 , *405*
Sports and outdoor activities.
  ⇨ *See* under individual cities
  and areas
Spynie Palace, *308*
Staffin Museum, *406*
Stewartry, *445*
Stewartry Museum, *195*
Stirling, *236, 239–245*
Stirling Castle, *18, 241–242*
Stoer Point Lighthouse, *389*
Stone circles and cairns, *21*
  Argyll and the Isles, 332
  Great Glen, 358
  Northern Highlands and the
    Western Isles, 394, 413, 415
  Orkney and Shetland Islands,
    419, 425, 429, 437
Stonehaven, *286–287*
Stonehaven Open-Air Swim-
  ming Pool, *287*
Stornoway, *409, 411*
Stranraer, *199–200*
Strath Suardal, *402*
Strathisla Distillery, *300, 302,*
  305
Strathspey Steam Railway, *364*
Stromness, *423, 425–427*
Stromness Museum, *426*
Stronachlachar, *253*
Sueno's Stone, *362*
Summerlee-Museum of Scottish
  Industrial Life, *160*
Sunbank House Hotel 🖫 , *260*
Sweetheart Abbey, *190*
Symbols, *5*

T
Taigh Chearsabhagh, *415*
Tall Ship at Glasgow Harbour,
  119
Tangwick Haa Museum, *439*
Tantallon Castle, *97–98*
Tarbert (Kintyre Peninsula), *329*
Tarbert (Outer Hebrides),
  413–414
Tartans, *404*
Taxes, *495–496*

Taxis, 478–479. ⇨ *See also* Transportation under specific cities and areas
Tea, 16, 129
Telephones, 485–487
Tenement House, 114
Tennents (bar), 145
Tentsmuir Forest, 208
Theater, 77, 142, 162, 180, 211, 223, 244, 260, 264, 279, 343, 357
Theatre Royal, 141
Thirlestane Castle, 178
Threave Castle, 193
Threave Gardens, 193–194
Three Chimneys ✕, 408
Three Hills Roman Heritage Centre, 180
Thurso, 393
Tigh na Coille: Aros, 403, 405
Time, 496
Timespan Heritage Centre, 395
Timing the visit, 12
Tipping, 496
Tiree, 344–345
Tobermory, 342–343
Tolbooth Arts Centre, 195
Tolbooth Kirk, 47
Tolbooths, 46, 195, 244, 279
Torridon, 381, 397–399
Tours, 497. ⇨ *See also* under specific cities and areas
Toy Museum, 408
Train travel, 479–481. ⇨ *See also* Transportation under specific cities and areas
Transportation, 12, 472–481. ⇨ *See also* under specific cities and areas
Traquair House, 184

Travel times, 12
Trinity Temple (Teampull na Trionaid), 415
Troon, 154–155
Trossachs, 15, 236, 245–257
Trotternish Peninsula, 405–406
Turnberry, 446

U

Ubiquitous Chip ✕, 133
Ullapool, 385, 387
Ullapool Museum, 387
Unicorn (ship), 222
Union Street (Aberdeen), 276, 278–280
Union Terrace, 279–280
Union Terrace Gardens, 279–280
University of St. Andrews, 210
Unst, 441–442
Unst Boat Haven, 441
Unstan Chambered Tomb, 429
Urquhart Castle, 370

V

Vane Farm Nature Reserve, 217
Vennel Art Gallery, 154
Verdant Works, 221
Visas, 494
Visitor Center of Glencoe, 376
Visitor information, 13, 498. ⇨ *See also* under individual cities and areas

W

Waterloo Monument, 171
Waternish Peninsula, 407
Weather, 12

Web sites, 498
Wedgewood ✕, 60
Weisdale, 438–439
West Highland Museum, 374
West Plean ⬚, 243–244
West Register House, 54, 55–56
Western Gailes, 446
Western Isles. ⇨ *See* Northern Highlands and the Western Isles
Wheatsheaf Hotel and Restaurant ✕, 177
Whisky, 23, 49, 235, 271, 300, 302, 303, 304, 305, 306, 315, 334, 349
Whisky Coast, 334
Whithorn, 198–199
Whithorn Priory, 198–199
Whithorn Story and Visitor Centre, 199
Wick, 394
Wick Heritage Cenre, 394
Wigtown, 197–198
Wigtown Book Festival, 198
Wildlife reserves. ⇨ *See* Nature reserves
Wood of Cree Nature Reserve, 196–197
Writers' Museum, 48, 49–50

Y

Yell, 440

Z

Zoo (Edinburgh), 54

PHOTO CREDITS

NOTES

ABOUT OUR WRITERS

Based in Dundee, **Nick Bruno** peddled breathable base layers, led jinxed coach tours across Europe, and translated Italian legalese before taking up travel writing and journalism. He has written for Fodor's for nearly a decade and has also authored four books about Italy. In recent years, feature writing, photography, and work for the BBC have helped Nick avoid a return to a proper job. For this edition, he updated Edinburgh and the Lothians as well as A Golfer's Country.

Mike Gonzalez is emeritus professor of Latin American Studies at Glasgow University and also writes regularly for the *Herald* and other publications on politics and culture. Mike's assignment for Fodor's was the Glasgow, Borders and the Southwest, Central Highlands, and Argyll and the Isles chapters. His travels took him to places familiar and less familiar, and included exploring a tiny island on Islay whose houses were once an imperial center and walking in a hidden sculpture park in the hills near Dumfries.

Shona Main grew up in Shetland; after moving to the mainland, she spent some informative years working on magazines for teenagers. She had a brief career in law and politics before she returned to writing. Now living in Dundee, Shona is a freelance contributor to newspapers and books and has just written her first work of fiction, which is based on a wind-flattened island community not unlike the one she grew up in. She updated Travel Smart Scotland as well as Fife and Angus, Aberdeen and the Northeast, and Orkney and Shetland.

Originally from Chicago, **Elizabeth Reeder** first visited Scotland while backpacking around Europe; after getting drenched in Glencoe and dried out on the sands of Morar, she was hooked. She has now lived in Scotland for more than 15 years and writes essays, stories, and novels. Her work is regularly broadcast on BBC Radio 4, and she is a lecturer in the Creative Writing program at Glasgow University. Elizabeth revised two chapters: the Northern Highlands and the Western Isles, and Around the Great Glen.